The Fighting Tigers II

Given by

BRUCE & KAREN SIMON

in memory of

Adrian "Kank" Klibert

3-31-89

Photograph by Rick Shinabery

The Fighting Tigers II

LSU FOOTBALL, 1893-1980

Peter Finney

Foreword by Paul Dietzel

Revised Edition

Louisiana State University Press
BATON ROUGE AND LONDON

Designer: Barney McKee
Composition: Kingsport Press and Service Typesetters
Typeface: Linotype Janson
Printer and Binder: Kingsport Press

LIBRARY OF CONGRESS CATALOGING IN PUBLICATION DATA
Finney, Peter.
  The fighting Tigers II.
  Includes index.
  1. Louisiana. State University and Agricultural
and Mechanical College—Football—History. I. Title.
GV958.L65F56   796.332′63′0976318   80-13030
ISBN 0-8071-0766-2

For Deedy
and to the memory of Jim Corbett

Contents

Foreword

WHEN I'm asked what makes LSU football unique, my answer cuts a number of ways. For one thing, there's the feeling here of playing football in what amounts to a basketball atmosphere, the feeling of playing in a stadium where your fans sit so close to the field that you have cheers in your lap. There is also the exhuberance of the fans, many of them Cajun, people with animated temperaments, people with a tradition for gracious socializing that helps make LSU football the great spectacle it is.

You can imagine the impact this climate of enthusiasm had on a young assistant coach from West Point. Coming from a region where fans, as a rule, are somewhat jaded, I discovered what total involvement was. The Saturday Night Syndrome in Baton Rouge amounts to an outdoor picnic for 76,000, a melting pot for Louisianians of all backgrounds and income levels.

As the Tigers begin their eighty-seventh season, they also begin a new era under a former Tiger great, Jerry Stovall. His is an era that was fated to begin with tragedy. But, from my position at the center of things, I have seen how a tragedy brings people closer together. No one who knew Bo Rein can possibly forget what a compelling individual he was, vibrant, straightforward, ambitious in the finest sense. Bo's Dad told me that his one great regret is that his son, through God's will, did not have the opportunity to realize his dreams at LSU. He told me, as only a father can, how proud, how excited Bo was to be LSU's coach.

Following the tragedy, there wasn't a doubt in my mind that Jerry Stovall was the only man for the job. Somewhat reluctantly, Jerry had put football behind him to work for me in athletic fund-raising, but without question the coaching fire inside continued to burn. As fate would have it, it was Jerry who introduced Bo around the state when Bo was getting his program off the ground, and later it was impressive to witness how the staff Bo Rein had assembled closed ranks behind the new coach.

Jerry Stovall may project a Sunday school image to some, but beneath a soft-spoken exterior, beats the heart of a tough competitor who has never backed away from a challenge. In a sense, Jerry spanned the last two coaching eras at LSU playing winning football for me and for my successor, Charles McClendon.

It now becomes Jerry's task to build on a tradition kept alive by Charlie Mac, a man's man, whose tremendous contributions to LSU football over an unprecedented eighteen-year span cannot be minimized. Mac brought the highest integrity to a program that had never borne the slightest hint of scandal. I am fully confident that Jerry Stovall will do the same at his alma mater.

The history of LSU football is the history of southern football. When intercollegiate football's power base was concentrated in the Northeast, in Ivy League country, the South was generally ignored. As southern football fortunes began to rise, LSU was at the forefront. In 1907 Coach Edgar Wingard packed his squad of thirteen Tigers on a boat and set sail for Cuba, the first American team to play a football game outside the continental United States. In 1924, when LSU moved to its new campus from a location near the downtown business area, the first two structures were a small cattle display building and, you guessed it, a football stadium, one seating fewer than 18,000. Seven years later, lights were installed, launching a night game tradition that has thrilled fans for nearly half a century.

LSU's football program has been the bellwether of the Athletic Department, which now includes eleven varsity sports for men and ten for women, placing the university sports program among the most well rounded in the country. Football at LSU has been marked by stability—in the last half century, only four men have coached Tiger teams—and by a winning tradition. From 1893 through 1979, the winning percentage has been .650, and over the past twenty-three years LSU has had twenty-two winning seasons and taken part in sixteen bowl games. Since 1957 the Tigers have ranked among the top ten in attendance, and since 1959 they've been on network television every year but one. These accomplishments contribute to the legend of LSU and the Fighting Tigers.

Peter Finney, chronicler of LSU sports for more than a quarter century, has watched LSU emerge as a national power. In *The Fighting Tigers* he told the story of LSU football from its 1893 beginning through the 1967 season. Out of print for many years, the first edition has become a collecor's item. Now, in *The Fighting Tigers II*, Finney picks up the story and carries it through the Charles McClendon era, giving Tiger fans the color, the excitement, the highs and lows, of eighty-six football seasons.

As you savor the contents of this volume, as you relive the golden moments, you come around to what I learned long ago: There's no place like Tiger Stadium on Saturday night!

PAUL DIETZEL, *Athletic Director*
Louisiana State University
January, 1980

The Fighting Tigers II

'For I'm in the rush-line, mother'

1893–1906

THE kickoff was at 3 o'clock on the afternoon of November 6, 1869, and the final score was Rutgers six goals, Princeton four goals.

Down through the years, this has become known as the game which launched American intercollegiate football, yet what transpired that fall day in New Brunswick, New Jersey, was more soccer than football, and primitive soccer at that. Primitive though it was, it lit a fire which swept through New England, then westward and finally south. Interest in the game (regarded by some as a mixture of prize fight, train wreck, and riot) was such that Dr. Charles E. Coates, a young chemistry professor from Baltimore, was somewhat surprised to find that there was no football team at Louisiana State University when he came to the Baton Rouge campus in 1893. Coates, later to gain recognition as an authority on sugar, had played football at Johns Hopkins and realized the esprit de corps value of the contact sport, especially at a school like LSU which was militarily oriented.

At that time, the university occupied what had been the old United States military post (now the State Capitol grounds), having moved there seven years earlier. Enrollment was just over two hundred, and had not yet become co-educational. When mild-mannered Charles E. Coates set about introducing the game to a skeptical student body, eighty-nine American colleges were fielding teams. In the East, where a fellow named Walter Camp was ramrodding things, the difficulty was making enough footballs to meet the demand. When Princeton played Rutgers in that first game, there were twenty-five men on a side, and nothing resembling an end run or a trap play. It wasn't until 1873 that running with the ball was allowed, and it wasn't until 1880 that Camp established the "scrimmage" line and set the number of players at eleven.

3

Dr. Charles E. Coates: He brought football to LSU.

Instead of dropping the ball between opposing lines, the team in possession would start play either by kicking it forward or kicking it backward to the quarterback. Although the quarterback couldn't run with the ball, he could pass it off, thereby enabling the offensive team to plan its action. Later, again thanks to the ingenious Camp, a system of "downs" was devised whereby, to maintain possession, a team had to do one of two things in three downs: gain five yards or be careful not to lose ten. As a player, halfback Camp of Yale had played a key role in the Eli's domination of the East, at a time when football heroes were easily

4   *The Fighting Tigers*

recognized by their bushy hairdos, chrysanthemum style, which they wore as a badge of honor.

In general, this was the picture when Coates issued an open invitation to LSU students to come out for a scrimmage in the fall of 1893. Later he recalled that there were "some mighty good-looking prospects" who turned out for the first practice. Assisting him was another young professor, H. A. Morgan, a veteran of the Canadian rugby wars. Morgan taught zoology and entomology and was destined, some years later, to become president of the University of Tennessee and one of the original directors of TVA. Working after classes with Harcourt Morgan, Coates taught the 27-man squad the rudiments of football as he knew them. The major offensive weapons were the "turtle back" and the "flying wedge." In the former, the ball carrier ran in the center of a circle formed by members of his team. The more widely known "flying wedge" was V-shaped, with the interference holding onto the belt of the man in front while the ball carrier took refuge in the middle.

Football at LSU was, of course, then in the caveman era. Not only were uniforms impossible to come by, but Dr. Coates spent a good part of his evenings nailing cleats into leather shoes. He wasn't the only coach involved in such extracurricular activities. In New Orleans, T. L. Bayne, former star quarterback at Yale and captain of the Southern Athletic Club, had lit a fire under Tulane. After selling students on the idea of forming a team, Bayne swung into action. He elected himself head coach, secured one of the few footballs in Louisiana, scheduled a game with his own Southern Athletic Club, hired the ball park, marked the football field, erected goal posts, printed tickets, sold them door to door, created a yell, selected Tulane's colors of olive and blue, inserted his brother Hugh into the Tulane lineup, assumed his regular duties as captain of the Athletic Club team, and refereed the game!

Despite this one-man whirlwind, the Southern Athletic Club and Tulane played in relative privacy in Sportsman's Park on the drizzly Saturday afternoon of November 18, 1893. The SAC team won, 12–0, but the university rookies were looking forward to the following Saturday and a game with LSU which Bayne had arranged.

During the week Bayne shuttled between New Orleans and Baton Rouge, assisting Coates and Morgan in coaching the LSU squad. "The LSU boys knew little or nothing about it," Bayne later recalled, "and Dr. Coates and I had to practice them plenty to get them started." This additional duty did not halt Bayne's ticket-selling chores, and this time, when he buttonholed friends to buy tickets at fifty cents each, the flavor of an all-university match suddenly became box-office magic. The game had caught on and an ecstatic Bayne informed Coates to expect a fine turnout.

The enthusiasm was contagious. The New Orleans *Times-Democrat* called football "the most exciting and interesting" of all college games. "As played at present," the newspaper said, "it is a great change from that played by our 'daddies,' who kicked the ball, while now the ball is kicked but little. . . . The football team consists of 11 men, seven of whom stand in line, one yard apart, facing the opposing team; this line is called the rush line, and is used to rush or crush against the line of the opposing side, and by surrounding and assisting the man with the ball and interfering and tackling the men of the opposing team, they endeavor to urge the ball forward."

One of the first sports cartoons to appear in a New Orleans newspaper (the *Daily Picayune*) pictured a husky football player looking down at his mother in much the same fashion as a soldier about to leave home to fight for his country. Captioned "Just Before the Battle," the drawing of "the football warrior on the eve of a great game" was accompanied by this poem:

> Farewell, mother; you may never
>   Press me to your heart again;
> For I'm in the rush-line, mother,
>   And more than likely to be slain.

JUST BEFORE THE BATTLE.

THE FOOTBALL WARRIOR ON THE EVE OF A GREAT GAME.

In Baton Rouge, pregame enthusiasm touched off a reaction in LSU's chemistry professor-coach. On the morning of the game Coates, quarterback Ruffin Pleasant, and a few of the other players went to town in search of ribbon to brighten the initial contest. S. I. Reymond's store had in stock a large supply of the trimmings for the approaching Mardi Gras season, so Coates and company bought out the purple and gold (the green had not yet arrived) from which were made rosettes and badges for students and fans who promised to follow the team. LSU's baseball team had defeated Tulane, 10–8, in the first intercollegiate meeting between the two schools in the spring of that year, and its members had worn purple and gold uniforms. So when the first LSU football special pulled out of Baton Rouge on November 25, 1893, it carried Dr. Coates's hardy outfit clad in gray jerseys with purple trim. Some three hundred War Skule devotees, including Colonel James W. Nicholson, the president, made the historic trip with the team.

In New Orleans, the day was cold and cloudy but that didn't stop the flow of carriages out Canal Street toward the New Basin Canal and Sportsman's Park. A crowd estimated at 1,500 to 2,000 witnessed the game. As captain Ruffin Pleasant, later governor of Louisiana, led the LSU team onto the field, the men were greeted with cheers punctuated by the sound of tin horns. And they heard this lilting yell:

> Rah! Rah! Rah!
> Rah! Rah! Rah!
> Louisiana! Louisiana!
> State U.V.

Waving banners and handkerchiefs saluted the Tulane players and their captain, John Lombard. The Tulanians likewise were spurred on by a yell—T. L. Bayne's own brainchild:

> Rah! Rah! Rah!
> Sis! Boom! Bah!
> Rah! Rah! Tulane!

Judging from newspaper accounts, no friendlier competition ever existed. LSU was given the privilege of naming the referee, and it designated Coates. Whereupon Tulane named Bayne umpire. There were two coin tosses in those days: LSU won the choice of goals, and Tulane won possession.

With Tulane in possession at midfield, Bayne's brother Hugh, a tackle, scored on the second play, a 30-yard run from the flying wedge behind the blocking of 220-pound Walter Castenado. Hugh was pushed and shoved across the foot-wide goal line by his teammates and got a bit of lime in his eyes, which no doubt caused him to miss the try for the extra point—or points. In 1893 teams were credited with four points for

Six of the first eleven. LSU's starting lineup for the 1893 game included, left to right, team captain Ruffin G. Pleasant (later governor), James Beard, Samuel Marmaduke Dinwidie Clark, Jr., Aaron Prescott, his brother Willis, and Edwin F. Gayle. Gayle, a Lake Charles attorney, is the only member of the team now living.

a touchdown, two for a goal after, four for a field goal and two for a safety. Bayne's touchdown gave Tulane a 4–0 lead, and by the time the two 45-minute halves had come to an end the host team had run up seven touchdowns and three conversions for a 34–0 victory. LSU, reflecting its inexperience, displayed a "wedge" that was "more showy than effective" and its deepest penetration—inside the Tulane 10—was halted by a fumble. For a picture of Gay Nineties football, ponder this goal line stand by LSU. Tulane recovered on the LSU 4-yard line and called for a wedge, whereupon the teams struggled back and forth for two minutes before referee Coates declared "down." Tulane had three more cracks at the goal, thanks to an LSU infraction, but wound up two yards shy of a score. Since the word "down," and not the halting of forward progress, determined the end of a play, the four Tulane plays consumed four minutes. Before the game, the players passed the word: "Don't stop if you hear a whistle—it may be a locomotive."

Both teams wore nondescript outfits with mismatched jerseys and stockings of various colors. Those who had $1.25 showed up in football breeches which were shapeless because of padding at the knees and hips. Some wore vests, tightly laced in front, which fit snugly from throat to hips. On some players, jersey sleeves alone were visible and these were padded at the elbows with leather shields. Players wore heavy-soled shoes and stockings over which were leather shields to protect the shin bones.

All this—and those bushy pompadours which men in the rush-line delighted in poking into the eyes of the opposition. A story is told that

one player (not from LSU or Tulane) wore a head guard of metal pointed in front, which fit over his head like a wig. He enjoyed chipping pieces out of his opponent's head until the other fellow complained to the referee about the concealed weapon.

No one employed any underhanded tactics in the LSU-Tulane inaugural. Tulane made no secret of the fact it had picked up several players from the Southern Athletic Club; LSU had a "ringer" in the person of Professor Morgan, who tripped and sprained his knee. Captain Pleasant was injured in the first half and was borne heroically from the field. A Tulane end was "knocked senseless." Hugh Bayne, who was having a field day, also was injured early but managed to stick it out until half time. He then left the ball park and took a carriage back to Tulane to attend a law lecture. LSU's offensive star was a 155-pound halfback by the name of Edwin Gayle who scared the Tulane crowd by almost breaking loose on several occasions. With the exception of the 220-pound Castenado, 155 pounds was about average, as these starting lineups for the 1893 game indicate:

Tulane	Position	LSU
Robelot (135)	LE	S. M. D. Clark (165)
Bayne (160)	LT	A. Brian (170)
Foster (160)	LG	E. A. Scott (175)
Castenado (220)	C	W. C. Smedes (190)
Guthrie (170)	RG	J. A. Roane (175)
Porter (150)	RT	A. Prescott (165)
Potts (150)	RE	W. C. Bates (165)
Lombard (145)	QB	R. G. Pleasant (150)
Lewis (135)	LH	J. Beard (155)
Johnson (150)	RH	E. F. Gayle (155)
Romeyn (150)	FB	W. B. Prescott (160)

LSU cadets who showed up for football practice in the fall of 1894. William C. Smedes holds the ball marked "LSU." Standing behind him, arms folded, is S. M. D. Clark, later named captain of the varsity. James Beard is stretched out on the ground in the left foreground, and Sam Dupree, Raphael Broussard, and Aaron Prescott stand third, fourth, and fifth from the left on the back row. The photograph on the opposite page, taken later the same year, shows the change from short military haircuts to the long hair that players of that era wore.

The editor of the Baton Rouge *Daily Advocate,* obviously disappointed if not surprised by the outcome of the game, wrote: "We do not blame the Tulane corps, nor do we for an instant charge them with unfairness, as our boys were aware of the conditions existing there before they consented to the game. But the game was not between similarly equipped teams, and a triumph on the part of our boys would have been the most remarkable victory in the history of athletics. And for the following reasons: Few of our boys have yet attained the majority—most of them being rather below than above eighteen. They come from the country, and until very recently have never seen a game of football played, and besides this, their military duties at the University have rendered it impossible for them to practice the game as much as is necessary to insure a good game." *

---

* The LSU catalogue for the 1893–94 session shows that the players listed in the starting lineup for the first LSU game were indeed "from the country." The following appear in the Roster of Cadets: Samuel Marmaduke Dinwidie Clark, Jr., of West Baton Rouge Parish; Alexis Brian, Grant Parish; Edwin Allen Scott, East Feliciana Parish; William Crosby Smedes, Vicksburg, Mississippi; James Andrew Roane, Lincoln Parish; Aaron Prescott, St. Landry Parish; William Cage Bates, Baton Rouge; Ruffin Goldstone Pleasant, Union Parish; James Beard, East Carroll Parish; Edwin Franklin Gayle, Pointe Coupee Parish; and Willis B. Prescott, St. Landry Parish. The complete list of players appears in the appendix.

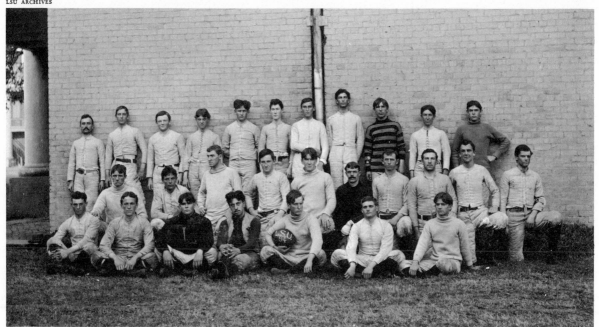

From these players the 1894 team was drawn. Left to right in the back row, John T. Westbrook, W. S. Slaughter, J. C. Conner, unidentified, Alexis Brian, W. J. Lewis, unidentified, William Nelken, Sam Dupree, unidentified, unidentified. Center row, E. A. Scott, unidentified, C. G. Young, Gordon B. Nicholson, Charles E. Chavanne, James Beard (who has grown a mustache since the picture on the opposite page was taken), L. A. Quirk, J. R. Salassi, Aaron Prescott, Raphael Broussard. Front row, J. E. Snyder, Hughes Arrighi, William C. Smedes, Coach Albert T. Simmonds (wearing Yale jacket), team captain Sam Clark, W. B. Mullins, Harry Gamble. Gamble, the last surviving member of the team, supplied the identification.

Coates was philosophical about his team's 34–0 whipping. "Barring the fact that we lost," he said, "everyone had a good time. We came home very tired, resolved to do better next year." The LSU special was hardly on its way back to Baton Rouge when he and several other school officials saw the need to hire a professional coach, and it wasn't long before A. P. Simmonds, an end on Yale's 1893 team, was engaged, following contributions of $300 from the university's cadet corps and a host of supporters.

There were some in Baton Rouge who had their doubts, however. The *Daily Advocate*, editorializing late in 1893 and again in the fall of 1894, said that the game of football should go. "Students," it said, "are sent to college to be educated into refined and intellectual gentlemen, and not to choose between having their necks broken in a hurly burly scramble, or escaping that, to be turned out at the end of four years burly and accomplished bruisers." The newspaper deplored "the spectacle of young men fracturing their shins, getting their jaws broken, their noses spread out all over their faces, and a half dozen ribs knocked clear through on the other side . . . ." The game, it said, "instead of being encouraged by our institutions of learning, should be strictly prohibited."

Even then the LSU team was practicing for its opening game of the 1894 season. The new coach whipped his 28-man squad into shape on LSU's first football field, located on the old parade grounds south of the Pentagon Barracks. When the team was ready to leave for its opener with the Natchez Athletic Club, Simmonds let it be known he was expecting "great things" in a brief talk to the cadets who lined the levee as the players walked aboard the steamboat *Royal*. As it developed, the trip was more eventful than the game. The *Royal* ran aground at Ford's Crossing, twenty miles below Natchez, and the steamer *Natchez* had to go to the rescue. As a result the LSU team arrived November 30, a day behind schedule. But captain Sam Clark and his men showed no ill effects from seven hours on the sandbar as they hung up a 36–0 victory.

The *Daily Advocate* assured its readers that "while the game was a strong one there was an entire absence of any display of brutality, and consequently there were no casualties . . . ."

Pride over the school's first win was short lived. Three days later, in its home opener, LSU suffered a 26–6 defeat at the hands of a more experienced Ole Miss team in a game that had one unique twist. When it was apparent that Ole Miss had it sewed up, Simmonds asked for, and received, permission to play in the LSU backfield. He proceeded to climax an 80-yard drive with a neat 45-yard run for LSU's only touchdown, a gallop which brought applause from Ole Miss players as well as LSU fans. When LSU closed out its three-game schedule with a 30–0 win over Centenary, Simmonds believed he had the nucleus of a good team for 1895.

He had no trouble getting his boys ready for the 1895 opening game, an October 26 date with Tulane. Under Coates, an admitted amateur at coaching, it was said that some members of the 1893 team who failed to receive a passing grade in chemistry had gone after him instead of the ball during practice. It was different with the swivel-hipped Simmonds. He was a taskmaster who taught his players not to tackle a man around the throat but around the legs. The fact that his squad was down to sixteen indicated he may have employed "survival of the fittest" methods.

Whatever the method, it worked. A crowd of 1,500 showed up at the parade grounds in Baton Rouge for the Tulane game and stayed to watch LSU avenge its 1893 defeat. With Simmonds' first string going the distance (at the time it meant they were 70-minute men), LSU wiped out an early 4–0 Tulane lead and came back with two touchdowns of its own to win, 8–4. A 16–6 victory over an improved Centenary, followed by a 12–6 win over Alabama—the school's first major victory—climaxed an unbeaten season. Fullback Sam Lambert, with two touchdowns, was the hero against Bama, a game played in the morning to allow the cadets to catch an afternoon train to the Atlanta Exposition.

The 1896 season, which found A. W. Jeardeau of Harvard inheriting Simmonds' coaching job, was eventful for more than one reason. The team swept through six games unbeaten, it won from Tulane on a forfeit, it scored a disputed 6–0 victory over the Southern Athletic Club, and it was the first team to bear the nickname "Tigers." As Coates related it, the name "Tigers" was logical if only because it was the custom to name university teams after animals—there were Tigers at Princeton, Bulldogs at Yale, Lions at Columbia. But there was more to it than that. During the Civil War, the Louisiana Tigers, composed of New Orleans Zouaves and Donaldsonville Cannoneers, had distinguished themselves in the Valley of the Shenandoah. So "Tigers" was a natural choice.

By 1896 football was beginning to undergo a change. The flying wedge was not allowed on the kickoff and other mass momentum was restricted. The basic formation was the old-fashioned T in which the quarterback squatted low behind the center, bent deeply at the knees and waist. In fact, he was so close to the ground he could look the center in the face. Plays were called by either numbers or letters, and the snap signal usually was the opening of the quarterback's fingers or an extension of his hands. The closest thing to a forward pass was the "quarterback kick," in which the quarterback dropped a soft punt into a certain area, timing it so one of his teammates would arrive as the ball hit the ground, could scoop it up and take off. Since it was a free ball—the

The 1890's football player in closeup. Phil Huyck, Sam Gourrier, and Ned Scott, like other LSU players of the period, donned sweaters, quilted pants, and shin guards and struck a pose in the studio of Lytle the photographer. The piece of equipment Huyck and Gourrier wear around their neck was apparently a nose guard.

opposition could advance it too—the quarterback kick was a dangerous play and was used sparingly. Guards and tackles, as well as backs, carried the ball and it was common to see runners pop through the line aided by teammates trying to push them free. Frequent also were head-on clashes of opposing backs with men on the rush-line, who sometimes began scrapping before the ball was snapped. The quarterback barked out his signals the minute the ball was dead, and his players lined up hurriedly in an effort to have the ball snapped before all of the opposition was onsides. What occurred then was a continuous flow of inelegant action.

After opening with a 46–0 win over Centenary, Jeardeau's 1896 Tigers invaded New Orleans for the third game in the Tulane series. With Tulane ahead 2–0 in the middle of the second half, a player named Brooke entered for the host team and the LSU captain, Ned Scott, immediately lodged a protest. He claimed the substitute was George Brooke, a star from Pennsylvania who was ineligible. Tulane maintained it was Brooke's brother. Scott said he would take his team off the field if Brooke remained in the game. Tulane captain Lou Genella refused to take Brooke out, claiming Brooke was eligible because he planned to enter law school shortly. The game officials upheld LSU's protest, declaring the game forfeited to the Tigers by a 6–0 score. When play was suspended, LSU had marched eighty-two yards to the Tulane 4-yard line.

The controversy was still raging when LSU returned to New Orleans a month later for a game with the Southern Athletic Club. Fullback Ed Robertson, high scorer for the season with forty points, scored the game's only touchdown to hand the club a 6–0 defeat, its first by a college team.

The big story of 1897 and 1898 can be told in two words—yellow fever. Because of an epidemic in 1897, LSU did not play its first game until December 20 when it handed the Montgomery, Alabama, Athletic Club a 28–6 beating. On January 8, 1898, a touring University of Cincinnati club downed the Tigers by a score of 26–0 in a game in which guard Phil Huyck sparkled in defeat. Huyck played so well that he was invited to return north with the Cincinnati team, but he declined the offer. No doubt prompted by the yellow fever, Jeardeau departed following the Cincinnati game, and the following fall team captain E. A. Chavanne of Lake Charles became head coach. A 37–0 victory over Tulane was all there was to the 1898 season, but it was enough to keep the Tigers talking for a year. LSU ran 111 plays from scrimmage, gained 726 yards, and didn't punt once. Tulane had the ball only on kickoffs and recovered fumbles.

John P. Gregg, a Wisconsin graduate, took over the LSU coaching

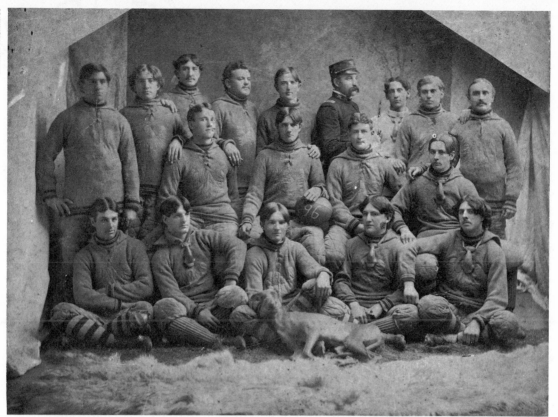

The 1896 team. Standing, from left, E. A. Chavanne, Wiltz Ledbetter, Justin Daspit, F. H. Schneider, James Harp, Lieutenant C. C. Gallup (commandant of cadets), Duncan P. Staples, A. T. Barbin, John T. Westbrook. Center row, Hughes Arrighi, E. A. Scott, Phil Huyck, W. S. Slaughter. Front row, George Schoenberger, Sam Gourrier, J. S. Atkinson, Gordon B. Nicholson (son of LSU President James W. Nicholson), Armand Daspit.

reins in 1899 and found himself with only three lettermen and a schedule that called for road games against Texas and Texas A & M within a three-day period. At the time, this was not an unusual schedule, but LSU simply wasn't up to it. Sewanee, the Southern champion, made history in 1899 by defeating five teams (Texas, Texas A & M, Tulane, LSU, and Ole Miss) in six days. The Tennessee Mountaineers, who took Sunday off between a 22–0 win over Tulane and a 34–0 conquest of LSU, held all of their victims scoreless. For Gregg's Tigers, it was just the opposite. They bowed to Ole Miss, 11–0, in the opener, were defeated by Sewanee, and then departed for the swing through Texas. On November 30 a heavy Texas team crushed them, 29–0, at Austin, and on December 2 Gregg's battered forces were no match for the Aggies, who ground out a 52–0 victory, the largest score run up on an LSU team to that time.

With the Tulane showdown approaching, the only points LSU scored (a 48–0 win over Lake Charles High in an exhibition game en route to Texas) didn't show up on the record. Tulane, however, looked like an even match. Like the Tigers, the Goats, as the Tulane team was

The 1897 team. Back row, from left, unidentified, Leopold Kaffie, Coach Allen W. Jeardeau, Thomas L. Sherburne, unidentified. Center row, W. S. Slaughter, G. B. LeSueur, E. A. Chavanne, team captain E. A. "Ned" Scott, Phil Huyck, John T. Westbrook. Front row, unidentified, Justin Daspit, W. B. Chamberlin, Gordon B. Nicholson, Armand Daspit.

called at the time, were winless and scoreless: on paper it appeared that neither team could win. But, to Tulane's dismay, everything jelled for Gregg's previously hapless club. The Tigers thrilled a crowd of 2,000 at the LSU parade grounds with the manner in which they handled a muddy football and executed double and triple pass plays. The final score of 38–0 didn't tell the whole story. LSU, sparked by the running of Huyck at tackle and the blocking of Ben Chamberlin, ground out 639 yards from scrimmage and held Tulane to 50. In the second half, the cadets ran seventy-seven consecutive plays, interrupted only by Tulane's kickoffs, and scored four touchdowns. Tulane didn't run a single play from scrimmage in the final half. This offensive display might have surpassed the 726 yards run up the previous year had not the game been called on account of darkness with nine minutes remaining. At the time, college teams were playing 25-minute halves, ten minutes shorter than the ones during the pre-1894 era.

E. A. Chavanne took over as coach for the second time in 1900 (he also served as commandant of cadets), and it fell to him to be linked with the greatest form reversal in LSU history. The Tigers opened the season with a 70–0 victory over Millsaps, a game highlighted by ten goals after a touchdown by O. W. McNeese. Three weeks later Chavanne took the team to Jackson, Mississippi, for a return match with Millsaps where it suffered a stunning 6–5 defeat. McNeese scored the LSU touchdown (worth five points) but missed the extra point. Between these two unusual clashes with Millsaps, the Tigers took a 29–0 whipping from Tulane and this time it was LSU which was saved by darkness from a more lopsided beating. The Tigers had possession of the ball only three times and managed to gain only 36 yards. Tulane, on the other hand, ran up 380 yards and scored five touchdowns.

MARIE CHAVANNE

Two of the early coaches, one homegrown, one imported. Edmond A. Chavanne, right, who had played for LSU in 1896 and 1897 and doubled as team captain and coach in 1898, coached the Tigers in 1900. He was succeeded in 1901 by W. S. Borland of Allegheny College, left.

Chavanne was succeeded in 1901 by another recruited coach, W. S. Borland of Allegheny, who was to remain for three years. Borland organized the scrub team and introduced a measure of discipline which resulted in a 5–1 record in his first year. A 28–0 loss to Auburn was the only blemish on an otherwise spotless record, although the 11–0 "victory" over Tulane was the result of a controversial forfeit. The Goats, using a player named Crandell whose participation was protested by the Tigers, scored three touchdowns, a point after, and a field goal for what would have been a 22–0 win. However, an LSU protest filed at the annual meeting of the Southern Intercollegiate Athletic Association

(SIAA) was upheld, and the 11–0 score went into the records. LSU-Tulane relations were suspended for two years as a result.

Borland's team fashioned a 6–1 mark in 1902 and laid claim to a conference co-championship. Actually, the 27–5 loss to a strong Vanderbilt team provided the most historic moment. The Tiger points came on a remarkable 45-yard field goal—a dropkick—by fullback Henry E. Landry, an LSU record. Previously, Landry's touchdown in the last minutes of an abbreviated 35-minute morning game gave the Tigers a 5–0 upset win over Texas, which defeated Sewanee and Oklahoma. In the final game, an 11–0 win over Alabama in Tuscaloosa, Landry turned in a gilt-edged performance. He won LSU scoring honors with twenty-eight points, a low figure that reflected new rules which further limited mass-formation plays. LSU laid claim to a co-championship on the strength of its win over Texas, conqueror of Sewanee, which in turn defeated Vanderbilt, 11–5.

In 1903 an iron-man schedule that called for four games in ten days wrecked Borland's final season at LSU. The Tigers had a 4–0 record and were unscored on when they invaded Starkville for a November 7 game with Mississippi State. State won, 11–0, on superior line play. Two days later, the Tigers were in Tuscaloosa for a game with Alabama. Bama won, 18–0. Two days after this, the Tiger team visited Auburn and came away a 12–0 loser. Then it returned to Baton Rouge for a November 16 meeting with Cumberland. The beefy Mountaineers from Lebanon, Tennessee, scored a crushing 41–0 decision and went on that year to share Southern honors. The final nail in Borland's coffin was an 11–0 defeat by the University of Mississippi in a game played in New Orleans. In the early stages of the game the Tigers drove seventy-five

Action shot of the 1902 game with Auburn.

LSU's 1905 team: Tulane launched an investigation. Standing left, Coach Dan Killian.

yards despite four fumbles. A fifth fumble, however, stopped them on the Rebel 5-yard line, a fitting climax to a frustrating campaign.

The 1904 season introduced Dan A. Killian, a Michigan alumnus, to the LSU coaching scene and was the occasion for the resumption of relations, at least temporarily, with the Tulane Goats. The game was played on November 19 before a crowd of 5,000 in New Orleans. In an interesting twist, Tulane was responsible for selling all of the tickets, LSU for collecting them at the gate. Admission was increased from fifty cents to one dollar—an indication that football was on its way. The game was a real thriller, with Tulane blocking a punt on the LSU 1-yard line for the only score in a 5-0 ball game. LSU marched fifty-three yards in the final moments and was on the Tulane 9-yard line when the game ended.

The Smith brothers furnished the big football news of 1905. After LSU scored a 5-0 win over the Goats, Tulane launched an investigation of Clarence and V. E. "Bob" Smith, a pair of imported halfbacks. A special *Olive and Blue* edition gave its version of the odd set of circumstances resulting in the Smiths' matriculation at the Ole War Skule: "LSU is blessed with two very fast backs from Albion, Michigan, who learned football through five years of hard work. They are farmers and manufacturers of potato crates who wanted to make a trip this winter. They came down to lend assistance to their friend, coach Killian. They were thinking of a trip west but Killian sold them on Mardi Gras so they came to Baton Rouge a week after Killian arrived. The Smiths will be back in Albion in the spring when the shipping of potatoes begins."

Tulane preferred official charges at a meeting of the SIAA in 1905, not only against the Smiths but against E. E. Weil, a tackle, and ends C.

J. McNaspy and John Griffith. Griffith, it was charged, came south with the Smiths. Weil was said to have played at Ruston, and McNaspy at a college out west. The SIAA referred the case to the association's vice-president for Louisiana, Mississippi and Texas, who happened to be Colonel T. D. Boyd of LSU. The protest was not allowed.

Football reached an important milestone in 1906. There had been 18 football deaths and 149 injuries during the 1905 season, and a ground-swell developed for a crackdown on the brutality of the game. When President Theodore Roosevelt, a champion of physical fitness, saw a photograph of Swarthmore lineman Bob Maxwell, black, blue, and bloody from a whipping at the hands of Pennsylvania, he threatened to ban football by presidential edict if steps were not taken to curb roughness.

It was because of the President's feelings that the first meeting of the National Collegiate Athletic Association's Football Rules Committee was held in New York on January 2, 1906. Out of it came four significant decisions: (1) a "neutral zone," the length of the ball, was created between the opposing lines; (2) a minimum of six men was required on the line of scrimmage; (3) first-down yardage was raised from five to ten yards; (4) the forward pass was legalized, but with restrictions.

Because the ball could be thrown forward only when the passer was five yards or more, laterally, from the center of the scrimmage line, the field was marked off lengthwise to help officials enforce the rule. The forward pass could be recovered once it was touched by a receiver. If it went out of bounds, it was awarded to the defensive team when it left the field. If caught behind the goal, it was a touchback and gave the defensive team a free kick from its end zone. One unusual note in the early days of the forward pass was that the receiver, and not the passer, utilized a ring of interferers so that he could catch the ball, usually thrown on a high arc like a punt. Establishment of a neutral zone cut down on the bloodshed while the six-men-on-the-line minimum further reduced mass plays and helped do away with "tackles back" and "ends back" formations.

LSU introduced the forward pass in its 1906 opener against the Monroe, Louisiana, Athletic Club October 19 on the parade grounds. In the first period, quarterback J. C. Muller caught a punt and, instead of running, tossed a pass to B. B. Handy. Seemingly, this was contrary to the rules then in force but the play was allowed nonetheless. This marked the uninspiring end of Killian's three-year coaching career. However, he left behind some pretty good football players who, as later events proved, needed only better organization, inspiration, and an athlete of some stature to rally around. LSU got one the following year.

'Doc was the hub
and we were the spokes'

1907–1909

HIS name was George Ellwood Fenton, but they called him "Doc" because his dad was a singer who traveled with one of the old-time Indian medicine shows selling patent medicine. The legend surrounding LSU's first football great has grown with the passage of time and, thanks to the chorus of superlatives from those who saw the artist perform, it will never die.

"I saw Jim Thorpe," says LSU President Emeritus Troy Middleton, "but Doc Fenton was better."

"Doc could do more with a football than a monkey can with a coconut," said teammate Marshall H. "Cap" Gandy. "He was the greatest field general who ever donned a uniform, a fellow who could punt on the run and catch the football one-handed. Doc was the hub of our team and we were the spokes."

"I believe Doc got more enjoyment out of football than anyone I've ever seen," said J. E. Thonssen, a fan of LSU from 1893 until the day he died.

Doc Fenton died February 8, 1968, but even in the twilight of his life he retained the twinkle in his blue eyes. His blond hair was gone, but he still had the look of a man hardened by athletic combat and one who thrived on competition. His athletic career began at St. Michael's College in Canada, where he gained some measure of fame for his soccer ability but gave no indication of future football talent. He later arrived at Mansfield Normal in his home state of Pennsylvania, unheralded yet bent on a career in athletics.

"The day I got to Mansfield," said Doc, "I put my name in for a backfield position. All of those were filled, so I had to change it to end so I wouldn't get left out." Fenton played end for four years and then got

The first of the LSU football greats—Doc Fenton.

an offer to play for Mississippi State. "A brother of a fellow called 'Big' Furman—he was one of my Mansfield teammates—was scheduled to leave to coach at State for the 1907 season," said Fenton. "I was one of the five men off our team he recruited to go with him and I was all for the idea."

This was the situation as Mansfield closed out its 1906 season. At that final game, however, a tall man with well groomed hair and a flower in his lapel was on hand to watch Mansfield play. "After the game," recalled Doc, "he came up and introduced himself. 'My name is Wingard—Edgar Wingard,' he told me. 'I'm the new coach at Louisiana University. How would you like to go to a Southern school?' " The direct approach impressed Fenton as much as Wingard's manners. He looked more like a preacher than a football coach, but he had an air of confidence about him which, to Fenton, spelled success.

"I told him about my offer from Mississippi State, but he told me not to make up my mind too quickly," said Doc.

Wingard began writing to Fenton regularly, and one spring day Fenton arrived at his home in Scranton, Pennsylvania, and found Mrs. Wingard talking to his mother. "As a speaker," said Fenton, "his wife was just as impressive as he was. She sure impressed my mother. Before she left, I promised to go down to Baton Rouge for a visit."

Wingard wasn't interested in the 165-pound Fenton alone. He also had his eye on John Seip, a 6-foot, 1-inch, 180-pound end from nearby Susquehanna, Wingard's alma mater. Thus, in the summer of 1907, Fenton and Seip headed south for a place they had never heard of on a visit. "I remember we stayed at the Grouchy Hotel," said Fenton. "Baton Rouge was a nice little town, but I have to be honest and say the thing that really sold me was the nickel beers. We had blue laws back home and Wingard was quick to point out they had blue laws in Starkville [Mississippi] too. Maybe he figured on the nickel beers all along. He did know that at Mansfield I had to promise not to chew tobacco after authorities found some juice in a bowl in my room. What it all added up to was Baton Rouge represented a nice change-of-pace."

When Mississippi State learned of Fenton's decision to enter LSU, "Big" Furman told Wingard he was going to prove Fenton was illegally recruited. "Luckily," said Doc, "I kept all of the letters Furman wrote me. They contained some mighty interesting offers. When Wingard read a few to Furman to refresh the Mississippi State coach's memory, he decided to lay off. The next year, State questioned my eligibility again. Furman had gotten his hands on some of the letters Wingard wrote to me when I was at Mansfield. Wingard played it cool. He and Furman figured they could wreck each other so they decided to trade letters—and there went the evidence."

Wingard was a graduate of Susquehanna. Although he claimed to have made quite a reputation as a player, there is no record of it. Once he became anchored at LSU, however, his coaching methods began to make quite an impression. He knew he had a stemwinder in Fenton, and he believed he had the raw material with which to build a pretty good ball club. His players were bigger than those on most Southern teams; not only that but they had the speed to go with the size.

Wingard leaned to the wide-open game and, in all of his practices, did everything he could to accentuate agility. Because of numbers and because he didn't want to leave the game on the practice field, his sessions were thorough but light. Sooner or later, the squad was split into sides for a game of soccer, to improve footwork and agility. Since linemen at the time could carry the football as much as backs, if the coach so desired, Wingard decided to play Fenton at an end. The new recruit gave an indication of what was to come when, in the 1907 opener against Louisiana Industrial Institute of Ruston, he ripped off a 90-yard scoring run, only to have it nullified by a penalty. After three weeks of practice, Wingard had Fenton and Seip at the ends, O. H. Noblet and Cap Gandy at the tackles, Willie Hillman and W. M. Lyles at the guards and R. L. "Big" Stovall at center. In the backfield there was two-year letterman S. W. Brannon at quarterback, C. C. Bauer and R. F. "Little" Stovall at the halves, and W. J. Hamilton at fullback.

Fenton returned all punts and could whip around and take reverses on plays from scrimmage. He did most of the passing (Wingard liked to put the ball in the air), but restrictive measures—the passing team was penalized fifteen yards if one of its players failed to touch the ball before it hit the ground—limited the overhead game. This happened to LSU twice in the LII opener, so for the rest of the season Wingard banked on his outside attack and his double and triple laterals to generate most of the offense.

In an ill-fated swing through Texas that season, superior Longhorn power resulted in two second-half touchdowns and a 12–5 victory for Texas, and it was the same case two days later when A & M prevailed, 11–5. The Tigers, who used but one substitute, scored at the very end on a 20-yard run by Seip.

After a 57–0 rout of Howard College, Wingard's crew scored their first win over Arkansas, 17–12. LSU fans were so deliriously happy afterward that they hauled the players aboard carriages and paraded them through downtown Baton Rouge. LSU had what was called a "Rooters Club," which did its best to whip the crowd into a frenzy; this wasn't too difficult since most of the onlookers followed the action by walking up and down the field.

Wingard could see the improvement in his team's next two victories—23–11 over Mississippi State and 23–0 over Ole Miss—but an invasion of Mobile for a meeting with Alabama produced a bitter 6–4 defeat. The Tigers had led by virtue of two safetys when the Crimson Tide turned an onside kick into an 85-yard touchdown. A week later highly regarded Baylor, the bookmakers' choice, invaded Baton Rouge, but Wingard had the Tigers rebounding. The game's opening play was the keynote. Fenton caught the kickoff and, instead of running with the ball, sent a 60-yard punt spiraling downfield. The Baylor safety, taken by surprise, fumbled the ball and "Little" Stovall picked it up and had the first touchdown in seventeen seconds: final score, 48–0.

That game was to have ended the 1907 season. However, circumstances decreed otherwise. Looking back, it is difficult to imagine how LSU's precedent-setting game against Havana University on Christmas

Tigers in Havana: 1907 team poses on the field before game with the University of Havana. Left to right, line, O. H. Noblet, H. E. Baldwin, R. L. "Big" Stovall, W. M. Lyles, Marshall H. "Cap" Gandy, John J. "Bill" Seip, Doc Fenton. Backfield, B. B. Handy, R. F. "Little" Stovall, R. O. Gill, C. C. Bauer. Standing in rear, Coach Edgar Wingard, W. F. Ryan, H. C. Drew.

Day, in 1907, failed to touch off a second war with Spain. The appearance of the first American college team on foreign soil came at a time when the Cuban situation remained touchy in the wake of the Spanish-American war. "Remember the Maine!" had not yet died away. U.S. Army garrisons were still stationed at Camp Columbia, and U.S. Navy vessels rode at anchor in the harbor where the hull of the sunken battleship was visible above the water. To make matters more explosive, Havana was football mad, the university team having run roughshod over every service team—Army, Navy, or other—in the area. With no more fields to conquer, Cuban officials turned to the United States in search of a prestige opponent. They found a willing one in LSU, and the invitation extended to Wingard was readily accepted, although it meant keeping his club in training for an extra month.

The international match caught the fancy of Tiger fans in Baton Rouge who quickly raised $2,000 for Wingard and company to take with them to Havana to wager. Upon arrival, LSU quickly discovered that Cuba was looking forward to the Christmas Day game as a sort of crusade. Americans residing there told Wingard that Havana officials were scouring the island for the biggest and meanest physical specimens they could find, operating on the theory that football was a game

1907–1909 25

entirely of brute force. Wingard's biggest problem was not in bringing his 13-man squad to an emotional peak—that was easy—but in protecting the members of the team from homesick Americans who showered them with hospitality. It was said that whenever two Americans met in Cuba the custom was to have a friendly drink, ordinarily a daiquiri, and something to eat, usually *arroz con pollo* (a rich concoction of stewed chicken and saffron rice), neither of which was an ideal training table item.

For some reason not explained, University of Havana authorities, at the last moment, felt the game would prove a financial flop and backed out of the promotion, leaving a vacuum into which quickly stepped a group of speculators who proceeded to peddle sideline seats to Havana aristocrats for ten dollars per ticket. Just as the 1893 Tulane-LSU inaugural in New Orleans had become a social event, so did the LSU-Havana match fourteen years later. Beyond this, it also attracted government and consular officials to say nothing of every United States soldier and sailor in the area.

It was the large cheering section of American servicemen—and their inflammatory yell—which made the occasion a possible powder keg. Before the game the chant began:

> Lick the Spicks, Kill the Spicks
> Rah! Rah! Rah! Louisiana!

When Wingard's 13-man "light brigade" ran onto the field for pre-game warmups, they noticed an odd sight on the Cuban bench—a

Flags fly over Almendares Park as Tigers play University of Havana.

LSU at the Havana goal line. The final score was 57–0.

number of large glass demijohns filled with wine. Every now and then one of the Cuban players, who were as large as advertised, would run over and take a swig of wine. Center of attention was a 300-pounder named A. C. Infante-Garcia who, it was reported, had been brought in especially to handle W. M. Lyles, the 200-pound LSU guard. Just before the opening whistle, Fenton gave Lyles a tip. "Hit that guy in the stomach with your head," Doc told him, "and he's done for."

The crowd of 10,000—the speculators inherited a gold mine—had hardly been seated comfortably when, on the first play from scrimmage, Lyles rammed his shoulder into the midriff of Infante-Garcia. Fenton chuckled when he told what happened. "The big guy spouted wine like an artesian well," he said. "I give you my word. We nearly had to swim to get out of there." No one was more surprised than Lyles, whose confidence skyrocketed. "Well, I'll be damned," he said. "Let's go to work." The sight of the supine 300-pounder touched off a 56–0 rout—ten touchdowns at five points each and six conversions. The home team never threatened.

W. F. "Pat" Ryan, an end on the 1907 team, said: "Every time we made a touchdown you'd have thought there was a flock of blackbirds flying across the field. Those sailors from the *Paducah* and the *Dubuque* would toss their blue hats in the air and chant their 'lick the spicks' battle cry." Fenton's incredible broken-field scampers and a 67-yard punt return by Seip kept the crowd enthralled. Because of Wingard's ingenuity, Fenton finished this and many another game with a jersey torn to shreds. It's possible Doc pioneered the tear-away jersey because, before every game, Wingard would soak Doc's woolen shirt in a mild acid solution to weaken the fabric, making Fenton a tough man to grab above the waist.

That night Havana was a madhouse. Wingard lifted curfew. Champagne flowed. Americans spent money on the players like it was going out of style. Homes were thrown open. Exclusive clubs feted them. The players' gray skull caps with the "L" on the front brought ten dollars each as souvenirs.

Years ago Doc Gandy (a native of Sabine Parish, Louisiana, he had gone on to become a veterinarian in Baton Rouge) recalled a "second game" in Havana between Christmas and New Year's and, if his memory was accurate, there was no question about the charges of professionalism leveled against the 1908 team. "We found we could make twenty-five dollars apiece," said Gandy, "so we made up two teams from the two squads and played again. We only had thirteen, so we loaned Havana a couple of men. We still won it, something like 20–0."

Fenton, who had won the nickname "The Artful Dodger" in the United States, caught the fancy of Cuban fans who hailed him as *El Rubio Vaselino*—"the Vaselined redhead"—as tough to catch as the proverbial greased pig. The first of the Pennsylvania coal boys to make good set a new LSU record of ninety-four points and fourteen touchdowns. Not bad for a 165-pound end who could hit the ground with his shoulder, bounce up, and keep going.

LSU's conquest of Cuba provided the tonic to make 1908 a season of great expectations. Wingard not only retained the nucleus of his 1907 club but made three significant additions. The Smith brothers were back, having laid aside their potato crates in Michigan, and a Mansfield teammate of Doc Fenton's, 180-pound Mike Lally, came south at Fenton's urging. Wingard, whose driving tactics during practice belied his Calvin Coolidge looks, made one important shift. He moved Fenton from end to quarterback. When Wingard finally settled on his starting lineup, it looked like this:

Right End—John Seip (183)
Right Tackle—O. H. "Baby" Noblet (230)
Right Guard—A. J. "Tommy" Thomas (176)
Center—R. L. "Big" Stovall (145)
Left Guard—Willie Hillman (172)
Left Tackle—Marshall "Cap" Gandy (175)
Left End—R. F. "Little" Stovall (139)
Quarterback—G. E. "Doc" Fenton (165)
Left Half—Clarence Smith (178)
Right Half—Mike Lally (170)
Full back—V. E. "Bull" Smith (171)

Wingard provided what he claimed were "exact weights" when stories began circulating that the Tigers had one of the heaviest teams in the country. From the coach's figures, his starting club averaged 168 pounds. If the LSU team was not the heaviest, it was obviously one of the oldest. The twenty-one-year-old Fenton was the youngest player, and halfback Clarence Smith, oldest half of the brother entry, was twenty-seven. Bob (also called "Bull") Smith was twenty-four. The pair had spent 1907 working around Baton Rouge.

What did Fenton think about being shifted to quarterback? "I didn't like the idea at first," Doc admitted, "but coach Wingard told me if I'd try, I could go downtown and buy some clothes. So for a $70 haberdasher's bill, I was a quarterback for the rest of my career."

The shift of Fenton to quarterback meant Doc would handle the ball on all offensive plays (the early version of the T was still in vogue) and be a threat in either direction. Although the Tigers approached the 1908 season with better-than-average credentials, the offensive whirlwind that swept aside ten opponents was nonetheless surprising. Wingard relied heavily on the lateral pass and the improvisations of magician Fenton. It was nothing for the Tigers to pitch the ball backward four or five times in one play as is done today in touch football.

Jim Halligan, a pioneer football official who worked all of LSU's 1908 games, maintained until the day he died that it was the finest team ever to come out of the South. "They had the lateral pass down to perfection," he said. "All of the backs were big, fast, triple-threat men who handled a football like a basketball. Fenton's knack of kicking on the run was fantastic. All of them were masters of the change of pace, stiff arm, blocking on the run."

Halligan recalled one incident in the Mississippi State game when three defenders were converging on Fenton from different angles. "Doc stopped on a dime," said Halligan, "and the three men ran into one another. Two of them were out cold."

Tommy Thomas, the fire-eating guard, said it was Lally who helped turn Fenton into a 1908 scourge. "Lally was the greatest blocker I ever saw," said Thomas. "He never left his feet, but got the opposition out of the way with shoulder or hip blocks. He had no peer in the open field. He and Doc were a great pair because they seemed to read each other's mind without signals. It was something like mental telepathy. When the occasion called for it, they could pass to one another or kick to one another."

In Wingard's version of the T, the Tigers lined up strong right or strong left. Fenton's head rested against the center's rear as he barked signals. When LSU was strong right, the line would unbalance that way with the two halfbacks and fullback lining up Indian file behind the left guard, who had shifted over. In tough-yardage situations, the pet play was "tackle over tackle," a maneuver in which the husky Noblet pulled out and, with the four backs leading the way, followed his interference over Gandy's position.

When the students learned that Wingard had exhausted the athletic funds (his recruiting was expensive), they took up a collection for new uniforms. The game was beginning to come into its own. The first indication had been the construction in 1906 of bleachers, which seated about eighty, on one side of the LSU playing field. A check at the end of that season, according to Dr. Edwin Whitaker, a medical student of 1906 vintage, revealed that the paid attendance was about one thousand. This was due in part to the ladies, who became more daring and began attending games with male members of the family. For the most part, the student body stood in a circle around the roped-off field, while a few businessmen, taking time off, drifted in from the commercial district on Third Street and paid for the privilege of standing around.

The 1908 season proved to be a season of glory—and controversy—at LSU. Writers had referred to the fall of 1907 as the "Ringer Season" in Southern football, one which came close to sounding a death knell for the sport in this section. Many felt that the advent of "ringers" —imported players who were paid to do a job—was the result

Seip and Gandy: Two of the spokes.

of the mailed fist which the Vanderbilt Commodores held over Dixie. Desperate alumni groups sprang up and the money vaults opened. Ringers came south in increasing numbers and, although rules were set up to keep the game pure, the practice continued in one fashion or another until 1920.

There had been rumblings about the squad Wingard had assembled, but nothing officially reached print until his Tigers began blazing a path through a ten-game schedule, the likes of which Dixie had never seen. It all started the afternoon of October 3 in Baton Rouge when LSU opened its season against the Young Men's Gymnastic Club from New Orleans. It quickly became evident that this was no ordinary college team. Lally's knack of blocking for Fenton, the elusiveness and ball handling of both, the crunching power of Clarence Smith all made the opposition seem like amateurs, which many thought was exactly the case. The New Orleans club, primarily a group of seasoned players, couldn't get near the LSU goal and were unable to halt the repeated sweeps of Lally and Fenton. The final score was only 41–0 because each half was mercifully cut to fifteen minutes.

Jackson Barracks, an Army team from New Orleans, was the next victim, and the feature of this affair, which ended 81–5, was the touchdown by the losers, the only one scored on the Tigers all year. It came

MR. AND MRS. JOHN J. SEIP, JR.

 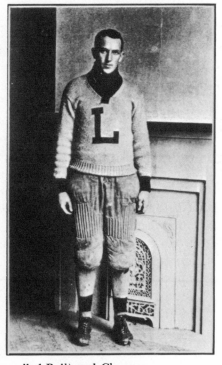

The Smith brothers—from left, Bob (also called Bull) and Clarence.

when the score was 48–0 and LSU was camped on the Barracks team's 5-yard line. On an attempted center buck, the ball popped into the air and into the arms of a fellow named Culligan. With a good head start, he streaked 105 yards (the field was 110 yards at the time) for what must be the longest fumble return in history. Lally's 60-yard scoring run was the longest of the afternoon for LSU, which again dazzled a crowd of about a thousand on its parade grounds.

Texas A & M, a contender in the Southwest, met the Tigers on October 17, 1908, before 1,500 fans in New Orleans' Pelican Park. For the price of a dollar (children under 14 fifty cents) fans could see a doubleheader—Baton Rouge High *vs* Boys' High of New Orleans in the opener and LSU *vs* A & M in the nightcap. After Baton Rouge shaded Boys' High, 6–5, Fenton and Lally went into what was by then a familiar act. One writer called Fenton "a marvel of speed who always kept his eye peeled for an opening." A 35-yard gallop by Lally wound up the scoring in a 26–0 victory, after which the A & M coach stated: "I regard LSU as one of the strongest elevens in the South." Wingard took the win in stride. "I expected LSU to win without too much difficulty," he said, "although the score was gratifying. The backs are working well but the line is not yet satisfactory."

A 55–0 rout of Southwestern Presbyterian University of Memphis was just the warmup Wingard wanted for a Halloween showdown with Auburn, then under the wing of the legendary Mike Donahue. In 1908 Donahue was in the fifth year of what was to be a glittering regime, and all of the preseason talk was whether Auburn, Vanderbilt, or Sewanee would win the Southern championship. The game was scheduled for Auburn, but during the week there was talk about moving it to either Mobile or Baton Rouge. A Mobile group was willing to put up a $375 guarantee! Baton Rouge made a $600 offer!

In Auburn it stayed, however, and when Wingard's Tigers left by train for the loveliest village of the plain so did a delegation of eight hundred rooters. "The game wasn't played on a football field," recalled Doc Fenton. "It was more like a sandhill. Fans were crowded all around the field and you had that hemmed-in feeling. A rope was the only thing that held them back." Up until this game LSU had been primarily a running team, chiefly to the outside. Wingard, feeling Auburn would concentrate on stopping the ground attack, sprang an aerial surprise. Fenton came out passing, and it wasn't long before he pitched a 25-yard completion and then one for thirty-five yards and a touchdown to Seip. Auburn got back into the game with a safety in the second quarter, but a third-quarter touchdown cinched it, 10–2.

Fenton retained a vivid picture of how Auburn got its two points. "I was kicking from behind my own goal," he said, "and an Auburn tackle broke through to block it. The ball was bouncing around so I picked it up and was getting ready to run it out of the end zone when a fan reached over the rope and cracked me over the head with a cane. It knocked me cold."

It was a rough game all around. Three Auburn players were knocked out and had to be carried off. Cap Gandy and an Auburn player got into a fist fight and both were ejected. "That Gandy had some temper," said Fenton, "and one of my jobs was to try and keep him cool. I forget what game it was, but he grabbed an opposing player one time and tossed him into an eight-piece string band just behind the ropes, busting most of the instruments. He was tossed out of that one too."

With LSU leading 5–2 at half time, Wingard pulled one of his psychological swifties. When the Tigers retired to a room near the field for their half-time talk, Wingard's wife was there to greet them. Her husband had been known for his rah-rah sermons, but Mrs. Wingard's plea for "dear old LSU" was said to be a real spellbinder. All during the talk, Auburn students pelted the tin roof with rocks. "That only made us madder," said Fenton. The ten points scored on Auburn (LSU muffed both extra-point tries) were the only points yielded by Mike Donahue's club that season.

When news of LSU's victory was flashed, people in other parts of the South were asking: "Who are these LSU people anyhow?" Grantland Rice, then writing for the Nashville *Tennessean*, felt he knew the answer. He wrote a by-line story charging the school with professionalism. Rice said he could prove that the Smith brothers, Seip, Fenton, Lally, and Gandy were imported and paid salaries to play football.

While Rice was firing his broadsides, Tulane came out with some charges of its own, charges growing out of attempts to arrange a Tulane-LSU game during the 1908 season. Whereas LSU wanted to play by the SIAA rules, Tulane insisted on a six-month rule: that is, no player entering school in the last six months would be eligible. Among others, this would eliminate the Smiths and Lally. When negotiations broke down, Tulane offered proof which, it claimed, showed how lax the SIAA was. It charged that Charles Cecil Bauer, a halfback on the 1907 team, was in fact Charles Ora Buser who had played for Wabash College in 1905. Tulane sent a detective to Buser's Indianapolis home and received a signed statement before witnesses that Wingard had lured Buser south as a "ringer." His name was changed, said Tulane, because he had played out his eligibility at Wabash. Pictures acquired from football magazines showed the Wabash Buser of 1905 and the LSU Bauer of 1907 to be one and the same. "Although this clearly violates an SIAA rule," said Tulane, "LSU remains in the good graces of the association."

Tulane also charged that John Seip had played at Susquehanna in 1906

The legendary 1908 team. Left to right, back row, Coach Edgar R. Wingard, W. M. Pollock, Bob Smith, R. O. Gill, Pat Ryan, J. A. Albright. Center row, mascot David Reymond, John J. Seip, Mike Lally, Doc Fenton, Clarence Smith, R. F. Stovall. Front row, O. H. Noblet, W. A. Hillman, R. L. Stovall, Tommy Thomas, and Cap Gandy.

and was brought south by Wingard when he took the LSU job. As for the Smiths, the charges brought by Tulane in 1905 (that the brothers had accompanied Coach Killian from Michigan) were revived. When a Tulane alumnus, who admitted he approached Wingard about taking the Tulane job in 1907, charged that Wingard promised him he "could bring in the players," the LSU coach wrote a letter in his defense. He said the Tulane man assured him: "I'll give you five hundred dollars more than you make at LSU to come to Tulane." Wingard didn't answer the charge about bringing in players but said: "If Tulane was willing to hire me away from LSU, it seems the only mistake I made was selecting LSU over Tulane."

And so the controversy waxed warm for the rest of the 1908 season. When "ringer" charges were submitted to the SIAA, LSU President

Thomas Duckett Boyd appeared at the December meeting and asked that a committee be appointed to investigate. The committee, making its report the following September, questioned the eligibility of only one man—Mike Lally. Lally, it seemed, had double-dipped during the summer. He had not only played baseball in Tonawanda, New York, but had also sung in a local movie house. When he was on the road with the team, he paid a local baritone to take his place. The fellow running the ball club paid Lally by check but, in this instance, Lally endorsed the check over to his singing substitute. It was this check that came before the SIAA and somewhat tarnished LSU's warbling halfback. As a result, Lally was dropped from the 1909 team. However, through some sleight of hand, he was later cleared of his professional stigma and was again eligible for football in 1910.

Meanwhile, Wingard's men proceeded to blaze through the last half of the 1908 schedule. Fenton and Lally blitzed Mississippi State, 50–0, and then reduced Baylor, a team which had beaten Tulane, 6–0, to rubble. Wingard's crew established an LSU record for a single game (actually two records), the 89–0 score and fifteen touchdowns. Based on the current point system, the final figures would have been 103–0. Apparently angry at the bad press his team was receiving, Wingard showed little mercy to the visitors from Waco. Fenton left the game for the first time after booting a field goal that made it 89–0.

The following week LSU made its second 1908 visit to New Orleans for what turned out to be the most controversial game of the season. At the time, controversy was the last thing LSU wanted, but the subsequent 32–0 victory over Haskell College of Kansas did nothing to improve U.S.-Indian relations. A crowd of three thousand, including baseball immortal Ty Cobb, was on hand at Heinemann Park on November 16, drawn by LSU's 7–0 record and the first appearance in New Orleans of the famed Indian school. Judging from reports, the officials made up for the scalping Sitting Bull handed General Custer at Little Big Horn. The Indians wept openly at the calls which repeatedly went against them, and it wasn't long before the game got out of hand.

Big Chief Baird got into a slugging match with "Little" Stovall, a fight that touched off a small riot. Throughout the second half LSU's 24-piece band and most of its nine hundred followers marched around the playing field. "Don't people here know how to run a football game?" asked Cobb of newsmen covering the event. Cobb, looking on from the sidelines, made repeated pleas of the officials to "open your eyes and watch those LSU men holding." Referee Jim Halligan later recalled it as "the roughest football game I ever saw." The other two officials were Tulane coach Joe Curtis and Joe Prichard of Vanderbilt, who became the LSU coach the following season. Said Prichard: "I said before the season LSU would have one of the best teams in the South. Now I'm sure of it."

LSU scored early after swarming over the Haskell ball carrier on the game's first play (one account said the Tigers were in on him before he got the ball). The Indians fumbled, LSU recovered and, several plays later, Clarence Smith faked a kick and ran for the first touchdown. The Tigers had a safe lead by half time and coasted home as penalty followed penalty. After the game, the Haskell coach said: "We were beaten because our men lacked the experience of the Louisiana veterans. I really don't care to say anything about our treatment by the officials. What's the use?"

The Tigers next went to Ruston to polish off Louisiana Industrial Institute in a methodical 22–0 manner. Wingard substituted freely because three days later LSU had a date in Little Rock with Arkansas, whose team was built around an Indian named Phillips, recruited from his happy hunting grounds in the Dakotas. As a crowd of five thousand looked on, a staunch Tiger defense frustrated the home team which couldn't muster a single threat. A 30-yard field goal was the only damage the Razorbacks could inflict in a 36–4 LSU victory. Fenton closed out in dazzling fashion, averaging forty-five yards on his punts, scoring two touchdowns, and booting six extra points. Lally contributed a sparkling 40-yard run which brought the crowd to its feet.

When the 1908 scores were totaled, they came to 442 points (508 by today's system) in 450 minutes of play. Amazingly, Wingard's outfit scored thirty-four times beyond the 20-yard line and eight times made gains of more than sixty yards. Fenton established four records: 125 points (132 converted), 6 field goals, 36 extra points and a 45-yard field goal from placement.

Because of the charges of professionalism, LSU was not the 1908 Southern champion of record. Auburn won the honor on the basis of a 6–0 victory over Sewanee, which tied Vandy, 6–6. Tiger fans, however, disregarded all of the "ringer" talk. Following the team's return home from Little Rock, there was a gala pep meeting, a civic banquet, and a night parade down Third Street led by Governor J. Y. Sanders, Mayor Wade Bynum and LSU President Boyd. Gold-handled umbrellas, gifts from Baton Rouge fans, went to Wingard and referee Halligan.

Twenty-five years later Doc Gandy, speaking at the silver anniversary celebration for the 1908 club, recalled the climate of the time. "The university was small then and the students close to the team," he said. "The town people supported us 100 percent and the alumni backed us in every possible way. We were taught the word 'Tiger' was a symbol to be respected, even feared . . . ."

Actually, the season ended on a note of sadness which had nothing to

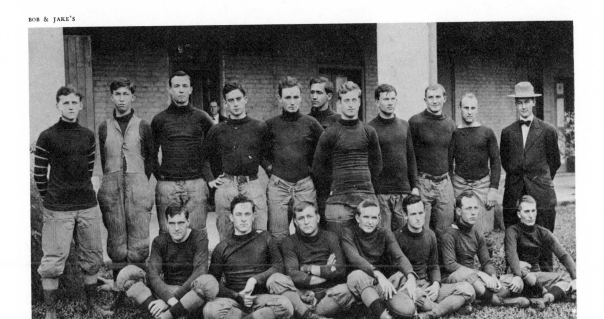

The 1909 team: End of an era. Seated, left to right, John J. Seip, W. M. Pollock, A. J. Thomas, R. L. Stovall, H. C. Drew, W. A. Hillman, R. F. Stovall. Standing, W. J. Phillips, M. A. Gosserand, J. O. Hall, A. M. McCollam, R. O. Gill, W. N. Falcon, Doc Fenton, L. R. Tilly, S. W. Brannon, Coach J. W. Mayhew, Manager James F. Broussard.

do with championships. Clarence Smith died on January 21 from ty-phoid fever contracted on the Arkansas trip. His body lay in state at Garig Hall and was escorted by six hundred cadets to the railroad station for the trip home to Michigan.

As the fall of 1909 approached, Edgar Wingard created the first big news when he announced his resignation to accept an assistant's job at Carlisle (producer of Jim Thorpe). The resignation came on the heels of a report by the SIAA charging Wingard with "grave irregularities" in the Buser-Bauer case (Will the real one please stand up?) and several others already cited. The association disqualified him from having any future connection with an SIAA team. So ended the stormy two-year regime of the man from Susquehanna—but the era of Doc Fenton had one more chapter.

When Vanderbilt's Joe Prichard stepped into the Wingard vacancy, he was banking on the added experience to maintain the momentum his predecessor had built. He knew Lally's absence would reduce Fenton's effectiveness, and he knew the loss of tackles like Gandy and Noblet would weaken the squad's defense. Prichard retained Wingard's wide-open attack and, relying heavily on Fenton, his team swept past its first three opponents in fairly impressive fashion—Jackson Barracks, 70–0; Ole Miss, 10–0; and Mississippi State, 15–0.

His moment of truth arrived October 30 in New Orleans, a historic date in that the LSU-Sewanee game was the only LSU game ever attended by a President of the United States. It was also the first time LSU ever changed coaches in midstream. For the Tigers, it was their first brush with Sewanee since 1899, when the Purple, a school with a student body of one hundred, burst upon the Southern scene. The Tennessee institution owed its advantage to a peculiar geographical and climatic condition. Because it was located in the mountains and the summer days were cool, Sewanee held classes during the summer (practiced football too, of course) and took its vacation during the winter months—after football. The fact that many Southern schools didn't open until October aided a team tuned by summer drills.

The Purple's superior execution was soon evident to the 6,000 fans who jammed Heinemann Park in anticipation of a good football game and a look at President William Howard Taft, on the last leg of a swing south. Sewanee's defense not only contained Fenton but the team's offense took it on a sustained drive for an early touchdown, to which was added a field goal (now reduced to three points) for a 9–0 halftime lead. "Big" Stovall put the Tigers back in the ball game when he blocked a Sewanee punt and turned it into a score. Fenton's kick made it 9–6, and there was lots of time left. Shortly afterward, play was suspended for five minutes as President Taft and his party entered—and it's a moot question as to whether this cooled off LSU. Taft stayed for only ten minutes of action but he watched the Purple put on a scoring drive—and score—just as he was leaving.

The 15–6 victory sent Sewanee on to an unbeaten season and another Southern championship. It sent Prichard, a preacher as well as a coach, to Africa as a missionary. Missionary work had long been uppermost in his mind, and the only reason he was serving as head coach, so the story goes, was because John W. Mayhew had no idea of either time or geography. A star halfback at Brown, Mayhew had been sent $150 by LSU alumni to pay his expenses to Baton Rouge. Everyone figured he would arrive before the season. However, instead of taking a train he went to New York and took a boat—a slow boat—headed for Galveston, Texas. Mayhew arrived in time to take over the club when both Sewanee and Prichard's missionary leanings combined to create a vacancy.

Since Prichard's resignation became effective after LSU defeated Louisiana Industrial, 23–0, a week after the Sewanee defeat, Mayhew's debut was against Arkansas; and it was less than spectacular. Doc Fenton hinted at the reason why the 1906 all-American halfback at Brown probably was not cut out for a coaching career. Said Fenton: "He spent his time trying to prove he was a better broken field runner than I was." Arkansas carved out a 16–0 victory in Memphis, and Tiger spirits had sunk so low that Mayhew luckily benefited from a scheduling mistake the following week. A 52–0 victory over Transylvania turned out to be an unexpected breather because, when negotiations were being conducted, LSU officials thought they were dealing with the University of Kentucky. Instead, they were corresponding with the State University of Kentucky, or Transylvania, at Lexington. Mayhew appreciated the error.

The curtain dropped on the Fenton era in Birmingham and it was John Seip, and not Doc, who got the headlines. The big end-turned-fullback cracked over for touchdowns in the first and second halves to spearhead a 12–6 upset, the Crimson Tide's only loss of the season. Fenton's only scoring was two extra points, but the slippery quarterback still wound up as 1909's leading scorer with fifty points. In three varsity seasons, Pennsylvania's—and Wingard's—gift to Tigertown scored thirty-six touchdowns and left a trail of bewildered tacklers. As Gandy put it, "Doc was the hub and we were the spokes."

'If we lose, I'll leave on a freight'

1910–1922

AFTER twinkletoed Doc Fenton stopped cutting capers, LSU alumni, accustomed to looking at football through rose-colored glasses, held to a perennial adage about the two great teams in LSU history—"1908 and next year."

"Next year" was a long time coming. The 1910–22 era produced some fine teams, but no unbeaten ones, and served mainly to keep a Tiger thirst alive for a championship that must have seemed like a mirage. Fans remained faithful, however—kept that way chiefly because of their heroes' success in whipping Tulane in an intrastate rivalry that was beginning to warm up.

This also was a time when the South was beginning to rise. Former Yale quarterback Mike Donahue at Auburn, Michigan guard Dan McGugin at Vanderbilt, and Pennsylvania's John Heisman at Georgia Tech were in the midst of building dynasties. Also, some semblance of order was being introduced into the game itself. By 1909 seven men were required on the offensive line; pushing or pulling the ball carrier, as well as interlocking interference, was outlawed; crawling was made illegal and so was the flying tackle.

At LSU the story was a sad one for Coach Mayhew, who suffered throughout 1910 from a shortage of good players, but a bright one for James K. Dwyer, a Pennsylvania alumnus who inherited a Mutt and Jeff combination that eased the loss of Fenton and company. Lawrence Dupont, a 5-foot, 7-inch, 165-pounder from Houma, Louisiana, was playing his second varsity year, and Tom Dutton, a 6-foot, 3-inch, 225-pounder from Minden, Louisiana, his first, when Dwyer arrived to take over as coach in 1911.

The early version of the T formation was still in vogue, and Dupont,

40

Dutton and Dupont: For Coach James K. "Pat" Dwyer, a winning combination.

whose younger brother John played on the same team, was gaining attention with some crafty ball handling and neat broken-field running. Dutton had come to LSU without any high school experience. He watched football rather than participated in it, but Dwyer took one look at him and decided he should do his looking from the field. Mayhew had struggled through a dismal 1–5 season in 1910, and when Dwyer's 1911 crew hung up five victories in a row Tiger fans smelled another 1908. However, injuries and the meatier portion of the schedule quickly shattered these dreams, sending LSU into its finale with Tulane with a 5–3 record.

At the time, the 1911 encounter was significant for two reasons. LSU was resuming football relations with its blood rival after a five-year lapse, and the Tigers were doing it on a new football field, having moved from the parade grounds to a location north of the Pentagon, where bleacher-type seats had been constructed on both sides of the gridiron. The kiss-and-make-up game found the newspapers going overboard in a pitch for "sportsmanship." LSU's James Broussard, faculty chairman of the Athletic Council, mentioned that "not only alumni and graduates but football lovers as well should see the game, because the state title was at stake and football relations were being resumed under the most auspicious circumstances." Baton Rouge was outdoing itself in stringing up "welcome" signs for the Olive and Blue followers, and the papers carried large ads telling of rates for special trains. Two dollars covered the cost of a round trip on an "oil burner" and a ticket to the game. Three Tulane students objected to the price and set out on foot.

About eight hundred Tulane fans boarded the train along with the team which carried with it a supply of "New Orleans water." The visitors weren't taking any chances, and one official said the "well-known properties of Baton Rouge water will hold no terror" for them. Whether or not the imported aqua had anything to do with it, on December 9 Tulane turned in an inspired performance before a crowd of 3,500 which braved heavy rain to watch a game on a field fenced off by barbed wire. Mud equalized Tulane's slightly favored position and the fourth quarter began with no points on the board. On the first play, Larry Dupont swept from the Tulane 24 to the 9, and on the next one, halfback W. M. Evans took a direct snap and swept around right end for the game's only touchdown, which was still worth five points. Once in the end zone, Evans kept going until he planted the ball squarely behind the goal posts to make Dupont's extra-point kick a formality. Keep in mind that the goal posts were on the goal line and the trick in scoring was to touch the ball down between the uprights if possible, because after a score the ball was brought out to the 2-yard line, where it was placed in a direct line from its point of entry. A score made near the sidelines, for example, gave the kicker an almost impossible angle.

Dupont had to wait five minutes before he made it 6–0 as the LSU stands erupted in prolonged cheering. Although LSU's stubborn defense allowed Tulane backs Semmes Walmsley and Sumpter Marks to

Tigers vs. Louisiana Industrials, the 1912 opener.

LSU cadets at depot to greet team that beat Arkansas, 1912.

break away several times, it held up during the final period. The Tigers
went the distance without a substitution. At the final whistle there was
handshaking, and the Tulane crowd paid captain Walmsley the tribute
of not only carrying him off the field but all the way to Tulane headquarters at the Mayer Hotel, possibly one of the longest football rides in
college history.

Football modernization continued in 1912 and brought the value of a
touchdown up to six points. The field was shortened from 110 to 100
yards; 10-yard end zones were added for the catching of forward passes;
the 20-yard distance restriction on passes was lifted; and a fourth down
was added. Tom Dutton, who spent his freshman year on the junior
varsity, was ready to contribute his blocking and defense to a ball club
that could never quite find itself. When it was at full strength, as it was
its first game of the season, when battling Auburn off its feet before
losing, 7–0, it was among the better outfits in the South. Auburn, which
tied Vandy, the Southern champ, didn't score on the Tigers until late in
the game. Dutton enjoyed a great afternoon against the Plainsmen doing
something unique. On defense he became a "roving" center, with free-
dom to follow the ball and sort out the ball carrier.

In the game against Mississippi College, LSU experienced a tough
break when captain Charley Reily, a tackle, broke a leg scoring a
touchdown. Two weeks later, end M. A. "Goose" Gosserand beat the
famous Roy Reigel by seventeen years with a wrong-way run that
resulted in a 7–0 Mississippi State victory. With the ball on the Tiger 20,
Gosserand was called on an end-over-end play. Back of the line, Goose
lost his bearings and set sail for the LSU goal. A State tackler nailed the

flying Frenchman just shy of the end zone in front of the goal posts. When Larry Dupont attempted to kick out on the next play, the ball struck the crossbar and bounced into the end zone where a State man recovered. There was some question whether or not it was a touchdown, and it took a wire to Walter Camp, who explained the ruling, before State's victory became official.

With a 3–3 mark going into the Tulane game, LSU needed a victory for a winning season. Tulane's stands were overflowing with a crowd of 4,000 when the home team grabbed a 3–0 lead on a 30-yard field goal by Carl Woodward, a kick which no doubt awakened the Tigers. In quick order, LSU's halfback A. J. Reid scored two touchdowns, one on a 30-yard run. Reid, the other half of Dwyer's one-two punch, was an acrobatic fullback from Lake Charles, Louisiana. This was before the days of the slants and spinner plays, and Reid made use of his somersaulting ability whenever the Tigers moved near the goal. A strong-arm man who could bend an iron bar, Alf Reid was so agile he could pull off a complete somersault running at full speed, hit on his feet and keep running. He sometimes entertained his teammates by walking the length of the field on his hands. LSU went on to register a 21–3 victory over Tulane, marred by one minor incident, grown funnier with age. Rookie tackle H. E. Bonvillian, told by Dwyer to "get in there and fight," took his coach literally. On the first play he poked the Tulane lineman opposite him in the face and was promptly ejected.

In 1913 it was a question of Dutton's and Dupont's coming into their own. Dutton won a berth on the all-Southern team, and Dupont scored fifteen touchdowns, the most ever made by an LSU player in regular-season play. Dupont got six of his touchdowns in a 40–0 win over Tulane, adding four extra points for a thirty-four total, an individual LSU record that still stands against the Olive and Blue. The 1913 season was also the season of the "kangaroo," a Dutton-Dupont version of the quarterback sneak, in which 5-foot, 7-inch Larry would crawl beneath the legs of the 6-foot, 3-inch center, who snapped the ball and pushed forward. It was a bread-and-butter maneuver in short-yardage situations.

Dutton had built up a reputation in track that was matched by his football prowess. As a sophomore he established Southern records in the shot, hammer, and 56-pound weight, his shot mark standing until the advent of Jack Torrance twenty years later. Georgia Tech coach John Heisman selected him for the all-Southern football team and gave him an honorable mention on the all-America squad. Oddly enough, Dutton claims the hardest game for him personally was the 1913 contest against Jefferson College of Convent, Louisiana, which was given a 45–6 whipping. "They had a 135-pound halfback that drove me nuts," he said. "I don't remember his name but I do know I couldn't tackle him. He ran

The 1913 team. Standing, left to right, Manager D. Y. Smith, W. C. "Little" Green, R. F. Walker, Phil Cooper, Art Klock, W. M. Evans, H. E. Walden, Coach James K. Dwyer. Center row, J. E. Crawford, George Spencer, Tom Dutton, Lawrence Dupont, A. J. "Alf" Reid. Front row, Floyd Spencer, T. R. Mobley, P. E. Harrison, H. V. Fluker.

circles around me. Later, he was ruled out because they discovered he was greasing his uniform. I would have hated to have met him under those circumstances."

Despite Dutton's all-Southern honors and Dupont's 108 points, it was a "near-miss" year for the Tigers who finished with a 6–1–1 record. The defeat was another 7–0 heartbreaker at the hands of Southern champion Auburn. LSU not only missed several regulars in the game at Mobile, but the Plainsmen made their touchdown after a penalty gave them a first down on the 5-yard line. The 40–0 win over Tulane was memorable for more than Dupont's 34-point afternoon. LSU wore numbers for the first time. Also, the automobile was beginning to replace the train as the major mode of transportation between Baton Rouge and New Orleans. "Since the college kids seem to own fifty per cent of the cars," said the *Times-Picayune*, "Tulane should be well represented in the state capital." The distance between the cities, via the River Road, was estimated as "something between 116 and 120 miles." Said the *Times-Picayune:* "Under present weather conditions, with a good car, it can be negotiated in perfect comfort in six hours."

Coach E. T. McDonnell (left, wearing Colgate jacket) and the 1914 team. Tommy Thomas stands at right. Holding the ball is Atherton "Skeeter" Gates.

E. T. McDonnell, an all-American at Colgate,* replaced Dwyer at LSU in 1914 and, as the season grew old, he probably wished he had remained at Jefferson College in nearby Convent. His Tigers had scored three warmup victories before entertaining Ole Miss. Against the Rebels, LSU marched to the one, fumbled, and a Mississippi player scooped up the ball and raced ninety-nine yards for a touchdown that ignited a 21–0 Reb win. If there was a turning point, that was it. Next week, little Jefferson College (Doc Fenton had succeeded McDonnell as Jefferson's coach) caught the Tigers with several key men injured and scared the daylights out of them before bowing 14–13. The following week in Dallas, LSU suffered the worst beating in its history. The Tigers had a 9–7 lead at half time when the roof fell in. The Aggies scored eight touchdowns and kicked seven goals in the last thirty minutes to walk off on the long end of a 63–9 score.

LSU took a 4–4 record into New Orleans for the Tulane game and from all indications it loomed as a tossup. Heavy rains brought the two teams even closer together and by half time the field resembled a sea of gumbo. Rain was still coming down when all of the eight hundred Tiger rooters, most of whom had made the trip on a fourteen-coach LSU special, spilled onto the field. R. B. "Billiken" Howell, who had won a football letter in 1909 and 1910 and later pitched for the Cardinals and Chattanooga, led the war-whooping rooters in a soggy snake

---

* He appears in the Colgate records as "MacDonnell."

dance. Students held aloft a mock Tiger whose mouth dripped blood as they charted their serpentine path through the goo. Minutes later they were joined by Tulane fans who appeared carrying a black coffin bearing the label "For a Tiger" as the Tulane band played a funeral dirge. It had all the appearances of innocent fun until the opposing lines gradually grew closer together for the "cheer of friendship." All of a sudden someone on the field tore down an LSU banner one of the marchers was holding and there was a king-size free-for-all. With the rain continuing to beat a steady tattoo, the mire thickened and the police, who had been watching from the sidelines, were reluctant to set foot in the ankle-deep mud. After five minutes the battlers became too tired and too wet. Both sides slowly retired to the grandstand, leaving the muck to the two teams. The crowd of 2,000 remained to the bitter end for a scoreless tie that was strictly anticlimactic to the half-time entertainment.

The only thing wrong with Coach McDonnell's last season at LSU—the 1915 season—was that someone scheduled Georgia Tech. John Heisman was under full steam in Atlanta and halfback Everett Strupper, one of Tech's immortals, was the scourge of the South. The Tigers were 3–0 going into the Tech contest, played at Heinemann Park in New Orleans, but it was soon clear they were no match for the visitors. In fact, the 36–7 whipping the Yellowjackets administered furnished but two bright moments for LSU. One was the touchdown drive—a three-play march of seventy yards which found Lee Himes passing to Mickey O'Quinn for the last thirty-five yards. The other came when Coach Heisman became involved in a row with the officials and protested so vigorously that he was escorted off the field and out of the ball park by the police as LSU fans applauded.

McDonnell, utilizing his depth, sometimes platooned his backfield depending on the situation. He had what he called his "beef brigade" in Joe Bernstein (190), Alf Reid (180) and W. C. "Poss" Green (180) and his speedsters in Bill Lewis, J. C. "Friday" Rodrigue, and Jerry Reagan. Phil Cooper, a full-blooded Indian from Tangipahoa Parish, was one of the South's top linemen, and he combined with fullback Bernstein (who led the interference) to make the tackle-over-tackle play a major offensive weapon.

Lewis Gottlieb, who served as student manager in 1915, vividly recalls the trip to Shreveport for the Tigers' annual clash with Arkansas. "We went by train from Baton Rouge to Shreveport traveling in what was known as a tourist sleeper," he said. "I remember the players slept two to each berth. C. C. 'Doc' Stroud, who was director of athletics at the time, ordered a horse-drawn buggy to take the players from the hotel to the stadium and by the time they got there all of them nearly had a heat stroke."

Gottlieb had held out for an automobile but the frugal Stroud won out. On another matter, Gottlieb also was balked by Stroud but the student manager outfoxed him. "The mosquitoes were bad and I wanted to buy some stuff they called 'Skeeter Skoot,'" Gottlieb explained. "Doc wouldn't hear of it. 'That's not for huskies,' he said.

"We had had a $400 gate for our game with Mississippi College so, thinking of the best interest of the team, I stole $5 and bought enough 'Skeeter Skoot' for the whole team for $3.50." Protected from the pests, quarterback Lee Himes fired scoring passes to Bill Lewis and Ray Edmonds to sew up a 13–7 victory.

A crowd of 5,000 gathered for the Tigers' finale with Tulane and everything pointed to an incident-free, although spirited, scrap. Both student bodies went on record as abhorring what had taken place the previous year and measures had been taken to see it didn't happen again. Someone should have gotten the message to the players. Two Tulane men were banished for slugging, as was guard R. H. Walton of LSU. That was bad enough. However, as Tulane was preparing to return home, Walton invited one of the Tulane players to settle their argument and this almost touched off another full-scale riot near the Tulane headquarters. So far as the game went, LSU settled the issue quickly with two first-half touchdowns, one by Reid and one by Lewis, on the way to a 12–0 decision. The Tigers, with McDonnell substituting freely, held off several frantic Tulane threats in the second half, and Tulane went away still looking for their first victory since 1904.

McDonnell had good reason to look forward to 1916 because he, better than anyone else, knew how good Mike Flanagan was. Flanagan stood a mere 5 feet, 7 inches and weighed a meager 146 pounds. Give him a football, though, and he was a broken-field virtuoso who revived memories of Fenton. Flanagan was an "importee," having played at Colgate, McDonnell's alma mater, had sat out his year of residency at LSU in 1915 and therefore was eligible the following year.

Mike fitted neatly into McDonnell's backfield that had A. W. "Dub" Baird at quarterback, Tom Henry at the other halfback, and Joe Bernstein at fullback. Tough, talented Phil Cooper, back at tackle and serving as team captain, was the mainstay of an experienced line. When the Tigers rolled over their first four opponents, the talk again was of "another 1908." LSU not only smashed Southwestern Louisiana, Jefferson College, Texas A & M and Mississippi College, but allowed only one score—a 60-yard run by Mississippi College's "Goat" Hale, considered by some as the finest runner the South ever produced. Tom Henry had scoring runs of seventy and thirty-five yards against the Aggies, Flanagan was slipping in and out of tackler's arms, and Baird, when he wasn't running, was kicking the enemy into hole after hole with an uncannily accurate foot.

Actually, the season did have the earmarks of "another 1908"—until Sewanee showed up in New Orleans for a game on October 28. The Tennessee outfit had played a scoreless tie with Kentucky the week before and the betting fraternity made the visitors a slight underdog to McDonnell's unbeaten crew. But the Mountaineers outclassed the heavier Tigers, 7–0, making an early touchdown stand up.

Sewanee, which had beaten LSU with President Taft watching in 1909 and caused the resignation of Coach Joe Prichard in mid-season, did it again. Two days after the 7–0 defeat, Professor T. W. Atkinson, head of the Athletic Council, announced that McDonnell's resignation had been accepted. No explanation was given, but sources close to the university said Atkinson felt the man from Colgate had done a poor job. McDonnell made no secret of his ill-feeling ("I feel I have a fine team and would have liked to continue."), and the subsequent furor created turmoil on the campus as LSU prepared for its annual game with Arkansas. Some players loyal to McDonnell were reported as having quit the squad. As tension mounted, Atkinson took the ball club to Coushatta to prepare for Arkansas and announced that Irving Pray, a part-time assistant, would serve as McDonnell's successor until a coach could be named. A graduate of MIT, Pray was a sugar chemist who headed for Cuba when the grinding season began there in November. He agreed to take over until duty called, and that was in two weeks.

JOHN FRED PRAY

Coach Irving Pray: LSU called him back twice.

When the Tigers invaded Shreveport on November 5, they were called "the coachless wonders" but they didn't play as though they lacked leadership. In the second quarter, the Razorbacks drove to the LSU 1-yard line, where they had a first-and-goal. Phil Cooper rallied his forward wall—center K. E. "Sweet Papa" Jones, tackle R. E. "Red" Rice, guards Art Klock and A. W. "Doc" Herbert, ends Mickey O'Quinn and J. C. "Red" Floyd—and, four downs later, Arkansas hadn't gained an inch. Dub Baird then booted the ball out of bounds on the Arkansas 40 with a 60-yard kick, to end the threat. To say that Cooper gave it the "old college try" on the goal line is a vast understatement. Against Sewanee the week before he had sustained a head injury. During the four-down stand he suffered a concussion and wound up in a Shreveport hospital, but not until after the game. In the third quarter, with the score still 0–0, Flanagan took a handoff from Baird on the Statue of Liberty and swivel-hipped seventy yards to a touchdown. Later, LSU pushed another touchdown across and, in the final period, Baird made it 17–0 when he drop kicked a field goal. Arkansas scored after Pray had yanked the regulars for a 17–7 final which represented a tremendous about-face after the Sewanee defeat. And the Tigers did it without the services of halfback Tom Henry, who had broken his leg against the Mountaineers.

Pray remained in charge for a 13–3 victory over Mississippi State and then turned over the reins to a young man by the name of Dana X. Bible. Bible, who was destined to write some glorious chapters at the University of Texas, had been "borrowed" by Doc Stroud from Texas A & M for the 1916 season only. It was his job to assist McDonnell and he performed admirably; in fact, when Stroud dropped the axe, Bible wanted a share of the blame for the loss to Sewanee.

So, with three games left (Mississippi, Rice and Tulane), the burden shifted to the young coach on loan. Ole Miss was easy, 41–0, but LSU needed a third-quarter touchdown on Baird's passing arm for a 7–7 standoff with Rice, a team that had clobbered SMU, 146–3, the previous week. The Owls also had beaten Tulane 23–13 and, while comparative scores apparently favored the Tigers, one Rice player put it this way: "To beat Tulane, LSU will have to bust the Minnesota shift."

The shift, brainchild of Dr. Henry L. Williams of Minnesota, had been brought to Tulane by another young genius named Clark Shaughnessy. Shaughnessy had taken over in 1915, and his long hours of instructions in the intricate maneuvers of a new technique were beginning to bear fruit. Williams' shift, sprung in 1909, was the first to shift both linemen and backs, sometimes twice before the ball was snapped. The idea was to outflank the defense.

Sterling W. "Buck" Gladden, reserve halfback on the 1916 Tigers, later recalled how it was the week of the Tulane game. "Every time Coach Bible would see one of his football players on the campus, he would stop him and say, 'He who hesitates is lost,' and then go on his way." Bible was one of the few men in the South who understood the shift, and he hammered away all week at the importance of the defense of shifting with the formation. Doc Stroud did all he could to paint a picture of gloom which was partly true. Baird, O'Quinn, and Rodrigue, the No. 2 fullback, were injured and weren't expected to play. Hungry for their first win over the Tigers since 1904, Tulane fans arrived early at Heinemann Park and soon the crowd of 7,000 became a sea of waving pennants. Everyone got their money's worth and went away wondering how great Eastern football must be if it allowed someone like Flanagan to slip away. LSU got limited duty from Rodrigue but it was without quarterback Baird and end O'Quinn. Still, because of Flanagan's offensive brilliance and an alert defense that reflected Bible's dedication to detail, the game ended 14–14, and everyone seemingly went home happy, including Governor Ruffin Pleasant, captain of LSU's 1893 team, and New Orleans Mayor Martin Behrman, on hand to root for Tulane.

Flanagan had scooted ten yards for a score in the first period and kicked the point to make it 7–0. After Tulane scored twice in the second quarter to go ahead 14–7, Flanagan broke loose on a 50-yard run and, several plays later, ran across for another touchdown. Lee Himes, filling in for the injured Baird at quarterback, booted the tieing point. In the second half Tulane checked Flanagan and LSU contained Shaughnessy's shift—and that was the story. Cooper, who refused to let head injuries keep him from his final collegiate game, won the toss for the game ball. Cooper took the souvenir with him to Cuba, where he had accepted a job as a sugar chemist, joining Irving Pray, who was already at work on the island.

In the spring of 1917 the United States entered World War I and the rush to the colors made it possible once again for colleges to play freshmen. While many schools abandoned their schedules, LSU followed the thinking of Georgia Tech's Heisman—that men in college could better serve their nation by remaining in school to await the call to arms. Heisman cited the Duke of Wellington, who maintained that the Battle of Waterloo was won on the football fields of Eton and Harrow.

So the Tigers played their eight-game schedule with as much enthusiasm as they could muster. For a time, it was believed Pray would return from his sugar duties in Cuba, but as fall approached the job fell to Wayne Sutton of Washington State. LSU had its share of freshmen which included quarterback R. L. "Rabbit" Benoit of Shreveport and halfbacks Clarence Ives and Perry Hague of Baton Rouge. In the line,

Sweet Papa Jones, Doc Herbert and Mickey O'Quinn were back, while Pete Dutton, brother of Tom, and John Fournet (now Chief Justice on the Louisiana Supreme Court) were among the more prominent new faces.

The opening game of 1917, a 20–6 win over Southwestern Louisiana Institute, served as the dedication of the Tigers' third playing site. Later known as State Field, it was located southwest of the Indian mound, now part of the State Capitol grounds. The 7,200-capacity wooden structure was made possible in large measure through the donation of three thousand dollars by Tiger fan H. V. Moseley.

After victories over Southwestern and Ole Miss, LSU lost its fifth straight decision to Sewanee on October 20 in a unique 3–0 game which must have set a record for scattershot field-goal kicking. Ten were attempted, four by the Tigers and six by the Mountaineers, and it wasn't until the last minute of play that the visitors connected from the 28-yard line. Sewanee's five consecutive wins over LSU, incidentally, is a record that still stands.

Going into the Tulane game, LSU had a 3–4 record but was given a shot against Clark Shaughnessy's crew, who had been blanked three times in succession after winning its first four. Although the Tigers enjoyed the home field edge and received top efforts from freshmen Benoit and Ives, Tulane scored in every quarter to win 28–6, the first victory over their bitter rivals since 1904. The victors' celebration began in Baton Rouge and continued all the way to New Orleans, where it was climaxed by the cancellation of classes. For Tulane, it had been a long time.

By 1918 colleges had lost much of their academic flavor: that is, they were then military schools turning out officers. The flow of casualty lists made any attempt at football half-hearted, so it was not a difficult decision for LSU to tuck away its gear until hostilities ended. When the school resumed football in 1919, it felt fortunate to be able to rehire Irving Pray. A native of Natick, Massachusetts, Pray, who stood a slender 5 feet, 10 inches, prided himself on turning out well-drilled ball clubs. He had been a prep school star and would have made it in college except for the fact that MIT did not have varsity football or baseball teams. He transferred to Harvard for his senior year (the one-year transfer rule made him ineligible for competition), and it was there that his close relationship with Eddie Mahan gave him a solid foundation in football basics and the art of teaching them. Pray's coaching career began in the Boston area, where he turned out top prep teams, and led later to his hiring by Mike Donahue in 1912 as an Auburn assistant. Pray later moved to Middlebury College in Vermont, where he was enjoying great success when the school dropped the sport at mid-season because of an accidental death of a team member. His academic training put him

Forerunner (Arkansas game, 1920) in papier-maché of Mike the Tiger.

in line for the position of a sugar chemist in Cuba, and it was his commitment there which had made it impossible for him to remain for the entire 1916 season. When LSU signed him (for $1,200) for the 1919 season, the arrangement was that he would remain for the eight-game schedule. Like most other coaches returning after the war, Pray greeted a combination of young men and returning veterans which required the touch of a psychologist. And that was a department in which the little man excelled.

Because of rules then in force Tom Dutton, a 1914 graduate, had a season of eligibility remaining, so he returned to LSU for postgraduate work and to serve as team captain for the second time. Overall, it was a mature ball club with depth. At the halfbacks, Clarence Ives and Buck Gladden (from 1916) were back to be joined by newcomers like Newton "Dirty" Helm, Reggie McFarland, and Fred Frey. Rabbit Benoit and Perry Hague were a one-two punch at quarterback.

Owing somewhat to the postwar climate, spirit seemed to be at an all-time high. "Shorty" Brannon, head cheerleader, was the most popular student in school. At pep meetings he would stand on the Garig Hall rostrum and quote stories from New Orleans newspapers about the "light" Tiger team—and then cite the actual weights of the huge linemen on hand. For some reason, Pray's LSU outfit was underrated right on down to the last game. Featured by the broken-field running of quarterbacks Benoit and Hague and a tough defense headed by Tom and Pete Dutton, John Fournet, Red Floyd and W. B. "Red" Hanley, the

Tigers swept past four opponents in a row, holding all of them scoreless.

Pray turned the team over to an assistant for the Ole Miss game (the third of the four opponents), feeling it was more important to scout next week's opponent, Arkansas. Buck Gladden scored both touchdowns in a 13–0 win over the Rebels, but reports that the Tigers "looked awful" prompted Pray to drill them three hours the following Monday. The morning of the Arkansas game in Shreveport on October 25, Pray welcomed an addition—fullback Joe Bernstein who had lettered in 1915 and 1916. Bernstein exchanged his Second Lieutenant's uniform for pants and a jersey and was in action that afternoon against the Razorbacks.

At the time, betting was widespread and there were few better wagering games than LSU-Arkansas. On this particular occasion, an oil field roustabout wearing red boots and a green vest wandered into the Shreveport hotel where fans of both teams were staying. "I want some action," he announced. "I'd like to bet on LS and U." When the man was told "chickenfeed bets" were not taken, he peeled off fifty $1,000 bills. Arkansas fans scattered to cover it. After the Tigers ground out a 20–0 victory, trainer Francis "Tad" Gormley handed each boy who played an envelope as they stepped onto the train. A reserve tackle, N. H. "Nap" Polmer, who had gotten in for one minute, opened his envelope on the train and took out a $20 bill. When Gormley saw him pacing up and down the car, he asked him what he was doing. "I'm trying to figure out," replied Polmer, "how much I would have gotten for sixty minutes."

LSU had its 4–0 record spoiled in Starkville where Mississippi State prevailed, 6–0, with a touchdown set up by a 60-yard punt return which, the Tigers claimed, came after the ball had been whistled dead. LSU blanked Mississippi College the following week, 24–0, and then entertained Alabama's "Thin Red Line," a term used in jest because Bama's linemen were anything but thin. For three quarters, the game was scoreless with Tom Dutton manhandling Bama's front. With one quarter remaining, however, Pray lifted him because his team was taking dead aim at Tulane the following week. Bernstein could have played against the Tide, but Joe, injured playing against Arkansas, was held out by Pray for the same reason—Tulane. In the last quarter, Bama broke through for twenty-three points but the loss left Pray undaunted.

The Monday before the Tulane game the LSU coach called his squad together in the law school. He pulled down the shades and proceeded to give a detailed report on Tulane's 7–7 tie with Georgia.

Clark Shaughnessy's Goats had compiled a 6–0–1 record to that point, but still all Pray did was belittle the Tulane club. Finally he pulled a piece of chalk out of his pocket, went over to a blackboard, and wrote

"21" in huge numerals. "That's how many points we're better than them," he said. "Now I'm going to show you how we'll do it." Pray went on to announce he was shifting Tom Dutton from center to tackle. "We're going to run Joe Bernstein behind Tom right at their tackle, Eva Talbot," said Pray. Bernstein hadn't played since a brief appearance against Arkansas, the day the 210-pounder returned from the service. He had been practicing right along, but Pray wasn't taking any chances of having him reinjured before he got a shot at the Goats.

Athletic Director Doc Stroud, at Pray's request, did his part by spreading "bear" stories about LSU injuries and the New Orleans press cooperated by reporting all he said. When the LSU special arrived in New Orleans, Tiger fans did a snake dance down Canal Street to their headquarters at the Grunewald Hotel. Heinemann Park was a splash of color by the 2:40 kickoff, but there was one surprise in the color scheme. Shaughnessy had formed a superstition about the traditional green, and he had his Tulane players outfitted in red jerseys. The home team was the solid betting choice, yet it wasn't long before LSU's power was evident. A 57-yard run by McFarland put Tulane in a second quarter hole and, following a poor punt, the "injured" Bernstein bucked across. Tulane got back in the game when Benny Smith intercepted a Rabbit Benoit pass and returned it sixty-five yards for a score. At half time, LSU led 7–6 on Pete Dutton's extra point.

The pile-driving Bernstein scored twice in the third quarter, an Ives-to-Ray Edmonds pass setting up one and a 35-yard run by Reggie McFarland setting up the other. McFarland scored to make it 27–6 in the final quarter and, with five minutes remaining, officials called the game on account of darkness when it became impossible to distinguish the players. Some Tulane fans felt it might have turned out differently had not Johnny Wight's 86-yard kickoff return for a touchdown been disallowed. An official ruled that he signaled for a fair catch (Wight said he was shading the sun from his eyes) and, instead of getting the score, Tulane was penalized. The call hardly influenced the outcome, however, because the day belonged to Pray's plotting, Bernstein's off-tackle jabs behind Dutton, and Ives's lofty punting. Trainer Gormley was given an assist for Bernstein's excellent showing. He taped the fullback's "good" knee as well as the injured one, being careful to allow the tape to show on the sound leg—a target for Tulane tacklers. Ives wound up as the high scorer on LSU's first postwar club with twenty-four points while Tom Dutton again won a spot on the all-Southern team.

One sidelight on the 1919 upset was the capture of the "Tiger coffin" following the game. Tulane students had prepared a mock Tiger, hangman's scaffold and coffin for ceremonies after an expected Tulane victory. When the game ended, however, the LSU cadet corps rushed across the field, destroyed the scaffold and carried the coffin back to Baton Rouge. The next day Third Street was the scene of a sad procession, a funeral ritual for the Tulane Goat. While the LSU band softly played the dirge, mourners followed the hearse to the parade grounds

Hearse leads funeral procession through downtown Baton Rouge to bury the Tulane goat, 1919.

where a black-faced parson delivered the oration. A military salute—three shots from a cap pistol—was fired as the coffin was lowered to its final resting place.

Football remained more of an avocation than a vocation for Irving Pray. When the 1920 season arrived he was devoting his time to sugar chemistry, and a fellow named Branch Bocock was head coach at LSU. Law missed an apt pupil in Branch Bocock. A graduate of Georgetown, he was a spellbinding orator. Above all, he characterized the famous line of Grantland Rice: "It's not whether you win or lose but how you play the game." During Bocock's regime, the cadet corps as well as the noncadet students and coeds watched football practice every day, and it was not unusual to see the practice field rimmed with as many as a thousand students. In the two years Bocock held the job, his midfield lectures to his squad were classics anxiously awaited by the students, especially those with theatrical leanings. Despite his unique approach to football and his refusal to place victory over integrity, his record is surprising. His Tigers went 5–3–1 in 1920 and 6–1–1 in 1921—but both years lost to Tulane. LSU officials, feeling he could play the game honorably and beat Tulane, asked for his resignation. To the end, Bocock was steadfast in his beliefs. Before the 1921 game with Tulane he was asked about LSU's chances. "I really don't care which team wins," said Bocock. "All I'm interested in is how we conduct ourselves on the field."

Bocock's LSU career began with double-header victories over Jefferson College and Louisiana Normal. The Tigers whipped Jefferson in the morning, Normal in the afternoon. This 1920 squad had lost some of its quality players of the previous season—the Dutton brothers, Bernstein, Edmonds, Fournet, Floyd, and B. "Gunboat" Smith. Among the backfield holdovers from 1919 were quarterbacks Benoit and Hague, halfbacks McFarland, Ives and the slim speedster, Dirty Helm.

It was Ives and Helm who were featured in 1920—Ives with his incredible punting and Helm with his blazing break-away speed. Dirty Helm came to LSU from Bunkie, Louisiana, High, and Tad Gormley, who handled the track team in addition to his duties as a trainer, had immediately seen his potential as a sprinter. "He had a pair of white shorts he liked to run in," said Tad, "and he was never able to keep 'em clean. So right away we started calling him 'Dirty.' Besides, it sounded better than Newton." Under Tad's guidance, Helm was SIAA sprint champion as a freshman, sophomore and junior, missing his last year because of a football injury. He won a football letter in 1919 and 1920 at end and then in 1921 and 1922 switched to halfback, where his speed was better utilized. In 1920 he drove the opposition daffy as a pass

Cheerleader Edna Arnold in action, 1921.

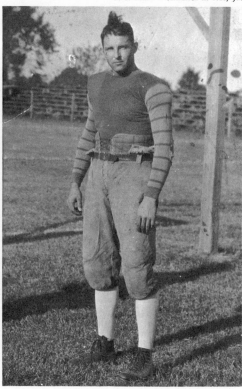

In the LSU backfield in 1920 and 1921 were Earl L. "Tubby" Ewen and Clarence A. "Fatty" Ives. Ives, one of the three four-sport lettermen in LSU history, was a spectacular punter. Ewen, high scorer in 1920, captained the team in 1922 and again in 1923.

receiver and, against Mississippi State, combined with Ives in a legendary play that almost pulled the game out of the fire. The Tigers trailed State 7–12 in the final quarter when Ives lofted one to Helm who was under a full head of steam. Helm was stopped dead in his tracks—after a gain of fifty yards and a pass that traveled at least sixty yards in the air.

Ives came into his own that season. The graduate of Baton Rouge High had lettered as a freshman in 1917 and had done so well in 1919 that he was voted the best athlete in what was his sophomore season. He retained the honor in 1920 and no one could raise a dissenting voice. During a scoreless tie with Texas A & M on a wet field at College Station, Ives booted one seventy-five yards and kicked three other punts that traveled more than fifty. Against Arkansas, following a goal line stand by the Tigers, he stood inches inside the boundary line and directly behind the goal posts (which were still on the goal line). LSU fan Nathan Weil, who was in Shreveport that day, never forgot what followed. "I was so scared," he said, "I put my head in my hands because I didn't want to look. I kept waiting for the 'bip' that comes when the ball hits the crossbar. When I didn't hear it, I got the courage to look up and, when I did, the ball was falling to earth around the Arkansas 30. It was an 80-yard boot, seventy yards from scrimmage. Fatty had so many 70-yarders I lost count but that was one I never forgot." It was the key play in a 3–0 Tiger victory.

Ives earned his nickname because of a bout with typhoid fever as a youngster. Confined to a wheelchair, he had lost weight at a fast clip but then steadily gained it back. He weighed 157 pounds during his first three seasons and 174 as a senior. Ives was given punting fundamentals by Afton Gates, mascot of the 1908 team. "He taught me the valve was the secret," explained Fatty. "In those days, the ball was inflated by mouth and the valve tucked under a piece of leather. By kicking away from the valve, it gave more momentum to your spirals." Gormley recalled that Ives was the first punter who booted spirals, rather than floaters, with any degree of consistency. "He kicked 'em so high," said Tad, "the safety man could have gone over and sat on a chair waiting for it to come down."

Ives was one of the three four-sport-lettermen in LSU history; the others were Norman Stevens and Charles Mason. When his kicks weren't gathering icicles, Fatty was a pole vaulter, a right fielder-third basemen, and a basketball guard.

When Bocock prepared to entertain Tulane in 1920, he was placing most of his faith in Ives's toe. Shaughnessy's Greenbacks (the name Goats had faded) were still smarting from that 1919 upset and, in seven games, had lost only to mighty Michigan. The fact that Benoit and McFarland were out with injuries put more of a burden on Ives because Bocock figured that if LSU was to win it would be a question of defense

DR. ROBERT N. HELM

Newton "Dirty" Helm, the great LSU sprinter from Bunkie.

Action on the LSU field, 1921. The bottom two photographs are of the game with Spring Hill.

and waiting for the breaks. Ives's toe held up admirably, but the Tigers could not contain Bill Dwyer and Benny Brown and left State Field thoroughly beaten, 21–0. LSU could make only thirty-six yards all afternoon against the 2-to-1 favored Tulanians and the only source of satisfaction was found at the box office.

The "Standing Room Only" sign went up early, and more than 1,000 fans were turned away after 7,300 were packed into the stands and in the area around the field. The largest Tulane special up to that time (the twenty coaches pulled by a single engine represented a half-mile-long caravan) carried 1,500 fans from New Orleans. Gross receipts were $17,300 and, after $1,600 in war taxes was deducted, the record $15,700 net was $2,500 more than had been taken in the previous year at Heinemann Park. It was more than double the largest previous Baton Rouge gate—$7,000 in 1917. After $3,000 for game expenses was deducted ($500 went to the officials), the balance was divided between the two schools. In fact, the turnstiles had clicked so merrily that stadium talk began in Baton Rouge and a move was discussed to raise $100,000 for a concrete structure.

The importance of the Tulane game—that is, winning it—was never more obvious than in 1921. Bocock had retained most of his key men and had added the box formation and single wing to the old-fashioned T. Two key additions were C. B. "Red" Hughes, a tackle just out of the service, and halfback Roland "Chesty" Kizer, a transfer from Arkansas. Generally, the starting backfield found McFarland at quarterback, Helm and E. L. "Tubby" Ewen at halfbacks and Ives at fullback. Ewen, a Nebraskan, had been the Tigers' top scorer in 1920. So Bocock entertained high hopes.

Following a 78–0 warmup win over Louisiana Normal, LSU won a weird 6–0 decision from Texas A & M—weird because the only score was the result of quick thinking by McFarland and a momentary letdown by the Aggies. A right end run was called but center L. C. Bourgeois, whose snap was supposed to lead the tailback to the right, snapped it to the left instead. McFarland ran back, scooped it up and, as his interference fanned out to the right, ran left sixty yards for a touchdown. Ives's punts were well covered by ends Jeff Curtis of New Orleans and Johnny Lewis of Opelousas, and as a result LSU was able to keep the Aggies bottled up. The win took on added significance later since A & M defeated Centre College ("Bo" McMillan and company) after Centre had pulled a miracle by whipping Harvard, an incredible feat at the time.

The Tigers then waltzed past Spring Hill, 41–7, to get ready for a game in New Orleans with Alabama. It turned into a bitter 7–7 standoff, Bama scoring in the third quarter and LSU in the fourth on a short buck by Ives after a long march. Ives's punting was simply spectacular (Bama made twenty-three first downs but always had to come a long way), and the running of Kizer, who had a 50-yard run cancelled by a penalty, was outstanding.

The following week against Arkansas, Ives gave a repeat performance in Shreveport as he consistently kept the Razorbacks penned up with his skyscrapers. Arkansas, worn out advancing the ball, succumbed, 10–7. A 21–0 win over Ole Miss set the stage for Bocock's second shot at Tulane, but it soon became another day of sackcloth and ashes. Shaughnessy's Greenbacks matched the 21–0 score of 1920, and they did it with the superb play of folks like "Brother" Brown, Morris Legendre, Paul Maloney, "Little Eva" and Ed Talbot. To be sure, Ives kicked them farther; he put a 50-yard spiral in Brown's hands and Brother carried it back eighty yards. Later, he returned another Ives punt fifty yards for a score as Tulane got ten men in front of the ball carrier.

The loss meant the end of Bocock—but there was one more game, December 3, against Mississippi State, a fitting valedictory for the strong-legged Ives. His 50-yard run set up the first touchdown; he passed to Fritz Spencer for the second; and he kicked the winning field goal in a tense 17–14 victory in Starkville. Ives booted one for seventy-five yards and finished the day with a 55-yard average. Luckily, LSU was able to get out of Starkville alive. With three minutes left, State

LSU fans march through streets of New Orleans before Tulane game, 1921.

scored on a "hideout play" that was good for sixty yards but the officials called it back for offsides. The men in the white shirts needed a police escort to leave the field and a full-scale riot nearly erupted.

When the season ended in 1921 the record showed 6–1–1, but this was overshadowed by Tulane 21, LSU 0. So the SOS call went out to Cuba, and Irving Pray, the old Tulane nemesis, heard it and accepted a $2,500 offer to return—but to what? Losses were heavy, particularly in the line. Ives's departure was enough to create gloom, but with him went such linemen as Johnny Lewis and Jeff Curtis at ends, Bob Hereford, J. E. "Pug" Steele, Red Hughes and Bobbie Davis at tackles, Bert Busse at guard, Pete Dutton at center. It meant Pray was greeted by an influx of new faces—Norman Stevens, Sam Thornton, Abie Bame, E. G. Blakewood, Luke Abramson, Gus Jackson, Bill Pitcher, A. D. Warner, and Seid Hendrix. Although a king-sized rebuilding job faced Pray, all of Third Street and most of the student body had an abiding conviction that the coach with an Indian sign on Tulane would be able to steer the Tigers through stormy seas.

An inkling of what was to come, however, became evident after an opening victory over Louisiana Normal of Natchitoches. The 13–0 score (LSU had won 34–0 and 78–0 the two previous years) indicated something was lacking. Sure enough, the next week Loyola of New Orleans invaded Baton Rouge and hung a 7–0 defeat on the Tigers to set in motion three weeks of disaster. In successive road games LSU lost 51–0 to SMU, 47–0 to Texas A & M, and 40–6 to Arkansas. Pray's crew returned home for a 25–7 win over Spring Hill but then came another losing orgy, 25–0 to Rutgers, 47–3 to Alabama, and 7–0 to Mississippi State. The Rutgers loss at New York's Polo Grounds marked LSU's first invasion of the East. Battered going into the game, Pray's Tigers suffered through one of the roughest games in the school's history (Rutgers was penalized 160 yards). Six LSU regulars were sent home with injuries, and two of them, halfbacks Dirty Helm and A. D. Warner, made the trip on stretchers. Ordinarily, this would have been bad enough, but the schedule called for LSU to meet Alabama three days later in Tuscaloosa. "Coach Pray," recalled halfback Chesty Kizer, "actually had to wire Baton Rouge for reinforcements. So some players came up from Baton Rouge to join the team for the Alabama game. We were so shorthanded I had to play in the position of the back who would carry the ball. Alabama had a linebacker named Probst. When we'd come up to the line to run a play, he'd holler across at me 'Bet you a coke, I get you!'—and he usually did."

The loss to State the following week sent LSU into the Tulane game with a 2–7 record and seemingly a hopeless underdog. As usual, Pray had an ace up his sleeve. Reggie McFarland was a quiet, methodical team man. He was handicapped by kidney trouble but kept it a secret. A keen student of the game, he was always in a bull session with his coach. The day he began preparing his club for Tulane, Pray gave quarterback McFarland a verbal thrashing in front of the squad and then announced he was dropping him from the team. Chins hit the floor. The unexpected move caught everyone by surprise (Pray's charge was lack of hustle) and left the team in an emotional turmoil. Pray then went to Edna Arnold, the head cheerleader, and laid out his plan. She was to spread the word around the campus about the raw deal McFarland had received and was to stir up student support for the quarterback, then approach Pray with the request that he be taken back. The LSU coach played his part to the hilt. He said he'd leave it up to the squad, knowing full well how the players would vote. With McFarland back in his good graces, Pray turned his thoughts to the game. Defensively, he made linebackers out of his speedsters, Helm and Warner, and gave them one simple instruction regarding Tulane's great Brother Brown. "Never try to tackle him on his sweeps," Pray told them. "Just run with him and try to force him to the sidelines." Offensively, Pray collaborated with Mike Donahue, who was all but signed as LSU coach for the 1923 season. Donahue gave his friend of long standing the rudiments of his famous "line-divide" formation, and Pray couldn't wait to spring it on the unsuspecting Greenbacks.

A crowd of 10,000, largest ever in the history of State Field, turned out for the game. Before the game the LSU coach had his team lounging on the floor of the old gym, and student manager Ran Williams remembered Clark Shaughnessy's walking through on his way to the field. "Go ahead," Pray told the Tulane coach, "we'll be out soon to give you a licking." Years later, Pray told Williams he always took keen delight in whipping Shaughnessy because of a cold shoulder Clark gave him during a meeting once in New Orleans. Pray had confidence in his psychological ability where Tulane was concerned. Before the 1919 game with his archrival, according to Fred Frey, Pray told the Tigers: "Boys, if you win I'm driving out of Baton Rouge in the biggest car I can find. If we lose, I'll leave on a freight train." It was his way of saying he bet a sizable chunk on LSU. In 1922 the story was that he bet his entire salary and got 10-to-1 odds. "I know he made a killing," said Chesty Kizer. "And he'd get mad if any of us tried to bet ten dollars."

The game got under way and Pray's wager didn't look too good. The fabulous Brother Brown took Tulane down the field by running one end and then the other. Pretty soon the Greenbacks had a touchdown and a 7–0 lead. "We'll get the next one," yelled Tiger center L. C. Bourgeois. LSU grabbed the kickoff and, with Kizer, McFarland and Gus Jackson eating up real estate, swept to the six from where Kizer slashed across.

Tiger cheering section at Tulane game: On Third Street there was bedlam.

LSU missed the point and Tulane led 7–6. Shortly before half time, a 20-yard run by Helm ignited another march which McFarland climaxed with a 3-yard jab up the middle. Again the Tigers missed the point and it was 12–7 at half time.

Despite LSU's ability to move the football and contain Brother Brown after his early success, Tulane still looked the winner. Early in the third period, however, LSU got another drive going as the line-divide continued to puzzle Shaughnessy's crew. When Jackson knifed over and LSU added the extra point, the score was 19–7 and, for the first time, it was apparent that Tulane would have to hurry to get back in the game. But what happened? On the kickoff, Tulane fumbled and the Tigers recovered on the Greenbacks' 28. On the first play, from a line-divide setup, Kizer broke through the 2½-yard gap existing between the center and the right side. He went the distance to make it 25–7 and, for all practical purposes, to sew it up.

In justice to Tulane, Florida had pretty badly crippled them the week before—center Eddie Reed was at less than half speed—and, when the Tigers were able to check Brown, it put too much of a burden on the rest. Brown, however, went down running. In the fourth quarter, as the sun began to set, he ran a punt back forty yards for a touchdown to lift the final tally to a more respectable 25–14. Pray had done it again, and today, many years later, the 1922 game ranks with the top form reversals in the long series.

The upset prompted some Tigerish prose from the typewriter of *Times-Picayune* sportswriter (and now Congressman) Eddie Hebert. Wrote Hebert: "A torn, patched and badly battered Tiger from Louisiana State University crawled from out of its lair early this afternoon, dragged itself onto State Field, and plunged into the waters of the Green Wave of Tulane to come forth healed and cured by a soothing 25–14 victory.

"Instead of a Tiger with drooping head, a proud stalwart Bengal marched with eyes straight and head forward into its den tonight with the first victory over the Olive and Blue in three years.

"Amen."

On Third Street that night there was bedlam. At Izzy Wolf's restaurant, at the old Istrouma Hotel, at Rafe Meyer's cafe, at the Brunswick pool hall, at the Community Club, on those forbidden streets back-o-town, they all yelled "Yea, Tiger." A story told by Tom Holland, perhaps apocryphal, has it that Colonel T. D. Boyd, in all his dignity, passed down Third Street arm-in-arm with his wife. "Martha," said Boyd, "I feel like cutting capers."

The memory of SMU, Texas A & M, Arkansas, Rutgers, Alabama, Mississippi State—and the 245 points they ran up to LSU's 72—had been obliterated in one afternoon. All that mattered was what had been engraved forever in the minds of the celebrators and in the record book—LSU 25, Tulane 14.

'I have no alibis to offer'

1923–1927

IN 1919 Irving Pray had been lured back from Cuba to coach the Tigers at a salary of $1,200 a year. Four years later Michael Joseph Donahue was paid $10,000 a year—more than the governor of Louisiana—to duplicate the magic he had worked at Auburn. And the five-year contract he was offered reflected the faith LSU officials had in the Irishman's getting the job done.

When Mike Donahue arrived at Auburn in 1904, the entire student body of four hundred turned out at the train station to greet the man they had been reading about. It was not too surprising that some jaws hit the ground when Mike—all 5 feet, 4 inches of him—stepped from the train. "This is a football coach?" they asked themselves. The answer to their question was a nineteen-year record of 101 victories, 37 defeats, and 6 ties, a record which, during one stretch, found Auburn winning 21 of 22 games and outscoring the opposition 597 to 13.

Donahue was born in County Kerry, Ireland, in 1876. He came to the United States a disciplined 14-year-old, the product of a school system which began classes at eight in the morning and let pupils go at six in the evening. "We had a half hour for lunch," said Mike. Donahue's family settled in Norwich, Connecticut, and when his dad died he had to work his way through a four-year classical course at Norwich Academy. Upon graduation, he worked for four years before borrowing $250 to enter Yale, where he soon began to toss his 142 pounds around. Before he left the ivy-laced campus, he had won letters in football, basketball, track, and baseball and was a member of the cross-country team which won the national championship.

No one made more of an impression on Mike than his football coach at Yale, none other than Walter Camp, whose contribution to the sport was monumental. In the four years quarterback Donahue was at Yale, Camp's Bulldogs won forty-five games and lost two, while Mike won fame for an airborne maneuver designed for short yardage. In those days handles were sewn into the pants of players, one on either side and one in the back. They were used either to hold on to the player in front or to pull him from the side. Picture the pint-sized Donahue taking a flip from his fullback and then running toward the center of the line. Just as he arrived, two Yale backs, one on either side, caught him by his handles and propelled him into the secondary. Understandably some landings were unhappy for the helmetless Mike.

In one game matching the varsity against the alumni, Donahue backed the line for the varsity and the legendary "Pudge" Heffelfinger, an all-American in 1889–91, for the alumni, marking one of the few times one linebacker (Pudge scaled 240) outweighed the other by 100 pounds. "He wasn't human on a football field," Mike recalled, "and no man could handle him." Camp's Bulldogs used the early version of the T (there were no pitchouts or forward passes) and usually pulled a tackle into the backfield, giving them five men behind the line. Harvard liked to pull a guard back while Princeton, the other member of the Big Three, made use of the man-in-motion, not away from the ball but toward the line of scrimmage. From a flanked position, the wingback would start toward the center on the snap signal and would then either block the opposing end, tackle, or halfback or swing deep and take a handoff from one of his backs. The fact that clipping was legal helped the play's effectiveness.

All of this had an effect on Donahue's thinking, as did the shift devised by Dr. Henry L. Williams, who coached Minnesota from 1900 to 1922. From it, John Heisman derived the idea for the so-called "Heisman jump," and Donahue, for his famed "line-divide," a formation that made Auburn a Southern powerhouse. As revolutionary as the "line-divide" was at the time, Mike remained a product of Eastern conservatism, whereas Dan McGugin, who dropped anchor at Vanderbilt in 1904, built his reputation on deception rather than power. Basically, McGugin's idea of defense was an irresistible offense, while Mike's idea of offense was an impregnable defense.

Donahue's "line-divide" baffled the opposition for years (Auburn was using it in 1910) before the enemy learned to concentrate four or five good linemen in front of the "I" made by two halfbacks, the fullback, and the quarterback, who lined up Indian file beind the center. On "line-divide-right" there was an end and a guard to the left of the center. Immediately to the center's right there was a gap of three and a half yards. In this gap, just off the line of scrimmage, were the two tackles. To their right, on the line, was a guard and an end. On the shift, both

Michael Joseph Donahue (and Mike, Jr.): $10,000 a year for the Auburn magic.

tackles moved into the line, leaving a split of some two yards. In the backfield, the quarterback would shift to a spot just behind the gap between the tackles; the right half, to a wingback spot; the fullback, to a spot behind the quarterback; the left half, to a tailback's spot. All signals were called by the quarterback, the numbers designating the players and where they were to go.

The fullback was the workhorse of the attack that generated great power up the middle, and it was not unusual for Mike to use as many as four in one game since the line-divide wore them out at a pretty fast clip. At Auburn, Donahue had turned out a flock of players who won national acclaim, among them Humphrey Foy, Frank Jones, Tom McClure, Walter Reynolds, John Pitts and Richard "Moon" Ducote.

Ducote, who caused a change in football rules when he booted a field goal using his helmet as a tee, was brought to LSU by Donahue as an assistant. Moon had gathered head-coaching experience at Spring Hill College in 1921 and 1922 and jumped at the chance to join his old teacher. Ducote had figured in a moral victory that propelled Donahue into the nation's eye, a 0–0 tie with Ohio State in 1917. The Buckeyes already had clinched what amounted to the Big Ten championship and they went to Montgomery expecting to take Auburn in stride. The invaders, who scored 292 points for the season, threatened only once, following a tremendous save by Ducote, who nailed a touchdown-bound ball carrier on the Auburn 15.

LSU officials, of course, were quite familiar with Mike's accomplishments, and the day following the 25–14 upset of Tulane, newspapers carried reports that LSU had spoken to Donahue about the head-coaching job. Mike had resigned at Auburn and quite obviously money was one of the reasons. His Auburn contract called for him to coach football, basketball, baseball, and track, serve as faculty advisor for social affairs, and oversee the mess hall. For this he was being paid $4,400 plus a modest fee for teaching a few classes. When an LSU committee headed by Colonel T. D. Boyd and including Professor T. W. Atkinson and alumni representatives Tom Dutton and J. Y. Sanders, Jr., waved a five-year pact worth $50,000, it was little wonder Mike jumped at it.

Donahue's signing became public shortly before Christmas, 1922. At the same time it was announced that Ducote and Doc Fenton would serve as assistants, Fenton being a holdover since he had aided Pray (without pay) during the 1922 season. LSU left no doubt of its intention to "go big time." A 35-man alumni committee was set up to play a part in reorganizing the athletic setup. Members were to be chosen each year on the day of the game with Tulane and their job was to confer with the president and athletic director from time to time, making recommendations when the necessity arose. Donahue realized the alumni group would have a large say in LSU policy if only because it had raised a portion of his $10,000 salary, but he tackled his new job with relish.

Despite Donahue's fame, LSU fans had no idea what kind of man to expect. The immediate impression in Baton Rouge was the same as it had been in Auburn—a man of 5 feet, 4 inches, with round face, blue eyes, and dark reddish hair. Donahue talked rapidly, in a sort of staccato-like bark. He walked briskly, taking unusually long strides for one so short of stature. In the summer and early fall, Mike was addicted to a stiff straw hat. During the season, after he discarded the straw, he would go bareheaded at home but on road trips he wore a regular brown or grey felt. Except for his interest in golf, he talked of little else than football, Mrs. Donahue, and the children.

The Donahue coaching staff, unofficial. From left, Tad Gormley, Moon Ducote, Third Street coach Izzy Wolf (his restaurant was a gathering place for players and fans), and Donahue.

Although Donahue was unfamiliar with the material he was inheriting from Pray, he not only passed up a chance at spring drills but also did not greet his LSU squad until September 15, two weeks before his 1923 opener against Louisiana Normal. His backfield was thin and inexperienced. McFarland was gone at quarterback. Helm was gone at halfback. There was no fullback of experience around except Charles Forgey, who had played only intercompany football in the cadet battalion. Lettermen reporting back received a shock when Donahue overlooked many of them in favor of green boys with larger physiques. Mike went for size and he liked to juggle. For example, he placed the inexperienced B. R. Vernon at center. At fullback, he had sophomores T. D. "Red" Fay and A. L. "Red" Swanson. Soon, however, Vernon became a guard as did Swanson. Fay played end as well as fullback. Mike continued to interchange throughout the season but basically he went with the following starting lineup: Ben Miller (163) and captain Tubby Ewen (178) at ends, J. E. "Buck" Steele (178) and Red Hughes (205) at tackles, Vernon (190) and L. R. "Tubbo" Matthews (210) at guards, L. C. Bourgeois (180) at center, Luke Abramson (167) at quarterback, Bill Pitcher (155) and A. T. "Shorty" Edmondson (150) at halfbacks, and Forgey (160) at fullback. Donahue's No. 2 backfield had Ike Carriere (140) at quarterback, Norm Stevens (165) and A. W. "Gus" Jackson (175) at halfbacks and Red Fay (190) at fullback.

An opening 40–0 victory over Louisiana Normal was more or less a shakedown cruise for Donahue. Mike still hadn't installed the line-divide, being content to stick with his A formation, another name for the single wing. Next week it was a somewhat different story. Southwestern of Lafayette invaded Baton Rouge and in the fourth quarter held a 3–0 lead. The afternoon belonged to a sandy-haired youngster who, some onlookers believed, seemed to pass with either hand. No one knew it at the time, of course, but they were getting their first look at Keener "Red" Cagle, then embarking on a glittering career destined to end on the plains of West Point. Cagle short-passed Donahue's crew to death, and it took a touchdown late in the game for LSU to get out alive with an uphill 7–3 victory. Said Donahue of his narrow escape: "SLI played November football and we played September football." Mike began installing his line-divide the following week, and a 33–0 decision over Spring Hill seemed to be just the tuneup for what he knew would be a real tester—Texas A & M. The Aggies were under the wing of Dana Bible, who had coached the Tigers for three games in 1916, and Bible was getting lots of mileage out of his two-team system, substituting by quarters. It worked to perfection against LSU. The Aggies took command at the outset, held the Tigers to a couple of first downs, and fashioned a workmanlike 28–0 decision. It's questionable whether Bible's platoon system overly impressed Donahue, but the next week against Arkansas in Shreveport Mike pulled his regulars in the second quarter after Jackson scored two touchdowns to give LSU a 13–7 lead. Before he knew what hit, Arkansas rammed over three touchdowns and had a 26–13 lead at half time. Ike Carriere caught a few passes from Stevens in the last half, but there was no more scoring.

Donahue's line-divide was moving the ball but it lacked the necessary goal line punch. A rain-drenched scoreless tie with Mississippi College followed the Arkansas loss and a week later Alabama slammed the Tigers, 30–3, to set the stage for the annual game with Tulane, still under the hand of Shaughnessy. LSU out-first downed the Tulanians, 11–3, but Tulane won by a lopsided 20–0, a victory that was a showcase for the fabulous Brother Brown. In the first quarter, the Tulane back, with the ball jammed against the west side, swept right end for seventy yards and a touchdown. Later Charles "Peggy" Flournoy pitched forty yards to Brown for a score when Tiger quarterback Luke Abramson collided with the goalpost trying to break it up. In the second quarter Ellis Henican put the icing on the cake when he recovered an LSU fumble and advanced it twenty yards for a touchdown (permissible in those days). Pitcher and Jackson ate up some real estate, but all to no avail.

When LSU dropped a closing 14–7 verdict to Mississippi State on December 1, it meant that Donahue's first season was 3–5–1. Still everyone felt better times were ahead. In the red shirt room that year was a crew that could hold its own with the varsity. There were the Weaver brothers, A. V. and O. L., from Natchitoches, a pair who had spent a couple of years at Georgia Tech and were now eligible; there were Joe Bonner and Sam Morgan, two good-sized linemen from Alabama; there was Opie Dimmick from Southwestern Louisiana Institute; Allen Connell, a transfer from Vandy; and Jack Clay, a prospect up from company football. These players, plus a new stadium abuilding on the present campus, made for a "wait-till-next-year" mood. The *Gumbo* took note of the new university taking shape south of Baton Rouge: "To old LSU, with all its customs, traditions, and hallowed memories, we dedicate this 1924 *Gumbo* in grateful love and lasting loyalty." Everyone was waiting for the first bright page in the Donahue era.

The 1924 opener did little to send fans into a frenzy. Spring Hill led the Tigers 6–0 at the half, and it took a late scoring drive engineered by quarterback Carriere and a dropkick by Bill Pitcher to pull out a 7–6

JUDGE OLIVER P. CARRIERE

The 1924 team. On the bottom row are three players later to serve as members of the LSU Board of Supervisors—quarterback Oliver P. "Ike" Carriere (fourth from left), guard A. L. "Red" Swanson (fifth from left), and halfback Bill Pitcher (fourth from right).

squeaker. Donahue fielded a beefy team that was a mixture of lettermen and red shirts. His normal starting eleven had Red Fay and Otto Weaver at ends, C. C. Campbell and Tubbo Weaver at tackles, Steele and Swanson at guards, Vernon at center, Carriere at quarter, Stevens and Jackson at the halves, and Connell at full. Because his line-divide was particularly punishing to the fullback, Mike had Forgey, Clay, and Fritz Spencer behind Connell. Slowly, his squad was beginning to get the hang of the power formation, and in a 31–7 victory over SLI and Cagle the week after the Spring Hill win the Tigers moved the ball as well as could be expected. It enabled Donahue to take an unbeaten team north to Indianapolis for a meeting which the influential Mike had arranged with the University of Indiana, scheduled for October 11. This was LSU's first and, to date, only football game against a Big Ten representative and the approaching intersectional contest had the campus in a tizzy. Because LSU was an unknown product in the Midwest at the time, a publicist was dispatched to Baton Rouge to send back accounts of the Tigers to boost the crowd. Donahue did some dispatching of his own, sending assistant Hugh "Gob" Wilson to scout the Hoosiers against De Pauw; Indiana won, 21–0, and, according to all reports, had one of the strongest clubs in the area. When LSU arrived in Indianapolis after a twenty-four-hour train ride the drumbeater who had built up LSU in the Indiana press met Donahue as he stepped off the train with the plea: "Please don't make me look bad." Saturday was "Dixie Day" in Indianapolis and the game pulled a crowd of 12,000, Hoosier rooters all. Back home, Tiger fans were gathered inside State Field to follow the action by wireless on the Gridgraph. The stage was aglow with Indiana crimson, LSU purple and gold, and the voice of announcer "Wild Bill" Graham who, depending on the returns, sent the assembly into groans or roars. Graham many times was "scooped" by a small group of students beside the scoreboard who, on hearing the message called out by the operator, leaped into the air and sailed their hats or sank to the ground with a mournful look. "Stevens struts through center, five ya-a-rds," Graham shouted as the drama unfolded many miles away. "Allen Connell goes through center for a touchdown!" Hats flew and cheers rang out.

The game turned into a 14-carat thriller. Indiana scored early when Carriere fumbled a punt and a Hoosier end picked up the ball and raced forty yards. Far from disheartened, LSU replied with a 60-yard drive climaxed by a 15-yard run by Connell. When the Tigers missed the extra-point try, they trailed 7–6 and moments later it was 14–6 when an Indiana halfback broke loose on a long touchdown gallop. In the third quarter Carriere recovered an Indiana fumble on the Hoosier 42 and two plays later Stevens stepped thirty-eight yards to make it a 14–13 ball

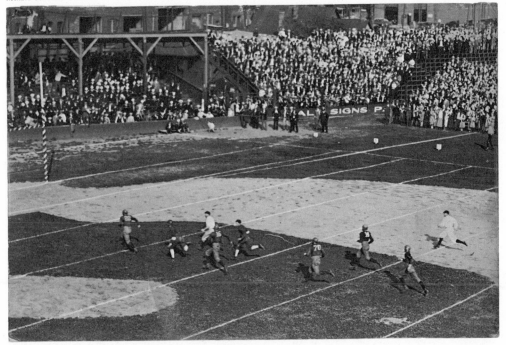

LSU man going for a touchdown at Indianapolis, 1924.

game going into the final quarter. A 67-yard march, gobbled up in small chunks and ended by Jackson's short sprint, put the visitors on top, 20–14. But Indiana had one shot left. With two minutes remaining, the Hoosiers moved to the LSU 1-yard line and had two downs to get it across. The Tigers tossed back the first assault and on fourth down Ben Miller broke through and nailed the ball carrier on the five. Miller had one more chore. Carriere called on him to punt—something he had never done before in varsity competition. Miller not only booted one to midfield but made the tackle as well, seconds before the final whistle.

Donahue was afraid to look as Miller punted, but once the horn sounded, the little Irishman bounded onto the field and wrung the hand of his grimy warriors. Ends Otto Weaver and Red Fay won special praise for their defensive work; Stevens, Jackson, Connell, Pitcher, Miller and Forgey for their running; and Carriere for his field general-ship. It remained for quarterback Opie Dimmick to contribute the game's most memorable play, a third-quarter interception in which the LSU back paused after catching the ball, turned to the stands, and yelled "Bound for Dixie!" His dramatic pause was just enough to allow him to be overhauled on the Indiana 6 and wound up costing LSU a touchdown. "Dixie" Dimmick's boo-boo was not only forgiven by Donahue in the flush of victory but it became the main topic of conversation on the ride home. Just as the Tigers were ready to depart, the private train of Democratic presidential candidate John W. Davis rolled into Indianapolis. One player shouted, "Fifteen long ones for Davis!"

Opie Dimmick

and, following the cheer, a smiling Davis stepped onto the platform to congratulate the team. "Your great battle," said Davis, "was typical of the great spirit of the Southland." LSU fared better than the Democratic standard-bearer. Davis carried Louisiana but lost to Calvin Coolidge by more than seven million votes.

Back in Baton Rouge, there was bedlam. Hordes of singing, pajama-clad students took part in a mammoth, two-hour snake dance down Third Street. When the team returned home on Monday, 1,400 students were at the station as the band played "Glory, Glory, Louisiana." Players received a victory ride through the business district.

Donahue gave assistant Gob Wilson's shrewd scouting job a large share of the credit for the upset. Wilson, who had played for Fielding Yost at Michigan and served as line coach under Mike at Auburn, had accompanied the Tigers to Indianapolis, passing up a chance to scout Rice, LSU's opponent the following week. Rice was then under the wing of John Heisman, who had moved from Georgia Tech, and Donahue felt his old rival had no secrets. He was vindicated as LSU defeated the Owls in Houston, 12–0, in a battle dominated by defense. One reason defense predominated (and this is something Donahue didn't realize until he took his team onto the field) was the unusually high grass. It was so high it slowed the ball carriers to a snail's pace and kept the roll of punts to a minimum. Ike Carriere engineered a scoring march in the first half and Gus Jackson picked off a Rice pass later in the game to sew it up. A knot of LSU fans made the trip to Houston, as did the LSU band. For those who were there, the picture of "Wild Bill" Graham, in gold pants, purple coat, and gold derby is still etched clearly in their memory. The 220-pound Graham had an on-again, off-again ten-year career as a student (1917–26) because side jaunts to such places as Tanganyika and Kenya continued to interrupt his studies.

Then Mike Donahue's Tigers, with a 4–0 record, turned their attention to Auburn. LSU's October 25 invasion of Birmingham left many Auburn fans with mixed emotions. The reception Mike received when the team reached the Alabama city made it clear he had lost none of his popularity at the school he served for nineteen years. Players whom Donahue had coached met the train and followed him to the roof of the Tutweiler Hotel where he sent the team through signal drills. Out at Rickwood Field a host of "War Eagles" gathered around the little Irishman to let him know they were "halfway pulling" for LSU. "Don't be silly," Donahue said, "pull for your school."

A crowd of 8,000 turned out to witness Donahue's "homecoming," a game in which the Donahue brand of football was clearly evident. Auburn, coached by Mike's longtime assistant "Boozer" Pitts, threw up a rugged defense that repeatedly tossed back LSU threats and allowed a second-quarter field goal to stand up for a 3–0 Auburn victory. Half-back Williams, whose toe was the difference, missed six attempts before he drop-kicked a 25-yarder.

Bill Pitcher and Norman Stevens spearheaded several LSU marches in the second half but the attacks bogged down near the goal each time. The afternoon's highlight, in fact a highlight in LSU football history, was a record 93-yard punt by Pitcher that traveled seventy-three yards in the air. Pitcher's kicking played a major role in the LSU defense, time after time putting the home team deep in its own territory. On the afternoon that Pitcher won undying fame with his foot, G. Caldwell Herget (later a distinguished jurist) won undying fame for his persever-ance. Early in the game Donahue called on Herget to "warm up," and the only place to do this in Rickwood Field was behind a fence outside the playing area. Donahue became so engrossed in the game he forgot all about his ball player, who continued to run up and down until half time.

Next week it was Arkansas in Shreveport, and this time the Tigers

Norm Stevens: One of the four-sport lettermen.

NORMAN STEVENS

Tiger Stadium, Thanksgiving Day, 1924: The work was hurriedly completed.

were unable to recover from an early siege of fumbleitis that gave the Razorbacks ten points in the first five minutes. It remained that way until the final minute when LSU avoided a shutout with a 55-yard march sparked by Stevens' passes to A. D. Warner and Ben Miller. Stevens bucked across for the touchdown, the extra point was added, and the final score was 10–7. The late touchdown drive brought an LSU rooter out of the stands—and onto the bench—for the first time! Huey Long wanted to be part of the show.

A record that two weeks before stood at 4–0 was now 4–2 and coming up was an unenviable trip to Atlanta—LSU's fifth road game in a row—to battle mighty Georgia Tech, which had passed from Heisman to Bill Alexander. Alexander was a sort of protégé of Donahue, so it was an easy matter to get LSU onto Tech's schedule. When Donahue sent his team through a practice session the day before the game in Grant Field, Alexander walked alongside chatting. When Tech took the field, Donahue accompanied the young coach as he shouted instructions. Someone asked Mike about coaches watching the opposition practice, and he said: "We both know what the other fellow is going to do. The team that executes its plays best will win. Fundamentals will always beat formations and trick plays." As it turned out Tech had no trick plays, but it did have a back named Doug Wycoff, and LSU tacklers left Grant Field black and blue from trying to tackle him. Ike Carriere, who weighed 138 to Wycoff's 215, tackled the Tech bruiser a few times, and ached for the rest of the game. Wycoff scored two touchdowns in the first half before LSU broke through with a Stevens-to-Red Fay pass to make it 14–7. This was unfortunate. Alexander not only had taken Wycoff out of the game, but he had put on civilian clothes and was watching the action from the stands. Alex told him to suit up at half time and he soon scored twice more to make it 28–7, the only time the 1924 Tigers were outclassed.

Donahue welcomed a breather the following week—a 40–0 victory over Louisiana Normal—as a means of gathering his group for "the old college try" ten days later against Tulane. It wasn't just any Tulane game. LSU was going to dedicate its new playing area on the new (but not yet occupied) campus south of the city. Work on the first stage of what we today know as Tiger Stadium had begun the previous January and it was hurriedly completed in time for the Thanksgiving Day clash. In fact, a section of the stands on one side had not been accepted by engineers and therefore was roped off.

Until then, the largest crowd ever to watch a game in Louisiana was approximately 12,000. Influenza caused Governor Henry Fuqua to miss the gala dedication ceremonies, but ex-Governor John M. Parker was among those in the record crowd estimated at 18,000. Colonel Theodore Roosevelt, son of the former President, was a guest of Governor Parker

ROSALIE DONAHUE DUKE

Action on the goal line in the first LSU-Tulane game in Tiger Stadium.

and acknowledged the cheers as Odette Alley led LSU rooters in "fifteen big ones."

All week before the game Donahue devoted the better part of practice to a surprise he was cooking up for the favored invaders who had a 7–1 record and a quick-striking backfield that included Lester Lautenschlaeger, Brother Brown, and Peggy Flournoy. Figuring that Shaughnessy would have Tulane prepared for the regular line-divide, Donahue put in the T formation off the line-divide, something he had not shown up to that time. Plans called for LSU to save it until the Tigers had the ball in Tulane territory, but when Tulane grabbed a 6–0 lead, quarterback Ike Carriere decided the time had come. Squatting behind the center, Carriere took the Tigers from the LSU 30 to the Tulane 10 in short, steady jabs as the Greenies seemed baffled by the new wrinkle. Three plays later the Tigers were inches short of a tying touchdown and, as Carriere was about to call a fourth-down play, Donahue sent fullback Fritz Spencer into the game. "When you see Spencer come in on the goal line," Donahue had instructed his quarterbacks beforehand, "call number 32." Carriere did, but the big fullback stumbled as he attempted to hit up the middle and was swarmed over at the 2-yard line. That was the game's turning point. Four plays later Flournoy punted out of danger, and Tulane intercepted a pass and went on to score on a pass from Lautenschlaeger to "Doc" Wilson. At half time Shaughnessy came up with the answer to the Tiger T. He had linebacker Harvey Wilson dive over the LSU center and smother Carriere before he could hand off.

Although Tulane's 13–0 victory threw a damper on dedication day, the year 1924 was significant in that it marked the start of big-time football in Louisiana. The day after the game Donahue sat around a table with assistant Gob Wilson, trainer Tad Gormley, and student manager Ran Williams counting gate receipts. The money taken in at the gate had been stuffed into two gunny sacks and locked in the athletic office overnight. After the bills and silver were counted, Donahue took the money downtown and put it in the bank. Besides launching big-time football in the state, the 1924 game also was the first Southern game to be broadcast, although on somewhat of an experimental basis. Buck Gladden, halfback letterman in 1919, handled the play-by-play as he walked up and down the sidelines relaying the action via his "mike" to a professor in the physics building. Word was then relayed to several Louisiana stations.

With the fall of 1925 and the move to the new campus came a new wave of optimism, a general expectation that the Donahue era would begin to pay dividends. This despite the loss of the Weaver brothers, Tubbo Matthews, and L. C. Bourgeois in the line, along with Bill Pitcher's gifted punting. Students and alumni were sky high on several newcomers—quarterback L. T. "Babe" Godfrey from New Mexico

Military Academy, E. H. "Hinky" Haynes from Jacksonville, Alabama, Normal, and guard Martin Flood. These and a few others, it was felt, would soon have Donahue back on top in the South and LSU with him. After two games—victories over Louisiana Normal, 27–0, and Southwestern Louisiana, 38–0—the forecasters looked good. Tiger enthusiasm was running so high that Alabama assistant Russ Cohen was caught up in the tide. Wallace Wade had sent Cohen to scout LSU in its first two games and Russ brought back glowing reports of the Donahue crew. When Wade arrived in Baton Rouge with the ball club, he got a first-hand look at the LSU personnel and felt Cohen had oversold the Tigers and been duped "by all that pep." He laid it on the line to Bama at its Istrouma Hotel headquarters after bawling out his assistant for reporting what he felt were emotions rather than fact.

Wade had confidence in players. When ball carriers like "Red" Barnes, "Papa" Pooley Hubert, and Johnny Mack Brown were clicking, it was something to behold. And Alabama clicked in Baton Rouge. The first time the Tide got the football, it sliced through Donahue's defense in short, steady gains—three, four, five yards at a clip—to score a touchdown within five minutes. Five more followed in an overwhelming 42–0 victory—the worst home defeat suffered by LSU until 1948 when Tulane won 46–0.

Donahue based his defense for Bama on some advice offered by Bill Alexander of Georgia Tech. "Concentrate on stopping Brown to the outside," Alex wrote Mike. "Don't worry about Hubert because you can stop him in critical territory." When Hubert spotted the LSU tackles playing abnormally wide, he simply hammered away at the middle. When the Tigers adjusted, Brown went to the outside. Lots of LSU money had showed before the game because Bama was considered a 21-point choice and the folks in Baton Rouge didn't feel anyone could be that good. Not only was the Tide's offense relentless but the defense was every bit as good. Allen Connell and Babe Godfrey, who had broken loose on some long scoring runs against Normal and Southwestern, were completely muffled. In fact, the Tigers wound up with one first down. Linemen Red Swanson and B. R. Vernon were knocked cold early and never returned. The defensive play of Connell and Ben Miller was about the only redeeming feature of a somber afternoon.

To say Alabama put a damper on 1925 is putting it mildly. On the next three weekends the Tigers squeaked by the LSU freshmen, 6–0, played a scoreless tie with Tennessee, and bowed to Arkansas, 12–0. A Godfrey-to-Haynes pass got LSU safely past Rice, 6–0, and a 70-yard run by Norm Stevens triggered a 13–0 win over Loyola to give Donahue a 5–2–1 record (if you count beating the freshmen) entering the Tulane game.

Because Tulane was busy building its new, 22,000-seat stadium, the game was played in Baton Rouge for the second year in a row. Shaughnessy's Tulanians, who made national headlines with a stirring intersectional win over Northwestern, had a 7–0–1 mark and were ruled a heavy choice. A crowd of 25,000 jammed into Tiger Stadium (end-zone bleachers had been added) and, for a half, it seemed that LSU had an outside chance of springing a major upset. In the first thirty minutes the Tigers had been able to contain Lautenschlaeger and Flournoy. In the third period, however, Tulane capitalized on a ruse that changed the tempo of the game. When Shaughnessy's club upset Northwestern ear-

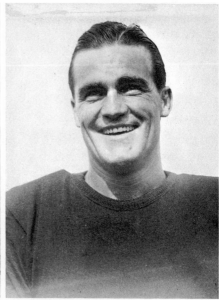

Two of Donahue's standouts—Jess Tinsley and Babe Godfrey.

lier in the season, Lautenschlaeger had completed eight passes in eight attempts, six to end Pat Browne. In the third quarter, with Tulane camped on the LSU 23, Lautenschlaeger flanked Johnny Menville to the left side. Hinky Haynes, Tiger defender, had been coming up fast to cover Browne and, this time, after taking the snap, Lautenschlaeger looked to Browne and yelled "Hey, Pat." Sure enough, Haynes came in and Lautenschlaeger fired a pass to a wide-open Menville to break the scoring ice. Early in the final period, Flournoy punted out beautifully on the LSU 1-yard line, and on the next play Tulane guard "Irish" Levy tackled Godfrey in the end zone for a safety. With a safe 9–0 lead, Tulane drove for a score late in the game and Flournoy climaxed the march with a four-yard run. The extra point made it 16–0 and Donahue was 5–3–1 for the season and 0–3 with his archrivals.

Mike retained most of his key offensive players for 1926, and the addition of two standout tackles, Jess Tinsley and Guy Nesom, again was responsible for rosy predictions in the early fall. The Tigers began with the same script, whipping Louisiana Normal, 47–0, and Southwestern Louisiana, 34–0, before getting into the meatier portion of the schedule. As it had been Alabama that brought Tiger fans to earth in 1925, so it was Tennessee, tutored by a young man named Bob Neyland, which helped temper the 1926 optimism. The Vols did not win as impressively as Bama had done the previous year, but their rhythmic attack carved out a 14–7 victory indicating young Neyland had a bright future ahead. A jarring tackle by Tinsley, causing a Tennessee back to fumble the ball, was responsible for the LSU touchdown which came on a 16-yard pass from Charley Mason to Haynes. The following week Mason had a foot, instead of a hand, in a 10–0 win over Auburn. He booted the Plainsmen into a hole with a 70-yard punt and the Tigers came charging back for a touchdown.

Feet, and luck, figured in a 7–6 loss to Mississippi State a week later in a game that seemed to be right out of Hollywood. State scored first and its try for extra point struck the crossbar but bounced over to make it 7–0. After Haynes scored for the Tigers, Nesom's place kick hit the crossbar and fell back into the playing field.

Donahue took his hardluck crew into Tuscaloosa seven days later for another meeting with Alabama, a team headed for its second straight trip to the Rose Bowl. For three quarters LSU, taking heart from the defensive play of Tinsley and Nesom, trailed by a thin three points before Bama's depth took its toll. In rapid succession, Tide tackle Fred Pickard burst through to block two LSU kicks and Wallace Wade's outfit turned them both into touchdowns. Alabama scored once more on the tiring Tigers to walk off with a 24–0 decision, a game, so the saying goes, that was closer than the score indicated.

Apparently Donahue's defense, long his trademark, had jelled. The Tigers closed out the season with three shutouts, beating Arkansas, 14–0; Ole Miss, 3–0; and Tulane, 7–0, for a 6–3 record, Mike's best in Tigertown. Against the Razorbacks, Mason returned a punt seventy yards for one touchdown and passed to Haynes for the second. In the Ole Miss game Nesom booted a 20-yard field goal in the second quarter which managed to stand up. So far as the Tulane game is concerned, Clark Shaughnessy is still being second guessed by some Wave alumni for following a practice initiated by Knute Rockne, whose "Four Horsemen" had just closed a glittering career. Rockne would start his second team ("shock troops" he called them), play them for a spell, and then bring on his first unit. Shaughnessy sprang this on the Tigers but it backfired, before a crowd of 22,000 on hand for the game in the new Tulane Stadium. With Tulane's reserves in the game, Allen Connell started an LSU drive with a 34-yard run, and several plays later Haynes bucked over from the one for the Tigers' first touchdown against Tulane in four years. Since more than three quarters remained, Tulane fans weren't too concerned. However, the LSU defense improved as the game wore on. Tulane mounted its most serious threat in the third period when it reached the LSU 1, only to be thrown back on fourth down by the mighty Jess Tinsley, practically a unanimous all-Southern selection, thus sewing up LSU's 7–0 victory.

By 1927 LSU fans, while optimistic, were wise enough not to allow "warmup" victories to go to their heads. The return of Otto Weaver, a 1924 standout at end, and the addition of G. A. "Nubs" Freeman, who had quit before the 1924 season began, were enough to create some preseason sunshine. Perennial optimists withheld judgment following a 45–0 win over Louisiana Polytechnic Institute and a 52–0 rout of Southwestern Louisiana, but when the Tigers went to Birmingham and played a 0–0 tie with Alabama, they could not restrain themselves. Although mud, the great equalizer, was present in quantity, the Tide had been held scoreless for the first time in thirty-one games. Also, it was the first time in three long and weary years that a Southern team had done anything but lose to Wallace Wade. When brilliant punting by Mason and a superb defensive job by Tinsley helped bring about the major surprise, Southern writers asked the question: Was this the end of Alabama's domination of Dixie?

LSU officials were sure it was the beginning, the beginning of a bright era for Donahue in Baton Rouge. They tore up Mike's existing contract (which had one more year to run) and wrote him a new six-year pact at $10,000 per season. The Tigers were roaring.

A week later, Donahue took his club back to Alabama, this time to Montgomery, where it turned back a stubborn bid by Auburn, 9–0. A

Cheerleaders Harry A. "Red" Taylor and Eileen "Little Mike" Donahue (Coach Mike's daughter), 1927. After Arkansas, there was not much to cheer about.

30-yard field goal by Nesom provided an early 3–0 lead and this was followed by a 60-yard scoring pass from Godfrey to Haynes. Godfrey was still in there pitching the following week against Mississippi State in Jackson. He tossed one into the flat to Percy "Bronco" Brown, a rookie halfback, who sped thirty-eight yards behind a blocking convoy for six points. The extra point was missed but Nesom later added a field goal to give Donahue a 9–0 lead which withstood a final-quarter touchdown by State.

The Tigers, with a 4–0–1 record, had four games remaining—Arkansas, Ole Miss, Georgia Tech, and Tulane. Could they go all the way? Baton Rouge thought so. You can imagine, therefore, the pall of gloom that settled over Louisiana's capital when the flash came from Shreveport's State Fair Grounds: Arkansas 28, LSU 0. Impossible? No. Unbelievable? Yes, but true. Arkansas had ripped Donahue's proud defense to shreds and talk of dissension immediately began circulating. Weaver and Freeman left the team, lending credence to rumors that some boys had broken training. Things went from bad to worse. When, on November 5, an up-and-coming Ole Miss club handed the Tigers a decisive 12–7 setback in Oxford, amid rumors of a rift between LSU authorities and Donahue, it looked like the end was nearing. The Tigers were never in the game. The Rebs took a 12–0 lead and were driving for a third when Tinsley grabbed a fumble and raced sixty-five yards to set up the Tiger touchdown. Against Tech, LSU held Bill Alexander's Yellowjackets to a 3–0 half-time lead but crumbled before superior numbers in the second half, bowing 23–0. Adding to the miseries was the misfortune which befell Tinsley. He was pouring in on a Tech ball carrier when he was hit from the side and suffered a broken leg. Donahue's world was coming apart at the seams. A month before, he was unbeaten—the toast of Dixie—with a new six-year contract in his pocket. Now his disintegrating ball club was 4–3–1 and it had to play "new look" Tulane without its best defensive player.

Tulane had changed coaches—Bernie Bierman taking over for Clark Shaughnessy—and that meant fewer "freakish formations" (the words of one observer) and more orthodox football. The game, before fifteen thousand in Tiger Stadium, was rated a tossup and boiled down to a question of LSU's being able to contain powerful Bill Banker, Tulane's all-Southern halfback. The Greenbacks drew first blood when Dick Baumbach passed forty-one yards to Eugene McCarroll and Banker promptly took it across from the 5. Pat Browne's place kick made it 7–0 after one quarter. In the second period a fake pass and run by Godfrey brought the Tigers to the Tulane 9 and, two plays later, Haynes scored from the 2. LSU missed the try for point. Later in the quarter McCarroll caught a touchdown pass to make it 13–6—and 13–6 it was at the final whistle, taps for Mike Donahue.

When the announcement finally came December 23, it came as no surprise. Said Donahue: "Three days after Thanksgiving, I felt I had enough of coaching after twenty-four years. I have no alibis to offer. The players worked hard and I received loyal support of trainers, coaches and staff."

His five-year record had been 28–19–3. What happened to the Donahue magic at LSU? Some observers felt the lovable little Irishman failed to grow with the game. Throughout his stay, Mike remained proficient in teaching defensive play, particularly for guards and tackles, and he held fast to the theory that fundamentals not formations win ball games. However, some felt he did not keep abreast of the changes in fundamentals, for example the changes in forward passing techniques, end play, and how to take full advantage of the roving center. In the 1920s speed, deception, and forward passing were coming to the fore and, for the most part, Mike stuck with the deception and forward-pass format of the 1910–20 era. Of perhaps greatest importance, Mike never relished recruiting, feeling the players would gravitate to LSU without any all-out campaign.

Donahue could have held LSU to its contract, but he chose to ask for his release and bow out gracefully. An accomplished golfer, he accepted the job as professional at the Baton Rouge Country Club, where he had won several tournaments. In 1929 he couldn't resist a call to return to football when Spring Hill beckoned. He remained at the Mobile school until 1937 when he returned to LSU, at the request of athletic director T. P. Heard, as director of intramurals. For the next dozen years he helped popularize golf at the university, and at one time had three thousand students taking lessons.

Donahue retired in 1949 and lived out his years in Baton Rouge, long enough to see himself become a charter member of football's Hall of Fame and to see LSU win a national championship. He died December 11, 1958, at the age of eighty-four.

Zipp Newman, veteran sports editor of the Birmingham *News*, paid Mike this tribute: "Mike Donahue was first a father and then a coach to his boys. They showed their love with gifts through all his life. He had taken some as poor farm boys from the farms and small hamlets—not only making fine football players out of them—but guiding them into successful accomplishments in business, science and medicine . . . the rich compensation in writing sports is to know and love teachers like Mike Donahue, Johnny Heisman and Dan McGugin. And see in the lengthening shadows the flower and fruits of the good in football."

'Call 1099! Call 1099!'

1928-1931

THE failure of Mike Donahue to lift LSU among the powers of Dixie football did not sour university officials on the possibility that gridiron prosperity was ahead. On the contrary, it merely whetted the appetite of the men in positions of influence, men jealous of the success Tulane had achieved under Clark Shaughnessy and Bernie Bierman. LSU still hungered for something which was beginning to seem phantomlike—the "championship team," an excuse to stand up and roar "I'm a Tiger." Thus it was no different in the winter of 1927 than it is today, and there was no difference in the thinking of athletic officials as to the best method of putting their school on the football map.

First you try a head coach who had proven himself in tough competition. LSU did this with Mike Donahue. Failing this, you go after an assistant at a school whose head coach is somewhat of a legend. LSU did this with Russ Cohen. Scarcely a month after the Tigers had played their last game under Donahue, LSU announced the hiring of the 32-year-old assistant under Wallace Wade at Alabama. Cohen had excellent credentials. Aside from his impressive work at Alabama, he had been captain of Vanderbilt's 1916 team which lost only to Alabama. Therefore, anyone who coached under Wade and played for Dan McGugin had been exposed to the titans of Southern football. McGugin gave his former captain the highest recommendation when he said: "If I were LSU I'd try to get Russ. He's high class and a great teacher."

There had been one report that LSU President T. W. Atkinson approached Don Miller, one of Notre Dame's Four Horsemen and then an assistant at Georgia Tech, on the prospect of joining LSU as an assistant under Donahue, with the idea of keeping Donahue and grooming Miller for the head job. Miller reportedly declined, whereupon

87

Russ Cohen, the coach with the Phi Beta Kappa manner, right, and his assistant, Ben Enis.

Atkinson decided a "new look" was in order. The man highly instrumental in Russ Cohen's coming to Baton Rouge was Phil Connell, president of the Louisiana National Bank in Baton Rouge and a close friend of Atkinson's. A Vanderbilt graduate, Connell recommended Cohen and had McGugin give Russ his blessing.

So it was that LSU cast its football future, in late December, 1927, with a ruddy-faced chap with blue eyes, bushy eyebrows, and red hair. Although Cohen had the stocky build of an athlete, his talk reflected exactly what he was—a serious, almost solemn Phi Beta Kappa, someone with a scholarly background who was at ease in intellectual company. He habitually dressed in brown suits with a brown cap to match. He wore horn-rimmed glasses and he managed to keep in shape by playing handball at every opportunity. Although some considered him a crepe hanger, with friends he was warm and friendly. He spoke with a soft Southern drawl, native to the states of Georgia, Alabama, and western

Tennessee where he had spent his earlier years. He was not afraid to talk, off the record, on any subject, particularly the stock market and politics. While not necessarily a straitlaced prohibitionist at heart, he had no use for alcohol or tobacco.

That is a brief personality sketch of the man LSU signed to a three-year contract to begin in the fall of 1928. Cohen brought in only one assistant, Ben Enis, who had played for Wade at Alabama. Rounding out the three-man staff was Harry Rabenhorst, who had served on Donahue's staff as football assistant, in addition to being head basketball and baseball coach. At the time, there were still no football scholarships as such. Players took odd jobs (some were janitors) as a means of working their way through school. Many of the athletes lived in cramped quarters under the stadium, others in fraternity houses, others in dormitories on the campus. Cohen inherited two fine tackles from Donahue—Guy Nesom and Jess Tinsley—along with N. A. "Fats" Wilson, a 220-pound guard of speed and agility. Frank Ellis was another key holdover at tackle. In the backfield, Hank Stovall and Percy Brown were returning while W. A. "Dobie" Reeves was among the promising recruits up from the freshman team.

Johnny Hendrix, another sophomore of note, ripped off a 52-yard scoring run in the opener against Southwestern and the Tigers were off to four warmup victories, SLI, Louisiana College, Mississippi College, and Spring Hill. It was at this juncture, with the Tigers 4–0, that a man named Huey Long first bubbled to the surface of LSU football. Huey was then in his first year as governor and, while his controversial days were ahead, he was beginning to see football as a political companion. Russ Cohen understood Long better than most Baton Rougeans; that is, he didn't work up a big "mad" over everything Huey said or did. Before the Arkansas game, for example, Cohen sensed the governor's enthusiasm when Long trooped out to a practice session, drew him aside and exclaimed: "Coach, we must beat Arkansas. Why? Because everybody in Shreveport hates me and I hate everybody in Shreveport."

It was a large order, of course, since Arkansas had beaten the Tigers, 28–0, the year before and the Razorbacks had another representative ball club. As it turned out, Long was unhappy, but not crushed, over a 7–0 defeat, the result of a 55-yard runback of an intercepted pass. In the opening minutes Bronco Brown brought the Shreveport crowd to its feet, running fifty-three yards on a "dead man" or "hideout" play that came close to putting LSU on the scoreboard.

The following week Brown made it into the end zone—on two occasions. With LSU entertaining Ole Miss, Brown grabbed a Rebel fumble and raced ninety-eight yards for a touchdown and he later rambled sixty-two yards on an end sweep to score again in a 19–6 victory that sent Cohen's Tigers against Georgia with a 5–1 record. On November 17 LSU met Georgia on Sanford Field in Athens, and the performance that day by captain Jess Tinsley was rated by some press box observers as "the best ever." Cohen considered the Haynesville strongboy the finest tackle he had ever seen—and he had seen quite a few at Vandy and Alabama. An awesome open-field blocker, Tinsley played weak side tackle and, on each play that went to the strong side, his job was to block the safety man. Cohen at one time thought of shifting Jess to strong side guard to provide better blocking for his power plays. Jess demurred. "When 10,000 fans are in the stands," he said, "that means 20,000 eyes will see me block the safety. No one would see me block in close." Against the Bulldogs, Tinsley was a tower of strength both on offense and defense as LSU scored a thrilling 13–12 victory which ranked among the best of the Cohen regime.

Georgia matched a touchdown by Dobie Reeves in the first period and then the home team took a 12–6 lead with a second-quarter score. It remained like this until the final minutes ticked away. Hank Stovall picked off a Georgia pass and returned it thirty yards to the Bulldog 6. Brown scored a moment later around the left side to tie it, 12–12, leaving the matter squarely to Guy Nesom. Here's how the winning point was described in 1928 sports prose in the New Orleans *Item:* "An insignificant batch of leather encasing a pumped-up mass of rubber coolly socked into the ether in the fourth period by the sturdy toe of Guy Nesom and which went hurtling through the bars accounted for the point which brought a scintillating 13–12 victory to Russ Cohen's Louisiana Tigers."

Back in Baton Rouge, fans were as steamed up as the writer. More than 250 traveled to New Orleans to welcome the ball club home. They cheered Russ Cohen—but they also reminded him Tulane was next.

Tulane, under the wily Bierman, came into the LSU game with a 6–3 record and was then on the threshold of three outstanding seasons—9–0 in 1929, 8–1 in 1930, and 11–0 in 1931. Aside from a great nucleus, Tulane had one of its all-time greats in Bill Banker. As the script unfolded, Banker figured in the game's most memorable play, a dash down the east sideline toward the north end where he was met by Hank Stovall and missed scoring, so said the officials, by a scant six inches. It was the closest either team came to a touchdown in a 0–0 tie that was particularly frustrating to Tulane fans, still waiting to celebrate a win over LSU in the new Tulane Stadium. In 1926 Mike Donahue's Tigers had spoiled the Green Wave's inaugural in its present football home which has since grown into the 80,000-seat Sugar Bowl. At that time the stadium seated 22,000. These stands were filled: in fact, a crowd officially counted at 24,332 spilled onto the field to watch the battle for

Louisiana supremacy. In the opening period LSU made its only threat, moving to the Greenie 7 where it had first-and-goal. From here Dobie Reeves carried the football four straight times but fell two yards shy of a score. Afterward the Tigers never got outside their 41.

Tulane made its big move in the third period, marching to the LSU 8 where it also had a first-and-goal. On first down quarterback Dick Baumbach was held for no gain. He was nailed back on the 16 on second, and on third down Baumbach lost two more, presenting Tulane with a fourth-and-18. With one shot left, Baumbach flipped a pass in the right flat to Banker, and Billy roared on down the sidelines—to his collision with Stovall. When the Tulane back wound up vaulting into the end zone, the home stands roared, but the official ruled he was knocked out inches short. Although Tulane had a 4–2 edge in first downs, the scoreless tie was regarded as a "moral" victory for Cohen's club, chiefly because it came on enemy soil.

The 1928 schedule called for one more outing, a trip to Birmingham for a game with Alabama. Wallace Wade, Russ's old boss, was having only mediocre success that year with five wins in eight games, so the game was anticlimactic for both teams, but not for Jess Tinsley. Playing without a helmet as was his custom, he climaxed a season that made him, along with Tulane's Bill Banker, a unanimous selection on the all-Southern team. Offensively, LSU could generate little steam and wound up losing a 13–0 decision that gave Russ Cohen a 6–2–1 record in his rookie year as head coach.

By the time the 1929 season began, Cohen had made an addition to his coaching staff that was to play a major role in the university's athletic

Harry Rabenhorst, a hometown boy who had played for Wake Forest, was first Donahue's and then Cohen's assistant.

future. Through a friendship that began when Russ was an assistant at Alabama and Bernie Moore an aide at Sewanee, Russ hired Bernie to help with football and serve as head track coach. Moore must have felt right at home because of a quantity of scatbacks on hand. Joining holdovers Percy Brown and Johnny Hendrix were W. E. "Billy" Butler and Sid "Snaky" Bowman, an all-stater at Hammond High who in 1928 had made the U.S. Olympic team in the triple jump.

It never took much to make Baton Rouge fans optimistic and as 1929 approached many looked back on the results of the 1928 game against the Tulane freshmen, a game won 6–0 by LSU, featuring Bowman as he ran Tulane plays back at the Greenies. These sophomores and some key

Top, Dobie Reeves, Hank Stovall. Bottom, Percy Brown, Charley Mason.

lettermen were all that were needed to paint a rosy picture. In the line were team captain Frank Ellis and W. D. "Red" Allen at tackles, Walter "Goat" Fleming and J. B. Luker at end, Estes Cole at center. Dobie Reeves was back to run and throw. Tom Smith was a sophomore fullback of note and Ed Khoury a promising tackle.

Looking back at records, the only thing that matters is the won-lost column. But to Russ Cohen, 1929 was always synonymous with Blue Cross. Injuries to key personnel dogged the Tigers every step of the way, so much so that Cohen was forced to juggle his lineup in virtually every game. Despite the injuries LSU was able to breeze past its first five opponents, but many lost sight of the fact that only two, Sewanee and Mississippi State, were considered in the major category and even these were below par.

Huey Long paid no heed to the caliber of the opposition. All that mattered to him was that he still was at outs with Shreveport and LSU had lost two in a row to the Razorbacks in their annual North Louisiana pilgrimage. When Long arrived in Shreveport for the game, he went to Cohen's hotel room only to find Russ nervously pacing the floor. "What's got you so worried?" he asked Cohen. "Arkansas," said Cohen. "I'm scared to death of Arkansas." With that, Long turned to one of his bodyguards and said: "Go take a look at that Arkansas bunch." A few minutes later, after a trip to the lobby where the Razorbacks were milling about, the bodyguard returned and told Huey: "They don't look so tough to me." Long told Cohen, "You see, they're not tough. So stop worrying."

But Cohen had cause for butterflies. Whereas Arkansas, a year before, had yanked the Tigers from their rose-colored paradise with a modest 7–0 victory, this time it was more like the roof falling in. With several regulars sidelined and with steady rain erasing LSU's speed advantage, the Razorbacks smashed Cohen's outfit 32–0, getting their first score in three minutes and then completely dominating play. Arkansas wound up with a 240–54 edge in total yardage and a 19–5 advantage in first downs.

Battered and bruised, the Tigers limped into Durham, North Carolina, the following week, the first major opponent to face Duke in its brand-new stadium. It was practically the same story, with LSU coming away a 32–6 loser. To get its lone touchdown, the team needed two penalties to advance the ball to the Duke 2 and, from there, it took Tom Smith three cracks to get the ball across. The next week, when the Tigers managed to break their tailspin with a 13–6 victory over Ole Miss, J. B. Luker scored the decisive touchdown—but broke an arm doing it.

Even at full strength, it was not likely that LSU had the tools to upset a Tulane team which had swept past eight opponents and was on its way to its first perfect season in history. Many felt the only advantage Knute

Rockne's unbeaten Notre Dame club of the same year had on Tulane was depth. Tulane's imposing first eleven had all-America Jerry Dalrymple and Jack Holland at ends, Charley Rucker and Elmer McCance at tackles, "Red" McCormick and Morris Bobinger at guards, "Preacher" Roberts at center, Dick Baumbach at quarterback, Bill Banker and Ike Armstrong at halfbacks, and Jack Pizzano at fullback.

On November 28 Huey Long, sitting in his Tiger Stadium box among the crowd of 23,000, had little chance to cheer as he witnessed a crushing 21–0 defeat with an inspired performance by captain Frank Ellis the lone redeeming feature. Armstrong grabbed a 16-yard pass from Banker, Armstrong and Dalrymple combined on a 58-yard passing play, and Preacher Roberts went all the way with an intercepted pass for three touchdowns. Cohen sprang the double wing on the Green Wave, but both the new formation and Bronco Brown were held in check.

Huey Long at the LSU-Tulane game, 1928: He would soon be calling the signals.

Suffering on the sidelines, Long told everyone within earshot that "Banker is too good a player to be at Tulane." Added the Kingfish, oblivious to any transfer rules: "He'll be playing for LSU next season." He wouldn't, of course, but Long was beginning to swing into high gear.

In the fall of 1930 Joe Almokary and Joe Keller joined holdovers Bowman, Butler, Reeves, Hendrix, and Smith in the LSU backfield. Khoury was developing into quite a tackle. Jess McLain had come up at center, Roy Wilson at end. Long's enthusiasm accentuated the preseason optimism, but, unlike 1928 and 1929, the 1930 season turned sour in a hurry. Following a shakedown cruise past three warmup opponents— South Dakota Wesleyan, Louisiana Polytechnic and Southwestern Louisiana—Cohen's club came a cropper. The Tigers journeyed to Co-

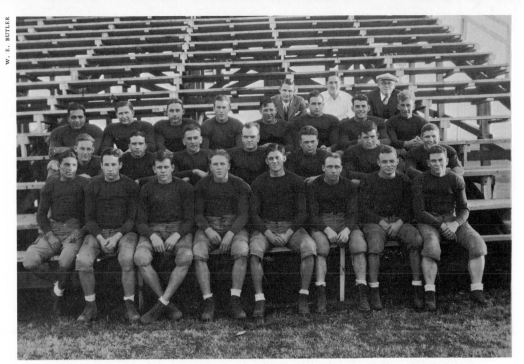

The 1929 Tigers. Left to right, front row, Johnny Hendrix, Dobie Holden, Les Peebles, Tom Smith, Sid Bowman, Louis Harrell, Billy Butler, Norwood Jones, Second row, Walter "Goat" Fleming, Percy Brown, Ben Landry, Bill Allen, F. H. "Teddy" Schneider, Bob Powell, Donald Ogden. Third row, Ed Khoury, Buck Staples, C. A. LeBleu, Ellis A. "Little Fuzzy" Brown, Estes Cole, J. B. Luker, Joel Pressburg, Dobie Reeves. Top row, team manager Jack Fraim, Haywood Moore (temporarily benched by an injury), and Coach Cohen.

lumbia, South Carolina, for a game with South Carolina, piled up a huge statistical edge, but came away beaten, 7–6. A 55-yard punt return by Bowman set up the LSU touchdown, which Hendrix scored from the 1, but Almokary missed the extra point. Tackle Bob Powell and end Roy Wilson were defensive standouts for the losers.

The next week in Jackson, Mississippi, LSU's Butler gave Mississippi State a touchdown with a fumble, but he then squared accounts with an 80-yard run to tie the score at 6–6. This LSU loss, 8–6, came in an unusual manner—when captain Dobie Reeves stepped back onto the end line to give State a safety while punting from his end zone. These two defeats deflated Tiger hopes in a hurry, and it is to Cohen's credit that he jacked up his squad in time for the annual clash with Arkansas which, next to Tulane, was the most hated rival on the Tiger schedule.

LSU prepared for its invasion of Shreveport with a 12–0 win over Sewanee, a game in which Butler scored both touchdowns, one on a pass from Almokary that can be credited to the Kingfish. To satisfy Huey, Russ Cohen put in a special play which he called 1099. In the dressing room before the game, Cohen told fullback Tom Smith, who called the signals, to look toward the bench if in doubt about when to call 1099. "If I have my hat off," he told Smith, "call 1099." As Cohen related the yarn years later, he nearly caught pneumonia because his head was bare.

"Time was running out and Smith still hadn't looked to the bench for the signal," said Cohen. Late in the game Long walked over to Cohen asking about the play. Russ told the Kingfish that Smith wasn't looking for the signal. With this, Long dashed down the sidelines yelling to Smith, "Call 1099! Call 1099!" Smith got the message, called the pass, and LSU scored its second touchdown.

LSU came out of the game in good shape and, for once, prepared to take on the Razorbacks with no key men on the sidelines. Not surprisingly, upon their arrival in Shreveport, Tiger fans found Arkansas rooters highly confident. Bolstered by three straight wins over LSU, they were offering fourteen points in hotel lobbies. Huey Long made his usual impassioned pregame plea and he deserted his customary box seat to walk the sidelines. It was Snaky Bowman who brought a smile to the Kingfish's face and dashed Arkansas' hopes with a fine exhibition of broken-field running. After the Razorbacks took a 6–0 lead, an Almokary-to-Luker pass tied it up. Powell then blocked an Arkansas kick, Reeves scored, Almokary kicked the point, and LSU fans went wild with a 13–6 lead. The Razorbacks drew up to 13–12, but a punt return by Bowman set up a short touchdown run by Reeves to make it 20–12 and ease the pressure. With time running out, Bowman, hurdling tacklers, broke loose on a scoring run to put the game out of reach, 27–12.

It was hotly contested all the way. At one stage, a 320-pound Arkansas tackle named Clark looked across at Ed Khoury and said: "Tighten your belt, big boy, I'm going to block this punt with you." He didn't.

"We were really keyed for the game," said Cohen, "and in the first half we ran up and down the field but had only a 13–12 lead. It seemed every time we got deep into Arkansas territory we got slapped with a penalty. Late in the second quarter we moved to the Arkansas five and Jim Perry tossed Jim Skidmore, our tackle, out of the game for slugging. Not only that but we were penalized half distance to our goal, back to around midfield."

It was a red-hot Kingfish who charged referee Perry at half time. "Do you know who I am?" asked Long. "Yes, sir, you're Governor Long," said the official. "That's correct," said Huey. "Now I want to say one thing. As governor, I protest your calls. I don't mind you penalizing LSU, but penalize us in midfield. Don't do it when we get down to the goal line." The referee smiled at Long's frankness, turned and walked away. He didn't call one penalty on the Tigers in the second half.

LSU returned home for a game with Ole Miss, a game which turned into a defensive battle won by the Tigers, 6–0. The only score came when Reeves cleverly faked a run, then passed to a wide-open T. D. "Dobie" Holden just inside the Rebel end zone.

The three consecutive victories lifted LSU's record to 6–2 and made some of the stronghearted hold out hope for an upset against Alabama, an unbeaten steamroller headed for the Rose Bowl. Cohen felt confident, not of victory but that he had his old head coach figured. Wallace Wade, he told his squad before they left for Montgomery, would do what he had done best all season—try to run the ball down his opponent's throat. It was a bad guess. Figuring the Tigers would be set to stop Bama's power thrusts, Wade relied almost exclusively on the forward pass, the result being a 33–0 rout. Adding insult to injury was the fact that Wade used his second and third string in the first half, holding out his first unit until the third quarter.

The Monday following the game, one newspaper said LSU President T. W. Atkinson and Coach Cohen had both been fired by the governor—which would have been a first. Huey made no secret of his intention to let Cohen go (his contract was up at the end of the 1930 season) and the morning of the season finale with Tulane went to Russ's hotel room predicting a Tulane victory by fifty points. Like Alabama, Bernie Bierman's Greenies were a powerhouse with seven victories and a single loss to Northwestern. Gamblers were offering as many as twenty-five points and 5-to-1 odds.

Although Long expected the worst, he kept close to Cohen and the team at the old Bienville Hotel in New Orleans. In the Tiger dressing room before the game, he was very much in evidence, his coat pockets bulging with tickets, as he paced up and down with his walking cane. Just before the Tigers left their dressing room for the pregame warmup, Huey decided on a pep talk.

"Do you know that Arkansas beat the Texas Aggies by a bigger margin than Tulane did, and that we beat Arkansas?" he began. "Keep that in mind." Having made his point on comparative scores, the Kingfish walked out of the room and onto the field in solitary grandeur. The scattering of applause from the crowd of 22,369 that greeted Long grew into a roar when the purple-clad Tigers followed Huey onto the gridiron. The Kingfish took his seat in a box on the LSU side, his plan being to spend the second half on the side of the enemy. It wasn't long before he was out of his seat. LSU received, gained one yard in two plays. Then, playing a third and nine from its 33, Dobie Reeves dropped back to punt. Reeves went through a smooth kicking motion, so smooth most of the fans thought he had booted the football. Instead, he flipped a lateral to Billy Butler circling behind him and outside the onrushing Jerry Dalrymple, Tulane's all-America end. Butler raced all the way to the Tulane 7 where he was brought down from behind by Hugh Whatley.

The faked kick and lateral was the brainchild of Ike Carriere, who had spent most of the season scouting the Green Wave. It was designed to take advantage of the hard-charging Dalrymple, who had blocked several punts during the year and was accustomed to spending a good bit of the time in his opponent's backfield. It worked perfectly, although the fleet-footed Whatley was able to overhaul Butler. Had Butler gone all the way, it's anyone's guess what might have happened. One thing that Butler's run did was lift Huey Long out of his seat. When Billy was glorybound, Huey cast his overcoat and cane aside, leaped over the rail of his box, and ran down the sidelines. With the Tigers camped on Tulane's 7, Huey fell to his knees, raised his clutched fists to the heavens, pounded the turf with his fists, and jumped up and down. It did no good. Tulane held, took over on the 4, and went on to carve out a 12–0 lead. Dalrymple caught a pass for the first score and Don Zimmerman scored the second on an 8-yard gallop.

At half time, Huey was in the dressing room looking after the Tigers. He requested lotion for Almokary's bruised eye, went around slapping backs, carrying towels. Although he had promised to sit on the Tulane side during the second half, he spent the third quarter in his LSU box. At the start of the fourth period, with LSU still trailing, 12–0, the Kingfish went over to the Tulane side. Midway through the final quarter Roy Wilson smashed through, blocked a Tulane punt on the Greenie 20, scooped up the ball, and took it across. The extra point made it 12–7 and LSU was back in the ball game. No sooner had the point been kicked than Huey raced straight across the field to exhort his heroes during the time that remained. With the initiative now squarely with the Tigers, Tulane was hard put to hold off LSU's bids for an upset in the closing minutes.

Shortly after the game ended, Long entered the LSU dressing room and asked for silence. Then he announced that Russ Cohen's contract was being renewed for three more years. That made Cohen the first, and possibly only, football coach who was rehired in a dressing room after being fired.

Cohen told Huey nothing but he did tell a newsman that he wasn't going to "jump at any offer." When Long read this the next day, he told Cohen he wasn't in the habit of offering men jobs and allowing them to think about it. "I'll give you thirty seconds," he told Russ. "Then get yourself another coach," came the reply. Shocked, Huey asked Cohen how much time he wanted. Two days, said Cohen. Terms were finally reached at the Mansion. After reading the contract, Long scratched out the $7,000 salary figure and added $500. As he handed Russ the document, he said: "You're the only man in Louisiana who has my name on a paper that I don't have his undated resignation."

The pivotal year in LSU football probably was 1931. Strangely enough, it was at a time when this country was beginning to feel the effects of the great depression that the university made a move which shaped its athletic future. The prime mover in LSU's decision to install lights for night football was Thomas Pinckney "Skipper" Heard, in 1931 the graduate manager of athletics, a man who might well be considered the father of the tremendous sports plant on today's Baton Rouge campus. Heard's connection with LSU dated back to 1924, when he served Mike Donahue as assistant student manager while a sophomore in the College of Agriculture. A student at Pitkin High in Vernon Parish, Heard had left high school at the end of his sophomore year to join the Navy, serving a two-year hitch, spent mostly laying mines in the North Sea. Upon discharge, he re-entered high school, received his diploma in 1920, and, after trying his hand at teaching, enrolled at LSU in 1922. Because Heard served well in the post of assistant student manager, Donahue named him student manager in his senior year and, upon graduation in 1926, Skipper became graduate manager. In this job he took most of the administrative burden from the shoulders of Russ Cohen and began to lay the foundation for an enviable football program.

"At this time we had scheduling problems attempting to avoid conflicts with Tulane and Loyola," recalls Heard. "We felt playing on

Thomas Pinckney "Skipper" Heard: In 1931, a man of vision.

Saturday nights not only would solve this but also make it possible for many of our fans, busy on a Saturday afternoon, to attend our games. For example, we had many well-to-do fans whose duties running nearby plantations made it impossible to get away on a Saturday afternoon."

The first lights, according to Heard, cost $7,500 and gave LSU as good a lighting system as any in the United States. When light standards along the east and west sides were erected, the stands also were heightened and lengthened to the goal lines, giving Tiger Stadium a concrete capacity of 20,500, an increase of 8,500 in permanent seats. Wooden bleachers still stood at each end of the field. "Night football," said Heard, "was fairly new and it became a tough job selling teams. This led to some big guarantees. To give you an idea, Vanderbilt got $10,000 in 1933, SMU received $7,500 in 1934."

This first addition to the stands in Tiger Stadium reflected the shrewd business sense of LSU's graduate manager. Later, through the grapevine, Heard learned that LSU president James M. Smith had $250,000 earmarked for dormitories. Armed with this knowledge, he proceeded to sell Smith on the idea that the president could have his dormitories in the stadium simply by raising the stands on both sidelines and extending them to each goal line. Explained Heard: "What it meant was, for $250,000, the president got his dormitories and we increased the seating capacity."

The 1931 season also was destined to blend tragedy with comedy. Besides having most of his key men return, Cohen greeted some highly-touted prospects, led by Jack Torrance, whose later achievements in putting the 16-pound shot and tossing the discus were coincidental to his potential as a tackle. He was recruited to play football. Arthur L. "Red" Swanson, a 1927 graduate, brought "Baby Jack" in from Oak Grove in the summer of 1930, watching over the 6-foot, 5-inch, 260-pound specimen lest he be swiped from the campus. In his freshman season Torrance not only displayed enormous power and agility but showed fine punting and place-kicking ability. Whereas Torrance was a known quantity, that is, he had played as a freshman and was on the campus, the athlete who really stirred the imagination as the fall approached was a halfback by the name of Art Foley.

Foley came into the LSU picture when someone handed Huey Long a newspaper clipping relating the heroics of a halfback at a junior college in New Mexico. Foley's feats, as told in the story, stimulated the Kingfish to such an extent that he dispatched Heard to seek him out and bring him back. Armed with the clipping, Skipper caught a train west to Eufaula, Oklahoma, home of this ball-carrying phenomenon, only to find that he and his family were vacationing in Mineral Wells, Texas. Heard located the Foley family, learned that Art liked golf and, being a dogged recruiter, went out and bought some clubs. "I played several times with Foley in Mineral Wells," said Heard, "and then followed him and the family back to Eufaula where we played some more. When I phoned Huey and told him Foley was crazy about the game, he sent him some new clubs."

By then Heard was fast friends with the halfback, and before he left Oklahoma, Foley promised he'd report in September to LSU where, as a junior college transfer, he would be eligible immediately. When fall practice began and Foley hadn't appeared, Long sent Heard back to Oklahoma. Skipper returned with the halfback in tow and brought him to Huey, who personally saw that he had fine campus accommodations.

Art Foley: His first game was also his last.

The Saturday after Labor Day, with Cohen staging his first scrimmage in Tiger Stadium, a limousine drove onto the field from an entrance on the east side. Out stepped Huey who opened the rear door—and then out stepped Foley. Long escorted the halfback over to where the team was huddled and turned him over to Cohen. With a wave to all of the writers present, Huey jumped back into his limousine and drove off, fully content that he had "delivered the mail."

Because of his late arrival, Art Foley was not ready for the September 26 season opener against TCU in Fort Worth, and it's quite possible he could have made a difference in a game that wound up 3–0 in the Horned Frogs' favor. The following week, however, with 7,500 on hand for the first football game under lights in Baton Rouge, Foley made Huey Long seem like a shrewd judge of talent. Spring Hill found the shifty speedster as elusive as quicksilver in the course of absorbing a 35–0 licking. He burst loose repeatedly, one time running fifty-six yards for a touchdown, and later returning a punt sixty-two yards for a second score.

Unfortunately, Spring Hill was Art Foley's first and last game for LSU. A few days later he became ill and an examination revealed a lung ailment. Two weeks later, on doctor's advice, Foley gave up football to return home where, it was hoped, the drier weather would enable him to recover. "Huey felt sorry for the boy and indebted to him," said Heard. "He presented him with a brand new Ford sports car to drive back to Oklahoma." However, Foley failed to improve and he died a few years later.

During the short time that Art Foley was in Baton Rouge he was a guest of the governor at the Mansion. With him—and they stayed on for some months after Art had headed home—were three other players, Ed Khoury, Billy Butler, and Sid Bowman. As Bowman recalls it, he was watching a movie on Third Street when in walked Khoury to tell him that Huey Long wanted to see him. "I thought it was all a joke," said Bowman, "but, sure enough, the governor was outside in front of the movie eating peanuts."

"I want you two boys to live with me at the Mansion," said Long. Then the Kingfish added: "And what's that little fellow's name?"

"You mean Billy Butler?" suggested Bowman.

"Yeah, that's him," said Long. "Tell him to come, too. You'll get a lot better grub at my place."

Butler recalls that suddenly he was called to the athletic office, where his clothes had been brought from his room in the Gym-Armory without his knowing it. There the governor informed him that henceforth he would be living in the Mansion. Butler says that the reason he and Khoury and Bowman were picked was that they had been injured in the game against TCU. The governor was going to look after them personally. "Why, I know more about medicine than those quacks," Huey told him.

So it was that a whole new world opened up for the LSU players. At the Mansion they discovered the governor's thirst for football information. He pumped them continually for some of the finer points—explanation of the various formations and trick plays. One evening he had eleven chairs brought into the ballroom and asked his house guests to demonstrate the single and double wing.

"Actually," Butler says, "it got so he was pretty good—very good, in fact. He could diagram plays and put up a defense. Later, when I had left school and was doing some coaching, I drew on some of his plays."

Butler shared the Green Room with Khoury, and Bowman and Foley (until Foley left) roomed together in the Blue Room. The players sat down with the Longs at every meal as part of the family and Huey saw to it that they drank quantities of sour milk. "Not buttermilk," Butler says. "Milk that had been allowed to sit out until it soured. Huey didn't believe sweet milk was good for you. So we drank gallons of sour milk—whether we liked it or not. And plenty of steak. Two meals a day we had turnip greens and cornbread and broiled steak and pineapple upside down cake." Khoury went into the Mansion weighing two forty and came out weighing three hundred.

The week after their win over Spring Hill, Russ Cohen's Tigers turned back South Carolina, 19–12, the highlights being a 40-yard scoring pass from Joe Almokary to Goat Fleming and the running of Amite's Neil Mixon. A week later, playing its third night game in a row (before 12,000), LSU whipped Mississippi State, 31–0, with Leroy Langley of Jennings doing most of the damage.

Other than the 76-yard run by Tom Smith that won the game, LSU's 1931 game with Arkansas is memorable for its travel plans. The Tigers left Baton Rouge with the idea of spending Friday night in Marshall, Texas, just across the state line from Shreveport. But Cohen figured without Huey. When the team departed Thursday evening by train, the plan was to disembark in Marshall the following morning, have a light workout, a good night's sleep, and then drive over Saturday morning for the game. Shreveport, Russ felt, was becoming overrun with Tigers and Razorbacks and therefore was too distracting. However, Long's reaction was simple: "We're not going to stay in Texas." Without telling Cohen or any of the players, he had the LSU special stop Friday morning in Shreveport. Because the squad had no hotel reservations in the city (Cohen had arranged accommodations in Marshall), Huey then spent most of the day moving guests out of the hotel to make room for "my team."

Long's pep talk before the game hinged on the importance of players "forgetting personal differences when facing a common enemy—Arkansas." It surely didn't do any harm. Fullback Smith, who gained 143 yards in ten carries, broke a 6–6 tie with his 76-yard gallop as LSU won a 13–6 thriller before 10,000. Bowman scored the first Tiger touchdown and Jess McLain was a defensive star.

A week later, LSU's 1.000 batting average under its Baton Rouge lights was broken. Sewanee sprang a double wing attack on the Tigers and went away a 12–6 winner. It's anyone's guess whether the Tigers were looking past Sewanee to the school's first and only meeting with the United States Military Academy. Maybe so, but LSU's performance at West Point did not indicate a team that was keyed up, even though Long did his share in the cheerleading department. A traveling squad of thirty left Baton Rouge aboard a special train on Wednesday, November 4, accompanied by a 150-piece band and two hundred fans, among them the governor's wife and his son Russell (Huey was having political troubles at the moment and was afraid to leave the state). Although Tiger fans represented a small portion of the 15,000-strong turnout, they raised a rumpus. The game itself, an LSU nightmare, still was much closer than the 20–0 margin the home team enjoyed. Dropped passes cost LSU two scores. While the Tigers were able to move the ball with trick plays that captured the imagination of the crowd, they were an unsure ball club.

The upshot of the West Point debacle was a public request by the LSU student newspaper, the *Reveille*, that Cohen resign. A 26–3 win over Ole Miss in Jackson on the way home did not calm the rumblings. Russ's only chance for redemption, as usual, was Tulane and the passing of Almokary and a 32-yard scoring run by Neil Mixon (who had helped humble the Rebs) did not take anyone's mind off Bernie Bierman's Rose Bowl express.

Tulane, in 1931, was the talk of the South. Texas A & M, a 7–0 victim, was the only one of nine opponents to get within a touchdown of the mighty Green team built around all-America halfback Don Zimmerman. Along with Zimmerman was Lowell "Red" Dawson at quarterback, Harry Glover at halfback, and Nollie Felts at fullback. Few of the crowd of 25,600 in Tulane Stadium gave LSU much of a chance. Even the Kingfish was subdued. The only question seemed to be when Tulane would make the announcement about playing in the Rose Bowl. Russ Cohen's Tigers enjoyed a brief moment of glory that afternoon which, after all these years, is still worth retelling. Early in the first period Almokary rifled a 15-yard pass to Tom Smith which the LSU fullback caught between Dawson and Glover, a couple of stunned defenders who wound up watching Smith hoof it forty yards to a touchdown. Incredible as it seemed, when LSU added the extra point to go ahead 7–0, it

1931 team captain Ed Khoury: Room and board at the Mansion.

marked the first time Tulane had trailed the Tigers since 1926 and the first time Bierman's Greenies were behind that season. But it merely was the signal for Tulane to roll. Spearheaded by the great Zimmerman, the Greenies went on to score a smashing 34–7 decision. Don picked up 104 yards in twenty carries while Tulane's stubborn defense limited LSU to 64 rushing yards and only one completed pass, the one Smith caught for a touchdown.

After it was over, Cohen, who had seen quite a few good teams said: "This is the greatest team I've seen any time, any place, anywhere."

Of course, Tulane's greatness (Southern California defeated the Greenies, 21–12 in the Rose Bowl) did not help save Cohen's job. A few days later, Russ and LSU came to a friendly parting of the ways and, thanks to the Kingfish's closeout offer and Cohen's daring, it turned into a bonanza for the former Vanderbilt end. As Russ had two years remaining on the $7,500-per-year contract he signed after the 1929 season, Long asked Cohen if he would agree to accept $7,500 cash and call it a deal. Cohen, who wanted to return to Vandy to assist Dan McGugin, jumped at the offer. He took the $7,500 and used it all as a down-payment on $40,000 worth of Chrysler stock. He later sold it for close to a half million dollars, which meant that, while he wound up a four-year regime with a 23–13–1 record, he scored a big victory in his personal war on poverty.

'Why can't I talk to the boys?'

1932–1934

BECAUSE Huey Long embraced LSU football with an alarming intensity, no coach could be blamed for regarding the vacancy created by Russ Cohen's departure cautiously. Newspaper stories of Long's activities were likely to make anyone reluctant to invade the kingdom of the Kingfish. After all, coaching alone was hazardous enough, but coaching, plus responding to the many moods of an armchair quarterback who held life-or-death power over your contract, was something else.

As an intelligent man, Huey Long realized that discipline would be the primary requisite in a successor to Cohen. Discipline—and a strong personality. LSU President James M. Smith asked Major Troy Middleton, then commandant of cadets at the university, if he thought Tennessee's Bob Neyland, a West Point graduate, might be interested. Middleton felt Neyland was out of the question. But there was a field artillery captain at the Academy, a man Middleton had never met but who was recommended by the departing Cohen, who might be available. So it was that President Smith and James Broussard, chairman of athletics, sought out Lawrence McChesney "Biff" Jones—with Huey's blessing, of course. Jones had been Army's head coach in 1927, 1928, and 1929. At the time, he was serving as assistant athletic director at the Academy and Broussard hoped he would like to get back into coaching at a school which prided itself on its cadet corps. On the telephone, Jones told Broussard frankly, "Huey Long worries me." Middleton interceded, telling Jones the newspapers had exaggerated Huey's influence, that he really was more interested in the band than the football team.

After some urging, Biff agreed to come to Baton Rouge (without any publicity) to look over the setup. He stayed with Middleton but, after a

Biff Jones talks to his squad, 1932.

brief visit, decided he wasn't interested, whereupon Broussard, greatly impressed with the man's military bearing and apparent flare for organization, asked him to spell out any conditions that might stand in the way. Jones wanted to be detailed to LSU as an instructor in military science so that he would not have to resign from the Army.

Since the latter was a military concern, it meant a trip to Washington for Smith and Broussard and a face-to-face meeting with General Douglas MacArthur, chief of staff and a close friend of Biff's, whose permission was necessary. Smith and Broussard were ushered into MacArthur's office and found the general seated behind a huge desk in a swivel chair smoking a cigarette. "How much are you going to pay Biff Jones?" MacArthur wanted to know. "Seventy five hundred dollars," said Broussard. "Okay, you can have him," snapped MacArthur. "You've got yourself a good coach, but don't ever come back and ask for any more favors."

A big-time staff was quickly assembled, with Jones actually having a hand in only two selections, trainer Frank Wandle and freshman coach Penn Dixon. Previously, Broussard had hired Burt Ingwerson, who had been let out at Iowa, and Emerson "Spike" Nelson, an assistant under Ingwerson. Ben Enis, line coach under Russ Cohen, was retained as was Bernie Moore, although in 1932 Bernie was assigned the post of intramural director in addition to his duties as track coach.

Huey Long boasted loudly of his "all-America staff." He prophesied that championships were ahead, and he promised not to tell his new head coach how to run the team. Biff was well received in Baton Rouge and, finding the state split into pro- and anti-Long factions, he was smart enough to keep out of the crossfire. There was the question, of course, whether Biff could sell the Kingfish on his methods. Cool and aloof,

Jones disdained incendiary pep talks ("They only incite players to do unsportsmanlike things.") for a factual analysis of the situation. "You've cried to them, coaxed them and cursed them," he told Huey with tact. "Now let's try it my way. We'll teach them how to play football, get them in good physical and mental condition, and then let them play it. It's their game and not a case of life and death." Huey wasn't sure about that, but he was going to play ball with his new coach.

Russ Cohen had served in the twin capacity of head coach and athletic director. However, because Biff Jones had teaching duties in the school's ROTC program in addition to his coaching job, the athletic directorship passed to T. P. Heard. Although Heard's title during the Cohen regime was graduate manager of athletics, Skipper had been carrying out athletic director's chores for some time, so he was merely inheriting a more important title.

LSU's new director moved swiftly; in fact, his early actions had far-reaching significance. "When Mike Donahue left LSU, there was $48,000 in the athletic fund," said Heard. "After Russ departed following the 1931 season, we had the same amount on hand. Before the new regime could put their hands on this money, I used it to recruit players and create jobs for the athletes. We were in the depths of the depression then and twenty-five cents an hour was pretty good money. The stadium had been built on cypress swamp land that was fit for nothing, so during the summer months athletes helped with a reclamation project. They assisted in draining the area surrounding the stadium, rice fields operated by the LSU experimental station."

Because Heard used athletic funds for recruiting and jobs for athletes, Biff Jones and his staff were carried on the Arts and Sciences payroll and stayed there until 1934, when the salaries were transferred back to the athletic department. More significant, unquestionably, was the initiation of athletic scholarships. In this Heard was a trailblazer. "The boys have been getting jobs and paying for their schooling out of the money they earned," he explained. "Some ran canteens, others picked up laundry, others cleaned dormitories. All in all, this was bad for morale and I felt a system of scholarships, open and above board, would end all this." The system started by Heard called for all athletes making a varsity squad to receive free room, board, fees, books, tuition, and ten dollars per month for laundry.

"Actually, this came at a good time because the effects of the depression were being felt, so athletes felt they were really fortunate," said Heard. "The boys realized that, to keep their free ride, they had to study and live by the rules. It made for a lot healthier situation all around."

Thanks to Huey Long's drive, facilities at LSU, as Biff Jones began to take over, were improving rapidly. The Huey P. Long Field House, with room for seventy athletes, was nearing completion. Already completed were eight handball courts, two squash courts, and a king-size swimming pool.

LSU in 1932 had an enrollment of 3,000 and when 105 hopefuls reported to Jones and his well-publicized staff for spring practice the ratio of candidates to students was far greater than today. Prior to the six weeks of spring drills, Huey Long let the players know he thought a lot of the new coach. "I'm a good advisor," said Huey, "but as soon as the coach tells me he's the boss and running the show, I think a lot more of him."

Jones's two major announcements in the spring were: (1) it would be his practice to name game-by-game captains instead of one before the season, and (2) LSU would operate out of the double wing. "Unless you have deception," he told newsmen, "you're wasting your time. We intend to have it here at LSU."

An erect 6-foot, 3-inch, 200-pounder with clear blue eyes that seemed to take in everything and with a strong chin that reflected determination, Jones impressed those around him with his poise and traits befitting an Army captain trained at West Point. "Prepossessing was the best way to describe him," said one observer. A congenial mixer at social functions, he was at ease on the banquet circuit, where he spoke with quiet force rather than with the dynamic flare of a Rockne. On the football field he was a drill master and expected results by operating on the John D. Rockefeller theory—organize, deputize, and supervise. Looking somewhat like a director on a Hollywood movie set, Jones was easy to find at any football game sitting in an elevated chair near the 50-yard line. Rarely did he stand or walk the sideline. Once in a while he would half rise out of his seat to signal a player or member of his staff, but for the most part he sat still in the saddle even during the fiercest set-to's.

For those fans who considered LSU players nothing more than a bunch of rough-and-ready guys spoiling for a fight, Jones changed the image with a "sportsmanship" approach. After a ball carrier had been tackled, LSU players helped him to his feet. LSU players also shook hands with incoming Tiger substitutes, and this sometimes became a production, because it was Jones who made it a practice of substituting by units each quarter. Another touch was the gaily colored water wagon of trainer Frank Wandle, a purple-and-gold oasis equipped with multiple drinking taps attached to flexible hoses which enabled all eleven men to slack their thirst simultaneously.

So far as the detailing of duties to his staff, Jones's main assistant, Burt Ingwerson, was put in charge of the line; Spike Nelson handled the guards and tackles; Ben Enis, the ends; and Penn Dixon, the freshmen. In 1932 Biff handled the backs but in 1933 he brought in Joel Hunt for that job. Bernie Moore handled Jones's scouting during the 1932 campaign, and when Dixon bowed out following the 1932 season because of ill health, Biff appointed Bernie freshman coach.

The squad Jones inherited from Cohen was proof enough of the latter's knowledge of material. Joe Almokary and Bert Yates alternated at tailback, George "Junior" Bowman and William Y. "Billy" Lobdell at quarterback. Joe Keller, so-so under Cohen, blossomed into a fine spinner back in Jones's double wing. John Kent became a fine center in the line where he alternated with Lloyd Stovall. Roy Wilson, shifted from end to guard, was a stemwinder. Goat Fleming and Frank "Spec" Moore were better than good at end; G. "Gee" Mitchell moved in at one guard post and no one could dislodge him; Bob Bannister, Jim Skidmore, and Jack Torrance began to jell at tackles. All recruited by Cohen, they seemed to hit their stride under Jones. Whether it was because of the introduction of the double wing or possibly the platooning of units by the quarters, it's anyone's guess. The fact remains that LSU's football team took on a "sound" look, giving Huey Long the opportunity to supply his special "hotcha" touch.

After Torrance booted a third-quarter field goal to give LSU a 3–3 standoff with TCU in the season opener, the Tigers invaded Houston to face Rice. The game promptly was subordinated to the antics of the

Rice, 1932: Quarterback Billy Lobdell carries.

governor of Louisiana. Dressed in white flannels, Huey led 150 purple-and-gold clad cadets on a march through downtown Houston. At various times he played the part of drum major, cheerleader, and water boy. Bert Yates's passing got the Tigers off to an early 6–0 lead, and when John Kent dumped a Rice ball carrier for a safety LSU had an 8–7 lead going into the final quarter only to lose 10–8 on a field goal in the fading moments.

They called him "Baby Jack": Oak Grove's 6-foot-5 Jack Torrance, right, with center John Kent.

Those were the last points scored on Biff Jones's ball club until a strong Centenary team broke a five-game streak six weeks later. Walter Sullivan scored three times in an 80–0 rout of Spring Hill; Lobdell and Yates sparked an easy 24–0 conquest of Mississippi State; the Tigers got two quick scores, one on a Yates pass, and then threw up a brick wall to whip Arkansas, 14–0. Jones cleared the bench as Sewanee fell, 38–0; and a 45-yard Yates-to-Fleming pass following a neat punt return by Bowman sank South Carolina, 6–0.

Centenary prevailed 6–0 at Shreveport, coming up with a defensive answer for the "Pop" Warner system, but the record was still 5–2–1 and prospects were bright for the first victory over Tulane since 1926. If the game with the Greenies had been played the following week, before the influenza had gotten to Tulane, the 1932 contest probably would have been a matter of little rehashing. However, there was a two-week break, and it seemed as though the virus timed its arrival perfectly, sidelining Don Zimmerman, Tulane's top back, and several other regulars. Two days before the game, a Tulane request for postponement was refused by the Tigers and LSU went on to score a 14–0 victory in what was regarded as the "influenza game." It was particularly pleasing to Huey because LSU's workhorse (he carried twenty-five times for a 4.6 average) was Joe Almokary, the Shreveport schoolboy whom Long had personally helped recruit. Almost a month later, in what amounted to a postseason contest, LSU closed its 1932 season in a Baton Rouge snowstorm bowing to a huge Oregon team headed by a ploughhorse named Mike Mikulak.

Soon after the December 17 loss to the Webfeet, Biff Jones had the Tigers in the midst of a grueling eight-week spring training session, the major problems being replacements for Fleming, Skidmore, and Wilson in the line and Keller at spinner back. Jones was getting his first close look at his 1932 freshmen, a crop largely recruited by Ben Enis with the assistance of Red Heard, the man who supplied the off-season jobs. "We had great recruiting years in 1932, '33 and '34," said Heard. "This is when we got the boys who formed the nucleus of the great bowl teams of the 1930s. Biff left the recruiting to his assistants, one reason being he felt he could deal with all incoming players on an impersonal basis."

An idea of the quality of the 1932 frosh crop was evident the following fall when Jones had seven sophomores on his first unit. At ends, Garland Pickett and Pete Burge alternated with Spec Moore and Bill Barrett. At tackles, Torrance and a hot-shot sophomore Justin Rukas were backed by A. B. "Pop" Nevils and Shelby Calhoun. At guards, Gee Mitchell had the company of two sophomores—A. D. Brown and Osborne "Butch" Helveston. At center, it was still Kent and Stovall. At quarterback, Billy Lobdell and Bowman shared time with sophomore Joe Lawrie. At blocking back, holdover Walter Sullivan had a competitor in newcomer Jess Fatherree. At spinner, Keller was gone, but Neil Mixon was returning for his last year and he faced a fight from sophomore Ernest Seago. It was the same thing at fullback where Bert Yates, the passing star of 1932, shared his position with a McComb, Mississippi, boy named Abe Mickal.

Gee Mitchell, Spec Moore, Walter "Goat" Fleming.

Jones felt that if the sophomores matured soon enough he would have the necessary depth to make a run at the Southeastern Conference crown: 1933 marked the formation of the new league out of what had been the old Southern Conference, which had included teams as far away as Virginia. By 1932, when it became apparent the latter had become too unwieldy for good competition, a division along geographical lines was agreed on by representatives of thirteen colleges—Alabama, Auburn, Florida, Georgia, Georgia Tech, Kentucky, LSU, Mississippi State, Ole Miss, Sewanee, Tennessee, Tulane, and Vanderbilt.

What LSU produced in the SEC's inaugural year was the school's most successful football team since 1908, a team which (unbeaten in its own conference) trounced Southwest champion Arkansas, laced Southern Conference co-champion South Carolina, and played a scoreless tie with unbeaten Centenary. Alabama, conference champion by virtue of a 5–0–1 record (compared to LSU's 3–0–2), played a 0–0 tie with Ole Miss, a club the Tigers walloped, 31–0. Ranked as high as fifth nationally by one poll, the 7–0–3 Tigers played before a record 128,000 fans—22,000 turning out for the Arkansas clash in Shreveport and 26,000 for the Tulane game in New Orleans.

For an opener, LSU turned in an impressive effort handing Rice a 13–0 defeat, the scores coming on a short run by Mixon and a 20-yard run by Stovall with a pass interception. After a 40–0 tuneup at the expense of Millsaps, Jones had his Tigers primed for what he felt would be a revenge victory over Centenary, a well-equipped team sparked by a

Workhorse Joe Almokary and passing star Bert Yates.

nifty runner in Shorty Oslin. With a partisan crowd on hand in Baton Rouge, LSU won everything but the ball game, leading 16 to 6 in first downs and 309 to 128 in total yardage. A 56-yard scoring pass from Mickal to Lobdell was called back and Torrance missed two field goal tries—all of which added up to a 0–0 scoreboard, the only thing that counted.

Bouncing back nicely LSU went to Shreveport the next week and scored twenty points in twenty minutes to hand a 20–0 convincer to Arkansas as the name Mickal crept more and more into the headlines. Abe pitched for two of the scores, forty-eight yards to Burge and fifty-seven to Fatherree. A week later, before a Homecoming crowd of 15,000 and a returning Russ Cohen (he was Dan McGugin's assistant), Mickal hit Fatherree again, this time for twenty-seven yards, as the Tigers scrapped hard for a 7–7 standoff with Vanderbilt.

Jones's two-team system and his fast-maturing sophomores produced a 30–7 victory over a fine South Carolina team, one that led 7–3 at half time but then faded to become a victim of substitution. Mickal's twisting runs marked the victory over the Southern Conference champions. LSU's easy conquest of Ole Miss was highlighted by burly Jack Torrance's lumbering 40-yard run with an intercepted pass, and a 21–6

The 1933 coaching staff. From left, trainer Frank Wandle, Bernie Moore, Joel Hunt, Burt Ingwerson, Biff Jones, Emerson "Spike" Nelson, Ben Enis.

decision over Mississippi State in Monroe sent the Tigers against Tulane with a 6–0–2 record.

Tulane, under the direction of Ted Cox, had started slowly but was coming fast with six victories in nine games, including impressive ones against Colgate and Kentucky. With backs like Preacher Roberts, John McDaniels, and sophomore Claude "Lil Monk" Simons, Tulane had the nucleus of the ball club that was to sweep it into the Sugar Bowl the following year. The day the Tigers came to town, the still-to-be-named Sugar Bowl stadium was rocking with prospects of an upset as Tulane grabbed a 7–0 lead on a Roberts-to-McDaniels pass. Early in the second quarter, however, with LSU threatening at the south end of the field, sophomore Mickal lofted what looked almost like a lob in tennis. To the standing crowd of 26,000, the ball appeared headed for a cluster of green jerseys. At the last instant, just inside the end zone and in the midst of three Tulane defenders, Pete Burge leaped up and pulled LSU from the jaws of defeat. The spectacular catch resulted in a 7–7 half time score—and that's exactly how it ended thirty playing minutes later.

Strange as it seems, there was one item on the 1933 schedule that upstaged LSU's game with its traditional rival—a December 9 game with Bob Neyland's Tennessee Vols and all-America halfback Beattie Feathers. For Jones, it meant a crack at a team coached by his 1915 West Point teammate. Neyland already was well established at Tennessee and

Pete Burge's miracle catch, Tulane game, 1933: One of the great plays of Tiger football history.

his 1933 outfit, with seven wins in nine outings, had only one conference defeat, a 12–6 setback at the hands of Alabama. Despite LSU's home advantage, Tennessee came in favored, chiefly because of Feathers, and it was cause for a rousing Baton Rouge celebration when the Tigers shut out Neyland and his all-American, 7–0, the first time in his seventy-seven games at Tennessee Neyland had been blanked in a losing effort. Yates, the Haynesville flash alternating with Mickal, outgained the entire Vol backfield, and Abe made the touchdown. With LSU having a 16–3 advantage in first downs, the score was much closer than the game indicated.

Jones's status zoomed with this closing victory and, as Biff looked toward 1934, it was difficult for even a well-disciplined Army captain not to feel enthusiastic about the upcoming season. Only four regulars were departing—Torrance, Mitchell, Kent, and Burge—and there was another bumper crop of sophomores moving in, headed by Gaynell Tinsley, an end, and three backs, Pat Coffee, Bill Crass, and J. T. "Rock" Reed. A sensation as freshman, Tinsley was considered by many the finest sophomore end in the country. He moved right onto the first unit, teaming with steady Jeff Barrett. Justin "Iron Man" Rukas (he played 502 out of a possible 600 minutes in 1933) teamed with Marvin Baldwin at tackles after an injury sidelined Shelby Calhoun. A. D. "Buck" Brown and Butch Helveston were the starting guards, backed by Ray Egan and Wardell Leisk. At center senior Lloyd Stovall divided time with sophomore Marvin Stewart. In the backfield, Jones was hip-deep in talent. The single-wing alignment had Joe Lawrie and Walter Sullivan at quarterback; Fatherree and Reed at halfbacks; Mickal, Yates, Coffee, and Crass at tailbacks; and Seago and Bill May at fullback.

Overall, it was a well-balanced, predominantly junior team which was called on to tackle the toughest LSU schedule to that time. For openers the Tigers picked the two toughest clubs in the Southwest Conference, Rice and SMU. In the curtain-raiser at Houston, the Owls had LSU down 0–9 with eight minutes left when Mickal kicked to the Rice 1. Rice promptly gave the Tigers a safety and it was 9–2 with about six minutes remaining. Rock Reed then upset Owl strategy returning a punt forty-five yards to set up a touchdown run by Seago. Mickal's kick made it 9–9, and so it ended.

Returning home, Jones prepared to defend against the famous "aerial circus" of Coach Ray Morrison, whose Mustangs had been driving the enemy daffy with forward passes followed by multiple laterals. It was a big game from a financial as well as a prestigious standpoint, in that athletic director T. P. Heard needed a $10,000 guarantee to lure the colorful visitors to Baton Rouge. This is offered as background to an early morning phone call Huey Long put through to Heard the Tuesday before the game. "How are tickets going?" the Kingfish wanted to know. "Not too good, Senator," replied Heard. "They've got a circus scheduled Saturday night and the conflict seems to be hurting the advance."

Later in the day, after doing some checking, Long asked to see the advance man for John Ringling North's Barnum and Bailey Circus. "Did you ever dip a tiger?" he asked the puzzled fellow. "Or, better yet, an elephant?" Then, as his visitor expressed open-mouthed amazement, Huey continued. "You know we have laws in this state, mister," said the Kingfish. "And the way I interpret them, every one of your animals will have to be dipped before they can cross the state line. We can't take any chances with disease."

In Texas at the time, the Ringling Brothers production was scheduled to move its tents into Baton Rouge, a move Long had decided to head off. Thumbing through Louisiana's sanitary code, with the help of a law student, he dusted off the little-known animal-dipping law. Emphasizing he had every intention of enforcing it unless the show was cancelled, Long watched as the shaken circus representative put through a call to North, who decided it would be unwise to call Huey's bluff. So he cancelled.

Ticket sales picked up and when Morrison turned loose his freewheeling ball club at LSU on Saturday night 20,000 were on hand, more than enough to get Heard off the financial hook. From the opening whistle, SMU grabbed the initiative, confusing the Tigers with hot-potato antics featuring a whirling dervish passer-ball carrier in Bobby Wilson. Wilson scored from fifteen yards out after taking a lateral to give the visitors a 7–0 first quarter lead. In the second period LSU began to move behind Mickal's passing, and a 32-yard heave, from Abe to Bill Barrett, helped make it 7–7 at half time. The Mustangs opened the aerial throttle in the third period, marched fifty-five yards for a go-ahead score and, when the visitors punted to the LSU 28 with less than three minutes remaining, the fans felt they'd have to settle for a 14–7 setback. On first down Mickal faded, let go a long one that barely eluded the fingertips of the streaking Sullivan. Second down, the ball went to Abe again and back he went—to the 20—the 15. Planting his feet firmly near the north end, Mickal arched a mighty toss diagonally across the playing field, one which carried a good sixty-five yards in the air. Incredibly, Sullivan had again slipped behind SMU defenders (perhaps because they felt no one could throw the ball that far), and Abe's bomb settled in his arms as he raced past the 30 near the east sidelines. Taking it in stride, Sullivan sped into the end zone without an SMU man within fifteen yards. Pandemonium reigned—until the Tigers lined up for the crucial extra point. Mickal had kicked sixteen in a row but, until his seventeenth floated over the crossbar at the south end, no one breathed easy. When it was officially 14–14, complete madness enveloped Tiger Stadium once again. That game still ranks among the most thrilling ones in LSU history—one which gave the Tigers momentum as they went deeper into a rough schedule.

A 70-yard return of the opening kickoff by Jess Fatherree sent LSU on its way to a 20–6 win over Auburn, and the following week, before 20,000 in Shreveport, Fatherree and Sullivan broke loose late in the game to produce a 16–0 victory over Arkansas.

LSU, which had then played 14 games in a row without losing one, began preparing for an invasion of Vanderbilt, one of the high spots on the schedule. Coach Dan McGugin, a titan in his profession, had announced he would retire at the end of the 1934 season, but he was putting forth a great final effort. His Commodores had swept four straight, and the game with LSU took on some national attention—a lot more when the Senator from Louisiana got into the act.

In Harnett Kane's book *Louisiana Hayride*, Huey Long's football image was treated thus: "Huey's football shows could not be kept out of the newspapers, no matter how much the newspapers hated Huey. They were spectacles in the Billy Rose-Roxy tradition: 2000 cadets, 200 musicians, 50 'purple jackets'—coeds in white pleats, blazers and 50 smiles—octettes of dancing boy and girl cheer-leaders and 50 sponsors in a row. And the star of the troupe, Huey, swinging, roaring, hightailing it at the head of the march. He led his boys and girls down the main streets of the invaded towns, razzled-dazzled over the field between halves and, remained, as usual, perilously close to the players during the game."

More than anything, Huey owed this image to the gala junket he

All aboard for Nashville: Huey Long and his Tiger "special."

promoted to Nashville in October, 1934. Early in the week Huey announced: "No student should miss this trip because of lack of funds." His first move was to talk to passenger agents of the Illinois Central Railroad regarding a modest fare for LSU students. Long was told that it was out of the question—a railroad could not lower its fares for a special group. Huey then simply bypassed the agents, and when he did, he made sure he was armed with a knee-shaking argument. "The bridges over which your trains travel in Louisiana," he told the president of the railroad, "are taxed at $100,000. Their value is $4 million. It would be a sad day for you if our legislature was to raise the assessment from $100,000 to $4 million." Huey had made his point. The railroad agreed to a $6 fare—not bad for a round trip that cost $19.

Once the fare was established, the Senator appeared on the campus, passing out close to $3,000 in loans of $7 per student, $6 for the fare, $1 for meals. Many students wrote IOU's on laundry slips. When depar-

The Senator from Louisiana (dark suit, light hat): He led his boys and girls down the main streets of the invaded towns.

ture time came at 6 P.M. on Friday, October 26, nearly 5,000 made the trip, including the 125-piece band, and 1,500 ROTC students. The five trains, of fourteen cars each, had the following labels: blue, for students; green, for students and friends; red, for cadets; orange, for general public and alumni; white, for cadets, band and coach; car 3164 for Huey and party.

All night long the Kingfish ploughed through his train, stopping to wave at small clusters of people gathered in small towns along the way. When the train stopped, Huey would step down, chat with the folks, give them a bit of music from his personal orchestra of eight hand-picked cadets. At times, he would talk railroading with the yard men, telling them what he thought of the railroads. Through the night he discoursed on a variety of subjects: his favorite was the shortcomings of college graduates. "Why, they can't even work fractions," said Huey. He gave an example to three students, and then proved his point by working out the problem himself.

He stepped from the train at 9 o'clock the following morning having had hardly a wink of sleep. With the words, "I feel like a fighting cock," he ordered his cadets in line for an immediate march through Nashville's business section. Huey was met by Nashville mayor Hilary Howse, the secretary to Governor William McAllister, and Coach McGugin. Long was dapper in a white flannel suit and tan hat. At the station he received a purple and gold ribbon which carried the words "Deputy Game Warden, Tennessee." He put this across his chest as he marched with his wife, son Russell, then sixteen, and Coach McGugin. "The only difference between me and Dan," said Huey, "is that he tells his team what to do before the game and I tell the LSU team what to do during the game." Declining an automobile, the Kingfish marched at the head of the parade which was to go on for two miles. Huey's every move was wildly cheered. Mayor Howse said that the welcoming committee along the line of the march was the biggest "since the boys came home from France." Saturday's Nashville *Banner* front page streamered: "Nashville Surrenders to Huey Long."

It was rumored that Huey might announce as a candidate for President on his "Share the Wealth" program, opposing Franklin D. Roosevelt in 1936. Reporters asked Long what he was going to talk about between halves (his four sound trucks were already on hand at Dudley Field). "I don't know," he said. "With such a reception here, I think maybe I should annex Mexico to Louisiana and then annex the United States to Louisiana." Huey had said he was merely paying a courtesy call in return for the visit Andrew Jackson and his Tennessee riflemen paid New Orleans in 1815. When the Senator halted the parade at the War Memorial building to conduct the LSU band in an impromptu concert, clusters of people gathered to hear Huey's favorites, "Lindy Lou," "Harvest Moon," "River Stay Away From My Door," and, for the home folks, "Vanderbilt Forever." Huey asked the crowd to join in singing and, between numbers, acted as water boy, passing out cups of water to band members. Although he had given away nearly $3,000 in loans to students earlier in the week, when it came time to feed the band, Huey had to borrow $150.

After changing into a dark blue suit, white shirt, and light grey hat, Long arrived at Dudley Field at 1:15, forty-five minutes before the kickoff, in an automobile decorated with purple and gold ribbon. Introduced to the crowd by Coach McGugin as "LSU's all-American football rooter," Long spoke briefly before the game. "We're the greatest team in the world at this time," the Senator said. And, with Biff Jones probably squirming, he added: "And anyone who thinks we ain't, we plan to meet 'em."

Huey called the shot: LSU played like "the greatest team in the world." With Mickal passing for an early touchdown and Bill Crass scoring twice, the Tigers romped, 29–0, handing Vandy its worst licking in fourteen years. Huey's half-time speech, because of the buildup, was somewhat of a disappointment. He made no presidential announcement but merely said LSU was settling an obligation it owed to the Nashville institution (Vanderbilt had scheduled the Tigers in 1933 when LSU was in search of high-caliber opponents for its nighttime home schedule). Actually, some of the half-time attention was diverted from the

Senator by the appearance of a solitary drunk trying to copy the intricate maneuvers of the cadet band.

The Nashville *Banner* liked the show. "The Louisiana Kingfish may be a political mountebank and rabble-rouser but his tremendous talent for showmanship made this city his debtor," commented the newspaper. "They say he is crude and blatant and pusillanimous and a lot of other long words that mean bad things, but the mental and physical tonic he dosed us with Saturday was pure and wholesome. When you amuse, entertain and excite as many people as the Kingfish did during his visit here, you have accomplished something bigger than yourself."

By now Huey was under a full head of steam and, once back home, he felt it due time to pay tribute to an athlete who had brought glory to the university. He decided to make Abe Mickal a *de facto* state senator. A premedical major and cadet colonel, Mickal was a product of athletics, an example of the athletic scholarship at work. Abe's family had come to the United States from Syria when the future football star was eight. The Mickals settled in McComb, Mississippi, and when Abe's dad opened a store, sports seemed out of the question. "He wanted all of his children to work," said Abe. "He was against my playing football in high school. I was holding the ball for the opening kickoff in my first high school game when my dad ran into the stadium and pulled me off the field. He said there was work to be done." Finally, the elder Mickal relented in the face of his son's heroics. The family's proudest moment came when Huey Long, stopping briefly in McComb, paraded down the main street with the Mickal clan.

To honor Abe, Long picked a time when the state legislature was in special session in Baton Rouge. While the center of interest focused on the house, the Kingfish ordered the senate to meet for the express purpose of naming Mickal as senator, no trick compared to the 44-bill package Huey was steamrolling through the legislature. Naturally, the newspapers jumped on the story.

LSU was in Washington, D.C., at the time for a game with George Washington University and even though Mickal was ailing from a knee injury in the Mississippi State game, he went along for the trip. Without Mickal's passing threat, the Tigers barely managed to get out alive, 6–0, thanks to a 62-yard punt return by Sullivan which set up a touchdown by Bert Yates, Abe's understudy. During the game, when Yates came in for Bill Crass, he was greeted by the George Washington players with "Hiya, senator," and Yates chuckled. However, when his helmet was jarred loose by a tackler who said sarcastically, "How did you like that, senator?" Bert brushed himself off and told the player: "Say, you got me wrong. My name's not Mickal. It's Yates."

Naturally, this latest move by Huey disturbed Biff Jones. He called

Abe Mickal: Huey made him a senator.

Skipper Heard when he read the newspaper story and said: "Look, I can't run a ball club like this. It's bad for morale." Heard relayed Biff's feelings to Long, who said: "Hell, Red, I'll make 'em all senators." But Heard explained: "Senator, this would only give our opposition that much more psychological ammunition to use against us." Also the technicality was pointed out that making a football player a state senator might technically jeopardize the player's amateur standing since senators received ten dollars per day. Huey finally gave up the idea and "Senator" Mickal's name was taken down at the State Capitol.

Long followed the Tigers to Jackson, Mississippi, where Tinsley and Rukas both blocked punts as LSU, with the regulars resting most of the way, registered a methodical 14–0 win over Ole Miss. Now the Tigers had a two-week rest as they prepared to defend their 6–0–2 record against the December 1 invasion of Baton Rouge by the Tulane club which had lost only to Colgate in nine games.

For sheer drama, no LSU-Tulane game, before or since, matched the 1934 meeting. To appreciate the buildup, consider the following:

1. The newly-formed New Orleans Mid-Winter Sports Association had $30,000 in pledges to launch the Sugar Bowl Classic, January 1, 1935. The winner, particularly if it happened to be Ted Cox's Green Wave, was a virtual cinch to be invited as the host team.

2. The Tulane team, a worthy successor to the school's Rose Bowl outfit of 1931, had Claude "Little Monk" Simons, the halfback who had won all-America recognition.

3. LSU had not lost in eighteen games and had never, under Biff Jones, been humbled by a Southeastern Conference school.

4. Senator Huey Long (a former Tulane law school student) was riding high politically. His bills to strip New Orleans of much of its power had recently been rubber-stamped by the legislature, and his junket to Nashville plus the "Senator" Abe Mickal incident remained the topic of conversation.

Traditional games of this kind between two excellent teams with excellent records and with more than school pride riding on the outcome usually fall short of expectations. The 1934 game, as it unfolded before a then record crowd of 31,620 in Tiger Stadium, exceeded them all. Seven special trains, carrying 8,000 Tulane fans, arrived on an ideal football afternoon, cool and crisp with little or no wind. Jones decided to start Bert Yates in place of Mickal, whose knee was heavily taped from the Mississippi State injury, and LSU, minus Abe, seemed listless at the outset. Grabbing the initiative, Tulane put on a march midway through the first period which Monk Simons climaxed with a 27-yard scoring pass to Dick Hardy. Tulane converted and the visitors led 7–0 at the end of the quarter.

Mickal's first appearance as the second quarter got under way seemed to give the Tigers a lift. It wasn't long before sophomore Tinsley burst through to block a kick by Simons and, as the ball bounced crazily around, Ernie Seago sprang out of a crowd of jerseys and headed twenty-three yards to an LSU touchdown! Or was it? Tulane players claimed the ball could not be advanced, and for several agonizing minutes it appeared the officials could not make up their minds. Finally, however, the signal was given, arms went up, and it was 7–6. LSU fans considered the next play automatic. Mickal came into the game with eighteen conversions in a row and only one miss in thirty tries in two seasons. But this time a groan went up from the west side as Abe's place-kick was wide of the uprights, leaving Tulane with a 7–6 lead at half time.

Mickal started the third quarter, and it wasn't too long before he delivered what had become almost commonplace—the bomb. With the ball on the LSU 45, Abe took a lateral from Sullivan, after Sullivan took a reverse from Fatherree, and rifled a 50-yard bullet (the ball never was more than fifteen feet off the ground) diagonally across the field to Jeff Barrett who had gotten behind Tulane's deep defender. Barrett took the ball on the run but was nailed from behind five yards short of a touchdown. Mickal took care of that on the first play, knifing off right tackle to make it 12–7. Again, however, Abe was wide with his conversion attempt, giving the Tigers a shaky five-point margin as the final period began. Mickal took the Tigers to the Tulane 8, where LSU missed a first down by inches and it was there that Tulane showed it was not ready to

Backfield star Jess Fatherree.

fold. Three minutes later, back on their 20, the Greenies got a second shot at a first down because of an offside penalty. Simons faded, hit Fred Preisser, and Fred went all the way to the LSU 28 before being hauled down by Mickal. The Tulane end got up. Mickal didn't. In obvious pain, Abe was carried from the field and placed near the LSU bench. A concerned Huey Long came over to whisper some words of encouragement. The big green team marched to the LSU 5-yard line and seemingly was headed for a touchdown. Just at that time, a pain-wracked Mickal was put on a stretcher and carried into the dressing room at the north end of the field his team was defending. It was strictly from Hollywood. As the stadium stood to applaud the departing LSU hero, the Tigers took heart, dug in, and, sparked by crippled linebackers Lloyd Stovall and Seago, halted Tulane on the 3. Yates punted from his end zone and, to no one's surprise, Tulane went to the air. No dice. So Simons punted deftly to the Tiger 3, where end Harold "Hoss" Memtsas downed the football. Three minutes remained. LSU ran two plays and then Yates dropped back again to kick his ball club out of trouble. Bert got his foot into a good one, and he aimed it smartly toward "Bucky" Bryan, and away from Simons who, with Bucky, formed a double safety. Running to his left on the LSU 45, Bucky suddenly pivoted and flipped a lateral to Simons crossing behind him. The sleight-of-hand fooled some Tigers, but not all. "I had been given a hard time all day by Tinsley and I thought I was in for another creaming," Simons recalled later. "Actually, I believe I was aided by some LSU players because they seemed to knock off some of the guys who had hold of me." At any rate, Simons ran through lots of traffic and made only one mistake. He slowed up near the end zone where a desperation tackle by Fatherree broke Monk's collarbone.

But Simons was in, and as Tulane fans went berserk on the east side a pall of gloom settled over the LSU section. Simons' mother fainted during her son's 45-yard run, LSU fans wept openly. Tragically, one Tiger rooter, overcome by the emotion of his team's 13–12 loss, died in the stands of a heart attack. LSU fans were too shocked for any post-game free-for-all. Leaving the stands, one weeping woman summed up what must still stand as the most bitter defeat of the ancient series. "If it had been anyone but those SOBs," she said dejectedly.

Every man a king.

Long, of course, was crushed and the Senator did not hide his feelings. "Biff Jones may not be the worst coach around," Huey told intimates, "but he sure ain't the best." Reportedly, the breach between Senator and coach widened the next week when Biff played Mickal against Huey's orders. The Tigers were in Knoxville for a game with Neyland's Tennessee Vols, who had won seven and lost two, close decisions to Fordham and unbeaten, Rose Bowl-bound Alabama. It turned into a rough afternoon. Tinsley was knocked out with a blow to the mouth. Sullivan was clipped and had to leave the field. Mickal was roughed on a punt and limped off the field. Even referee Moon Ducote was a casualty. Tennessee pulled it out 19–13 in the final two minutes on a fake pass off the Statue of Liberty.

These back-to-back defeats, after a string of stunning successes dating back to 1932, set the stage for the dressing room showdown between two strong-willed men in the final game of the 1934 season. Oregon, paying its second visit to Baton Rouge in three years, jumped off to a 13–0 lead in the first half, the Webfeet being benefactors of a listless LSU exhibition. Coach Jones was about to begin one of his clinical half-time talks—more reason than emotion—when Huey, accompanied by Edmond Talbot, United States referee in bankruptcy for Eastern Louisiana, appeared at the dressing room door. The Senator motioned a puzzled Jones over to the door and asked, "Can I talk to the team?"

"No," was Jones's curt reply.

"Who's going to stop me?" demanded Long.

"Well," shot back Jones, "you're not going to talk."

"Well, I'm sick of losing and tying games," said Long. "You'd better win this one."

Jones flushed with anger. "Well, Senator, get this: win, lose, or draw, I quit."

"That's a bargain," said Long as Jones shut the door.

Shaken, Long tried to convince a cluster of people outside the dressing room that his intentions were to help, not hurt, the football team. "Ain't I part of the organization?" he asked. "Why can't I talk to the boys? Why do we have to spot the other team two touchdowns?"

A pro-Jones man told the Senator: "Why don't you run the band and lay off the football team?"

Inside, Biff turned emotional for the first time during his LSU regime. He asked the players to win the game for Biff Jones. It was another Hollywood script. In the third quarter, a hobbling Mickal tossed a touchdown pass to Jeff Barrett, Seago kicked the point, and it was 13–7. Dressed in a blue suit and pink shirt, Huey didn't make an appearance until midway through the third period. And, when he did, he sat on the end of the bench and was unusually quiet. He didn't cheer the touchdown. Nor did he cheer when Fatherree raced thirty-nine yards to make it 13–13 or when Seago booted the winning point in a 14–13 victory.

The comeback did little to soothe Jones. He informed LSU President James M. Smith of his intentions. Because talk of the verbal clash quickly spread, Long was asked for a statement. "I don't know whether I want to have the Army assignment of Captain Jones extended," he said. "When it was about to end last year, I had it extended another year. I haven't been asked to extend it and I don't know whether I want to have it extended."

With a day to cool off, Jones and Long had second thoughts. But, when a detailed version of what took place hit the newspapers, neither wanted to back up publicly. Biff told Heard he regretted the incident and, several days later, after his resignation was official, he and Heard went to see the Senator. "They had a friendly chat," said Heard. "The last thing Huey said was: 'Biff, if I can ever do a favor for you, please let me know.' They shook hands and parted friends."

'You gotta be lucky to be a good coach'

1935–1947

AS the 1934 season drew to a close, Huey Long's disatisfaction with LSU did not involve the football team alone. In fact, weeks before the verbal flareup that resulted in Biff Jones's resignation, the Senator was intent on "doing something to improve the band." So intent was he that he decided to steal the orchestra leader from the Blue Room of the Roosevelt Hotel in New Orleans.

Castro Carazo's "kidnapping" typified the way in which the Kingfish went about things. "One day, as I was going from the elevator to the Blue Room," said Carazo in recalling the incident, "Huey was waiting. 'Where you headed?' he asked. 'I'm on my way to the matinee for high school children, Senator,' I told him. 'Well,' he snapped, 'I just want you to know Seymour Weiss has fired you and I've hired you. You're the new band director at LSU.'" Since Long and Weiss, top man at the Roosevelt, were close friends, Carazo knew the Senator had arranged everything and there would be no problems. "I had known the Senator for some time and realized he usually got what he went after," said Carazo. "I was content with my job at the Blue Room but, mainly because of Huey's enthusiasm, I looked toward my new job as a challenge."

The musician was accustomed to Long's challenges. "One day Seymour Weiss called and told me Huey wanted to see me in Baton Rouge right away," said Carazo. "Weiss turned over his car and chauffeur and, after a quick trip, I arrived at the Heidelberg Hotel at 11:30 at night. When I went to the Senator's suite, I saw that he was sleeping, so I went to an adjoining bedroom and dozed off. Around 3 A.M. I felt someone shake me. It was Huey and his first words were, 'I need a campaign song. Let's start working.' Huey ordered coffee and then he and I began working from hotel stationery on the desk. I had a melody in mind and, when he told me he wanted the song called 'Every Man a King,' I wrote the music in half an hour. I played it and he liked it. By 5 A.M. he had written the words and he told me to whistle the tune while he sang. Two hours later, after some polishing, we had the words and music on one sheet.

"This, it turned out, was only the beginning. Huey wanted it orchestrated for broadcast that night over radio. This meant sheet music for forty musicians who had donated their services. So I scooted back to New Orleans, ordered paper from Werlein's, and had the orchestration ready for 7 P.M. At 8:30 a vocalist sang 'Every Man a King' over the air."

Castro Carazo

Carazo was a guest of Long's at the Oregon game in 1934 and when Huey asked for a critic's appraisal of the LSU band Carazo told him: "There's a sameness to the music it plays. I feel they should try to break away into something new, something different." The Kingfish told his new band leader matter of factly: "I want the best college band in the country. You'll have all the scholarships you want and you'll travel in air-conditioned Pullmans." The morning after Carazo's appointment was announced, the new band director, on Huey's request, was in the Senator's office at 5 A.M. "He called for President Smith and Major Middleton," said Carazo. "When they finally arrived—they must have been used to early morning calls—he told me, in their presence, that the three men in the room were the only ones I'd ever have to answer to. 'Do what you think is necessary,' he told me. And that was the end of the meeting."

While Carazo was filling one position that Long felt needed bolstering, the resignation of Biff Jones had left him with an unexpected headache—and the necessity of more meetings. Long seemed determined to land a big-time coach. However, in all of his talks with T. P. Heard the LSU athletic director recommended Bernie Moore, head track coach, freshman football coach, and scout. "I felt Bernie knew the material and knew the situation at LSU as well as anyone," said Heard. "He had impressed Biff in three short years with his scouting and also with his handling of the frosh. But Huey had 'big-time' on his mind. First he felt out Clark Shaughnessy, who wasn't interested, and then he arranged a meeting with Frank Thomas of Alabama at the Roosevelt Hotel. Alabama was on its way to the Rose Bowl and, in a talk that was supersecret, Thomas agreed to come to LSU for a $15,000 salary, plus salaries of $7,500 for two assistants of his choosing. Thomas shook hands on the deal but emphasized he wanted to inform Alabama authorities. 'If any hint of this talk gets into the papers,' he told Huey, 'the deal is off.'"

According to Heard, Long agreed. "He sent me to the West Coast with Alabama to send back reports that everything was status quo. I called him first from San Antonio and then from Phoenix. Talking to him the second time, I realized the situation was changing in Baton Rouge. 'Bernie Moore looks better to me all the time,' he told me. When I got to Los Angeles, the story was in the paper: 'Kingfish Appoints Moore Head Coach.' What happened was Huey called Dan McGugin, a fellow he really respected, for his recommendation. Dan recommended Bernie and that was good enough for the Senator."

Huey had promised LSU fans a coach who had gained national recognition and the appointment of Bernie Moore, in a way, fulfilled that promise. During the summer of 1933 Bernie had taken a five-man track team to Chicago and brought back the NCAA championship to Baton Rouge and an overjoyed Huey Long. This accomplishment simply added weight to McGugin's recommendation.

"I lost some friends when Huey appointed me," Moore recalled later. "They figured I was Huey's pet, and they didn't much like him. I was never his pet, but I wasn't his enemy either. I understood him. I also learned never to discuss anything with him unless I knew more about it than he did."

Long had been elected governor in 1928, the year Moore arrived at LSU as an assistant to Russ Cohen. Bernie's coaching career had begun eleven years before, at Winchester, Tennessee, High where he handled all sports and taught English ("May the Lord forgive me for what I did to the language."). The youngest of fourteen children born to a missionary Baptist preacher, Bernie (he was named Bernice) played college football and baseball at Carson-Newman College in Jefferson City, Tennessee. It was in track, however, that he gained fame of a sort. With no cinder path on which to practice and no uniforms to wear, he and his teammates once decided on a little night practice, a workout which the city constable broke up by arresting the entire team for running in their underwear.

After seeing combat in World War I, Bernie returned to find many of his college debts waiting, a situation that prompted him to give up thoughts of medical school and turn to coaching. Following successful stints at Winchester and a prep school in East Texas, he went to Mercer University (where, among others, he coached Wally Butts) and then to Sewanee. When the LSU offer came from Cohen in 1929, he jumped at it.

"You gotta be lucky to be a good coach," Bernie once said. "It so happened that everywhere I went I inherited a good bunch of boys." Specifically, this perhaps applied best to the material he fell heir to in his first season at LSU. The 1932 freshman crop, which included men like

Bernie Moore: His selection surprised a few.

Mickal, Fatherree, Barrett, Seago, Rukas, Helveston, was in its final year. Joining these seniors were such outstanding sophomore prospects as Charles "Pinky" Rohm, Art "Slick" Morton, Paul Carroll, and Bernie Dumas. The only fly in the ointment was Mickal's multiple injuries which were destined to slow him throughout the season. At this left halfback spot, however, Moore could fall back on Bill Crass and junior Pat Coffee. Seago handled most of the quarterback duties. Fatherree had

Rohm behind him at right half, and Rock Reed and Junior Bowman alternated at fullback. In the line, the brilliant Tinsley teamed with Barrett at ends; iron-men Carroll and Rukas were at tackles, Wardell Leisk and Butch Helveston at guards, and Marvin "Moose" Stewart at center.

Since Burt Ingwerson had resigned upon learning he was not in line for the head job, Moore worked with a four-man staff—Ben Enis, chief assistant; Spike Nelson, in charge of the line; Joel Hunt, in charge of the backs; and J. B. Whitworth, freshman coach. Moore assumed command of this football operation fully conscious that Huey was willing to contribute. "He called McGugin and asked for a play that would score every time," said Moore. "McGugin explained what he called 'Number 88' to Huey and Huey passed it on to me."

In the early fall of 1935 Moore had his talent-wealthy squad hitting hard for a September 28 opener against Rice. Long had come from Washington to Baton Rouge for a special session of the legislature, and took the opportunity to check with Moore on the team's progress. "I told him things were shaping up!" said Moore. "I also suggested he go to Hot Springs to take a rest so he'd be in shape for the season. But he said pressing legislation made his presence necessary."

Meanwhile Castro Carazo, with an unlimited budget, had completed preliminary spadework for a band that would soon number 242. He and Huey, in a two-hour session at the Capitol, had combined to write "Touchdown for LSU" which, hopefully, would be played many times during the next three months. Also, they had pooled their efforts on another ditty, "Miss Vandy," which Long, still glowing over the treatment he received in 1934, planned to take with him on a return trip to Nashville in October.

Huey envisioned additional football songs, and it was with this in mind that he chatted with Carazo at the Capitol on Sunday, September 8. He talked also about one of his dreams. "I want to start a school in New Orleans where kids can go for music only," he told his visitor. "And I know where I'm going to get the money." Carazo sat chatting as the Senator signed papers and discussed business with aides and legislators.

"He was in and out of the office most of the day," said Carazo. "When my wife came to pick me up at 5 o'clock, I was dead tired. I went home and went straight to bed. I was sleeping peacefully when my wife woke me with the startling news: 'It's on the radio. Senator Long has been shot.'" Three days later, thousands flooded the grounds of the Kingfish's skyscraper. Castro Carazo and his LSU band, with drums muffled and playing "Every Man a King" in a minor key that changed Huey's rousing campaign song into a moving dirge, led the cortege from the Capitol's bronze doors to a vault which laborers had prepared by working around the clock. Today a statue of the Senator stands above the vault, which lies in front of the Capitol.

With Huey at rest, Bernie Moore never felt obligated to use No. 88. Also, he did not feel tied to the two-formation system of Biff Jones; that is, he was planning to make the single wing his basic attack while using the double wing sparingly. He would rely more on power, less on deception. Moore hewed to Jones's two-team idea although he used it somewhat differently. Generally, Bernie followed a rather set system—first team for first quarter, second team for second quarter, first team for third quarter, second team for fourth quarter. Jones usually made his substitutions shortly before the end of the quarter so that he could get the first team back into the game in case of trouble.

In the 1935 curtain raiser against invading Rice, LSU's depth, while in evidence, was not enough to carry the day. Spearheaded by Bill Wallace, the Owls grabbed a 10–0 lead in the first half and then were forced to hold off repeated assaults by the Tigers in the last two periods. In the third quarter Rock Reed went twenty-three yards for a touchdown on a spinner play, but it was nullified by an offsides penalty. The great Tinsley got the Tigers on the scoreboard in the fourth quarter when he blocked a punt which Justin Rukas recovered on the Owl 1. Son Seago scored, added the point and it was 10–7 with half a quarter remaining. With two minutes left and LSU on the move, Bill Crass stumbled while fading for a pass. In came Mickal, still hampered by that "trick" knee. Abe rifled one straight and true, in search of a sprinting Jeff Barrett, but at the last instant Wallace swiped it to put the game on ice. There was no way of knowing it at the time, but the opening day crowd of 19,000 was watching LSU lose its last regular-season game until midway through the 1937 campaign—a string of twenty-three without a defeat.

The string began on October 5 as the Tigers spotted Texas a first-quarter score, then roared back for an 18–6 victory, cracking a 6–6 deadlock in the final period, when Reed returned a punt and Fatherree an interception for touchdowns. With their single-wing timing improving, the Tigers next week gave New York City a display of overall power, featuring Mickal, who passed for the first two scores and kept Manhattan College in the hole with his quick kicking. Sophomore Pinky Rohm got into the act in the third period, catching a 31-yard pass from Pat Coffee and racing fifty-three yards for a touchdown. The 32–0 decision reversed earlier New York City defeats at the hands of Rutgers and Army and would no doubt have been a field day for the late Kingfish, who had planned another "economy" trip for LSU students and a march down Broadway.

Moore's maturing "shock troops" enabled LSU to escape an Arkansas ambush in Shreveport a week later when Pat Coffee led the second stringers on a fourth-quarter march which the powerful Rohm climaxed with a 17-yard scamper on a reverse. The score put the Tigers ahead, 13–7, but they had to hold the Razorbacks on the four to preserve the victory.

From Shreveport to Nashville—and a meeting with improved Vanderbilt. This time it was the old head, Mickal, who pulled it out and in dramatic fashion. The Commodores looked as though they would make a 2–0 lead (Bill Crass was nailed for a second quarter safety) stand up until Abe's passes began clicking in the third quarter. Starting from midfield, he hit Tinsley with two successive tosses, drew Vandy's defense in with a center buck, and then stepped back and flipped to Barrett for the touchdown, and a 7–2 victory.

A stiffening defense, one which held Auburn's great Billy Hitchcock

All-America Gaynell Tinsley: As a freshman, the varsity couldn't handle him.

to zero yardage in sixteen carries, carried the Tigers to a 6–0 victory over the Plainsmen, but the score didn't come until Coffee passed to Barrett in the fading moments.

After three cliff-hangers Moore, an all-American worrier, was able to breathe easier, but only a little, as his ball club took the measure of Mississippi State (which had beaten Army) by a 28–13 score on touchdowns by Reed, Barrett, Crass, and Rohm. This was a prelude to an invasion of Athens and a collision with Harry Mehre's Georgia Bulldogs who had lost only to Alabama in seven games. The 1,200 LSU cadets who made the trip came home with everything but the goal posts, which happened to be cemented in the ground. After a 13–0 defeat, which was no indication of how lopsided things were, Mehre called the Tigers "the best team that ever played on Sanford Field." Crafty Son Seago called the play that swung the tide when, after halting Georgia on the six in the opening period, he sent Mickal into punt formation. Standing in the end zone Abe, in a variation of the Statue of Liberty, handed the ball to Fatherree who snaked 105 yards (actually, 94 yards from the line of scrimmage) to a touchdown that knocked the wind out of the home team. In the final quarter Crass raced twenty-three yards to the second touchdown. Carroll, Rukas, and Stewart played sixty brilliant minutes, especially on defense, as LSU finished with a 15–2 edge in first downs.

Moore substituted freely the following week in a 56–0 rout of SLI, making sure not to risk injury before the Tulane finale seven days ahead. Thanks to that 7–2 conquest of Vanderbilt (leaving the Commodores with a 5–1 record in SEC play) the Tigers needed a victory over the Greenies to wrap up an undisputed conference championship. Graduation had cut into Tulane's Sugar Bowl champions, but it was still a Tulane-LSU game (anything could happen), and it was being played in New Orleans. With 31,000 looking on, the thrice-beaten Green team began like it meant business, driving to the Tiger 24 in the opening period, but that was it. Gathering steam, Crass passed to Barrett to give LSU a 7–0 halftime lead before the floodgates opened. Mickal, facing Tulane for the last time, had a hand in three of four third-quarter touchdowns, running for one and passing to Barrett and George Bowman for the other two. Rohm stepped fourteen yards for the other, and in the last period Coffee bucked across to make it 41–0, biggest score of the series. The first downs were 23–3. Scoop Kennedy, writing in the New Orleans *Item*, spoke appropriately for all Tulanians when he said: "They beat us in the air, on the ground, everywhere, as the lazy sun went down." As the sun set behind the west stands, LSU students, despite electrically charged wires and defending Tulane troops, managed to pull down the goal posts, a job that took about thirty minutes. When Tiger fans let go with a yell, a staggering Green Wave rooter was

Familiar scene in the thirties: Tigers attack, Greenies defend goal posts.

leaning on an iron rail beneath the stadium. "Good God," he moaned, "they scored again."

While LSU broke many hearts in New Orleans, the Sugar Bowl welcomed Bernie Moore's 9–1 outfit with open arms, and feeling ran high for the impending January 1 clash with TCU and all-America Sammy Baugh. The Tigers had an all-American of their own in the incomparable Tinsley and wound up putting seven men on the Associated Press's first three all-SEC teams: Tinsley, Fatherree, and Crass on the first team, Mickal and Rukas on the second, Stewart and Barrett on the third. Moore never wavered in his evaluation of Tinsley. "He's the greatest lineman I ever saw," said Bernie, "someone who could have made all-America at any position. He was so tough he made blockers quit. When Gus was a freshman, Biff asked me to bring over the frosh so the varsity could work on punt protection. He was at left end. The ball was snapped. Gus rushed, knocking the blocker into the punter. They lined up a second time and he did the same thing. Biff was pretty hot, so he ordered it a third time. Darn if Gus didn't do it again. Biff turned to me and said: 'Take that damn team back where it came from.'"

The LSU-TCU Sugar Bowl, matching the undisputed champions of the SEC with the Southwest runner-up, was billed as a passing duel between "Slingin' Sam" and Abe Mickal. Already a legend, Baugh had completed 101 passes for 1,293 yards and nineteen touchdowns as the Horned Frogs won eleven and lost one (to Rose Bowl-bound SMU) during regular season play. He had thrown for touchdowns in all but two games, and in the 20–14 loss to the Mustangs he completed seventeen of forty-three passes for 172 yards.

As it happened, the elements turned the Baugh-Mickal duel from passing to punting, a kicking exhibition which even today ranks as the most dramatic in the history of the classic. It rained in New Orleans during the last three days of 1935, and when the teams squared off on January 1 it rained again, turning Tulane's field into a huge platter of gumbo. At that time football equipment added fifteen pounds to a player's weight, and when his leather helmet, woolen jersey, and awkward padding became soaked the load increased appreciably. With this in mind, it's difficult to imagine how the mud-caked Mickal, who shared kicking duties with Bill Crass, averaged forty-five yards in eight kicks, while Baugh, more incredibly, kicked fourteen times for a 47-yard average. One punt of Sammy's was particularly memorable. With the rain pouring down, he stood in his end zone and sent one booming fifty-six yards, out of bounds on the LSU 44.

In that January 1 game, won by the Horned Frogs by a World Series score of 3–2, the Tigers threatened several times, once getting to the 6-inch line, where Crass was halted by TCU's all-America center Darrell Lester who fractured his shoulder making the stop. Following this second-quarter goal line stand, Baugh dropped back deep into the end zone and, crowded by Tinsley, shot a hurried pass out to the right which

TCU field goal that won the 1936 Sugar Bowl game.

fell incomplete in the end zone, an automatic safety putting LSU ahead 2–0. Minutes later TCU recovered a fumble on the LSU 45 and drove to the 17. There, with Baugh holding, Taldon Manton booted a "line drive" field goal from the 26-yard line. Even the LSU rooters cheered the wobbly boot that stood as the thin margin of victory. Statistics were almost as close. LSU outgained the Frogs 166–162. The Sugar Bowl crowd of 35,000, added to the 177,000 regular-season total, lifted LSU's attendance over 200,000 for the first time.

Ironically, at this time in the mid-thirties, with the country still struggling to recover from the depression, the abundance of football beef on hand in Baton Rouge was staggering. The best gauge was the transition from 1935 to 1936. Bernie Moore could lose four backs of quality (Mickal, Seago, Fatherree, and Bowman) and two ace linemen (Barrett and Rukas) and still not blink. Why should he? Left behind at the old homestead was material enough to carve two equally talented ball clubs from a roster he rated superior to anything he ever had as a coach. In the first line, there were Tinsley and Bernie Dumas at ends, Clarence "Pop" Strange and Paul Carroll at tackles, Wardell Leisk and Marvin Baldwin at guards, Marvin Stewart at center. Spelling this front, Moore had Basil Myrick and Mickey Mihalic at ends, Gordon Lester, Eddie Gatto, and Harry Farmer at tackles, Oscar Matlock and Blythe Clark at guards, Dick Gormley at center.

If anything, the backfield was richer. Senior Bill May alternated with sophomore Barry Booth at quarterback, Pat Coffee shared tailback with Bill Crass, Guy "Cotton" Milner shared wingback with Pinky Rohm, captain Slick Morton shared fullback with Rock Reed.

All of this was the cream which surfaced after talent was picked from a huge army of recruits. "When I was a freshman in 1934," said Bernie Dumas, "I was one of twenty-two ends. We suited out eleven teams. It was the custom to bring in around 125 freshmen each fall. The boys who made the squad got a free ride, those who didn't either had to pay their own way or drop out." Aside from scooping up Louisiana talent, LSU recruited successfully in Arkansas, Mississippi, and Texas. In the 1935 Arkansas game, for example, Dumas and six of his teammates from El Dorado, Arkansas, High faced the Razorbacks.

As the 1936 opener approached, Castro Carazo had his entertainers cranked up, including the popular drum and bugle corps made up of freshman and sophomore military students. Naturally, expectations were high and they nearly went out of sight when the Tigers met Rice, the only team to beat them in 1935, in the curtain raiser. Rock Reed, whose touchdown run was nullified the year before, streaked fifty-eight yards to a first-quarter score and the Tigers were off to a 20–7 win. After the Owls tied it, 7–7, Morton raced twenty-six yards to set up a short jab by

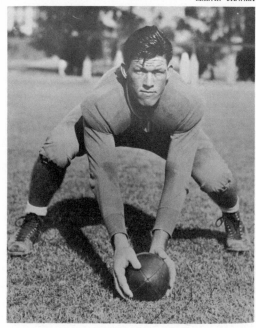

Moose Stewart: Man in the middle.

Coffee, and later Tinsley rushed the passer, knocked the ball from his hands, picked it up and ran it over.

A miserable performance the next week in Austin—six fumbles in the first half—resulted in a 6–6 tie with Texas, the only blemish on the 1936 record. Morton's fumble paved the way for a Longhorn touchdown but the Tiger back later made amends by running for the Tiger score. "This game, oddly enough, was the turning point," said Moore. "Everyone seemed determined to do a better job because we knew we had the ability."

LSU's overwhelming power quickly became evident as the season unfolded:

Georgia (47–7)—Milner, Reed, Crass, Rohm pulverized the Bulldogs in an awesome display—Forrest "Spec" Townes, the great hurdler, picked up a blocked punt to account for the Georgia touchdown.

Ole Miss (13–0)—The Tigers took to the air, with Coffee tossing thirty-three yards to Tinsley, Crass thirty-six yards to Rohm.

Arkansas (19–7)—A Razorback team which was later to capture the Southwest title didn't score until the fading minutes. Milner and Crass climaxed drives with short runs and then Crass broke loose on a 75-yard gallop for the third touchdown.

Vanderbilt (19–0)—In an important conference game which meant national recognition for the winner, the Tigers invaded Nashville to win impressively. After Rohm scored in the second quarter, he caught the Commodores napping by tossing his first pass of the season, a 34-yarder to Mihalic, to set up a Crass-to-Morton touchdown pass. The last Tiger score came on a 20-yard pass from Coffee to Dumas.

140   *The Fighting Tigers*

Mississippi State (12–0)—Rohm went forty-five yards in the second quarter while Coffee passed twenty yards to Tinsley in the fourth quarter.

Auburn (19–6)—With a crowd of 25,000 on hand at Birmingham, including 5,000 Tiger rooters, Reed capped a 72-yard march in the second period, Milner dashed ninety yards off tackle behind the blocking of Tinsley and Mihalic, and Coffee passed fifteen yards to Tinsley. Auburn scored with twelve seconds left.

Southwestern Louisiana (93–0)—This Tulane tuneup resulted in the biggest score in LSU history, a 14-touchdown orgy which marked the debut of Mike the Tiger (Mike I) in Baton Rouge.

Tulane (33–0)—A 47-yard Coffee-to-Tinsley pass started the rout before a crowd of 48,000, largest turnout up to that time in Southern football history. Milner ran thirty-two yards, Tinsley caught two more scoring passes and Rohm stepped thirty-one yards to account for the other points.

Of the 9–0–1 Tigers, Georgia coach Harry Mehre said: "They're on a par with Alabama's 1934 club with better balance, more speed and more power. I've never seen a better looking squad. They must have at least twenty men over six feet weighing more than 215 pounds." In capturing their second straight undisputed SEC title, the Tigers finished as the No. 1 team in both the Deke Houlgate and Williamson systems and as the nation's No. 2 club (behind Minnesota) in the Associated Press ratings.

With 281 points, the Tigers led the nation in scoring, and Tinsley, all-American for the second year in a row, led all ends in scoring and finished second in the balloting for the country's most valuable player. The Associated Press named both Tinsley and Leisk to its No. 1 all-SEC team; Stewart and Coffee made the second; Carroll, May, and Crass the third.

Not since 1908 had fans had so much to crow about, and this time, in addition to an unbeaten ball club, there was a live mascot and the South's largest football arena. Mike I was a 9-year-old Royal Bengal Tiger when he was purchased for $750 in Little Rock, as a result of a fund drive initiated by physical ed instructor W. G. Higginbotham. Housed for the first season in Baton Rouge's City Park zoo, Mike soon moved to swankier living quarters, a steam-heated home (complete with a tree on which to sharpen his claws) built just outside Tiger Stadium. The handsome mascot, who put away twelve pounds of meat daily, was named for trainer Mike Chambers, a lovable 249-pounder who, as a tackle at Illinois, helped clear the way for "Red" Grange. Born in New Orleans, the Irishman served as Olympic trainer in 1928 and was brought to LSU in 1935 by Bernie Moore following a tour of duty at

Trainer Mike Chambers and namesake. LSU's first tiger mascot was housed in City Park zoo until a steam-heated home was built for him.

Georgia Tech, where he handled the Jackets' 1929 Rose Bowl team.

The addition of 24,000 permanent seats, following the completion of the north end, had raised the stadium's capacity to 45,000. Completed by seven hundred workers as a WPA project, the new north end also added 250 rooms for students, plus 21 others to be used as stadium offices. Dedication ceremonies attracted a number of notables, including President Roosevelt's confidant, Harry Hopkins. These ceremonies, as well as a broadcast of the 1936 game with Tulane, were carried coast to coast.

From the West Coast, incidentally, was to come LSU's Sugar Bowl opponent, little-known Santa Clara, then trying to gain recognition among the Pacific Coast Conference Rose Bowl aristocracy. Good enough to knock off bigger-name schools in its area, Santa Clara leaped at the opportunity to come south for a crack at the unbeaten Tigers. Bernie Moore worked his squad behind closed doors in Baton Rouge and the Tigers arrived in Tulane Stadium on January 1, 1937, a 4-to-1 favorite (point spreads were not yet popular) to take the visitors. Surprisingly, the sluggish Tigers were never in the ball game against a club they possibly underestimated. Coach Buck Shaw's Broncos jumped to a 14–0 lead in the first period, watched LSU make it 14–7 thirty seconds before half time, moved out 21–7 with a third-quarter score, and then, with substitutes in the game, allowed a last-quarter touchdown and came away a 21–14 winner.

Tiger Stadium: Before . . .

. . . And after the north end was closed in 1936. At dedication ceremonies the band saluted Louisiana's governor.

Tiger forward wall in 1936: John Mihalic, Paul Carroll, Oscar Matlock, Moose Stewart, Wardell Leisk, Eddie Gatto, Gus Tinsley.

This postseason embarrassment was the last game for players like Tinsley, Leisk, Stewart, Baldwin, Strange, Crass, Coffee, Reed, and May. In fact, Moore was losing thirteen of his first twenty-two, and he looked to 1937 knowing he would have to bank heavily on sophomores. But Bernie didn't find the cupboard bare. No fewer than seven sophomores—headed by an end named Ken Kavanaugh and a triple-threater named Young Bussey—figured in the scheme of things as Moore, following his 1936 tactics, continued to use the single wing and to bank on sheer power. Moore shifted Rohm from right half to left half—that is, tailback—and made the flashy Bussey (who was plucked from Houston) Pinky's understudy. Jimmy Cajoleas, a rookie from Warren Easton High School in New Orleans, worked his way in the quarterback post behind Barry Booth. J. H. "Jabbo" Stell, from Shreveport's Byrd High, alternated with Milner at right half. And Jake Staples lent depth to fullback which already had Morton, the 1937 captain, and Roy Joe Anderson. Kavanaugh, a 6-foot, 3-inch, 205-pounder from Little Rock, Ogden Baur, and Larry King terminated Moore's worries for a few seasons as far as ends were concerned.

The squad was almost 80 percent sophomore, and when the Tigers opened against Florida ends Bernie Dumas and Jack Gormley were the only seniors in the starting lineup. The rest were juniors—tackles Ben Friend and Eddie Gatto, guards Blythe Clark and John H. Smith, and center Dick Gormley. The opening 19–0 conquest of Florida turned into a smashing debut for sophomore Bussey, who scored two touchdowns as the Tigers ran up 346 yards and held the Gators to 30. Rohm, playing tailback for the first time, contributed a touchdown and a 72-yard quick kick.

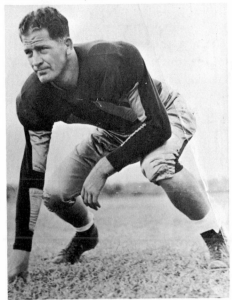 

Two of Bernie's boys: Clarence "Pop" Strange and high-kicking Young Bussey.

A week later, tailback Pinky Rohm made a deeper impression in a 9–0 decision over Texas. First he kicked out on the Longhorn 1 and moments later he returned a Texas punt sixty yards for the game's only touchdown.

A crowd of 20,000 in Houston, including Louisiana's Governor Richard Leche and 5,000 LSU rooters, was on hand for the Tigers' 13–0 win over Rice, a victory memorable for one of those "Hall of Fame" moments. LSU held a shaky 7–0 lead in the third quarter when Rice drove inside the Tiger 1, giving every indication it would become the first team to score on LSU in 1937. However, "Red" Vickers, attempting to hit the left side, was met head-on near the goal, the ball popped out of his hands, and, in the words of an eyewitness, "Kavanaugh plucked it out of the air like he'd pick an apple off a tree." Kavanaugh carried his 205 pounds one hundred yards, leaving a string of Owls in his wake and dashing any Rice hopes.

With a 3–0 record and its goal line still uncrossed, LSU next week scored its eighth win in a row over the Rebels, breaking loose for three touchdowns in the final quarter for a 13–0 decision. This set the stage for a critical SEC showdown the following Saturday between two unbeaten contenders, LSU and Vandy. For the Tigers, it meant the fourth straight year they would be playing the Commodores at Nashville's Dudley Field, scene of three successive LSU victories. Vandy had beefed up under the slick handling of Ray Morrison, who had succeeded Dan

McGugin in 1935, and, as Moore took his Tigers north, he said, in a tribute to the imaginative Morrison, "I'm expecting the unexpected." Bernie didn't have a long wait. In the first three minutes, after an exchange of punts, the Commodores got the football near midfield. Vandy lined up normally but then, in the words of spectator Lewis Gottlieb, long-time LSU backer, "there was a pileup in the line and, all of a sudden, there was this fellow running down the sidelines."

LSU had become the victim of the "hidden ball" and, although the play was later ruled illegal, in 1937 it not only ruined the Tigers' string of defensive zeroes but turned out to be the only blot in an otherwise perfect season. Vandy kicked the extra point to take a 7–0 lead that stood until the final three minutes when Young Bussey went on a passing rampage, finally hitting Jabbo Stell on a 19-yard scoring play. By this time the crowd of 18,000 had forgotten all about the 39-degree weather. As Bussey prepared to hold for Barry Booth's extra point try, everyone was standing, but what happened then was almost as unexpected as Vandy's touchdown play. Center Bill Warmbrod snapped the ball high over Bussey's outstretched hands, Booth had no chance to kick, and the score forever stood 7–6 in favor of the Commodores.

This dramatic upset, in the most dramatic manner imaginable, made the "hidden ball" play a topic of conversation nationally. Greer Ricketson, who ran fifty yards unmolested as the Tigers chased the wrong man, spent the following week posing for publicity shots with the ball

Hidden-ball play tricks Tigers: Greer Ricketson, all alone, heads for Vanderbilt touchdown.

stuffed in his jersey and his pants. Down through the years, the most popular theory was that the Vandy quarterback wedged the ball into the leg of the squatting tackle, who waited a few seconds and then took off for the end zone.

As Ricketson related the facts, the events leading up to the play were as fascinating as its execution. Morrison, realizing he would need a surprise to shake up what looked like an impregnable LSU defense, took a suggestion from assistant Henry Frnka, who had come to Vandy after a stint at Greenville, Texas, High. In 1933 Frnka's team had used a trick play to win the state championship, and when Henry outlined it for his boss Morrison decided to put it into the game plan. "Things were so hush-hush during practice," said Ricketson, "half the squad didn't know about it. Every day Coach Morrison would take the eleven starters to one end of the field and carefully go over each assignment. We were pledged to secrecy, told to keep it from the other squad members."

The final cloak-and-dagger touch was added by the name Morrison gave the play. When the opportune moment arrived, Vandy quarterback "Dutch" Reinschmidt was to say but two words in the huddle: "Henry Frnka." Before it was called, the officials were to be told what to expect to avoid any controversy. "We had the ball near midfield playing a second and four," said Ricketson. "We lined up in the T and Reinschmidt took the ball from Carl Hinkle, our center, and placed it on the ground behind Bill Hays, the left guard. I had shifted from right tackle to right guard. I pulled out to join the interference as Reinschmidt, faking ball possession beautifully, swept wide to his left. LSU followed him.

"Just as I got behind Hays, I fell down as if I were blocked. After a three-count, I picked up the ball and ran down the right side of the field. I thought I'd be tackled any instant and didn't learn until later LSU had no idea where the ball was until it heard the roar of the crowd. Following the game the question arose as to whether my knee was touching the ground when I picked up the ball. It wasn't."

Because he planned to use it again, the cagey Morrison deleted the play from film he had taken of the game. "We tried it the following week against Georgia Tech and it didn't work. Then we tried it on Tennessee and it backfired. One of their linemen jumped over our guard and fell on the ball."

Vandy's victory ended a streak of thirteen straight conference wins by the Tigers and, although the flag was at half-mast in Baton Rouge, LSU had too much talent to fold. The Tigers went on to wallop Loyola, 52–6, Louisiana Normal, 52–0, and Mississippi State, 41–0, until Auburn tested them before bowing, 9–7, with 35,000 fans watching in Birmingham. This left Tulane, building again under Red Dawson, in the

Pinky Rohm: Looking for the end zone.

path of an LSU club that still had a shot at a share of the title since unbeaten Alabama had Vandy remaining. The Tigers found the Greenies anything but a soft touch this time; in fact, it took a questionable scoring play to pull out a 20–7 decision. A crowd of 38,500 watched as LSU, trailing 6–7, went for a field goal from the Tulane 4. Jimmy Cajoleas, however, fumbled the snap from center and then gave the impression that he was going to run with the ball. At the last instant he fired over the middle, into a knot of players, and Larry King came up with the ball for a Tiger touchdown. There was some discussion whether the Tigers had an ineligible man downfield but the score stood. Pinky Rohm later tacked on a third touchdown, his eighth of the season, which tied him with teammate Jabbo Stell for conference scoring honors.

Many observers still consider Rohm, who owed his nickname to a healthy reddish complexion, the finest all-around back in LSU history. At Fortier High in New Orleans, Pinky won six varsity letters—three in football, three in track. On the record, his future looked better in track than in football, because he had established a New Orleans schoolboy mark in the hop step—47 feet, 11 inches—and later, in a national high school meet in Chicago, took off on a 24-foot, 8-inch broad jump, only to finish behind a 25-foot-plus leap by a youngster named Jesse Owens.

Rohm's football at Fortier did not lift many eyebrows, for Pinky devoted most of his time to blocking, but a year at Riverside Military Academy in Georgia, where he came into his own as a ball carrier, put a flock of schools on his trail. After visiting Alabama, Pinky returned home one afternoon to find a limousine parked out front. "Huey Long was in the front room chatting with my mother," he said. "And she already had my bags packed. A few minutes later, I was on my way to Baton Rouge with the Senator."

Rohm was acting captain of the LSU team for the 1937 Tulane game and, before the coin toss, he made a deal with Tulane's co-captains Norman Buckner and Norman Hall. "We agreed the captain of the winning team could cut out the seat of the other captain's pants as a souvenir," said Pinky. After the game, Rohm braved a shower of football shoes as he entered the Green Wave's dressing room, borrowed a pair of scissors from "Big Monk" Simons, the Tulane trainer, and deftly removed the seat of Hall's football trousers. Pinky has preserved the memento, forerunner to the famous Tulane-LSU "rag."

Rohm won a spot on the Associated Press's second all-SEC team (tackle Eddie Gatto was a first-team selection), and sophomore Bussey, with 404 yards running and 731 passing, joined LSU's 1,000-yard club. The victory over Tulane gave the undisputed conference champions of 1935 and 1936 a 5–1 SEC record, but this time the Tigers finished behind Alabama (6–0) which managed to squeak past Vandy, 9–7.

A total of 193,000 watched the 1937 Tigers and this figure would soon jump to past 200,000 when the 40,000 for the Sugar Bowl encore with Santa Clara was tacked on. "We never seemed to get cranked up for the Sugar Bowl," said Moore. "And, remember, we met some pretty good teams." The unbeaten Broncos of 1937 were better than "pretty good." Twice they slammed the door in LSU's face with goal line stands that preserved an early touchdown and ultimate 6–0 victory, marking the first time in fifty games that LSU was held scoreless.

In a way, this goose egg was ominous. It ushered in Bernie Moore's "dark ages," a span during which LSU would not contend for the conference championship, making it more an era of incidents and individuals than of teams. The 1938 campaign (six wins and four losses), for example, is remembered chiefly for one event—a lulu of a free-for-all, fondly referred to today as "the big blowout," following a rough-and-tumble finale with Tulane. As the home team, one with three wins in a row over its archrival, LSU did not gain status from the free-swinging melee that came on the heels of a 14–0 defeat. Bob "Jitterbug" Kellogg,

Big blowout of 1938: From fists to frozen sugarcane sticks.

turned down by the Tigers because he was "too small," and Fred Cassibry scored the Tulane touchdowns in a game that had 161 yards in penalties. In the fourth quarter both teams were punching openly although the main go seemed to be between Tulane's center Bernie Smith and LSU's Bussey.

First round in the postgame fight was touched off when someone hit Claude "Big Monk" Simons, Tulane trainer and the father of the Wave's 1934 star. Quickly, both teams rushed together like clashing armies, and eventually mascots, cheerleaders, and water boys were caught up in the punchfest. Despite several renditions of "The Star Spangled Banner," fighting continued long after the players had left the arena. From one side of the field to the other, like a giant tidal wave, the battlers flowed as LSU fans defended their wooden goal posts, or anything else they could think of. Fighting actually was in progress until moonlight, with small skirmish groups battling with frozen sugarcane sticks in nearby fields. Bernie Moore watched it all from the tunnel at the north end of Tiger Stadium. "There must have been 15,000 people on the field throwing punches," he recalled. "After a while no one paid any attention to the national anthem. One thing I'll never forget. When the fighting was at its peak, a little blond cheerleader ran out of the milling throng over to where I was standing. Her clothes were torn and she was bleeding from a cut on the face. 'Coach,' she told me, 'ain't we having fun?' Then she turned right around and ran back to join those crazy folks."

The 1938 fight prompted action on the student-body front, a proclamation that made three points: (1) the football field was neutral and off limits to students; (2) a rectangular flag of purple and blue cloth bearing the Louisiana seal would be awarded to the winner; (3) the presentation would take place at a banquet of the two student councils after the game. Some called it a "truce flag," but after a 1942 free-for-all (not as

150   *The Fighting Tigers*

violent as the one in 1938) it was called the "rag"—a name which stuck.

More than anything else, 1939 was the year of Ken Kavanaugh. Outscored by the opposition for the first time since 1923, the 4–5 Tigers produced their second all-America end in three years in the spectacular pass grabber from Little Rock. Ken set a record for consecutive touchdowns by an individual—seven—and he set a record for points scored by a lineman—54. In a 26–7 victory over Holy Cross in Worcester, Massachusetts, when the 37-man LSU squad became the South's first football team to travel by air, Ken caught three touchdowns tossed from sophomore Leo Bird and scored a fourth by intercepting a lateral. He tied Tennessee's Bobby Foxx as the most valuable player in the SEC, won the Knute Rockne Memorial trophy as the year's outstanding lineman and, most significant, finished second to Iowa's Nile Kinnick in the balloting for the Heisman trophy. "Kavanaugh," said Moore, "was a pass completer rather than receiver, simply because he'd catch passes no one else could get to."

Kavanaugh had shared all-SEC honors with tackle Eddie Gatto in 1938 and with guard J. W. Goree in 1939, but the year after his departure LSU was without an all-conference player for the first time since the SEC organized seven years earlier. The redeeming features of 1940, (6–4); 1941 (4–4–2); and 1942 (7–3) were the victories over Tulane, victories which enabled Moore to survive the howling wolves. It was a time when the university, having been rocked by political scandals, was trying to regain prestige, and because of indifferent success on the football field many wanted walking papers handed Moore and his seven assistants. Critics pointed to $100,000 athletic department deficits in 1938 and 1939, arguing that Bernie's championships in 1935 and 1936 were won by material recruited by Biff Jones. "We called on Moore when no one else wanted the job and he gave us two championships and almost a third," said Bernie's backers. "The record calls for a change now," said the anti-Moore segment. And so it went.

For Bernie, those Tulane conquests might well have been lifesavers. In 1940 the Tigers won, 14–0, by setting up a defense for Tulane's power and waiting for the breaks. In 1941 they took the bull by the horns with a gambling passing attack. The play that turned the tide—and opened the mouths of a record throng of 50,764 in Tulane Stadium—was a screen pass. When the ball was snapped, the Tiger line stepped aside and allowed the Greenies to converge on Leo Bird. When the green shirts were within a yard, he flipped the ball over their heads to a blocking back named Steve Van Buren standing a yard behind the line of scrimmage. Van Buren, behind a wall of interference, rambled sixty-two yards before being caught from behind. LSU didn't score on the play,

Ken Kavanaugh, the pass grabber from Little Rock. At right, Kavanaugh is shown receiving his All-America certificate from Bernie Moore. The others in the picture are Mrs. Maggie S. Smith of Wilson, the No. 1 Tiger supporter of that period, and LSU President Campbell B. Hodges.

but, emboldened by the success of this maneuver, the Tigers gambled their way to a 19–0 decision. A year later, when the Greenies, then under Monk Simons, used a 6–3–2 defense to guard against Bird's passing, Bird quick-kicked instead, paving the way for an 18–6 victory.

The kicking star of 1942, however, and possibly any other year, was a sophomore from Lake Charles High named Alvin Dark. Against Ole Miss, the Tigers were playing a fourth-and-long yardage from their 20. "Thud" went Alvin's foot into the ball, sending it sailing some seventy yards, over the safety man's head and out of bounds near the Rebel 10. Then an incredible thing happened. The ball was brought back to the 20 and a 5-yard penalty paced off against Ole Miss. LSU had wiped out a 70-yard punt for an offsides penalty. Seething on the sidelines, Bernie Moore sent in a substitute for captain Walter Gorinski as Dark dropped back once again. Before Moore could question Gorinski, he was following the flight of another skyscraper which again flew over the safety's head to go out of bounds on the Ole Miss 3, seventy-three yards from scrimmage. "You see, coach," said Gorinski, anticipating Moore's question, "I was just showing my confidence in Alvin."

That afternoon, the slim tailback had scoring runs of seventy and

LSU was the South's first team to fly when it went north to face Holy Cross in 1939. Standing, left to right, Leo Bird, Charley Anastasio, Roy Joe Anderson, Coach Moore, Young Bussey. Kneeling, Ogden Baur, Irving Campbell, J. W. Goree, Bernie Lipkis, Jake Messina, Ralph Whitman.

forty-six yards in the 21–7 victory, ending any doubt he might be too small, at 160 pounds, to play college football. The first time he got a chance he dashed twenty-five yards for a score against Texas A & M. Next week he passed for two touchdowns against Mississippi State. And then came Ole Miss. Dark was LSU's top scorer in 1942, as was Sulcer Harris, one of the finest broken-field runners ever to come out of Baton Rouge, the year before. In Moore's judgment, there's no telling what his twosome might have accomplished had not World War II intervened. "Dark was a fun-lovin' boy," said Moore, "but if some guard missed a block, ol' Alvin would tell him, 'Better start getting the job done or it's going to be you and me after the game.'" Back from the service in 1946, Dark went to Moore to discuss a $40,000 bonus offer he had from the Boston Braves. "I told him to take it before he changed his mind," said Bernie.

In many ways 1943 was the strangest football season on record. With World War II at its height, American football made an appearance on every continent of the globe. Not only that, but the action, which began with the college all-star game in August and continued until the last of the armed service championship games the following March, made for an eight-month campaign. Naturally, the question arose as to whether football should be emphasized or de-emphasized during wartime and, addressing himself to it, Lou Little of Columbia University had this to say: "Play football. Play it hard and intensively with an even more

Alvin Dark takes off. He loved the coffin corner.

savage will-to-win than in peacetime. Play intercollegiate football as much as the speeded-up educational programs which have accompanied the nation's war effort will permit. Play high school football exactly as it has been played—but play it harder."

Beyond doubt, the backbone of American football in 1943 was the U.S. Navy, with its famed preflight and physical training courses, V-5, V-7, V-12, and Navy ROTC. This program was responsible for two of the four SEC teams which played formal schedules—Georgia Tech, ultimate Sugar Bowl winner, and Tulane. LSU and Georgia were civilian outfits made up of 16- and 17-year olds and those rejected for military service. Vanderbilt played an informal schedule of five games while the conference's seven other members, Tennessee, Mississippi State, Ole Miss, Alabama, Auburn, Florida, and Kentucky, decided to sit it out.

To any LSU fan of the era, 1943 meant one thing only: Steve "Moving Van" Van Buren. Born in British Honduras, red-headed Steve was brought to New Orleans as a youngster. His size (a puny 127 pounds) seemed to dictate against any football ambitions. In his third year at Warren Easton High, a team reject because of lack of weight, he packed his books, stayed out of school until the following season and built himself up to 168 pounds. Because Warren Easton had a veteran all-prep backfield, senior Steve made first string at end, playing opposite a fellow named Lou Thomas. On the way home from watching Warren Easton defeat Holy Cross in 1939, Ike Carriere, quarterback under Mike

Donahue and later a scout for Russ Cohen, offered a ride to a young man with a duffle bag slung over his shoulder. Van Buren identified himself and, after being praised by Ike for some fancy stepping on end arounds, revealed he had no plans to attend college. "Why? Can't you run?" asked Carriere. "Mister," said Van Buren, "I'm the fastest man on the team." Then Ike asked, "What about your grades?" Replied Van Buren, "I'm above 90," and he added that he was 6 feet, 168 and just turned seventeen.

"Son, if what you say is true, you've got yourself a scholarship to LSU," Carriere told him.

Upon questioning, Warren Easton coach Johnny Brechtel backed Van Buren on all counts and indicated he found it hard to believe no one had given Steve a tumble. So Ike called Bernie Moore and said, "Coach, I've got a Warren Easton end for you." "You mean Lou Thomas wants to come to LSU," inquired Bernie. "No, but Steve Van Buren does," Moore was told. Even over the telephone, Moore's disappointment was noticeable (Thomas would have been quite a catch) but he agreed to go along with Carriere. Ironically, Thomas not only wound up at Tulane, but, like Van Buren, in the backfield as well.

Steve played end for a spell as a 1941 sophomore, but Moore later shifted the tough, muscular boy to blocking back in the single wing— simply because he had a flock of ball carriers with impressive credentials.

Steve Van Buren against Georgia Tech: In '43 and '44, a "Moving Van."

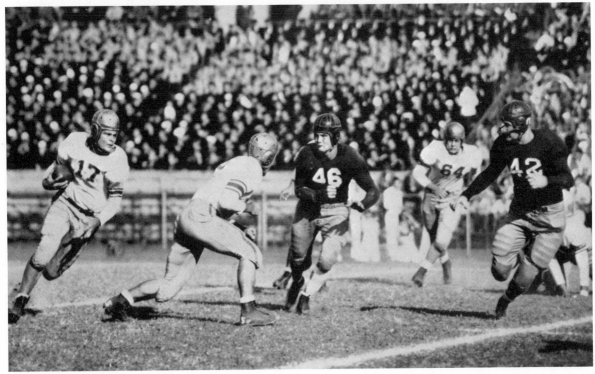

Van Buren, by now 6 feet, 1 inch and 207, performed his chores effectively and conceivably would have slipped out of LSU unnoticed (his one shining moment was with that screen pass in the 1941 Tulane game) had not Moore found himself without a tailback for 1943.

Having inherited the job by default, Van Buren went on to finish second nationally in rushing with 847 yards and top the SEC with ninety-eight points. It wasn't all that simple. "When Steve learned he'd have to pass and punt, as well as carry the ball," said trainer Marty Broussard, "he worked as long and as hard as any athlete I've ever known. He'd carry the ball forty times on a Saturday and the next day he'd be out working again, passing and punting. You'd never see him in the training room."

LSU had a young guard, Felix Trapani, who caught passes and shagged punts for Van Buren on those Sundays when he'd work in the morning, have lunch, and then work in the afternoon. "For fifty yards," said Broussard, "Steve was as fast as any back I've ever seen at LSU. After two steps, he'd be full speed." Van Buren was rejected by the army for defective vision—for a while, there was concern that he might lose sight in one eye—enabling him to join a squad made up mostly of boys under eighteen.

The Georgia football team that LSU opened with in Baton Rouge that year was composed entirely of freshmen (except for one junior) and the two fuzzy-cheeked outfits were locked in a 27–27 standoff going into the final two minutes when Van Buren broke loose to give the Tigers a 34–27 victory. A 28–13 loss to Texas A & M and its "kiddy corps" was mixed with wins over Rice, LSU Army Specialists, Georgia (a second time), and TCU before Georgia Tech and its V-12s scored a crushing 42–6 decision. Because bowl pickings were slim, the Orange Bowl lined up the Tigers for a rematch with Texas A & M, then sat back and hoped for the best as LSU closed out against Tulane. However, in another ironic twist, Dub Jones, who had played for LSU the previous season, sparked the V-12 Greenies to a smashing 27–0 victory, leaving the Orange Bowl stuck with a 5–3 ball club, but also with Steve Van Buren.

With gas rationing in effect, Moore's squad went to Miami by train and in automobiles, thanks to fuel stamps saved by Tiger rooters. A crowd of 27,000 forgetting, for a few hours, the Germans and Japanese, watched Van Buren run and pass (to Burton Goode) for first quarter touchdowns and, then, in the third period, sew up an ultimate 19–14 victory with a 63-yard scoring gallop. It was Steve's sixteenth touchdown of the season, an LSU record that still stands. When the Tigers returned from Miami—in eighteen used cars purchased by long-time booster Lewis Gottlieb—Van Buren was hailed for his awesome prowess; yet some remained skeptical, wondering whether he might be a wartime flash in the pan who owed his reputation to the imbalance of competition. When Van Buren played with the Philadelphia Eagles of the National Football League (Bernie Moore called him "a genius with an inferiority complex"), he removed all doubt as he rewrote the record book. His quick starts, combined with well disciplined power, shoulder fakes, and a smooth, diesel-like stride made him the scourge of the pros. Moore chuckled when he recalled the calculus whiz who, because of his shyness, later backed off from testimonials and spent most of his time fishing. "He probably was the greatest running back in SEC history, and I used him as a blocking back until his last year," said Bernie. "Folks down in Baton Rouge will never quite get over it."

Nor will connoisseurs of the college game get over the seemingly endless parade of football players in and out of Baton Rouge. As Van Buren made his exit, LSU reached into Texas—in fact, into a university dormitory at Austin—for one Yelverton Abraham Tittle. "What other school could lay claim to such a coup?" explained a coach, once ticking off LSU football greats. "They lose a phenomenal runner and get a phenomenal passer, athletes who were all-time standouts in the professional game."

Like Steve Van Buren, Y. A. Tittle worked to develop the talent with which he was blessed. "I remember him going out in the back yard to hang up an old tire as a target," said older brother Jack Tittle, who had played for Tulane before his more publicized brother was picked off by the Tigers. "He'd throw at it by the hour. And he didn't take the easy way out. He'd get that tire swinging and still hit it on the button. Y.A. appointed his young brother Don as his pass catcher. He'd tell Don the only way he could play football was to run and the best way to do that was to shag passes. He also had another deal with Don. Y.A. had an ice route around town and had to get up around three in the morning. So he'd pay Don ten cents to get up and cook breakfast for him."

Through the years Jack Tittle has tried, without success, to live down the fact his younger brother went to LSU. "I did my best to keep the coaches posted on Y.A.'s progress in high school," he said. "Even told them about all the offers he was receiving. I simply feel my alma mater didn't try hard enough. He received a brochure but no personal letter was sent nor did anyone contact Y.A."

Obviously, Y.A. took devilish delight in beating the Green Wave. His career total against Tulane was forty-two completions in fifty-six passes and eight touchdowns. As a 1944 freshman, he completed thirteen of seventeen, including his first twelve in a row, as the Tigers prevailed, 25–6. In 1945, as a T quarterback, he clicked on eleven of thirteen in a 33–0 rout. He hit six of eight in the 41–27 win of 1946 and wound up by completing ten of eighteen in a 6–6 tie in 1947.

Patriarch of the Tittle clan, Y.A., Sr., warmed up to football gradu-

A leaping Y. A. Tittle: Strong arm and, at the time, lots of hair.

ally, losing an early coolness toward the game when friends would stop to congratulate him on his sons' playing. Y.A. came by his tag because his dad decided he wanted a "junior" after a William and a Jack.

Once at LSU the name Yelverton Abraham became famous, even before the passer did. Intrigued by the initials after checking publicity forms, sports information director Jim Corbett asked Tittle about it and got a terse reply. "That's my name—all of it," said Y.A. Curious, Corbett checked with the registrar and discovered, sure enough, the entrance application carried the initials, not the full name. For the moment, Corbett was satisfied, but when it became obvious to any amateur observer that the boy from Marshall would soon be something special, Corbett decided to call the courthouse in Marshall. "I requested information on a Y. A. Tittle and was told there was no one by that name," said Corbett. Then the man on the other end added: "But we do have a Yelverton Abraham Tittle." Next day Corbett confronted Tittle with the long handle, and the player said: "I'd appreciate it if you'd lay off using it." Instead, publicity-conscious Corbett laid it on as college football's most exciting name.

Just how this highly-touted schoolboy passer got to LSU in the first place is a story with a cloak-and-dagger flavor. In fact, had the FBI been sports oriented, LSU assistant coach Red Swanson would have been on its "most wanted" list in 1944. That fall, before the season had gotten under way, Swanson drove on to the University of Texas campus at Austin, entered the men's dormitory and told Tittle, then curly-haired and seventeen, to "start packing." Swanson and Y.A. made only one stop—at Houston to pick up a back named Jim Cason—then headed straight for Baton Rouge, stopping only for gas.

Although it strained the relationship between Bernie Moore and Texas coach Dana Bible, Swanson's lightning stab into the Lone Star State (raids of this kind were fairly common) has to go down as one of the school's most lucrative recruiting trips on record. Four years later, Y.A. and the swivel-hipped Cason were among a flock of Tiger backs to sign pro contracts. Tittle left behind four passing records, most of his hair and—almost—his pants. Herman Lang, a fixture in the LSU training room since the early 1930s, recalled that Tittle felt his helmet had something to do with his receding hairline. "Y.A. always wanted something to put in the helmet," said Lang. The Texan also sought out specialists to see what could be done to preserve the precious fuzz, but it was only a matter of time before he became the Yul Brynner of football.

If Y.A.'s lack of hair was a source of embarrassment to him, it was mild compared to the celebrated "falling pants" episode in the 1947 Ole Miss game. Tiger Stadium was packed the night that Tittle, in a key conference game, picked off a Charley Conerly pass and made tracks for the end zone. One Ole Miss player grabbed Y.A. by his belt and, as Tittle yanked away, the belt broke and his gold pants began a slow descent. Guard Charley Cusimano, who was out in front of Y.A. looking for someone to block, heard Tittle yell: "Hold it, hold it." Cusimano looked to see Tittle trying to pull up his trousers and run at the same time. Since Tittle might have gone all the way, it was a crucial play because Ole Miss wound up a 20–18 winner and went on to claim the SEC crown in Johnny Vaught's first season as head coach.

The start of the Tittle era three years earlier actually was as embarrassing—for LSU fans—as losing your pants in public. The 1944 record (2–5–1) had represented LSU's worst season since 1910 but the raw material on hand indicated it was only a matter of time before an improvement. While Van Buren had been virtually a one-man gang in 1943, Y. A. Tittle was just another bright name among a promising rookie crop. Ray Coates, who had sparked Jesuit of New Orleans to the high school state championship in 1943, was on hand along with Dan Sandifer, star of the Byrd High team which had lost to the Jesuit High Blue Jays in the finals. Then there was Houston's "Slim Jim" Cason, all of sixteen years old.

Bernie Moore, who also had Gene "Red" Knight, red-haired sophomore from Bossier City, Louisiana, and Elwyn "Ripper" Rowan (later a star at West Point), stuck with the single wing. Rowan was the high scorer, and Knight won a third-team all-SEC berth along with guard Gerry Bertucci in a season best remembered for a thrilling 27–27 opening tie with Alabama (eventual Sugar Bowl entry), and a closing 25–6 win over Tulane, highlighted by Tittle's pinpoint passing. All of the defeats—by Rice, 14–13; Texas A & M, 7–0; Mississippi State, 13–6; Tennessee, 13–0; and Georgia Tech, 14–6—found the Tigers game but coming up short.

The maturing 1944 freshmen (frosh remained eligible for varsity competition until 1946) and the decision to junk the single wing for the T formation was responsible for a 1945 turnabout—a 7–2 record and a near miss at a major bowl. Realizing that someone like Tittle, who wasn't blessed with an abundance of speed, would be far more effective under center than at tailback, Moore and his staff spent some time at Cornell, where Ed McKeever was head coach. McKeever passed on the basics of the formation and the play book, results of an association with Frank Leahy, first at Boston College and later at Notre Dame where McKeever had served as head coach in 1944.

Back home, Moore settled on a backfield that had Tittle at quarter, Coates and Sandifer at halfbacks, and either Bill Montgomery or Knight at fullback. Cason was available at halfback as was Willard Landry and a freshman from Baton Rouge, Harrell "Rip" Collins. The unique twist during the 1945–47 T formation period at LSU was that halfback Coates, not quarterback Tittle, called the plays. Y.A. was the signal caller only when Coates was not in the ball game.

In the line were Clyde Lindsey and Bill Kellum at ends, Earl Tullos and Fred Land at tackles, Herd Miller and Felix Trapani at guards, and captain Andy Kosmac at center where he alternated with Mel Didier. Behind quarterback Tittle in the balanced T were halfbacks Coates and Sandifer and fullback Knight. Cason, Landry, and Montgomery supplied ample depth for a stable of ball carriers that finished with 2,725 rushing yards, second only to the national champion, Army.

In an opening 42–0 defeat of Rice, Cason made LSU history by scoring three touchdowns in a 13-minute span, but this easy win only helped make the Tigers an easy mark the following week for Rose Bowl champion Alabama. Gilmer passed LSU dizzy as the Tide coasted to a 26–7 victory. At this stage the Tigers could have folded or jelled. They jelled. On each of the next five weekends, LSU scored three or more touchdowns, winning four in a row (including a 32–0 upset of Georgia and Charley Trippi) before losing to Mississippi State, 27–20. In the latter, with the Tigers on the march, State picked off a Tittle pass with

Put them all together and they spell TIGERS. Dan Sandifer, Y. A. Tittle, Ray Coates, Jim Cason, Rip Collins, Al Heroman.

five minutes remaining to break a 20–20 tie.

The season's most dramatic victory came the following week before 27,000 at Grant Field in Atlanta. With Knight hobbled by an injured leg, LSU marched eighty yards for a first quarter score but Tittle, taking over Knight's kicking chores, missed the extra point. It was still 6–0 in the final period when Tech scored and then went ahead 7–6 with less than five minutes on the clock. Montgomery returned the kickoff thirty-six yards to the Tech 39 and the Tigers were on the move. In short chunks Montgomery, Coates, and Sandifer moved to the Yellow-jacket 21 where the home team braced, leaving the Tigers with fourth-and-eight. There was a minute left when Red Knight, who had been used sparingly, limped into the ball game. Considering Knight's condition, Tech had every reason to expect a fake when Coates knelt on the Tech 30 to hold for a field goal. As the teams lined up, Clyde Lindsey told the Tech end opposite him: "Let's don't waste our time buttin' heads. That cripple can't kick." Incredibly, the player agreed and both watched as Knight put his foot into the ball which sailed squarely through the uprights from a wicked angle. LSU, by a 9–7 score, had its first victory in history over Georgia Tech.

Tittle, who played sixty minutes against Tech, had a red hot arm as the Tigers closed with a smashing 33–0 conquest of Tulane before 52,636 in New Orleans. When the Sugar Bowl selected Oklahoma A & M (No. 5) to play St. Mary's College (No. 7), LSU, shut out of the top ten, packed its gear despite offers from three minor bowls. Guard Felix Trapani and Knight were AP all-conference selections for a team which led the nation in first downs (134) and established a conference record for rushing.

Smitten with the T formation, Bernie Moore in 1946 faced a task familiar to all other major college coaches regarding personnel: evaluating service veterans along with returning lettermen. Moore had nine of eleven starters back in harness on a squad made up of twenty-eight service returnees, plus twenty-two 1945 lettermen and incoming freshmen. He stuck with a backfield that returned intact—Tittle, Coates, Sandifer, and Knight, but five servicemen joined 1945 starters Clyde Lindsey and Fred Land in the line. They were tackle Ed Champagne, guards Fred Hall and Wren Worley, center Sheldon "Buck" Ballard, and end Abner Wimberly. Walter "Piggy" Barnes was another veteran ticketed for heavy duty at tackle.

The 1946 campaign began on a wet note in Houston with the Tigers squeaking by Rice, 7–6, on a soggy extra point by Holly Heard. Heard added the point after a touchdown by Willard Landry and later Charles "Chuck" Schroll and Jim Cason teamed to block the Owls' place-kick attempt following a last-minute score. With Piggy Barnes winning national acclaim, LSU made it two in a row at the expense of Mississippi State when "Shorty" McWilliams, a wartime star at Army, was nailed behind the goal line by the huge Tiger tackle. Barnes jarred the ball loose and then recovered for the deciding six points. Seven days after, in a 33–9 victory over Texas A & M, three freshmen grabbed the headlines: speedy Al Heroman, bulldozing Zollie Toth, and rookie end Mel Lyle. Heroman scored twice and set up two more with dazzling broken-field runs, breaking open a game that was close at half time.

The honeymoon came to a temporary halt the next week when Georgia Tech, avenging Knight's field goal of 1945, invaded Baton Rouge and left with a seemingly lopsided 26–7 victory. With five minutes left, LSU trailed only 12–7, but, trying to pull it out with desperation passes, the Tigers had two interceptions returned for scores.

Playing a week later, LSU's team shook Knight loose for thirty-six yards in the first half, going on to a 14–0 victory over Vanderbilt that set the stage for a tough back-to-back assignment: Ole Miss and Alabama. In the first half of this double header, Charley Conerly's pitching had the Rebels in front 14–7 at half time before Tittle swept the Tigers ahead 27–21. LSU sewed it up finally, 34–21, when Jeff Burkett returned an interception thirty yards.

Stars of the forties: Clyde Lindsey and Gene "Red" Knight.

As the Alabama game approached, the campus cry was "Beat Bama for Bernie!" And this the Tigers did in an afternoon of thrills that kept a crowd of 47,000 out of their seats most of the game. After spotting the Tide a 7–0 lead, Tittle picked off a Bama pass and raced sixty-five yards for a score. The point was missed and it remained 7–6 until seconds before half time when end Jim Loftin intercepted a toss by Harry Gilmer. As he was tackled, Loftin lateraled to Sandifer, who picked up a six-man convoy on way to a touchdown, the play covering eighty-two yards. Again the point was missed, so it was 12–7 going into the third period when LSU suddenly broke loose. Before Bama knew what hit, Collins galloped thirty-two yards, Tittle passed twenty-five yards to Sandifer, and Coates crashed over from the 1 to make it 31–7. Gilmer collected his forces for two late scores but the 31–21 setback, first LSU win over Alabama in thirty-seven years, was thoroughly impressive, projecting the Tigers into the national picture for the first time since the 1930s. LSU got outstanding line play from tackles Ed Champagne and Hubert Schurtz, guards Wren Worley and Herb Miller.

With a bowl invitation looming, the Tigers won a 20–7 decision over Miami and then marched into New York's Yankee Stadium to take the measure of Fordham, 40–0. The Sugar Bowl kept the 8–1 Tigers on the hook, pending the outcome of their Tulane finale. Tittle didn't give the Green Wave a chance. In the first half, he hit six for six for 127 yards and three touchdowns, and later LSU drew off to a 41–13 lead only to have a late Tulane rush cut the final score to 41–27. Oddly, all ten touchdowns were made by freshmen. For the Tigers, Al Heroman and Jeff Adams each got two, Mel Lyle and Dale Gray one apiece.

The closing win lifted LSU to eighth spot in the final AP ranking but the Sugar Bowl, looking for a match for unbeaten, third-ranked Georgia, went for ninth place North Carolina and a Charley Trippi-Charley Justice showdown. Passed over for the Sugar Bowl, the Tigers accepted a waiting Cotton Bowl invitation to meet Southwest champion Arkansas. Individually, Tittle was an all-SEC choice by the United Press, guard Wren Worley by the AP, and tackle Piggy Barnes wound up on the all-America team selected by sportscaster Bill Stern. On New Year's Day, 1947, in Dallas, however, the top individuals on both teams were overshadowed by the weather. A helpless Chamber of Commerce could only shake its head at the combination of ice, snow, sleet, and rain which only the foolhardy fan braved. LSU rounded up several oil drums, filled them with charcoal and started a fire to produce some on-the-field heaters. To keep the players' feet warm, athletic director Heard purchased twenty-five bales of hay which were spread out in front of the bench. In the stands some of the more imaginative fans, who walked through foot-deep snow in the aisles, built their own fires, and erected signs "Ten Cents To Warm Up." Billed as a match between Tittle and Clyde "Smackover" Scott, the game ended in a scoreless deadlock but with LSU holding a 15–1 advantage in first downs and a 271–54 edge in total yardage. Harry Rabenhorst, who recalls it as the only game in memory in which all of the LSU linemen wore gloves, retains a vivid picture of Bernie Moore on the sidelines. "The cold brought tears to everyone's eyes," said Rabenhorst. "I went up to Bernie one time and, sure enough, the tears had frozen on his cheeks."

Later that year, Moore's tears had nothing to do with the weather but rather with a disappointing 5–3–1 season which had everyone asking what had happened. As far as Bernie was concerned, it was simply a matter of injuries. By early November, 1947, eleven players who were regulars at one time or another were on the shelf. Jim Cason hurt his knee before the opener and was out for three weeks. Ray Coates, another knee victim, missed the last half of the season. Tittle twisted his ankle early in the year and reinjured it several times. Zollie Toth, the sophomore fullback coming on fast, was another midseason casualty. The brightest spot was the performance of Rip Collins, whose punting and ball carrying won him a berth in an all-SEC backfield that included Charley Conerly, Harry Gilmer, and Shorty McWilliams.

A 21-point final quarter by Georgia, resulting in a 35–19 victory started the Tigers' downhill slide and, six weeks later, a 21-point first quarter by Alabama (the Tide won 41–12), managed to keep the flag at

Brrrr: LSU 0, Arkansas 0 in the 1947 "Ice Bowl" in Dallas.

half-mast. Most embarrassing moment, however, came when Henry Frnka's underdog Tulane team (it had only won two games), held LSU to a 6–6 standoff before 66,342 in New Orleans, a then record crowd for the classic. Tittle passed to Ray Bullock a second before intermission for the Tiger score; Tulane matched it in the third quarter and then held the visitors on the 1-inch line in the final period.

LSU's disappointing season became more of a sore spot with Tiger fans (especially those who disregarded injuries) when four backs won starting jobs with the pros the following fall—Tittle with Baltimore, Cason with San Francisco, Sandifer with Washington, Coates with the New York Giants. During the career of this foursome, ten other LSU players eventually wound up on a pro team—Jeff Burkett, Hubert Schurtz, Piggy Barnes, Ed Champagne, Abner Wimberly, Bill Schroll, Rip Collins, Ray Collins, Zollie Toth, and Ken Konz.

The incomparable Tittle left five LSU records: passing yards in a career, 2,517; completed passes in a career, 166; touchdown passes in a career, 21; total offense in a career, 2,619; touchdown passes in a season, eleven in 1946.

Although Moore first said it in jest—"When Tittle leaves, so will I"—the words were more a prophecy than a joke. In December he planned to return the following fall, but two months later, in February of 1948, the SEC, shopping for a commissioner, selected the native of Jonesboro, Tennessee.

Biff Jones's successor, the only coach in history to win national championships in track and football, watched his football teams win eighty-three, lose thirty-nine, tie six and play in five bowl games—a record he later claimed hid lots of anguish.

"The truth is," he said, "I worried too much. I had to walk when I worried. I used to walk the streets of Baton Rouge all hours of the night, wondering what I was going to tell my players before the game, wondering about my defense and offense, wondering how certain players would take defeat if it came. Some boys just aren't built to take much of a beating."

How much of a beating can a coach take? "There are wolves the nation over," said the departing Moore. "And there are all species of 'em. Elsewhere the wolves howl the night long. In Baton Rouge and Louisiana they howl all night and all day."

But Bernie Moore survived 'em all.

'It would not be fair to expect miracles'

1948–1954

IN North Louisiana, Homer is fourteen miles south of Haynesville and somewhere in between lies Ruple, a tiny dot off Highway 79 not big enough to qualify as a whistle stop. Looking back, the surprise is not that a small farming town produced the successor to Bernie Moore. Coaches have come from humble diggings, all right, but when LSU on March 10, 1948, selected Gaynell Tinsley, it shocked alumni expecting to welcome a "name" coach to Baton Rouge. From the time Moore announced he was resigning to accept the commissioner's job, names like Bear Bryant, Frank Leahy, Bobby Dodd, and Bud Wilkinson were tossed around as newspapers joined in the guessing game.

While in most cases the guessing was pure speculation, one night during the interim period Bernie Moore drove up to Jim Corbett's home and, acting mysteriously, invited the sports publicity director to accompany him for a ride across the Mississippi River bridge at Baton Rouge. "On the other side," said Corbett, "we had a rendezvous with another automobile. It was real cloak-and-dagger and I had no idea what was going on. Finally, Coach Moore told me to get into the other car because there was someone I should meet. I recognized Red Heard and Lewis Gottlieb, who then introduced me to the mystery man—Bob Woodruff, head coach at Baylor."

Woodruff was the choice of some influential Tigers, and it was quite logical for Corbett to feel he was meeting Bernie's replacement. Woodruff, however, was unable to secure a release from his Baylor contract, whereupon the Board of Supervisors began thinking of hiring an LSU man, a turn of events which automatically introduced three names into the picture—Red Swanson, Jess Fatherree, and Gus Tinsley. After serving as head coach at Southeastern Louisiana College, Swanson

T. P. Heard and Gaynell Tinsley: Coach Gus gives the word.

had joined the LSU staff in 1938 as freshman coach and four years later had been promoted to line coach. Fatherree, whose exploits as a defensive ace and a ball carrier in the 1930s won him entry to his school's Hall of Fame, replaced Joel Hunt as backfield coach in 1942 after coaching at Lyon High in Covington and at Southeastern. Tinsley was serving the second of two hitches at his alma mater. Following two all-pro seasons with the Chicago Cardinals, he became end coach in 1939. In 1943 he entered the Navy, received a medical discharge because of a "football" knee, and returned to his home area to take over as head coach at Haynesville High. By 1945 he was back at LSU as end coach for the last three years of the Tittle and Moore era.

Although Tinsley admitted he was surprised when the board picked him, more surprising was Gus's winding up at LSU in the first place. "When I was a senior at Homer High," he said, "I was approached by Tulane and had every intention of going there. The Homer coaches, Preacher Roberts and Hugh Whatley, were Tulane men and when I visited the campus I really liked it." It was at this point that Joe Farrar, principal of Haynesville High and an LSU graduate, suggested Tinsley accompany two Haynesville boys, Rock Reed and Doug Callender, to

LSU "just to look around." Tinsley recalled, "He told me I could go on to Tulane but asked me to stop and pay LSU a visit on the way. So I packed my bags with the idea of winding up in New Orleans, but I never got past Baton Rouge. The fellow who sold me on LSU was Major [Frank] Wandle, the trainer under Biff Jones. After he made his pitch, I decided I didn't want to go any farther."

Because of his heavy North Louisiana accent, Gus Tinsley was regarded as "a big country boy," something he made no effort to hide. He had a quick smile and his nose, pushed flat and to one side after being broken at LSU, gave him the rugged looks of a friendly boxer. He had won all-America honors in 1935 and 1936 as a 6-foot, 3-inch, 215-pounder, famous for tackling, blocking, and stripping the ball carrier of interference. In 1937, when the College All-Stars defeated the Green Bay Packers, 6–0, before 84,560 in Chicago, Tinsley caught a 22-yard pass from Sammy Baugh and then ran twenty-five yards more for the game's only touchdown. All-pro for two years with the Chicago Cardinals, he was considered the finest defensive end in the game. When "Bronco" Nagurski named Gus to his all-time all-America team, he said: "Never have I seen an end who could do everything so well."

As a coach, Tinsley translated words into action, and during his apprenticeship under Moore it was nothing to see him get down with the linemen and bounce them around the practice field until they got the message. "Had to keep an eye on him," recalled Bernie, "to make sure he wouldn't put any of the players out of action."

The man who became the second alumnus to coach LSU in its fifty-five-year football history (E. A. Chavanne was the first) agreed to year-to-year employment at a starting salary of $12,500 and, to the surprise of some, requested that two former Tigers who had been in the running, Fatherree and Swanson, remain as his assistants. They agreed. Tinsley also brought in Clyde Funderburk from Southeastern Louisiana College to aid with the line, he named Guy "Skipper" Hays, one-time coach at El Dorado High in Arkansas, end coach, and he selected Roy Wilson of Fair Park High in Shreveport, an all-Southern lineman at LSU, to handle the guards. Ed Walker, who had served on staffs at Iowa, Columbia, Ole Miss, and Princeton, stayed on to coach the freshmen.

The day after Tinsley's appointment was made public, Bernie Moore, at a testimonial in his honor, warned LSU fans about the new coach's first season. "It would not be fair to Gus to expect miracles," said Bernie. "The schedule he faces is as tough as any in the country." This was true—one writer commented the only opponent Red Heard missed was the Russian Army—and it was true also that, with Tittle, went much of the cream. Tinsley had to open with Texas (then a Southwest power under Blair Cherry), and close with Tulane, at its peak under Henry Frnka. In between, the Tigers had Rice, Texas A & M, Georgia, North Carolina (and Charley Justice), Ole Miss, Vandy, Mississippi State, and Alabama.

To say the least, opposition such as this helped make Gus Tinsley's debut disastrous and made it difficult for Tiger fans, accustomed to the success of the Tittle years, to accept such lopsided defeats. It was not only that 1948 produced a 3–7 record, but LSU allowed the opposition a grand total of 271 points—still a record—and could score only 99 in ten games. Six players, and this is another record, tied for high point honors with twelve points—Rip Collins, Kenny Konz, Mel Lyle, Bill Schroll, Zollie Toth, and Abner Wimberly.

From the outset, a 33–0 pasting by Texas, it was obvious that Tinsley faced a long autumn. Not even victories over Rice, 26–13, and Texas A & M, 14–13, could lift the cloud. Texas got its fifth touchdown when a Tiger defender deflected a pass into the enemy's hands and, in the one-point decision over the Aggies, LSU made its winning score when Ebert Van Buren (brother of Steve) fumbled the ball, only to have Konz scoop it up and ramble twenty-seven yards, setting the tone for a weird season. Four crushing defeats followed—22–0 to Georgia, 34–7 to North Carolina, 49–19 to Ole Miss, and 48–7 to Vandy—before LSU managed to stay in a ball game, and this turned into another frustrating evening. LSU rolled up 359 yards, nineteen first downs, and permitted Mississippi State to cross midfield but once, and still lost, 7–0. The only

Abner Wimberly: He held up his end.

bright spot, and only conference victory of the season, was a 26–6 conquest of Alabama, highlighted by Charley Pevey's touchdown passes, fifty-four yards to Mel Lyle, forty-seven yards to Billy Baggett.

It was a drizzly, dismal afternoon when Henry Frnka brought his Tulane troops to Baton Rouge and, for most of the 43,418 fans who braved the weather, the game was dismal too. Quick-starting Eddie Price sparked a 46–0 Green Wave romp, a milestone since it was the worst LSU ever suffered at the hands of its ancient rival. When all was said and done, the only crumbs left for the Tigers in 1948 were picked up by end Abner Wimberly, named to the all-SEC's second team, and captain and center Ed Claunch, a third-team selection.

Considering Tinsley's year-to-year status, it is remarkable that he was able to survive, and especially in the face of another concerted move by at least one influential Tiger to bring in Bob Woodruff. Red Heard, who had become the dominant personality in the LSU athletic setup upon Bernie Moore's departure, supported Tinsley but, eyeing the new rules liberalizing substitution, made a move which he felt would strengthen the staff. He hired Ed McKeever as backfield coach and Norman Cooper as line coach, two men with sound credentials and familiar with schooling offensive and defensive specialists.

As backfield coach at Boston College and at Notre Dame under Frank Leahy, McKeever had developed such stars as Charley O'Rourke, Angelo Bertelli, and Johnny Lujack. He joined Leahy's staff after three years as halfback at Texas Tech, moving to Notre Dame with Leahy in 1941, following Boston College's 19–13 Sugar Bowl upset of Tennessee.

Tinsley's staff: Alf Satterfield, trainer Marty Broussard, Ed McKeever, Norm Cooper, Ben Enis.

Well-versed in the T-formation, McKeever took over as head coach of the Fighting Irish in 1944, moved to Cornell as top man in 1945, and then to the University of San Francisco. In 1948, he became head coach of the Chicago Rockets professional team. When the Rockets failed financially at the end of the season he was in the market for a job, and Heard beckoned.

A Little All-America center at Howard College in Birmingham, Cooper came to LSU after coaching at Vanderbilt and Kansas, and had had before that, a brief playing career with the Brooklyn Eagles. In 1948 he moved from Vandy and "Red" Sanders to Kansas, where he helped mold one of the finest lines in the Big Seven, one which led the Jayhawks to a 7–3 season. Cooper brought in his own assistant, Alf Satterfield, all-SEC tackle for Vandy in 1946.

As the 1949 campaign approached, there were a number of questions facing Tinsley: (1) How would quarterback Charley Pevey return, following a shoulder separation in the spring game? (2) If Pevey could not play, would Kenny Konz and Carroll Griffith, both converted halfbacks, pick up the slack? (3) Would the 1948 freshman team, with standout backs like Lee Hedges and Jim Roshto, provide help? (4) Would junior college graduates like Aubrey Anding, an end from Tyler, Texas, and George "Nick" Roussos, a guard from Santa Ana, California, live up to expectations?

Because of a disastrous 1948, none of the experts expected much from the Tigers; in fact, LSU and Auburn were leading candidates for the SEC cellar in all preseason speculation. "What was accomplished in 1949 was accomplished by everyone pulling together," said Tinsley. "Primarily, it was the same bunch we had the year before and the schedule was just as tough, maybe tougher. We took advantage of all the good bounces and the players never stopped believing in themselves."

Here's the story of Cinderella:

Kentucky (0–19)—"Bear Bryant had a mighty fine team, make no mistake about that," said Tinsley, "but we never quite recovered from an early shock given us by that sophomore quarterback, Babe Parilli. They put a flanker out, we made a mistake in our secondary coverage, and they had a touchdown in three minutes." A few minutes before half time Parilli struck again with another bomb, after which the Wildcats settled down to defensive football.

Rice (14–7)—"I think this game set the tone of the season," said Tinsley. "The pegs began to fall into place." One peg in particular was Kenny Konz. Against Kentucky he had played his last game as quarterback. Konz was moved to safety, and Carroll Griffith, the senior who had sparked a 70-yard drive against the Wildcats, was elevated to the starting club where he was expected to alternate with Pevey, given the

Ray Collins: The best defensive tackle Gus
ever coached.

medical okay. Tinsley found himself with a healthy situation at right
half where sophomore Chester Freeman and junior Billy Baggett held
forth—and an even healthier one at left half with Lee Hedges, Dale
Gray, and Jim Roshto, and at fullback with Zollie Toth, Ebert Van
Buren, and Billy West. The line was beginning to take shape. On offense
there was Captain Mel Lyle and Ray Bullock (backed by Aubrey
Anding) at ends, Harold Voss or Ed Coyne and Charley Cusimano at
tackles, Jim Shoaf and George Roussos at guards, and Joe Reid at center.
On defense Armand Kitto, Jess Yates, Sam Lyle, and Warren Virgets
gave Cooper depth at the ends. Ray Potter and Ray Collins were at
tackle, Allen Hover and Dick Bradley at guards, Jack Cole and Billy
West at linebackers. Roshto, a standout against Kentucky, loomed as a
fine defensive halfback prospect. Baggett and Van Buren spelled one
another at the other halfback, while Konz and Dale Gray were being
worked at safety. Rice came to Baton Rouge on a rainy Saturday night
with a ball club rated the finest in the Southwest. In the first quarter
halfback Gordon Wyatt shook loose on a 71-yard scoring run to make it
7-0, setting the stage for what probably was, as Tinsley indicated, the
turning point of 1949. The Tigers fumbled but held, thanks to a remarkable defensive save by Roshto, who tipped away a sure touchdown.
Another fumble and Rice recovered on the LSU 17. Four plays later,
the Tigers took over on the 9. A third fumble. Four plays later, after
vicious tackling by Hover, Collins, Voss, and Anding, Rice turned over
the ball on the 23. In the third quarter, with Pevey handling the ball

beautifully, the Tigers moved eighty-five yards for the tying touchdown. A 27-yard run by Van Buren after being sprung loose by Cusimano's key block highlighted the march, which wound up surprisingly. With the ball on the Owl 5, Freeman swung wide to the left, was hit on the 4 and fumbled. The ball bounced over the goal line, and when the officials sifted through the pileup Cusimano came up grinning with the football. "I sort of helped it into the end zone with my foot," said Charley. Finally, LSU turned its only break of the game into a winning touchdown. Roshto recovered a fumble on the Rice 11 in the fourth quarter, and four plays later Freeman sped around left end, outracing three Owls in the run for the end zone flag. With five completions in six passing attempts in the second half, Pevey showed he had recovered from springtime surgery. Hover was picked as the SEC's lineman of the week. Said Tinsley: "The Rice game taught a lesson we were to profit from later on: 'Bad breaks can be overcome.' "

Texas A & M (34–0)—This time the bad breaks came before the game. Defensive tackle Potter was lost indefinitely with injuries and safety Gray, permanently because of a technicality on eligibility. Another rainy night produced a gumbo setting but the Tigers proved to a crowd of 25,000 that they were good mudders. Using forty-four men, everyone who dressed, LSU combined tough defense and an offense that hummed despite the elements. Van Buren, with 121 yards in fourteen trips, and Pevey, with two scoring passes, were the attacking stars.

Georgia (0–7)—"We planned to throw the football," said Tinsley, "but Bernie Moore didn't help." Moore? For the second week in a row, the SEC commissioner ruled an LSU player ineligible. This time it was pass-catching Ray Bullock whom the Tigers had counted on in their Georgia preparations. The midweek ruling sidelining Bullock seemed to turn the Tigers, in the unfriendly surroundings of Athens, into a club unsure of itself. Spending most of the game on defense, LSU turned back every threat but one.

North Carolina (13–7)—How wet was the field? "Well," noted one observer wryly, "there was a three-inch drop in the Mississippi River over the week end." Whatever the intention, it seems LSU overdid the job of sprinkling its football field and its upset of Charley Justice and the Tar Heels, snapping a winning streak of twenty games, can never be separated from the postgame dispute. A year before, Carolina had smashed the Tigers, 34–7, and, toward the end, actually was ridiculing LSU's ineptness. Now, before a home crowd of 43,000, the chance for revenge arrived. In the second quarter Carl Snavely's single wing was at its effective best as the Tar Heels hammered ninety-eight yards to a score, a drive which began with Konz kicking dead on the Carolina 2. The 7–0 lead held until the fifth play of the second half when Roshto, departing from his normal defensive duties, took a pitchout, started wide to his right, cut back, and then swung outside to streak twenty-seven yards to a touchdown as Coyne and Mel Lyle eliminated Justice. Griffith's miss on the extra point only served to prolong the agony. Angered by an official's ruling (on a Carolina pass), LSU halted a Tar Heel drive on its 18 as Sam Lyle made a great fourth-down tackle. From there the Tigers, with Zollie Toth as the workhorse, paraded eighty-eight yards to the winning score. With the band swinging into "Tiger Rag" on every first down, LSU needed fourteen plays, the last a 1-yard jab by the charged-up Toth who netted seventy-four yards in twelve carries, compared to forty-eight in eleven for all-America Justice. Following the touchdown, hysteria reigned, hats flew, fans embraced one another and the glistening field became subject for debate. When the controversy arose, athletic director Heard said: "LSU would have beaten North Carolina on a muddy field, snowed-in field, or on concrete." Since it hadn't rained in Baton Rouge for two days, Tinsley explained that Carolina had practiced so long on Friday night, the ground attendant left before the Tar Heels finished. After the visitors left, a team manager sprinkled the field. On Saturday morning, the attendant, not knowing the field had been watered, sprinkled it again. Asked to comment on the "mechanical showers," Coach Snavely, back home in Chapel Hill, said: "The LSU game is history."

Ole Miss (34–7)—More revenge. In view of the Rebels' smashing 49–19 victory in 1948, the game represented a 57-point turnabout. Again it was Toth, with 102 rushing yards and two touchdowns, who wrecked the visitors. Behind 7–6 after a first quarter interception, the Tigers scored three times during an 11-minute, second-quarter spree. Zollie made LSU's first two touchdowns, Pevey passed to Hedges for the third, Baggett scored the fourth after a punt return of sixty-seven yards, and Billy West, a linebacker, hung up the last one on a 55-yard dash. To do the job, the Tiger defense had to contain stampeding John Dottley, heading for a record 1,312-yard rushing season. Dottley managed eighty-two yards but Johnny Vaught's whirlwind attack could not dent the LSU end zone. Bradley, Kitto, and Konz, with two interceptions, were the standouts.

Vanderbilt (33–13)—Still more revenge—this time a 61-point turnabout when the 48–7 defeat of 1948 is placed alongside 33–13. The chilling defensive exhibition—the Tigers limited the Commodores to twenty-three yards on the ground—was characterized by one seven-play span when five Commodore players limped from the field. Bone-rattling tackling caused fumbles on the Vandy 14 and 12, paving the way for two scores in the first 13 minutes. The Commodores lost six of eight fumbles during the cold evening; in fact, after it was over, the students were too numb to cheer.

Mississippi State (34–7)—After three aroused performances, Tinsley feared a letdown—and got one—although you wouldn't guess it from the score. Despite a homecoming crowd of 32,000, the Tigers lacked sharpness and seemed uninspired. Baggett dashed thirty-three yards for the first touchdown, and Konz stepped twenty-nine for the second as LSU quickly established its superiority. A pass from Pevey to Hedges clicked just before intermission, and in the third period Pevey sneaked over after Ray Collins blocked a Vandy kick. West closed out the scoring seconds before the final horn.

Southeastern Louisiana College (48–7)—The tuneup for Tulane turned into a clear-the-bench ball game with LSU running up 516 yards in total offense. Tinsley, dissatisfied with the performance of a club obviously looking forward to Tulane, ordered his first and second stringers behind the scoreboard in the second half to push blocking machines. As the crowd of 19,000 left the stadium, he put the squad through a series of wind sprints. Tinsley also had a reserve halfback, Erwin Baylot,

Cinderella seniors. Standing, Jeff Adams, Zollie Toth, Sam Lyle. Kneeling, Carroll Griffith, Charley Cusimano, Charley Pevey.

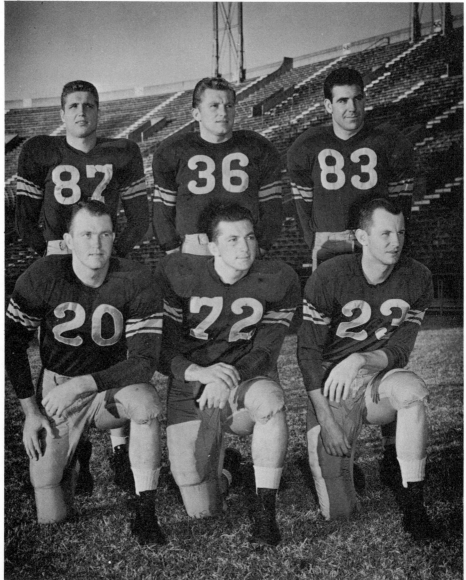

A week before—someone knew the score.

paged over the stadium's loudspeaker in the second quarter. Baylot, who had not dressed out, was told to report to the dressing room at half time and, answering the call, made a third-quarter appearance.

Tulane (21–0)—The "mad painters" may never be known, but documentary evidence of their crystal-gazing exists. A week before the game, some farsighted LSU students invaded New Orleans and splattered an incredible prediction—LSU 21, TU 0—on the ramps in Tulane Stadium. At the same time, several agricultural students from the Baton Rouge campus stole into the Sugar Bowl under cover of darkness and sprinkled the field with ice cream salt that, one week later, spelled out LSU in 15-yard-high letters between the 30-yard lines. Tulane responded with raids of its own—"46–0"—brushed in green at several spots on the LSU campus, recalling the humiliating Tiger defeat of 1948. With a team considered superior to the 1948 club, Tulane already had clinched the SEC championship, and Coach Henry Frnka had been told that an invitation to the Sugar Bowl was automatic should the Green Wave win. Tulane sought to ease the memory of the 46–7 whipping at the hands of Notre Dame, and the experts figured the Greenies, built around all-America fullback Ed Price, a one-touchdown favorite to do it.

"A coach can never really tell when a ball club is ready, but the best medicine so far as I was concerned was that bus ride to New Orleans," said Tinsley. "It gets a team to thinking. Two hours is just long enough. The ride in 1949 was silent and I could feel that the boys, win or lose, would give a good account of themselves. I think they realized if they didn't, Tulane was good enough to run them out of the stadium. So we had a little fear going for us too. The one fear of a team being keyed up is a bad break. The higher you are, the more you are deflated if something doesn't go right for you early in the game. On the other hand, a good break will send you through the roof."

On this occasion, before a then SEC-record crowd of 79,292, LSU struck with lightning quickness in the opening minutes when Konz stepped ninety-two yards with a Tulane punt, and, after that, watched Tulane play left-footed football. Kenny grabbed the punt after the first Tulane series and, running out of the south end, headed along the east sidelines right past the LSU bench. Chased in vain after several key blocks, he wound up in the end zone a few yards from Mike the Tiger's cage. The native of Weimar, Texas, who learned his light-footedness playing six-man football in high school, said: "When I caught the ball and looked up I didn't see a single Tulane man on his feet. I just turned a little to the right and made my way downfield. Everyone near me was knocked down. Fact is, some of our guys blocked two men."

The Greenies never quite recovered. In the third quarter they collected themselves for a march that reached the Tiger 12. There, however, an inspired defense tossed Tulane back twenty-three yards in four plays, and on the next play Hedges sprinted sixty-five yards on a quick opening play over guard as a Tulane halfback was faked out of position by clever ball handling. "All I had to do," said Hedges, "was run like hell." LSU added the *coup de grace* in the final period after an interception by Konz. Baggett took it over from the 6-inch line and, when LSU added the twenty-first point, it represented a 67-point switch over the 1948 result.

"No team I've ever seen played as close to 100 percent of its capabilities as this 1949 bunch did against Tulane," said Tinsley. "On every tackle, it seemed like we had four men or more around the ball. Konz played the greatest game at safety I ever witnessed."

Late Saturday night Red Heard was busy on the telephone in New Orleans. Under an existing SEC rule, to be eligible for a bowl game a conference team had to win 75 percent of its ball games. Although the Tigers had beaten three conference champions (Rice, North Carolina, and Tulane), their 4–2 SEC record left them with a percentage of .667. Anticipating the possibility of an LSU victory, Heard had begun contacting school heads Friday and by 7 P.M. Saturday he had the necessary majority to waive the rule and permit LSU to accept a Sugar Bowl invitation.

LSU's Cinderellas made good reading as 1950 approached. Seventeen players shared in scoring thirty-four touchdowns. Carroll Griffith, with two touchdowns and twenty-seven extra points, was the leading scorer with thirty-nine. The touchdown leader was Baggett (six) and he was followed by Hedges (five), Konz and Toth (three), Van Buren, West and Mel Lyle (two), Roshto, Jim Barton, Bullock, Pevey, Freeman, Joe Shirer, Cusimano, Virgets, and Charley Gaudin (one). Ed McKeever held up Van Buren as an example of unselfishness, for the most part sacrificing ball-carrying for defense. Sam Lyle and Al Hover won first team all-SEC recognition at end and guard, tackle Ray Collins and Zollie Toth landed spots on the second team. Line coach Cooper classified defensive guard Dick Bradley, who played over the center, as "the most underrated lineman in the conference."

In appraising his Cinderellas, Tinsley said: "I think maybe the only player you could classify in the 'great' category was Ray Collins, the best defensive tackle I ever coached. If I had to pick two players who personified the 1949 bunch, however, it would be Charley Pevey and Armand Kitto. Pevey couldn't throw the ball across the living room and I don't believe he could bust a glass with a pass. But he got the job done, he moved the team, and they believed in him. Now about Kitto, we had to do a little lying about his weight. We listed him at 170 to protect him. He was closer to 150. You just couldn't run around him—maybe you could run at him, no one ever tried—but not around him. Block him and he'd bounce up like a rubber ball."

In Baton Rouge grog shops and hamburger havens, the 1949 Tigers were embraced as hairy Cinderellas as Baton Rouge ascended into what passes for athletic paradise, but this time paradise was scheduled to come to a screeching halt. In fact, the clock, rather than striking twelve for Cinderella, exploded!

"We reached an emotional peak in the Tulane game we could not expect to regain," said Tinsley. "And I'm not sure if we had played our Tulane game in the Sugar Bowl it would have been good enough to handle one of the all-time great football teams."

That team was Bud Wilkinson's Oklahoma Sooners, of course, and even the hammer and tong society on Third Street, openly dissatisfied with Tinsley at the start of the season, admitted their LSU darlings were "in tough" on New Year's Day, 1950. Ranked second to Notre Dame, the unbeaten Sooners had run up 3,202 yards rushing and allowed but 556. Scorning the platoon system, Wilkinson instead alternated two lines at 8-minute intervals with everyone going both ways. Two future head coaches, all-America tackle Wade Walker and end Jim Owens, were among the Okie standouts up front, while Darrell Royal, who hop-scotched around before becoming a fixture at the University of Texas, was a quarterback who made Wilkinson's split-T a savage weapon.

In sunny, 75-degree weather 83,000 fans saw Cinderella go up in smoke after a first-quarter threat was repulsed by a red-shirted defense that got better as the afternoon wore on. The Sooners used the halfback

VIRGETS   HEATH   THOMAS

Nightmare in New Orleans: The clock strikes 12 for Tigers as Sooners romp, 35–0, in 1950 Sugar Bowl.

pass to make it 7–0 in the second quarter and, moments later, went thirty-seven yards after recovering an LSU fumble. Any chance of a comeback (Oklahoma was an eight-point favorite) faded early in the third quarter when fullback Leon Heath streaked eighty-six yards on a split-T quickie, going the distance without a hand being laid on him. As the Tiger defense wilted, Oklahoma added two fourth-quarter scores, winding up with 286 rushing yards to LSU's 38. Survivors told a grim story. "It wasn't the size so much," said Armand Kitto, "but the speed that went with the size."

LSU fans wrote off the 35–0 Sugar Bowl defeat as a bad dream. With the approach of fall, they looked to "coach of the year" Tinsley to make use of reinforcements from a star-studded freshman team to take up the slack created by the graduation of ends Sam Lyle and Ray Bullock, tackles Ray Collins, Joseph "Red" Baird, and Charley Cusimano. The Tigers had lettermen at every position and looked particularly solid in the middle with holdovers Harold Voss, Moose Potter, Ed Coyne, Al Hover, Jim Shoaf, Dick Bradley, Nick Roussos, and Joe Reid, student body president.

If there was a question mark, it was at the worst possible position—quarterback and this proved Tinsley's undoing in what amounted to a "riches to rags" story. Halfback Lee Hedges was given a try at the spot vacated by Charley Pevey and Carroll Griffith, but when this move didn't work out, the quarterback post was turned over to sophomore Norm Stevens of Picayune, Mississippi, son of Norman Stevens of the 1922–25 Tiger teams. By the end of the year, Stevens was sharing time with Jim Barton, a junior from Marshall, Texas. Elsewhere, Tinsley was

Ken Konz: All-around Tiger.

deep in ball carriers. Aside from Hedges there was Ken Konz, Jim Roshto, Bill Baggett, and Chester Freeman at halfback, captain Ebert Van Buren and Billy West at fullback.

Because they were never able to get consistency at quarterback, the 1950 Tigers wound up as the South's most disappointing team. Tinsley's club was consistently inconsistent—completely inept one week, losing to underdog Georgia Tech in Tiger Stadium; a ball of fire the next, battling favored Georgia to a 13–13 tie in Athens. The Tigers did manage to put sharp back-to-back efforts together, pounding Ole Miss 40–14 behind the running of Baggett and Hedges and smashing Vandy, 33–7, by throttling the Commodores' Bill Wade-to-Bucky Curtis passing threat.

In true Tinsley fashion, LSU saved its best for Tulane. Henry Frnka's Green Wave was better than a touchdown choice over a team which took a 4–4–1 into New Orleans. Loser only to Alabama and Notre Dame, Tulane had won five in a row, helping pull a crowd of 68,670 into Sugar Bowl stadium. What the fans saw was an LSU defense headed by Paul Miller and Ray Potter hold Tulane to 143 yards on the ground and 80 in the air, the Wave's lowest of the season. Trailing 7–0 in the third quarter, Baggett, who picked up 617 yards during the year, swept thirty-one yards to a touchdown, and minutes later Jim Barton punched across another, following a fumble recovery by Jim Roshto deep in Tulane territory. For awhile it looked like the Tigers had a 14–7 upset sewed up, but the Greenies, capitalizing on a poor punt, drove sixty-seven yards in the final two minutes to pull out a 14–14 tie.

Jim Roshto, Harold Voss, Chester Freeman.

If there is one word for Gus Tinsley's reign as LSU head coach, it would have to be "unpredictable"—something readily apparent over the 1949–51 stretch. From Cinderellas in 1949 to bums in 1950, the Tigers in 1951 regained a measure of prestige despite a man-eating schedule designed by athletic director Red Heard and despite the loss of a host of veteran linemen. Remembering that in 1951 colleges adopted platoon football, some unusual ingredients went into a 7–3–1 season: a junior college transfer, George "The Terrible" Tarasovic of Bridgeport, Connecticut, who won a defensive berth on the Newspaper Enterprise Association all-America team, as well as one on the all-SEC team; and two Bogalusa freshmen (freshmen were eligible because of the Korean War), guard Sid Fournet and quarterback Cliff Stringfield, who contributed handsomely. Fournet, who started every game for the offensive team, won a second-team all-SEC berth, while Stringfield spelled Stevens at quarterback and won three games with his place kicking—Rice, 7–6; Mississippi State, 3–0; and Tulane, 14–13.

Two of LSU's defeats came at the hands of national powers, unbeaten Georgia Tech (25–7) and Maryland (27–0), conquerors of national champion Tennessee in the Sugar Bowl. The other was the result of three passing bombs by Vandy's Bill Wade, resulting in a 20–13 Commodore victory.

Otherwise, Tinsley's ball club prevailed with a surprising defense that held everyone but Tulane to one touchdown or less. After a lackluster 13–0 opening win over Mississippi Southern, the Tigers went into Mobile and upset Alabama, 13–7, to win Tinsley the national "Coach of the Week" honors. A defense headed by Tarasovic and 165-pound linebacker Caswell Brown put the clamps on Bama's Bobby Marlow. Jim Barton passed to Warren Virgets for one LSU score and Leroy Labat, the "Black Stallion" from Lutcher, scored the other after runs of thirty-one and twenty-one yards by Jim Roshto. The Bogalusa rookies took turns playing hero. After Stringfield helped produce a 7–6 decision over Rice, Fournet came up with the big play that sank Georgia, 7–0, in Athens, LSU's first win over the Bulldogs since 1945. Sid cracked through to block a third-quarter punt by Zeke Bratkowski, which Billy West picked up and carried over for the touchdown. To protect this lead, the Tiger defense had to beat back two late Georgia drives.

A 28-yard run by Labat got the Tigers a 6–6 standoff with Ole Miss and after Wade riddled the secondary for a Vanderbilt victory, Stringfield booted a 19-yard field goal to turn back State.

A 45–7 conquest of outclassed Villanova pushed LSU's record to 6–3–1 and made the Tigers favored over Tulane (which had won four and lost five) for the first time since 1947. The game was a 14-carat thriller that had 41,766 in Tiger Stadium panting at the end. LSU shot to a 7–0 lead in the early minutes when Charley Oakley scored after Ed Coyne recovered a Greenie fumble. It stayed like this until Max McGee scored for Henry Frnka's Wave following recovery of a Labat fumble. Comeaux missed the extra point, however, and the Tigers kept the lead.

When LSU marched sixty-one yards with the kickoff (Hedges scored and Stringfield made it 14–6), the Tigers appeared to have it salted away. At this time, Frnka made good use of his surprise weapon, a spread formation featuring Les Kennedy's herculean passing. Kennedy sent a 57-yard bomb to Ray Weidenbacher to set up a touchdown. Trailing 14–13, Tulane was again flirting with the LSU end zone as time ran out.

Deke Houlgate, national authority in rating teams, voted LSU "the most successful team in America," an honor that toned down, but did not silence, the sniping on Third Street. While there was no open break between the two, a sort of "cold war" atmosphere existed between

Paul Miller, George Tarasovic, Norm Stevens, Jr.

Leroy Labat breaks loose on touchdown jaunt against Tulane, 1952.

Tinsley and assistant Ed McKeever. In many quarters, McKeever and Cooper received a lion's share of the credit for the Cinderella season, a fact Tinsley resented. The "cold war" ended after the 1951 season when McKeever and Cooper resigned.

The most memorable thing about 1952 was the introduction of a letter-number system, an innovation that came at an opportune time in that it diverted some of the attention from the scoreboard. The Tigers parlayed another awesome schedule, a young squad, and forty-one fumbles (they lost twenty-four) into a 3–7 record. Under the letter-number system, brainchild of Jim Corbett, ends, guards and tackles wore E, G and T, respectively, followed by a number from zero to nine. The right side wore even numbers, the left side odd. Centers, quarterbacks, left halfbacks, right halfbacks, and fullbacks were identified by C, Q, L, R, F and an accompanying zero-to-nine numeral.

Rice, Kentucky and Tulane were the only teams unable to solve this novel LSU equation. The Tigers drew some consolation from the fact that five of their opponents won spots in the top ten, but it was not enough to erase another fact: LSU failed to win a home game for the first time since 1894.

Highlights were few for a ball club that entered eight of ten games as the underdog. Oddly enough, the Tigers scored back-to-back upsets early in the season, whipping Rice, 27–7, with Sal Nicolo scooting ninety-four yards for one of the touchdowns, and then handing Bear Bryant one of his worst defeats during his eight-year stay at Kentucky,

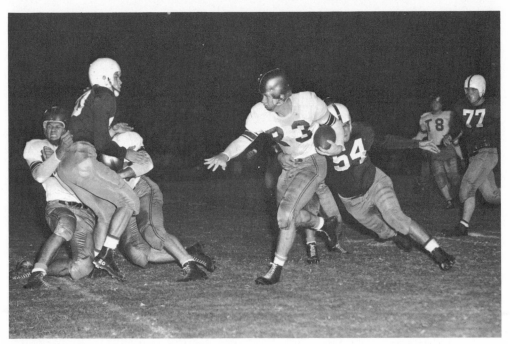

Al Doggett on the loose against Bama, 1952.

34–7. Norm Stevens passed for two touchdowns against the Wildcats and Jerry Marchand scored two.

Because LSU came up to its annual scrap with Tulane after being blitzed by Georgia, Maryland, Ole Miss, Tennessee, and Mississippi State, the Tigers invaded New Orleans an eight-point underdog to the Greenies, who were coached for the first time by "Bear" Wolf. With Max McGee the offensive spark, Tulane had a 5–4 record and the notion that LSU was ripe for picking. But not for long. Tinsley kept the Tigers in the dressing room until ten minutes before the kickoff, a psychological move that quickly paid off. With the game less than two minutes old, Leroy Labat rambled thirty-three yards for a touchdown, bouncing off several Greenies on the way. Early in the second quarter, Marchand stepped fifty-four yards for another score and with fifteen seconds left before halftime, Stringfield booted a 22-yard field goal to make it 16–0. The score stayed that way and once again Tinsley had won the game he needed most. The victory took some of the sting out of a miserable season, one Tinsley partially attributed to the loss of senior quarterback Norm Stevens.

With 1953 came the end of unlimited substitution, and as Gus eyed the return to one-platoon football he found himself with several talented two-way players—halfbacks George Brancato and Charley Oakley, fullbacks Jerry Marchand and Russ Gautreaux, tackles Sid Fournet (a bona-fide all-America candidate) and Paul Miller, guard Gary Dildy (another Bogalusa recruit), and sophomore end Joe Tuminello of Brookhaven, Mississippi, who had caught eight passes for sixty yards while lettering as a freshman. Aspiring rookies were headed by 225-

pound freshman halfback Lou Deutschman, who rewrote the record book at Holy Cross in New Orleans; fullback Tommy Davis, a high school all-American who had sparked Fair Park (Shreveport) to the state championship; and quarterback Win Turner, who had won a flock of honors at Istrouma in Baton Rouge. Turner was expected to add depth at quarterback where Cliff Stringfield and Al Doggett, a converted halfback, gave Tinsley some cause for optimism.

As it turned out, LSU was typically Tinsley in 1953, losing as the favorite, winning as the underdog. Oddly enough, the Tigers went through six games before losing, then seemed to fall apart before regrouping for their final two games. Form took an awful licking from the start. Highly-touted Texas came to Baton Rouge a solid choice and left badly-beaten, 20–7. Doggett, who had had only a week's work at quarterback, ran the club like a veteran. Favored Alabama, upset by Mississippi Southern the week before, was still the favorite over an LSU team that went to Mobile, fell behind 0–7, and got out with a 7–7 tie on the sparkling running of Brancato.

The Tigers next won as expected, over Boston College, 42–6, featured by Oakley's 60-yard scoring run, but a week later they were fortunate to escape with a 6–6 tie against underdog Kentucky. Still fumbling around (they dropped a dozen passes), the Tigers managed to whip Georgia in Athens by intercepting Zeke Bratkowski three times. Continuing on their unpredictable path, they allowed an underdog Florida outfit to come up with a 21–21 standoff, when Doggett's sharp passing was offset by a sieve-like defense. With a 3–0–3 record after six games, LSU apparently was in a position to make a stretch run but Ole Miss popped the bubble in a hurry. Before a crowd of 45,000 in Baton Rouge, the Rebels used a deadly passing game engineered by quarterbacks Lee Paslay and Jimmy Patton for a 27–16 victory. A 49-yard run by Marchand and a 73-yard gallop with an intercepted pass by Deutschmann accounted for the LSU touchdowns.

Tinsley was unable to rally his forces. Underdog Tennessee completely outplayed the Tigers in Knoxville, winning in convincing 32–14 fashion, and the next week Mississippi State dealt LSU its third straight loss, 26–13, even though it lost all-America Jackie Parker in the first half when the score was 13–all. Understudy Bobby Collins was State's hero. Somehow, the Tigers, resting some of the wounded for the Tulane finale, managed to squeak past Arkansas, 9–8, thanks to a 22-yard field goal by freshman Tommy Davis, whose foot was destined to play a major role in future history at LSU.

Because Tulane was in the early stages of self-imposed de-emphasis, LSU's closing 32–13 victory, highlighted by Jerry Marchand's three touchdowns, lost some of its importance. It was a glowing exit by the

Jerry Marchand:
Talent and courage.

5-foot, 8-inch, 185-pounder, a member of his school's Hall of Fame. A transfer student from Notre Dame, the Catholic High (Baton Rouge) graduate led the Tigers with 697 rushing yards and was voted his team's most valuable player. LSU trainer Marty Broussard, not easily impressed, rates Jerry's 1953 performance against Georgia as the most courageous he has ever witnessed at the university.

"We kicked off to Georgia," says Marty, "and, on the first defensive play, Jerry took a lick that fractured his upper jaw, shattering his four middle teeth right at the gum. He came to after a moment and I wanted to take him out but he wouldn't hear of it. So I put what we call a steri-pad—it's made of gauze and cotton—into his mouth to protect the upper gum and he played with it the rest of the game. Didn't miss a play."

Jerry wound up with a third-team berth on the all-SEC team, Joe Tuminello won a spot on the second team, and Sid Fournet was a unanimous all-SEC selection and a second-team all-America choice. While he won no honors, Al Doggett, who played his high school football at Homer, Louisiana, High, ended Tinsley's quarterbacking worries by completing sixty-eight passes for 822 yards, more damage in one season than the great Y. A. Tittle was able to accomplish.

Understandably, with men like Marchand, Oakley, and Brancato gone, Tinsley was banking heavily on the 180-pound Doggett and on 225-pound Lou Deutschmann, whose freshman performance indicated great things ahead. But fate intervened. During a spring practice scrimmage, Deutschmann suffered a crippling injury to his left leg which ended his career as a ball carrier. To this day Gus Tinsley, who many feel was the finest all-around football player in LSU history, rates Deutschmann "the finest ball-carrying prospect I ever saw." Tinsley says "prospect" because Deutschmann never had the opportunity to blossom. "It got so in practice," said Tinsley, "our defensive backs would find it convenient not to be around when Lou ran toward them. I'll never forget the day he was hurt. He had run for about fifteen touchdowns. The last time he had just scored on a long run—he actually carried a player the last 10 yards—and was standing up in the end zone when someone ploughed into him." The impact shredded ligaments in Lou's left leg and doctors had to drill five holes in the bone to stitch them together.

Deutschmann's loss to the offense—he was to play tackle in 1954—came at a time when the heat was beginning to build around Tinsley. After the win over a Tulane team that managed only one victory in 1953, Baton Rouge *Morning Advocate* sports editor Bud Montet wrote: "We go on record and state that the 1953 football season at LSU has been a failure, a poor year and little cause for celebration. Hooray, we beat Tulane, but so did eight other ball clubs." Montet said the team did not keep training and repeatedly beat itself. He said LSU's "wishy-washy policy" called for a new deal.

In a way, there was a new deal, one which, it turned out, proved rather costly for the university. At the NCAA meeting in January, 1954, Fred Russell, sports editor of the Nashville *Banner*, reported LSU as being on the verge of hiring Bear Bryant, who apparently was dissatisfied at Kentucky. Bear was leaving, but he was headed for Texas A & M, not Baton Rouge. Before this matter was resolved, however, there were repercussions from Russell's story in Baton Rouge, the upshot being an 8–5 vote by the LSU Board of Supervisors granting Tinsley a new three-year contract at $12,500 per year, which would continue through January 31, 1957. Said Tinsley after the vote: "I'm happy the board saw fit to stabilize the athletic program after some of the rumors we have had."

Tinsley was not the only target in LSU's athletic department. T. P. Heard had scored a personal victory in his fight to enlarge Tiger Stadium to 67,500, a face-lifting job that was completed for the 1954 season. But the addition was secured at the temporary expense of a new library, which gave the battle an academic-versus-athletic flavor. It all began quite innocently enough at the 1950 session of the legislature. At the time, LSU was seeking money for expansion of the medical school in New Orleans and a library on the main campus, considered by university officials to be the primary needs. Simultaneously, there was a group interested in enlarging Tiger Stadium, which had a capacity of 42,500. The desires of both groups seemed to merge in a bill providing a $6

After the library fight, LSU had a 67,500-seat "bowl"—but Gus had trouble filling it.

million bond issue based on the excess revenues of the corporation franchise tax which included these three items, plus a gym for what was then Northeast Junior College under LSU.

When the act was written (and behind the scenes could be seen the hand of athletic director Heard), it stipulated that medical school expansion should come first, the stadium next, the Northeast Junior College gym (cost of which was not to exceed $300,000), and then the library. This meant that the state was giving LSU $5.7 million for the medical school, stadium, and library in that order. While plans went ahead for the medical school (a contract of $3.4 million was let), the stadium project was held up when the Korean War prevented a steel allocation. When the original estimate of stadium expansion was pegged at $1.5 million, only $800,000 remained for the library, whose cost was over $4 million. This, then, was the background.

At the 1952 session of the legislature an effort was made to change the dedication, that is, to place the library ahead of the stadium. A bill along these lines, however, was reported unfavorably by the education committee, on the grounds that one legislature should not upset the decision of a prior legislature. Later, however, the 1952 legislature approved a bill which would dedicate the surplus, after the stadium, to construction of a school for veterinary medicine, a move that virtually eliminated the library from the picture.

Stadium proponents pointed to the shifting of the 1950 game with Tulane from Baton Rouge to New Orleans because Tiger Stadium was inadequate. The 1949 game in New Orleans had drawn 79,292, a record at the time, and in 1950 a crowd of 68,760 had watched the archrivals play in Tulane Stadium. Opponents contended that LSU's 42,500-seat stadium was seldom filled more than once every two years (for the Tulane game) and that with more seats available fewer season tickets would be sold. Looming large, of course, was the issue of scholarship versus athletics. In an effort to head off the stadium enlargement in February, 1953, a group of LSU alumni produced, among other statistics, figures on football attendance in Baton Rouge.

Total Season Attendance, 1946–50

	Paid Attendance	Average Per Game	Student, Comp. Tickets	Average Total Attendance
1946—7 games	159,750	22,680	6,500	29,180
1947—5 games	137,428	27,485	6,500	33,985
1948—6 games	130,469	21,745	6,500	28,245
1949—7 games	148,003	21,143	6,500	27,643
1950—6 games	107,206	17,868	6,500	24,368

Game Attendance 1951

	Paid Attendance	Student, Comp. Tickets	Total Attendance
Mississippi Southern	8,526	6,500	15,026
Rice	25,826	6,500	34,326
Mississippi State	10,876	6,500	17,372
Maryland	18,415	6,500	24,915
Ole Miss	25,962	6,500	32,462
Vanderbilt	9,923	6,500	16,423
Tulane	34,700	6,500	41,200

Game Attendance 1952

	Paid Attendance	Student, Comp. Tickets	Total Attendance
Tennessee	20,617	6,500	27,117
Georgia	23,328	6,500	29,828
Alabama	20,129	6,500	26,629
Texas	31,093	6,500	37,593
Mississippi State	9,371	6,500	15,871

The group pointed out that only three Southeastern Conference colleges then had stadiums larger than LSU, and that by contrast all but one had larger and newer libraries with more books. In 1953 the LSU library had seats for 540 and room for 300,000 books, whereas the University of Texas library had seated 1,800 and had space for 2,000,000 books. Newspapers throughout the state began firing editorial broadsides. The Shreveport *Times* charged that the original act of 1950 giving the stadium priority over a library was "slipped through the Earl Long legislature by the athletic department without any request, recommendation or approval from LSU itself." The New Orleans *Item* said legislators "have not only a right but a duty to reverse any mistakes by their predecessors—particularly mistakes involving the virtual waste of $2 million."

In a heated six-hour session on February 28, the Board of Supervisors voted 7 to 6 to accept a bid of $1,242,342 for a stadium addition, one that would increase the capacity to 67,500 by closing in the south end of the horseshoe-shaped stadium to make it a bowl. In October, 1953, the board gave a $4-million library priority in an $18-million building program, and five years later, after Governor Robert F. Kennon's administration secured the money from mineral leases of state-owned land, the building was dedicated.

Heard's victory in the stadium-library fight had something of a backlash effect on Gus Tinsley: it left him with 22,000 more seats to fill at home games. When the Tigers dropped their first four in a row in 1954, attendance fell alarmingly and rumors grew in intensity, even though Tinsley's team managed to win five of the last seven to finish 5–6.

LSU was never in the ball game against Texas; in fact, it took a 44-yard run by Vince Gonzales to let the Tigers escape, 20–6. Then, in succession, Bart Starr's passing produced a 12–0 victory for Alabama, a last-minute fumble handed Kentucky an unexpected 7–6 win, and the speed of Billy Teas paved the way, 30–20, for Georgia Tech. Characteristically, when the picture looked darkest, Tinsley sprang his annual surprise—this time shocking a favored Florida team that had beaten Georgia Tech and Kentucky. The Tigers prevailed in impressive 20–7 fashion but only 25,000 were on hand in Baton Rouge, reflecting a declining interest in a club that had dropped four straight and beaten only Texas Tech. Setting up all three touchdowns with his passes, Al Doggett hit his stride for the first time.

The upset of Florida did not signal an LSU comeback. It was merely a case of LSU's firing then falling back. The next week, Ole Miss spoiled Homecoming while taking the air route for a 21–6 win, and two weeks later, after LSU disposed of outclassed Chattanooga, 26–19, the Tigers hit the skids, losing 25–0 to Mississippi State as Art Davis scored all four touchdowns. With crowds of 11,000 for Chattanooga and 20,000 for State, LSU profited by its scheduling. Luckily, the Arkansas

Left, Joe Tuminello displays 1952 equation; right, All-America Sid Fournet out of battle dress.

game was played in Shreveport, where Razorback fans helped swell the turnout to 33,000. For the second season in a row, the Tigers outpointed the Hogs—this time 7–6 on Doggett's extra point with twenty-eight seconds left in the first half.

A week later Doggett was again the man of the hour after a hopelessly underdog Tulane team (one which had won only a single game) grabbed a 13–0 half-time lead and seemingly was headed for one of the biggest upsets of the series. In the third quarter a spectacular catch by Gonzales of a Win Turner heave set up a touchdown that came moments later on a Turner-to-Tuminello pass. Doggett converted. Then, in the final quarter, Gonzales lofted his first pass of the season, a 45-yarder to end John Wood that set the Tigers up on the Tulane 12. Again Turner hit Tuminello for the touchdown and again Doggett converted to allow Tinsley's club to get out of New Orleans a shaky 14–13 victor.

The season's brightest note perhaps was the postseason laurels scooped up by Sid Fournet who was winning his fourth varsity letter. In becoming LSU's first bona-fide all-American since Ken Kavanaugh, Fournet was a first team selection of United Press, International News Service, Newspaper Enterprise Association, *Look* and *Collier's*. The Associated Press placed him on the second team. Bogalusa's gift to the Tigers made a sweep at the LSU football banquet, receiving awards as permanent team captain, most valuable player, and as the varsity member playing the most minutes. The man Tinsley calls "the greatest all-around lineman I ever saw at LSU" had been an all-state tackle as a junior at Bogalusa and an all-state fullback as a senior. As a 205-pound freshman, Sid quickly asserted himself as a starting offensive guard, missing the most minutes played award by a scant sixty seconds. "As a sophomore," said Tinsley, "he reported at 230 but could still outrun all of the lineman. Linemen like Sid don't happen along often."

The question now was: Would Gus Tinsley be able to outrun his critics? Although rumors persisted following the win over Tulane, it looked as though Gus apparently had weathered another storm when, according to reports, those opposing him on the Board of Supervisors could not muster the required votes to buy up his contract. When LSU announced later in December the signing of "Doc" Erskine, an assistant at Marquette, as an addition to Gus's staff, prospects of Tinsley returning for 1955 seemed bright indeed.

In early February the dam broke. President Troy Middleton called a special meeting of the LSU board which took double action: Tinsley's contract was bought up and T. P. Heard was retired after twenty-three years as athletic director. Why was Tinsley, whose seven-year record was thirty-five wins, thirty-four losses, and six ties, being ousted? "For the good of the university's athletic program," said board chairman Lewis Gottlieb.

The sudden clean sweep, which Dan Hardesty, sports editor of the Baton Rouge *State-Times*, labeled "Operation Ouster," had an interesting background. Several days before the scheduled meeting of the Board of Supervisors, LSU's Athletic Council met and voted to recommend to the board that Tinsley be fired for cause, a move that would justify terminating his contract (which still had two years to run) without pay. Wrote Hardesty: "That was where the plot thickened. As every follower of LSU athletics knows, Red Heard has had his critics—and many of them—for years. Whether they were right or wrong in the present case is beside the point . . . the fact was some people wanted to get rid of Tinsley and others wanted to get rid of Heard. . . . Heard sent his resignation to the Board of Supervisors and, of course, there were the usual denials later that it was demanded."

Representing the Athletic Council before the board, Dean J. G. Lee presented charges against Tinsley, charges accusing him of failing to comply with recruiting instructions. Any student with lower than a C average recruited by the Tigers had to have a letter from his high school principal indicating the athlete was capable of doing satisfactory work in college. Among those in question was one C. J. Alexander of Donaldsonville. Tinsley, however, was able to produce transcripts of grades, and, in the case of Alexander, produced not only a letter from the Donaldsonville principal but the principal himself. Unable to fire Tinsley for cause, the board, with Heard's request for retirement before it, took what may have been its only way out: it voted to accept Heard's request for retirement and to fire Tinsley—with full payment, of course, of the $25,000 coming to him under his contract.

Summed up Hardesty: "It must be made clear to anyone puzzled about all this talk of recruiting issues and assorted items that the real reason back of the entire ouster was the same old story—Tinsley didn't win enough games. Nobody is going to follow the story that Tinsley was to be fired because he didn't bring enough scholars to the university—that was merely a means toward an end."

Tinsley was relieved of his duties as of February 5, 1955. His $12,500 salary was paid up to the end of his contract period, January 31, 1957, in the usual monthly installments. Under fire almost from the start, the all-America end who returned to coach at his alma mater could not overcome a suicide schedule—and possibly his "country boy" image, which many felt made him ineffective as a disciplinarian. "Gus Tinsley was too nice a guy for his own good," said LSU's President Middleton.

Heard's retirement brought many tributes to a man who fathered the athletic plant which LSU boasts today. Said Bill Keefe, sports editor of the *Times-Picayune:* "Heard had been the first college athletic director to fly football teams on long hops; he had been the first to conceive the idea of fitting dormitories into a big football stadium and he was the first athletic director in the South to eliminate 'breathers' from the schedule. Red encountered lots of opposition when he talked Huey Long into getting the big Tiger Stadium with its living accommodations for 1,000 students; he weathered a storm of protest when he spearheaded the drive for an athletic dormitory; he ran into a tempest when he campaigned for the enclosure of the north end of the stadium and the construction of a new press box. Many of those who fought him on all these moves and who were defeated have been bitter and they will hail with delight the decision to retire him."

Ironically, the dismal 1954 crowds in the 67,500-seat Tiger Stadium were perhaps the biggest sign of the crying need for a coaching change. In pushing for a bigger stadium, Red Heard proved to be a little ahead of his time—but not by too many years.

'We're No. 1 !'

NO sooner had the Board of Supervisors disposed of the Red Heard–Gus Tinsley matter than board member Ike Carriere headed for the coaches' offices in Tiger Stadium to report to the men most affected by the departmental shakeup. Quite understandably, Tinsley's assistants were concerned about their future, a future they felt would best be served by the promotion of a staff member. "They were about to vote among themselves," recalls Carriere. "They had their slips of paper ready and had agreed that the assistant receiving the most votes would receive the backing of the staff. I advised them not to go through with it. First I told them it was the board's feeling no one on the staff would be selected, so any candidate they might propose would be in competition with the man chosen by the board. Furthermore, I told them if they followed my advice, one of the conditions the new coach would have to accept would be that he must retain Tinsley's entire staff."

While the staff pondered this turn of events, Carriere telephoned President Middleton. "General Middleton not only backed me up," said Carriere, "but he requested that I pass on to the staff this bit of information: Charley McClendon [defensive coach who had joined Tinsley's staff in 1953] would be acting head coach and Harry Rabenhorst acting athletic director until both jobs were filled."

When Carriere returned to the room where the staff had gathered, they told him they had decided to go along with his advice. He then told them of his conversation with Middleton. Shortly thereafter, a screening committee headed by Sterling W. "Buck" Gladden and including two other board members, Carriere and Horace Wilkinson, and three faculty representatives, Dr. John Floyd, Dean Arthur Choppin, and Dr. Henry V. Howe, was set up by the board and the hunt was on.

Some of the applicants—official and unofficial applicants, that is—made the committee blink. They included Jim Tatum of North Carolina; Red Sanders of UCLA; Bear Bryant of Texas A & M; Ara Parseghian of Miami of Ohio; Ray Graves and Frank Broyles, assistants at Georgia Tech; Ben Martin, assistant at Navy; Paul Dietzel, assistant at Army; Stan Galloway of Southeastern Louisiana College; Perry Moss, assistant at Miami; Chuck Purvis, assistant at Illinois; and Ed McKeever, former LSU assistant who had entered private business in Baton Rouge. Graves and Broyles had been recommended by SEC commissioner Bernie Moore. Tatum, Sanders, and Bryant were not formal applicants but had expressed interest to certain board members or persons close to the university. However, when the committee applied its guidelines to the list of prospects, the number dwindled considerably. At the urging of Carriere, five points were set down. The board would NOT consider: (1) a high school coach, (2) an LSU assistant, (3) anyone who coached or played in the pro ranks in 1954, (4) a head coach under contract, (5) a head coach who had been fired, (6) an SEC assistant.

Although this trimmed the candidates to a half dozen, members of the board were still skeptical of Carriere's claim: "We'll have a coach in ten days." However, less than a week after the ouster of Heard and Tinsley, six interviews were set up over a two-day period. The first day's schedule had Galloway, Martin, and Dietzel; the second, McKeever, Purvis, and Moss.

"I was anxious to meet this West Point assistant whose name I found difficult to pronounce," said Carriere. When Earl Blaik's 29-year-old line coach walked through the door to keep a 1 P.M. appointment, he smiled and said as he headed for his seat in the board room: "I hope this is not a duplication of my Kentucky experience." A year before, when Bear Bryant left Kentucky for Texas A & M, Dietzel had been given verbal assurance that the job in Lexington was his. Here's what happened: Blanton Collier, assistant for the Cleveland Browns, accepted the Kentucky post but told officials he wanted to personally tell Paul Brown, head coach of the Browns. Collier flew to Cleveland where the persuasive Brown apparently talked him out of leaving. Collier phoned Lexington and told Kentucky officials he had decided to stay with the Browns. Kentucky then notified Dietzel to fly to Lexington (he had been the Wildcats' No. 2 choice) to sign a contract. When the plane carrying Dietzel from New York to Lexington was airborne, Collier had a change-of-heart: he wanted the Kentucky job after all. When Dietzel landed, he received the sad news.

So impressed was the president of Kentucky by this tall blond with an unsettling poise and a 24-carat smile that he recommended him to Troy Middleton when the LSU vacancy occurred. Dietzel's name landed among the candidates, however, because of a phone call made by board chairman Lewis Gottlieb to Biff Jones, former LSU coach who was still close to the Army football scene. On the possibility that Jones might be interested in the athletic directorship at LSU, Gottlieb contacted Jones, who politely declined. "Well, then," asked Gottlieb, "who would you recommend for head coach?" Suggested Biff, "Why don't you look into this Dietzel fellow."

A few days earlier Jones had received a call from Dietzel expressing interest in the position. Dietzel telephoned Jones at the urging of Charley McClendon, who had served with Dietzel on Bryant's staff at Kentucky. So the timing was perfect. The day Jones recommended Dietzel to Gottlieb, Biff phoned the young assistant and told him to expect a call, adding: "When it comes, act properly surprised." The call came and Dietzel then received the reluctant blessing of Earl Blaik, who had already lost two assistants. "You go down there," Blaik told Dietzel, "and, if you can get the job, you take it." Early in the interview, when Dietzel learned the new LSU coach, as a major condition, must retain Tinsley's staff, he balked. Realizing a promise had been made to the assistants, the unruffled Dietzel pulled a stack of cards from his pocket and went over the background of each coach. "It was obvious," said Carriere, "he had done his homework." As Dietzel went on to outline his football philosophy, Dr. Howe handed Carriere a note: "Ike, this is your boy."

Following the interview Dietzel returned to West Point, only to be called back several days later by the screening committee which had decided he was the man. It was at this point that an eleventh-hour appeal on behalf of Ara Parseghian by the athletic director of Miami of Ohio provided an interesting footnote. "We were prepared to recommend Dietzel to the Board of Supervisors," said Carriere, "when we learned Dietzel had been rapped by the athletic director at his alma mater. We felt we should check it out. So President Middleton placed a long distance call to John Brickels, the athletic director at Miami. I got on an extension and we began to question Brickels on Paul Dietzel. According to the word we received, he had said something to the effect that after a while Dietzel would wear thin. Brickels began to hedge and said he had nothing against Dietzel. Rather, the point he wanted to get across was that Ara Parseghian was the best man for the LSU job.

"This led me to the obvious question. 'If Coach Parseghian is as good as you say he is,' I asked him, 'why are you recommending him to LSU?' His reply was: 'We're not going to be able to keep him and I'd like to see him at a major football school.' We asked him if Parseghian was under contract and he said he was. So then we explained we were not considering any head coaches under contract. 'We'll gladly release him,' said Brickels. But President Middleton insisted it was against our guidelines and that ended the conversation."

When Dietzel learned of the Brickels matter, he was furious but he soon cooled down. The screening committee recommended him to the board—Carriere spoke for fifty minutes on why Dietzel was the man for the job—and, by the time he was named Tinsley's successor on February 16, his selection had been predicted by Bud Montet in the Baton Rouge *Morning Advocate* and Bill Keefe in the *Times-Picayune*. "Because of the Army angle I'd venture the prediction that Dietzel will be the next Tiger coach," wrote Keefe on February 15. "General Middleton's opinion is so highly regarded by all connected with LSU and his Army contacts so strong I don't think it out of order to call the shot on the new Tiger coach."

On February 15, 1955, Dietzel was named coach. He was signed to a three-year contract at $13,000 a year—$500 a year more than Tinsley was receiving when the end came. "If there is one watchword," the new coach said at his first press conference, "it is enthusiasm. I would like to see enthusiasm on the part of the players. I hope to see a fireball brand of football."

At twenty-nine, Dietzel was the youngest member of his staff, which included first assistant Charley McClendon (Kentucky, 1950); Carl Maddox (Northwestern Louisiana, 1932); Clarence "Pop" Strange (LSU, 1937); George Terry (College of the Ozarks, 1932); Abner Wimberly (LSU, 1949); Doc Erskine (Loyola of New Orleans, 1926); and Bill Peterson (Ohio Northern, 1946). With the exception of line coach Will Walls, who resigned after being the subject of a head coaching petition by LSU players, all of Tinsley's staff returned. The only new face was Peterson, whom Dietzel brought in as offensive line coach from a high school in Ohio. "At our first staff meeting," said Maddox, "Paul made it plain that all of us were being retained. After that it depended on whether or not we did the job. He called us all in individually and was cordial yet businesslike."

Delayed because of the coaching shakeup, spring practice began three weeks after Dietzel got the job. Eighteen lettermen were among the seventy-four prospects, including eight seniors and seven junior college transfers.

Spring drills had been under way for two weeks when LSU ended the hunt—it was a one-man hunt—for athletic director. Thirty-five-year-old Jim Corbett, a 1944 graduate of Southeastern Louisiana College in Hammond and former sports publicity director at LSU, left a job as sports coordinator for the National Broadcasting Company to return to LSU for a five-year contract at $10,000 annually. From the beginning, Corbett had been the leading candidate and, when he was assured secu-

Paul Dietzel: New face in Tigertown.

rity via faculty status, he accepted a cut in salary to have a hand in revamping the athletic department. Corbett's appointment gave LSU athletics a vibrant image, an image projected by two men who battled their way toward fulfillment of lifetime ambitions through sheer dedication.

"I wanted to be a coach ever since I was a little boy," said Dietzel. "When I was a little boy, we had a kid football team that challenged everyone in sight. We had no equipment, no shoulder pads. We wore two sweaters. For an extra tough game, we wore three sweaters." When Dietzel was a ninth-grader in Mansfield, Ohio, the first junior high team in the history of the town was organized. Dietzel played center and the same group played together right on through their senior year when Mansfield won the state championship.

Football started Dietzel thinking of college, since his father, a skilled mechanic, did not have the means to further his son's education. Dietzel turned down scholarship offers to Ohio State and Tennessee, choosing instead Duke, where he played freshman football before the Air Force called him in March, 1943. After receiving his wings as a B-29 pilot, he married his high school sweetheart, Anne Wilson, a cheerleader at

Dietzel's first staff. Standing, Abner Wimberly, Ray Didier, Pop Strange, Dietzel. Kneeling, George Terry, Bill Peterson, Charley McClendon, Carl Maddox.

Miami of Ohio. Interested in the future services of the 6-foot, 3-inch, 215-pound center, Miami coach Sid Gillman corresponded with Dietzel throughout the war and, following a tour of duty that included twelve missions over Japan, Dietzel enrolled at Miami, where he went on to become a Little All-America center while completing an accelerated premedical course in two years.

He graduated with honors in February, 1948, and was all set to enter Columbia Medical School (he had paid a room deposit), when he received a letter from Gillman, who had left Miami to become line coach at Army under Earl Blaik. "When I got Sid's letter," said Dietzel, "I forgot about med school." He served as plebe line coach and, after a year, followed Gillman to Cincinnati where he coached the defense. In 1950, Bear Bryant beckoned from Kentucky, and Dietzel, anxious to broaden his coaching background, spent an inquisitive two years as assistant before returning to Army in 1952 as offensive line coach. Later he handled the defensive line and was set to become cadet backfield coach when the LSU position opened.

"I learned something different from each of the coaches I served under," said Dietzel. "Gillman gave me the foundation. Bryant taught me the name of the game is knock. And Colonel Blaik taught me organization. If I don't make good at LSU, I'm no coach."

The Jim Corbett story was one of quiet perseverance. When Jim was three months old his father, a mechanic, died and Jim was sent from Arlington, Massachusetts, city of his birth, to Woburn, Massachusetts, to live with his grandparents. He flashed his first sign of promotional genius when it came time to attend high school. Since money was a scarce item in the household and Jim had his sights set on Austin-Cate, a private school in Maine, the matter called for some study. Upon learning Austin-Cate was offering football scholarships covering all fees but $300, Corbett put the following proposition to school authorities: "If I can get you three football players willing to pay $400 instead of $300, will you accept me free of charge as part of the package deal?"

They agreed and Corbett set out to land three recruits, explaining to them and to their fathers exactly what he had in mind. Three fathers, impressed by the young man's ingenuity, agreed—and Corbett attended Austin-Cate. Jim finished out his schooling at Arlington High, holding part time jobs, evenings and weekends, one of which was as a "stringer" for the Boston *Herald* and *Globe*. Hell-bent on a college education, he learned of an insurance man in Quincy whose hobby was to put football prospects in touch with colleges, large and small. Out of this association, Corbett was invited, in the fall of 1940, to try out for the football team at Southeastern Louisiana College in Hammond. After receiving permission from his grandparents and his mother, Jim began a hitch-hiking trek south, working one time as a trucker's helper, another time for ten days in a bottling plant.

No worse for wear, he arrived on the Southeastern campus, made the freshman team, which assured him tuition, food, and shelter. Once football was over, he worked weekends in a soft drink plant and for a frozen food concern, wrestling 200-pound blocks of ice. During a preseason scrimmage in his sophomore season, he aggravated a high school leg injury, an unfortunate turn of events which would have removed a less determined fellow from the scholarship rolls. Realizing his playing days were over, Corbett, resilient as ever, didn't wait for an opening, but made his own. He convinced officials the school was not receiving adequate sports publicity. "Let me continue on scholarship as publicity director on a trial basis," he suggested. The "trial" lasted through January, 1944, when Jim graduated from Southeastern, after receiving a medical discharge from the Marines (the football injury) the previous year.

Corbett had considered coaching. Instead, he answered the call of the

Jim Corbett: He sold a product he believed in.

Associated Press bureau chief in New Orleans, then searching for someone to break in during the manpower shortage. After a year he per-
suaded his AP boss to transfer him to the state capital—a move that was
to alter his career. He was just becoming accustomed to his spot in the
Capitol press gallery (Jimmie Davis was the new governor) when, in
August, 1945, LSU had an opening for sports publicity director. Corbett jumped at the opportunity.

Except for a two-year stint in 1948–50 with a food freezing concern
in Hammond, Jim handled sports publicity at LSU until, in early 1953,
he joined NBC as coordinator of its college football series, a position he
held when the athletic shakeup came in Baton Rouge. "Why are you
leaving a job in television that pays $14,000 a year for one that will pay
$10,000?" he was asked by board member Carriere. "Because," said Jim,
"I've always wanted to be an athletic director."

Corbett and Dietzel formed a dynamic twosome as they crisscrossed
Louisiana selling LSU. "We sold a product we believed in," said Corbett. "We'd drive as much as two hundred miles to speak to as few as ten
persons."

Addressing audiences in 1955, Dietzel made it a point to open his coat
to show he had nothing up his sleeves. "I'm no magician, you know,"
he'd say. "All I can promise LSU is hard work and honesty with the
team." Visiting events like the St. James Parish Free Fair, which some-

times drew as many as 20,000, he would march through the barns and exhibits, greeting children, exhibitors, and farmers grooming hogs and cattle. It was always: "Hello, I'm Paul Dietzel, football coach at LSU. We have a mighty fine school up there and we want your boys and girls."

Dietzel was frank in discussing his football philosophy to attentive crowds. "I don't appreciate the cute type of football player," he said. "In fact, I don't like cute football. I don't like backs with fancy footwork. They're the kind who have you third-and-23 every time you look up. I'm looking for the slashing runners, the kind who get the extra yard on sheer courage. We'll use the Army-T and we'll throw the ball—but not because we're seven points behind. We won't get wild out there. Our aim is to elevate LSU football to a high plane in the SEC. We want our football to be so efficient that high school kids will be proud to come to LSU."

Spring practice was in its early stages when Dietzel shocked alumni and fans by dropping Lou Deutschmann from the squad. In 1954 the 235-pound fullback, hobbled by a leg injury, had been switched to tackle, where he saw enough action to win a letter. Under the new regime, Deutschmann was ticketed for fullback, but, when he missed a practice because of a conflicting baseball workout, he became a celebrated victim of Dietzel's disciplinary ax. From the spring to the fall of 1955, LSU's attrition rate was high; team membership dwindled from seventy-four to forty-three the week of the season opener against Kentucky. Dietzel inherited a squad with eighteen lettermen, only eight seniors and, significantly, seven junior college transfers. Wealthy at guard, he shifted Enos Parker to tackle and had four dependable hands left, juniors Don Scully, Paul Ziegler, Ted Paris, and sophomore Ed Cassidy. The 205-pound Parker had a 265-pound running mate at tackle in Earl Leggett, and at center there was 220-pound Durwood Graham. At the ends were senior Joe Tuminello, three-year letterman and all-conference candidate, and sophomore Billy Smith. Scully, Leggett, and Graham were transfers from Hinds Junior College, at the time something of an LSU farm club, one which, in 1955, was allowing a fullback named Jimmy Taylor to become eligible.

Quarterback Al Doggett, 1954 offensive leader had departed, but the Tigers had a solid although slow backfield that included three game seniors, halfbacks Chuck Johns and Vince Gonzales and fullback O. K. Ferguson. In Doggett's spot, Dietzel alternated Matt Burns, a junior who had played sparingly the year before, and a sophomore passing whiz, M. C. Reynolds.

Because Dietzel had served as an assistant at Kentucky and almost landed the coaching job Blanton Collier held, a touch of drama was

JOE MAY

Launching the Dietzel era: Joe May streaks 96 yards with kickoff to spark 19–7 upset of Kentucky.

added to the opener, one which attracted a crowd of 39,000—far short of 67,500 capacity, yet still some 12,000 over the 1954 home average. For openers, the script left little room for improvement. Snapping out of the huddle like a drill team, the Tigers went seventy-nine yards in sixteen plays with the opening kickoff. Burns passed thirteen yards to Gonzales for the touchdown. LSU kept its 7–0 lead until the third quarter when the same combination, Burns to Gonzales, clicked on a 28-yard scoring play. At this point the Wildcats began to play like a team with twenty-two lettermen and one listed among the favorites for the SEC crown. The Cats cracked LSU's defense to make a new ball game out of it, 13–7, but then a 5-foot, 9-inch, 170-pound junior from Shreveport took over. Joe May grabbed the kickoff on the 4 and, running like a frightened deer, zipped straight upfield ninety-six yards to assure Dietzel a successful debut. Collier, SEC coach of the year in 1954, paid tribute to his hosts: "LSU came to play."

The Monday following the 19–7 upset, Dietzel, still in the clouds, received a sobering—in fact, prophetic—telegram from a coaching colleague. It said simply: "Remember, Paul, it's a short trip from the penthouse to the outhouse." A week later, in the Cotton Bowl, Dietzel made the trip. That year they called Bear Bryant's Texas Aggies "the best team money can buy." Whatever it was, it was an easy twenty-eight points better than LSU. John David Crow, a 210-pound halfback Bryant had snatched off the Tiger campus, ran seventy-seven yards for one score and spent the evening bouncing off tacklers. LSU's ineptness was best illustrated when Billy Smith kicked dead on the Aggie 1—and the Aggies promptly marched ninety-nine yards.

From this point, 1955 for LSU was generally a case of lack of depth and speed. Against Rice before 51,000 in Houston, a pass from Reynolds to Gonzales in the last twenty-two seconds got the Tigers a 20–20 standoff; in fact, LSU missed a chance to win when Durwood Graham hurried his place kick. Back home for the first time in two weeks, LSU was greeted by its largest crowd in history, 61,000, drawn by a rekindled spirit and Georgia Tech, the nation's fourth-ranked team. The Tigers scrapped but could not get past the Tech 22. Bobby Dodd's outfit did only a mite better, "Toppy" Vann passing forty-six yards to Gene Volkert for the game's only points.

Down 18–0 to Florida in the fourth quarter, the Tigers scored twice and were driving again when time ran out in an 18–14 thriller. Ole Miss

Durwood Graham misses the extra point with twenty-two seconds remaining and the Tigers settle for a 20–20 tie with Rice, 1955.

was even wilder. With 42,000 looking on, Eagle Day hit on ten of sixteen passes and two touchdowns as the Rebs took a 29–13 lead into the final quarter, only to have Reynolds (seventeen of thirty for 199 yards) spark a comeback that fell three points short, 29–26. Maryland, No. 1 in the country at the time, was simply too powerful in a methodical 13–0 win in College Park, the one redeeming feature for LSU being Chuck Johns going ninety-four yards in seventeen trips against a fearsome Terp defense.

On Homecoming night, LSU at last caught someone as battered and as slow afoot as it was. The result was a 34–7 victory over Darrell Royal's Mississippi State Maroons, LSU's first Homecoming win since 1949, its first over State since 1951, and the worst defeat, up to that time, suffered by a team of Royal's. It was a dreadful night for the Maroons, in that LSU's Larry King picked off a stray lateral and stepped eighty-seven yards with twenty seconds left.

A week later Dietzel enjoyed his third victory, 13–7 over Arkansas in Little Rock, but it was such a bruising game he wondered if it was worthwhile, since Tulane was enjoying an idle weekend. Leggett and Tuminello harassed the Razorbacks all afternoon while Johns dashed sixty-five yards for one score, Ferguson twenty yards for the other.

Better than anyone, Dietzel realized the recruiting value of his first brush with Tulane. LSU, 3–5–1 at that stage, was a one touchdown favorite over a Greenie team that was 5–4. At Tiger Stadium, with a crowd of 55,000 looking on, Andy Pilney's Green Wave turned two LSU mistakes into a 13–0 lead before the Tigers could muster any kind of offense. When it was able to crank up a drive, LSU went seventy yards in thirteen plays with Ferguson taking it over. Durwood Graham kicked the point but a holding penalty nullified it—and Graham missed the next one. It was 13–6 going into the final quarter when Reynolds warmed up to carry the Tigers forty-nine yards, the last twenty-one on a pass from M.C. to Johns. Needing the point to tie, Dietzel pointed to a surprised Gonzales, who proceeded to calmly put it through the uprights. "Carl Maddox told me if we ever really needed a point to let Chico kick it," explained Dietzel afterward. "He was one of the best pressure athletes I've ever seen."

Despite its record, LSU wound up with two all-conference perform-ers—end Joe Tuminello ("He was our captain and he led by action, not words.") and tackle Earl Leggett ("He's an all-American and I don't often say that about a boy before he graduates but he deserves it.") Because LSU was such a smash at the turnstiles—the Tigers drew 241,000, best in the South, to five home games, compared to 167,000 for six home games in 1954—Dietzel's original three-year contract was torn up and another written for four years at $14,000 per year. "I wouldn't

Earl Leggett dresses out for his last game.

swap my job here for six other coaching jobs anywhere," said Dietzel.

When the 1956 season unfolded, he may have had some second thoughts. Leggett, Scully, Ziegler, and Parker gave the line stability, but the loss of Johns, Gonzales, and Ferguson removed the heart of the Tiger attack. Although Dietzel knew him by reputation only, Jimmy Taylor, who had played at Hinds Junior College in Mississippi in 1955, was scheduled to be the man to take up the offensive slack. A high school all-American at Baton Rouge High, Taylor had spent an auspicious 1954 season on the LSU frosh team but came a cropper in the classroom. This resulted in his re-entering Hinds after a talk with LSU's president. Middleton called in the fullback and put the question to him straight: "Jimmy, if you were sitting in my chair, what would you do?" Taylor answered, "I'd throw me out of school." Middleton promised Taylor he'd be welcomed back to LSU if he made the proper credits at Hinds.

Taylor met his wife, Dixie Jo Pyron of Natchez, at Hinds. Under age, they forged their parents' signatures and eloped. Afterward Jimmy spent the afternoons hitting the line; Dixie, a good student, taught her husband how to hit the books. Nothing came easy for Taylor. When he was ten his dad, an invalid, died, and his mother worked in the alteration department at a Baton Rouge laundry to educate her three sons, of whom Jimmy was the second. Jimmy worked his way through high school delivering newspapers on a bicycle, tossing two routes which got him up at four in the morning and after class kept him occupied until 6:30 in the evening. Many believe that Taylor owed his abnormal leg drive—and his balance—to his days as a newsboy.

As a 170-pound junior at Baton Rouge High, Taylor was used exclusively on defense because the school had runners like Ronnie Quillian and Tommy Bookman ahead of him. When he was a senior, he blossomed as a tailback in the single wing and was scooped up by Gus Tinsley after being wooed by a flock of schools.

Jimmy was 5 feet, 11 inches and a solid two hundred when he reported to LSU for the second time in the fall of 1956. "The fact that

Jimmy Taylor: He earned the respect of "The Great White Father."

he missed spring practice," said backfield coach Carl Maddox, "really put him behind. He spent the early part of the season trying to find himself and we spent it simplifying the offense."

In the first five games, Taylor scored only eight points, but in the final five he scored fifty-one to lead the SEC with fifty-nine. While Jimmy was busy finding himself, LSU dropped six in a row, the first a 9–6 thriller to Texas A & M, perhaps Bear Bryant's best team during his stay at College Station. The Aggies, who went on to an unbeaten season, jumped off to a 9–0 lead before 61,000 in Tiger Stadium and then had to fight off a last-quarter comeback by the Tigers. Sophomore J. W. "Red" Brodnax capped an 84-yard march with a 10-yard run after which the Tigers recovered an onsides kick. When time ran out, LSU was on the Aggie 26. With fifty-six yards in a dozen carries, Brodnax outgained all-America candidate Crow.

The all-out effort against A & M left a thin LSU club easy prey for its next five opponents—Rice, Georgia Tech, Kentucky, Florida, and Ole Miss. Frank Ryan's pitching and the incredible catching of Buddy Dial helped Rice frustrate the flu-ridden Bengals, 23–14; after Taylor put

Taylor over the top in 1956: Jimmy 7, Tulane 6.

LSU ahead 7–6 in the first quarter, powerful Georgia Tech made it a final 39–7 on Grant Field; the Tigers bowed 14–0 to Kentucky, failing to generate any semblance of an offense; they lost to Florida, 21–6, and to Ole Miss (which had trailed 17–14 at half time) by a final score of 46–17.

It was against the Rebs that Taylor arrived. With sixty-one yards in fifteen carries, he scored all of his team's points. The following week, when LSU snapped its losing streak with a 13–0 conquest of Oklahoma A & M, Taylor had 104 yards in a dozen carries. In the next game LSU did its best to make an all-SEC back out of Mississippi State sophomore Billy Stacy. In the course of a 32–13 win, Stacy gained 77 yards running, he passed for 59, kicked for a 43-yard average, returned five punts for 80 yards, two kickoffs for 42, scored three times, and passed for another.

At this stage, a one–seven record had some alumni howling but, like the cavalry from Fort Dodge, Jim Taylor came to the rescue of his coach, a man he called "The Great White Father." He sparked a 21–7 upset of Arkansas, gaining 170 yards, including a 70-yard touchdown jaunt. Then, in the finale against a favored Tulane team which had a 6–3 record and victories over Ole Miss and Mississippi State, Taylor was LSU's one-man show. Jimmy overcame a 6–0 Tulane lead with a touchdown and extra point in the second half. Also, he caught Claude Mason from behind to save a score and intercepted a pass on the LSU 8 to prevent another touchdown.

"The 1956 season was so tough," Jim Corbett liked to say, "even Mike couldn't take it." Well-nigh indestructible, Mike I had lived for twenty

A mighty yawn from Mike III.

years, having survived a tiger-napping by Tulane students and assorted ailments until pneumonia did him in during the 1956 losing streak. Said Corbett: "I received a call early one morning that Mike had passed away. I decided to sit on it for awhile and put Mike on ice, figuring, if the word got out, even the strong-hearted would give up hope. When we finally won a game, Mike's death was announced."

Mike II was born in the Audubon Park Zoo (in the shadow of the Tulane campus) but survived only the 1957 season. When he died of pneumonia in May, 1958, Corbett, after striking out in Detroit and Brooklyn, found Mike III in the Seattle Zoo. Like Mike II, he was purchased for $1,500 (raised by the students) and flown to Baton Rouge by Flying Tiger Airlines, arriving just in time for the national championship season.

Dietzel was building toward 1958; in fact, one 1956 result that made a

3–7 season palatable was LSU's 44–20 victory over the Ole Miss freshmen. He had made a recruiting sweep signing, among others, Max Fugler, 6-foot, 1-inch, 195-pound center from Ferriday, Louisiana, and three homegrown prospects—halfback Johnny Robinson of University High, quarterback Warren Rabb of Baton Rouge High, and halfback Billy Cannon of Istrouma.

Cannon was the prize catch. "He's either the strongest sprinter or the fastest shotputter in the country," said one coach of the 6-foot, 1-inch, 196-pounder who in the spring of 1958 ran a 9.4 100-yard dash and tossed the 16-pound shot 54 feet, 4½ inches, first athlete in history to put together such a double.

It was sheer fate that the paths of Cannon and Dietzel crossed at LSU. The odd set of circumstances which led Dietzel from West Point to Baton Rouge have been related. Less known is the fact that, had it not been for World War II, Cannon undoubtedly would have played his college football at Ole Miss. Billy was born in Philadelphia, Mississippi, an Ole Miss hotbed, in 1937, but when he was five the family moved to Baton Rouge, where his dad took a war defense job.

Cannon was christened Billy Abb for Abb Deweese, lumber company executive in Philadelphia who employed Billy's dad and helped build his home. "I worked a farm in the winter and worked in Mr. Abb's lumber mill in the summer," said Harvey Cannon, Sr. "Billy was our second child and he was supposed to be a girl. When he was ten he used to sneak off to watch Istrouma practice. One of his childhood idols was Paul Miller, who played a lot of tackle for the Tigers. He knew all of the plays and just loved football. When he was in the ninth grade, he was still smaller than the other kids in the neighborhood, so when school ended, he brought home his report card and told us he flunked. My wife cried and then Billy explained he put down the wrong answers on purpose so he'd be big enough to play football when he entered Istrouma. The first year at Istrouma he weighed 138 pounds but played only a little. The next year he was 175 and made all-state."

Billy's high school heroics in track and football were legendary. One time he made five touchdowns in one half against Baton Rouge High. Another night against Bogalusa, on a fake punt, the line opened a hole on the right side, but Billy ran around left end for a touchdown. He left Istrouma with a record-equalling 9.7 in the 100 and a new record in the 12-pound shot, 57 feet, 4 inches.

"I always wanted to go to LSU," he said the day Dietzel beat a raft of other schools battling for his services. Actually, it would have been an upset if he had gone anywhere else, because his dad had been working at LSU since 1952 and had watched his oldest son, Harvey, Jr., go through LSU on a track scholarship.

Billy himself had spent Saturday nights during football games selling soft drinks in Tiger Stadium. "The first game my daddy took me to was LSU-Mississippi State. For weeks afterward, I made out like I was Shorty McWilliams. And I can remember Charley Conerly, too. I would try to pass drinks, make change, and keep my eye on the playing field."

Cannon owed his bowl-'em-over physique to weight training, as did his 1957 sidekick Jimmy Taylor. Alvin Roy, who operates a Baton Rouge health studio, remembers the day Cannon, a 168-pound Istrouma sophomore, walked into his gym. "Fuzzy" Brown, the Istrouma coach, decided to put in a weight training program in 1954, the day after Baton Rouge High walloped him. After he did, his team went through forty-one games without losing to a Louisiana team. You could see Billy expand. He was 187 as a senior and 193 by the time he entered LSU. He was right at 200 for his sophomore season. When Billy reached 200, he could press 270 pounds—and that was only 12 pounds off the Olympic record at that time.

As the 1957 season approached, the prospect of Cannon and Taylor in the same backfield had LSU fans starry eyed. In right-half Red Brodnax, Dietzel also had another tough runner and surefire blocker, and in quarterback Win Turner, returning after sitting out 1956, an unspectacular but dependable performer. "In 1956, we had to dream up ways of moving the football," explained Dietzel. "We used flankers and spreads. By the time we faced Tulane, we had straightened out and won without doing anything fancy." Dietzel's intentions for 1957 were to try to move it without any gimmicks, but that depended on how well the line jelled. The right side with end Billy Smith, tackle Al Aucoin, and guard Ed Cassidy was solid, but there were holes on the left that needed filling, created by the departure of Leggett, Scully, Parker, Ziegler, and Graham. Dietzel planned to use alternate units ("You can't play football today with a bunch of iron men.") but he feared the drop-off between the first and second teams. Apparently, the prognosticators did too, because, despite the fact Taylor was a proven quantity and Cannon had all the earmarks of a superstar, LSU was picked to finish last in the SEC.

The week of the opener against Rice half of the ball club came down with the flu, but this was forgotten when Taylor scored twice to give the Tigers a 14–0 lead in the second quarter, a lead that King Hill cut to 14–7 at half time with a touchdown pass. But the bug took over and Rice dominated play, walking out of Baton Rouge a 20–14 winner. For the conference opener with Alabama the following week, only 32,000 showed in Tiger Stadium and they went away spreading the word on Cannon. He was for real. After Taylor scored and Brodnax took a pass from Turner to make it 14–0, Billy showed the home folks his dazzling speed for the first time as a varsity player. He zipped around end and simply outran his pursuers on a 53-yard gallop. A few minutes later, back to punt on fourth down, he juggled the snap and again out-legged every red jersey in hailing distance on a 73-yard scoring run.

Cannon embroidered on this reputation seven days later in Lubbock, Texas. Just before half time, Johnny Robinson caught a pass to send LSU to the dressing room 7–7 with a highly-charged Texas Tech club. Then came the fireworks. In the third quarter Cannon took a pass in the flat and seemed to hurdle tacklers as he blitzed fifty-nine yards down the sidelines for a score. The Tigers missed the point, and when Tech scored its second touchdown it nudged ahead 14–13. Afterward, everyone was second guessing the Red Raider coaches for what happened next. They kicked off to Cannon. Billy took it on the 3 and charted a course straight up the middle. By the time he reached midfield, the race was over. Billy's 97-yard sprint which gave LSU a 19–14 win came on the heels of Russia's launching of Sputnik 1, as leading sportswriters compared Sputnik and Cannon. There was no question that Billy had LSU fans in orbit.

A record crowd of 63,000, almost twice as many as were on hand for Alabama, turned out for Georgia Tech's invasion of Tiger Stadium fully expecting Cannon to keep his hot hand. Obviously, Bobby Dodd had his club outside-conscious, so instead of watching Cannon sweep the flanks, the fans saw Taylor pummel the middle for three touchdowns in a 21–13 upset. When Cannon scored twice and Taylor once next week in a 21–0 conquest of Kentucky, LSU found itself with a 4–1 record, 3–0 in the SEC.

Gradually lack of depth took its toll, resulting in four straight defeats.

J. W. Brodnax picks up yardage against Texas Tech, 1957.

Despite a 99-yard kickoff return by Brodnax, longest in LSU history, the Tigers wilted in dropping a 22–14 decision to Florida. They were out-hustled by Vandy, 7–0, in Nashville; dropped a tough 14–12 battle to Ole Miss in Oxford; and took a 14–6 whipping from Mississippi State in Baton Rouge. In many respects, the loss to Ole Miss was LSU's finest effort of the season, except, perhaps its closing 25–6 triumph over Tulane.

Rated as a heavy underdog to the Rebels, the Tigers jumped to a 6–0 lead on a 60-yard run by Taylor. After Ole Miss went ahead 7–6, Cannon slipped Brodnax a reverse on a punt return, and as all of the Rebels ganged Billy, Red raced untouched fifty-three yards and LSU led 12–7. In the fourth quarter, Bobby Franklin fired a touchdown pass to Don Williams for the winning points. The Tigers were driving as the game ended; in fact, Cannon caught a pass on the Ole Miss 15, only to have a holding penalty nullify it and keep LSU out of field goal range.

When a 4–1 team becomes 4–5, alumni talk, and as Dietzel approached the Tulane windup, he was conscious of the barbs. "If I don't win this game," he confided to a friend, "I'm through as a football coach." With a flare for the dramatic, he was possibly overstating the case, but not by much. Tulane was coming into the game with a 2–7 mark and it was coming into Tiger Stadium. So LSU had better win. For the second year in a row, it was Taylor who wrecked Andy Pilney's Greenies, this time with touchdown runs of forty-eight and thirty-two yards, giving him a 1957 total of eighty-six points (tops in the country) and 762 yards (tops in the SEC). Taylor's LSU swan song was memorable—171 yards in seventeen carries.

A few weeks later, Green Bay made the consensus all-America back its No. 2 draft choice. "With the ball under his arm," said Dietzel, "Jimmy Taylor is the finest player I've ever seen."

From the glory days of Doc Fenton, the cry of those perennial LSU optimists had been "1908 and next year." However, if this hunger for an unbeaten team was to be satisfied in 1958, it would be over the red faces of sportswriters and sportscasters taking part in the Associated Press' preseason poll. With only fifteen lettermen and three seniors returning from a team which had won five and lost five, not to mention an all-America fullback as well, no one expected LSU to get any first-place votes. But one might have figured on a little more than five points, good only for 35th spot.

No. 35 suited Paul Dietzel just fine. He knew what he had in Billy Cannon, and after spring drills he was convinced the wing-T, which had carried Forest Evashevski and Iowa to the heights, was suited to what he had on hand. "We are less experienced than we were in '57 and we're not as large," said Dietzel, "but we are faster. We hope to take advantage of our breakaway runners, Cannon, Robinson, and [Don] Purvis, and we hope to make use of quarterbacks who can run as well as pass, Rabb and [Durel] Matherne. This is the first time we'll have quarterbacks who'll be respected as runners."

The big change in the spring was expected—shifting 200-pound Red Brodnax from halfback to fullback. This move gave Dietzel a No. 1 backfield of Rabb, Robinson, Cannon, and Brodnax, backed by a second unit of Matherne, Purvis, Donnie Daye, and Tommy Davis. Daye was a sophomore from Ferriday, Louisiana; Davis a 24-year-old veteran returning after a stint in the army.

No more than single wing plays run with a man under center, the wing-T seemed to take hold nicely during drills; in fact, Dietzel was pleased to see the deception it offered in the way of counters, reverses, men-in-motion. Deception made up for the lack of size up front where the tackles were in the neighborhood of two hundred pounds. When fall practice began, Dietzel had every intention of alternating two units, both of which would play both ways since, under the substitution rules then in force, a player could re-enter a game only twice each quarter. "The 1956 Ole Miss game, more than anything else, taught me the value of depth," said Dietzel. "When you're ahead 17–14 at half time and lose 46–17, you learn something. At staff meetings in the fall, however, it seemed we had only sixteen boys we felt we could trust as two-way players. The more we looked at our squad, the more we came to the conclusion we had players, after our first eleven, who could play one way. Finally we decided to put together two units and work them one way about 80 percent of the time in practice. Actually, we had no idea if we'd be able to get away with it in a ball game so we decided to play it by ear."

The second week of September, the squad listings drew more than a cursory glance. Typed in red letters in column one were the words "Chinese Bandits," in column two, the word "White," and in column three, the word "Gold." Later, through a misunderstanding on the part of a sportswriter, "Gold" was shortened to "Go."

"Our first unit always worked in white jerseys," Dietzel explained, "so the name was no surprise. The team we decided to play on offense worked only in gold jerseys so that was no surprise either. But the Chinese Bandit label for our defensive group that worked in red jerseys took some explaining." At a squad meeting after the breakdown into three units, Dietzel told of his feeling toward two-platoon football when he was assisting Sid Gillman at Cincinnati. "I was trying to come up with something to brighten the practice days of our defensive team when I came across a line in the comic strip 'Terry and The Pirates.' One sinister Oriental character said something to the effect that 'Chinese

The first Bandits. Back row, Andy Bourgeois, Darryl Jenkins, John Langan, Merle Schexnaildre, Henry Lee Roberts, Hart Bourque. Front, Mel Branch, Emile Fournet, Tommy Lott, Duane Leopard, Gaynell Kinchen.

bandits are the most vicious people in the world.' So I decided to call the defensive club Chinese bandits and the kids seemed to take pride in their name. I hope you will, too."

At mealtime, the coaches began to notice that the players on each team were beginning to gravitate toward one another. "We were still playing it by ear," said Dietzel with a September 20 opener against Rice in Houston bearing down. Although there was some shuffling of positions once the season began, here's how LSU lined up in 1958:

White Team

	Age	Ht.	Wt.	Class	Ltr.	Hometown
LE Billy Hendrix	22	6-0	185	Sr.	2	Rayville
LT Lynn LeBlanc	20	6-2	201	Jr.	1	Crowley
LG Larry Kahlden	22	6-1	210	Sr.	2	Weimar, Tex.
C Max Fugler	21	6-1	203	Jr.	1	Ferriday
RG Ed McCreedy	20	6-1	195	Soph.	0	Biloxi, Miss.
RT Charles "Bo" Strange	19	6-1	202	Soph.	0	Baton Rouge
RE Mickey Mangham	19	6-1	192	Soph.	0	Kensington, Md.
QB Warren Rabb	21	6-0	190	Jr.	1	Baton Rouge
LH Billy Cannon	21	6-1	204	Jr.	1	Baton Rouge
RH Johnny Robinson	20	6-0	185	Jr.	1	Baton Rouge
FB J. W. Brodnax	22	6-0	202	Sr.	2	Bastrop

Go Team

	Age	Ht	Wt	Class		Hometown
LE Scotty McClain	20	6–2	180	Jr.	1	Smackover, Ark.
LT Dave McCarty	21	6–2	200	Jr.	0	Rayville
LG Al Dampier	20	6–1	201	Soph.	0	Clayton
C Bobby Greenwood	20	5–10	195	Soph.	0	Lake Charles
RG Mike Stupka	21	6–0	205	Jr.	0	Bogalusa
Manson Nelson	20	5–9	185	Jr.	0	Ferriday
RT Jack Frayer	21	6–2	210	Jr.	0	Toledo, Ohio
RE Don Norwood	20	6–3	202	Jr.	1	Baton Rouge
QB Durel Matherne	21	5–11	188	Jr.	0	Lutcher
LH Don Purvis	20	5–7	160	Jr.	1	Crystal Springs, Miss.
RH Donnie Daye	19	5–10	184	Soph.	0	Ferriday
FB Tommy Davis	24	6–0	204	Jr.	1	Shreveport

Chinese Bandits

	Age	Ht	Wt	Class		Hometown
LE Andy Bourgeois	20	5–10	174	Soph.	0	New Orleans
LT Mel Branch	21	6–1	210	Jr.	0	DeRidder
LG Emile Fournet	20	5–11	195	Jr.	0	Bogalusa
C John Langan	21	6–3	183	Jr.	1	Carbondale, Ill.
RG Tommy Lott	20	5–9	188	Jr.	1	Texarkana, Ark.
RT Duane Leopard	20	6–2	205	Jr.	1	Baton Rouge
RE Gaynell Kinchen	20	6–3	196	Soph.	0	Baton Rouge
QB Darryl Jenkins	20	6–1	163	Soph.	0	Franklinton
LH Henry Lee Roberts	19	6–0	172	Soph.	0	North Little Rock
RH Hart Bourque	20	5–8	165	Soph.	0	Gonzales
FB Merle Schexnaildre	22	5–9	182	Jr.	0	Houma

Looking back on 1958, there were three significant aspects on the three Tiger teams: (1) none of the so-called thirty-four "starters" weighed more than 210 pounds; (2) the right side of the White Team line was all-sophomore; (3) among the first thirty-four were seven juniors who failed to letter in 1957.

Biggest White Team surprise was Mickey Mangham who came to LSU with the idea of studying petroleum engineering. All-county as a guard on the Bethesda-Chevy Chase, Maryland, high school football team, Mangham went out for the freshman team and became one of the top ends, but was offered no scholarship. In the spring of 1958, Dietzel was still not conscious of Mickey's being around. He once remarked: "Everytime I asked Abner Wimberly about a certain end, he'd say something like: 'He's doing all right but this Mangham's really something.'" First, it was "Who's Mangham?" and, before the end of spring practice, it was "Mickey, you've got a scholarship."

Bo Strange, an all-American at Baton Rouge High, teamed with Lynn LeBlanc to form the lightest tackle combination in the SEC. Son of assistant coach Clarence "Pop" Strange, a tackle in 1935–37, Bo expected to be compared to his dad and Bandit guard Emile Fournet expected the same treatment in regard to his older brother Sid, the 1954 all-American. Both held up their end.

The city of Baton Rouge was delirious over the No. 1 backfield which was three parts homegrown. "I'll never forget how Cannon, Robinson, and Rabb worked on their own during the summer," said Dietzel. "They were out practically every day tossing the ball around and polishing their ball handling. When they reported in the fall, they formed a classic backfield, handling a new formation with poise and confidence. Each came from a different high school—Billy from Istrouma, Johnny from University High, and Warren from Baton Rouge High—but they were united by one simple ingredient: pride."

It rained in Houston throughout the day on September 20 and, although the showers ceased by the time Rice and LSU opened their football seasons before a damp crowd of 45,000, the underdog Tigers had reason to believe the slow footing would blunt their biggest advantage, speed. The assumption was incorrect. Scoring once in each quarter and displaying unusual September poise, LSU impressively whipped a team which had beaten it two years in a row. During the course of a

The 1958 White Team. Standing, Johnny Robinson, J. W. Brodnax, Warren Rabb, Billy Cannon. Kneeling, Mickey Mangham, Bo Strange, Ed McCreedy, Max Fugler, Larry Kahlden, Lynn LeBlanc, Red Hendrix.

26–6 victory, there were repeated illustrations of the three factors which were to characterize LSU in 1958—speed, deception, and pursuit. "I don't know if I've ever seen a team with more overall speed," said Alabama's Bear Bryant, on hand to scout the Tigers, his opponent the following week in a game that was to mark his return to his alma mater. "Everyone expected the backfield to have it but the line had it too—and on a wet field." When Bryant was asked if the wing-T helped LSU, Bear replied: "I think LSU helps the wing-T."

In command from the start, the Tigers punched forty-nine yards in ten plays for the first touchdown; traveled thirty-seven yards in seven plays for their second; got their third after a 30-yard punt return by Cannon to the Rice 5; and went thirty yards for the last one after Mel Branch recovered an Owl fumble. Rabb swept end from the 9 for the first score and swept it again, this time from the 7, for the last score. Brodnax jabbed two yards for the second touchdown and Robinson took it across in the third quarter following Cannon's punt return, a return Billy set up moments earlier when he punted dead on the 1-foot line. On the return, Cannon waited until a group of blue-shirted Owls relaxed. Then he stepped in, scooped up the football, and raced past a host of wide-eyed Ricemen. LSU made use of the halfback pass, Robinson to Cannon, and unveiled a new wrinkle that confused the Owls, sending a flanked halfback in motion toward the football and behind the remaining backs.

Dietzel was not going overboard. "If I said I wasn't pleased, I'd be lying," he said. "We made some foolish mistakes but we covered them up with hustle." He cited as the most pleasing prospect of opening night, "the way the second and third group performed." The White Team, Go Team and Chinese Bandit labels were not being used publicly yet. "Actually, there was still plenty of shifting going around," said Don "Scooter" Purvis. "For example, I played some with the Go Team and some with the Bandits against Rice. So did Hart Bourque." Actually, the "birth of the Bandits" was at hand.

| LSU | 7 | 6 | 6 | 7 | – | 26 |
| Rice | 0 | 0 | 0 | 6 | – | 6 |

Mobile was all tensed up on September 27. Bear Bryant had come home, so it was only natural—considering his rebuilding jobs at Kentucky and Texas A & M—for Alabama faithful, who longed for a return to the glory days under Wallace Wade and Frank Thomas, to expect an instant miracle.

Bear had inherited a 2–7–1 ball club from "Ears" Whitworth, but when the Crimson Tide ran onto the field for its pregame workout it was obvious the players were ten feet in the air. Bear had them pumped for a super effort and he had come up with a few gimmicks. One was a quick shift into an unbalanced line; another was to number an end in the 40 instead of 80 series to confuse the defense. Playing like a bunch of wild men, the underdog Tide carried the fight to LSU during a scoreless first quarter and in the second period were presented with sudden good fortune. Cannon broke through the middle for thirteen yards but, hit hard on the 50, Billy fumbled, and Bama back Duff Morrison grabbed the ball in mid-air and raced to the Tiger 5 before being chased out of bounds. Dietzel then made perhaps his biggest gamble of 1958. He took out his first unit and sent in the Bandits. Four plays later, having gained only a yard in three downs, the Tide booted a field goal into end zone seats which, a bit later, collapsed just as LSU's offense had.

The second half was all LSU. "We went to the counter play and to double reverses off the wing-T, something we hadn't showed against Rice," explained quarterback Warren Rabb. Faking to Cannon and handing to Robinson and then reversing the procedure, Rabb had Bama's defenders going for the first man through on an eleven-play drive that covered sixty-seven yards. The payoff came when Warren fired a 9-yard pass to Robinson who made a leaping catch between two red shirts. Cannon, who picked up eighty-six yards in twelve carries, scored in the fourth quarter on a crunching run of twelve yards, after being sprung loose by Larry Kahlden's block.

"Now we know we're a fourth-quarter team," said Dietzel, who had asked the players for a victory over Bryant "as a personal favor." Bear, whose Crimson Tide could not get beyond the LSU 41 other than on Morrison's run with the fumble, grumbled: "We lost because they knocked our butts off."

| LSU | 0 | 0 | 7 | 6 | – | 13 |
| Alabama | 0 | 3 | 0 | 0 | – | 3 |

Johnny Robinson on the receiving end against the Crimson Tide, 1958.

BILLY CANNON

Coming into Tiger Stadium for its first home appearance against Hardin-Simmons, LSU had been jumped from sixteenth to thirteenth in the Associated Press rankings and dropped from thirteenth to seventeenth by United Press International. A crowd of 45,000 turned out and was quickly treated to a pair of sharp first-quarter scoring drives, one for sixty-five yards engineered by Rabb, another for forty-three directed by Durel Matherne. Both quarterbacks did the scoring.

Early in the second quarter, Sammy Baugh's pass-happy visitors swept ninety-five yards to a touchdown, traveling almost exclusively by air. Just before intermission, with the score 13–6, the Tigers got a 20–6 cushion on an 11-yard gallop by Cannon which came after LSU took possession when a Cowboy punter fumbled the snap. The Tigers played indifferently in the second half and, after it was over, Dietzel declared: "This is a good one to get behind you. It's always tough trying to convince anyone Hardin-Simmons has a good team."

LSU	13	7	0	0	–	20
Hardin-Simmons	0	6	0	0	–	6

The Tigers still had not impressed the pollsters enough to crack the top ten—the AP had them eleventh, UPI fifteenth—when they moved the show on the road once again, this time to the Orange Bowl for a game with Miami. At LSU headquarters, one bellhop mistook Chinese Bandits Bourgeois and Bourque for high school players. They were soon more appreciated. Before a turnout of 40,614, the Tigers dazzled a much larger Hurricane club with offensive speed and defensive pursuit. In the opening quarter Purvis jitterbugged fifty-one yards to a touchdown to launch a 41–0 rout. In the second quarter Rabb passed fifteen yards to Billy Hendrix and in the third Brodnax cracked over from the three after which Rabb passed to Mangham for a two-point play, LSU's first under the new NCAA rule. A 20-point fourth quarter—Cannon scored once and Tommy Davis twice—completed the whitewash.

It had been a banner evening for the No. 2 offensive unit and, when a writer heard Dietzel refer to it as his "Gold Team," he misunderstood—which is how the "Go Team" was born.

LSU	6	7	8	20	–	41
Miami	0	0	0	0	–	0

Not since 1937 had an LSU team won four games in a row. The smashing victory over Miami elevated the Tigers to ninth place in both AP and UPI polls, and a record Baton Rouge turnout of 65,000 (it beat the 1957 crowd for Georgia Tech) welcomed the team back home for its annual scrap with Kentucky. A Wildcat team which the week before yielded stubbornly to top-ranked defending national champion Auburn by an 8–0 score, soon found itself surrounded by Tigers. LSU swept fifty-nine yards the first time it got the football, Brodnax scoring from the 1. After the visitors tied it, 7–7, the Tigers went fifty-three yards in six plays with Rabb passing the last eighteen yards to Hendrix.

Then the three Tiger teams took their toll. In the third period Mickey Mangham recovered a fumble on the Kentucky 24 and, two plays later, Cannon sprinted nineteen yards for a score. Later in the quarter Matherne pitched five yards to Don Norwood to make it 26–7 after which Cannon tacked on a 2-yard touchdown run in the final quarter.

"Last week we went out and whipped Auburn's line," said Coach Blanton Collier. "Tonight we wilted." Kentucky halfback Bobby Cravens said: "Before any team can beat LSU, they've got to find the ball." Obviously, the Wildcats had problems. In the first half the Tigers ran outside, setting two backs as flankers. In the second half, when Kentucky became outside-conscious, Cannon, who wound up the evening with 108 yards, killed the visitors up the middle.

Talk of White Team, Go Team, and Bandits suddenly dominated everyone's conversation. Salesman Dietzel was having himself a field day. He read the Bandits a letter from one of their honorable ancestors, who had played on the not-so-famous defensive unit Paul coached at the University at Cincinnati. A Memphis disc jockey wrote a Chinese chant which was introduced at a pep rally the night before the Homecoming game against Florida. The windup went: "Gonna stop a TD . . . chop-chop. . . ."

"We have confidence in the Bandits," said Dietzel. "They kept coming up to me and saying Kentucky hadn't made a first down on them, something the White Team couldn't say." Dietzel revealed statistics showing how the three-team idea allowed the Tigers to keep fresh troops in the game. With the exception of Hardin-Simmons, Billy Cannon and company played for little more than half the game. The minutes-played breakdown went like this:

	White Team	Go Team	Bandits
Rice	30	14	16
Alabama	35	12	13
Hardin-Simmons	42	8	10
Miami	30	19	11
Kentucky	33	13	14

LSU	7	6	13	6	–	32
Kentucky	7	0	0	0	–	7

Beating Kentucky impressively jumped the Tigers to fifth in the UPI ratings and to third in the AP, highest any LSU team had been since 1937. Assistant George Terry warned that Florida, a team which had lost only to Mississippi State, would not be worn down by LSU's manner of substitution. "They used forty-six players against Tulane," said Terry. Clearly, it was a question of the Tigers' being able to handle a line which had a decided edge in size and experience.

A Homecoming crowd of 63,000 (the Tigers had yet to play to a sellout) gathered to see if Dietzel could break his Florida jinx, three losses in three tries. Before the Kentucky game, Dietzel said: "The game that worries me most is Florida. Why? Well, because I know the boys will get ready for Kentucky because of the game they played against Auburn. They'll be up for Ole Miss and State because they know what to expect from them. But Florida is going to be a tough selling job."

It was tough all right. In a game in which defense held the upper hand, Cannon cracked through for second-quarter touchdown. Billy capped a drive which he ignited with a 32-yard punt return by running over all-America tackle Vel Heckman on a fourth-and-one situation. LSU managed to protect its 7–0 lead until the Gators mounted a drive midway through the fourth quarter and clicked on a 14-yard scoring pass. With a 7–7 tie in prospect, the Bandits forced a Florida punt and Darryl Jenkins fair-caught the football on the Gator 43. From there it was Cannon's knifing through tackle on runs of eight, four, and seven yards that carried the ball to the Gator 19. Earlier in the quarter, Dietzel got

BILLY CANNON

Florida, 1958: Cannon runs over Gators on a fourth-and-one situation to score LSU's only touchdown.

Tommy Davis off the bench and told him to start warming his kicking leg. Later, during the LSU drive, Charley McClendon went over to Davis and asked if his leg was warm. "If I warm it any more," said the 23-year-old veteran, "it'll fall off."

When Florida braced on its 19, Dietzel waved Tommy into the game. With 2:59 showing on the clock, a nonchalant Davis told Warren Rabb to "just tilt it back a little," and he then booted a perfect three-pointer, touching off a wild demonstration among the Homecoming throng. After it was over, Dietzel said: "If there's a better college football player in the United States than Billy Cannon, I'd like to see him. His blocking was vicious and he saved a touchdown in the first quarter when he nailed a Florida runner after a run of thirty-one yards. This is definitely the finest team we've played so far."

| LSU | 0 | 7 | 0 | 3 | – | 10 |
| Florida | 0 | 0 | 0 | 7 | – | 7 |

On Monday morning, newspaper offices throughout the state were badgered by Tiger faithful demanding "Who's No. 1?" It was like waiting for election results. When the final precinct was heard from, sure enough, LSU had made it, made it, that is, in the eyes of the sportswriters and sportscasters voting in the AP poll. Third behind Army and Ohio State after beating Kentucky, the Tigers swept past both teams, the Cadets losing ground when Pitt played them to a 14–14 tie. It was a different story over at UPI, a poll conducted by a board of college coaches. Unimpressed with the victory over Florida, UPI kept the Tigers in fifth place, all of which put LSU students to work on Tuesday when a large group turned out to hang the wire service in effigy.

What did Dietzel think of the No. 1 rating? With one eye on Ole Miss, he said: "I think any coach wants his team to be No. 1. It gives it that much more pride in its accomplishments." Unbeaten in six games, Johnny Vaught's Rebels were ranked sixth by the AP and UPI, setting the stage for the first sellout in the history of the 67,500-seat Tiger Stadium. Some 15,000 end zone seats were put on sale Monday and gobbled up within two hours. At 4 A.M., there were more than a hundred people lined up outside the ticket office. The early sellout naturally increased the demand. Some people were willing to swap television sets for tickets. One fan in particular made an offer of $800 for "eight good sideline seats."

On Wednesday the Baton Rouge campus was "bombed" with "Go to Hell, LSU" leaflets, whereupon 3,000 students marched into practice to cheer the team. The following day, no doubt taking the hint, 1,500 Ole Miss students interrupted Rebel drills.

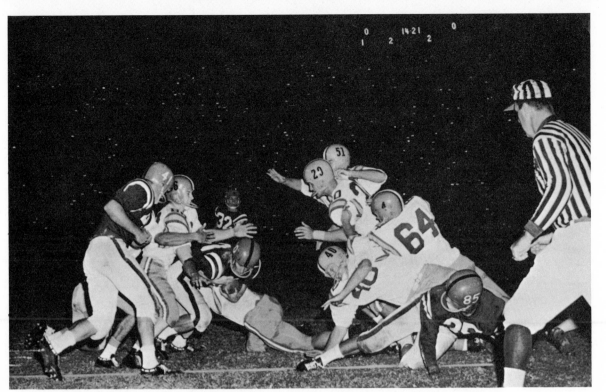

Ole Miss, 1958: Tigers, led by Mickey Mangham, halt Bobby Franklin at the goal line, the first of five futile Rebel tries.

The tense atmosphere greeting the 8 P.M. kickoff was readily apparent. Keyed to a fever pitch, LSU surprised the Rebs on the first series of downs when Rabb rifled a 40-yard pass to Robinson who had beaten the Ole Miss secondary. Johnny dropped it right in front of the LSU bench. If the game illustrated anything, it underlined a standby psychological stimulant used by many a football coach, which says: "When the going gets tough, the tough get going."

For LSU, it got tough at the start of the second quarter when Ole Miss halfback Kent Lovelace slashed to the LSU 2-yard line, from which point the Rebs had four cracks at a touchdown. On the first play quarterback Bobby Franklin, behind a huge Ole Miss line, jabbed to the 1-foot line and was promptly confronted with a painful decision: LSU was offsides. Did Franklin want to play a second-and-goal from the 1-foot-line or a first-and-goal from the 1? Bobby took a look at the football twelve inches away from the chalkline and decided to decline the penalty. He felt no team could deny Ole Miss twelve inches in three tries. On second down Franklin sent Lovelace up the middle where he was greeted by the proverbial stone wall. On third down Bobby called on Charley Flowers, a bruising junior fullback, who barely made it back to the line of scrimmage. On fourth down, with everyone in the stadium on their feet, it was Lovelace again off tackle, but the Tigers penetrated and he was snowed under on the 2. Somehow LSU had held. When Dietzel graded the movies the following day, he still found it hard to believe. "When you get shoulder-to-shoulder in an eight-man goal line defense, you can't afford a mistake," he said. "We didn't make one. Max Fugler made key tackles on two downs. When they sent Flowers up the middle, the line held and Cannon met him head on and knocked him back. Another time Rabb came up after the initial stop was made and halted progress. It was an incredible effort."

After that goal line reception, Johnny Vaught's Rebels were never the same. They battled but seemed to lack their first-quarter fire. Late in the second period the Tigers recovered a fumble on the Ole Miss 21. This time Dietzel found himself confronted with a decision when LSU reached the Rebel 4 with a fourth-and-goal and only thirty seconds left in the half. Instead of trying for a field goal, Rabb decided to throw for it, rolling out to his left. When Ole Miss blanketed the receivers, he decided to run. Guard Marvin Terrell hit Rabb on the 2 and apparently had him nailed when end Warren Ball, in hot pursuit, hit Warren from behind, carrying everyone into the end zone with his momentum.

With a 7–0 lead, LSU threw up a porcupine defense in the second half and was the picture of an ultraconservative ball club. With five minutes left, the Go Team launched a drive which quarterback Durel Matherne climaxed with the same play on which Rabb had scored, an option around the left side. This time Matherne got into the end zone on his own power.

Losing to Dietzel for the first time in four games, Vaught said: "We played better in this game than we did in beating Texas 39–7 in last season's Sugar Bowl. LSU took advantage of the breaks which is what you're supposed to do."

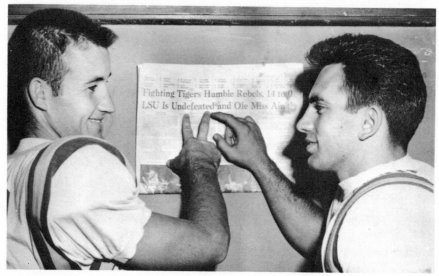

Warren Rabb and Durel Matherne: Their touchdowns did it.

It was the first time Ole Miss had been blanked in fifteen games and Dietzel never ceased to marvel at the defense. "One time Fugler tackled the quarterback and made him pitch," he said. "Then he got off the ground and tackled the ball carrier. He actually made two tackles on the same play." Dietzel also cited the performance of Bandit tackle Mel Branch. "Once he spun out of a double-team block, hit the quarterback, made him fumble and then fell on the football after a chase. The Bandit effort was truly amazing. After each play, all eleven men seemed to be within three yards of the ball."

According to Dietzel, Ole Miss's plan was "to butt us out of there." He continued: "This year we had the manpower to match them. We stopped them on the outside because our ends kept their feet. Branch, LeBlanc, and Mangham did great jobs. They tried the run-pass option eleven times but they only threw three times because we had the pass covered." With no completions in three attempts, it was perhaps the only time in Ole Miss history the Rebels failed to hit on at least one pass.

LSU	0	7	0	7	–	14
Ole Miss	0	0	0	0	–	0

Baton Rouge, of course, was in a state of delirium. Everyone seemed to be too busy celebrating when the UPI refused to come around, keeping once-tied Army with its Lonely End in first place and lifting the Tigers to second. At Jack Sabin's Goalpost Restaurant, on the fringe of the campus, the advertisement went up: "Confucius say: Join Chinese Bandits—Keep Spirit Rolling." Sabin offered 1,000 free coolie hats "to ancestral followers nation number one team" and had to buy another 1,100 to satisfy customers. Bowl talk began and athletic director Jim Corbett was forced to announce he could not accept ticket orders because no agreement had been made with anyone, not yet. Bowl talk, of course, worried Dietzel who feared a post-Ole Miss letdown against Duke.

In the first quarter, he had cause to worry. Duke stopped a Tiger drive and then mounted one of its own—a 63-yard march in ten plays that sent the visitors ahead 6–0 and cast a pall over the 63,000 souls in Tiger Stadium. On the first play after the kickoff, however, LSU traveled sixty-three yards in one play, a pass from Rabb to Cannon. Billy outraced the Blue Devil secondary, gathering the ball in on the 25 and loping over for the score.

"We were handling them easy," said Duke guard George Dutrow, "and they seemed to lack enthusiasm but, when they hit that pass, they took on new life and were a different club." After the demoralizer which tied the score 6–6, Duke made three second-quarter mistakes which put it out of the game:

1. Bandit guard Emile Fournet broke in to block a quick kick which Gaynell "Gus" Kinchen recovered on the Duke 2. Dietzel, to the delight of the fans, left the Bandits in the game and fullback Merle Schexnaildre scored quickly on an off-tackle smash.

2. A penalty followed by a poor kick gave the Tigers the ball on the Duke 35, and in four plays Red Brodnax made it 20–6 from the 1.

3. Mickey Mangham recovered a fumble on the Duke 40 and, five plays later, Rabb passed eight yards to Red Hendrix to make it 28–6.

Still charged up, LSU came out in the third quarter, ran Cannon wide twice, and then sent him in motion. When the Blue Devil halfbacks flew to the outside to meet Billy, Robinson darted off tackle on a quickie and went forty-five yards to score. Although its doom was sealed, Duke battled back for two touchdowns and then watched Cannon step twenty-five yards and Matherne run eight to put the finishing touches on a 50–18 victory. This was Duke's most lopsided defeat since Davis and Blanchard sparked Army to a 48–13 victory in 1945. "We've met bigger teams, physically stronger teams, but never anyone quite so fast," said Coach Bill Murray. "Definitely, they're deserving of No. 1."

LSU	6	22	8	14	–	50
Duke	6	0	6	6	–	18

Even though the Blue Devils actually outgained LSU—353 yards to 285—UPI finally conceded, possibly because Duke had beaten Illinois and lost to Notre Dame by a scant 9–7 margin. Because the Tigers now were unanimously acclaimed the nation's top college team, Dietzel didn't need the reminder he received from a headline in the Shreveport *Times*—"Tigers Now Occupying Precarious Pinnacle"—to remind him that Mississippi State spelled trouble.

Actually, everything coming up to the Saturday night kickoff in Jackson's Hinds Stadium looked gloomy. Afternoon rains had left the field looking like soup and Wade Walker's Maroons, with a 3–4 record, came bouncing onto the field like a team with nothing to lose. In a hole from the start, the Tigers had the ball for only seven plays in the first quarter, starting from their 5 twice and from their 12 on another occasion. After fumbles gave State four scoring chances, the Maroons finally cashed in, claiming a Cannon bobble on the Tiger 22 with Billy Stacy scoring two plays later on an 11-yard end sweep. The extra point was wide but, on the muddy Mississippi battleground, six points looked like a boxcar figure.

It took a sudden change of fortune in the third quarter to put LSU back in the game. Captain Red Hendrix pounced on a Stacy fumble on the Maroon 34 and, on the first play, Brodnax shot up the middle for fourteen yards. In short jabs, the Tigers nudged the ball to State's 5

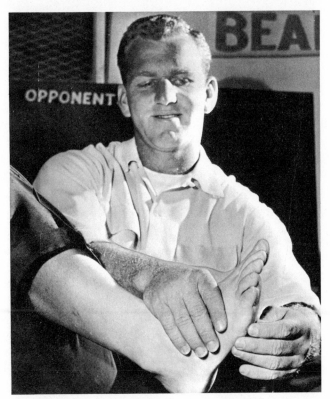

Tommy Davis—and the most important foot of 1958.

where LSU faced an excruciatingly tense fourth-and-goal situation, one of national championship proportions. Rabb rolled out to his left and, just for an instant, spotted Hendrix in the end zone sprinting for the sideline. "It hit my right hand," said Red, "and I was able to control it. Then I pulled it into me and just hugged it." Stacy, who saw the play developing, had the senior end from Rayville covered or thought he did. "I had my hand up," he said, "but Rabb put the ball just over my fingertips."

This left the matter completely up to Tommy Davis. "I hit it squarely," he said. "It didn't go as high as they usually do but it got over that bar and that's all that counts." That night, it was all that counted.

Rabb moaned about the conditions. "We planned to go wide and throw the ball, but the mud changed all that. We had to stick to simple stuff." Dietzel felt lucky to get his mud-caked team out of Jackson with its streak still intact. Looking at the scoreboard as he was leaving the stadium, he said: "What does it matter—7–6 or 70–6?"

| LSU | 0 | 0 | 7 | 0 | – | 7 |
| Mississippi State | 0 | 6 | 0 | 0 | – | 6 |

A Tulane team which had played spotty football in winning three and losing six was in a classic ambush position as the last hurdle in LSU's race toward a national championship. With talented Richie Petitbon at quarterback, Andy Pilney's Green Wave had played Texas and Ole

Miss off their feet before losing, had upset Navy, and had defeated Alabama the week before Bama upset Georgia Tech. However, Tulane's undoing came against Vanderbilt—not in the game itself but on the train ride home from Nashville. Feeling low after a 12–0 defeat, Greenie halfback Claude "Boo" Mason told Cro Duplantier of the New Orleans *States-Item:* "We'll beat LSU because they'll choke." Previously, Dietzel had said: "The Tigers are easy to get up for Tulane. They like to play the Greenies because they know many of the boys and this always makes for a heated rivalry." When he read Mason's quote in the *States-Item*, Dietzel suddenly realized how easy his selling job would be. Mason's slip resembled the proverbial red cape in the hands of the matador; in fact, the word "choke" was so powerful that all Dietzel needed during the week was gentle reminders. Partly because Tulane enjoyed the home field advantage in Sugar Bowl Stadium, but mostly because Tulane had shown flashes of excellent football, the unbeaten Tigers were favored by only a touchdown.

LSU's ranking, combined with the Deep South's oldest rivalry, resulted in a record SEC crowd of 83,221, a record which figures to remain since Tulane inadvertently sold 200 extra end zone tickets. For the first half, it seemed that LSU might break it open, but the Greenies were living up to the advance billing given them by Bear Bryant who said: "They're the best defensive team I've seen this season." The Tigers took a 6–0 lead to the dressing room—a drive climaxed by a 5-yard run by Cannon—but the opening thirty minutes of action was highlighted by the punting of Tommy Davis, who averaged fifty-three yards on four kicks and once, standing on his 15, punted into the Tulane end zone.

The dam burst early in the third period when the Tigers put the rush on Petitbon, and Max Fugler cut in front of the Tulane left end to intercept on the Wave 40. Max returned ten yards and, in eight plays, Rabb scored by faking to a halfback and bootlegging it around right end from the 8. Two more third-quarter scores quickly followed—a 34-yard run by Robinson and an 8-yard gallop by Cannon to make it 27–0. Tulane mistakes paved the way for each touchdown and the end wasn't in sight. Five fourth-period touchdowns finished the burial rites. Purvis took a screen pass from Matherne and zigzagged fifty-four yards; Robinson made a breathtaking catch of a 45-yard toss from Rabb; Johnny then stepped thirty-four yards with a Tulane punt; moments later, he caught a 23-yard toss from Rabb; and, with time running out, Cannon turned end for forty-five yards, his longest run of 1958. When you toss in a couple of two-point runs by Cannon, a two-point catch by Mickey Mangham, and extra points by Purvis and Davis, you get 62 points.

The biggest victory margin in a series which began in 1894 was aided by interceptions and fumbles, to say nothing of Boo Mason's quote. As the score mounted in the final period, the Tigers stood along the east sidelines yelling "Choke! Choke! Choke!" As far as Tulane was concerned, the unkindest cut came when Dietzel sent Cannon back into the game along with the White Team late in the fourth quarter. Naturally, Tulane fans viewed this as nothing more than a move to pour it on, yet Dietzel explained afterward it was not his intention to humiliate the Green Wave.

"The Go Team and Chinese Bandits could not re-enter the game late in the fourth period," he said. "We played every available man and, near the end, I found that our White Team were the only ones eligible to re-enter. I did not want Tulane to score and therefore did not want to play the Go Team on defense or the Bandits on offense."

The explanation did little to remove the sight of Cannon running for that last score against a team offering only token resistance, a victim of its own mistakes and LSU depth. Tulane finished with eighty-one yards in total offense. Cannon's 117 yards lifted his 1958 total to 686, putting him behind Steve Van Buren, Jimmy Taylor, and Jerry Marchand for rushing yardage in a single season.

LSU	0	6	21	35	– 62
Tulane	0	0	0	0	– 0

Postseason honors quickly flowed. For the first time in history, the AP named three backs from one team—Cannon, Robinson, and Rabb—to its all-SEC team. UPI cited two Tigers, Cannon and Fugler, who also were named to the *Look Magazine* all-America team selected by the Football Writers. Unanimous all-American and "player of the year," Cannon finished second in the balloting for the Heisman Trophy behind Army senior Pete Dawkins.

When the AP and UPI closed their polling booths on the 1958 season, the results looked like this:

AP

	1st Place Votes	Points
1. LSU, 10–0	139	1,904
2. Iowa, 7–1–1	17	1,459
3. Army, 8–0–1	13	1,429
4. Auburn, 9–0–1	9	1,396
5. Oklahoma, 9–1	10	1,200
6. Air Force, 9–0–1	2	800
7. Wisconsin, 7–1–1	13	797
8. Ohio State, 6–1–2	3	571
9. Syracuse, 8–1–0	1	340
10. T.C.U., 8–2		311

1.	LSU, 10–0	29	331
2.	Iowa, 7–1–1	4	275
3.	Army, 8–0–1	1	255
4.	Auburn, 9–0–1		224
5.	Oklahoma, 9–1		174
6.	Wisconsin, 7–1–1		170
7.	Ohio State, 6–1–2		117
8.	Air Force, 9–0–1	1	75
9.	T.C.U., 8–2		74
10.	Syracuse, 8–1		64

In the voting of both wire services—AP by 212 sportswriters and broadcasters, UPI by 35 leading coaches—the Tigers' landslide was one of the largest in history, as was Dietzel's selection as SEC coach of the year (in the annual poll by the Nashville *Banner*) and college coach of the year (by the football coaches). Close to 500 of the 618 voting members of the American Football Coaches Association put Dietzel first, second, or third on their ballots.

When the L Club honored the national champion Tigers two weeks before a Sugar Bowl match with Atlantic Coast Conference Clemson, the surprise of the evening was the naming of Red Brodnax as the winner of the Roberts-Eastland Award as the team's most valuable player. The surprise, in which the hand of Dietzel could be seen, was designed to "share the wealth." Red Hendrix was named permanent team captain, Max Fugler cited for most minutes played (an average of thirty-five per game), Tommy Lott as the varsity letterman with the highest scholastic average, Mickey Mangham as the sophomore with the highest average as a freshman.

Dietzel, meanwhile, was reaping rewards of his own. After the Tulane game he received a new five-year contract at $16,500 per year, replacing one for $14,000 which had been scheduled to run through February, 1960. Now, no doubt as a symbol of cementing the former Army assistant to Tigertown, the L Club announced it would build a swimming pool in Dietzel's backyard. "I think someone would have to drag me by both feet to get me out of Baton Rouge," said the head coach, accepting the backyard addition and applause for a national championship. President Troy Middleton, who said he watched LSU's last unbeaten team perform in 1908, declared: "I've been waiting forty-nine years for this season. But remember, there's still one game left."

That would be the twenty-fifth annual Sugar Bowl, the end of the glory road for the 1958 national champions, a game which according to Billy Cannon, "was won by a pass the Lord threw." Actually, there was

Victory in the Sugar Bowl: Cannon passed, Mangham caught, and the Tigers escaped with a 7–0 win over Clemson.

a touch of hoopla, nostalgia, and sadness to the silver anniversary presentation. LSU had been unsuccessful in four previous Sugar Bowl games, but Tiger fans eagerly gobbled up as many of the 80,000 tickets as they could, confident their heroes would live up to their 17-point favoritism. The nostalgia was provided by Monk Simons, president of the New Orleans Mid-Winter Sports Association, whose 1934 punt return beat LSU and whose kickoff return sparked Tulane to a victory over Temple in the inaugural Sugar Bowl; the sadness by the death, the previous November, of general manager Fred Digby the man who spearheaded the early fight for the post-season classic. On Dietzel's first meeting with Digby, the new LSU coach said: "How would you like LSU to play Army in the Sugar Bowl three years from now?" Had third-ranked Army not stuck to its bowl ban, the match might have come off.

With a team that had lost only to South Carolina and Georgia Tech in ten games, unranked Clemson was sitting in the gap for the nation's No. 1 team. Wisecracking Frank Howard kept his Carolina bunch loose ("My boys play like a bunch of one-armed bandits.") and all Clemson needed to keep it close was a couple of breaks. They got one early in the first quarter when Warren Rabb came up with a fractured right hand.

The next one came in the second quarter when Red Brodnax cracked into the end zone only to lose the football. Red claimed he was across the goal line when he lost control of the ball, the officials said no, and, because Clemson recovered in the end zone, the visitors not only saved a touchdown but got possession on the 20.

Finally, in the third quarter, the breaks went for LSU. Duane Leopard came up with the ball on the Clemson 11 in a scramble after a wild pass from center. "Our center caught a handful of grass, the ball stuck and then slipped out of his hand, hitting one of our backs on the leg," said Howard. LSU lost a yard and then Cannon swept end for three. With a third-and-eight from the 9, Cannon took a handoff from Durel Matherne, ran to his right, and passed deep into the end zone to a sprinting Mangham. "I threw it and prayed," said Billy. "I was looking for Robinson but they had him covered—then I spied Mickey and let go."

But it wasn't over yet. In the fourth quarter, after LSU had repulsed two Clemson drives, the visitors launched another from their 17, one which didn't stop until the Bandits dug in on the LSU 24. In a wild dressing room, Dietzel said: "God bless the Bandits. They were out-weighed some fifteen pounds per man but they never played more courageously than they did on that final drive."

The White Team, however, provided the individual defensive stand-out in 202-pound tackle Bo Strange. "Clemson aimed three-fourths of its attack at Bo," said Dietzel. "Those big linemen knocked him back ten yards sometimes, but he kept coming off the deck to make the tackle."

The game-ending horn was welcome for more than one reason. It not only meant a perfect season and ended LSU's Sugar Bowl drought, but, because the long, pressurized campaign had drained the players emotion-ally, the final horn was much like the school bell announcing summer vacation.

LSU	0	0	7	0	–	7
Clemson	0	0	0	0	–	0

When football classes resumed the following autumn, the pressure of being a defending champion, one whose losses were scant, hit the Tigers long before their September 19 opener with Rice. Picked 35th the year before by the AP, LSU in 1959 was an overwhelming choice to retain its No. 1 position, a prediction reflected in season ticket sales.

Mainly through the selling efforts of Jim Corbett, season tickets, beginning in 1955, had showed a steady if slight increase. A whirlwind tour of the state by the "new look" athletic department resulted in a sale of 6,243 in 1955, followed by 8,551 in 1956, 9,211 in 1957 and 9,318 in 1958. The fact that the national championship year showed a jump of

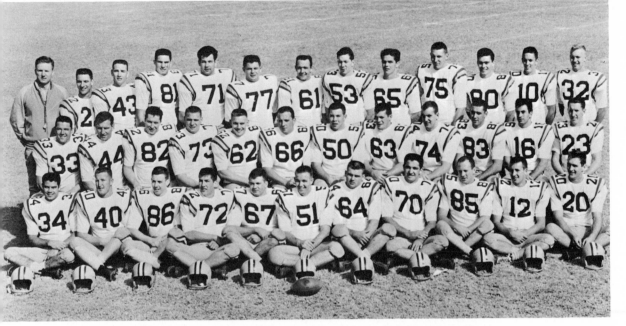

The Champs: Back row, Coach Paul Dietzel, Hart Bourque, Merle Schexnaildre, Gus Kinchen, Duane Leopard, Carroll Bergeron, Tommy Lott, John Langan, Emile Fournet, Mel Branch, Andy Bourgeois, Darryl Jenkins, Henry Lee Roberts. Middle row, Donnie Daye, Tommy Davis, Don Norwood, Jack Frayer, Manson Nelson, Mike Stupka, Bobby Greenwood, Al Dampier, Dave McCarty, Scotty McClain, Durel Matherne, Don Purvis. Bottom row, Johnny Robinson, J. W. Brodnax, Mickey Mangham, Bo Strange, Ed McCreedy, Max Fugler, Larry Kahlden, Lynn LeBlanc, Billy Hendrix, Warren Rabb, Billy Cannon.

only 107 gave some indication of what a long shot Dietzel's ball club was. Since it's an American tradition to get in on a good thing, LSU scored its first season-ticket breakthrough in 1959, selling a whopping 31,242—a sale termed by Corbett "the best rain insurance there is."

As the man who gave the three-team system to collegiate football, Paul Dietzel was in great demand as a public speaker during the summer of 1959. He and his staff cranked out a book aimed at high school and college coaches, *Winged T and The Chinese Bandits*, and by that time only those under an iceberg were not familiar with White Team, Go Team, and Bandits.

So the 1958 question, "Does LSU have enough depth to go with a celebrated backfield?" became, in 1959, "Can the Tigers repeat?" As Dietzel explained it, the season ahead hinged on one thing in particular. "We were practically injury-free last year," he said, "and we only lost nine fumbles in 11 games. So the breaks went our way. You not only have to be good. You have to be lucky."

The battle cry Dietzel brought with him from Army in 1955—"The Fourth Quarter Is Ours"—was classically illustrated during the championship year, reflecting how three teams wore down the enemy. Total score by quarters looked like this after eleven games:

LSU	39	68	77	98	–	282
Opponents	13	15	6	19	–	53

Offensively, the Tigers not only gained momentum as the game progressed but, defensively, only one of four second-half touchdowns (the one by Florida) was of any consequence. The other three were scored after the opposition's doom had been sealed. If anything, LSU figured to be stronger defensively because of experience. Max Fugler had beefed up to 217 and Bo Strange was up to 212. The lone White Team losses were Red Hendrix, Larry Kahlden, and Red Brodnax. They were being replaced by Scotty McClain (Go Team), Emile Fournet (Bandits) and Donny Daye (Go Team).

Perhaps the biggest loss was Go Team fullback Tommy Davis who decided to give up a final year of eligibility to play with the 49ers. Dietzel did not discourage the ex-Fair Park star who was twenty-five at the time. With Daye and Davis gone from the Go Team backfield, room was made for two promising sophomores, halfback Wendell Harris from Baton Rouge High, and fullback Earl Gros from Terrebonne.

Billed as "the next Cannon," Harris was winning games for Baton Rouge High with his place kicking when he was only a freshman. Like Cannon, the 5-foot, 10-inch, 185-pounder was a sprinter and, though he lacked Billy's speed, he had a deft change of pace and great balance. Gros came to LSU with far less experience than Cannon, having played no varsity football until his junior year. "I saw this big boy in school," said Terrebonne coach "Buck" Seeber of the 6-foot, 1-inch, 215-pound Gros, "and knew he had to be a football player."

Two other sophomores moved on to the Bandits—Roy Winston, an Istrouma all-stater taking over Fournet's post as guard, and Tommy Neck, a redshirt from Marksville, moving into a halfback spot vacated by Henry Lee Roberts who chose to pass up football. Another Tiger who called it quits was Tommy Lott, who yielded his Go Team guard berth to sophomore Rodney "Monk" Guillot of New Orleans.

As the opener with Rice approached, one to be televised nationally, college football's defending champions looked like this:

White Team	Go Team	Chinese Bandits
LE Scotty McClain	Jim Bond	Andy Bourgeois
LT Lynn LeBlanc	Dave McCarty	Mel Branch
LG Emile Fournet	Monk Guillot	Roy Winston
C Max Fugler	Bob Greenwood	John Langhan
RG Ed McCreedy	Mike Stupka	Manson Nelson
RT Bo Strange	Jack Frayer	Duane Leopard
RE Mickey Mangham	Don Norwood	Gus Kinchen
QB Warren Rabb	Durel Matherne	Darryl Jenkins
LH Billy Cannon	Don Purvis	Tommy Neck
RH Johnny Robinson	Wendell Harris	Hart Bourque
FB Donnie Daye	Earl Gros	Merle Schexnaildre

For thirty minutes in its nationally televised opener against Rice, college football's defending champions sent an awful picture into America's living rooms. Because of an offense that sputtered and stalled, Rice took a 3–0 half-time lead before the Tigers could mount any kind of steady attack. "I believe the boys were too wound up," said Dietzel. "All last season we lost only nine fumbles. Now, in one game, we lost four."

At the start of the third period the White Team turned on the juice as Cannon sprinted seventeen yards around right end behind a key block by Fournet. While the defense was holding the Owls to a net gain of forty yards in the last two quarters, the Tigers tacked on two touchdowns and a 33-yard field goal by Harris in the final period. A 32-yard pass from Rabb to Schexnaildre brought one score and a 2-yard jab by Neck, the other. Owl coach Jess Neely shook his head at LSU's speed. "You have to be conscious of stopping them on the outside or you're in deep trouble," said Jess.

Whereas television held the opening crowd to 48,000, a turnout of 65,000 was on hand the following week to see the Tigers continue their shakedown cruise through the Southwest Conference. What the fans saw was more of the same: inconsistent offense and great defense. Actually, LSU grabbed a 10–0 lead over TCU in the second quarter on a 29-yard field goal by Harris and a 45-yard pass, Rabb to Robinson, and then settled down to trench warfare.

Tackle Bo Strange, recalling a goal line stand in which he played across from all-America Don Floyd, said: "It was a case of big butts and elbows." With a chance to get back in the game in the fourth quarter, TCU could not push it across in four tries from the 6. On third down, Cannon met the ball carrier at the goal line and knocked him back. LSU's experience was beginning to show defensively. Rice could gain but forty-nine yards rushing, TCU only ninety. But where was the offense?

The question was still being asked after a 22–0 victory over Baylor before 33,000 on a wet field in Shreveport but Johnny Bridgers, the beaten coach, saw enough to convince him. "There are many things about LSU that makes it great," he said, "but the most impressive thing is pursuit. They call 'em Tigers. Well, they're more like bees." Sophomore halfback Ronnie Bull added: "Every time I was tackled and looked up, there were eight of 'em around me."

The only impressive offensive display came on a six-play, 76-yard White Team march with the opening kickoff. First, Cannon went for thirty-five, Robinson for seventeen and, finally, Rabb shot an eight-yard touchdown pass to Daye. In the second quarter Billy picked off a Baylor pass and streaked fifty yards to make it 12–0, Harris added a 26-yard field goal (his third in three tries), and Matherne tacked on another score on a three-yard pass to Norwood. With a 22-point lead, LSU spent the final half frustrating the pass-happy Bears who wound up with thirty-two yards on the ground, seventy-nine in the air.

"I think it's ridiculous to hear some fans say we haven't cut loose yet." Those were the sentiments of Paul Dietzel after his top-ranked ball club went to 4–0 at the expense of Miami, 27–3. There was one person, Hurricane coach Andy Gustafson, who felt the Tigers not only had cut loose but actually poured it on his beaten football team. "The guys you meet on the way up, you meet on the way down," said Andy, who felt the Tigers got greedy near the end because of national polls. "Dietzel's day will come."

At half time LSU had a precarious 7–3 lead, thanks to a 5-yard run by Cannon. Robinson scored on a 12-yard dash in the third quarter. In the final period Norwood took a pass from Matherne and Rabb swept it on an 8-yard rollout. It was the last score which nettled Gustafson, ending a drive which Cannon highlighted by running thirty-two yards with a screen pass. The sight of Billy toppling his worn-out athletes was too much for the Miami coach who, for the moment, conveniently forgot a 75–7 whipping he dealt hapless Fordham in 1954.

By this time, on a national as well as Southern level, the annual LSU-Ole Miss showdown couldn't come quick enough. Dietzel saw back-to-back trips to Kentucky and Florida as potential booby traps and, when he was able to survive them with a couple of 9–0 victories, he realized his 1959 defense was for real.

The Tigers limited Kentucky to 117 yards, Florida to 169, jumping into a lead in both cases and then playing it cozy. Against the Wildcats, Rabb passed to Robinson for five yards and Harris booted a 39-yard field goal. Against the Gators, Cannon capped a drive with a 1-yard buck while Wendell booted one for 27 yards. These victories cleared the decks, as the cliché goes, for Halloween night—a moment of truth with an unbeaten Ole Miss team which had steamrolled six opponents in a row and which held a No. 3 ranking. On the way from the football field to the airport in Gainesville, LSU's chartered bus passed a billboard advertising a local insurance company. Somewhat prophetically, it said: "Let Cannon Protect You."

Paul Dietzel always seemed to welcome the challenge of meeting Ole Miss, possibly because it allowed him free rein with his "gimmicky" approach in preparing a team psychologically. On Madison Avenue, when the ad boys are searching for a slogan, the war cry is "Let's run it up the flagpole and see who salutes." For the Rebels, Dietzel always tried to have something special on top the flagpole; in fact, for the Ole Miss game of 1959, he rolled out his heavy artillery. First, a newspaper story quoting Rebel fullback Charley Flowers declaring he "would outgain

Cannon" became wall-to-wall reading in the Tiger dressing room. On Thursday, the LSU campus was "bombed" by a plane carrying "Go to Hell LSU" leaflets. Taking note of the incident, Ole Miss coach Johnny Vaught recalled that Dietzel was a B-29 pilot during World War II and commented: "I thought his flying days were over." On Friday, LSU players were greeted by a larger-than-life mural of a hairy gorilla, done in living color by Dietzel and wearing, of course, Flowers' No. 41. Friday night, as is the custom before home games, the team attended a movie in the projection room under Tiger Stadium. For that occasion, Dietzel selected "Kiss Me Deadly," featuring heroic private detective Mike Hammer. It was tailor made to relieve the tension.

All during the week Dietzel was more concerned about proper psychology—"You have to build toward a peak and not reach it too

A Souvenir: Halloween, 1959.

soon."—than about tactics. LSU's one bit of strategy was running its wing-T plays from an unbalanced line, a change that was to cause the Rebels a measure of concern.

Halloween, 1959, was a warm (73 degrees), muggy (100 percent humidity) evening. There was an almost misty air to Tiger Stadium, giving the battleground a dramatic setting long before the capacity crowd of 67,500 had filled every seat. Two hours before the 8 P.M. kickoff, Paul Dietzel, wearing slippers, stretched out on a couch in his office, alone and meditating. Johnny Vaught, trying a new experiment in acclimating his team to Tiger Stadium, brought them onto the field at 6:30 in street clothes. They inspected the turf, then strolled over to their bench where they sat for twenty minutes listening to LSU students chanting "We're Number One."

Bob Khayat's kickoff to Johnny Robinson helped break the tension and some of the fans were beginning to try to enjoy the game when

Cannon, cracking over the middle for fifteen yards, fumbled the ball away on the LSU 21. The Rebs got a first down at the 8 and were third-and-goal at the 3 when Mickey Mangham nailed Jake Gibbs for a 2-yard loss. Vaught waved in Khayat, and Ole Miss had a 3–0 lead midway through the opening period. Cannon's fumble was to be the first of four for the Tigers, and each one either killed a drive or set up the Rebels in scoring territory. With time running out in the second quarter, Earl Gros bobbled on the LSU 29 and, six plays later, Ole Miss had a first down on the 7. On the last play of the half, however, Bandit end Andy Bourgeois stopped quarterback Bobby Franklin on a rollout and it was still 3–0.

As the third quarter began, Cannon brought the crowd to its feet when he picked off a Gibbs pass on the LSU 49 and returned it to the Ole Miss 36. The significance of the play was simply this: Vaught wasn't going to put the ball in the air anymore—unless an emergency arose. The Rebs protected a 3–0 lead by blocking a field goal attempt by Harris, and the next three times when Ole Miss got the football, Vaught had Gibbs punt on first down. His strategy on a damp field was obvious: he was banking on his superb defense and felt that LSU, given the ball, might continue to fumble.

While the Rebs played it ultraconservatively, the Tigers were gambling. On four-and-nine from the Reb 35 with a minute left in the third period, Cannon faked a punt and was smeared for a yard loss, a play which, under the circumstances, seemed like a last gasp from a national champion.

As the final period began, Vaught had no reason to doubt his "let-LSU-make-the-mistakes" strategy. Playing a third-and-seventeen from the Old Miss 42, Johnny ordered Gibbs into punt formation. Battle-weary from the punishing blows he had taken and rankled by that first-quarter fumble, Cannon dropped back to the 5-yard-line awaiting what he felt would be another skyscraper by Gibbs whose second-half kicks traveled fifty-two, fifty, forty-five, and forty-seven yards. This one went forty-seven yards, too, skidding inside the 20 until, at the last moment, it took a high bounce into Cannon's arms on the LSU 11.

Trying to chart a treacherous course near the east sideline, Cannon was hit at the knees by Richard Price at the 19. Billy struggled loose. At the 20 Jerry Daniels, with a clear shot, grabbed Billy near the shoulders, but by the 30 he had slipped from the shoulders to the ankles. At the 40 Mangham threw a block and suddenly Cannon was at midfield—so close to Vaught that the Ole Miss coach could almost reach out and touch him. Gibbs was still very much in the picture. He eluded a block by Fournet and then made a lunge at Billy on the 45. For a moment Gibbs held on, but Billy shook free and all he could see in front of him were chalklines. "When I saw Johnny Robinson looking back for someone to block," said Billy, "I felt this was it—just don't stub your toe, I told myself."

Oblivious to the tremendous roar during his 89-yard journey, Cannon became conscious of an exploding Tiger Stadium as soon as he crossed the goal line. "I seemed to hear everyone at once," he said. "I don't think I got hit much harder in the game than I did by my teammates in the end zone. I was lucky to get out alive."

There was a moment of excruciating suspense among those fans with the presence of mind to spot a red handkerchief near midfield. It lasted until the referee's arms went up, the first official sign that Ole Miss had been in motion on the punt and LSU had declined the penalty. When Wendell Harris kicked the extra point to make it 7–3, a glance at the scoreboard showed that ten minutes exactly remained. Then Vaught came up with a surprise of his own: he chose third-string quarterback Doug Elmore, a sophomore, to lead the Rebel charge. No one thought he'd lead it so well. Starting from their 32 after the kickoff, Ole Miss, sticking to the ground, marched through the Bandits for four consecutive first downs. When the Rebs reached the 23, Dietzel sent the White Team back into the game in a classic do-or-die situation.

Four plays later, the fired-up Elmore skirted end to the 7 for a first down. Ninety seconds remained; everyone was standing and seemingly out of their minds. George Blair hit right tackle for two yards. Elmore, on a keeper, jabbed at left tackle and knifed to the 2 before Donnie Daye halted him. Jim Anderson hit the middle and was stopped cold on the 2. This brought up fourth-and-goal at the 2—and once again sophomore Elmore called on himself. Once again he headed over left tackle where he was first met by Rabb and then by Cannon on the 1. With

Rabb and Cannon halt Ole Miss's Doug Elmore one yard from Promised Land.

THE RUN, Halloween night, 1959. Sequence starts top right on opposite page.
Frames are to be viewed from top to bottom and right to left. In Frame 1 Cannon
fields the ball on the bounce. Frames 3 through 8 show him running by and
through several Ole Miss players between the 19 and 30-yard lines. Cannon
eludes Jake Gibbs in Frames 13 and 14 and has clear sailing for the final fifty
yards. He passes Coach Johnny Vaught (in dark suit) on the 50.

eighteen seconds left, Cannon was merely helping insure the immortality of his superhuman 89-yard punt return, a run which in later years would have been lost in the agate type had Elmore made that final yard.

In the dressing room, a cross between a Turkish bath and the tunnel of love, the most appropriate quote of the evening came from Go Team guard Mike Stupka, who put his arm around an exhausted Cannon and said simply: "Thank you, Billy." If LSU fans had known what was going through Billy's mind as Gibbs's fourth-quarter kick bounced toward him, there would have been an outbreak of heart seizures. "Until that last second, I wasn't going to field it," he said. "I was going to let it roll. Gibbs didn't kick this one as long as the others and it was sort of dribbling toward me. Ole Miss was covering well and I didn't feel like taking chances—but right at the end, it took a high bounce and came right to me."

Dietzel echoed the sentiments of every witness when he called Cannon's run "the greatest I have ever seen on a football field." Veteran Nashville sports editor Fred Russell minced no words when he wrote: "For its fury, suspense, and competitive team performances, Louisiana State's 7–3 heart-throbber over Ole Miss was the fullest and finest football game I've witnessed in 31 years of sports reporting."

Naturally, Ole Miss second-guessers were out in force—with Vaught the obvious target. Why were the Rebels kicking on first down? Why didn't Ole Miss kick a field goal at the end of the first half, since it then would have needed only another at the end for a 9–7 victory? Actually, Vaught's strategy was sound—until Cannon shot it full of holes. The White Team made only two of LSU's seven first downs (Ole Miss had thirteen); in fact, Cannon and company never had the ball for more than five plays in a row. All of which made the defeat more galling for the Rebels to swallow.

The afternoon after Halloween night, a relaxed Cannon was telling about how nice it was to get back on friendly terms with his wife and children. "The week of a game, especially one with Ole Miss, I'd get irritable, snapping at everyone," said Billy. "You can tell when a team is ready. Before the game, we were all sitting around like a bunch of rattlesnakes. I noticed some of the coaches looked worried, but I told them 'Don't worry, we're gonna win'—I said it just to be talking. I was wound up like a clock. Sitting in the dressing room afterward is the emptiest feeling you can imagine. Warren Rabb and I took the wives out for some celebrating when we still didn't feel normal. I think I fell asleep around four but I remember the boy throwing the paper around six. I was glad to see daylight. Don Purvis told me he, Don Norwood, and Bo Strange didn't sleep a wink—they just waited for the sun to come up.

Really, though, how can you celebrate about Ole Miss when Tennessee's sitting home just waiting to knock us off?"

Cannon's sentiments had been shared by his coach who pegged the Vols as the most likely booby trap before the season. At that time, Bowden Wyatt's club had a respectable 4–1–1 record, losing only to Georgia Tech, 14–7. The Vols not only would be catching the Tigers in an obvious "letdown" week but they would have the benefit of the home field—and a Homecoming crowd. While Dietzel eyed the trip to Knoxville anxiously, he felt confident about a defense which had kept LSU's goal line uncrossed for thirty-eight quarters. Not since Mississippi State's Bill Stacy scored on an 11-yard rollout in the second quarter of the eighth game in 1958 had anyone put the ball in the Tigers' end zone.

"If we can only put that goose egg up there next to Tennessee," said Charley McClendon on the bus ride to Shields-Watkins Field, "we've got nothing to worry about." A temperature in the twenties—a far cry from the 73 degrees and 100 percent humidity of Halloween night—sent Dietzel shopping Saturday morning for long underwear for his squad. Not only that but the Tigers for the first time donned their purple-and-gold woolen stockings. "I'll never forget," said Bandit end Bourgeois, "bundled up like that made me feel like a pro."

And the Tigers played like pros that afternoon, with no sign of any letdown. Possibly the best explanation of the story told by the lights on the scoreboard—lights which stayed on through the night, saying simply Tennessee 14, LSU 13—is the old bromide: The operation was a success but the patient died. The Tigers out-blocked and out-attacked a team that prided itself on the primitive approach to football, winding up with a 19–9 edge in first downs and a 334–112 advantage in total offense. But the scoreboard was all that mattered. It said LSU was No. 1 no more and its nineteen-game winning streak had been shattered by the famed Tennessee treatment.

For example: the Vols intercepted two passes, both by wingback Jim Cartwright. He brought one back fifty-nine yards for a third-quarter touchdown (breaking LSU's streak at forty touchdown-less quarters in a row) to erase a 7–0 Tiger lead. The Vols also recovered two fumbles—the first on LSU's 30 to set up their winning touchdown, the second on the Tennessee 18 to end any hope of a last quarter comeback.

Both Cannon (122 yards) and Robinson (115 yards) outgained the entire Tennessee team. Billy put his team ahead in the second quarter when he dashed twenty-six yards off tackle on one of those textbook plays. With the score 7–0 in the third quarter, Dietzel faced an agonizing decision with a fourth-and-goal on the Vol 5. With the ball squarely between the uprights, he called on Harris for a field goal. "I simply felt," said Dietzel, "the ball game would have been over if we could make it 10–0." But Harris missed and the Vols were given new life. Minutes later, however, LSU was on the move again. The Tigers had moved to midfield, thanks in part to a pass from Rabb to Cannon in the left flat. Now Warren called the same pass to his halfback, this time to Johnny Robinson. As Rabb rolled to his right, he spied Robinson in the open and fired. Somehow there wasn't enough behind it and the ball was on a collision course with wingback Cartwright, who had allowed Robinson to get behind him. A leaping interception by the wingback, a futile drive at Cartwright's feet by Robinson, and, in the twinkling of an eye, Jim was speeding past the LSU bench on the first trip into the LSU end zone in forty quarters.

Silent most of the afternoon, Tennessee's Homecoming crowd came alive and, for the first time in 1959, LSU lost its poise. The Go Team went into the game and Earl Gros promptly fumbled the ball over to the fired-up orange shirts; it seemed inevitable that they would score again. Sure enough, in less than two minutes, they went thirty yards and, when Cotten Letner booted his second extra point, it was 14–7.

All of a sudden, like a rookie golfer who finds himself leading the U.S. Open, Tennessee lost its cool, too. Billy Majors fumbled a punt he should not have tried to handle and, in what seemed like Christmas in November, Ed McCreedy recovered on the Vol 2. Durel Matherne (Rabb had injured his knee on the first play of the fourth quarter) sneaked across to make it 14–13 and Harris began to trot onto the field with the kicking tee. But Dietzel called him back. In went guard Mike Stupka with a two-point play—Cannon off tackle—a play even the Tennessee cheerleaders expected, but one which LSU had used with awesome effectiveness all afternoon. With Stupka leading the charge, Cannon knifed off tackle as the Vols spread out to protect the outside. Tackle Joe Scheffer penetrated and slowed Billy a little. Then guard Wayne Grubb hit him head-on, but Cannon kept going. Linebacker Charley Severence turned him in and then Majors came up to halt progress at the goal line. "I'll go to my grave believing I was over," says Cannon. But linesman Bob King of Missouri, in the only decision that counted, flashed the "no good" sign.

By no means were the Tigers dead. Emile Fournet pumped new life into his team when he blocked a punt and set LSU up on the Vol 27. The Tigers drove to the twelve and once again the call was Cannon off tackle. This time the exchange between Matherne and Cannon was faulty, Cannon left the ball behind him, and an orange jersey got it on the 16. "I've watched that play over and over in the film," said backfield coach Carl Maddox, "and the sad part about it was Billy could have walked in. There wasn't a Tennessee man standing at the point of attack.

If we had made that score or even kicked a field goal, no one would ever have remembered the two-point gamble."

Dietzel had no regrets over the try for two. "We were the No. 1 team in the country," he said. "We were playing to win, not tie. It might have been our last chance. We just happened to miss a key block on the play."

Like tributes to a dead man, bouquets flowed. Wyatt said: "I don't know if there's ever been a back on this field as good as Cannon." General Bob Neyland, watching from the press box, said Robinson "reminds me of Bobby Foxx, our wingback in 1938, '39 and '40." Nationally, the Tigers won praise for their gallant try for two. Thousands turned out for a thunderous welcome home at Ryan Field. "It was nice," said Cannon, "but there's nothing anyone can do to make you feel anything but rotten."

LSU's first loss in nineteen games not only dropped the Tigers out of first place (the Tigers fell to third behind Syracuse and Texas) but left them without their No. 1 quarterback for remaining games against Mississippi State and Tulane. Rabb, nursing a sprained knee, wasn't missed in a 27–0 conquest of State, a game in which Matherne threw touchdown passes to Robinson and Purvis. In the Tulane finale, however, LSU needed all the help it could get against a team it had smashed 62–0 the year before.

Sputtering throughout against an aroused Green Wave that had won only three games, the Tigers had a 14–0 lead on runs of forty-five yards by Cannon and twenty-two by Gros before Tommy Mason made a game of it by returning a punt fifty-nine yards for a Tulane touchdown. With time running out, it was 14–6 when Tulane's Phil Nugent carried a kick by Cannon to the LSU 36. Mason chewed up twenty-four yards in four plays and then had to retire with an injury. At this point, Dietzel substituted the Bandits for a tired White Team, keeping Fugler in as linebacker. Three plays later Max batted down a "touchdown" pass of Nugent's to preserve a shaky victory.

It was also a costly victory. Harris suffered a broken arm which would keep him out of any postseason game, and at the time LSU's postseason plans were a matter of statewide speculation. The Sugar Bowl fanned the flames for a rematch with Ole Miss to assure a meeting of the nation's second and third ranked teams. The Rebs' smashing 37–7 win over Tennessee vaulted them past LSU and set the stage for an encore—if the Tigers were willing. Dietzel did not welcome the idea of playing a team he had already beaten—no coach does—and, as a result, leaned to a match with fifth-ranked Georgia, the surprise SEC champion. But behind the scenes Ole Miss had accepted a no-strings-attached invitation to the Sugar Bowl before its 7–3 defeat Halloween night. This meant the Rebels were in one corner no matter what, and any possibility of an LSU-Georgia game was eliminated.

At the Quarterback Club meeting in New Orleans the Monday following the Tulane game, Dietzel said that the squad, which was divided on playing in a bowl game, would vote that night. Mainly on a plea from athletic director Jim Corbett, the Tigers voted to give Ole Miss a second shot, a decision which left Dietzel "shell shocked." When he discovered there was no turning back, he said: "The boys wanted to play in a game in which they had a chance to regain No. 1. If Syracuse loses (it had a December 5 game with U.C.L.A.), our meeting could be for the championship." It was all so much window dressing. Dietzel dreaded the thought of New Year's day not only because he would be playing someone with the psychological edge but because he knew he would have a handicapped Rabb and no Harris. Then, a week before the game, Johnny Robinson suffered a fractured hand.

From the moment the match was made, Louisiana-Mississippi fans became so steamed up that it all made for one of the hottest-selling Sugar Bowls in history. Although the game could be seen on television in New Orleans, those with tickets were willing to trade them for items ranging from a used car for twenty-five sideline seats, to refrigerator repairs for one ticket. One man with a 1952 Cadillac and four new tires was willing to swap it for sixty tickets. In the classified section, a one-ticket married couple asked for baby furniture; a two-ticket man asked for a case of whiskey (bonded, if you please); a three-ticket man wanted a table-model TV; a four-ticket man, a 14-foot fiberglass boat; a six-ticket man, a frost-free upright freezer; a ten-ticket man, a washer and dryer or used station wagon.

After it was all over, many of the 83,000 customers were wondering why they went to all the trouble. To paraphrase a familiar sports cliché, the score of the 1960 Sugar Bowl game was closer than the game indicated. Three salient features of Ole Miss's 21–0 victory were: (1) The Rebels had a 373–74 edge in total offense. (2) LSU did not cross midfield until there were eight minutes left in the game and then got no farther than the Ole Miss 38. (3) Billy Cannon, with a brand new Heisman trophy on his shelf, netted eight yards in six tries.

"I really don't think it was a case of our playing so poorly," said Dietzel in a postmortem. "Ole Miss was simply terrific. That touchdown pass just before the half broke our backs."

With thirty-eight seconds left in the second quarter of a scoreless game, Ole Miss was on the LSU 43. As Jake Gibbs faded behind good protection, the Rebels got four men deep on the Tigers with Jake finding Cowboy Woodruff wide open down the middle for an easy score—the first touchdown pass thrown on LSU in fourteen games.

For Paul Dietzel, a sour Sugar.

With a 7-point cushion, Ole Miss continued to hold the upper hand in the second half and, for unhappy Tiger fans, the end could not come soon enough. When it did, Cannon finally made it into the end zone—that is, he signed a professional football contract under the goal posts to play with the Houston Oilers of the American Football League, scheduled to begin play the following fall. A three-year pact worth a reported $100,000 included service stations and an automobile, a gift from Bud Adams, millionaire Oiler owner. Cannon's signing touched off a court fight between the National and American leagues because, said Pete Rozelle, general manager of the Los Angeles Rams, "we have a legal, valid and binding contract with Cannon."

When the smoke cleared, it was obvious that Cannon as well as Johnny Robinson, who had signed with the Detroit Lions, were pros when they played in the Sugar Bowl. The Ram suit attempted to establish the validity of a contract Cannon signed with the Rams in Philadelphia, one dated November 30, 1959. The Ram contract called for Billy to receive $10,000 the first season, $15,000 in 1961 and 1962. Also, Billy had received a $10,000 bonus for signing, plus $500 expense money for traveling from Baton Rouge to Philadelphia where he traveled incognito, registering at a hotel under the name "Peter Gunn." Cannon returned the bonus check and expense money to the Rams on December 30, after he made a verbal agreement to play for the Oilers. When the courts decided in favor of the Oilers in a celebrated test case, it gave the new league impetus and went a long way toward helping it survive the incubation period.

A runaway winner in the balloting for the Heisman Trophy, Billy had taken a December 9 handoff from Vice President Richard Nixon at New York's Downtown Athletic Club to become the most honored player in LSU history, all-America, back of the year, etc. Those eight yards in six carries in the Sugar Bowl were an unfortunate exit for him and the 1959 club, but nothing, not even 21–0, could ever blot out the memory of Halloween night.

For LSU fans the hardest part of 1960, which featured a fall match between Richard Nixon and John F. Kennedy, was waking to the fact that Cannon, with 1,985 yards and 165 points in three seasons, was gone. The heritage he and the twenty other departing lettermen left behind, however, was a rich one, a winning tradition Dietzel felt would rub off on his "wide-eyed sophomores." A 7–7 spring game underlined the feeling the Tigers would bank heavily on defense until the young team members—eighteen of the first thirty-three were sophomores including the entire Go Team—learned to move the football.

Dietzel's three-deep shaped up like this:

White Team	Go Team	Chinese Bandits
LE Andy Bourgeois	Bob Flurry	Gene Sykes
LT Bob Richards	Don Estes	Bob McDonald
LG Roy Winston	Dexter Gary	Dan Hargett
C Bo Strange	Gary Kinchen	Dennis Gaubatz
RG Ed McCreedy	Ed Habert	Monk Guillot
RT Billy Booth	Rodney Guillot	Fred Miller
RE Mickey Mangham	Jack Gates	Gus Kinchen
QB Jimmy Field	Lynn Amedee	Darryl Jenkins
LH Jerry Stovall	Bo Campbell	Tom Neck
RH Wendell Harris	Ray Wilkins	Hart Bourque
FB Donnie Daye	Earl Gros	Steve Ward
	Charley Cranford	

As the September 17 opener with Texas A & M approached, Dietzel did his best to curb newsmen's enthusiasm over the practice performances of Jerry Stovall, the all-stater from West Monroe. So as not to alert the Aggies, he continued to list little Hart Bourque on the White Team at right halfback, keeping Stovall at the No. 2 left half spot behind Harris. Actually, Stovall was so impressive with the ball under his arm, it was no difficult decision for Dietzel to shift Harris from left half (his spot in the spring) to right half and move Stovall to the post vacated by Cannon. This was no gamble at all compared to the quarterback spot where redshirt halfback Jimmy Field, a product of University High in Baton Rouge, was groomed to fill Warren Rabb's position. "We were well off at halfback," Dietzel explained, "and Field was such a fine athlete, and leader, he had to play somewhere."

It took Jimmy a while to grow into the job he was introduced to in the spring of 1960, but Stovall was a smash from the start. In an opening 9–0 win over Texas A & M, Jerry turned in a dazzling defensive play that tipped the scales in LSU's favor, retreating twenty yards while fending off blockers to nail a touchdown-bound Aggie on a punt return on the Tiger 19. Moments later, after two Stovall punts (one went for sixty yards, the other went out on the Aggie 11), LSU was camped on the visitors' 28 and went in for the score. "Stovall's debut was as impressive as any I've ever seen by a sophomore," said Dietzel.

From the opener, it was obvious the Tigers were going to have trouble moving the football, creating the impression the defense might have to do most of the scoring. In 1960, however, it was too much to ask. The Tigers, for example, gave up only two touchdowns in the next four games and lost all four. Bourque fumbled a punt to pave the way for a 7–3 Baylor victory. Georgia Tech kicked two field goals and then surrendered an intentional safety to wind up a 6–2 winner. Kentucky won by the World Series score of 3–0. And Florida, with Larry Libertore dashing sixty-six yards on the opening play from scrimmage, won 13–10 on field goals of thirty-five and forty-seven yards.

Earl Gros and Wendell Harris: Inside and Outside.

"Uncle Paul" charms the viewers. Caricaturist's view of the Quarterback Club, which also starred emcee John Ferguson, the Voice of the Tigers, and Baton Rouge sports editor Bud Montet.

LSU's miseries were reflected in the Tiger Stadium crowds—51,528 turned out for Florida—and it was hard to find anyone who gave Dietzel's crew much of a chance as it prepared to invade Oxford for the annual brush with Ole Miss. This was one of Johnny Vaught's finer teams, one which had won six games in a row and was ranked second nationally. The Rebels were a confident three-touchdown choice; in fact, many of the 34,000 fans on hand at Hemingway Stadium felt the home team would be able to score at will. But an LSU defense headed by captain Bo Strange sobered Ole Miss in a hurry. It was 0–0 at half time and in the third period the home team managed to nudge ahead, 3–0, on a 38-yard field goal by Allen Green. In the final quarter, however, the all-sophomore Go Team suddenly came alive, moving forty-eight yards behind quarterback Amedee for a touchdown. On a third-and-nine situation, Amedee ran thirteen yards to keep the march alive and, then, with the ball on the 1, he faked a dive play to Cranford and handed to Wilkins, who shot into the Ole Miss end zone. When Harris missed the extra point (he had missed a first-quarter field goal try from the 11), Dietzel wasn't overly concerned about his 6–3 lead, since he felt the Rebels still needed a touchdown to win.

With one shot left, an injured Jake Gibbs built a fire under his club and, starting on the Ole Miss 21, began a race with the clock. In one minute, twenty-five seconds, Gibbs moved the Rebels from the 21 to LSU's 25. With thirty-eight seconds left, Vaught called time and

Dietzel was amazed to see Green trot onto the field with the kicking tee. The big lineman sent a 41-yard field goal (kicked from the 31) squarely through the uprights and Vaught had his "Mexican standoff."

"If someone had told me before the game, it was going to wind up in a tie I would have been elated," said Dietzel. "Now it almost feels like we lost." In the end, the tie was the only blemish on the record of a team that wound up in the Sugar Bowl. It also marked the third regular-season game in a row that Ole Miss had failed to score a touchdown on LSU. "The big thing," said Dietzel, "was that it proved to the boys they could move the football. Our offense should pick up."

It did. With Amedee pitching for three touchdowns, the Tigers smashed South Carolina, 35–6, the following week, winding up with 359 yards in total offense. After holding on for a 7–3 decision over Mississippi State, LSU blanked Wake Forest and Norman Snead, 16–0, and faced Tulane with a winning season hanging in the balance.

With a terror in all-SEC halfback Tommy Mason, Andy Pilney's Green Wave was only a two-point underdog to the invading Tigers and it was a game Pilney had pointed his club for all season. Starting off, Tulane was the picture of a charged-up club, taking the opening kickoff and marching from its 42 to the LSU 30, where Mason fumbled. A second Tulane fumble set up the Tigers on the Wave 38 and Amedee scored seven plays later on an 8-yard run. In the second quarter, the Tigers swept fifty-five yards with Lynn running the last yard and, in the third period, Steve Ward blocked a kick to set up a 33-yard field goal by Tommy Neck.

"You might say we won by getting the breaks," said Bourgeois, "but we went into the game feeling we could wear Tulane down and that's just what happened. It's a great lift to know you'll always be fresh out there. Keeps you hustling."

A great catch by Mason of a 33-yard pass from Phil Nugent in the final period saved Tulane from a shutout and, for awhile, the Tigers felt that the six points in a 17–6 victory might have cost them their only slice of glory in a 5–4–1 year. But they did not. The fifty points allowed by LSU were the fewest by any major college team. With only thirty-four yards in ten carries, Mason could attest to LSU's toughness.

If 1960 taught Paul Dietzel anything, it increased his belief in the value of three teams. Many had felt that in 1958 and 1959 the all-around talent of the White Team was the chief reason for almost back-to-back national championships. The 6–6 tie in Oxford against a superior Ole Miss outfit—the game in which the all-sophomore Go Team came alive—and the strong finish convinced him there would be more dividends ahead.

Because Dietzel gambled with eighteen sophomores in 1960, he went

Roy "Moonie" Winston: Homegrown all-American.

into 1961 with a battlehardened squad that had room for only nine rookies in its first three teams. The only major losses, ends Bourgeois and Mangham, guard McCreedy, and fullback Daye, left LSU looking like this in the fall:

White Team	Go Team	Chinese Bandits
LE Gene Sykes	Danny Neumann	Rob Hucklebridge
LT Don Estes	Ralph Pere	Bob Flurry
LG Roy Winston	Dexter Gary	Bob Richards
C Dennis Gaubatz	Gary Kinchen	Dan Hargett
RG Monk Guillot	Eddie Habert	Steve Ward
		Ron Pere
RT Billy Booth	Rodney Guillot	Fred Miller
RE Jack Gates	Bill Truax	Mike Morgan
QB Jimmy Field	Lynn Amedee	Dwight Robinson
LH Jerry Stovall	Bo Campbell	Tommy Neck
RH Wendell Harris	Roy Wilkins	Buddy Soefker
FB Earl Gros	Charles Cranford	Buddy Hamic

At the time, Dietzel had a good idea that he had assembled a wealth of talent, but he probably wouldn't have guessed that fifteen of his teams' members would wind up playing professional football. The 1961 success was a matter of Gaubatz's coming of age as a center, Winston's playing all-America football at guard, Miller's becoming a destroyer on the Bandits, Field's blossoming as a quarterback, and Gros's maturing as a fullback. Harris and Stovall did not fall into the surprise category. They merely played to their potential, which is saying quite a lot.

It had taken LSU six games to straighten out in 1960. In 1961 it took just seven quarters. The opening 16–3 loss to Rice before 73,000 in Houston was costly enough but, luckily for the Tigers, they seemed to consolidate all their mistakes into one game. Trailing 0–6, Harris dropped a pass in the end zone and later Stovall fumbled to set up Rice's second score, a touchdown which came on a play (a pass to the fullback down the middle) the Owls borrowed from the LSU playbook. "We have lost a battle," said Dietzel, "not a war."

But next week, in Tiger Stadium, LSU fans began to wonder. After three quarters, the Tigers trailed underdog Texas A & M, 7–2, when Harris, a doubtful starter because of a bruised leg, tightroped down the west sidelines sixty-two yards to the go-ahead score. A fine block by Jimmy Field sprang Wendell loose and he went on to make a brilliant run. "We had to prove to ourselves we could come back in the fourth quarter," said Dietzel.

With unbeaten Georgia Tech coming up, Harris snapped LSU out of its doldrums just in time. Bobby Dodd was bringing his Yellowjackets to Baton Rouge (the second time during Dietzel's regime) and it was a trip he viewed with apprehension. "There's no place tougher to play than Baton Rouge," said Bobby. What about South Bend? "Believe me, it's not as tough as Tiger Stadium." What LSU did on a clear October evening was combine the advantage of playing before 66,000 screaming fans ("It was like the Colosseum in Rome—and we were the Christians," said Dodd.) with a near-perfect game to produce a 10–0 gem that went a long way toward making a cohesive unit of the 1961 squad. "In all my career," said Dodd, "I've never seen a team better prepared to stop us. The pass rush and coverage was the best I've ever seen."

Tech quarterback Stan Gann, whose bombs had demolished Southern Cal and Rice, wound up with a total offense of one yard. The visitors netted eighty-six yards rushing and only seventy passing (forty-four in one play).

A key play helped Dietzel silence critics of his conservatism, those who claimed it was foolish to punt on third down inside your 30. Billy Lothridge, standing on his sixteen, fumbled the fourth-down snap while in punt formation and LSU was in business when the Tigers trapped him. In two cracks, Gros blasted to the 1 and then Field faked to Earl and followed him across. An interception by Bandit linebacker Buddy

Hamic set up a 22-yard field goal by Harris shortly before the half. LSU then dug in.

Tech's back was broken by a third-quarter goal line stand in which the Jackets had two shots from the 1, only to be denied on jarring tackles by Harris and Stovall. "Before you can lead," said Dietzel, "you have to perform." Now, all of a sudden, he had a flock of leaders on his hands. His job on the goal line and his punt return against A & M increased Harris's stature. Stovall regained his punting touch. Winston was all over the field. Amedee juiced up the Go Team as he had done the year before. And Field scored the touchdown that he needed to start believing in himself. His confidence booming, the man written off by many Tiger fans in 1960 followed up Tech by sparking the Tigers to a 42–0 conquest of South Carolina, running for ninety-five yards (more than any quarterback of the Dietzel era), completing five of six passes and piloting the White Team to three touchdowns.

It left LSU with two high hurdles before Ole Miss, first Kentucky and then Florida. The way the Tigers handled them illustrated their all-around class. The Kentucky game turned into a Baton Rouge spectacular. When the White Team bogged down near the end of the first period, Amedee took the Go Team half the field, pitching the last two yards to Neumann after faking Cranford into the line. Moments later, Campbell broke off tackle on a 59-yard scoring run to send the Tigers out to a comfortable, or so they thought, 14–0 lead. Dramatically, Kentucky struck back on a 77-yard scoring pass from Jerry Woolum to Tom Hutchinson for one score and got another on a march highlighted by Woolum passes. With the score tied 14–14 and time running out in the second quarter, the Tigers went into the shotgun with Amedee pulling the trigger. In less than one minute, they swept seventy-seven yards, setting up a field goal by Harris with thirty-eight seconds left. Having regained the psychological edge, LSU dominated the second half, prompting one Wildcat to remark: "It was more like playing five teams than three." Hutchinson, who faced Ole Miss two weeks earlier, said: "Ole Miss paced themselves like a bunch of pros, playing like they knew they'd win. LSU came at you from all sides like a bunch of wild men. They made their own breaks."

Muffled by a porcupine defense, Florida crumbled, 23–0, before constant pressure. In the second quarter, Wilkins—the Go Team was still hot—dashed thirty-three yards for one score, and Dwight Robinson intercepted a Gator pitchout and stepped twenty-five yards for another. To finish the job, Harris kicked a field goal and Neumann took a 17-yard pass from Amedee.

At this point in the fall of 1961, it was time again for fans to fasten their seatbelts. For the third time in four years the LSU-Ole Miss game was going to have national implications. In fact, if Minnesota tripped top-ranked Michigan State on the afternoon of November 4, the night game in Baton Rouge would send LSU against the No. 1 team in the United States. Ole Miss was not only unbeaten but unchallenged. By Johnny Vaught's own admission, LSU had become a crusade. "We're going to Baton Rouge," he said, "with every bit of determination and energy we can muster. This year we did not play Arkansas the week before. [Instead the Rebels had warmed up by crushing Vandy, 47–0.] We're not crippled and we're well rested. This team believes in itself and the boys don't believe anyone can whip 'em. We have a dozen seniors who were in that Halloween Night game. And a dozen juniors who played against LSU last year. It makes no difference that we've won six games so far this season. It's what we do next Saturday that counts."

If any team had cause to crusade, Ole Miss was that team. For example: (1) The Rebels had not crossed LSU's goal line in regular season play since 1957. (2) Vaught, who had never had a perfect season, would have had two had it not been for the blemishes left by the Tigers in 1959 and 1960.

Spicing the hostile climate was Perry Lee Dunn, Ole Miss's No. 3 quarterback (behind Doug Elmore and Glynn Griffing), who had been signed by Vaught in Oxford while Paul Dietzel cooled his heels in Dunn's Natchez home. It was clearly a recruiting coup for one of college football's winningest coaches.

With two teams of equal striking power, Ole Miss passed for fourteen of its thirty touchdowns and had one of its finest fullbacks in history in Billy Ray Adams, who had run for six touchdowns. Since the Rice debacle, the Tigers had begun to look like a football team, but the manner in which the Rebels handled its opposition—scoring 204 points to 13 for the enemy—made them a touchdown choice despite the home field advantage Tiger Stadium afforded.

Ole Miss didn't need any last-minute lift, but the Rebels got one just the same when they arrived for a Friday afternoon warmup. LSU students chanting "Go to Hell, Ole Miss, Go to Hell" surrounded the bus and it was some time before the team could get into the dressing room. Saturday afternoon the melodramatic touch was added when Minnesota DID upset Michigan State, making Ole Miss exactly what the banners carried into Tiger Stadium decreed: "We're No. 1." In sixty minutes of almost unbearable drama, LSU removed the apostrophe. Afterward the classic symbol of Old Miss's downfall was the red-shirted warrior who stood alone looking up unbelievingly at the electric lights which had etched the story for posterity: LSU 10, Ole Miss 7. The Tigers had done it again. Actually, it was Wendell Harris 10, Ole Miss 7—but you got an argument out of the senior halfback if you made a point of it. "If there was ever a team victory," said Harris, "this was it. It was a question of big plays by many different people."

If the screaming throng of 68,000 could have reached a consensus, it would have been that LSU beat a superior team with a series of clutch performances and with a trap that caught the Rebels going the wrong way. Overall, it was the finest Ole Miss club that Vaught, to that time, had sent against the Tigers, one better than the LSU staff anticipated. Ole Miss ran sixty-nine plays to forty-three for LSU, outgained the Tigers 322 yards to 213 and out-first-downed them 21–10, but still they lost. Why? Because Ole Miss was able to score only once in the six times it crossed midfield while LSU, which crossed midfield only three times in sixty minutes, twice put points on the scoreboard.

There were seven crucial spots which paved the way for the Rebels' demise:

1. A 37-yard field goal by Harris following a drive from the LSU 20 the first time the Tigers got the football.

2. A 57-yard run by Jerry Stovall which brought the Tigers from their 20 to the Rebel 23.

3. A diving catch by sophomore Billy Truax of a fourth-and-five pass by Lynn Amedee which kept the touchdown drive alive.

4. The seven-yard scoring run by Harris around left end behind a key block by Monk Guillot.

5. A third-down interception by Steve Ward which killed a fourth-quarter drive on the LSU 16.

6. A first-down fumble recovery by Gene Sykes on the LSU 34 which stifled Ole Miss's final bid.

7. The punting of Danny Neumann who, substituting for a bruised Stovall, kicked four times for a 45.2 average.

"I hope the boys on the 1958 and '59 teams will forgive me," said Dietzel, "but this is the greatest victory I've ever been associated with."

It was the run by Stovall, reminiscent of the Halloween gallop by Billy Cannon, which turned the game around. Until Jerry broke loose, it looked as if Ole Miss's touchdown seconds before half time had deflated the Tigers. But Stovall's burst around the right side suddenly changed everything. LSU sent Harris in motion to the right. Jimmy Field started out the same way but handed to Stovall coming to the left. A couple of good blocks sprang him loose. Moments later, LSU's drive seemed destined to fizzle out when the 6–5 Truax came up with a miracle catch of a fourth-down pass on the Ole Miss 12. "I barely got my fingers under it," said Billy. "As I stumbled forward, I pulled the ball into my chest." It was LSU's only completion of the evening.

Two plays later, Guillot leveled Ole Miss' Lou Guy, and Harris sped into the end zone untouched. It was the same play, run to a different side,

Ole Miss falls in 1961: Monk Guillot levels Lou Guy and Wendell Harris sprints across for the winning touchdown.

that Stovall had used to tilt the momentum in LSU's direction. "Both times," said Dietzel, "we caught them going the wrong way."

As matters developed, the Sugar Bowl also caught LSU going in the opposite direction. LSU's upset of Ole Miss lifted Paul Dietzel's club into fourth place behind Texas, Alabama, and Ohio State. When the Tigers went to Chapel Hill and blanked North Carolina 30–0 with ridiculous ease, the Sugar Bowl moved toward an Alabama-LSU match. But this time the Tigers weren't buying. Jim Corbett announced LSU would not play in the Sugar Bowl; in fact, the Tigers pointedly declined an invitation for the New Orleans classic, a game in which they had played twice in the last three seasons. Corbett's next move was to engineer a favorable vote by the Board of Supervisors, one which would clear the way for LSU's participation in a postseason game against a racially-mixed team. The fourteen members, meeting as a committee of the whole, reaffirmed a 1956 policy of scheduling athletic contests with "major institutions of this and other sections of the country."

With everyone speculating on where LSU would spend New Year's Day, a Mississippi State team with a 5–3 record slipped into Baton Rouge and came close to springing an embarrassing upset. With three minutes left, the Maroons trailed 7–6 but were driving for a possible winning touchdown or field goal when Earl Gros turned into a ragin' Cajun.

A loser pays off: Rebel fan Ted McCullough gives Tiger fan (and one-time Tiger) Jake Staples a ride up Third Street after 1961 game.

First, the senior fullback intercepted on LSU's 22 and returned the ball to the Tiger 48. On the next play, he burst through the middle and rambled all the way to the 2-yard-line. In two cracks, Earl was over, LSU had a shaky 14–6 victory and could go back to bowl business.

The day after, the players voted to accept an invitation to the Orange Bowl (racially-mixed Colorado and Kansas were the possible foes), an invitation tendered the Tigers in view of the Board of Supervisors' ruling. Since LSU had Tulane remaining, it could not officially accept until after its final game.

The finale was not much of a game. With 63,500 on hand at Tiger Stadium, the Miami-bound Tigers recovered a Green Wave fumble on the opening kickoff, had a touchdown in two minutes and were off to their second crushing victory since 1958. Late in the afternoon, the shadows were long in Tiger Stadium and the scoreboard frozen at LSU 62, Tulane 0, when Andy Pilney turned from a postgame handshake with Paul Dietzel and walked, head bowed and alone, to join his beaten team. As Andy made his way through the milling, victory-flushed LSU throng, a small boy sailed a paper airplane toward the Tulane coach, which hit him on the shoulder and spiraled to the ground. In a way, it was a symbol of life and football, both of which, in a split second can be a peak of exaltation and a ravine of gloom. The big difference is, in coaching, your successes and failures are shared by thousands. You are cheered on the mountaintop and cussed in the valley. Andy Pilney was the classic illustration.

You might say November 2, 1935, and November 25, 1961, were the opening and closing parentheses in a life devoted to a game which Army's Earl Blaik described as "violent chess." As a Notre Dame halfback in 1935 playing against Ohio State before 81,000 in Columbus, Pilney, with superb passing and fearless running, had helped the Irish erase a 13–0 Buckeye lead in the final fourteen minutes and go on to an 18–13 victory regarded by many as the finest comeback in football history. At the finish, Pilney was not around. Rather, he was lying on a stretcher with torn ligaments sustained on a dazzling broken-field run to set up the winning touchdown. He heard the news of the Notre Dame victory in an ambulance and wept. Now, twenty-six years later, Andy Pilney was walking the last mile, his only consolation being that a coach, whatever his record, can gain strength from the fact he is a braver and better man then any of his critics.

As LSU began to make plans for an Orange Bowl meeting with Big Eight champion Colorado, Andy Pilney was not the only head coach out of a job. Several days after Navy defeated Army, Paul Dietzel picked up his Baton Rouge *Morning Advocate* to learn that Dale Hall, Earl Blaik's successor after the 1958 season, had been fired. Dietzel looked across at his wife and said: "Honey, better start packing." As Dietzel was to explain later, he felt the question of his future had been answered. He had been approached by Army after his national championship year of 1958 but declined the offer, feeling he had not accomplished what he had set out to do. Also, he did not relish following Blaik.

In 1961, however, he felt the challenge was gone in Baton Rouge and, admittedly, the former West Point assistant had long been dazzled by the glamor of the Army job. The same day he learned of Hall's dismissal, Dietzel placed a long-distance call to Joe Cahill, sports publicity director at West Point, indicating interest in the job. Several days later the athletic director at the academy called Dietzel, who said that if Army was interested in him, he would first have to speak to Jim Corbett to get permission. Corbett impressed upon Dietzel the fact that he still had four years remaining on his contract. "Paul," said Corbett, "I don't want you to leave but, if you want to leave, I'll release you from your contract." With this, Dietzel flew to New York during the Christmas holidays to meet General William Westmoreland, superintendent of the academy, at the International Hotel near Kennedy Airport. They discussed the job and Dietzel told the general that, if details could be worked out, "this is what I'm looking for."

The story that Dietzel was in contact with Army officials broke while LSU was in Miami winding up its Orange Bowl preparations. The man

Final touchdown in the Orange Bowl—and the final game for Paul.

who had said many times "I'll never leave LSU" found himself in a delicate position. He was forced to label reports he would accept the West Point job "a silly assumption" while making sure word of his departure did not have an adverse effect on his ball club. Ever the psychologist, Dietzel turned a headline in a Miami paper—"LSU to Give Coach Goodbye Win"—into a pregame pep talk in which he stressed the team was not playing for Paul Dietzel but for LSU.

Colorado didn't have much of a chance. The Tigers won comfortably, 25–7, with Roy Winston playing like the all-America guard he was and the White Team, Go Team, and Chinese Bandits dominating most of the afternoon. The jubilant Tigers carried Dietzel from the field, but, back in Louisiana, the real fun was about to begin. Ike Carriere, the board member instrumental in landing Dietzel in 1955, was telling everyone Dietzel should not be released. Although he was not then a member of the LSU board, Judge Carriere buttonholed board members and expressed his feelings. He felt that there was only one honorable thing to do: refuse to release Dietzel from his contract and then fire him.

On January 5, 1962, Corbett went before the LSU board and requested that Dietzel be granted his release. "There is no reason," said Corbett, "to keep a man who does not want to stay." After heated discussion, board member Tom Dutton introduced a motion that Dietzel not be released from his contract. It lost by an 8–5 vote.

It was a relieved Dietzel who faced the press after the verdict. "Deep in my heart," he admitted, "I've always wanted to be head coach at West Point." About his "I'll never leave LSU" statements, Dietzel said: "When I said it I meant it because I never dreamed I'd have the opportunity of coaching the Cadets. I realize I should never have made such statements. It was a mistake."

Dietzel said that in January, 1959, when he was offered the Army job, it would have been "presumptuous" of him to discuss the position, since he had just signed a five-year contract. Also, he said, he was swayed by President Troy Middleton who decided, at the time, not to retire. In January, 1962, Middleton's retirement was at hand; he would be succeeded on February 1 by Dr. John A. Hunter. Dietzel's departure came only a few days earlier.

"I feel I can contribute something at West Point," he said. "The academy is not a university but an institution, one which has produced men like MacArthur and Eisenhower. I've always admired the Cadets and what they represent. Being able to give them a football team they can be proud of thrills me. I accept it as a tremendous challenge." Because Dietzel was leaving behind a squad that was dominated by juniors and sophomores, he felt he was not deserting the ship. "If LSU were down," he said, "I might feel differently."

For many LSU fans, it was an emotional time. Paul Dietzel was leaving behind a 46–23–3 record. In the last four of his seven seasons, his team had won a national championship, won one SEC title and shared another, and finished among the nation's top four teams three times. Meanwhile, The Long Gray Line was preparing to welcome the new coach with open arms. Try as they might, the fanatical fans he was leaving were finding it hard getting used to one thing—there would be Chinese Bandits at West Point.

'I've had the monkey on my back'

1962–1968

ALTHOUGH many missed the classic irony, it was there on the same sports page in early January, 1962: one story dealing with a member of the LSU Board of Supervisors talking about coaches who regard a contract as "just another piece of paper," while elsewhere a dispatch from Lexington said: "Blanton Collier, who faced an almost impossible task of replacing Paul 'Bear' Bryant, was fired yesterday as head coach at the University of Kentucky. The University's athletic board voted to buy out the remaining three years of Collier's contract." It was ironic, of course, because in 1954 Paul Dietzel would have had the coaching job at Kentucky had not Blanton Collier experienced a last-minute change of mind. Eight years later, a victory-flushed Dietzel was packing for West Point and 55-year-old Collier, in Lexington, was lamenting the fact he had "no immediate plans."

The irony was not lost on New York columnist Red Smith, who accused Noah Webster of "goofing off" in his definition of "sanctity." Observing that the dictionary defines the word as a "religious binding force; as in sanctity of an oath," Smith wrote that Webster "fails to add the obvious example: 'As in sanctity of a contract with a coach whose teams win football games.' This is important because saintliness and godliness are coachly attributes only when the team gets invited to the Orange Bowl. There is no sanctity of a contract with a coach whose team loses half its games." In requesting release from his contract, Smith said, Dietzel was "only recognizing a fact of life."

Once Dietzel had departed, leaving behind a lot of bitterness, the only fact of life that mattered to the Board of Supervisors was finding a replacement and, here again, the firing of Collier played a major role. The day Dietzel was granted his release his No. 1 assistant, Charley

McClendon, was in Lexington being interviewed by his alma mater. Suddenly the man who a few years earlier had come within a whisker of landing the Navy job found himself in an enviable position. Kentucky offered him the head coaching post and, with no contract obligations binding him to LSU, he could have accepted on the spot. Instead, he telephoned Jim Corbett to apprise him of the situation. Corbett, McClendon learned, had been named a committee of one to find Dietzel's successor, so now it became a matter of Jim's wishing McClendon well at Lexington or hiring him as head coach at LSU. "Charley," said Corbett, "come on back to Baton Rouge and we'll talk."

And talk they did—all day Sunday, January 7, in Corbett's home. "We discussed all aspects of the job," said Corbett. "It was a frank, free-wheeling conversation in which Charley and I exchanged views." By sundown Corbett felt this 38-year-old native of Lewisville, Arkansas—someone he said "contributed heavily to LSU's football success"—deserved a chance. The chance came in the form of a four-year contract at $18,000 a year, an offer acceptable to the board and to McClendon. "No use expressing how happy I am to have the opportunity to coach LSU," said McClendon. "The way I feel, the music has started, so my job is to keep in step. I was in on the organization of the three-team setup and it's been good to LSU. So there's no sense in changing it."

Of most immediate concern to McClendon was the task of selecting a staff. Following Dietzel to West Point were George Terry, Larry Jones, Bill Shalosky, and Charley Pevey. At the NCAA meeting in Chicago, however, Pevey had a change of heart and decided to stay on as Charley's first assistant. Then, in short order, LSU's new head coach added Doug Hamley, head coach at LaGrange, Louisiana, High; Dixie White, assistant at Arkansas; Bill Beall, assistant at Rice; and John North, assistant at Kentucky. Along with holdovers Taylor McNeel, former Louisiana Tech quarterback, and Don Purvis, this was the makeup of Charley McClendon's staff for his first season as head coach.

Charles Youmans McClendon, the new man in Baton Rouge, was not cut from the same cloth as his predecessor, and he made no pretense that he was. "The worst mistake any coach can make is not being himself," he said. "I'm no spellbinder, so my conversation will be brief and simple." McClendon kept it simple. He sprinkled his Arkansas-accented chatter with "gosh knows," his unbelievable honesty startled many newsmen, and he made no attempt at histrionics. He was "just plain Charley," an image that reflected his origin. McClendon's birthplace, the tiny community of Lewisville, was eighty miles from Fordyce, first home of Bear Bryant. "Fordyce was so far back in the country," Bryant was fond of saying, "that, when we moved, all we had to do was throw

Charley McClendon: "The worst mistake any coach can make is not being himself."

water on the fire and call the dogs." Lewisville was little different.

McClendon's middle name came from Dr. William Youmans, a friend of the family who delivered the McClendon brood—Charley, six brothers and a sister. "I was the last one," said Charley. "Doc Youmans saved my life and my mother's, too, so she figured it was the least we could do." A regular childhood activity was baseball and basketball games against families of other communities, the site of which was any unoccupied cow pasture. "We had a hot series with a group from Hope, a town about twenty miles from Lewisville," said Charley. "Because there were only eight of us, we'd recruit a cousin or two for baseball games."

It was a long time before the youngest McClendon entertained any football ambitions. Following graduation from high school, he worked for Phillips Petroleum before enlisting in the Navy in 1943. After a 1946 discharge, he entered Magnolia Junior College on a basketball scholarship, and it wasn't until three years later that he turned his football talents into a free ticket to Kentucky. "A friend recommended me to Coach Bryant," says Charley. "Fortunately, I played with some fine teams. We went to the Orange Bowl when I was a junior and to the Sugar Bowl in my senior year. I stayed on as an assistant during the 1951 season when we went to the Cotton Bowl."

In 1952 McClendon left Kentucky for Vanderbilt, going there with the idea he would be an end coach (he played defensive end at Kentucky) on the staff of Bill Edwards. He wound up in charge of the defensive line. "I didn't like the idea of leaving my alma mater," said McClendon. "Looking back, I realize Coach Bryant recommended me to Vandy because he knew the job paid more money. I was making $2,800 at Kentucky coaching the freshmen, that is, the freshmen who weren't good enough to make the varsity. At that time, you could play varsity ball as a freshman. Anyway, I liked it at Kentucky and liked working for Coach Bryant. When I learned the assistant's job at Vandy was going to pay $4,800, I put it to Coach Bryant that I didn't see how I, as a newly married man, could turn the job down, sort of hinting for a boost in pay. I'll never forget Bear's words: 'If I wanted to pay you more, I would.' I got the message. He wanted me out on my own and I've never regretted it."

Charley also didn't regret being put in charge of Vandy's defense. "It seemed I was always at the blackboard drawing X's and O's," he said. McClendon's experience came the painful way. The Commodores limped through a 3–5–2 season and, when Tennessee scored a crushing 46–0 victory, it was common knowledge, but not official, that Bill Edwards would be replaced. "Of course, this meant job-hunting for the assistants," said McClendon. "Here I was in my first season away from Kentucky and already the immediate future looked shaky. But I was lucky once again. Bear called Coach Tinsley to recommend me. More important, however, was a call by Fred Russell of the Nashville *Banner* to Red Heard. Fred gave me a big buildup and the next thing I knew, Red Heard contacted me. It was shortly before Christmas that I accepted the LSU offer for $6,500—$2,000 more than I was making at Vandy. What a Christmas present."

Twenty-nine, 6 feet, 2 inches, 210 pounds, the jovial Scotch-Irishman impressed everyone with his attention to detail and his tirelessness. Although he built LSU's 1953 defensive line into one of the most respected in the SEC, the 159 points allowed by the Tigers was frustrating. The

1954 season, even though it produced all-America Sid Fournet, brought more frustration to a defense that yielded 173 points. When Dietzel appeared on the scene, his healthy respect for McClendon was immediately apparent. He turned over to Charley all of the defensive planning and within three years LSU became one of the stingiest teams in the United States, allowing the enemy an average of 4.57 points per game from 1958 through 1961.

When did McClendon feel he was ready to become a head coach? "Around 1958," he said. "As I missed out on certain jobs, I began to get particular. I made up my mind I wanted to stay in the South and coach at a major school."

Before McClendon made that decision, he had experienced his biggest heartbreak. In 1959 he left Annapolis convinced he would succeed Eddie Erdelatz as Navy coach. "I was under the impression the job was mine," he said. "When I got back to Baton Rouge, however, there was a terse telegram telling me officials at the academy had decided on an assistant on the staff, Wayne Hardin. It hit me like a kick in the stomach. It was the lowest moment of my life."

In trying to analyze a coach's approach, McClendon says he always has been a firm believer in teaching what you know best. "There is no one best way to do something in football," he says. "For example, LSU and Alabama handle their defensive alignments differently but both have gotten good results. Bama likes the eight-man front, we like the five-four. It isn't what you do but how well you do it. The only constant thing in football is material. You can't win without it. And you can't win with it unless you have good morale."

McClendon didn't need anyone to tell him about the material he inherited, least of all Paul Dietzel. When Dietzel got to West Point, he went out of his way to emphasize the raft of talent he left behind. Not only that, but he verbally bestowed on Jerry Stovall the 1962 Heisman Trophy. It got so bad McClendon had to telephone his former boss, who knew better than anyone else talk like this was only adding to the burden of a first-year coach.

Seven 1961 seniors were missing—Harris, Gros, Winston, Booth and Monk Guillot from the White Team, Neck and Richards from the Bandits. But twenty-six lettermen were returning, including quarterbacks Jimmy Field and Lynn Amedee. The manner in which Field and Amedee performed during a sparkling 10–1 season—Lynn's total offense was 617 yards, Field's 438—would have been enough to satisfy most fans that the pair should be back at their jobs in 1962. Not LSU's fans, however. Occasionally, well-meaning alumni get on a "kick," and in the spring of 1962 many happened to be on a "Pat Screen kick." They felt the 180-pound sophomore from Jesuit High in New Orleans was good enough to step right into the quarterback post, moving aside two seniors. So the question greeting rookie head coach McClendon at every turn was: "Are you going to red-shirt Screen?"

The spring game didn't help Charley's problem any because the gifted sophomore steered the Golds to a 21–20 win over the Purples, running for thirty-three yards in seven carries and completing seven of eleven passes for eighty-seven yards. Privately, McClendon made it clear he wasn't going to "throw Screen to the wolves" by playing him before he was ready. Publicly, he said: "We don't red shirt anyone just to be red shirting. If a boy's ready, and we have a place for him, we play him."

When the shuffling was completed in the fall, McClendon had only one major surprise in his three teams, and, again, this was not too much of one because sophomore halfback Danny LeBlanc from Lake Charles High as a freshman had demolished tacklers, preferring to run over, rather than around, them. In fact, his reckless ways as a ball carrier led many to feel there was no way to keep him out of the lineup. Unlike Screen, who found himself behind two seniors, LeBlanc benefited by the departure of Wendell Harris and moved into the right half slot on the White Team.

LSU's three-deep for 1962 looked like this:

	White Team	Go Team	Chinese Bandits
LE	Gene Sykes	Danny Neumann	Bob Flurry
LT	Don Estes	Ralph Pere	Charles Simmons
LG	Rodney Guillot	Jerry Young	Remi Prudhomme
C	Dennis Gaubatz	Gary Kinchen	Ruffin Rodrigue
RG	Rob Hucklebridge	Eddie Habert	Jim Turner
RT	Fred Miller	Willis Langley	Milt Trosclair
RE	Jack Gates	Bill Truax	Mike Morgan
QB	Jimmy Field	Lynn Amedee	Dwight Robinson
LH	Jerry Stovall	Bo Campbell	White Graves
RH	Danny LeBlanc	Ray Wilkins	Buddy Soefker
FB	Steve Ward	Charley Cranford	Buddy Hamic

After an opening 21–0 victory over Texas A & M, it was obvious McClendon was going to stick to LSU's tried-and-true formula; defense is the best offense. The Aggies were unable to get past the Tiger 21 and were out of the ball game when Stovall returned the second half kickoff fifty-eight yards to set up LSU's second touchdown. Generally, the Tigers played like an experienced club, seemingly content to go through the motions before an overflow of 68,618 that gave a roaring welcome to "Hey Fightin' Tigers," a new fight song inspired by Jim Corbett.

A week later, against a Rice team that was better than a two-touchdown underdog in Tiger Stadium, the Tigers were more frustrated than

Jerry Stovall with his wife.

fighting. Wily Jess Neely found himself in one of those nothing-to-lose positions and the relaxed manner in which his Owls refused to panic against a superior team reflected this feeling. Most embarrassing of all, however, was the way in which a 19-year-old sophomore, playing his first varsity game, treated LSU's secondary. Walter McReynolds looked more like a quiz kid than a quarterback. Actually, the fact that he was far-sighted made him oblivious to the Tigers' pass rush. He completed thirteen passes for 179 yards, including one for a touchdown in a 6–6 standoff. The Owl touchdown was on a "couldn't happen" play which completely shocked LSU and all of the 64,500 in Tiger Stadium. Rice was playing a fourth-and-twenty-seven on the LSU 30 and McClendon sent in a substitute to alert the Tigers to expect a screen pass. Sure enough, McReynolds drifted back and, at the last second, flipped the ball to wingback Gene Fleming in the right flat and then, as Tigers stumbled and fell, Fleming skipped down the sidelines to a touchdown.

Because Rice missed the extra point, LSU had a chance to go ahead in the third period when Stovall cracked over from the 6 but Field bobbled the ball on Amedee's extra point try. Later, in the fading moments, another bobble—this one by Danny LeBlanc on the Owl 10—wiped out LSU's last opportunity to escape embarrassment.

His team's stuttering performance against Rice set up McClendon's first moment of truth as a head coach. This moment came in unfriendly surroundings—and before a national television audience. Unbeaten Georgia Tech had Grant Field going for it and a pitch-and-catch combo in Billy Lothridge and Billy Martin that had already taken care of Clemson and Florida. Tech always managed to bring out the best in LSU and this time, with the home team favored by a touchdown, it was no exception. With a defense headed by Fred Miller, the Tigers carried the fight to Tech in a scoreless first half and then the fireworks began.

Stovall gathered in Lothridge's second-half kickoff on the 2 and LSU had its familiar return set up—he would run to the 15, fake a handoff to Field who had his back turned to the onrushing Jackets and then take off. When LSU unveiled this play in its 1961 opener, Stovall, after a run of fifteen yards, handed the ball to Amedee who, in turn, pitched to Ray Wilkins running laterally from left to right. Wilkins ran all the way to midfield against the befuddled Owls. From that time, however, the handoff was faked to the quarterback. "We've had good success because they've got to spread out to protect the sidelines in case of a handoff," said McClendon. "This helps open the middle."

Although Tech had seen film of Stovall's 58-yard return against Texas A & M on the identical play, Bobby Dodd's club was still outside-con-

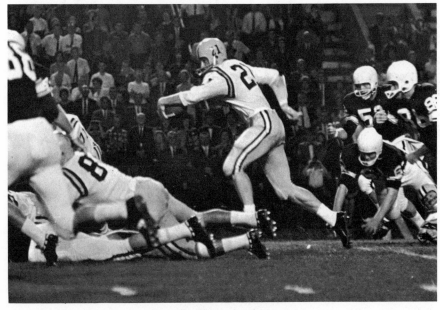

Stovall tears off yardage against the Texas Aggies, 1962.

scious on this particular occasion—perhaps too much so. Stovall repeated what he had been doing since the 1961 Rice game: he faked to Field and, suddenly, found a huge hunk of daylight. Without a hand being laid on him, he sprinted up the field, was in the clear at the LSU 40, veered slightly to the left, and pranced into the end zone like a drum major.

The drama had only begun. Lothridge finally got Tech cranked up on a 83-yard march which ended with Billy passing ten yards to Martin and then kicking the tying point. On the next kickoff, Charley Cranford came within a step of breaking loose and was finally nailed on the Tech 48. With Amedee taking over for an injured Jimmy Field, the Tigers moved to the Tech 7 in seven plays where, on fourth down with 4:35 left, Lynn booted a field goal to make it 10–7. The thrills weren't over. With a minute left, Joe Auer made a diving catch of a Lothridge pass to take Tech from its 20 to midfield. Later, with twelve seconds showing on the clock, the same Auer raced fifteen yards past the LSU secondary but dropped a Lothridge bomb at the LSU 10.

Characteristically, the Tigers had said it with defense and they did the same thing the next three weeks, beating Miami and George Mira, 17–3; Kentucky, 7–0; and Florida, 23–0. Mira—"He must have eyes in his ears," said Gaubatz—completed fourteen passes for 168 yards, but LSU managed to keep the Hurricanes out of its end zone. Stovall fractured a 3–3 tie with a 26-yard run up the middle and Danny LeBlanc iced the game with a 10-yard scoring run on which he carried three Miami tacklers weighing 610 pounds across the goal line. "The thing about Danny is," said Stovall, "no one knows just how good he is."

The Kentucky game was almost a replica of the 1959 battle with Tennessee. LSU had a 23–4 edge in first downs, a 363–108 advantage in total offense, and it had the ball for seventy-nine plays compared to thirty-three for the Wildcats. At the end, however, all the Tigers had to show for their work was a fourth-quarter score by Stovall, and LSU was lucky to get it. Stovall fumbled on the University of Kentucky 5 but Steve Ward recovered, and then Jerry took it across three plays later.

It would not be accurate to say Jerry Stovall made LSU fans forget Billy Cannon, but the way he played against Florida made one fan observe: "There was only one Cannon but there's only one Stovall too." In smashing the Gators, 23–0, for the second year in a row, Jerry (1) ran and caught passes for 65 of a 77-yard march to set up a first-quarter field goal; (2) caught a 16-yard touchdown toss from Jimmy Field in the third period; and (3) scored on a slashing 6-yard run in the fourth period. According to Coach McClendon, his defense and blocking was "the most vicious this season by one of our backs."

Apparently, the Tigers had arrived just in time. Their defense seemed to increase in ferocity each week, the Go Team had found itself, and

Stovall was showing signs of being a legitimate Superman. If anything, statistics showed that no Tiger back—Cannon included—had been as effective against Ole Miss, preparing for its annual Tiger Stadium invasion, as the senior halfback from West Monroe. In two games against the Rebels, Jerry carried for 190 yards in thirteen rushes, a fantastic 14.6 average.

Winless in regular season since 1957, Ole Miss fans were beginning to wonder if there was such a thing as a jinx. Particularly galling to Johnny Vaught was the fact that LSU had ruined perfect seasons for his Ole Miss teams in 1959, 1960, and 1961. In 1961, Vaught had spoken of a "crusade." Now, with another outstanding club, one that was ranked sixth, two notches below the Tigers, he was as silent as the Sphinx. Except for the 21–0 Sugar Bowl victory, which, in some respects, was a hollow one, Vaught's teams seemed to fail in the clutch against LSU. Ole Miss never played badly against the Tigers but, to some, it seemed the sight of LSU made Ole Miss abandon its reckless role and become archconservative, which was not characteristic of the Rebels.

This time Vaught decided to shoot the works. On the second play of the game, quarterback Glynn Griffing rifled a long pass—the first of thirty-one—to halfback Lou Guy who had gotten behind the LSU secondary. Guy dropped it, but as far as the Rebels were concerned, it set the tone of the game. And what a game! Glynn Wilburn Griffing succeeded where former Rebel quarterbacks—folks like Bobby Franklin, Jake Gibbs and Doug Elmore—failed. And the amazing thing was that he did it by only a 15–7 score. It should have been much worse.

The Rebs wound up with a 23–6 edge in first downs and a 393–107 advantage in total offense. Actually, the turning point came just when it seemed LSU might be pulling out of a first-half daze. Jerry Stovall smashed over with 2:27 left in the second quarter and Amedee kicked the point to make it 7–0. But the Rebels then blitzed sixty-one yards in twelve plays, eleven of them passes, beating the half-time clock by sixteen seconds. The payoff was a 10-yard pass to A. J. Holloway. Holloway caught the ball on the 5, was hit, squirmed loose, and barely made it into the end zone. There seemed to be disagreement between the two officials on the spot—one apparently felt Holloway's knee hit on the 1—but it was still six points. When Griffing fumbled the snap, LSU was able to take a 7–6 lead into the dressing room, but the Tigers left the field with a deflated look. Just how deflated no one realized until the second half. In the final two quarters Ole Miss rushed for 144 yards and held LSU to minus 21. Overhead, the Rebels went for eighty-seven yards, LSU for ten. Ole Miss had thirteen first downs to LSU's one and that came via a penalty. It seems incredible that Ole Miss could manage only nine points but it is possible they got tired moving the football.

In the face of LSU's collapse, all sorts of stories cropped up, the major one being reports of a fight among the players at half time. Not so. It's quite possible LSU left its game on the practice field, although the probable answer was supplied by Griffing, who accounted for 213 yards of Ole Miss's 393 yards of total offense. Said the senior quarterback: "We simply got tired of losing to these folks."

For Charley McClendon, with a severe case of post-Rebel blues, it became a case of salvaging the rest of the season, that is, TCU, Mississippi State, and Tulane. Not surprisingly, it was done with defense because, although no one knew it at the time, Ole Miss was the last team to put the ball in LSU's end zone. Twice in the last quarter of the TCU game the nimble hands of Dwight Robinson knocked down "touchdown" passes by Sonny Gibbs to preserve a 5–0 victory. "We got a field goal," said Jim Corbett after the game, "and then we told the boys to run up the score." TCU was the first team to keep Stovall from scoring, but the next week, in a 28–0 win over State, Jerry scored twice in a Jackson, Mississippi, downpour to push his 1962 touchdown total to ten. State did not get a first down until nine minutes into the third quarter.

For the finale, McClendon found himself a five-touchdown favorite over the Greenies, coached for the first time by Tommy O'Boyle, Andy Pilney's successor. Tulane's 0–9 record was reflected in the slim crowd of 37,811 in Sugar Bowl Stadium, and for Green Wave fans on hand it was like Camelot—they experienced a brief moment of glory. Tulane enjoyed a 3–0 lead until LSU made it 7–3 in the second quarter, and then the Tigers went on to add four touchdowns and a field goal in the last half for a 38–3 victory. If Jerry Stovall had been rough on Ole Miss, Lynn Amedee emerged as Tulane's archnemesis. In three games against the Greenies, Lynn rushed for 174 yards and four touchdowns, passed for 286 yards and two touchdowns, and kicked a field goal. Amedee's splurge made him LSU's total offense leader for the third year in a row, and gave Texas an extra problem in the Cotton Bowl.

Jim Corbett formally accepted an invitation to the Dallas classic after the Tulane game, one matching the seventh-ranked Tigers and the fourth-ranked Longhorns, a team which Coach Darrell Royal called "the most criticized undefeated club in history." They had been tied by Rice but had handed Arkansas its only defeat of the season in the final thirty seconds to win the Southwest Conference crown. Everything pointed to a low-scoring game; in fact, one Texas writer, reviewing the close-to-the-vest philosophies of McClendon and Royal, suggested a 12–6 score, six safeties to three safeties. LSU had yielded but thirty-four points in ten games while Texas, sparked by all-America linebackers Johnny Treadwell and Pat Culpepper, surrendered fifty-four. Mainly on the strength of Stovall, the Tigers entered their first Cotton Bowl since the memorable "Ice Bowl" of 1947 as a slight favorite and, if there

Cotton Bowl-bound Tigers. Front row, Johnny Mercer, Milton Trosclair, Charley Cranford, Steve Ward, Dennis Gaubatz. In back, Willis Langley and Billy Truax.

was any question about LSU's being ready to play, Fred Miller answered it on the first scrimmage play of the afternoon. He knifed through and nailed the Texas ball carrier for a 6-yard loss. From that moment, LSU set the tempo with a stubborn defense that sent the proud Longhorns down to only their second defeat in twenty-seven games.

With eight seconds left in the second quarter, Amedee, after passing the Tigers into position, booted a 23-yard field goal to crack the Cotton Bowl record. Lynn recovered the second-half kickoff on the Texas 37 after Sykes and Gaubatz jarred the ball loose from the ball carrier. Four plays later, Field went twenty-two yards for a touchdown and Amedee made it 10–0. Finally, in the fourth quarter, after his touchdown pass was nullified by a penalty, Amedee proceeded to break his two-quarter-old Cotton Bowl record when he booted a 37-yard field goal, the icing on a 13–0 victory.

The game's outstanding back credited two moves by the LSU staff as vital to the victory. "We put in a new play which looked like a sweep to one side but wound up as an off-tackle play to the other side," said Amedee. "This caught their quick linebackers going in the wrong direction. We also gave them the appearance of the sprint-out pass but we'd

Quarterbacks Jimmy Field and Lynn Amedee.

stop and hit the end down the middle." It was a glittering finish for the Istrouma graduate who was passed up by both NFL and AFL. Meanwhile, Stovall was signing with the St. Louis Cardinals for a contract worth $75,000, while LSU's other all-America, Fred Miller, signed a lucrative pact with the Baltimore Colts.

For McClendon, rounding out a 9–1–1 season, the game eclipsed the Georgia Tech victory as a matter of prestige. Typically, McClendon spoke glowingly of his eighteen seniors, saying: "The thing that impressed me most was that goose egg next to Texas."

Defensively the 1962 Tigers became the stingiest of the Dietzel era— "Dietzel era" because McClendon admittedly was inheriting a senior ball club put together by his predecessor. Although Charley would be playing Dietzel recruits for three more years his 1963 squad, including eighteen lettermen and heavily loaded with sophomores, was generally considered to be more of a test for McClendon as a head coach. It would be a rebuilding year, a year that not only would usher in the "McClendon era" but the "Pat Screen era" as well. Although a 9–1–1 record would be acceptable to almost anyone, there were still those critics who insisted McClendon could have beaten Rice and Ole Miss by making use of Screen. McClendon was not the only one who disagreed. So did Screen. "I don't care what anyone says," explained Pat, "it was the best

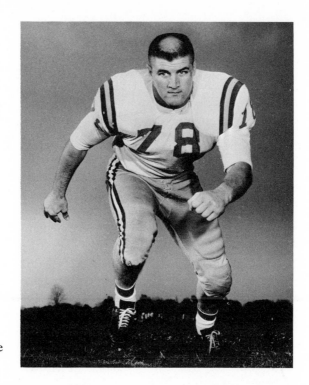

All-America Fred Miller: He signed a pact with the Colts.

thing that ever happened to me." He felt the tips he picked up sitting next to Field and Amedee on the bench were invaluable. "They'd explain in detail a particular problem; they'd tell me what they were trying to do and why. On the telephone I guess I delivered more messages than Western Union. But listening to the conversations with Coach Pevey in the press box and Coach North in the end zone, you learned what to look for. I realized I wasn't ready. The coaches tell me I won't understand how fast the SEC really is until I get out on the field under fire."

Screen had been personally recruited by Dietzel, and rumors circulated in 1962 that he would drop out of LSU and transfer to Notre Dame if he were red-shirted. "Ridiculous," said Pat. Actually, Screen was smitten with LSU long before his graduation from Jesuit. By his own admission, one of the most embarrassing moments of his life was the time he attended the 1960 LSU-Ole Miss game in Oxford as a guest of Johnny Vaught. Screen was seated on the Rebel bench when Stovall broke loose on a 42-yard run in the first quarter. "I jumped off the bench and began to cheer Jerry on when I realized where I was," said Pat. He sat down red-faced.

Screen was not the only athlete sitting on the Ole Miss bench that day to wind up in Tigertown. Joe Labruzzo of Lockport and Don Schwab of Thibodaux had expected to fly into Oxford in a private plane provided by Vaught. The plane developed engine trouble, landed in Jackson, and the two players proceeded to Oxford by automobile. They arrived in the second half but had gotten well acquainted during the trip. Vaught spoke to both prospects individually and had Schwab, a short-legged fullback, virtually sold. The 5-foot, 8-inch, 160-pound Labruzzo, with a wind-assisted 9.6 hundred-yard dash to his credit, wasn't thinking about attending college at the time. But when Schwab made known his feelings about Ole Miss, Labruzzo tried "to pound some sense into him" about state pride. He sold Schwab on LSU and Don signed with Ray Didier. Later, when Schwab learned Labruzzo was giving Tulane serious consideration, he talked Joe into LSU. "I went because I knew I'd have a friend there but I still didn't think I could make the team," said Labruzzo, a hero in the town of Lockport.

Screen, Labruzzo, and Schwab were among the more highly-touted red shirts scheduled to figure vitally in the success of a young squad that possibly was going to have to reshape its three-team thinking, because the 1963 season brought with it a new substitution rule aimed at restoring the two-way player. According to the new rule, an entire team could be sent in when the clock was stopped, EXCEPT on fourth down and when the ball changes hands. That was a pretty big EXCEPT, virtually forcing coaches to prepare everyone both ways. "You're going to have to have everyone ready both ways," said McClendon before the season, "because you can't anticipate injuries."

Just how prophetic those words were McClendon had no way of knowing at the time. Preparing for the Texas A & M opener, he was planning to stick with the three-team idea, more or less playing it by ear to see if it would stand up against the new rules. When McClendon announced his starting lineup, Labruzzo was surprised to find himself at left half on the White Team; in fact, he figured the coaches "were playing around trying to get us to work harder." A nervous Labruzzo not only started before a Tiger Stadium sellout of 68,000 but dazzled the Aggies with an 83-yard punt return in the second quarter that sent the Tigers on to a 14–6 victory. Joe fumbled the punt on his 17 and by the time he picked it up the Aggies were spread out. He began a zigzag course, setting up blocks with a deft change of pace, and, once free, ran like a scared rabbit.

Considering opening-game pressure ("When I ran out on the field and those people began yelling, I never thought I'd get out alive," said Labruzzo.), LSU's sixteen sophomores, of the thirty-four players who saw action, passed with flying colors. Screen ran the White Team with confidence, Billy Ezell took the Go Team on a 51-yard scoring march, and Schwab accounted for twenty-six of those fifty-one yards. Unquestionably, Labruzzo was the darling of the opening-night crowd. Born in New Orleans, Joe moved to Larose, Louisiana, when he was twelve and later attended Lockport High where, after a fabulous career, his jersey was retired by Coach Dudley Hillman. He ran fifty yards or better at least forty times in his last two high school seasons, and in his final shot against archrival Larose he scored five times and gained 327 yards. Lockport had to add temporary bleachers to its 1,600-seat stadium during his last season. Little wonder Labruzzo was still in a daze over the reception he received from the 68,000 Tiger Stadium customers. "Lockport," he said, "was never like this."

As far as McClendon was concerned, 1963 had the appearances of a roller-coaster ride. Sure enough, next week against a more experienced Rice team in Houston, the Tiger roller-coaster dipped as LSU, for the first time, ran up the Blue Cross flag. Had it not been for a last-quarter passing blitz by Screen, Rice would have won 21–0 instead of 21–12, but it wasn't the defeat that disturbed McClendon so much as the injuries. Go Team guard Dave Strange was lost for the season with an injured knee, while fullback Buddy Hamic, Bandit tackle Ernie Maggiore, and White Team tackle Ron Pere had twisted ankles, which made them doubtful against unbeaten Georgia Tech.

In 1961 and 1962, unbeaten Tech teams had answered many questions for LSU, serving as an early-season springboard to successful seasons. This time, because of LSU's youth, Charley didn't know what to expect but he soon found out—and so did Bobby Dodd. "Pat Screen," said Dodd after a bitter 7–6 defeat, "is probably the best running quarterback we'll see this year. As long as he's healthy, LSU will be tough." Screen awed Tech with ninety-four yards in sixteen carries, including a touchdown run of four yards, and several other Tigers awed McClendon with clutch plays that preserved a dramatic victory. Tech got its six points on two field goals by Billy Lothridge and the visitors could have easily gotten more. But, Buddy Soefker crashed through a wall of blockers to nail Lothridge and prevent a second-quarter touchdown; Ruffin Rodrigue hurtled through the air to block a fourth-quarter field goal try by Lothridge; Danny LeBlanc came from nowhere to tackle Joe Auer on a touchdown-bound screen pass; and Billy Truax tipped, and then intercepted a Lothridge pass to foil Tech's final bid.

McClendon had seen enough to be encouraged, and even the most pessimistic of Tiger fans had to agree with Dodd's observation on Screen: "As long as he's healthy, LSU will be tough." Less than a week after Dodd said this, Pat Screen was not healthy—for football. LSU led Miami, 3–0 in the fourth quarter, on a 20-yard field goal by Doug Moreau when Pat called on Danny LeBlanc on a power sweep around the left side. Screen blocked the Miami end with his right shoulder and explained afterward: "I felt a sharp pain and knew right away something was wrong. If I moved my arm just a little, my shoulder hurt. I took myself out of the game." X-rays revealed a separation of the right shoulder and, for Pat Screen, who had run up 401 yards in total offense in less than four games, this meant his 1963 season had ended in the Orange Bowl. It meant, too, that the burden now shifted to sophomore Billy Ezell of Greenville, Mississippi, whose status was accurately described by Jim Corbett. "Ezell is cast in one of those unfortunate roles," said Jim. "If he fails, fans will say Pat Screen would have succeeded. If he succeeds, fans will say Pat would have done it better. Billy Ezell cannot win."

Ezell did win next week: he piloted the Tigers to an impressive 28–7 win over Kentucky before another Tiger Stadium sellout, but the victory left Charley McClendon "the unhappiest coach with a 4–1 record who ever lived." The price for whipping the Wildcats was fullback Buddy Hamic, out for the season with a knee, and Labruzzo, out for a week with a sprained elbow. Because Buddy Soefker had sprained an ankle against Tech and hadn't played since, it meant McClendon had lost the backfield (Screen, Labruzzo, Soefker, and Hamic) that started the A & M game. "I've been here ten years and can't remember such a rash of injuries," said McClendon.

The injuries came at a time when LSU was preparing to invade Gainesville for a game with a Florida team that had beaten Alabama and lost only to Tech in five games. To the surprise of many, LSU left the favored Gators and a record Homecoming crowd of 48,000 a little sadder, and Billy Truax left them goggle-eyed in the course of a 14–0 upset, marking the third year in a row the Tigers hung a goose egg on

Pat Screen: For him, the 1963 season ended in Miami.

Florida. "Lineman of the Week" Truax stopped one Florida drive with a leaping interception, he killed another on the LSU 9 by blocking a pitchout and then recovering it, and he made key blocks on both 1-yard touchdown jabs by Schwab. "I've never seen an end make so many big plays," said McClendon.

It would have been a good idea to save some for Ole Miss. After a scoreless tie against Memphis State, Vaught's Rebels had rolled to four impressive victories and owned a No. 3 ranking when it came to Tiger Stadium for an afternoon, televised battle. The question for LSU, which was entering the game a four-point underdog, was whether it could move the ball on the ground against a ponderous Ole Miss front as it had against Kentucky and Florida. The answer was a resounding "no"; in fact, it took Ole Miss fan Dizzy Dean to best sum up his team's crushing 37–3 victory. "Pardner," said Diz, "I saw Ole Miss play two perfect games and they played 'em both against LSU—in the Sugar Bowl and here today. We ain't made a mistake in neither game."

LSU made its first mistake in the early moments. All week long, the Tigers had worked on their version of a quick-kick. The idea was to rush out of the huddle, have left end Danny Neumann line up in the halfback spot, give him a quick snap, and have him kick the ball before the Rebels could react. Backed up on its first series, the Tigers decided to

Tigers vs. Rebels, 1963: Joe Labruzzo's 81-yard punt return. Ole Miss guard Stan Hindman (top of picture) will stop him at the 1.

try it. Everything worked smoothly. Ole Miss didn't realize Neumann was kicking until he got the snap, but Robbie Hucklebridge blocked the wrong man, Whaley Hall roared in, blocked the punt, and Ole Miss had the ball on LSU's 12. Moments later, it was 7–0. It was here the Tigers put together their only drive of the ball game, a 71-yard march highlighted by Ezell's running and climaxed by Doug Moreau's 41-yard field goal. But that was it. Ole Miss responded with a 67-yard drive to make it 14–3, and by half time it was 23–3. Ole Miss demonstrated its complete superiority in the third period when Labruzzo got loose on an 81-yard punt return, only to be overhauled by guard Stan Hindman on the 1. Four plays later the Tigers wound up back on the 6. "I heard Hindman coming and looked back," lamented Labruzzo. "Then I tried running harder instead of relaxing. When I did I strained, broke my rhythm and lost my speed. I was tired too because I hadn't run hard since hurting my arm and missing the Florida game." Actually, had Labruzzo scored, it would have made little difference. Ole Miss enjoyed a 343–144 edge in total offense, explained this way by McClendon: "Last year against Glynn Griffing we came in too reckless and were too easy to block. This time we played it too soft."

The lopsidedness of the Ole Miss victory made everyone wonder if LSU could regroup for its final three games. The following week the Tigers were still in a daze for two quarters, trailing TCU, 14–7 with a 46-yard scoring run by Schwab the only redeeming feature. In the second half, however, the battle cry was "Viva Labruzzo!" Held together with adhesive tape and gauze, the 165-pound Lockport comet whipped the Horned Frogs, 28–14, with three touchdowns just when it looked as though he'd spend the last two quarters in a sling. "I can't remember anyone playing a second half like Joe considering the handicaps he was under," said trainer Marty Broussard. "Joe's left elbow was still swollen from the Kentucky game. On top of that, he had a nerve condition in his thigh. Early in the second quarter, he knocked down his shoulder and had to leave the game."

Back on the field for the third quarter, Joe forgot all of his ailments once he heard the roar of 67,000 in Tiger Stadium. Three plays after Bill Bass recovered a fumble on the TCU 17, Labruzzo zipped ten yards for the tying score. Later he capped an 81-yard drive with a 3-yard shot and, to wrap everything up, he streaked forty-five yards in the fourth quarter, leaving his path strewn with horizontal Horned Frogs.

Little Joe was still battling next week against Mississippi State in Jackson. State scored to take a 7–0 lead with 1:25 left in the game when Billy Ezell rallied the Tigers with a whirlwind 51-yard scoring drive, the touchdown coming with fourteen seconds left on a 6-yard pass from Ezell to Doug Moreau. A key play in the march was a 20-yard pass to

Labruzzo. Moments later, Joe was banished for scuffling with 214-pound Justin Canale of State. "I busted a signal and ran across the line of scrimmage," said Joe. "He got me around the head and wouldn't let go. All I was trying to do was shake loose."

The last-minute Tiger blitz brought a crowd of 46,500 to its feet in Memorial Stadium, leaving McClendon with a one or two-point decision. With Doug Moreau 13-for-13, the Tigers had what looked like a cinch tie but McClendon decided to go for the win. "Because of the way we came back," he said, "I felt I would be cheating the boys by playing for the tie." The two-point play was a down-and-out pass to Truax. "I should have hit Truax sooner but their end was putting pressure on me," explained Ezell. "I had to keep running toward the sidelines, and when I finally threw, he was almost out of the end zone."

The 7–6 defeat left LSU with a 6–3 record and with flickering bowl hopes. The week wasn't out when hopes were flickering everywhere. The day before the LSU-Tulane game, President Kennedy was fatally shot in Dallas, and for awhile there was question whether the game would be played. As the home team, LSU decided to play, but after the Tigers won, 20–0, before a tomb-like crowd and accepted an invitation to play Baylor in the Bluebonnet Bowl, assistant coach Scooter Purvis explained the feelings of everyone. "Football comes from in here," said Purvis, patting his stomach. "Maybe the players didn't realize it but both teams left a little behind. You can't have something like this happen and not have it affect young men." The 55,000 spectators showed little emotion as LeBlanc put the Tigers ahead in the first quarter. Moreau added two third-quarter field goals, and Schwab ended the scoring with a 66-yard run in the fourth quarter. LSU wound up with 314 yards rushing, Tulane with minus 1.

In the Bluebonnet Bowl, LSU discovered how the other half lived. With Don Trull completing twenty-six of thirty-seven passes, Baylor put together 430 yards in total offense to LSU's 116 and had a 27–4 edge in first downs. Incredibly, the Bears needed two last-period touchdowns for a 14–7 victory before 50,000 frozen fans in Houston. Even after Baylor went ahead, Labruzzo brought the crowd to its feet with a 72-yard kickoff return to the Baylor 24 but the Bears held. When the end came, Trull was on another aerial blitz. As Labruzzo thumbed through his game program afterward, he probably spoke for most of his teammates when he said: "I'd sure like to get that guy's autograph."

When McClendon ran a postseason check on his Blue Cross express, he discovered that eight players missed varying portions of the regular season: Don Ellen (nine games), Dave Strange (eight), Pat Screen (six), Buddy Hamic (five), Buddy Soefker and George Haynes (three), Ruffin Rodrigue (two), and Joe Labruzzo (one). This rash of injuries, particularly Screen's shoulder separation, plus the loss of hard-running Danny LeBlanc who had left school, prompted McClendon to abandon his tight formation for a more wide-open pro look for 1964. The thought of Screen's shoulder becoming unhinged on a power sweep led the LSU staff to a flanker-type attack in which there would be more finesse than power.

The key move, which McClendon kept secret until the Texas A & M opener, shifted Doug Moreau from end to flanker where his talents as a pass catcher would be put to use. This meant the Tigers would have only three running backs, Screen, Labruzzo, and Schwab, but that would be enough if LSU could loosen up the defense.

LSU's injuries didn't end with the Bluebonnet Bowl. In the spring Moreau and end Kenny Vairin underwent shoulder operations; linebacker Mike Vincent was recovering from a broken leg, Schwab and Rodrigue from knee operations. Danny LeBlanc's loss was somewhat offset by the return of Charley Simmons to play tackle in a White Team line that included 240-pounder George Rice and Remi Prudhomme. McClendon was sticking with the three-team system, but there was to be less two-way playing by members of the White Team. Among the promising sophomores coming up were a couple who had won spots on

Rice, 1964: With two minutes left, Moreau kicks field goal to win, 3–0.

the Go Team, halfback Gawain DiBetta and end Billy Masters, and Bandit tackle Tommy Fussell.

When McClendon finally got a look at his flanker-type attack in a 9–6 opening win over Texas A & M, it seemed the Tigers had gone from three yards and a cloud of dust to fifteen yards and a fumble. While running up 293 yards against a tough Aggie defense, LSU fumbled the ball away three times, and the only touchdown was the result of a fumble recovery by Fussell after a blocked kick. "I think we may keep our opponents loose," explained McClendon afterward, "but this team is going to keep the LSU coaches loose too."

Moreau's 34-yard field goal provided the winning points in the opener, and a week later the junior from University High in Baton Rouge kicked a 28-yarder with two minutes left, to beat Rice, 3–0. LSU was still moving the ball well between the twenties—it ripped the Owls for 271 yards—but it was bogging down in the tough yardage territory.

With the Tigers primed for another crack at Florida and Steve Spurrier in a battle of unbeatens, Hurricane Hilda swept in from the Gulf, causing an eleventh-hour cancellation. The arrival of Hilda gave the Tigers the week off but failed to add any goal line punch to its flanker offense. Against North Carolina, LSU amassed 319 yards in total offense but did not get its first touchdown until late in the third quarter. Moreau added two field goals and in the fourth period caught an 18-yard scoring toss from Screen to complete a 20–3 victory.

Screen had missed the second quarter after being leveled on a pass attempt and, although no one realized it at the time, he had played his last game of 1964 at full speed. By this time, Billy Ezell had been accustomed to waiting in the wings. The year before, he had taken over from Screen and now he was doing the same thing, and with the same results. Now, against Kentucky in dimly-lit Stoll Field in Lexington, Ezell engineered two field goal drives and two for touchdowns, scoring the last one himself on a 19-yard run. The key play, however, was provided by White Graves who, with the Wildcats threatening to erase a 10–7 LSU lead, intercepted a pass on the goal line and raced a hundred yards for a game-breaking score (the final score was 27–7). If Graves' gallop did anything, it put the focus on the major reason for LSU's 4–0 record—a surprising defense. The pro-type attack was getting most of the publicity, yet the fact remained the Tigers had surrendered only two touchdowns in four games. This reliance on defense hit home the week after the win over Kentucky when LSU entertained Tennessee in an afternoon, regionally televised game in Tiger Stadium. The Vols managed only six first downs and seventy-five yards in total offense—and never got past midfield in the second half—but were still able to get out of town with a 3–3 tie. LSU threatened, but lacked goal line punch.

Moreau's seventh field goal of the season got LSU its standoff, yet in the second half Doug missed three attempts inside the 30 (he was dead tired from running pass routes) and Schwab was halted by the Vols on the 1-foot line.

A tie with a team it had been favored to beat by more than a touchdown was not the best tonic in the world with Ole Miss coming up. With losses to Kentucky and Florida, Johnny Vaught was in the midst of one of his poorer seasons. Still many felt it was simply a question of the talent-wealthy Rebels pulling themselves together. In the first period, LSU looked the part of a six-point favorite, and Screen looked as though he had forgotten about his heavily-taped knee as he took the Tigers seventy-seven yards before Moreau settled for a field goal. Ole Miss replied with a 69-yard drive to go ahead 7–3, and then the wind seemed to come out of the Tigers when Screen, who had completed nine of ten passes in the first quarter, hobbled to the sidelines in the second period.

When the Rebs added a fourth-quarter field goal, the situation looked hopeless. More than a few of the 68,000 fans were leaving the stadium when Buster Brown stood on the LSU goal line and booted to Doug Cunningham on the Reb 47. Suddenly, Providence smiled. Don Ellen knocked an Ole Miss blocker into Cunningham and a surprised Doug lost control of the football. When John Aaron claimed it for the Tigers, there were seven minutes left. Six plays later found LSU camped on the Ole Miss 19, facing a second-and-ten. "I called a 'flanker circle route,' " Ezell explained, "which called for Billy Masters to go downfield ten yards and buttonhook." Masters had other ideas. "I started downfield," he said, "but when I noticed the Ole Miss defensive man running in, I took a sudden notion to keep running." Because he "took a notion," Masters wound up ten yards in the clear, Ezell spotted him, and, incredibly, it was 10–9 Ole Miss with three and a half minutes remaining. "If there had been more time, I might have kicked," said McClendon, "but I knew no one would have been satisfied with a tie." George Rice agreed, declaring: "I believe if someone had thrown a kicking tee on the field, I would have thrown it back."

Everyone was standing now and, as Ezell prepared to call the two-point play, there occurred what amounted to an ecumenical prayer meeting. Sitting in a wheelchair just off the grass in the north end was Pat Screen, a Catholic, saying a silent prayer for Baptist Ezell. Behind interfaith blocking, Billy rolled to his right, watched Masters buttonhook to the inside, and then saw Moreau fake inside and break for the sidelines. Ezell's pass was tipped by defender Tommy Luke, but Moreau grabbed the deflected ball on his fingertips and planted both feet six inches inside the boundary line before his momentum carried him out of bounds. The score was 11–10.

Billy Ezell to Doug Moreau: LSU goes for the win over Ole Miss, 1964—and gets it, 11–10.

"I didn't know we had it until I heard the roar of the crowd," said McClendon. Admittedly, hero Moreau was in some sort of twilight zone. "Before the game," he said, "Pat Screen and I were talking about heaven, wondering what a 'vision' is like. Now I think I have an idea. When I was leaving the field, I closed my eyes and I think I had one."

If Charley McClendon had a vision, it was of Bear Bryant and his unbeaten, third-ranked Crimson Tide. McClendon was bringing his 5-0-1 Tigers, rated eighth nationally, to Birmingham's Legion Field for the BIG game of 1964. It came at a time when both No. 1 quarterbacks, Pat Screen and Bama's Joe Namath, were nursing injured legs, setting up a prospective duel between the No. 2 men—Billy Ezell and Steve Sloan.

LSU fans making the trip must have gotten some inkling of what to expect before the game. Dark clouds hung overhead and a misty rain fell—until Bryant made his entrance. Then, as if by magic, the clouds parted and sunshine cast a mantle of gold on the field. There was a feeling of impending drama.

LSU struck first when Moreau crossed up the Tide's secondary. With Bama alert for the buttonhook, Doug faked short and went deep to take a 13-yard pass from Ezell and send the Tigers into a 6–0 lead. Doug's miss on the extra point loomed big when Bama went ahead 7–6 later in the period, but LSU responded with a 75-yard push climaxed by Moreau's 35-yard field goal, to go to the dressing room with a 9–7 lead.

A long drive followed by a field goal on the first play of the fourth quarter sent the Tide back into the lead, 10–9, and set up the game's turning point which came early in the final period. Screen, making a token appearance, fired a pass in search of Moreau (who wound up on the ground), and the ball landed in the arms of defender Hudson Harris, who sped thirty-three yards to a touchdown. Twice afterward, LSU drove to Bama's 11 where tackle Frank McClendon became an archnemesis. The 6-foot, 3-inch, 231-pounder got his meaty paws in the way of four Ezell passes, to do more than anyone to protect his team's 17–9 lead in a quarter when LSU ran forty plays to Bama's ten. Anticipating questions on Frank McClendon, the LSU coach said before anyone could ask: "He's no kin of mine."

As it was, LSU lost little prestige in the 17–9 loss to a team that went on to win the national championship. Once more it became a matter for Charley McClendon to rally his ball club for the stretch, which this time included Mississippi State, Tulane, and Florida. A 76-yard touchdown run by Marc Rhoden of State on the first play of the game awoke LSU in time for two Ezell-to-Moreau scoring passes in a 14–10 victory, and a mental lapse on the part of Tulane, with seconds left in the half and a 3–0 lead, allowed the Tigers to tie the score and go on to a 13–3 win.

But the hurricane-delayed finale with Florida was another matter. Part of the trouble, of course, was the fact that LSU had accepted a Sugar Bowl invitation after beating Tulane and the game would be anticlimactic. Other contributing factors, however, were Steve Spurrier and the goal line punch which haunted the Tigers throughout 1964. In losing 20–6 to the Gators, LSU again banked on the toe of Moreau whose two field goals gave him thirteen for the season and made him SEC scoring champion with seventy-three points. Statistics told a grim story. Of the twenty-one times LSU was able to get inside its opponents' 10-yard-line, it scored only five touchdowns. In 1963, using the tighter formation, the Tigers got inside the enemy's 10 on eighteen occasions and scored fourteen touchdowns.

In the Sugar Bowl, with an opportunity to erase the Florida nightmare, LSU faced the finest one-two punch the East had seen since the days of Glenn Davis and Doc Blanchard. Syracuse's halfback-fullback twosome of Floyd Little and Jim Nance had scored twenty-five touchdowns between them, fourteen more than the Tigers, so it was clearly a matter of containing them or losing.

As it turned out, LSU contained them effectively but still had to scrap for a 13–10 victory. The Orangemen got their only touchdown in the

Remi Prudhomme, UPI all-American, 1964.

first quarter on a 35-yard run with a blocked kick and, after George Rice nailed Little for a safety, Syracuse added a field goal to lead 10–2 at half time. In the first two periods it was a question of Screen's and Ezell's missing open receivers as the Tigers continued their scatter-shot passing which, against Tulane and Florida, showed two completions and three interceptions in twenty-two attempts.

Suddenly, in the third period, the law of averages caught up with the quarterbacks. On a "wide-and-go" route—one he had used to shake loose in the first half, only to be overthrown—Moreau streaked behind the Syracuse secondary, and this time Ezell laid the ball in his arms on a 57-yard scoring play. Billy then rifled the ball to Labruzzo on a two-point play and it was a 10–10 ball game. With the score still deadlocked in the last quarter, Screen found daylight at right end, stepping twenty-three yards for a first down, and later he hit Labruzzo down the middle on a 35-yard pass that put the ball on the Syracuse 19. The Tigers jabbed it to the 11 and on fourth down Moreau kicked his fourteenth field goal of the season to win the game and the outstanding player award.

The AP honored Moreau, Rice, and Granier on its offensive team and Vincent on its defensive club; the UPI, which made no offensive-defensive distinction, selected Prudhomme. Since Granier and Prudhomme were two of the only six seniors on his Sugar Bowl champions, Coach McClendon looked ahead anxiously to 1965 when he could welcome thirty-two lettermen in addition to some talented sophomores, quarterback Nelson Stokley and halfbacks Jim Dousay and Sammy Grezaffi.

But he wasn't standing pat. For the second year in a row he decided to make a change in LSU's offensive alignment; this time it involved a radical shift—making a strongback of end Billy Masters. With Danny LeBlanc back in the fold after a year's absence, the strongback formation was simply a return to a power attack that figured to add more goal line punch. In his new role, the 6-foot, 5-inch, 230-pound Masters would be used for his blocking and pass-catching ability, the equivalent to a wingback in the single wing. McClendon was retaining the I-formation, with Labruzzo backed by Dousay at tailback, and Schwab and LeBlanc alternating at fullback. "This offense," said McClendon, "will free Moreau for split-end duty where he won't be called on to do the blocking he did as a flanker."

Fully recovered from his knee operation, Screen liked the strongback alignment because, as he put it, "you have power to both sides." In the flanker setup, he said, "you had only two backs other than the quarterback who could run with the ball. Now we have three. And, in one respect, we still have a flanker in our split end." As a flanker Moreau set an LSU record with thirty-three catches for 391 yards and four touchdowns.

In 1965, because of more liberalized substitution rules, coaches were able to return to specialization and McClendon was able to put together one of the biggest offensive lines since he had been at LSU. He had

Tackles Dave McCormick and George Rice.

Dave McCormick (250) and Tommy Powell (238) at tackles, Don Ellen (225) and John Aaron (225) at guards, Walter Pillow (215) at tight end and Barry Wilson (200) at center. Defensively, the Tigers had John Garlington (215) and Ernie Maggiore (215) at ends, George Rice (255) and Tommy Fussell (230) at tackles, Mike Duhon (215) at middle guard, Mike Vincent (200) and Bill Bass (195) at linebackers, Jerry Joseph (175), Billy Ezell (180), Lenny Neumann (170) and Beau Colle (195) in the secondary. Ezell was being groomed both ways: as a defensive back, primarily because McClendon had senior Screen and sophomore Stokley working at quarterback, and, he was receiving enough offensive work to take over in case of an emergency.

LSU's strongback attack was going to receive its first test against a Texas A & M team under new management—that of Gene Stallings, former Alabama assistant. Always tough defensively, Stallings had the Aggies souped up for his coaching debut, and the result, a 10–0 LSU victory, was virtually a carbon copy of the 1964 game. On that occasion, Fussell had recovered a blocked kick for the only LSU touchdown. This time it was Maggiore who blocked and recovered an Aggie punt for six points. Moreau added a field goal just as he had done the year before, but this one was a 46-yarder which broke a record by Doc Fenton that had stood for fifty-seven years.

What about the strongback offense? LSU, it turned out, was its own worst enemy. Successive 15-yard penalties wiped out a first-half threat; in fact, one erased a 40-yard touchdown pass from Stokley to Masters. And back-to-back illegal procedure infractions killed a threat in the second half. McClendon poured fifty-one players into the game, including nineteen sophomores, and was pleased mostly by the play of a No. 2 offensive line that included four rookies.

"We may not look as spectacular as we did last year," said McClendon, "but we're simply out to win football games. Alabama fans told me last year what a crowd-pleasing team we had. That's because we threw forty passes and lost."

To Charley McClendon, at least, it seemed that no fan will ever be completely happy. His Tigers had just won its second game, 42–14 over Rice, the most points an LSU team had scored since 1961, and the nagging question was: What happened to the pass defense? For those seeking Utopia, forty-two points did not offset the 290 yards surrendered to the Owls, even though Rice had seldom been so thoroughly beaten. "All this proves," explained McClendon, "is that defense is going to win for you more than offense and I say this after our offense won for us."

Labruzzo sent the Tigers on their way, setting up the first score with a 51-yard punt return and, after the Owls pulled to within 14–7, Joe broke the game open by running a punt back eighty-two yards for a score. Then it became a question of LSU's establishing its running game first, after which the passing (which showed eight completions in eleven attempts) fell into place. More and more, the poise of sophomore Stokley, all-stater from Crowley, was becoming evident. He picked up eighty-four yards running, thirty-six in one chunk to set up LSU's second score. He definitely was on the move.

Unfortunately, so was Steve Spurrier. A week before, Steve and the Florida Gators were upset by Mississippi State, and now, before a home crowd of 47,592, he staged a characteristic Spurrier air show to beat the Tigers, 14–7. It was a combination of two LSU fumbles (by Schwab and Labruzzo which killed drives inside the Gator 10) and the improvised passing of the Florida quarterback. On the first Gator score, Spurrier spotted his receiver on reaching the line of scrimmage and released a 22-yard pass that caught the LSU secondary coming up to protect against the run. He did the same thing on a key play in an 86-yard march for the second touchdown.

While Spurrier was flashing his all-America credentials, Nelson Stokley, with forty-four yards rushing, fifty-six passing, and field generalship that took the Tigers to their touchdown, was staking claim to the No. 1 quarterbacking job at LSU. Added responsibility merely brought out the best in the Crowley sophomore as he went on an impressive three-week tear. Nelson had a hand in three of LSU's five touchdowns in a 34–27 win over Miami; he ran fifty yards for one and passed twenty-five yards to Doug Moreau for another as the Tigers whipped Kentucky, 31–21; and he passed and ran for two scores as the Tigers humbled South Carolina, 21–7.

All of a sudden, LSU not only was 5–1 and fifth ranked, but Stokley had become No. 2 on LSU's all-time total offense list for one season, 234 yards shy of the record Young Bussey established in 1937.

Here's how they stood:

	Run	Pass	Total
Young Bussey (1937)	404	731	1,135
Nelson Stokley (1965—6 games)	433	468	901
Al Doggett (1953)	33	822	855
Pat Screen (1964—8 games)	202	561	763
Warren Rabb (1958)	33	591	624
Lynn Amedee (1961)	132	485	617
Lynn Amedee (1962)	118	475	575
Jimmy Field (1961)	199	239	438

Because he was respected as a runner—he had an average of six yards per carry—Stokley had completed 64 percent of his passes, thirty-two of fifty. Just how much LSU had come to depend on this 5-foot, 11-inch, 170-pounder was evident when the Tigers made their fateful trip to Jackson to play Ole Miss. On LSU's sixth play from scrimmage, cutting back on a quarterback keeper, Stokley's knee collapsed—and so did the Tigers. As far as McClendon was concerned, Boris Karloff could not have come up with more of a horror script. Shortly after Stokley limped from the field, Labruzzo fumbled on the LSU 2 and Ole Miss wound up with a field goal. To make amends, Joe raced ninety-seven yards with the kickoff but the touchdown was wiped out by a penalty. Finally, in the third quarter, Labruzzo fumbled the second half kickoff, on the 6; the Rebels quickly had a 16–0 lead and an eventual 23–0 victory.

A week later, against Alabama, a team in search of its second national championship, LSU was still in a state of shock. Instead of reaching down for something extra with its No. 1 quarterback on the sidelines, the heavyweight Tigers were pushed all over Tiger Stadium by the lightweight Tide which struck early on a 45-yard touchdown toss by Steve Sloan to Dennis Homan and went on to embarrass LSU, 31–7, before 50,000 fans and a regional television audience.

In two weeks, LSU went from a 5–1 ball club to one seemingly on the point of disintegration, and, apparently, the major force keeping the Tigers from silently fading away was the comeback of Pat Screen. Thrust into the shadow by Stokley, Screen helped build a fire under LSU in engineering a 37–20 conquest of Mississippi State and a closing rout of Tulane by what Tiger fans had now come to regard as a traditional score, 62–0. Although still lacking his sophomore zip, Pat regained his confidence in the last two games and LSU seemed to lift with him. Against Tulane he started the scoring with a 4-yard run and went on to complete eight of ten passes for two touchdowns.

If Screen was adept at steering LSU to closing victories, Jim Corbett, by then an old hand in postseason dealing, deftly engineered the Tigers into a Cotton Bowl match with unbeaten Arkansas. When the Orange Bowl picked Alabama and Nebraska and the Sugar Bowl chose Florida and Missouri, it left only once-beaten Tennessee as a possibility for Dallas. But the Vols, 6–1–2 at the time, had a late game with UCLA and Cotton Bowl officials didn't want to take the chance.

Corbett politicked for the built-in rivalry which an Arkansas-LSU game would provide, and he predicted, because Arkansas was the opponent, that a healthy Louisiana crowd would follow the Tigers to Dallas. Of course, humiliation was a risk—but one Corbett figured worth taking. Arkansas had won twenty-two games in a row, the Razorbacks had two all-Americans in offensive tackle Glen Ray Hines and defensive tackle Lloyd Phillips, and they had won ten spots on a 23-man all-

Southwest Conference team. Versatile and speedy, the Hogs thrived behind quarterback Jon Brittenum who passed for eight touchdowns and ran for six more.

Because the wire services had decided to suspend their vote on a national champion until after the bowl games, Frank Broyles, whose Hogs held a No. 2 ranking behind Michigan State (UCLA's Rose Bowl foe), didn't have to remind his squad what was at stake. But he was worried, naturally. "Charley McClendon's sitting behind a rock with a great football team," said Broyles. "Don't let that 7–3 record fool you."

While the old story is true—"On a given day, any team can beat, etc. . . ."—LSU's lopsided defeats at the hands of Ole Miss and Alabama made the Razorbacks a solid nine-point favorite and they remained that way right up to kickoff time. Obviously, LSU was in an ideal psychological spot, but sometimes little things happen to add coals to the fire. On their way out of the lobby of their Dallas hotel, the LSU players crossed the path of several red-suited Arkansas rooters. "Look," shouted a woman, loud enough for everyone to hear, "they're going to show up for the game." If Charley McClendon had planned it himself, he could not have done a better job.

LSU was ready, no question about that, but was "ready" good enough? On a first quarter drive, 87 yards in eleven plays, Arkansas matched its press clippings as the clever Brittenum mixed passes with rollouts and off-tackle thrusts to push the football into the end zone. The payoff was a pass to split-end Bobby Crockett who made a circus catch and then tightroped down the sidelines on a 16-yard play. In the second quarter, Arkansas was touchdown-bound again but a fine tackle by Mike Robichaux forced a field goal attempt from the 33 which was wide and gave LSU the ball on the 20. According to McClendon, the Tigers went into the game determined to "sink or swim with Pat Screen." But now McClendon, in an on-the-spot decision, decided to let Stokley test his heavily-bandaged knee. Nelson was only in for seven plays but, before he reinjured himself running a keeper, he had moved the ball to the LSU 40.

Now it was Screen's turn, and if there was any doubt good fortune was riding with the Tigers it came on Pat's second play. After running eleven yards, Screen rifled the ball to Masters on a pass which, for the moment, looked as though it would be intercepted and probably would have been incomplete had it not been tipped into Masters' arms for a 14-yard gain. With the ball on the Hog 35, LSU began blocking. Dousay carried three times for eleven yards, Labruzzo once for five, and Masters once for three to put LSU on the 16. No one among the record 76,500 Cotton Bowl crowd could have called the next four plays. Labruzzo hit left tackle for seven, he hit it again for two, a third time for

Joe Labruzzo plunges through opening made by linemen Walter Pillow, John Aaron, and Don Ellen for first down in 1966 Cotton Bowl game against Arkansas.

four, and then for three yards and a touchdown. Moreau's kick tied the score at 7–7 with four minutes left in the half.

Then Providence smiled a second time on LSU. On the first play following the kickoff, Brittenum injured his shoulder, and two plays later, his understudy, Ronny South, fumbled and Bill Bass recovered on the Arkansas 34. Smelling blood, Screen ran for three, passed to Moreau for twelve and then, incredibly, pulled out his earlier script. From the 19, 170-pound Joe Labruzzo hit left tackle five times in a row—for three, eleven, two, two, and finally one yard—and LSU had taken the lead with eighteen seconds left in the half.

That was the end of the scoring but not the drama, as a Tigerish LSU defense, highlighted by Jerry Joseph's fourth-quarter interception, beat back Arkansas' threats and protected a 14–7 victory, the greatest post-season conquest ever by an LSU team.

McClendon and Corbett at Dallas: Moment of victory.

For McClendon, it was more than an upset. The year before, La-bruzzo had fumbled on the one in a 7–6 loss to Mississippi State. Earlier in 1965, Joe had bobbled on the two to cost LSU an apparent touch-down against Florida. Criticism was heavy both times, pointing to the folly of running a little man on the goal line. Now McClendon—and Labruzzo—had eloquently silenced these critics in an almost unbeliev-able manner. "If we had missed blocks," explained Charley, "these plays would have looked awfully unimaginative. But we didn't." Screen ex-plained it this way: "We had two good blockers on the left side in McCormick and Ellen and we also were running away from their big tackle Lloyd Phillips. Also, I believe Arkansas had a hard time finding Joe behind a big fellow like McCormick."

McCormick was voted the game's outstanding lineman and Labruzzo, the outstanding back. Sitting in the dressing room trying to keep a straight face, the 5-foot, 9-inch senior said: "This is the greatest victory since Lockport beat Larose."

LSU was still bathing in the afterglow of its Cotton Bowl victory when a surprising off-season development resulted in a make-believe script: Because of a mutual disenchantment, Paul Dietzel was leaving West Point to take over as head coach and athletic director at the University of South Carolina. When the announcement came in early April, LSU fans circled September 17 on their calendars, a date more than five months away, but one on which Dietzel would take his Game-cocks into Tiger Stadium. The showdown had all of the dramatic ingredients—fate, irony, opportunism—which combined to make the 1966 season opener a milestone in LSU football history.

Dietzel's second coming, so to speak, was going to be eleven years after his telephone call to McClendon and Charley's suggestion that Dietzel apply for the LSU job. It was coming seven years after McClendon narrowly missed landing the Navy job and five years after Dietzel headed for West Point. "For the first time I can remember," said McClendon, "no one is talking about Ole Miss or Alabama. They're beginning to sound like coaches—they can't get past the opening game."

With nine offensive regulars departing (center Barry Wilson and strongback Billy Masters were all that remained from the Cotton Bowl starters) and six defensive regulars gone, McClendon faced a rebuilding year despite the fact he was retaining twenty-eight of fifty lettermen, the largest crop of monogram winners in LSU history. The big question, of course, was how well Nelson Stokley, an all-SEC selection on the sophomore team, would emerge from his shoulder operation. With Screen and Ezell gone, LSU's quarterbacking operations fell to Stokley and two sophomores, Freddie Haynes and Trey Prather. And, if Nelson could regain his 1965 form, the Tiger backfield would have Stokley at quarterback, Jim Dousay at tailback, Masters at strongback, and Gawain DiBetta, who alternated with Masters in 1965, at fullback.

For a while McClendon would have to live with an offensive line that had to prove itself and, until it did, defense would have to do the job. LSU had the nucleus of a solid defense built around what Charley called his "dynamic duo," ends John Garlington and Mike Robichaux. Middle guard Mike Duhon was returning and at tackles were lettermen Tommy Fussell and John Demarie. With Jerry Joseph, Sam Grezaffi, and Lenny Neumann back, the secondary was heavy on experience, and at the important "linebacking" spot LSU had a couple of lettermen in Benny

Griffin and Mike Pharis but, more significantly, an outstanding sopho-more in George Bevan. "George Bevan is as fine an athlete as we've ever had at LSU," said McClendon. "He was a fullback at Baton Rouge High but I honestly believe he could make all-conference at any position he chose to play." It wasn't going to be long before the 5-foot, 11-inch, 190-pound Bevan began to make noise.

In view of the way it ate up the Arkansas defense, there would be no tinkering with LSU's strongback offense. McClendon wasn't going to tinker with anything, but he reminded LSU that Paul Dietzel was coming to Baton Rouge with thirty-five lettermen and "ten times better material than he left behind at Army." A two-touchdown underdog, dramatist Dietzel enjoyed striking the pose of the sacrificial lamb being led to the Tiger Stadium slaughter, a lamb he predicted "would receive the longest standing boo in LSU history."

According to officials involved, all kinds of "historical" records would be set. Jim Corbett, for example, remembering some of the classic Ole Miss games, claimed the South Carolina battle would eclipse those and provide "the most dramatic and emotion-packed night in our history." In addition to the bitterness Dietzel left behind was the fact that Dietzel and McClendon no longer were bosom buddies. First Paul seemingly had gone out of his way "to put the hat on" the 1962 Tigers and then, a week before his return to LSU, he wrote in *Sports Illustrated:* "In 1962 we were going to have more than 30 lettermen back and there wasn't any way I could coach them badly enough to lose." Dietzel explained the personal coolness this way: "Charley has held a grudge ever since I did not include him in my plans at West Point. The reason I didn't was I knew he'd get the LSU job."

As someone who had won twenty-nine of forty regular season games and three of four bowl games, McClendon could well consider himself the least-known successful football coach in the country and, because in the minds of many he was still basking in Dietzel's shadow, no coach ever faced more of a MUST WIN situation. Actually, Dietzel had a hand in selecting South Carolina as an LSU opponent. In 1959, Corbett showed him a list of possible future foes. Dietzel suggested the Game-cocks, and Jim later signed for a four-game series—1960 and 1961, 1965 and 1966. As soon as Dietzel announced acceptance of the South Caro-lina post, the LSU game became an instant 67,500 sellout and "Maul Paul" signs began appearing all over the state. One Tulane fan, admitting to mixed emotions, said "I'd like to see LSU win this one, 62–0." Dietzel told everyone who would listen that LSU was going to humiliate him, and, pointing to a "Countdown To D-Day" reminder in the Baton Rouge *State-Times*, Paul liked to say: "The D doesn't stand for De-Witt Clinton."

McClendon had a difficult time trying to keep himself and his team from getting overly emotional. Leaving the practice field after a Thursday workout, Charley punched his right fist into his left hand for emphasis: "I've never wanted to win a football game more than this one. You can't imagine how it's been, coaching in the shadow of that guy. I've had the monkey on my back for four years. I've tried to be realistic about this game but I can't. I've never been so worked up over anything. I've tried to keep from overcoaching and getting the boys wound up too much."

When the moment of truth finally arrived the evening of September 17, the historic "boo" Dietzel predicted was instead a mini-boo, virtually drowned out by the roar that greeted LSU which timed its arrival on the field with that of the Gamecocks. After such a buildup, any game figured to be anticlimactic and LSU's 28–13 victory was no exception, although the visitors, trailing 0–7 in the first quarter, caused a ripple of excitement with a shotgun attack that carried them seventy-six yards to a touchdown. Mike Robichaux blocked the kick and LSU led, 7–6. Then the Tigers, who put together a fourteen-play march for its first score, drove to a 13–6 half-time lead in sixteen plays. In thirty minutes, LSU had fifteen first downs and 205 yards rushing.

In the third period Jack Dyer recovered a blocked Carolina punt for a touchdown and, when the Tigers clicked on a two-point play, it was 21–6. Again, the Gamecocks stirred up the crowd when Bobby Bryant

An agonized Paul Dietzel returns to Tiger Stadium. The Big Boo never developed.

returned a kick seventy-seven yards but, when the try for two missed, LSU enjoyed a comfortable 21–12 lead going into the final period. It would have ended that way had not Carolina gambled on a fourth-down pass from its eighteen in the final moments. The Tigers took over, and on the game's last play Haynes ran two yards for the touchdown. Ordinarily, the brightest spot for McClendon would have been the performance of Stokley, who finished as LSU's top rusher with seventy-eight yards in fifteen carries including a touchdown run of eleven yards. But this time, for Charley McClendon, it came after the postgame prayer when Mike Pharis, one of the co-captains, pitched the game ball to Charley with a terse speech: "You're our coach. We've forgotten all about Paul Dietzel."

Maybe so, but misfortune hadn't forgotten Charley McClendon. For him, lightning didn't strike twice but four times—and each time it hit his No. 1 quarterback. In an almost incredible parallel, Nelson Stokley's junior season ended on the first play of the fourth quarter when the Tigers became a 17–15 upset victim at the hands of an old nemesis, Rice. Starting his final season as head coach, shrewd Jess Neely had the Owls primed, and LSU played into his hands with a lackluster performance that suffered even more when Stokley suffered a shoulder separation. At the time, LSU enjoyed a 15–10 lead, the result of a field goal and two touchdowns. The first came on a 42-yard run by John Garlington, who grabbed a Rice fumble in midair, and the second, on a 6-yard pass from Nelson Stokley to Tommy Morel. At the start of the last quarter, as Nelson completed a pass to Masters, he was hit and made a one-point landing—on his shoulder. The Tigers, behind Freddie Haynes, went on to set up a 34-yard field goal for Ronnie Manton, but LSU was called for delay of game on the play and Manton then missed a 39-yarder. Rice then drove for its winning touchdown.

The loss was one thing, but losing Stokley for the season, as he had lost Screen as a sophomore, made McClendon feel like the proverbial black cat. Screen and Stokley had suffered identical injuries in reverse order. With Pat, it was his shoulder and then his knee. With Nelson, his knee and then his shoulder. "The lick Screen took on his shoulder and the one Stokley received were almost identical," said trainer Marty Broussard. "Both were freak accidents. There's no way else to explain it."

Broussard said that when Stokley learned the extent of his injury, he was on the verge of hysteria. "No one can appreciate how much that young man worked to get in shape for the 1966 season," said Marty. "It wasn't the pain worrying him as much as the thought of a whole season going up in smoke after less than two games." Stokley had undergone a knee operation the previous January and, according to Broussard, he was back in the training room within twelve days to begin rehabilitation. "This went on for four months, until school was over," said Marty. "He was in the training room twice a day, every day. During the summer he'd come in from Crowley periodically for special treatment. That's why it was so hard for him to take."

By now McClendon should have been shock-proof. He merely turned the job over to the 5-foot, 9-inch, 165-pound Haynes and hoped for the best. Haynes went on to give his best, but overall the effort was something else. In fact, the Tigers were fortunate to get by with a win and a tie the next two weeks. They nipped an excellent Miami club, 10–8, on two tremendous defensive plays in the second half, one by Mike Robichaux and the other by George Bevan who ran clear across the field, waded through a convoy of blockers, and nailed a touchdown-bound ball carrier. Against Texas A & M, Haynes took the Tigers sixty-five yards to a touchdown but, after that, the Aggies tied it 7–7, completely dominated play in the second half, and missed a field goal when LSU held for three downs on the 1-yard line.

A 30–0 victory over Kentucky, featured by an 80-yard punt return by Sammy Grezaffi, provided only momentary relief for the three most harrowing weeks of McClendon's regime. Returning from Lexington to a sellout Homecoming crowd to play unbeaten Florida, and get a final crack at all-America Steve Spurrier, LSU failed miserably. Unable to muster any semblance of an offense, the Tigers were picked apart by Spurrier and seemed fortunate to get out with only a three-touchdown difference after falling behind 21–0.

In bowing to Ole Miss, 17–0, LSU put together a more gallant effort, one ruined by allowing the Rebels a quick 75-yard touchdown pass, two costly fumbles, and a horrid kicking game. In losing 21–0 to Alabama, the Tigers could not get past the Tide's 44 and needed a superb defensive performance (Bama scored once on an interception and again on a last-minute giveaway) to keep the score what it was.

For the first time in ten years (since the 3–7 season in 1956) LSU was faced with the prospect of a losing season; but defense, an improving Freddie Haynes, and the twinkling toes of Tommy "Trigger" Allen turned 3–4–1 into 5–4–1.

Running up 304 yards in total offense in whipping Mississippi State, 17–7, only served to set the stage for one of the more dramatic LSU-Tulane games of recent times. Coach Jim Pittman, Mississippi State graduate and a long-time aide to Darrell Royal, combined a new spirit, a standout quarterback, and a softer schedule, to pump new life into the Greenies. A year before, the third 62–0 whipping in eight years put the skids under Tommy O'Boyle, clearing the way for Pittman who, many felt, would either lift the school's football fortunes or end intercollegiate football on Willow Street. Under Pittman, the Greenies already had clinched their first winning season in ten years and were only a three-point underdog to a team which, the year before, had scored nine touchdowns against them.

An 82,307 sellout in Sugar Bowl Stadium was the kind of LSU-Tulane game that had athletic directors Jim Corbett and Rix Yard smiling all the way to the bank. Although the Tigers were not going bowling for the first time since 1960, their $160,000 slice of the Tulane pie—$45,000 more than an SEC team can keep from a postseason game—would go a long way toward balancing the books. This is the main reason Corbett always said it was good business to have Tulane competitive, that is, competitive enough to put fans in the seats but not competitive enough to win. In 1962, for example, when Tulane entered the LSU game with an 0–9 record and only 37,811 turned out in the Sugar Bowl, it meant each team's check was less than half of what it was in 1966.

As far as McClendon was concerned, of course, the less competitive Tulane was the better for the Tigers. Because the Greenies had beaten A & M and tied Miami, he had no trouble cranking the Tigers for one of their better efforts of the season, a 21–7 victory in which the mistake-haunted Tigers did not lose a fumble, throw an interception, or allow penalties to cripple scoring opportunities. Never were raw speed and individual ability more glaringly apparent than on the four touchdowns made in this dramatic renewal of a traditional series.

For example:

1. In the first period Trigger Allen, who became the No. 1 tailback only after injuries slowed Jim Dousay and sidelined Maurice LeBlanc, grabbed a Haynes pass in the flat and turned a routine gain into a 45-yard scoring play, faking two Tulane defenders, and outrunning a third with a display of his 9.8 speed.

2. In the second quarter Sammy Grezaffi, a 9.6 back, swept right end on a wide reverse and raced twenty-two yards to the Tulane 10. Two plays later Allen leaped into the end zone from the two.

3. In the third quarter, with the ball at the LSU 19, Greenie quarterback Bobby Duhon checked a pass and then literally flew around right end, winning the race to the end zone.

4. On the kickoff Grezaffi, finding his path blocked up the middle, braked at the 25 and then, on sheer speed, raced to the LSU 49. On the next play Allen turned one of those unimaginative off-tackle plays into a 51-yard touchdown by reversing his field and again outrunning the Tulane secondary.

McClendon's fifth straight win over his recruiting rival meant more to him personally than any of the others, if only because it vindicated his faith in the 5-foot, 9-inch Haynes whose 144 yards in total offense compared favorably with Duhon's 160 and gave him 836 for the season, putting him fourth on LSU's all-time list.

If Charley McClendon felt vindicated by Freddie Haynes, he believed also that his most emotional season in Tigertown—one which began with the return of Dietzel and ended with a Tulane team many felt would end eighteen years of frustration—was behind him. "From the first game to the last," Jim Corbett told the L Club banquet two days after the Tulane game, "Charley McClendon faced intolerable odds—a man with little to win and much to lose." Then Corbett, eying the start of recruiting season, added: "We have a lot to look forward to."

Tragically, Jim Corbett had little more than two months to look forward to. Going out, as was his custom, at full speed, he suffered a fatal heart attack January 29, 1967, as he prepared to leave New Orleans to attend a meeting in New York. Tributes flowed from a shocked press. Said Dan Hardesty of the Baton Rouge *State-Times:* "There are times when a typewriter is a wholly inadequate instrument. This is one of

Corbett and prize catch Butch Duhe: Last hurrah for the Boston Irishman.

those times. My typewriter will put down on paper any words in the English language if I can but think of the words I want and hit the proper keys, but this I find most difficult to do in attempting to express my feelings upon the sudden loss of my closest friend and a great man in the world of sports."

Bill Carter of the Alexandria *Daily Town Talk*, recalled the 1964 LSU-Alabama game, one the Tigers lost 17–9. "After leaving the press box," wrote Carter, "Jim could travel only a few rows of steps before heartbreak forced him to take an isolated seat in that vast Legion Field stadium in Birmingham. As I passed, he looked up, his eyes glistened with tears, and said, 'We tried, Bill, we gave it everything we had.' This was the Jim Corbett I'll always remember."

Corbett's legacy was pinpointed by Furman Bisher of the Atlanta *Journal*. "Take a football weekend in Baton Rouge, a Saturday night in Tiger Stadium on the campus of Louisiana State University, and you might come to the conclusion there is really nothing quite so important in the Cajun world. Jim Corbett created these nights. LSU had played football on Saturday nights before he arrived as athletic director in 1955. But nobody had developed such an idea of merchandising those nights as Corbett did. He made every Cajun believe he was a misfit if he didn't have a ticket every Saturday night the Tigers played football at home."

The hand of Jim Corbett is best reflected in the following 20-year statistics, illustrating how he helped build attendance starting in 1955 and how he helped keep it healthy:

Season	Coach	Size of Stadium	Season Tickets Sold	Record	Average Home Attendance
1947	Moore	45,000	No Record	5–3–1	38,000
1948	Tinsley	45,000	No Record	3–7	36,000
1949	Tinsley	45,000	No Record	8–2	28,000
1950	Tinsley	45,000	No Record	4–5–2	27,000
1951	Tinsley	45,000	No Record	7–3–1	26,800
1952	Tinsley	45,000	No Record	3–7	33,800
1953	Tinsley	67,500	No Record	5–3–3	35,500
1954	Tinsley	67,500	No Record	5–6	27,800
1955	Dietzel	67,500	6,243	3–5–2	47,894
1956	Dietzel	67,500	8,551	3–7	35,626
1957	Dietzel	67,500	9,211	5–5	49,532
1958	Dietzel	67,500	9,318	10–0	59,113
1959	Dietzel	67,500	31,242	9–1	62,471
1960	Dietzel	67,500	24,031	5–4–1	53,150
1961	Dietzel	67,500	29,666	9–1	63,583
1962	McClendon	67,500	32,978	8–1–1	66,284

Season	Coach	Size of Stadium	Season Tickets Sold	Record	Average Home Attendance
1963	McClendon	67,500	34,512	7–3	65,235
1964	McClendon	67,500	34,545	7–2–1	63,440
1965	McClendon	67,500	35,000	7–3	63,621
1966	McClendon	67,500	35,000	5–4–1	63,868
1967	McClendon	67,500	35,127	6–3–1	62,105

By the time of Corbett's death, night football, which had gotten a modest start before a crowd of 12,000 in 1931, had grown into a king-size product which, in 1965, brought an estimated $2,774,930 into Baton Rouge, a figure the Chamber of Commerce reached by averaging the money spent by local fans and the 145,000 visitors who attended seven home games. LSU football is woven so deeply into the fabric of Louisiana's capital city that there might be a minor depression among restaurants, motels, department stores, and beauty salons should it suddenly disappear.

The Chamber of Commerce's estimate is that a visitor staying overnight will spend $15, excluding the price of his ticket, $10 if he doesn't stay over. Another estimate is that ten thousand chickens surrender their lives for every LSU home game—fried for motorists and those who bus to Tiger Stadium; fried, broiled, baked, etc., for restaurants; fried and in salad for pregame and postgame parties. Bourbon and scotch business is up at least 50 percent on football Saturdays. Considering a sellout crowd of 67,500, arrests for drunkenness are minimal.

Not surprisingly, when the Tigers win, off-the-field management receives far fewer complaints than it does following a defeat. When LSU loses, it seems that traffic moves slower, there were splinters in the seats, there was no ice in the Cokes, the hot dogs were cold, and the hamburgers tasted like leather.

Jim Corbett saw the "spirit of Tiger Stadium" as something that was built in. "Because LSU grew up with Baton Rouge and Baton Rouge with LSU," said Corbett, "there is a stronger personal identity with the players than is found in most metropolitan areas. Local following of home boys in places such as Lutcher, Reserve, Thibodaux, Gonzales, and so on stimulates civic pride and these small communities carry this enthusiasm with them to Baton Rouge on Saturday night. What we have is the Great Society of Equality at work—the doctor, the lawyer, the farmer, the plant worker, the society matron—they all band together in a single social strata. In Baton Rouge, the focal point of everything, the average fan doesn't seem to have a good week in his job if the Tigers lose."

The merchandising genius behind what became the South's most celebrated Saturday night syndrome was warm and gracious, a man of extraordinary ability, sparkling Irish wit, someone who manifested an extraordinary sense of being alive. "James J. Corbett," he would say extending a hand to a stranger. "You know—after the fighter." For the better part of his forty-seven years, Jim Corbett was a fighter whose restless thrust of mind never abated, someone who lived life intensely, as though he knew it would be a short one. When he died, he was administering an athletic budget that exceeded $1.5 million.

On the national scene, Jim Corbett the consummate politician was just as effective. Because he was able to penetrate to the heart of an issue and then place it in a larger context, he battled aggressively for a sane television approach by the colleges and was instrumental in hammering out legislation that protected college football from encroachment by the pros. He saw the rise of professional football as a tremendous challenge but one he looked forward to with relish. "They're mentioning my name for the domed stadium job in New Orleans," said Jim a few days before he died. "I'm not interested in anything like that or in a front office job with the New Orleans Saints. I'm a college man and I always will be."

Corbett expressed deep concern at the barbs being hurled at Charley McClendon. "I feel partly responsible because I made the schedule," he said. "I'd like people to look at the brutal schedules Mac has taken on, consider his injuries at quarterback, total up his record for five years, and then compare that record to the first five years of Bear Bryant, Frank Broyles, Darrell Royal, and Ara Parseghian."

Characteristically, Jim Corbett went out fighting—winning and losing but still under a full head of steam. Two days before his death, he politicked for removal of the SEC's 140 limit on scholarships, and lost. He spent the next day beaming over a prize catch—quarterback Herman "Butch" Duhe of Holy Cross in New Orleans. When Duhe signed with the Tigers, it was the last hurrah for the Boston Irishman.

Corbett's death cast a pall over the coming 1967 season. And Nelson Stokley, LSU's senior quarterback from Crowley, was still a question mark as the Tigers began fall practice. To recap briefly, Stokley was blossoming as a sophomore in 1965 when he damaged the outside cartilage in his left knee against Ole Miss and was out of action except for a brief appearance against Arkansas in the Cotton Bowl. A year later he separated his right shoulder in the second game of the season and underwent an operation. And in a scrimmage during the 1967 spring practice, he was tackled by linebacker George Bevan, damaging the inside cartilage on the same left knee. Another operation. "It was the lowest moment of my life," said Nelson. "I had worked hard to build up my shoulder and then my knee goes. Everything seemed to be coming apart. It caught me in the middle of exams and my weight dropped from 175 to 155."

Charley McClendon still believes that nine out of ten athletes faced with Stokley's medical history would have called it a day. Not Nelson. After his third operation in two years, he was back in the training room for another rehabilitation program. He married campus beauty June Hamic in June, 1967, and spent part of his honeymoon running in the sand along the beach to build up his left leg.

At the time, no one, not even Stokley, knew whether he'd last one play, let alone one season. He was already a senior with only eight full games at quarterback behind him. This was the major reason all of the preseason polls left the Tigers out of the top twenty, put them in the

Nelson Stokley:
The word was "courage."

middle of the SEC, and predicted they'd be lucky to come up with a winning season.

Aside from the cloud over Stokley, LSU was coming off a 5–4–1 season minus seven defensive starters, including the middle of its line. All of these elements prompted *Playboy* magazine to forecast a 2–8 season for the Tigers, who had perhaps their toughest schedule in history, meeting Rice, Texas A & M, Florida, and Miami in one stretch and Tennessee, Ole Miss, and Alabama in another. Barry Wilson, one of the dozen seniors, enjoyed reading the death notices. "We're going to surprise a lot of people," he said. "I say this because we went through the best spring practice since I've been at LSU. You could sense the new attitude. You can't be an in-and-out player and expect to win in our league. Football games are won just as much by how you act off the field as on the field."

Before the season the seniors went to McClendon as a group and promised to come to him as a group with any gripes during the season. "Before we had gone as individuals," said Wilson. "Now, if anyone had a problem or a question as to why something wasn't being done, it was going to be a matter for all of the seniors to relay to Coach McClendon. I think this was the turning point of our season."

Tactically, the Tigers went to a split-back offense, employing wide receivers to each side to utilize backfield speed and the pass-catching of junior Tommy Morel. The opener against Rice provided a hint of what was to become "The Year of the Extra Point." Making its bow under Bo Hagan, Rice, behind quarterback Bobby Shelton, dominated the first half, and led 7–0 until two third-quarter touchdowns gave the Tigers a 13–7 lead. After the first score sophomore Ray Hurd missed the extra point, allowing the Owls to grab the lead in the final period on a 15-yard run by Shelton, one in which he suffered a shoulder separation as he landed in the end zone. This set the stage for a dramatic 75-yard drive which Glenn Smith climaxed with a seven-yard touchdown run, giving LSU a 20–14 victory with twenty-nine seconds remaining.

The squeaker did not win many converts, if only because the Tigers allowed Rice 454 yards in total offense and had a serious hole shot in its defense when it lost linebacker George Bevan for the season. "The week of our game with Texas A & M," said Wilson, "Coach Mac spent most of the time with the defense and the change was remarkable. The Aggies didn't score until late in the game."

The Tigers, meanwhile, were beginning to feel more at home in their new attack. A ten-play, 80-yard drive—all on the ground—produced the first touchdown and another for 78 yards in which Stokley mixed running and passing, Nelson hitting Tommy Allen for the last nine yards. A 37-yard field goal by Hurd was insurance in the 17–6 win.

Trigger Allen running and Eddie Ray blocking, against Florida, 1967.

The absence of Steve Spurrier—LSU had hit 0-for-3 against him—no doubt boosted Tiger confidence when it came time to go to Gainesville, yet McClendon, in his wildest dreams, did not envision a 37–6 rout of the Gators. "We were not that much better than Florida," insisted Mac. "The ball just bounced right for us for a change." After Sammy Grezaffi's 42-yard punt return set up a 43-yard field goal by Hurd, Sammy recovered a fumble on the Gator 10 and Stokley sprinted in for the touchdown to give the Tigers a 10–0 first quarter lead. Two more field goals, for thirty-two and thirty-seven yards, boosted the advantage to 16–0 by half time, and then a 50-yard dash by Stokley ("We caught the defense out of position," said Nelson.) made it 23–0 and put the game out of reach. Before it was over, the Tigers turned two interceptions into touchdowns to add frosting to the cake.

It looked good for LSU, returning home to face Miami of Florida (*Playboy*'s selection to win the national championship), but the question was how long would the sleeping giant remain asleep? Upset by Northwestern and Penn State before managing to slip past Tulane, the Hurricanes carried a 1–2 record into Tiger Stadium but by half time proved to the 67,000 customers they had indeed awakened. A smothering defense and crunching offense gave the visitors a 17–3 half-time lead in a game in which LSU showed little sign of life. In the third quarter, however, a Grezaffi punt return lit a spark that led to a 33-yard scoring pass from Stokley to Trigger Allen. A muff of the extra point halted momentum

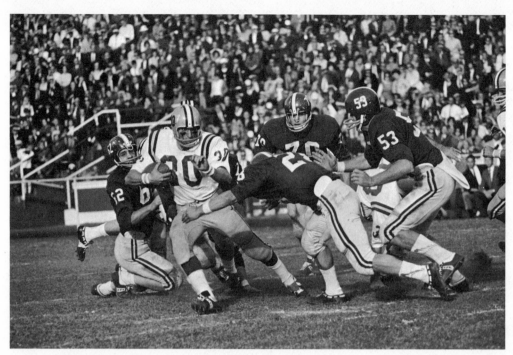

What made Sammy run? Grezaffi on a punt return.

until Gerry Kent picked off a Miami pass to pave the way for a 23-yard scoring run by Kenny Newfield. With the score 17–15, LSU went for two and missed, but the Tigers still had a quarter left. Hurd's moment seemed to be approaching when Stokley took his team from the LSU 35 to the Miami 10. However, on second-and-eight, Nelson found himself shut off at right end and suddenly turned to beat a retreat. He was overhauled on the 24 for a 14-yard loss. On third down, Nelson sent a pass into the end zone, but Miami intercepted, to wipe out any chance of a fourth-down field goal try by Hurd.

"If you look back," says Charley McClendon, "you're in trouble." Against Kentucky a week later, the Tigers suggested they were having trouble shaking off the Miami game when the Wildcats jolted them to life at the start of the second half. LSU enjoyed a 9–0 lead when Dickie Lyons returned the third-quarter kickoff ninety-five yards for a score. In short order, a 51-yard punt return by Grezaffi set up a touchdown and, moments later, the Tigers marched eighty-four yards to put an eventual 30–7 victory out of reach.

This meant LSU was 4–1 on its first trip to Knoxville since 1959, the year Tennessee snapped an eighteen-game winning streak. On this occasion, a Vol team, which had beaten Alabama the week before, was a touchdown choice and it looked every bit of it as it took a 7–0 halftime lead.

A third-quarter Tennessee touchdown made it 14–0 and once more it was the fast-stepping Grezaffi who helped shake up the Tigers, returning the Vol kickoff one hundred yards to tie an SEC record. With this swing in momentum, LSU mounted an 80-yard drive in the fourth quarter which Stokley ended with a 14-yard scoring run. Hurd's kick tied it, 14–14, but back came the Vols, aided by a 15-yard penalty, with a 33-yard field goal by Karl Kremser that flew over the uprights with 1:05 seconds left. Then back came the Tigers. In twenty-nine seconds, Stokley moved his club to the Tennessee 20, where Coach McClendon faced another agonizing decision. It was second and eight and the Tigers had no time outs left. After a sideline conference with Stokley, McClendon decided to go for a 37-yard field goal and a 17–17 tie. "The ball was in good position," he said. "I remembered what happened against Miami when an interception took us out of the game. So I didn't want to risk it. The boys had made a great comeback and didn't deserve to lose." Hurd's kick was long enough, but it was wide to the right.

Two days later, because of the timing, some LSU fans got the wrong impression from a story under the headline: "Hurd Disciplined for Rules Infraction." It almost seemed that the Covington sophomore was being dropped from the squad for missing the field goal. Rather, he was being disciplined for breaking curfew, and McClendon made the decision after unanimous approval of his seniors. "It wasn't a serious thing," explained Barry Wilson, "but everyone felt Roy Hurd should be punished."

This meant LSU would be without its No. 1 place-kicker for the Ole Miss game, and the turn of events in Jackson a few days later was fate at its worst. The Tigers fumbled eight times—once into the Rebel end zone—but, with 3:22 remaining, they had a chance to break a 13–13 tie with an extra point. Twice before, they had struck back to tie the score, marching sixty-three yards in the first period and, finally, with Stokley clicking on key third- and fourth-down plays on five straight series of downs, moving eighty yards with Newfield running the final eight yards. But Steve Daniel, who had booted the first extra point, kicked this one off to the right and for the second week in a row LSU had been frustrated by a place-kick.

This frustration reached a kind of a peak seven days later before a sellout crowd in Baton Rouge. Bear Bryant's once-beaten, once-tied Alabama Crimson Tide met the Tigers in a game dominated by defense. All of the fireworks were saved for the fourth quarter, when Bear Bryant's once-beaten, once-tied Crimson Tide went fifty-one yards to grab a 7–0 lead with thirteen minutes to go. Defensive back Jimmy Gilbert returned an intercepted Kenny Stabler pass to the Bama 10, but Tommy Allen fumbled at the 1 to erase what looked like LSU's last scoring chance. Moments later, however, with Eddie Ray gaining most of the key yardage, it became a 7–6 ball game when Allen darted over

Defensive end John Garlington, a 1967 all-American.

from the 4. Incredibly, for the third straight week, the place kick sailed off to the right. This time it was not the kicker, the reinstated Roy Hurd, but the holder, Freddie Haynes, who bobbled the snap and was unable to get the ball in position. "The ball came at me end over end," said Haynes. "I fumbled it and, when I finally put it down, Roy was well into his kicking motion. He had to start over and, by then, his timing was off."

McClendon said he didn't go for two points because "it's not good strategy to go for two with more than seven minutes left. With two minutes left, it's a different story. I've never seen more losses in one season stemming from the place kick. That's the difference between our national championship year of 1958 and this year. If we would have made all of our place-kicks, we'd be on top."

Bryant's fourth win in a row over his former defensive end left LSU with a 4–3–1 picture—but did not put the Tigers out of the bowl picture. In fact, LSU's luck took an incredible turn for the better and the team wound up in a major bowl 80 miles from home.

In quick order on November 18, three Sugar Bowl eligibles lost— North Carolina State to Clemson, Auburn to Georgia, and Ole Miss to Tennessee. Later that day LSU happened to stage one of its most impressive offensive shows in history in the course of a 55–0 rout of Mississippi State. The Tigers rolled up 630 yards, 34 first downs, controlled the ball for 90 plays and, on the twelve different occasions they got the football, they put it in the end zone, although one touchdown was nullified by a fumble and another by offensive pass interference. Split end Tommy Morel caught eleven passes for 152 yards and three touchdowns, all new LSU records.

The smashing victory boosted LSU into the Sugar Bowl against the country's only unbeaten, untied club—Wyoming, sixth ranked in the AP poll. Announcement of LSU's Sugar Bowl acceptance and installation of the Tigers as a 28-point favorite over Tulane placed Jim Pittman's Green Wave in an ideal psychological spot.

For a half, it looked as though the Tigers would win by at least four touchdowns. But, leading 28–7, Charley McClendon said he felt a letdown in his bones. "I took my coat off expecting a fight and I thought the kids would get the idea," he said, "but they didn't until Tulane was breathing down our necks." After the Tigers bogged down on the Wave 22 at the start of the third quarter, Tulane marched seventy-eight yards for a score and then went thirty-eight yards after receiving a fumble to make it 28–21. LSU went fifty-five yards to stretch it to 34–21 but the Tigers fumbled on their 7, and the Greenies shoved it across to bring Tulane back into contention at 34–27. A punt return by Sammy Grezaffi and a 15-yard penalty set up a late-game march for the clincher in a wild 41–27 ball game.

With 156 yards passing and 57 on the ground, Stokley wound up with 1,238 yards in total offense, a new LSU record. His 213 yards against the Wave was just shy of the 217 record Pat Screen picked up against Alabama in 1965. Stokley was highest among the "dedicated dozen" McClendon called "the finest bunch of seniors we've had at LSU since I've been here." Throughout the season, McClendon let the tributes flow for Stokley, center Barry Wilson, guard Bill Bofinger, tackles Terry Esthay and Allen LeBlanc, and tailback Jim Dousay of the offensive unit; and for end John Garlington, middle guards Ronnie Manton and Ron Jeter, linebacker Benny Griffin, tackle Jack Dyer, and safety Sam Grezaffi of the defensive unit.

"All I want them to keep in mind," said Mac at the L Club banquet the week after the Tulane game, "is that we have one left."

In a way, the Sugar Bowl characterized the pitfalls of 1967, winding up as sort of a blend of the Miami, Ole Miss, Alabama, and Tennessee games. The Tigers looked like losers, then they looked like winners, there was a missed extra point, and at the fadeout they were hanging on for dear life. Only, this time they wound up on the right end of the score. Glenn Smith, the fellow who got his team off to a winning start with a touchdown in the last twenty-nine seconds against Rice, came off the bench once again to pump life into a Tiger which Wyoming left for dead in the first half. For two quarters, few LSU teams have looked as frustrated, and the statistics best told the story. The Tigers not only trailed, 0–13, on the scoreboard, they trailed 1–11 in first downs, and 38–215 in total offense. "At half time," said McClendon, "it was a question of character. I had complete confidence in the football team."

Explaining first-half miseries, Barry Wilson said: "We had never played on slippery footing once during the season. The field turned up a little sloppy and it upset our plans to block Wyoming low. Because we weren't able to get solid footing, they merely pushed us off and got to the ball carrier. They were also able to put a lot of pressure on Nelson. At half time, we decided to hit 'em higher, and we decided to take advantage of their pursuit by starting to the outside and then running back against the grain."

Just when many LSU fans were thinking of drowning their New Year shame in firewater, Glenn Smith brought them out of their seats. At the time, facing a third-and-seven from the LSU 23, Stokley was an incredible one-for-thirteen in the passing department. Smith trotted in with a play from the bench and Nelson hit him down the middle on the LSU 40. Glenn, spinning off a tackler, raced to the Wyoming 38, a 39-yard gain. Few games have ever changed so dramatically on one play. Smith popped through on gains of five and six yards and, three plays later, facing another critical third-and-nine situation, Stokley, now oozing confidence, speared Jim West on the Cowboy 12 for a first down. Nelson swept left end to the 1 and Smith bulled across to make it a new ball game.

Stokley in action against Wyoming in the 1968 Sugar Bowl.

The touchdown came with only two minutes left in the third period, and when the Tigers took over once again, on the LSU 48, you had the inevitable feeling they'd put it in the end zone. It took nine plays, which included determined running by Smith, a couple of key end sweeps by Stokley, and two exceptional catches by Tommy Morel. Tommy made his first one a fingertip job and went out of bounds at a 45-degree angle on the Wyoming 35. The second was for the score and Tommy nabbed this one at his knees with Cowboy defenders draped around him. "I ran a post route and Nelson rifled a strike," said Morel. Since Hurd had converted after the first touchdown, the touchdown tied it up, 13–13, but, sure enough, this time Hurd sent his kick wide, reviving familiar nightmares for Charley McClendon.

This time, however, it became a nightmare with a silver lining, at the moment Benny Griffin picked off his second interception of the game and returned it twenty-four yards to the Wyoming 31. Three plays later, it was Stokley to Morel, fourteen yards and six points. "I think they were looking for me to run the post route again," said Tommy. "So I faked inside, turned outside, and Nelson got me the ball. All I had to do was step into the end zone."

McClendon's trial wasn't over. Wyoming got the ball, with thirty-nine seconds left, on its 18 and, after passing for a first down to the 28, Paul Toscano threw a pass that could have been intercepted by any one of three LSU backs. Instead, the ball was deflected into the arms of tight end George Anderson who suddenly saw nothing but daylight. LSU's Barton Frye gave chase, nailing Anderson on the LSU 23. Time was ticking away and Wyoming, with no timeouts remaining, quickly tossed an incomplete pass to stop the clock. The Cowboys stopped it, but were penalized to the 28 for illegal procedure. One second showed on the clock. Toscano faded, and, not surprisingly, went for his best receiver, Gene Huey, who was racing across from right to left. Huey caught the ball on the 5 and was stopped in his tracks by Gerry Kent.

"When I saw Anderson take off with the football," said Frye, "I started running for my life. I don't know if I can run that fast again." Jerry Kober, with thirteen tackles, and Griffin with eleven, were tops for LSU. John Garlington lived up to his all-America press notices at defensive end and won a tribute from one-time defensive end McClendon: "He's the finest I've seen since I've been at LSU." Glenn Smith, playing before a hometown crowd, was the first sophomore to win the Sugar Bowl's most valuable player award. The Holy Cross High product said: "If Wyoming had beaten us, I wouldn't have been able to go home."

As it developed LSU was the SEC's only postseason winner, what with Georgia, Alabama, Tennessee and Ole Miss losing in the Liberty,

Harry Rabenhorst, who came to the LSU athletic staff in 1925, retired in the spring of 1968. In addition to his contributions to LSU football as backfield coach, freshman coach, and scout, Rabenhorst served as basketball and baseball coach, and succeeded Jim Corbett as athletic director.

Cotton, Orange, and Sun Bowls. "There's no question in my mind Wyoming is SEC caliber," said McClendon. "I just can't say enough for our seniors and for the courage of Nelson Stokley." Stokley's second-half performance, typifying the way he overcame frustration, moved *States-Item* columnist Pie Dufour to suggest that LSU award a trophy in Nelson's honor to the football player displaying the most perseverance during his college career.

As it turned out, the Sugar Bowl victory was a going-away gift for departing athletic director Harry Rabenhorst, who had served LSU since 1925, the last few months as successor to Jim Corbett. At seventy, Rabenhorst was preparing to retire in April. It was his impending retirement that gave the Wyoming game added significance in the mind of Charles McClendon. In two weeks the Board of Supervisors would be selecting a new director of athletics, a post McClendon had come to regard as a security blanket. He realized members of the board were as emotional as any other fans about the success of the football team. He realized, too, that no one was as emotionally charged as Governor John McKeithen, LSU's No. 1 cheerleader and longtime close friend of the coach.

So, with Wyoming behind him, and seemingly with the governor in his corner, McClendon felt he was an odds-on choice in what was a two-horse race: the football coach and the director of the Student Union, Carl Maddox. Following the win over Wyoming, there was a report that McKeithen had promised McClendon his support. However, when the board met, McKeithen adopted a hands-off stance, and, after a long meeting, the decision was to maintain the policy of keeping the head coaching job and the athletic director's separate. Carl Maddox, backed by President John Hunter, was named director of athletics at a salary of $23,500. Charles McClendon was given a new five-year contract and a raise in salary from $23,500 to $25,000.

In announcing its decision, the board said Maddox had "demonstrated administrative and executive ability in his position as director of the LSU Union and has the athletic background." The fifty-five-year-old native of Nachitoches, a graduate of Northwestern State College in math and physics, had later received a master's degree in physical education at LSU. Before coming to LSU as backfield coach under Gus Tinsley in 1954, he coached high school teams at Franklin, Louisiana, Gulf Coast Military Academy at Gulfport, and at Greenville, Mississippi. He remained an LSU assistant under Paul Dietzel until 1960 when he became the director of the Union, which was then in the planning stages.

As for working with McClendon, his rival for the post, Maddox anticipated no problem. "Any wounds will heal," he said. "I have no scars, but then, of course, I got the job. I guess Charley did bleed a bit. But we've had each other's confidence over the years. We coached together and are friends. I'm confident we can work together." Whereupon, Maddox returned to his duties, administering an athletic program, and McClendon returned to the job of winning football games.

Before the Tigers teed it up in '68 the head coach was having a chat with Maurice LeBlanc, a tailback who was being shifted to split receiver. McClendon was wondering if LeBlanc could handle the pressure of the new position. LeBlanc assured him, "Coach, I never worry about pressure. If I do anything wrong, they won't blame me. They'll blame you."

It spoke volumes for the life of a coach, especially one who had snapped the longest winning streak in the country when his Tigers beat Wyoming in the Sugar Bowl, and who was now opening the season against Texas A&M, which had the longest string at the time—eight games, including victories over Texas for the Southwest title and over Alabama in the Cotton Bowl.

The Tigers were going to have to do it without Nelson Stokley, who had graduated, and manage with a watch-charm-sized quarterback named Fred Haynes, a 5–8, 160-pounder, who, said McClendon, "is the only quarterback I can remember who was booed in the spring." So there was Haynes, in the opener, running in and out of the arms of maroon-shirted Aggies, sometimes disappearing from sight. His knack for running the option was vital in the 13–12 victory, thanks to Mark Lumpkin's extra point; thanks also to a goal-line tackle by Carlos Rabb and Gerry Kent, which knocked the ball loose from the touchdown-bound Aggie, the ball going out of the end zone for a game-saving touchback.

Two subsequent Southwest foes, Rice and Baylor, were easier touches, sending the Tigers into Orange Bowl Stadium, 3–0, against a Miami team that had been waxed the previous week by Southern Cal and O. J. Simpson.

It turned out to be one of the most nightmarish evenings in McClendon's career, a 30–0 defeat in which the Tigers completely lost their poise. They managed to regroup during the next two weeks, Mark Lumpkin's educated toe getting two field goals in a 13–3 decision over Kentucky and a deciding 37–yarder in a 10–7 win over TCU.

All of this sent LSU into the first chapter of the Archie Manning series with a 5–1 record. Manning's reputation had preceded him to Tigertown. The running, throwing redhead out of Drew, Mississippi, was so impressive as a freshman that he became the first true sophomore to start at quarterback for the Rebels since 1949, an honor denied Eagle

Charley Mac and Carl Maddox in New Orleans, making predictions for 1968.

Day, Raymond Brown, Perry Lee Dunn, Jake Gibbs, and Glynn Griffing.

Manning's Tiger Stadium debut was right out of the Clark Kent-in-the-telephone booth. Before an SRO crowd of 69,337, Manning was a superman in red and blue, completing twenty-four passes for 345 yards and taking the Rebels 76 yards in the final three minutes for a storybook, 27–24, victory.

This time Ole Miss made up for the tipped 2-pointer that gave the Tigers an 11–10 win in '64. On the payoff touchdown from the Tiger 9 yard line, LSU's Craig Burns tipped the ball, only to see it fall into the arms of Stan Hindman, who didn't catch sight of it until he was in the process of falling backwards into the end zone.

It climaxed a spectacular offensive evening that was a virtual standoff, 458 yards for Ole Miss, 454 for LSU. The Tigers lost Fred Haynes in the first quarter with a dislocated wrist, but lefty Mike Hillman, a junior from Lockport, came off the bench to get LSU in front 17–3 early in the second quarter. Seemingly on the ropes, Ole Miss was jerked back to life by Manning who connected on a 65-yard bomb to Floyd Franks. An interception by Ole Miss's Glenn Cannon set up a touchdown that made it, 17–17, and set up the wild finish that followed.

Ordinarily a model of conservatism, Johnny Vaught gave Manning free rein. With the Rebels ahead, 20–17, and only six minutes left,

Archie was passing from his own 15. After one completion, however, LSU's Don Addison wrestled the ball away from Vern Studdard near midfield and LSU promptly marched to a 24–20 lead which many felt had sewed up the game. All it did was send Manning, one of eight sophomores on the Ole Miss offensive team, back to the telephone booth for another quick change. Said Charles McClendon: "He's the best Ole Miss quarterback I've ever seen."

In a situation like this, the Alabama game, in Birmingham the following week, was almost an anticlimax. McClendon went into it 0–4 against his former coach and came out 0–5 when the Tide won an ordinary game, 16–7. Touchdown underdogs, the Tigers led 7–6, and in the fourth quarter had a chance to take a 10–7 lead when Lumpkin missed a 24-yard field goal attempt. The miss eased the pressure on Bama, which tacked on another touchdown and was off to an 8–2 season.

To remain in minor bowl contention, the 5–3 Tigers had to win the final two, and they did, shading Mississippi State, 20–16, and crushing Tulane, 34–10. In the State win, the Bulldogs were gypped out of a down near the LSU goal and had to settle for a field goal. Still, it took an 87-yard march in the fading moments to win, Hillman crossing up State by running the last 11 yards on a second-and-1 situation. A 12-point underdog, the Green Wave was simply outmanned, mustering a mere 96 yards on offense to 506 by the Tigers.

While Tulane was finishing 2–8 under Jim Pittman, the 7–3 Tigers were booked into Atlanta's Peach Bowl against the 8–2 Florida State Seminoles. Ordinarily, this would have been just another postseason attraction to fill nighttime TV. However, since Bill Peterson was the FSU coach, it had an extra dimension, especially for Charles McClendon. Brought out of the high school ranks by Paul Dietzel, Peterson was a pass-oriented coach whose name always seemed to pop up when McClendon was being "fired" by alumni.

Peterson had a standout pitch-and-catch combo in quarterback Bill Cappelman and receiver Ron Sellers, so there wasn't any question about what the Seminoles planned to do. Early on, FSU got some unexpected help when LSU fumbled the opening kickoff, allowing the Seminoles to lead 7–0 only fifteen seconds into the game. It wasn't until the lead was 13–0 that Craig Burns got the Tigers started with a punt return, the first of 24 straight points by LSU.

Then Cappelman and Sellers struck back with 14 points of their own to give the Seminoles a 27–24 lead with six minutes remaining. What this did was put the burden on Mike Hillman, who began moving his club downfield, only to face a third-and-19 inside the Seminole 30. Hillman put the ball in the air, and, somehow, some way, senior end Tommy Morel outfought a cluster of defenders for it, getting the first

McClendon and Coach Lloyd Eaton after the Tigers defeated Wyoming in the 1968 Sugar Bowl.

down by a scant yard. It was almost anticlamatic when Maurice Le-Blanc ran it in for the winning score (30–27). And it was nerve-wracking when Barton Frye, in the final seconds, saved the game by tipping a pass out of the arms of Ron Sellers.

The most interesting statistic is that the "conservative" McClendon outgained pass-happy Peterson in the air, 233–221, a stat that could be attributed to Hillman going 16-for-19 and the LSU rush, headed by nineteen-year-old Buddy Millican, the defensive MVP, sacking Cappelman eight times.

Starting in the preseason top twenty, the '69 Tigers were now nowhere to be seen. In the SEC, where Ole Miss was the composite choice, LSU was picked no higher than fifth. It was going to be a year of surprises on the field and off.

The good news was that linebacker George Bevan, whose crunching deportment on defense belied his cherubic choirboy looks, was alive and well. Bevan sparkled as a sophomore in '66. In the opening game of '67, he ruptured an achilles tendon. He was operated on the next day; the tendon did not heal. A second operation the following May cleaned out the troubled area, and there was a third operation, in which tendons were taken from Bevan's thigh and sewed into his ruptured achilles.

A shade under 6 feet and weighing 190, Bevan could run the 40 in 4.7. "When he put on an LSU uniform," said trainer Marty Broussard, "it was an inspiration to the squad." On the squad were a crop of wide-eyed sophomores, including defensive back Tommy Casanova and a pass catcher named Andy Hamilton.

No LSU team sailed through the first half of a schedule in more impressive fashion. By mid-October, the Tigers not only were 5–0, the closest anyone could get was Miami, a 20–0 loser. With Bevan and junior linebacker Mike Anderson, a couple of hometown products, on the prowl, the first four opponents could muster only 87 yards rushing. Auburn, with an offense averaging better than 425 yards, playing LSU for the first time in twenty-seven years, would be a different matter. The 4–1 Plainesmen would allow LSU to find out just how good it was.

The regionally televised game out of Tiger Stadium began with an opening salvo. A study of the films showed Auburn safety Buddy McClinton flying in on sweeps. On LSU's first play from scrimmage, quarterback Mike Hillman pitched to tailback Buddy Gilbert, giving the impression of a left end run. Suddenly, Gilbert, after running a few steps, stopped and lofted a pass to an all-alone Andy Hamilton, who gathered it in, waltzed into the end zone, to complete a 62-yard scoring play. Ordinarily a split back, Hamilton lined up as a tight end, coming out of the huddle with his hands covering his number as a means of avoiding detection.

The mood of the crowd of 68,000 changed quickly. Pat Sullivan engineered two touchdown marches, and it looked like a 14–7 Auburn halftime lead until Hillman began ad libbing. With thirty seconds left,

Mike Anderson stops Mickey Zofko in the Auburn game, 1969.

Andy Hamilton, Ole Miss game at Jackson, 1969.

Hillman rolled out to his right. "I was supposed to hit Eddie Ray," he explained afterward, "but they held him up. I got boxed in and had to come back left. Jim West was a blocker on the play. He blocked, then drifted out, and I got the ball to him."

The second-half drama involved the third-quarter score that put LSU ahead, 21–14 and, in the final period, the biggest play in a 21–20 LSU victory, which said something about George Bevan. Bevan was beaten by Auburn halfback Mickey Zofko for the third score. Seconds later, he was making amends, knifing between two Plainesmen to block the extra point with his forearm.

What this did was give an extra dimension to LSU's visit to Jackson the following week for the annual scrap with Ole Miss. McClendon's surprising Tigers were 6–0 and ranked eighth. The Rebels, beaten by Kentucky, Alabama, and Houston, were 3–3 and unranked. LSU was a 7-point favorite. Archie Manning welcomed the challenge.

As the shadows lengthened in Memorial Stadium, one Ole Miss. fan turned to another and said: "I'll give you $5 to rent your Archie button for the last quarter."

Manning was in the process of taking Ole Miss to its second straight 3-point decision over the Tigers, this one 26–23, a game, incredibly enough, he dominated more than the 27–24 thriller a year earlier. To do it, he overcame an aggressive defense with a bewildering assortment of scrambling moves. More than half of his 22 completions went to secondary receivers, many of whom were running alternate routes as Manning ran for his life. "Not counting the Ole Miss game," said

George Bevan, "we only missed 19 tackles all season. Against Ole Miss, we missed 18 and I bet Archie was responsible for 15."

On one 9-yard scoring pass, Archie ran 30 yards behind the line before releasing the ball. In the third quarter, with the Rebs trailing, 23–18, Manning faced a third-and-16 at the LSU 28. He passed for 15, then sneaked for the first down. Three plays later, he faced third-and-10 at the LSU 11. He passed for 10, then sneaked for the score. And then ran it across for 2 points to give Ole Miss a 3-point lead.

Mike Hillman rallied his troops, moving the Tigers from their 20 to the Ole Miss 23. With 65 seconds left, it was fourth-and-8. McClendon faced an agonizing decision: field goal for a tie or a first down to stay alive for a winning score. Nine years before, faced with a similar situation in Oxford, Johnny Vaught went for 3 and a 6–6 tie, the only blot in a 10–0–1 season. This time Mac told Hillman: "You took us this far. Now take us in." The play was a pass to tight end Bill Stober. Stober was hit from three sides as Hillman's pass came to him, the ball and the ball game tumbling away.

At the start of Alabama week, McClendon faced another decision: the best way to get the team geared up after two tough games in a row, playing a coach he had never beaten in five meetings. Mac's decision was to shorten practices and take a bunch of fresh players into Birmingham where Bear Bryant's 5–2 Tide, which had beaten Ole Miss in a wild 33–32 shootout, was a 10-point underdog.

The idea was to beat Bama with ball control. As it turned out, the Tigers rushed the football sixty-two times, compared to twenty-eight for the Tide, but quarterback Scott Hunter was a threat to the end. After Hunter threw a fourth-down, 37-yard pass to narrow LSU's lead to 13–9 with six minutes remaining, Bryant out-smarted himself, going for an on-sides kick that LSU recovered at midfield and promptly marched to a 20–9 lead.

Gambling wasn't over. Passing deep into its territory on fourth down, Bama put together a drive that made it 20–15 with ninety seconds to go. This time Bama's on-sides kick was recovered by Chaille Percy. On fourth-and-a-foot at the Bama 45, there were still forty-six seconds left. McClendon decided to go for it. Allen Shory, a 5–9 workhorse, who wound up as the game's top rusher with 118 yards in twenty-six carries, made it.

And Charles McClendon became the first of Bear Bryant's former players to beat him in a regular season game.

The season's biggest surprise was ahead: a decision in South Bend and a miscalculation by a man who would be voted coach of the year. Charles McClendon was handling the behind-the-scenes politicking for a postseason berth. When the Tigers crushed Mississippi State, 61–6, to up their record to 8–1, McClendon felt he had a strong hand. But he reckoned without the glamour of a Notre Dame playing in its first bowl game since the days of the Four Horsemen.

McClendon was hankering to meet the winner of the Texas-Arkansas game in the Cotton Bowl. Even though the Irish were heading for an 8–1–1 season, they had the pick of the Orange and Cotton bowls should they choose to discard a self-imposed bowl ban. Mac banked on another no vote by Notre Dame. But the school, feeling the money pinch, and realizing it didn't have to share a bowl with anyone, voted yes. It chose the Cotton over the Orange because it felt the Southwest winner would finish higher in the rankings than unbeaten Penn State, which had already been lined up for Miami.

Miami was planning a Penn State-Tennessee match, but Archie Manning ruined these plans when he engineered a stunning 38–0 upset, a game that not only shocked the Orange but impressed the Sugar. When Tennessee came tumbling down, the Orange quickly grabbed 8–1 Missouri, best in the Big Eight. And Tennessee, heading for 9–1, quickly grabbed a Gator Bowl invitation to play Florida, heading for 8–1–1.

This left the Sugar Bowl a choice among LSU, Ole Miss, and Auburn to meet the Texas-Arkansas loser. It selected Archie Manning and a 7–3 ball club over one that had to beat Tulane to finish 9–1. Some members of the Sugar Bowl committee were irked that LSU did not show interest in New Orleans until Notre Dame shut the door in Dallas.

The irony was obvious. LSU had been to the Cotton Bowl with a 7–3 club. Now it was going to sit home for the holidays with a 9–1 record, best ever by a Charles McClendon team. The Tigers could have gone to the Sun or Bluebonnet but, at a team meeting, the vote was not to play anyone without a comparative national ranking, which, at that time, was No. 10.

A closing 27–0 victory over Tulane, one in which the Greenies were held to minus yardage on the ground, was devoid of any drama and no doubt an anticlimax to the bitter bowl picture.

Said one Tiger coach: "Before the season everyone was saying LSU wasn't going anywhere this year. They didn't mean it that way, but that's the way it turned out."

In early September, Charles McClendon was talking about the impending three-way battle for quarterback on his 1970 team, a battle involving senior Buddy Lee, who had understudied Mike Hillman the year before; junior Butch Duhe, who had lettered as No. 3 quarterback; and sophomore Bert Jones, up from the freshman team.

"These things," said the coach, "take care of themselves."

When he said this, McClendon had no inkling what hand fate would play. Herman Duhe, Jr., a twenty-one-year-old product of Holy Cross

High in New Orleans, was personally recruited by athletic director Jim Corbett, who died of a heart attack two days after signing the blue-chip prospect. When he was signed, the speculation was he would be coming of age as a quarterback just in time for the two-game series with Notre Dame, a '70 date in South Bend, a '71 date in Tiger Stadium.

During the summer of '70, Duhe kept fit on a construction job and by running four miles a day. Although he was bothered by severe headaches, he never changed his routine. He faced the fall brimming with confidence. Duhe dressed out for a Monday practice but remained on the sidelines with a severe headache. The next morning, when the headaches persisted, he was hospitalized. In three hours, he was dead of a brain hemorrhage.

"When one of your players dies," said Assistant Coach Charley Pevey, "it's like a death in the family." Watching his son blossom, Herman Duhe, Sr., was reliving his life as a high school star at Reserve. "I've never known a father who wanted his son to succeed as Mr. Duhe did," said assistant coach Doug Hamley, who helped recruit Butch. Mr. Duhe never had the opportunity to attend college, so here was Butch doing the things he always dreamed of doing. He spent a large part of the summer running pass routes and acting as Butch's holder on place-kicks."

The tragedy lingered. As McClendon put it, "It's impossible to shake something like this. You try to get the players' minds off it, but you don't know whether you're getting through."

Ronnie Estay tackles Ole Miss's Archie Manning for a safety, 1970.

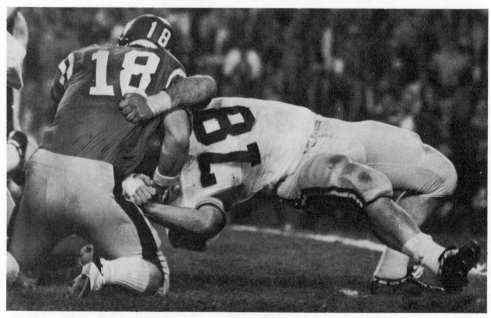

There was a foggy climate to LSU's opener against the Texas Aggies. Trailing by a point in the fourth quarter, the Tigers took a 15–13 lead on a field goal by Mark Lumpkin. They held the Aggies for four downs and took over at the Aggie 19 with a minute and a half left. Four plays later, with 45 seconds remaining, another Lumpkin field goal made it, 18–13.

School seemed to be out for A&M. But it wasn't. On third down, from the Aggie 21, quarterback Lex James put up a long one in search of split Hugh McElroy. LSU defender Paul Lyons had McElroy covered, but instead of playing it soft, Lyons went for the interception—and didn't get it. McElroy gathered in the football and crossed the goal line with 13 seconds on the clock. The Tigers were a 20–18 loser.

At this stage, McClendon's 0–1 team needed some help and got it—from the schedule. Rice, Baylor, and Pacific did not qualify as stemwinders, nor did Kentucky, victimized 14–7. The four-game cruise that brought the Tigers into a road game against Auburn enabled McClendon to establish his two-quarterback system—Lee No. 1, Jones No. 2—with an offense that had an easier time making third-and-13 than it did third-and-3. "I'd like for both of them to start running more on the option," said McClendon. Auburn, he felt, would have to be whipped in the trenches.

It was going to be LSU's first visit to Auburn since the unbeaten, untied Tigers of 1908 came away with a 10–2 win. At this stage, Auburn was 5–0 and No. 6 in the country. Quarterback Pat Sullivan was averaging almost 9 yards every time he ran or passed the football. The Plainsmen not only were averaging 35 points a game, they were comparable to the Army juggernaut of Davis and Blanchard. Also, they had the SEC's best pass defense and the third-best defense overall. It was no surprise when the home team was called a 13-point favorite.

With this in mind, what happened that afternoon in Auburn ranked up there with the Cotton Bowl upsets of Texas and Arkansas. Since neither the Longhorns nor Razorbacks were two-touchdown favorites, it was a bigger upset.

A muddy track produced a quick break—when Ronnie Estay recovered a fumble on the game's first play—and LSU was in front to stay on a soggy pass from Lee to Andy Hamilton. They added a touchdown in the second quarter when Jones took the team 85 yards with Art Cantrelle scoring. And they added 2 points in the final period when Estay, Buddy Millican and John Sage nailed Sullivan for a safety. All this while, Auburn had to content itself with three field goals. Although the Tigers didn't plan it, they got 2 points on an ad-lib play from a place-kick alignment an extra point alignment in which Lumpkin, the kicker, wound up passing to Paul Lyons, his holder, after a fumbled

Mac celebrates winning the SEC crown after a 61–17 win over Ole Miss earned the Tigers an Orange Bowl berth, 1970.

snap and a mad scramble. And they added two more, legitimately this time, in the final period when Ronnie Estay, Buddy Millican, and John Sage nailed Sullivan for a safety.

All the while, Auburn had to content itself with three field goals, which helped set up a dramatic finish. With a chance to tie, the home team, cheered on by a homecoming crowd of 63,000 watching from under umbrellas, needed a touchdown and a 2-pointer. It got its chance when it reached the LSU 3 on fourth down. In a battle of wits, Pat Sullivan called an audible when he spotted an inviting hole between LSU end Art Davis and tackle John Sage. Mike Anderson left the gap as if inviting the run, but on the snap of the ball he filled it. He met the ball carrier, Wallace Clark, at the 1 and stopped him cold with a shoulder-high tackle. Said Sage: "He would have scored if Mike hadn't hit him in the chest." McClendon called it "the finest one-on-one tackle I've ever seen."

As challenges go, the next one was Bear Bryant and Johnny Musso, the "Italian Stallion." It was not a good year for Bryant whose Tide was limping along with a 5–3 record, but, with the game in Birmingham, they went to the post a 3-point favorite. It was a good year for Musso, the SEC's leading rusher.

In a game that should have been more lopsided, McClendon made it two in a row over Bear, 14–9, one in which the Tiger defense limited the Italian Stallion to 44 yards. A year before, LSU finished first in rushing defense nationally, yielding 38 yards per game. At this stage, they were still on top, having given up an average of 47 yards on the ground, doing it with only two returning first stringers.

Gone from the seven-man defensive line-backer front of '69 were Jerry Kober, Donnie Bozeman, Fred Michaelson, Bill Thomason, and all-American, George Bevan. Only Mike Anderson and John Sage remained, joined by Davis, Estay, Millican, Lou Cashio, and Richard Picou, a 193-pound walkon.

A thinking man's tackle, the 6–3, 220-pound Sage was a cadet colonel in the ROTC who, because of his quickness, seldom got knocked off the line of scrimmage. On Bama's first scrimmage play, he shed a blocker and nailed Musso for a 1-yard loss, setting the tone of the game. Anderson, the other key, was a 6–3, 225-pounder McClendon called, "the strongest linebacker I've ever had at LSU." Anderson wanted to play the middle in '70 but his coach kept him on the strong side, explaining: "Everytime they run away from Mike, we've got 'em outnumbered."

It was a defense that hadn't allowed a rushing touchdown all season, one characterized not by size, but blinding quickness. All of which added to the boxer-slugger confrontation for LSU's first-ever game against Notre Dame, November 21, in South Bend. Playing the Irish there means you're not only up against awesome physical specimens, but also the intangibles—Knute Rockne, Pat O'Brien, the Gipper, a Warner Brothers orchestra.

Ronnie Estay pressures Joe Theismann in South Bend.

It so happened that Notre Dame had one helluva team. Winners of eight straight, Ara Parseghian's club was ranked second behind Texas, featuring the No. 1 offense in the country, one averaging 541 yards and a staggering ninety-four plays from scrimmage, thirty more than the opposition. It featured quarterback Joe Theismann and defensive behemoths like Walt Patulski (6–5, 250), Mike Kadish (6–5, 263), and Greg Marx (6–5, 260). In Las Vegas you could get LSU and 14 points.

"Notre Dame may beat us," said McClendon, "but they sure won't scare us." Richard Picou admitted he was somewhat apprehensive when he watched the Irish run onto the field. "They were so big," he recalled, "I thought someone had made a mistake and we were playing the Green Bay Packers."

On Notre Dame's first offensive play, Theismann, hoping to take advantage of LSU's quickness, threw a screen pass which looked as though it would go for a long gain. But Picou roared in from his linebacker post, hit the ball carrier, knocked the ball loose, and LSU recovered at the Irish 31. Later, with the Irish playing a first-and-goal at the LSU 3, Picou again separated the ball from the ball carrier and recovered. Later still, the Irish went for it on third and 1 near midfield. John Sage made the stop inches short. On fourth and inches, the Irish gambled and called another running play. No gain.

On four series in the third quarter, the Irish failed to make a first down and wound up with one yard in total offense. In the fourth quarter, Bill Norsworthy intercepted a Theismann pass to set up a 34-yard field goal try that was blocked.

All afternoon Tommy Casanova was covering Tom Gatewood, the nation's No. 2 receiver, one-on-one. In the first half, Gatewood caught four passes for 21 yards. In the second half, Casanova shut him out.

The game turned on a questionable pass interference call in the fourth quarter with the Irish facing a third down at their 17. While the SEC official closest to the play signaled an incompletion, a Big Ten representative upfield tossed the flag on John Nagel, giving the Irish life near midfield. This was followed four plays later by a punt (one of twenty-two in the game) which angled out on the LSU 1-yard line. When LSU kicked back, the Irish marched to the Tiger 7 where it faced a third-and-goal. Theismann decided to go to Gatewood. Covering perfectly, Casanova moved in front of the receiver in the end zone and had two hands on an apparent interception but couldn't hold on. On the next play, Scott Hempel kicked a 24-yard field goal for the only score of the afternoon. The stat sheet made heroes of the Tigers. A Notre Dame offense averaging 541 yards was limited to 227. An Irish running game averaging 304 was held to 78, only 30 of which came in the heat of battle.

Said Theismann: "I've never seen a better defense in my three years at Notre Dame. The quickness was amazing, the way they covered screens and pursued on sweeps. And the rush didn't give you much time to throw." He was sacked six times. Possibly Theismann's failure to score on the LSU defense cost him the Heisman which went to Jim Plunkett of Stanford.

For LSU the balm for losing was an invitation to play Nebraska in the Orange Bowl, a bid that hinged on the Tigers beating Tulane and Ole Miss. The Greenies were catching the Tigers in an ideal spot—after Notre Dame, before Ole Miss—in Tulane Stadium. LSU jumped to a 20-0 lead and, obviously showing a letdown from its South Bend visit, wound up as an uninspired 26-14 winner, capitalizing on two Tulane fumbles and an interception. Chris Dantin scored three times for the Tigers but it was a 1-yard run by Tulane's Dave Abercrombie that figured more in postgame conversation. It was the first rushing touchdown given up by LSU in twelve games.

In this case, Tulane was soothed by an invitation to play Colorado in the Liberty Bowl, thanks to a tackle by linebacker Rick Kingrea, a Baton Rouge High product. Had Kingrea not stopped Art Cantrelle at the 1 late in the game, LSU would have been a 33-14 winner and the Liberty probably would have looked elsewhere.

Since the Orange Bowl invitation hinged on beating Ole Miss, McClendon wasn't out of the woods yet, even though Archie Manning was coming to Baton Rouge with a plate in his left arm, fractured in early November. The year before Manning's heroics cost LSU a major bowl invitation, the conference championship, and a perfect season. Now the Tigers would have to whip the Rebels to lay claim to the SEC title.

LSU began with a case of the jitters, fumbling three times in the first quarter, one leading to a Rebel touchdown, another killing a Tiger drive. A 46-yard Lee-to-Hamilton pass put the home team ahead for good, 14-10, a 61-yard punt return by Tommy Casanova made it 21-10. But it was not until Ronnie Estay nailed Manning for a safety shortly before halftime that Tiger partisans felt secure. It was like bagging the Indian chief.

The final 61-17 tally, most lopsided of the series, produced 811 yards by a Tiger team, including three scoring punt returns, two by Casanova, one by Craig Burns. Hindered by a 7-pound cast on his left arm, Manning completed twelve passes, but threw two interceptions and was minus-25-yards on the ground. "I feel like we had the weight of the stadium on us," said McClendon afterward, thinking how close his team had come to a 10-0-1 season—the last second foul-up in the Aggie opener and the dropped "interception" by Casanova in South Bend.

LSU was on its way to meet a bonafide 10–0–1 club in third-ranked Nebraska. On his last trip to the Orange Bowl in '61, McClendon had been a spear carrier for Paul Dietzel. Now he was returning as LSU field marshal and as SEC coach of the year. Although the Tigers went to Miami with no legitimate shot to win the national title—they were No. 7—they found themselves in the midst of a day of dizzying upsets on January 1. After Notre Dame upset No. 1 Texas in Dallas, Stanford did the same to No. 2 Ohio State in Pasadena, all of which made it a crusade for Bob Devaney's No. 3 Cornhuskers. The kickoff was delayed until the Rose Bowl score was posted, and the impact was obvious as Nebraska took the field before a sellout crowd of 80,000. "They looked 12 feet off the ground," said Richard Picou. "They realized they'd be number one if they beat us." LSU began as if it had a championship at stake. Two fumbles in the first quarter paved the way to a 10–0 Nebraska lead, the scores coming in less than a minute, one on a 15-yard drive. That wasn't the only bad news. On the first series, the Tigers lost their bread-and-butter runner, Art Cantrelle, who had outrushed nine of LSU's opponents. But LSU settled down. Chris Dantin picked up some of the slack on offense and the defense hung tough, enabling two field goals by Lumpkin to shave the margin to 10–6. When Buddy Lee connected with Al Coffee on a 31-yard scoring strike late in the third quarter, another upset loomed even though Lumpkin missed the extra point to leave it at 12–10.

But the mighty Cornhuskers would not be denied. They powered 76 yards at the start of the final quarter, getting it in small chunks against a grudging defense. However, before quarterback Jerry Tagge sneaked the final yard, Nebraska got a quick-whistle break when John Sage separated Joe Orduna from the ball. "I hit him high and the ball came loose," said Sage. "It was definitely a fumble." But the officials ruled otherwise. A Nebraska defense, which limited the Tigers to 38 yards on the ground, saved the game with two interceptions, one near the end off Bert Jones. All-American Mike Anderson felt that eight days of regimentation in Miami Beach took something out of the overall effort. "It was a change from what LSU had done before when a more relaxed approach was taken. It wasn't much of a fun trip and I think our performance showed it."

You couldn't take anything away from Nebraska. As Coach Devaney put it after the 17–12 win, trying to head off any claim 10–1 Notre Dame might have to the title: "I think even the Pope would vote us No. 1." The final tally showed Nebraska No. 1, Notre Dame No. 2, and LSU No. 7, matching the highest finish ever by a McClendon team in the AP poll.

It isn't often a football team goes into a season overlooking its first nine opponents but that's the way it was for LSU in the early fall of '71. Notre Dame was coming to Baton Rouge November 20, and every Tiger, from Gonzales to Bunkie, from Kaplan to Hahnville, had it circled in red.

The Tigers figured to have trouble putting an early defense together since Ronnie Estay was the only member of the '70 front returning, but the linebackers and secondary looked solid. Estay was out of rabbit-hunting, crayfish-eating, pole-fishing, bank-walking, French-talking country, having grown up in Larose, the heart of what Cajuns enjoy calling "coonass country." The area had produced Joe Labruzzo, hero of the '65 Cotton Bowl. At 6–1 and 230, Ronnie Estay was a lot bigger than Joe. The year before, Estay owned the unique distinction of throwing two Heisman candidates—Archie Manning and Pat Sullivan—for safeties. McClendon was now calling him "the finest tackle we've had here since Fred Miller." Estay's contribution went beyond tackling. He snapped on punts and was a member of the field goal, extra point, and kickoff teams.

Offensively, the strongest item going into the season was the first-cousin combo from Ruston—Bert Jones and Andy Hamilton—and the running of senior workhorse Art Cantrelle. With powers like Colorado and Alabama and Notre Dame scheduled to come to Tiger Stadium, some prognosticators felt a sweep was possible. To increase Tigertown fever, Tommy Casanova's picture graced the cover of *Sports Illustrated*'s college football issue.

The rose-colored paradise of anticipation came to an abrupt halt. Whether the Tigers were too much concerned with Fighting Irish talk, whether Colorado was determined to avenge an embarrassing Liberty Bowl loss to Tulane, the facts were that the Buffaloes were big enough and good enough, to blow LSU out of Tiger Stadium. While LSU's air game came to dropped balls and missed receivers, the defense to missed tackles, Colorado controlled the line of scrimmage, and a half-back named Charlie Davis rushed for 174 yards, the most any one runner gained against LSU.

The 31–21 romp of Davis and the Buffaloes was a shock to Tiger egos—egos fattened the past two years by the best rushing defense in the country. "Maybe we spoiled some people," said McClendon, "but you can't lose seven starters and expect to be as good." As big a surprise as the Colorado score was what was happening at quarterback. Paul Lyons, a defensive back in '70, had taken the No. 1 job from blue-chipper Bert Jones, who had thrown three interceptions in the opener. Explained McClendon, "We're going with the quarterback who can move the team." What he really meant was the quarterback who can best run the option, which the 5–10, 180-pound Lyons could do.

Lyons won "back of the week" honors for directing a 37–0 win over Texas A&M, and a week later he set a single-game total offense record of 304 yards—139 of it running—in a 38–28 visit to Wisconsin, a game witnessed by a capacity crowd of 78,000. Rice, Florida, and Kentucky fell, and the operation seemed to be running smoothly as a young defense matured. Then, all of a sudden, everything seemed to go up in smoke. The Tigers went to Jackson a three-touchdown favorite over an Ole Miss team that had been trounced by Alabama and Georgia and seemed to be troubled by a department shakeup. The Rebels were under a new coach, Billy Kinard, who got the job when his brother Bruiser Kinard was victorious in a power play over Johnny Vaught, whose choice was Bob Tyler, then an assistant on the Ole Miss staff. When Billy Kinard won the nod, Bruiser was elevated to athletic director. Tyler joined the Alabama staff and eventually found his way to Starkville. So much for office politics.

In this case, politics was forgotten. After the 61–17 humiliation of the previous year, Kinard had an easy time getting his club ready. Before LSU woke up, the Rebels were on top, 21–0, which was enough of a cushion to hold off a Tiger rally for a 24–22 win.

The shock came at a bad time. After 6–5 and 6–5–1 seasons Bear Bryant decided to get serious again. He was taking an 8–0 team into Tiger Stadium, a team which had gone to the Wishbone and steamrolled to 400 rushing yards a game. Emotion being what it is, a Tiger defense that had been slipshod against Ole Miss turned tiger. Against an LSU team that had the ball for seventy-six plays, compared to fifty-two for the Tide, Alabama needed an errorless game to win, 14–7. They got the points on two first-half field goals and a short scoring drive in the third quarter before LSU marched 69 yards for its only score. "I'm happy as hell to get out of here alive," said Bryant on snapping a two-year drought against LSU.

Even though the Tigers were 6–3 after an easy win over Mississippi State, and seventh-ranked Notre Dame had lost only to Southern Cal in nine games, LSU was a 1-point favorite on a red-letter day. The frenzy engulfing Baton Rouge climaxed a twelve-month wait, and it seemed to eclipse fervor for Ole Miss epics of the late '50s and Paul Dietzel's return in '66. One reason was that the game would be nationally televised during primetime, a showcase in which Cajun pride was squarely on the line.

Charles McClendon made his most important decision in the dressing room before the game. Bert Jones would start at quarterback. The game was only minutes old when the Tigers struck, Jones going to Andy Hamilton for a couple of 36-yard completions and a 7–0 lead. Then the Tiger defense turned the south end of the stadium into some kind of LSU Stalingrad, the same standoff that stopped Ole Miss in '58 and again in '59.

In this instance, the Irish faced a favorable situation—fourth with 4 inches to go for a first down, 1 foot for a touchdown. Behind an offensive front that averaged close to 260, Notre Dame sent Andy Huff off the right side. Skip Cormier, a 205-pounder, penetrated to make the initial contact. Then Lou Cashio, a 205-pound linebacker, fought through a double-team block to stand up Huff, as Lloyd Frye, another 205-pounder, finished him off short of a first down.

The drama then shifted to the north end. With the Irish playing a fourth-and-2-feet at the Tiger 10, sophomore cornerback Norm Hodgins nailed quarterback Cliff Brown for a 3-yard loss. Later, on a fourth-and-1 at the LSU 3, Frye separated an Irish receiver from the ball to end the threat.

There was more. The first of two interceptions by Warren Capone, another sophomore, helped give the Tigers a 14–0 half-time lead, and a picturebook interception by Tommy Casanova stopped an Irish touchdown. LSU went from a fumble recovery by Hodgins to a 21–0 lead in the third quarter, the first touchdown scored on Notre Dame in the second half of the '71 season.

Andy Hamilton takes a touchdown pass after outwitting Notre Dame's Clarence Ellis, 1971.

All-American Tommy Casanova and tackle Ronnie Estay flank Charlie Mac at press day in Baton Rouge, 1971.

In the meantime, the Ruston cousins, Jones and Hamilton, were having a ball playing pitch-and-catch. Hamilton was having a field day with the Irish secondary and, on LSU's final TD, he turned defensive ace Clarence Ellis completely around as he gathered in a pass from Lyons.

As the final seconds in a 28–8 victory ticked away, fans tore down the metal goalposts, and the floor of Tiger Stadium became a surging sea of humanity. No one was going to argue with McClendon's assessment: "Gentlemen, there has never been a bigger victory in Tiger Stadium." Dorothy Faye McClendon agreed. "Since Charles has been head coach, I considered the Cotton Bowl win over Arkansas the best, followed by the Cotton Bowl win over Texas. Now I have to put this one on top."

"In this game," explained Tommy Casanova, "you knew the whole state was behind you. It's probably like this in the Olympics when you're representing your country." In a sense, Louisiana had stood off college football's version of *National Geographic*, the cream of Texas, Pennsylvania, Illinois, Connecticut, New York, Ohio, Iowa, Michigan, New Jersey, Wisconsin, Maryland, California. The victory went to Jennings, Ruston, Amite, Crowley, Franklinton, Gonzales, Rayville, Larose, Lutcher, Morgan City—the places that produce the Picous, Estays, Cormiers, Joneses, and Hamiltons.

When Andy Hamilton caught six passes, two of them for touchdowns, in a 36–7 win over Tulane, he was setting an LSU record for regular-season receptions (45), scoring passes (9) and tying a record for career touchdowns (24). It meant the Tigers were going to El Paso, and a Sun Bowl meeting with Iowa State, on some kind of Cajun high. Sixteen players would be playing their final game for LSU, and when the Texas sun came up that Saturday morning on the Sun Bowl, it looked as though Charles McClendon might be coaching his final game at LSU.

For several weeks, McClendon had been mulling an offer from Texas A&M, one that would pay him a reported $100,000 a year for ten years, a million-dollar package. Looking for a replacement for Gene Stallings, Aggie officials were putting the pressure on McClendon with their million-dollar package. Although the story broke the morning of the game, it had no apparent effect on the team, which dusted off State, 33–15, behind the bulls-eye throwing of Bert Jones. A 12–for–18 afternoon for 227 yards and three touchdowns made Jones an easy Most Valuable Player winner.

The victory quickly took a backseat as McClendon discussed his situation with Governor John McKeithen following the game. The result was a five-year contract, renewable for five years at the end of each of the five-year periods. McClendon also was granted control of Broussard Hall, something he felt was necessary to maintain discipline on his football team.

In the summer the talk was in terms of a national championship. Looking ahead to '72, Charles McClendon found it difficult to understand. "After all, we lost six players from our starting defense and seven from our offense, and this included Ronnie Estay, the best college tackle in America, Tommy Casanova, Andy Hamilton, and Art Cantrelle."

But these debits were offset by one fact—Bert Jones would be returning for one more season. It was good enough for *Sports Illustrated*, which, in its annual issue on college football, planted the kiss of death squarely on the cheek of the Tiger: LSU was picked to finish No. 1. Said *SI*: "By early November, when they confront their two toughest opponents—Ole Miss and Alabama, the Bengals should be a vote-grabbing 6–0 . . . their chances for a national title have seldom seemed better." As for Jones, the magazine cited his 60–for–90 completions in the last six games, for nine touchdowns, and no interceptions.

It would have been an upset had Bert Jones turned into anything but what he did—a 6–3 ½, 205-pound quarterback with a bazooka arm. His father, Dub, owned the distinction of playing for both LSU and Tulane. When Dub went on to fame as a professional and later as a pro assistant, Bert, the third of five sons, spent some of his youth in the training camp of the Cleveland Browns, watching people like Jim Ninowski and

Mac with Bert Jones and Paul Lyons, his two top field generals, 1972.

Frank Ryan. He also grew up with a natural throwing motion and a buggywhip arm. "I remember my grandfather holding me on his knee, teaching me how to throw the knuckler," Bert recalled. "He was really something. When he was at Tulane, he'd pitch doubleheaders, the first game righthanded, the second lefthanded."

This was the climate in which Jones blossomed, an athletic family that championed backyard games in Ruston. Oddly enough, when Jones finished a spectacular career at Ruston, he still found himself in the shadow of Shreveport's Joe Ferguson, all-state quarterback at Woodlawn High. McClendon, and Governor McKeithen, made the big pitch for Ferguson—and lost. So, in effect, LSU got Bert Jones, who would have gone elsewhere had Ferguson chosen Tigertown, as something of a consolation prize.

"Bert came to LSU strong-armed and strong-willed," said McClendon. Most of the time, the two were on different wavelengths, McClendon looking on a quarterback's ability to run the option as more of an overall asset than the knack of throwing the dropback pass.

It all came down to one simple fact: Jones was tailored for the pro game, and McClendon would never go to the protype attack, regardless of the quarterback's talents. Later, with the Baltimore Colts, Bert would say that the highlight of his college career was "getting out." Mac would say: "Bert wasn't the most coachable player I've ever had." The two had crossed swords in the Orange Bowl when sophomore Jones shook off a play from the bench, and proceeded to throw an interception that killed a drive in the 17–12 loss.

As for Jones, he didn't particularly relish serving his sophomore apprenticeship under Buddy Lee, but he didn't like losing the battle to Paul Lyons for most of his junior season. He had to close with three stellar performances—Notre Dame, Tulane, Iowa State—to win it outright.

Picking up where he left off, throwing bullets, Jones had no problem keeping it. After three games—Pacific, Texas A&M, and Wisconsin—he had six TD passes while a young defense, headed by linebacker Warren Capone, was coming together. The first major test for the 4–0 Tigers came when Auburn, also 4–0, visited Tiger Stadium. In the two weeks previous, Shug Jordan's Plainsmen had snapped the longest existing winning streaks—first Tennessee, then Ole Miss. Thanks to Auburn, LSU's eight-game string was now No. 1. For McClendon, beating Auburn meant something else. It would give him his eighty-fourth victory, more than any coach in LSU history.

As it turned out, few were easier than No. 84. With Jones going 10-for-14, three of them for TDs, the Tigers coasted, 35–7. With six games left, Bert had already matched Y. A. Tittle's career record of twenty-three scoring passes.

The biggest touchdown of them all was yet to come. When the Tigers scored a "letdown" 10–0 win over Kentucky, it was only the second time (1969 was the other) a McClendon team had won its first six in a row. To make history, they had to beat Ole Miss, which came to Baton Rouge with a 4–3 record and as a 14-point underdog.

From the start, there was no indication that the solidly favored home team was going to blow out the Rebels. Ole Miss pounced on a Bert Jones fumble and drove to a 3–0 lead, compliments of a 42-yard place-kick by Steven Lavinghouze, who was to figure prominently in that evening's drama before a overflowing house of 70,502. Jones promptly got his team in front, 7–3, scoring on a keeper from six yards out, after which a Rusty Jackson field goal made it, 10–3. But the Rebels were hanging tough. Quarterback Norris Weese engineered a drive before halftime that produced a second Lavinghouze field goal, and it was a 10–6 ballgame.

When Weese took the Rebels 69 yards to a third-quarter touchdown and Lavinghouze tacked on another 3-pointer, this one from 40 yards, Ole Miss not only had a 16–10 advantage, but the momentum as well. They had it right up to the moment the strong-footed Lavinghouze stood over a 27-yard attempt in the final period, a field goal that would have put Ole Miss out of reach. When the kick went wide, it was an opening that would haunt the visitors, even though the Tigers could do nothing on the next series.

When Weese punted into the end zone, with 3:02 remaining, the countdown began. On first down from the 20, with two Rebels hanging on to him, Jones threw a 23-yard strike down the middle to Gerald Keigley. Chris Dantin ran for 5, but Reb All-America Ben Williams broke in to sack Jones for a 9-yard loss. Jones then threw to Dantin for 12, bringing up a fourth-and-2. Back stepped Jones, rifling a dangerous sideline pass to a small target—5-8 Jimmy LeDoux—but one that went for 10 yards to keep the drive alive.

When Bert threw to tight-end Brad Boyd for 8 yards and Boyd scrambled out of bounds, fifty-nine seconds remained. On second-and-2, McClendon decided to go for broke. On a variation of the flea-flicker, tight-end Boyd wound up throwing long to LeDoux, who had beaten the Rebel secondary and managed to get his hands on the ball in the end zone, but couldn't hang on. On third-and-2, Dantin got 1. On fourth down, he got 6, to the Ole Miss 24 yard line.

It was nitty-gritty time. Jones went to Keigley on first down, and although the pass picked up 4 yards, Keigley couldn't get out of bounds to stop the clock. LSU had to call its last time out with ten seconds on the clock. Jones elected to go to Keigley again, this time down the middle. Keigley was leveled before the ball arrived and the interference call gave LSU a first down on the Ole Miss 10. A first down, in this case, didn't mean much. Only four seconds remained.

Again Jones went into the heart of the Rebel secondary, stepping back and rifling one down the gut to LeDoux. When defender Mickey Fratesi broke it up, Ole Miss fans immediately went into a celebrating frenzy—until they looked up at the clock. It showed .01. It was more like .0001, but there was time for one more play—from the 10-yard line.

The call was "halfback flat," one the Tigers had worked on during the week to use in 2-point situations—after a touchdown. This time they needed 6 points. With three receivers out to the left side, tailback Brad Davis was slotted between the split end and split back. On the snap (the final horn sounded immediately) the split end and split back ran curling patterns toward the inside. Brad Davis ran for the flag in the southeast corner of Tiger Stadium. Jones was going to Davis all the way. "When I turned inside," explained split-end Keigley, "I kept screaming for the ball to take the heat off Brad." When Jones threw, Davis lost the ball in the lights, and then, he explained, "I sort of felt for it, and juggled it, and I was going backwards into the end zone, right at the flag." He held on. It was 16–16. Rusty Jackson looked upon his winning place-kick this way: "Sure there was pressure, but how could I miss after the way Bert took the team downfield?"

What impressed McClendon most was his quarterback's cool demeanor under fire. "When Ole Miss called a time out before the last play to get the defense straight, Bert came over like someone who was enjoying every second of it. He was completely unruffled. After he got the play, he gave me one of those 'don't worry coach' looks, winked, and ran back on the field. It was really something."

The twenty-one-year-old had moved his team 80 yards in thirteen plays, with only one timeout at his disposal. Some looked upon that drive as upstaging Billy Cannon who was watching his first Ole Miss game since Halloween Night of '59. Sitting in the north end he watched the crucial field goal miss by Steven Lavinghouze go wide by "that much," Cannon said, as he held his hands one foot apart. "It's still a game of inches," he added, "and seconds."

Which is about all the time the 7–0 Tigers had to celebrate. Waiting next week in Birmingham would be 8–0 Alabama. It was going to be another test of defensing the Wishbone, run by a team McClendon said "was every bit as big as the Notre Dame team we played." Running mostly behind 270-pound tackle John Hannah, Bama was more red elephant than Crimson Tide, good enough to be a 7-point favorite.

As it turned out, the turning point of the 35–21 Alabama victory was LSU's failure to have recruited Terry Davis out of Bogalusa. Running the Tide Wishbone flawlessly, Davis enjoyed a big-play afternoon, converting key third-down situations. Jones lost no stature in defeat, even though he had lost his key receiver, Gerald Keigley, through a practice injury the day before the game. He threw well, long and short, and his two interceptions were on passes that bounced out of the hands of receivers.

After the Tigers handled Mississippi State the next week, 28–14, they accepted an invitation to meet Tennessee in the Bluebonnet Bowl, taking no chances of getting shut out as was the case in '69. A week later in Gainesville, heavy rains virtually shut out both teams in a water-logged 3–3 standoff memorable on two counts: Juan Roca of the Tigers missed eight of nine field goal tries, succeeding on one incredible 45-yarder; cornerback Mike Williams caught Florida's Nat Moore from behind, running him down on the LSU 1, and then recovered a Gator fumble on the next play, to save the day.

In the ever-tightening series with Tulane, it was Tiger defensive back Frank Racine who saved the night, as LSU won, 9–3, in a game of field goals before a breathless crowd of 85,372, breathless because the Green Wave fell a yard short of ending a winless string dating back to 1949. As Bert Jones had won against Ole Miss, Tulane quarterback Steve Foley sparked a last-minute Tulane drive, passing and scrambling his team to the Tiger 5. With six second left, and no time outs, Foley rolled out to his right and hit halfback Russell Huber who quickly found himself in a one-on-one situation with Racine. Racine wrestled his man down with a two-handed tackle on the 1-yard-line as the final seconds ticked away.

The Bluebonnet Bowl was a matter of too little, too late. Behind a scrambling Condrege Holloway, Tennessee raced to a 24–3 halftime lead before the Tigers warmed up on Jones's passing and Davis' running. It was 24–17 with two minutes left, and Jones had his team marching again when his final pass was broken up on the Vol 10, leaving the all-time record with Tennessee at that point 1–13–2.

When you reflect on it, Bert Jones's stay at LSU was merely a matter of marking time before heading off into the sunset, to discover a new day and a new career in the National Football League. Jones was tailored for the professional game of pocket passing, and no sooner had he been gobbled up by the Baltimore Colts in the draft than Tiger fans turned their thoughts to the dawn of a new era—the Mike Miley era.

One thing for sure, Miley, a blue-chipper out of East Jefferson High in New Orleans, would have to live up to his name, Miracle Mike. He was taking over as No. 1 quarterback minus varsity experience at the position, also minus a full spring practice, a time he'd spent playing shortstop on the baseball team. Coming to LSU, he was said to create more problems for the defense than Bert Jones, who didn't have Miley's quickness, or Paul Lyons, who didn't have his arm. But Miley spent his sophomore year pass defending and returning punts and was now going to get his baptism of fire under center behind a virtually new offensive line, on a young football team, one with only seven seniors among the first twenty-two.

In the Bert Jones era, offense had carried the show. As '73 arrived, the feeling was the defense would have to hang on until a young offense matured. Charles McClendon would not have to wait long for an answer. Colorado, which had embarrassed him in the '71 opener, was coming back to Baton Rouge a 2-point favorite, along with Charlie Davis. This time the Tigers were ready. As the defense, featuring such artists as Steve Cassidy and Mike Williams, Bo Harris and Gary Champagne and Warren Capone, held the Buffaloes scoreless into the third quarter, Miley finally cashed in on a 30-yard, third-down scoring pass to Ben Jones, brother of Bert, to send the Tigers on their way to a 17–6 upset. The victory set the tone for the next two months. It was not only a baptism for Miley, but for a freshman running back named Terry Robiskie as well.

McClendon's jubilation was tempered by his awareness that he still had a young team and that inconsistency can be a frailty of youth. A week later he had an example: three fumble losses and two interceptions by the offense, but still a 28–23 win over Texas A&M, the game-saver being a spectacular pass deflection by sophomore cornerback Mike Williams in the final moments to prevent a winning score.

The shakedown cruise continued. After Rice and Florida were handled easily, the Tigers went to Auburn and won, 20–6, limiting the home team to 90 yards on the ground, 14 in the second half. Offensively, the yeoman effort came from junior tailback Brad Davis who rushed for 58 yards, set up a touchdown with a 24-yard pass, scored another on a 28-yard reception, and distinguished himself on special teams. The letdown that followed was not surprising, although in this case the Tigers had enough time to erase a 14–0 Kentucky lead and win going away, 28–14, from a team that was a three-touchdown underdog.

Kentucky was sandwiched between Auburn and another McClendon Armageddon, a visit to South Carolina to play Paul Dietzel's Gamecocks. Never at a loss for names, Dietzel called his stadium the Cockpit, one that would be filled with 54,000 screaming Carolina fans. Carolina was 4–2 on the season sparked by a Veer quarterback named Jeff Grantz, who resembled Miley in more than one way; he not only was gifted in running the option, but his first love was baseball. Grantz was coming off a game against Ohio University in which he won back-of-the-week with 260 yards in total offense. Offense figured to predominate, and did.

As sustained thrills go, there have been few to match it. LSU finished with 260 yards in total offense. Offense figured to dominate, and did. 33–29 victory. All evening, it seemed, Miley and Grantz played a game of one-upmanship. Down by two touchdowns early, Miley got the Tigers ahead 26–22 in the final period, only to have Grantz respond with a drive that made it 29–22, with less than four minutes remaining. Then bedlam. Miley began marching his team, the big play coming as he scrambled like a rabbit before hitting Ben Jones on a 47-yard pass play that set up a Miley touchdown with a minute left. When the horn sounded, Grantz was scrambling in the vicinity of the Tiger 12-yard-line.

Immediately speculation began on how such a draining performance would affect next week's biggie in Jackson against Ole Miss—before a national television audience. The Rebels were limping along, 4–4, under Johnny Vaught, who had replaced Billy Kinard three games into the season. Because McClendon trailed Vaught, 2-6-1, in head-and-head showdowns, talk of an upset (LSU was a nine-point choice) was prominent. LSU had not beaten Ole Miss in an afternoon game in Jackson since 1934. All week long, Jackson disc jockeys played the song "One Second Blues," growing out of the Bert Jones-to-Brad Davis "miracle" of a year before. Flag-waving Rebels felt Vaught had gone one-up before the kickoff. While LSU waited to make an appearance, Ole Miss seniors were carried onto the field by their dads. Moments later, Brad Davis began an un-psyching job on the Rebels, breaking loose for a long gainer. A 51–14 rout was on. For the first time, Charles McClendon had won his first eight games. He made it nine straight against Mississippi State, which brought up 9–0 LSU vs 9–0 Alabama in Tiger Stadium. Alabama was No. 2, LSU No. 7 in the AP poll, making the game the most significant in Baton Rouge, from a national standpoint, since '59 when the No. 1 Tigers faced No. 3 Ole Miss.

Bear Bryant's Tide had accepted an invitation to play Notre Dame in the Sugar Bowl, and LSU would face unbeaten Penn State in the Orange Bowl. The game was set for national television on Thanksgiving night. Penn State coach Joe Paterno called McClendon and said: "I'll be pulling for you." McClendon needed all the help he could get. Bama's Wishbone was averaging better than 500 yards. It had a crafty quarterback in Gary Rutledge and a punishing runner in Wilbur Jackson. Bryant hinted, "This could be my best team ever." It was good enough for the oddsmakers who installed the visitors a 12-point favorite. "To win," said McClendon, "we'll have to control the football."

LSU did just that—and lost 21–7. Why? Because Alabama made the big plays and no mistakes. The Tigers ran seventy-seven plays to Bama's fifty-three and enjoyed a 21–11 edge in first downs. LSU fumbled once to kill a drive, fumbled again on its 19 to set up a 19-yard scoring run by Rutledge. Bama got another on a 49-yard pass when Tiger coverage broke down and another on a 77-yard pass when Mike Williams tripped covering a receiver. A 40-yard run by Brad Davis saved LSU from a shutout. In effect, LSU took away Bama's big weapon. Wilbur Jackson was held to 24 yards. But the quarterbacks ran for 109 yards. Bama passed only six times, missing on the first one, hitting the next five. It was a victory for the Wishbone. And Bear Bryant's eighth win in ten games against his former pupil.

Tulane was another matter. Charles McClendon was 11–0 against his arch rival. Everything indicated McClendon would keep his own winning string intact as well as that of the Tigers, who had not lost to the Green Wave since 1948, back when McClendon was playing for Bryant at Kentucky. The Tigers were going to New Orleans (the second year in a row because of a scheduling wrinkle) off three fine efforts while the Greenies were going in off an embarrassing 42–9 loss to Maryland. From what the oddsmakers had seen, it was enough to make LSU a 12-point favorite over a team with an 8–2 record.

Before a blow was struck, the setting in Tulane Stadium was memorable. The largest crowd ever to see a football game in the South—86,598—was rocking long before the kickoff. All tickets had disappeared early in the season, with Tulane enthusiasm fanned by the close call of

'72. The game was of particular interest to the New Orleans crowd, which had watched the high school progress of Mike Miley at East Jefferson and Steve Foley at Jesuit.

When the story was written, it wasn't so much a battle of quarterbacks as a high tide of emotion. In the past, Tulane teams had gone against LSU emotionally charged, but this bubbling inside had a way of dissipating via a fumble, an interception, a glaring error. On this night, the Greenies went in on an emotional wave that continued to grow until it reached tidal proportions. It was the case of Tulane making every big play, never allowing a superior team to get up a head of steam. On fourth-and-inches of a scoreless game, Brad Davis was stopped cold. Trying to get a drive going near the end of the half, Mike Miley overthrew an open man, giving Tulane the ball. Then it happened. Terry Looney, Foley's understudy, threw a 36-yard touchdown pass to Darwin Willie nineteen seconds before halftime.

But there was a half to go and the Tigers were far from out of it. LSU recovered a Steve Foley fumble at midfield and drove to the 11. Brad Davis bulled to the three for a first down, only to have it nullified by a procedure penalty. On third-and-7, Miley, rolling left, was sacked by Mark Olivari for a 13-yard loss. Roca then missed a field goal try from 46 yards.

Still steaming, the Greenies finally put it away when Doug Bynum raced 53 yards to the LSU 1 to set up the final score in a 14–0 victory, as big as any in Tulane history. As the final seconds ticked away, Tulane fans poured onto the field. The goalposts came down. Meanwhile, the winning coach, Bennie Ellender, made his way to a victorious dressing room. Oddly enough, he was a member of Tulane class of '48, graduating the year of his alma mater's last football win over LSU. "Winning," he said, "is not having to say, 'wait till next year.'"

Despite the enormity of the loss—"This is something I'll have to live with the rest of my life," said Warren Capone—Charles McClendon had no problem bringing his club out of its stupor. An 11–0 Penn State team was waiting in Miami with Heisman winner John Cappeletti. As it turned out, LSU's only consolation was that Brad Davis outgained the All-American running back, 70 yards to 50, as the Tigers lost the Orange Bowl, 16–9.

After jumping off to a 7–0 lead, the Tigers watched the Lions score 16, one touchdown coming on a 72-yard pass play. The turning point came when LSU was trying to get back into a 16–7 game with two minutes remaining in the half. Miley marched his team 75 yards to the State 5. Although a field goal would have put them within striking distance, the Tigers gambled on a touchdown and came away empty. Despite giving up a second-half safety on a bad snap, Penn State had all of the breathing room it needed to finish the season 12–0. The Lions also came up empty, finishing fifth in the final AP poll behind champion Notre Dame, a 24–23 winner over Alabama in the Sugar Bowl.

There was no way of telling at the time, but LSU was finished with bowl games for three seasons, the first time this had happened since Paul Dietzel put the Tigers on the national map in the late 50s. In a way, the '73 season—nine victories followed by three defeats—symbolized a falloff in recruiting that had begun several years earlier. Beginning in '71 Tulane under Bennie Ellender began to make inroads in the battle for Louisiana talent, enough to make a dent. Aside from LSU losing Mark Olivari and Mark Jones to Tulane, there were Alabama, Mississippi State, Colorado, Oklahoma, and Texas A&M slipping in to cart off prospects, not to mention Grambling, a perennial power among the black schools.

The irony of it all was the seeds sown in the early '70s suddenly hit home in 1974, which, on the Chinese calendar, was the Year of the Tiger. For LSU, it was also the Year of the Veer and the Year of the Fumble.

When LSU could make but two touchdowns in the last twelve quarters of the '73 season, McClendon began giving serious thought to junking his I-formation. "We had won nine games in each of the last five seasons, and here I was thinking of making a change," he said. He decided on the Veer chiefly because of Mike Miley and a wealth of ball carriers headed by Brad Davis and Terry Robiskie. The big question was quarterback. When Mike Miley signed a professional baseball contract after spring practice, McClendon reluctantly decided to stay with the Veer, the feeling being the Veer would succeed or fail on the split-second decisions of senior quarterback Billy Broussard and sophomore quarterback Carl Trimble. The heart of the defense, McClendon felt, was in good hands, those of tackles Steve Cassidy and Adam Duhe.

The first result—a 42–14 conquest of Colorado—turned out to be a mirage. In its debut, the Veer produced 437 rushing yards, including 14 gains of 10 yards or more. The fact the Tigers did not complete a pass didn't sound any alarms. Carl Trimble had broken loose on a 58-yard run, LSU's longest in eleven seasons.

A week later, Texas A&M popped the balloon. Fearing no threat from the pass, the Aggie defense crowded the line of scrimmage and went away with a well-earned 21–14 upset. LSU completed one pass. Suddenly, the Tigers became a bewildered football team, stumbling to a 10–10 tie with outclassed Rice, losing to Florida and Kentucky. The second win in history over Tennessee and a 24–0 pasting of Ole Miss did not erase the Tigers' inconsistencies. One pertinent stat: after six games, LSU had fumbled thirty times and lost nineteen. The year

Mac and All-American safety Mike Williams, before the 1974 season.

before, in eleven games, LSU had fumbled seventeen times and lost nine.

Alabama, unbeaten again, was merciful in a 30–0 rout of the Tigers in Birmingham. It could have been 50–0. When Mississippi State sneaked by, 7–6, it left McClendon with a 3–5–1 record, meaning he would have to whip Tulane and Utah to avoid his first losing season. Utah was no problem. But the Greenies, which had started fast and then stumbled, pushed the Tigers to the limit, before bowing, 24–22. Knocked out twice, Billy Broussard returned with a dozen stitches to close a facial wound and led a decisive fourth-quarter drive that shattered Tulane hopes for two in a row. The most telling aspect of a 5–5–1 season rested in one statistic: LSU had lost twenty-nine of forty-nine fumbles.

Whatever the reason—McClendon insisted it was not completely the fault of the Veer—LSU was junking the offense popularized by the University of Houston. In the Year of the Tiger Plus One, LSU was going back to the I-formation. While Mac felt departing running backs Brad Davis and Steve Rogers were tailored for the Veer, the I formation, he felt, was more suitable for junior Terry Robiskie and a freshman from Galveston, Texas, by the name of Charlie Alexander. For Robiskie, moving to Tiger Stadium from the tiny confines of Second Ward High in Edgard, Louisiana, was a significant change. He was an all-everything quarterback for the all-black Class-A school, a well-chiseled 6–3, 205-pound athlete with a punishing, straight-up running style. He played immediately as a freshman, and by '75 he was coming into his own, acting as a model for Alexander, the new rookie.

In the return to the I-formation, quarterbacking would be in the hands of redshirt sophomore Pat Lyons, 6-foot, 1½-inch brother of Paul. Youth characterized the '75 squad, one with fewer seniors—twelve—than any of McClendon's previous clubs. In this case, the problem was a squad dominated by freshmen, sophomores, and juniors would be opening in Lincoln, Nebraska, against the highly touted Cornhuskers. Were the Tigers up to it? They were. But the performance turned out to be another mirage. A defense headed by Steve Cassidy and Ken Bordelon was superb, holding Nebraska to a 10–7 decision even though the home team had the advantage of recovering four fumbles.

Since the Cornhuskers were sixth-ranked, the feeling was the young Tigers would be able to mix it with anyone, especially in their Baton Rouge backyard. But this theory was quickly shattered by Texas A&M and Florida. The Aggies, big and quick, chopped up the Tigers 39–8, and after LSU managed to stagger past Rice, 16–13, in Shreveport, Florida came into Tiger Stadium and administered a 34–6 crusher. Against these two Wishbone teams, McClendon's club resembled broom sticks fighting tanks. As long as the Tigers had been playing in Tiger Stadium, they never lost back-to-back home games by 31 and 28 points. Suddenly the gap in personnel had become obvious. The Aggies and Gators represented bumper recruiting crops. Four years earlier, LSU had beaten Florida, 48–7. The worm had turned.

Even though a loss at Tennessee was followed by victories over Kentucky and South Carolina, the Tigers were now flirting with their first losing season in nineteen years as they invaded Jackson to play Ole Miss. The match between the 3–4 Tigers and 3–5 Rebels was rated a tossup, and that's exactly how it turned out. Trailing 13–10 in the fading moments, Ole Miss faced a fourth-and-2 at the LSU 16 and decided to pass up a field goal and go for 6 points. Quarterback Tim Ellis rolled right and hit tailback Michael Sweet, who won the footrace to the end zone. Tiger linebacker Terry Hill complained about being illegally screened on the play (movies showed he was "picked" by another Rebel receiver), but that didn't erase the touchdown.

A week later, Alabama marched into Tiger Stadium a 17-point favorite (it was biggest underdog an LSU team had been at home since World War II) to assure the Tigers of their first losing year since the 3–7 record of '56. LSU surrendered grudgingly to a Crimson Tide team that would finish 10–1 and whip Penn State in the Sugar Bowl. Behind 17–10 with a quarter to go, LSU faced a fourth-and-goal at the Bama 4. Disdaining the field goal, McClendon sent in a pass play in which only one receiver was sent out. Despite the precaution, Pat Lyons was sacked from the blind side by a safety blitz, ending the last Tiger threat. Bama went on to win, 23–10, dropping the Tigers to 3–6 with Mississippi State and Tulane remaining.

After State prevailed, 16–7, McClendon's only salvation was to whip Tulane. It would be the first game of this ancient series to be played in the Superdome. As matters unfolded, however, that was not the major story. Reports were circulating that Bennie Ellender, whose Greenies were 4–6 on the year, would be fired after the LSU game, regardless of the outcome. Whether an upset would have saved him (LSU was a 4-point favorite), we'll never know. Tulane was never in it. The Tigers rushed to a 21–0 halftime lead and won going away, 42–6. LSU intercepted six passes and Tulane finished with 6 yards' rushing. LSU ran seventy-three plays, Tulane twenty-one. Bennie Ellender, who had broken a twenty-five-year famine for his alma mater two years earlier, was out of a job.

"It's none of my business," said McClendon in the winning locker-room, "but they'd be foolish to get rid of Bennie after the job he's done under trying circumstances. Who'll they get that's any better?"

Tulane wound up with Larry Smith, an assistant at the University of Arizona. And Ellender, who had been given a ten-year contract after the '73 win over LSU, wound up with a $360,000 settlement to be paid at the rate of $2,000 a month over the next fifteen years.

Although LSU's 4–7 finish produced the usual backbiting, McClendon survived, pushing ahead into '76 with an offense built around

Defensive tackles Adam Duhe and Steve Cassidy await the '75 season after making 136 solo tackles on record for '74.

senior tailback Robiskie and senior tackle Adam Duhe, who, although built like a man—6-4 and 245—would not officially reach manhood, his twenty-first birthday, until the day LSU closed out its season against Utah. McClendon looked on the Cajun out of Reserve as a composite of standout Tiger tackles. He had more tiger in him than George Rice. He was quicker than John Demarie (who had made it in the pros), taller and faster than Terry Estay, taller, faster, and quicker than Steve Cassidy. At 235, Cassidy ran the 40 in 4.9. At 245, Duhe ran it in 4.8.

For the second year in a row, Nebraska was the opening opponent, this time in Tiger Stadium, this time as the preseason No. 1 pick in the AP poll, making the Cornhuskers the first No. 1 team to visit Baton Rouge since Tennessee in 1939. Although LSU held Nebraska to its lowest total offense total of the '75 season (156 yards) in the 10–7 loss in Lincoln, the visitors came to Baton Rouge a 13-point favorite. They were fortunate to leave with a 6–6 standoff. Mike Conway, who had kicked second-half field goals of 35 and 18 yards, watched a 44-yard attempt go wide by inches in the final seconds.

Was the opener misleading? Not exactly. It said two things about the '76 Tigers: the defense would be good; the passing game would not. A one-handed offense would haunt LSU for the rest of the season. With a chance to upset Florida, a last-minute pass misfired, the Gators winning, 28–23. Dominating Kentucky early in the game, LSU watched an interception light a fire under the Wildcats who went on to win 21–7. The Tigers gained most of their 301 rushing yards between the twenties. In the air, they were six-for-24 with two interceptions.

In what was the brightest spot of the season—a 45–0 blitz of Ole Miss —passing wasn't necessarily important. It was a case of the Tigers exploding—Alexander ran for 138 yards, Robiskie for 129—and the Rebels bungling: five lost fumbles and three interceptions. In a series that began in 1894, there had been only one more lopsided score, a 46–0 LSU win in 1901.

As impressive as it was, the victory had no carryover effect. Keeping mistakes to a minimum, Alabama was never in any serious danger, gliding to a 28–17 win as the Tide defense limited Robiskie and Alexander to a combined total of 115 yards. When Mississippi State jumped to a 21–0 lead and held on for a 21–13 decision, it became a familiar tune for McClendon: beat Tulane to salvage some pride.

The 17–7 victory was less than artistic. While the Tigers' defense effectively smothered the Greenies—Tulane was minus-43 on the ground—the offense managed only two touchdowns against a defense that had been shredded much of the season. Individually, the highlight was an 84-yard evening by Terry Robiskie, making him the first runner in Tiger history to rush for more than 1,000 in a season. Terry finished with 1,117 yards.

The major question was not statistics. It was, simply, could Charles McClendon survive after going 5-5-1, 4-7 and 6-4-1? His job was in the hands of the Board of Supervisors, which met and produced the following items: In a straw vote, the Board was 10-5 for McClendon's dismissal. This was followed by a heated discussion in which board members Camille Gravel, Jr., and Jerry McKernan went to bat for McClendon, emphasizing that to buy up the head coach's contract would adversely affect LSU in the state legislature. Finally, the offer to McClendon was for him to accept a two-year contract (a reduction from the existing four-year arrangement) and the Board would vote to retain him as coach. McClendon accepted, agreeing, in effect, to coach in '77 and '78 for a salary of $37,600 a year.

He was banking on a good team, featuring Charlie Alexander, and a favorable schedule to change his fortunes. Come '77, the Tigers would be playing the four teams that beat them in '76—Alabama, Kentucky, Florida, and Mississippi State—in Tiger Stadium, these in addition to Rice, Oregon, and Wyoming. The road schedule was not imposing: Indiana, Vandy, Ole Miss, and Tulane.

By the time autumn arrived, there were three tragic reminders that winning football games is a small, unimportant part of the overall scheme of things. In January, Mike Miley was killed in an automobile accident in Baton Rouge. In 1972, Joe Labruzzo, hero of the '65 Cotton Bowl, died of a self-inflicted gunshot wound. And in August, with the Tigers about to start fall practice, Carl Otis Trimble drowned while tubing with friends in the Tchefuncte River.

For McClendon, as it had been in the cases of Trey Prather and Butch Duhe, each tragedy brought a telephone call. And memories. It was easy for a coach to recall a Mike Miley at his football zenith, that night in South Carolina when he rallied the Tigers again and again against Paul Dietzel's Gamecocks. It was easy to remember Labruzzo grinding out the yardage in the upset win over Arkansas. And it was easy to remember Carl Trimble dazzling Colorado with his speed as a Veer quarterback in the opening game of '74.

Now it was '77, and last season's memories were of Charlie Alexander, a 6-1, 215-pound junior blossoming at such a fast pace that no less an observer than Jerry Stovall was constantly awed. Alexander came to LSU as a raw diamond. Because of track, he missed spring football practice at Galveston Ball High throughout his high school career. In his senior year, he averaged but seven carries a game, this compared to the thirty and forty times a game Terry Robiskie carried the ball in his final season as a schoolboy. "He has everything you're looking for in a running back," said Stovall, "which is speed, quickness, and toughness." Alexander had twice run 9.4 as a high school senior. In the spring of '72, pro scouts were blinking at his time for 40 yards—4.4 seconds.

By the third game, opponents were blinking as Alexander always seemed to be battling for tough yardage because of a series of circumstances: he was a marked man behind an inconsistent offensive line and a woeful passing game. He was running in crowds. On opening day, when the defense fell apart in the final period, allowing Indiana to score a 24–21 upset, Alexander gained 115 yards. Playing briefly in a 77–0 rout of Rice, he gained 155. Playing more in a 36–14 conquest of Florida, he picked up 170. The amazing thing was that except for one run of 34 yards, Charley's bursts were in the 15-and-under category.

Alexander was making a run of 8 yards an adventure, bouncing off linemen and linebackers like a hard rubber ball. He was reminding longtime Tiger watchers of a cross between Jim Taylor and Billy Cannon. He had Cannon's speed, but with more quickness and more of a stutter step. And he had Taylor's knack for stinging tacklers, also for giving the limp leg, then taking it away. When Cannon first saw Alexander's massive thighs, which he kept incased during games in skin-tight rubber pads, he said, "Compared to you, I was a skinflint."

Alexander needed all the weight he could carry to withstand the pounding. In Nashville, Vandy jumped out to a 15–0 lead, whereupon Charlie ignited a 28-point spurt with a 23-yard gallop, one of three touchdowns. It was LSU's first out-of-state victory since a win over Ole Miss in '73. With ineffective passing a recurring problem, not even "Alexander the Great," who failed to gain 100 yards for the first time in the '77 season, could make much headway against an awesome Kentucky defense. The anchor of this defense was All-American end Art Still who ran 52 yards with a blocked field goal to take the Tigers out of a game that wound up, 33–13, with Alexander gaining 88 of his team's 162 yards.

Oregon was a 237-yard cakewalk for Alexander, all of which made Ole Miss concentrate its guns the next week on stopping No. 4. This the Rebels did, holding Charlie to 61 yards, but, as it turned out, the Rebels had so many troops up front, quarterback Steve Ensminger was able to find wide-open receivers as the Tigers erased a 21–0 deficit to emerge a 28–21 winner in Jackson. Steve ran for 2, threw for another.

This set up, before the season, what looked as though it might be a game for the SEC title—the annual showdown with Alabama. The second-ranked Tide held up its end and, in a nationally televised game from Tiger Stadium, overcame a testy LSU defense and their own four fumbles to prevail, 24–3. Alexander had to scratch for his 110 yards in twenty-two carries, chiefly because the passing game, which had been effective the week before, reverted to form. In the air, the Tigers were three-for-15.

Against Mississippi State, Alexander got enough daylight to break a 43-yard run that set up a winning field goal in the final three minutes, sending the Tigers against Tulane on a one-game winning streak, also with an invitation to play Stanford in the Sun Bowl. LSU made the Sun sweat. The Greenies were coming into this one on anything but a high note, having lost to Rutgers, 47–8, the previous week, dropping their record to 2–9. But this was a new deal. With Tulane loose and with LSU pressing, the home team scored twice in the last minute of the first half (on a pass and a blocked punt) to lead, 17–7. It was 17–13 in the final quarter when freshman Chris Williams took a handoff on a punt return and raced 60 yards behind a wall of blockers for a 20–17 LSU win before 72,000 in the Superdome. The Tigers were driving for another at the finish. Alexander toted the football a record forty-one times, his 199 yards erasing the one-season SEC rushing record held by John Dottley of Ole Miss.

Charley added to the total in a 66–7 walk over Wyoming, and in a 24–14 loss to Stanford in the Sun Bowl he still managed to set a pair of records for the postseason game: thirty-one carries and 197 yards. This was not enough to offset the 269-yard passing of Guy Benjamin, the nifty catches of Jim Loftin, on a day when the Tigers were seven-for-23 in the air, with three interceptions. Sort of the epitaph of an 8–4 season in which one man, with minimal aerial assistance, netted 1,686 yards in 311 carries. "Charlie," said Jerry Stovall, "earned his letter."

At this time, growing pains were boosting the capacity of Tiger Stadium for a fourth time, to 76,092. The last addition had come in 1953 when the south end was closed in, raising capacity from 46,000 to 67,720. During the sixties, athletic director Jim Corbett commissioned a feasibility study on enlarging Tiger Stadium capacity to 100,000. It never got beyond the study stage. However, in 1971, Carl Maddox decided it was time to move ahead, his feelings triggered when 10,000 new season ticket applications arrived the first day for the mere 500 available seats. "It's getting to the point," Maddox observed, "where our graduates cannot see the football team play."

In the fall of 1972, a new study presented to the Board of Supervisors showed that an addition of 10,000 seats would cost $7 million. Insufficient funds put the project on the back burner. A second study was made in which it was stated that approximately 7,500 seats could

The addition to Tiger Stadium, which cost over $10 million and seats 7,500 fans, was first used at the season opener with Indiana in 1979.

be added for $6 million. In May of 1974, the board gave the green light. However, when bids came in a year later, the board learned a 7,500-seat addition would cost $10,120,000.

At this point, the LSU administration, not the athletic department, began looking for assistance from the state legislature. The upshot was a subsidy of $5 million. This subsidy, along with monies from three other sources, got the stadium project off the ground. The sale of 750 seats in the VIP, or Purple Section, of the addition raised $1 million, that is, fans donated $1,500 for the right to buy one seat on a seasonal basis for ten years. The athletic department dipped into its cash reserves for $1,250,000 and backed a bond sale for an additional $3.5 million, representing an annual note of $288,000 for twenty-five years, this money coming from football revenues.

Work by Southern Builders, Inc., began in August of '75 with an announced completion date of July, '77. Because of construction delays, the addition was not accepted until September 16, 1978, narrowly beating the deadline for the season opener with Indiana.

Awaiting the advent of Charlie Alexander's last year in an LSU uniform turned out to be the liveliest off-season since the sacking of Gus Tinsley and Red Heard in the clean sweep of '55, a coup d'etat that ushered in Paul Dietzel as head coach.

Now, twenty-three years later, Tiger fans looked on as the saga

The 1978 defensive backfield included Marcus Quinn, James Britt, Willie Teal, and Chris Williams.

entitled "The Second Coming of Paul" unfolded. Returning as the new director of athletics, replacing the retiring Carl Maddox, Dietzel's selection over such candidates as Joe Dean, the LSU basketball star of the 1950s, was controversial in many quarters for obvious reasons. After having said, "I'll never leave LSU," he had indeed left for Army following the '61 season. To many fans this should have precluded his return in any capacity, forever.

But return he did, championed in the early stages by board member Charley Cusimano of Metairie, Louisiana, later by enough members of the Board of Supervisors to carry the day. Said Cusimano, "In the final analysis, Paul got the job because he sold himself to some Board members who had to be convinced he was the man for the job."

Dietzel's long-standing relations with some of his players from the '55–'61 era helped significantly; these players actively lobbied his case while Dietzel was still serving as AD at Indiana. More than anything, Dietzel's return heightened the irony in the twists and turns of a Paul-and-Charley Mac script. Charley McClendon had campaigned for the AD job when it went to Carl Maddox in a two-horse race. Now he would wind up serving out the string as LSU coach under the man he helped get the coaching job in '55. Shortly after the firing of Tinsley and Heard, assistant coach McClendon had received a call from assistant coach Dietzel at Army, inquiring, not about the vacancy at LSU but about one at the University of Cincinnati, then hunting a replacement for Sid Gillman. When Dietzel finished talking about Cincinnati, McClendon made the suggestion: "What about LSU? Get someone at Army to recommend you down here and see what happens." Dietzel did just that and the rest is history.

Although Dietzel was never a declared candidate for the job as Maddox's successor, the Athletic Committee of the LSU board recommended him to the seventeen-member body. Of the ten men on the committee, Dietzel received nine votes. In two hours of discussion called "open and lively," committee members spoke up. Cusimano recalled one of Dietzel's first statements when he came to the university in '55. "He said, 'I'm going to make every boy in Louisiana want to go to LSU.'" Cusimano suggested, "If you talk about unity, who's better than Dietzel? He did it once before." Committee member James Peltier of Thibodaux carred the same theme. "When Paul Dietzel walks into a room, he makes things happen. The alumni and friends of LSU need to be brought together, and he's the man who can do it quicker than anyone." Said board chairman Jerry McKernan of Baton Rouge, "After everyone had spoken, it was apparent that Coach Dietzel was the man for the job. After analyzing all the candidates, you have to recognize Coach Dietzel is widely acclaimed as one of the nation's outstanding athletic directors."

For Dietzel, his return marked his fifth move since his departure. Following his tour at West Point (1962–1965), he was coach and AD at South Carolina (1966–1974), commissioner of the Ohio Valley Conference (1975) and AD at Indiana (1976–1978).

An added irony this time was he would officially be taking over his AD duties from the outgoing Maddox the week following LSU's opener against Indiana. The team McClendon was preparing for his seventeenth season was one that returned nine starters on offense, five on defense, good enough to win the Tigers a spot in most top-twenty preseason polls. In a nutshell, hopes were based on an offensive line returning intact that would ease the job of Alexander, two quarterbacks of contrasting assets in David Woodley, the runner, and Steve Ensminger, the passer, and a maturing defense which had been sprinkled with freshmen the previous year.

The opening before a record crowd of 78,534 was anything but auspicious. A year before, Indiana rallied late for an upset. Now, it seemed, the Hoosiers might do the same. The Tigers were penalized ten times for 129 yards, enough self-inflicted wounds to keep the Hoosiers in the game. When the visitors pulled to within, 24–17, with a fourth-quarter score, then drove to a first down on the LSU 12 in the final minutes, the natives became restless. Suddenly, Lyman White came up with a big play, deflecting a pitchout that resulted in a 22-yard loss. On the next play, Tommy Frizzell's interception killed the threat. Charlie Alexander earned every one of his 144 yards against a keying Indiana defense.

Rather than improve off a ten-penalty game, the Tigers seemingly dug a deeper hole the next week. LSU played so poorly in nipping an inept Wake Forest club, one that lost five fumbles, it was later reported that the girl friends of the LSU players left in the third quarter. The effort against another weakling, Rice, was considerably better. Alexander's 144 yards in the 37–7 victory gave him 3,295 yards in total offense for his career, moving him past Bert Jones. For the first time since '73, LSU was 3–0.

A week later, the Tigers were 4–0 as they dominated Florida, 34–21, rushing for 315 yards while holding the Gators to 38 on the ground. It was a performance that matched the preseason clippings, one the Tigers were able to sustain for the first two quarters of a crucial SEC meeting with Georgia. In the first half, LSU not only led the unbeaten Bulldogs 17–7, it had a 225–127 edge in total offense. Looking like a team that was on its way to a 5–0 start, the Tiger balloon was abruptly punctured. Lindsay Scott took the second-half kickoff on his 1 and ran right past everyone in a virtuoso effort that changed the complexion for good. From that point, Georgia dominated as the Tigers suffered a complete collapse, offensively and defensively. The Bulldogs' 24–17 win sent them on the way to challenge for the SEC title and left LSU looking for its second wind.

Charlie Alexander takes flight over Alabama, 1978.

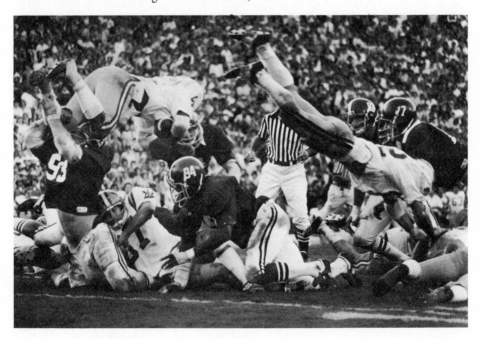

Mac congratulates Vince Dooley after Georgia upset the
Tigers, 1978.

Judging from the next two games, the Tigers had come out of their
second-half swan dive. They crushed Kentucky, 21–0 in Lexington,
running and passing as the Wildcats gang-tackled Alexander, who finished with 64 yards. Then, before a regional TV audience, Charlie broke
the chains, in a 30–8 win over Ole Miss, running for 147 yards and two
TDs, including a scoring run of 64 yards.

It sent the revived Tigers against their nemesis in apparently a good
frame of mind. Alabama is always tougher at Legion Field. But this
LSU team had won in Gainesville and Lexington and, with the Georgia
nightmare fading, looked like it was ready to give the Tide a run for it.
For a half, the Tigers more than held their own. Woodley took his
team 58 yards in seven plays to make it 7–0 and it appeared Chris
Williams, returning an interception 79 yards, had made it 14–0. But a
clip erased it and no one will ever know what LSU could have done
with a two-TD lead. While Bama was faking a punt to keep a scoring
drive alive, the Tigers were having a 46-yard field goal by Mike Conway
nullified by a penalty. This combined to give Bama a 14–10 lead at
halftime in a game that had the appearance of one that could go either
way.

But, in a Georgia replay, the Tigers turned into second-half pump-
kins, Bama outscoring them 17–0, as Bear Bryant went home a 31–10
winner. After the Tide drove to a field goal, Chris Williams fumbled
a punt on his 2 to set up a Bama TD, which was all the help Bama
needed to make it eight in a row over the Tigers.

LSU fans soon had something to take their minds off this annual nightmare. Something, too, that made the rest of the season an anti-climax. Out of Tigertown came the announcement. Paul Dietzel, after conferring with Charles McClendon and wife Dorothy Faye, had rec-ommended to the Board of Supervisors that McClendon's contract as head coach be extended through the 1979 season after which time, said Dietzel, "I will recommend a new head football coach . . . the best avail-able from among the ranks of proven head collegiate football coaches."

The McClendons had met with Dietzel the Wednesday before the Alabama game, at which time the director of athletics outlined his plan. Dietzel pointed out, in a memo to Chancellor Paul W. Murrill, that ex-tending McClendon's contract would allow the coach to fulfill a long-time dream—serve as president of the American Football Coaches Asso-ciation—and allow McClendon to finish his long career "in dignity and good taste."

The announcement also included something else: following the '79 season McClendon would be offered the post of administrative assistant to the director of athletics for a period of two years.

An unusual aspect to the entire matter was that when the announce-ment was made at a press conference, neither Dietzel nor McClendon attended. McClendon later noted he was happy to be given another year but, asked if there was any resentment over being "retired," said, "This is a private affair."

At the time, Charley Alexander's Heisman hopes were dimming—he had gained only 46 yards against Alabama and would pick up only 57 yards in a 16–14 loss to Mississippi State. The loss was not only LSU's but the Liberty Bowl's as well, the Memphis committee having extended the Tigers an invitation win-or-lose-or-draw prior to the game.

After a miserable first half, in which State led, 13–0, Alexander cli-maxed two long marches with short scoring runs. Ultimately, the Tigers lost to a 21-yard field goal early in the final period. But, in reality, they were victimized by a poor defensive effort, one which allowed State, a passing team, to run up 219 yards on the ground. Did the McClendon announcement have an effect on the lackluster performance? "I don't think so," said split-back Mike Quintella. "We just didn't play worth a damn."

A week later, Tulane brought the Tigers out of their doldrums, but only for a spell, in a 40–21 LSU win punctuated by twenty-five pen-alties. Just when it appeared the Tigers would coast, after leading 27–7 at halftime, the Greenies blocked two of John Adams' punts in less than three minutes, both resulting in touchdowns, that made it 27–21. It remained for Charlie Alexander to recapture the elusive "Mr. Momen-tum." He turned a third-and-1 short-yardage play into a 64-yard TD, bouncing off three defenders before breaking into the open. An interception by George Cupit in the fading moments set up the coup de grace.

The Tigers warmed up for a Liberty Bowl match with Missouri with a Letdown Bowl win over Wyoming, a game in which the underdog Cowboys jumped out to a 17–3 lead only to lose, 24–17, to a second-half surge.

It was, more or less, the same script three weeks later in the Liberty. Missouri rushed to a 20–3 halftime lead, running up 233 yards in total offense, after which LSU returned with a couple of second-half scores triggered by Alexander heroics. But it wasn't enough. Alexander finished with 133 yards, Missouri with a 20–15 win, leaving the 8–4 Bayou Bengals out of the final top ten for the sixth year in a row.

For Charles McClendon, his final season began with a Colorado High, a 44–0 blitz of the big, but slow, Buffaloes under new coach Chuck Fairbanks. One idea of LSU dominance is that Colorado never moved inside the Tiger 46, had its ball carriers tackled eleven times for losses, and finished with only 21 yards on the ground. LSU, meanwhile, was using ten backs, including four quarterbacks. Said Fairbanks: "We could have played LSU for a month and I don't think we could have scored."

It was not the kind of test that allows a coach to find out how good his team is, nor was next week's 47–3 cakewalk past Rice, in which the Tigers, playing flawless football jumped to a 27–3 half-time lead on drives of 60, 92, 63, 70, 60 yards. After it was over, Mac said: "Please let me savor this for an hour before I start thinking about Southern Cal."

Going from undermanned Rice to overmanned Southern California was like going from the Little League to the majors in one jump. Out west some observers were calling this perhaps the finest USC team ever, better than the ones with O. J. Simpson and Anthony Davis. It had a Heisman candidate at tailback in Charles White, a gifted quarterback in Paul McDonald, both of them operating behind an offensive line bigger than some professional teams, with at least a couple of first round prospects. In the preseason polls, the Trojans were a strong No. 1, a position strengthened by easy victories over Texas Tech, Oregon State, and Minnesota.

"It's quite likely," said McClendon the week of the game, "this is the most talented team ever to play in Tiger Stadium." For that moment, the first meeting of the Tigers and Trojans, Tiger Stadium rocked with a record crowd of 78,322, a crowd that stayed to the bitter end.

The drama built steadily. USC went ahead with a first-quarter field goal after which Steve Ensminger came off the bench to take the Tigers to 9 second-quarter points, a touchdown on a 13-yard pass to LeRoid Jones, a 32-yard field goal by Don Barthel. The Trojans missed a field

Touchdown Tiger celebrates another score.

goal try at the end of the half and missed another following a third-quarter drive when the Tiger defense stiffened inside the 20. With pressure mounting, David Woodley took LSU on a march that carried as far as the USC 3 before the visitors rose up and threw the Tigers back, bringing a 28-yard field goal from Barthel to make it 12–3.

Southern Cal's No. 1 ranking was clearly on the line. With the home crowd screaming, Paul McDonald managed to move his team 57 yards in six plays, White making the touchdown on a 4-yard run up the middle, cutting the Tigers lead to 12–10 with just under ten minutes remaining.

When LSU recovered a fumble at the Trojan 26, it looked as though the Tigers might put it out of reach. But a call for offensive pass interference and a sack of Woodley forced a Tiger punt. With four minutes left, it was clearly do-or-die for dear old Troy. Three plays later, on a third-and-9 at the USC 36, McDonald was rushed, barely managing to get rid of the football as he went down. A penalty flag was dropped. The ruling: a call against Benjy Thibodaux for touching the facemask of the USC quarterback. "When the play began," McClendon was to say later, "I relaxed because I knew Southern Cal would be called for jumping before the snap. That's what I thought the flag was for." Game film bore out McClendon's contention, a Trojan lineman had jumped, but it went undetected. The penalty gave USC a first down. The Trojans marched on. With thirty-two seconds remaining, McDonald passed 8 yards to Kevin Williams, a 5–8 speedster who lined up at tight end, for the go-ahead score.

LSU wasn't dead yet. With time running out, Ensminger moved the Tigers to the USC 30. LSU was out of time outs and had only eight seconds to cover 30 yards. A pass from Ensminger brushed the fingertips of a streaking Willie Turner as he raced into the end zone. With two seconds left, Ensminger lofted a high one in search of a leaping Lionel Wallis, who went up in a cluster of red shirts, the ball bouncing away. All of which made it official: USC 17, LSU 12.

For intensity, few, if any, LSU teams of the past could surpass this effort for a simple reason: it was LSU's discipline that kept it from being blown out of Tiger Stadium. At the end, the student section was not only packed, but the students were standing, shouting, "LSU, we're proud of you."

Le Roid Jones celebrates TD against USC, 1979.

Fans could only wait to see how much the intense effort against the Trojans took out of McClendon's team. Winless University of Florida held a 3-0 advantage late into the third quarter before freshman Jesse Myles scored on a 16-yard run, his first of two touchdowns in a 20-3 victory. "Before the game," said McClendon, "the kids kept telling me not to worry, that they were ready. But Florida just flat knocked our britches off."

Coming after USC, Florida was a big hurdle in the emotional scheme of things. Next came Georgia, off to a disappointing 1-3 start, yet still one of the best bets to challenge Alabama for the SEC title. Since losing to the Bulldogs in Tiger Stadium had put a damper on the '78 season, McClendon had reason to feel his team would be poised for a solid effort. It wasn't. The Tigers fumbled, tackled sloppily, and committed costly penalties. When a kickoff return by Chris Williams set up a touchdown just before the half, to make it 7-7, there was reason to feel LSU might prevail "between the hedges" in the Bulldog den in Athens. It was an incorrect assumption. A fumble early in the third period set up a Georgia score, the Bulldogs got another on a drive, then held off the Tigers in the final quarter for a 21-14 win. Fumbles killed two chances for a third score late in the game.

The loss to Georgia triggered one in-squad move. Figuring they needed something to "get psyched," a group of players, including Steve Ensminger, showed up for the Kentucky game with the "mohawk look" —clean shaven heads save for a ribbon of hair down the middle. It didn't help. Charged-up Kentucky carried a 19-10 lead into the fourth quarter against an LSU team that continued to sleepwalk. An 80-yard march got the Tigers back into the game, but to win it, the Tigers needed a fumble recovery at the Wildcat 10 to push across another score in a sweaty-palmed 23-19 win.

Except for brief flashes, the Tigers had not played with any degree of intensity since USC. Now they had someone to stir the juices—unbeaten Florida State. Before a regional TV audience, and a crowd of 69,197 in Tiger Stadium, LSU took command after the visitors grabbed an early 7-0 lead. The Tigers moved in front, 13-7, and were seemingly headed for another score when Jesse Myles fumbled near midfield. Immediately, Seminole quarterback Jimmy Jordan hit a streaking Hardis Johnson for a score that gave FSU a 14-13 half-time lead. Whatever intensity the Tigers may have picked up quickly evaporated. Jordan, who passed for 312 yards and three TDs, threw a 40-yard scoring strike in the final period as the Seminoles went on to a 24-19 win, one some observers called the biggest in the history of the school.

In years past, LSU-Ole Miss had been a glamour game on the national scene. Not this time. LSU went to Jackson 4-3, Ole Miss 2-5.

The stake was pride. For a long time, it looked as though it would be Rebel pride. Ole Miss led 17–0 and, later, 24–14, going into the final six minutes. It was Hokie Gajan who lit the fire when he turned a short pass into a 52-yard score. With spirits perked, Tracy Porter grabbed an Ole Miss punt and darted 49 yards to set up the go-ahead touchdown on a short run by Porter. The Rebels and quarterback John Fourcade had a little more than two minutes to do something about LSU's 28–24 lead. They did. With less than a minute remaining, the Rebels were on the LSU 9. Fourcade threw an incompletion, then scrambled to the 3. On third down, he lofted a pass into the end zone. Out of a host of jerseys, the hands of Willie Teal prevailed. He came down with a backpedaling interception just inside the back of the end zone. "When Willie went up," said McClendan, "he looked ten-feet tall." It was a game-saver Mac will long remember since it meant he would leave LSU with a 9–8–1 edge over the Rebels.

It came at a time the Tigers needed a lift, or an aspirin. Coming up next was the second No. 1 team in six weeks to visit Tiger Stadium. Bear Bryant's Crimson Tide would be shooting for its eighteenth straight and would be showing LSU maybe the finest all-around defense in the land. The big flap the week of the game concerned television. Paul Dietzel, deferring to the wishes of his head coach, turned down a request that the kickoff be moved up to midday and telecast nationally. McClendon, feeling he needed all the advantages at his disposal, wanted his last crack at Bama under the lights.

On a rainy, cold evening, it turned into a classic battle of trench warfare in which LSU's defense rose to Southern Cal heights to limit the visitors to a lonely 27-yard field goal in the third period, the only score of the game. The farthest LSU got was Bama's 42. "We've now played two No. 1 teams and unbeaten Florida state," lamented McClendon afterward. It doesn't seem like justice. Someone up there musn't like me."

Someone liked him enough to make his Tiger Stadium swan song a rousing success, a 21–3 win over Mississippi State, the 136th win of his career. Steve Ensminger engineered two drives that gave the Tigers a 14–0 half-time lead. In the final period, Dave Woodley hit Orlando McDaniel on a 75-yard scoring play to ice Mac's goodbye victory. The players gave their coach a triumphant ride out of the stadium. Mac shed a few tears as he said: "People are always asking me what team I remember most. Now I can tell them. I will remember this team because they've done more with less than any of the others. They've milked their ability dry game after game and I'll never forget 'em."

He had to milk 'em for one final effort against a Tulane team riding the crest of an 8–2 season, which made this renewal of the ancient ri-

After scaring the Bear, a last handshake.

valry a toss-up in the eyes of the oddsmakers. Not only was the Green Wave entering with the better record, it had one of the hottest passers in the country in Roch Hontas, and it had an extra week to prepare.

The kickoff had been moved up because the game was selected to be telecast as one of that day's regional attractions. As the drama unfolded before a Superdome crowd of 73,496, it became obvious it would be a long afternoon. After an opening LSU drive, it was all Hontas who passed with deadly accuracy for three first-half scores, giving Tulane a comfortable 24–0 lead. After a third-quarter fencing match, the Tigers got on the board with less than nine minutes left, added one more, and were knocking on the door at the finish. But it was a simple case of too little, too late as the Wave prevailed, 24–13, for its second victory in thirty-one years. "Tulane was a deserving winner," said Mac. "You might say they took our tears away. I'm just happy we've got one left. Something to look forward to."

McClendon's finale, in the Tangerine Bowl against 8–3 Wake Forest, brought the tears back in what turned out to be an emotional farewell. It was the Deacons' misfortune to become swept away in the emotional wave, the Tigers exploding from the locker room to take a 24–0 lead, and eventual 34–10 victory, behind the crackling play of David Woodley, who hit on eleven of nineteen passes for 199 yards, rushed for 68 more and accounted for three TDs.

This one was one shortly before the kickoff when Mac cleared the room of assistant coaches and talked to his team. His voice choking, McClendon said, "When I came here, I never thought I'd be at LSU twenty-seven years. I knew this day would come. As you become a grown athlete, you push it back. But it's here . . ." Then, eyes brimming, he concluded: "I've never done anything. Anything I have you gave me, you and those assistant coaches out there. I'll give my right arm for those people. And tonight I'm asking you to do the same thing for them. There's no tomorrow. . . . God bless you all."

Two hours later, McClendon and his departing staff, were carried from the field in Orlando, having closed one more chapter in LSU football history. The McClendon legacy: a record that read 137–59–7, most wins by a Tiger coach; national coach-of-the-year once, Southeastern Conference coach-of-the-year twice; one conference championship; thirteen bowl games in eighteen seasons; seventeen first-team all-Americas; fifty-three first-team all-SEC players; six academic all-Americas.

A trace of bitterness surfaced in remarks McClendon made during his visit to San Francisco as one of the coaches in the East-West game. "The pressures coaches are coming under is unreal," said McClendon. "There's the whole gambling aspect, the point spread. I've been called a hero when I've lost and beat the spread and a bum when I've won and not beaten the spread."

He said his "retirement" was the work of a few who were frustrated by his inability to beat Alabama. "If they're thinking about being a national champion, they better think of getting into trouble. Maybe that's what they want. Some people don't seem to care about being on probation."

McClendon didn't mind citing Billy Cannon as one of the instigators in his demise. "Billy is anti-McClendon," said the coach. "I'm not upset with Billy, but Billy is upset with me, and I really don't know why."

He said he wasn't dropping his head as he took his leave. "I'll probably be dead before the next man wins as many games as I have. I'm not being cocky, just honest. I can do more for the next guy than he can ever do for himself, because I can tell folks this is what you better do for the guy or you gonna have him out of there just like you had me. The good will always outweigh the bad. Probably the greatest disappointment is what my family has had to suffer through. I'll never be envious of the next coach. I hope he wins every game. But, buddy, he will pay the price."

Tragedy and
a New Beginning, 1980-

WHEN Charles "Bo" Rein was presented to the Board of Supervisors on November 30 as the successor to Charles McClendon, he talked of being willing to pay the price, whatever it might be.

Fate decreed it would be the ultimate price. Forty-two days later, the Bo Rein era had ended, closing the shortest and most tragic chapter in LSU athletics. Starting to Baton Rouge from Shreveport after a day's recruiting, Rein and the pilot of a private plane perished following an eerie journey of 1,000 miles, a journey that ended when the aircraft plunged into the Atlantic Ocean 100 miles off the Virginia coast. The twin-engine, eight-seater had picked up Rein for what was to be a 57-minute flight to Ryan Airport. Shortly after takeoff, the pilot, Lewis Benscotter, was instructed to head east to fly around some bad weather. Then the mystery began. When the plane began climbing above its assigned altitude, there was no response when contact was attempted. Over North Carolina, two Air Force fighter planes intercepted the plane whose course indicated it was flying on automatic pilot. When these jets, running low on fuel, returned to their base, another fighter, piloted by Captain Daniel Zoerb, flew out of Langley Air Force Base in Virginia to take up the chase.

Zoerb picked up the plane at 41,000 feet out of Norfolk. He reported seeing a red glow from inside the cockpit, apparently from the instrument panel. He made three passes, gave all of the standard intercept signals, but got no response. Finally, aproximately 100 miles east of Cape Charles, Virginia, at 12:24 a.m. Baton Rouge time, the Cessna Conquest 441, 1,400 miles off course, ran out of fuel, went into a steep dive, and crashed into the Atlantic. Zoerb made a pass after the plane hit but saw no signs of wreckage, only an oil slick.

Athletic director Paul Dietzel

In all probability, the mystery will never be solved. The speculation is that either the pilot was stricken or a problem developed inside the cabin, due to lack of pressure or carbon monoxide.

The tragic news hit few harder than Paul Dietzel, who had chosen Rein from a list of "proven head coaches," ending more than a year of speculation. The man who became LSU's twenty-fourth football coach was a thirty-four-year-old product of Ohio State and, for the last four years, head coach at North Carolina State. He was called "probably the best young coach in the country" by Woody Hayes, who coached him in college, and was called "a highly educated over-achiever" by Frank Broyles, on whose staff he served at Arkansas.

Whether you consider it fate, or the hand of God, sudden death first brings disbelief, then shock, followed by an awareness that life goes on. Two days following the fatal crash, the Board of Supervisors accepted Paul Dietzel's recommendations that Jerry Stovall succeed Rein. Although Stovall admitted it was a lifetime ambition of his to coach his alma mater, he told his first press conference: "I would give up any job, I would give up my right arm if it meant Bo Rein could come back. I love LSU but the loss of Coach Rein makes the conditions sorrowful."

The thirty-eight-year-old Stovall, a native of West Monroe, was a three-year varsity star with the Tigers. In his senior season of '62, the ace running back was voted player of the year in the SEC and finished second in the voting for the Heisman Trophy behind quarterback

Bo Rein, LSU head coach for only forty-two days.

Terry Baker of Oregon State. A first-round selection in the NFL draft by the St. Louis Cardinals, he played there for nine years, winning all-pro honors twice, before joining Paul Dietzel's staff at South Carolina. After three seasons, he left to become an assistant under McClendon in '74, remaining through the '78 season, after which he left coaching to become head of the Varsity Club. "I left coaching," he explained, "but I did not leave football. I left coaching because I felt, if I couldn't be head coach at LSU, I didn't want to be a head coach anywhere else."

Stovall, who handled the offensive backs for McClendon, invited the assistants assembled by Rein to remain. All but two did. Moving quickly, Stovall brought in Pete Jenkins with the title of assistant head coach and defensive line coach. Jenkins, thirty-eight, had been defensive line coach at Florida. His other addition was Bob Gatling, forty-four, to

Jerry Stovall, LSU star, '61; all-pro safety for St. Louis Cardinals, '69.

handle the quarterbacks. Gatling had served the last three seasons on the staff at Wyoming.

They joined the men handpicked by Bo Rein: George Belu, forty-one, offensive coordinator and offensive line; Darrell Moody, thirty-two, running backs; Bobby Morrison, thirty-five, linebackers; Greg Williams, thirty-three, defensive coordinator and defensive backs; Bishop Harris, thirty-eight, defensive ends; Steve Regan, thirty, receivers; and Otis Washington, thirty-eight, offensive line. All but Washington, who coached St. Augustine High School in New Orleans to three state championships, were on Rein's staff at North Carolina State.

Dietzel said Stovall was "qualified in every way." "He's young, tough, aggressive, articulate, a great recruiter with superior integrity. Under the circumstances, he was my only choice. Jerry Stovall is LSU through-and-through."

Stovall, who received a four-year contract, at a salary of $42,000-a-year, announced he would be using the Veer, the same offense Bo Rein planned to install. He said that in recruiting, there would be "no bound-

Head coach Jerry Stovall meets the press for the first time.

aries," adding, "with one of the finest programs in America, academically as well as athletically, there's no reason why LSU cannot be sold to young men all over the country."

As for Stovall the person, he said this: "I'm a Christian who believes there is a right way and wrong way to do everything. The man who influenced my life more than anyone, other than my father, is Paul Dietzel. As a player, I knew he cared about me. We never lost touch over the years. I'd like to be the same kind of coach he was, the kind who loves his players, but is also demanding of them."

A staunch member of the Fellowship of Christian Athletes, Stovall explained he had to discipline himself to the fact he would not coach again. "I had prepared myself to serve LSU in a fund-raising capacity," he said. "But the Lord works in mysterious ways, ways we will never comprehend."

On a day he was scheduled to be in St. Louis to represent LSU and the Varsity Club before the FCA, he was standing instead before the Board of Supervisors, and the media, as LSU's twenty-fifth football coach. He would be only the third alumnus to hold the job. E. A. Chavanne coached his alma mater in 1898 and again in 1900. And then there was Gus Tinsley, who was in charge from 1948 to 1954. Bo Rein would have been the first man with head coaching experience to get the job since Biff Jones arrived in 1932, Stovall following a list of assistants who took a step up in Tigertown—Moore, Tinsley, Dietzel, McClendon.

It had to be especially nostalgic for Dietzel who first remembers Stovall as "that skinny little runt from West Monroe." Jerry began making noises as a slender 6-2, 170 pounder. And, in his first varsity game, when his prized sophomore waded through a convoy of Texas Aggies to make a game-saving tackle on a punt return, Dietzel knew he had something special. "Jerry Stovall never knew what it was to do anything half-speed," his coach liked to say. "He was an inspiration by his performance on the field—and off the field. He's the kind of man a father would like his son to be."

As LSU football enters the eighties, and a new era, Jerry Stovall is a man with a man's job. "I'm more of a man for having known someone like Bo Rein," he said on the bittersweet day he was named coach. "My wish is that I can accomplish what I'm sure Bo would have accomplished. My apprenticeship has been a long one. And, goodness knows, I love this school."

Sources and Acknowledgments

Two major sources—interviews and newspaper files—provided most of the information for this book. Another invaluable source, especially for LSU football's early years, was H. Warren Taylor's *Forty-two Years on the Tiger Gridiron*, published in 1936 by Otto Claitor, Baton Rouge. Mr. Taylor also contributed vital post-1936 information in an interview.

LSU football became my regular beat for the New Orleans *States* in 1953, and material from that time on was easily available. Going back to 1893, however, and bringing the story forward made a search of the following newspapers necessary: the Baton Rouge *Morning Advocate* (and its predecessor the *Daily Advocate*), Baton Rouge *State-Times*, New Orleans *Daily Picayune*, New Orleans *Times-Democrat*, New Orleans *Times-Picayune*, New Orleans *Item*, New Orleans *States*, New Orleans *States-Item*, and LSU's student newspaper, the *Reveille*. *The Gumbo* was also an invaluable source of information—and supplied a number of photographs which could not now be found anywhere else.

In addition to *Forty-two Years on the Tiger Gridiron*, Fuzzy Woodruff's *A History of Southern Football, 1890–1928*, published (in three volumes) in 1928 by the Georgia Southern Publishing Company, proved a useful source, as did the *Encyclopedia of Football* (New York: Ronald Press, 1960).

Anecdotal material was provided by interviews—personal or by letter—conducted from 1964 to 1968 with the following: Russ Cohen, Biff Jones, Bernie Moore, Gus Tinsley, Paul Dietzel, Charley McClendon, Sidney Bowman, Judge Oliver P. "Ike" Carriere, Ray Coates, Charley Cusimano, Al Dark, Bernie Dumas, Tom Dutton, Frank Ellis, Doc Fenton, Chief Justice John B. Fournet, Clarence Ives, Roland Kizer, Abe Mickal, Pinky Rohm, Jake Staples, Bill Pitcher, Y. A. Tittle, J. E. Thonnsen, Castro Carazo, T. P. Heard, Harry Rabenhorst, General Troy Middleton, Ran Williams, Mrs. Charles E. Coates, Lewis Gottlieb, A. L. "Red" Swanson, Tad Gormley, W. E. Butler, Jim Corbett, Bud Montet, Dan Hardesty, John Ferguson, W. I.

Spencer, Marty Broussard, Ace Higgins, Bud Johnson, Bill Keefe, Harry Martinez, Hap Glaudi, Bob Roesler, Buddy Diliberto, and Tom Fox.

I am grateful to all of these for the help which they gave so generously. I am also grateful to those who supplied photographs, or who helped with the identification of photographs: Mr. Edwin F. Gayle (the last surviving member of the 1893 team), Mr. Harry Gamble (who played in 1894 and 1895), Mrs. Charles E. Coates, Harry Rabenhorst, Mr. and Mrs. John J. Seip, Jr., Jake Staples, and the many others whose names appear in the photo credits. I would also like to acknowledge the help given by the LSU Department of Archives, LSU's Office of Information Services (with special thanks to Oscar Richard), the Sports Information Office, and the Office of Alumni Affairs. I also thank Ruth Hubert, Barney McKee, and Charles East of LSU Press, whose devoted attention to the book went far beyond the call of duty.

For their assistance in the 1980 revision of this book, I am grateful to Paul Manasseh, director of the Sports Information Office at LSU; and at LSU Press, Martha Hall, managing editor, and Joanna Hill, production manager.

PETER FINNEY

Appendix

375

Bud Montet's All-time LSU Team

Bud Montet, sports editor of the Baton Rouge *Morning Advocate*, ha watched LSU football since 1925. Bud agreed to select his all-time Tige₁ team as a part—perhaps a controversial part—of this history of the sport at LSU.

"This team might not meet with popular approval, but the players I've selected excelled not only in ability but in leadership, toughness, and those little things that set them ahead of others of equal ability," said Bud.

"The switch from the 60-minute man to platoon football makes selection difficult. I selected only players I saw play, which should explain why Doc Fenton is not included."

Following are the best whom Bud has watched, with an occasional personal comment:

ENDS—Gaynell Tinsley. "Without a doubt, the best college football player I ever saw. He did things in the thirties that the pros are just now getting around to doing."

Ken Kavanaugh. "A great pass catcher."

TACKLES—Justin Rukas. "Best blocking tackle I ever saw."

Ed Champagne. "Quickest tackle I ever saw."

GUARDS—J. W. Goree and Roy Winston

CENTER—Marvin Stewart

QUARTERBACK—Y. A. Tittle

RUNNING BACKS—Steve Van Buren. "My choice as the greatest runner ever to play for LSU."

Billy Cannon

Jimmy Taylor

Charles Alexander

KICKER—Pinky Rohm. "Great punter and best kicker I ever saw. A gifted broken-field runner, I'd pick him as the fifth back on any Tiger all-star team."

MODERN LSU FOOTBALL RECORDS
Individual Records

TOTAL OFFENSE

Most Plays

Game: 46 (11 rushing, 35 passing) by Pat Screen vs. Alabama (11-6-65)

Season: 312 (311 rushing, 1 passing) by Charles Alexander (1977)

Career: 857 (855 rushing, 2 passing) by Charles Alexander (1975-1978)

Most Yards Gained

Game: 304 (139 rushing, 165 passing) by Paul Lyons vs. Wisconsin (9-25-71)

Season: 1,703 (1,686 rushing, 17 passing) by Charles Alexander (1977)

Career: 4,052 (4,035 rushing, 17 passing) by Charles Alexander (1975-78)

Most Yards Gained Per Game

Season: 154.8 (1,703 yards in 11 games) by Charles Alexander (1977)

Career: 121.5 (2,308 yards in 19 games) by Nelson Stokley (1965-67)

Highest Average Gain Per Play

Game: (Min. 20 plays) 10.9 (240 yards on 22 plays) by Bert Jones vs. Auburn (10-14-72)

Season: (Min. 800 yards) 7.6 (917 yards on 121 plays) by Nelson Stokley (1965)

Career: (Min. 1,500 yards) 5.7 (2,308 yards on 403 plays) by Nelson Stokley (1965-67)

Most Touchdowns Scored and Responsible For

Season: 18 (scored 4 and passed for 14) by Bert Jones (1972)

Career: 40 (scored 40) by Charles Alexander (1975-78)

RUSHING

Most Rushes

Game: 43 (231 yards) by Charles Alexander vs. Wyoming (11-26-77)

Season: 311 (1,686 yards) by Charles Alexander (1977)

Career: 855 (4,045 yards) by Charles Alexander (1975-78)

Most Rushes Per Game

Season: 28.3 (311 in 11 games) by Charles Alexander (1977)

Career: 19.4 (855 in 44 games) by Charles Alexander (1975-78)

Most Yards Gained

Game: 237 (31 att.) by Charles Alexander vs. Oregon (10-22-77)

Season: 1,686 (311 att.) by Charles Alexander (1977)

Career: 4035 (855 att.) by Charles Alexander (1975-78)

Most Yards Gained Per Game

Season: 153.3 (1,686 yards in 11 games) by Charles Alexander (1977)

Career: 91.7 (4035 yards in 44 games) by Charles Alexander (1975-78)

Highest Average Gain Per Rush

Game: (Min. 5 att.) 17.7 (106 yards in 6 att.) by Jim Benglis vs. Texas A&M (9-18-71)

(Min. 10 att.) 17.5 (192 yards in 11 att.) by Billy Baggett vs. Mississippi (11-4-50)

(Min. 15 att.) 9.7 (155 yards in 16 att.) by Charles Alexander vs. Rice (9-24-77)

Season: (Min. 75 att.) 7.9 (667 yards in 85 att.) by Gene Knight (1946)

(Min. 125 att.) 5.7 (876 yards in 155 att.) by Charles Alexander (1976)

(Min. 200 att.) 5.4 (1.686 in 311 att.) by Charles Alexander (1977)

Career: (Min. 225 att.) 5.9 (1,337 yards in 226 att.) by Billy Baggett (1948-50)

Most Touchdowns Scored by Rushing

Game: 4 by Charles Alexander vs. Oregon (10-22-77)

Season: 17 by Charles Alexander (1977)

Career: 40 by Charles Alexander (1975-78)

Longest Scoring Rush 94 yards by Sal Nicolo vs. Rice (10-4-52)

FORWARD PASSING

Most Passes Attempted

Game: 35 (15 comp.) by Pat Screen vs. Alabama (11-6-65)

Season: 199 (103 comp.) by Bert Jones (1972)

Career: 418 (220 comp.) by Bert Jones (1970-72)

Highest Percentage of Passes Completed

Game: (Min. 5 att.) 1.000 (9 of 9) by Fred Haynes vs. Baylor (10-5-68)

(Min. 10 att.) .917 (11 of 12) by Nelson Stokley vs. Miss. State (11-11-67)

(Min. 12 att.) .778 (14 of 18) by Y. A. Tittle vs. Tulane (12-2-44)

Season: (Min. 50 att.) .640 (32 of 50) by Nelson Stokley (1965)

(Min. 100 att.) .561 (60 of 107) by Mike Miley (1973)

Career: (Min. 300 att.) .541 (171 of 316) by Mike Hillman (1967-69)

(Min. 400 att.) .526 (220 by 418) by Bert Jones (1970-72)

Most Passes Completed

Game: 18 (32 att.) by Bert Jones vs. Alabama (11-11-72)

Season: 103 (199 att.) by Bert Jones (1972)

Career: 220 (418 att.) by Bert Jones (1970-72)

Most Yards Gained (Passing)

Game: 242 (18 of 32) by Bert Jones vs. Alabama (11-11-72)

Season: 1,446 (103 of 199) by Bert Jones (1973)

Career: 3,255 (220 of 418) by Bert Jones (1970-72)

Most Touchdown Passes

Game: 4 by Steve Ensminger vs. Rice (9-24-77)

Season: 14 by Bert Jones (1972)

Career: 28 by Bert Jones (1970-72)

Longest Scoring Pass Play

82 yards by Steve Ensminger to Carlos Carson vs. Georgia (10-14-78)

PASS RECEIVING

Most Passes Caught

Game: 11 (152 yards) by Tommy Morel vs. Miss. State (11-18-67) and Charles Alexander (94 yards) vs. Kentucky (10-21-78)

Season: 45 (854 yards) by Andy Hamilton (1971)

Career: 100 (1,995 yards) by Andy Hamilton (1969-71)

Most Yards Gained

Game: 201 (5 rec.) by Carlos Carson vs. Rice (9-24-77)

Season: 870 (39 rec.) by Andy Hamilton (1970)

Career: 1,995 (100 rec.) by Andy Hamilton (1969-71)

Most Touchdown Passes Caught

Game: 5 by Carlos Carson vs. Rice (9-24-77)

Season: 10 by Carlos Carson (1977)

Career: 18 by Andy Hamilton (1969-71)

Most Consecutive TD Passes Caught: 6, Carlos Carson (5 vs. Rice 9-24-77 and 1 vs. Florida 10-1-77)

PUNTING

Most Punts

Game: 13 (519 yards) by Leo Bird vs. Tennessee (11-1-41)

Season: 81 (3,147 yards) by Al Doggett (1952)

Career: 169 (6,623 yards) by Rusty Jackson (1972-74)

Most Yards Punted

Game: 519 (13 punts) by Leo Bird vs. Tennessee (11-1-41)

Season: 3,147 (81 punts) by Al Doggett (1952)

Career: 6,623 (169 punts) by Rusty Jackson (1972-74)

Highest Average Per Punt

Game: (Min. of 5) 51.3 .359 (359 yards on 7 punts) by Billy Cannon vs. Mississippi (11-9-57)

(Min. of 10) 47.3 (473 yards on 10 punts) by Jerry Stovall vs. Mississippi (10-29-60)

Season: (Min. of 30) 43.1 (1,593 yards on 37 punts) by Leo Bird (1939)

(Min. of 45) 42.9 (2,228 yards on 52 punts) by Eddie Ray (1967)

(Min. of 60) 42.1 (2,696 yards on 64 punts) by Jerry Stovall (1960)

Career: (Min. of 125) 41.2 (6,039 yards on 153 punts) by Eddie Ray (1967-69)

(Min. of 160) 39.2 (6,623 yards on 169 punts) by Rusty Jackson (1972-74)

Longest Punt
    76 yards by Ray Coates vs. Rice (10-7-44)

INTERCEPTION RETURNS
Most Pass Interceptions
    Game: 3 by Craig Burns vs. Mississippi (12-5-70); Jerry Joseph
            vs. Kentucky (10-16-65); Kenny Konz vs. Tulane (11-26-49);
            Chris Williams vs. Rice (9-30-78)
    Season: 8 by Craig Burns (1970), and Chris Williams (1978)
    Career: 12 by Craig Burns (1968-70)
            Charley Oakley (1951-53)
Longest Scoring Interception Return
    100 yards by White Graves vs. Kentucky (10-17-64)

PUNT RETURNS
Most Punt Returns
    Game: 7 (86 yards) by Young Bussey vs. Tulane (11-27-39)
            7 (42 yards) by Sammy Grezaffi vs. Mississippi (11-4-67)
    Season: 41 (369 yards) by Sammy Grezaffi (1967)
    Career: 79 (905 yards) by Sammy Grezaffi (1965-67)
Most Yards Returned (Punts)
    Game: 145 (3 ret.) by Joe Labruzzo vs. Rice (9-25-65)
    Season: 539 (35 ret.) by Pinky Rohm (1937)
    Career: 905 (79 ret.) by Sammy Grezaffi (1965-67)
Longest Punt Return For Score
    92 yards by Kenny Konz vs. Tulane (11-26-49)

KICKOFF RETURNS
Most Kickoff Returns
    Game: 5 (58 yards) by Robert Dow vs. Vanderbilt (9-9-76)
    Season: 23 (598 yards) by Robert Dow (1975)
    Career: 70 (1,780 yards) by Robert Dow (1973-76)
Most Yards Returned (Kickoffs)
    Game: 148 (4 ret.) by Robert Dow vs. Tennessee (10-11-75)
    Season: 598 (23 ret.) by Robert Dow (1975)
    Career: 1,780 (70 ret.) by Robert Dow (1973-76)
Longest Kickoff Return For Score
    100 yards by Sammy Grezaffi vs. Tennessee (10-28-67)

TACKLES
    Game: 17 by Lyman White vs. Alabama (11-10-79)
    Season: 109 by Lyman White (1979)

SCORING
Most Points Scored
    Game: 30 by Carlos Carson vs. Rice (9-24-77)
    Season: 104 by Charles Alexander (1977)
    Career: 254 by Charles Alexander (1975-78)

Most Touchdowns Scored
    Game: 5 by Carlos Carson vs. Rice (9-24-77)
    Season: 17 by Charles Alexander (1977)
    Career: 40 by Charles Alexander (1975-78)

Most Field Goals Made
    Game: 4 by Mike Conway vs. Kentucky (10-21-78)
    Season: 14 by Mike Conway (1978)
    Career: 33 by Mike Conway (1975-78)

Longest Field Goal
    53 yards by Juan Roca vs. Rice (10-7-72)

Most PATs By Kicking
    Game: 10 by Bobby Moreau vs. Rice (9-24-77)
    Season: 39 by Jay Michaelson (1971)
    Career: 92 by Mark Lumpkin (1968-70)

Most Consecutive PATs By Kicking
    Game: 10 by Bobby Moreau vs. Rice (9-24-77)
    Season: 25 by Mike Conway (1977)
    Career: 42 by Mike Conway (1976-77)

Most Points Scored By Kicking
    Game: 13 by Mike Conway vs. Kentucky (10-21-78)
            Jay Michaelson vs. Texas A&M (9-18-71)
            Roy Hurd vs. Florida (10-7-67)
    Season: 68 by Mike Conway (1978)
    Career: 187 by Mike Conway (1975-78)

TEAM RECORDS
SINGLE GAME OFFENSE

TOTAL OFFENSE
    Most Plays: 99 vs. Tulane (11-22-69)
    Most Yards Gained: 746 vs. Rice (9-24-77)
    Highest Average Gain Per Play: 7.9 vs. Vanderbilt (10-27-45)
RUSHING
    Most Rushes: 83 vs. Wyoming (11-26-77)
    Most Yards Gained: 503 vs. Oregon (10-22-77)
    Most Touchdowns Scored Rushing: 8 vs. Tulane (11-25-61)
    Highest Average ain Per Rush: 8.0 vs. Vanderbilt (10-27-45)

PASSING
    Most Pases Attempted: 56 vs. Tulane (11-24-79)
    Most Passes Completed: 22 vs. Baylor (10-3-70)
    Most Passes Had Intercepted: 6 vs. Tennessee (11-4-39)
    Most Passes Attempted Without Interception: 36 vs. Mississippi
        (10-30-71)
    Highest Percentage Of Passes Completed:
        (Min. of 10 att.) .846 (11 of 13) vs. Tulane (12-1-45)
        (Min. of 20 att.) .750 (18 of 24) vs. Miss. State (11-15-69)
        (Min. of 25 att.) .724 (21 of 29) vs. Miss. State (11-18-67)
    Most Yards Gained: 357 vs. Baylor (10-3-70)
    Most Touchdowns Passes: 5 vs. Tulane (11-30-46)

PUNTING
    Most Punts: 17 vs. Tennessee (10-31-42) and vs. Miss. State **(11-9-40)**
    Most Yards Punted: 664 vs. Miss. State (11-9-40)
    Highest Average Per Punt:
        (Min. of 5) 51.3 (7 for 359 yards) vs. Mississippi (11-9-57)
        (Min. of 10) 47.3 (10 for 473 yards) vs. Mississippi (10-29-60)

INTERCEPTIONS
    Most Passes Intercepted: 8 vs. Villanova (11-24-51)

PUNT RETURNS
    Most Punt Returns: 13 vs. Tulane (11-27-37)
    Most Yards Returned Punts: 205 vs. Mississippi (12-5-70)

KICKOFF RETURNS
    Most Kickoff Returns: 7 vs. Texas (9-20-52); vs. Vanderbilt **(11-6-48)**;
        vs. Mississippi (10-30-48); vs. Texas (9-18-48); vs. Alabama **(11-22-
        47)**; vs. Georgia Tech (11-7-43)
    Most Yards Returned (Kickoffs): 162 vs. Vanderbilt (11-6-48)

SCORING
    Most Points Scored: 77 vs. Rice (9-24-77)
    Most Touchdowns Scored: 11 vs. Rice (9-24-77)
    Most PATs Scored by Kicking: 11 vs. Rice (9-24-77)
    Most PATs: 11 vs. Rice (9-24-77)

    Most Field Goals Scored: 3 vs. Tulane (12-2-72); vs. Texas A&M
        (9-18-71); vs. Texas A&M (9-12-70); vs. Mississippi (11-1-69); **vs.**
        Florida (10-7-67)

MISCELLANEOUS
    Most First Downs: 35 vs. Miss. State (11-15-69)
    Most Yards Penalized: 184 vs. Florida (10-28-61)
    Most Fumbles Lost: 6 vs. Rice (9-28-74); vs. Georgia (10-18-52); **vs.**
        Texas (9-20-52); vs. Rice (10-6-51)

SINGLE GAME DEFENSE

Fewest Yards Allowed, Total Offense: 26 vs. Mercer (10-19-40)
Fewest Yards Allowed, Rushing: Minus 43 vs. Tulane (11-20-76)
Fewest Yards Allowed, Passing: 0 vs. Alabama (11-6-71); vs. Missis-
    sippi (11-1-58); vs. Alabama (9-29-58); vs. Texas Tech (10-16-54);
    vs. Mississippi (10-17-42); vs. Louisiana Normal (9-19-42); vs. Au-
    burn (11-18-39); vs. Texas (10-2-37); vs. Florida (9-26-37)
Fewest First Downs Allowed: 1 vs. Mississippi (10-17-42)

TEAM SEASON RECORDS

TOTAL OFFENSE
    Most Plays: 872 (1977)
    Most Yards Gained: 4,542 (1977)
    Highest Average Gain Per Play: 6.7 (1945)
    Most Yards Gained Per Game: 412.9 (1977)
    Most Touchdowns Gained by Rushing and Passing: 47 (1977)

RUSHING
    Most Rushes: 675 (1973)
    Most Yards Gained: 3,352 (1977)
    Highest Average Gain Per Rush: 6.8 (1945)
    Most Yards Gained Per Game: 304.7 (1977)
    Most Touchdowns Rushing: 35 (1977)

FORWARD PASSING
    Most Passes Attempted: 295 (1979)
    Most Passes Completed: 139 (1969)
    Most Passes Had Intercepted: 19 (1956, 1954, 1951, 1941, 1940)
    Most Yards Gained: 2,061 (1979)
    Most Yards Gained Per Game: 188.7 (1969)
    Most Touchdown Passes: 20 (1971)

LSU STATISTICAL LEADERS

(Year-By-Year)

RUSHING LEADERS

Year	Player, Pos.	Att.	Yds.	Avg.
1937	Young Bussey, hb	97	371	3.8
1938	Jabbo Stell, hb	78	277	3.6
1939	Charley Anastasio, hb	79	287	3.6
1940	Adrian Dodson, hb	142	556	3.9
1941	Walter Gorinski, fb	88	280	3.2
1942	Alvin Dark, hb	60	433	7.2
1943	Steve Van Buren, hb	150	847	5.6
1944	Elwyn Rowan, fb	69	288	4.2
1945	Gene Knight, fb	85	667	7.8
1946	Gene Knight, fb	95	473	5.0
1947	Rip Collins, fb	73	315	4.3
1948	Rip Collins, fb	58	277	4.4
1949	Billy Baggett, hb	87	481	5.5
1950	Billy Baggett, hb	119	778	6.5
1951	Leroy Labat, hb	152	574	3.8
1952	Al Doggett, hb	71	382	5.4
1953	Jerry Marchand, fb	137	696	5.1
1954	Chuck Johns, hb	88	408	4.6
1955	O. K. Ferguson, fb	117	465	4.0
1956	Jimmy Taylor, fb	117	552	4.7
1957	Jimmy Taylor, fb	162	762	4.7
1958	Billy Cannon, hb	115	686	5.9
1959	Billy Cannon, hb	139	598	4.3
1960	Jerry Stovall, hb	65	298	4.5
1961	Earl Gros, fb	90	406	4.5
1962	Jerry Stovall, hb	89	368	4.1
1963	Don Schwab, fb	108	553	5.1
1964	Don Schwab, fb	160	683	4.3
1965	Joe Labruzzo, tb	103	509	4.9
1966	Jimmy Dousay, tb	104	441	4.2
1967	Tommy Allen, tb	106	535	5.0
1968	Kenny Newfield, fb	85	441	5.2
1969	Eddie Ray, fb	115	591	5.1
1970	Art Cantrelle, tb	247	892	3.6
1971	Art Cantrelle, tb	133	649	4.9
1972	Chris Dantin, tb	165	707	4.3
1973	Brad Davis, tb	173	904	5.2
1974	Brad Davis, rb	169	701	4.1
1975	**Terry Robiskie, tb**	**214**	**764**	**3.6**

RUSHING LEADERS (Cont.)

1976	Terry Robiskie, tb	224	1,117	5.0
1977	Charles Alexander, tb	311	1,686	5.4
1978	Charles Alexander, tb	281	1,172	4.2
1979	Hokie Gajan, tb	134	568	4.2

PASSING LEADERS

Year	Player, Pos.	Att.	Comp.	Yds.	TD
1937	Young Bussey, hb	78	35	712	8
1938	Young Bussey, hb	52	18	285	1
1939	Leo Bird, hb	77	35	574	7
1940	Leo Bird, hb	55	20	246	2
1941	Leo Bird, hb	76	27	358	3
1942	Alvin Dark, hb	106	40	556	5
1943	Gene Knight, hb	51	19	190	1
1944	Y. A. Tittle, qb-hb	62	36	552	3
1945	Y. A. Tittle, qb-hb	77	35	404	3
1946	Y. A. Tittle, qb-hb	95	45	780	13
1947	Y. A. Tittle, qb-hb	96	49	789	4
1948	Charlie Pevey, qb	99	37	607	5
1949	Charlie Pevey, qb	86	36	521	6
1950	Norm Stevens, qb	108	42	551	4
1951	Jim Barton, qb	75	29	417	1
1952	Norm Stevens, qb	97	52	583	2
1953	Al Doggett, qb	142	68	822	4
1954	Al Doggett, qb	104	34	459	2
1955	M. C. Reynolds, qb	115	51	660	6
1956	M. C. Reynolds, qb	70	30	385	1
1957	Win Turner, qb	41	16	231	2
1958	Warren Rabb, qb	90	45	591	8
1959	Warren Rabb, qb	65	33	422	4
1960	Lynn Amedee, qb	67	31	438	4
1961	Lynn Amedee, qb	94	40	485	2
1962	Lynn Amedee, qb	63	24	457	2
1963	Pat Screen, qb	38	22	194	1
1964	Pat Screen, qb	99	55	561	1
1965	Nelson Stokley, qb	50	32	468	3
1966	Fred Haynes, qb	91	39	424	2
1967	Nelson Stokley, qb	130	71	939	4
1968	Mike Hillman, qb	118	64	787	5
1969	Mike Hillman, qb	167	93	1,180	8
1970	Buddy Lee, qb	138	73	1,162	6
1971	Bert Jones, qb	119	66	945	9
1972	Bert Jones, qb	199	103	1,446	14
1973	Mike Miley, qb	107	60	978	7
1974	Billy Broussard, qb	103	41	700	1
1975	Pat Lyons, qb	168	72	457	4
1976	Pat Lyons, qb	133	54	685	3
1977	Steve Ensminger, qb	159	71	952	9
1978	David Woodley, qb	153	79	995	3
1979	Steve Ensminger, qb	174	80	1,168	5

RECEIVING LEADERS

Year	Player, Pos.	No.	Yds.	TD
1937	Ken Kavanaugh, Sr., e	11	310	4
1938	Ken Kavanaugh, Sr., e	17	294	5
1939	Ken Kavanaugh, Sr., e	30	470	7
1940	Odell Weaver, e	7	139	1
1941	Dudley Pillow, e	16	214	2
1942	Jim McLeod, e	15	278	1
1943	Carroll Griffith, wb	6	67	0
1944	Dan Sandifer, hb	10	241	1
1945	Clyde Lindsey, e	11	147	0
1946	Sam Lyle, e	7	162	3
1947	Ray Bullock, e	12	188	2
1948	Abner Wimberly, e	10	197	2
1949	Sam Lyle, e	20	268	2

RECEIVING LEADERS (Continued)

Year	Player			
1950	Warren Virgets, e	25	455	3
1951	Warren Virgets, e	17	263	1
1952	Jim Mitchell, e	17	209	0
1953	Jerry Marchand, fb	13	192	1
1954	Joe Tuminello, e	13	181	3
1955	Chuck Johns, hb	14	217	3
1956	J. W. Brodnax, hb	13	123	0
1957	Billy Cannon, hb	11	199	1
1958	Johnny Robinson, hb	16	235	3
1959	Johnny Robinson, hb	16	181	4
1960	Jerry Stovall, hb	12	114	0
1961	Wendell Harris, hb	10	177	2
1962	Jerry Stovall, hb	9	213	1
1963	Billy Truax, e	10	112	1
1964	Doug Moreau, se	33	391	4
1965	Doug Moreau, se	29	468	3
1966	Billy Masters, sb	24	241	1
1967	Tommy Morel, se	28	404	3
1968	Tommy Morel, se	42	564	2
1969	Lonny Myles, se	43	559	4
1970	Andy Hamilton, sb	39	870	6
1971	Andy Hamilton, sb	45	854	9
1972	Gerald Keigley, sb	27	433	7
1973	Brad Boyd, te	16	259	3
1974	Brad Boyd, te	18	275	2
1975	Carl Otis Trimble, sb	16	177	2
1976	Carl Otis Trimble, sb	14	211	2
1977	Carlos Carson, se	23	552	10
1978	Carlos Carson, se	27	568	2
1979	Carlos Carson ,se	39	608	2

TIGER ALL-AMERICAS (29)

Gaynell Tinsley, End	1935-36
Ken Kavanaugh, Sr., End	1939
George Tarasovic, Center	1951
Sid Fournet, Tackle	1954
Jimmy Taylor, Fullback	1957
Billy Cannon, Halfback	1958-59
Max Fugler, Center	1958
Roy Winston, Guard	1961
Jerry Stovall, Halfback	1962
Fred Miller, Tackle	1962
Bill Truax, End	1963
Remi Prudhomme, Guard	1964
George Rice, Tackle	1965
Doug Moreau, End	1965
John Garlington, Defensive End	1967
George Bevan, Linebacker	1969
Mike Anderson, Linebacker	1970
Tommy Casanova, Cornerback	1970-71
Ronnie Estay, Defensive Tackle	1971
Bert Jones, Quarterback	1972
Warren Capone, Linebacker	1972-73
Tyler Lafauci, Guard	1973
Mike Williams, Safety	1974
Charles Alexander, Tailback	1977-78
Robert Dugas, Offensive Tackle	1978

ABC-TV/CHEVROLET PLAYERS-OF-THE-WEEK

OFFENSE	DEFENSE
Andy Hamilton, 11/20/71	Ronnie Estay, 11/20/71
Michael Miley, 11/3/73	John Wood, 11/11/72
Steve Ensminger, 10/29/77	Steve Cassidy, 11/3/73
Charles Alexander, 11/4/78	Kenny Bordelon, 11/1/75
Carlos Carson, 10/27/79	John Adams, 11/4/78
	Willie Teal, 11/24/79

LSU MILESTONES

VICTORIES

No.	Year	Score	Opponent
1	1894	36-0	Natchez AC (A)
50	1908	55-0	SW Tennessee (H)
100	1919	39-0	SW Louisiana (H)
150	1929	58-0	SW Louisiana (H)
200	1936	12-0	Mississippi State (H)
250	1945	32-0	Georgia (A)
300	1954	20-7	Florida (H)
350	1962	21-0	Texas A&M (H)
400	1968	34-10	Tulane (A)
450	1974	24-22	Tulane (H)

DEFEATS

No.	Year	Score	Opponent
1	1893	0-34	Tulane (A)
50	1917	0-9	Mississippi State (H)
100	1934	12-13	Tulane (H)
150	1950	0-35	Oklahoma (Sugar Bowl)
200	1963	12-21	Rice (A)
250	1977	14-24	Stanford (Sun Bowl)

LSU ACADEMIC ALL-AMERICA

1959—Mickey Mangham, E	1973—Tyler Lafauci, G
1960—Charles Strange, C	1973—Joe Winkler, DB
1961—Billy Booth, T	1974—Brad Davis, RB
1971—Jay Michaelson, KS	1977—Robert Dugas, T
1971—Tommy Butaud, T*	*Second Team

ALL-TIME TIGER STADIUM CROWDS
(through 1979)

No.	Attendance	Opponent	Date	Score
1.	78,534	Indiana	9-16-78	LSU, 24-17
2.	78,322	USC	9-29-79	USC, 17-12
3.	78,073	Florida	10- 6-79	LSU, 20-3
4.	77,197	Wake Forest	9-23-78	LSU, 13-11
5.	75,876	Tulane	11-25-78	LSU, 40-21
6.	74,934	Rice	9-22-79	LSU, 47-3
7.	73,708	Alabama	11-10-79	Ala., 3-0
8.	73,120	Ole Miss	11- 4-78	LSU, 30-8
9.	71,495	Kentucky	10-15-77	Ky., 33-13
10.	71,296	Kentucky	10-20-79	LSU, 23-19

OUTSTANDING SEC BLOCKER

(Selected by the Birmingham QB Club)
Billy May, 1936
J. W. Brodnax, 1958

BLUE-GRAY BOWL MVP SELECTIONS

Ken Kavanaugh, Sr.—1939
Dan Sandifer—1947
Kenny Konz—1950
Leroy Lebat—1952
Jerry Marchand—1953

SENIOR BOWL MVP SELECTIONS

Jim Taylor—1958
A. J. Duhe (MVP—Defense—South)—1976

ABC-TV/CHEVROLET LINEMAN-OF-THE-YEAR

Ronnie Estay—1971

LSU's MVP/TOP SCORER (SINCE 1933)

Year	Most Valuable	Leading Scorer	
1933	John Kent (Center)	Abe Mickal, Back	(38)
1934	Walter Sullivan (Back)	Walter Sullivan, Back	(36)
1935	Jesse Fatherree (Back)	Bill Crass, Back	(36)
1936	Gaynell Tinsley (End)	Gaynell Tinsley, End	(48)
1937	Pinky Rohm (Back)	Pinky Rohm, Back	(54)
		Jabbo Stell, Back	(54)
1938	Dick Gormley (Center)	**Ken Kavanaugh, Sr.**, End	(31)
1939	Ken Kavanaugh, Sr. (End)	Ken Kavanaugh, Sr., End	(54)
1940	J. W. Goree (Guard)	Adrian Dodson, Back	(42)
1941	Bernie Lipkis (Center)	Sulcer Harris, Back	(36)
1942	Walter Gorinski (Back)	Walter Gorinski, Back	(36)
1943	Steve Van Buren (Back)	Steve Van Buren, Back	(98)
1944	Charlie Webb (End)	Elwyn Rowan, Fullback	(18)
1945	Gene Knight (Fullback)	Gene Knight, Fullback	(51)
	Clyde Lindsey (End)		
1946	Fred Hall (Tackle)	Al Heroman, Halfback	(30)
		Gene Knight, Fullback	(30)
1947	Y. A. Tittle (Quarterback)	Zollie Toth, Fullback	(30)
		Rip Collins, Fullback	(30)
1948	Abner Wimberly (End)	Six Players Tied	(12)
1949	Ray Collins (Tackle)	**Carroll** Griffith, Quarterback	(39)
1950	Ken Konz (Halfback)	Ken Konz, Halfback	(45)
1951	Jim Barton (Halfback)	Leroy Labat, Halfback	(30)
1952	Norman Stevens (Quarterback)	Jerry Marchand, Fullback	(42)
1953	Jerry Marchand (Fullback)	Jerry Marchand, Fullback	(48)
1954	Sid Fournet (Tackle)	Vince Gonzales, Halfback	(24)
		Chuck Johns, Halfback	(24)
1955	O. K. Ferguson (Fullback)	Vince Gonzales, Halfback	(32)
1956	Paul Ziegler (Guard)	Jimmy Taylor, Fullback	(59)
1957	Jimmy Taylor (Fullback)	Jimmy Taylor, Fullback	(86)
1958	J. W. Brodnax (Fullback)	Billy Cannon, Halfback	(74)
1959	Billy Cannon (Halfback)	Billy Cannon, Halfback	(44)
1960	Charles Strange (Center)	Wendell Harris, Halfback	(34)
1961	Wendell Harris (Halfback)	Wendell Harris, Halfback	(94)
	Earl Gros (Fullback)		
1962	Jerry Stovall (Halfback)	Jerry Stovall, Halfback	(66)
1963	Robbie Hucklebridge (Guard)	Donald Schwab, Fullback	(36)
1964	Richard Granier (Center)	Doug Moreau, Flanker	(73)
1965	Joe Labruzzo (Halfback)	Doug Moreau, Split End	(59)
	Doug Moreau (Split End)		
1966	Mike Duhon (Guard)	Tommy Allen, Tailback	(32)
	Gawain DiBetta (Fullback)		
1967	Nelson Stokley (Quarterback)	Roy Hurd, Kicker	(31)
	Sammy Grezaffi (Safety)		
1968	Tommy Morel (Split End)	Mark Lumpkin, Kicker	(40)
	Gerry Kent (Defensive Back)		
1969	George Bevan (Linebacker)	Mark Lumpkin, Kicker	(62)
	Mike Hillman (Quarterback)		
1970	Mike Anderson (Linebacker)	Mark Lumpkin, Kicker	(53)
	Buddy Lee (Quarterback)		
1971	Andy Hamilton (Splitback)	**Jay Michaelson, Tight End**	(72)
	Ronnie Estay (Defensive Tackle)		
1972	Bert Jones (Quarterback)	Rusty Jackson, Kicker	(46)
	John Wood (Defensive Tackle)		
1973	Tyler Lafauci (Guard)	Rusty Jackson, Kicker	(46)
	Warren Capone (Linebacker)		

LSU's MVP/TOP SCORER (Cont.)

Year	Most Valuable	Leading Scorer	
1974	Mike Williams (Defensive Back) .... Brad Davis (Running Back)	Brad Davis, Back	(54)
1975	Steve Cassidy (Defensive Tackle) .... Greg Bienvenu (Center)	Terry Robiskie, Back	(62)
1976	Terry Robiskie (Back) .... Dan Alexander (Defensive Tackle)	Terry Robiskie, Back	(72)
1977	Kelly Simmons (Back) .... Steve Ripple (Linebacker)	Charles Alexander, Back	(104)
1978	Charles Alexander (Back) ...... Kent Broha (Defensive Tackle)	Charles Alexander, Back	(96)
1979	David Woodley (Quarterback) .... Steve Ensminger (Quarterback) .... Willie Teal (Safety)	David Woodley (QB) 42 Don Barthel, Kicker	(42)

COACHES RECORDS

Years	Coach (Alma Mater)	G	W	L	T	Pct.
1893	C. E. Coates (Johns Hopkins)	1	0	1	0	.000
1894-95	A. P. Simmons (Yale)	6	5	1	0	.833
1896-97	A. W. Jeardeau (Harvard)	8	7	1	0	.875
1898-1900	E. A. Chavanne (LSU)	5	3	2	0	.600
1899	J. P. Gregg (Wisconsin)	5	1	4	0	.200
1901-03	W. S. Borland (Allegheny)	22	15	7	0	.682
1904-06	D. A. Killian (Michigan)	16	8	6	2	.571
1907-08	Edgar R. Wingard (Susquehanna) .	20	17	3	0	.950
1909	J. G. Pritchard (Vanderbilt)	4	3	1	0	.750
1909-10	J. W. Mayhew (Brown)	10	4	6	0	.400
1911-13	J. K. Dwyer (Pennsylvania)	25	16	7	2	.680
1914-16	E. T. McDonald (Colgate)	22	14	7	1	.659
1916	Dana X. Bible (Carson-Newman)...	3	1	0	2	.667
1916-19-22	Irving R. Pray (MIT)	20	11	9	0	.550
1917	W. Sutton (Washington State)	8	3	5	0	.375
1920-21	Branch Bocock (Georgetown)	17	11	4	2	.706
1923-27	Mike Donahue (Yale)	45	23	19	3	.544
1928-31	Russ Cohen (Vanderbilt)	37	23	13	1	.635
1932-34	Lawrence M. "Biff" Jones (Army)	31	20	5	6	.742
1935-47	Bernie H. Moore (Carson-Newman)	128	83	39	6	.672
1948-54	Gaynell "Gus" Tinsley (LSU)	75	35	34	6	.507
1955-61	Paul Dietzel (Miami of Ohio)	73	46	24	3	.651
1962-79	Charles McClendon (Kentucky) ..	203	137	59	7	.691
*1980-80	Robert "Bo" Rein (Ohio State)	0	0	0	0	.000
1980	Jerry Stovall (LSU)					

*Coach Rein was killed in a tragic air accident in January, 1980.

86 Seasons, 25 Coaches		784	491	258	41	.650

SEC MOST VALUABLE PLAYER
(Selected by the Birmingham QB Club)

Sid Fournet (lineman), 1954
Jimmy Taylor (back), 1957
Billy Cannon (back), 1958
Jerry Stovall (back), 1962
Terry Robiskie (back), 1976

SEC MOST VALUABLE PLAYER
(Selected by the Nashville Banner)

Ken Kavanaugh, Sr., 1939
Billy Cannon, 1958
Billy Cannon, 1959
Jerry Stovall, 1962
Charles Alexander, 1977

LSU PLAYERS IN PRO FOOTBALL

Alexander, Chas.—Bengals, 1979-
Alexander, Dan—Jets, 1977-

Baggett, Billy—Texans 1952.
Barnes, Walter—Eagles 1948-51.
Barrett, Jeff—Dodgers 1936-38.
Bordelon, Kenny—Saints 1976-
Brancato, George—Cardinals 1954.
Branch, Mel—Texans 1960-62; Chiefs 1963-65; Dolphins 1966-68.
Brodnax, J. W.—Broncos 1960.
Burkett, Jeff—Cardinals 1947.
BURRELL, Clinton—Browns, 1979-
Bussey, Young—Bears 1940-41.

Cannon, Billy—Oilers 1960-63; Raiders 1964-69; Chiefs 1970.
Cantrelle Art—49ers 1976-
Capone, Warren—Cowboys 1975; Buccaneers 1976; Saints 1976
Casanova, Tommy—Bengals 1972-1977
Cason, Jimmy—49ers 1948-52, 54; Rams 1955-56.
Champagne, Ed—Rams 1947-50.
Coates, Ray—Giants 1948-49.
Coffee, Pat—Cardinals 1937-38.
Collins, Albin Harrel (Rip)—Cardinals 1949; Colts 1950; Packers 1951.
Collins, Ray—49ers 1950-52; Giants 1954; Texans 1960-61.
Crass, Bill—Cardinals 1937.

Davis, Brad—Falcons 1975-1976
Davis, Tommy—49ers 1959-70.
Demarie, John—Browns 1967-76; Sea Hawks 1976-
Duhe, A. J.—Dolphins 1977-

Estes, Don—Chargers 1966.

Fournet, Sid—Rams 1955-56; Steelers 1957; Texans 1960-61; Titans 1962; Jets 1963; Broncos 1964.

Friend, Ben—Rams 1939.
Fussell, Tom—Patriots 1967.

Garlington, John—Browns 1968-1977
Gaubatz, Dennis—Lions 1963-64; Colts 1965-69.
Glamp, Joe—Steelers 1947-49.
Gorinski, Walt—Steelers 1946.
Graves, White—Patriots 1965-67; Bengals 1968.
Gros, Earl—Packers 1962-63; Eagles 1964-66; Steelers 1967-69; Saints 1970.

Hamilton, Andy—Chiefs 1972-74; Saints 1975.
Harris, Bo—Bengals, 1975-
Harris, Wendell—Colts 1962-65; Giants 1966-67.
Hodgins, Norm—Bears 1974; Packers 1975-

Jackson, Rusty—Rams 1976, Bills 1978
Jackson, Steve—Raiders 1977-1978
Jones, Bert—Colts 1973-
Jones, W. A. "Dub"—Seahawks 1946; Dodgers 1946-47; Rams 1948-49; Browns 1949-55.

Kavanaugh, Ken, Sr.—Bears 1940-41, 1945-50.
Kingery, Wayne—Colts 1949.
Konz, Kenny—Browns 1953-59.

Land, Fred—49ers 1948.
Leggett, Earl—Bears 1957-60, 1962-65; Rams 1966; Saints 1967-68.
Leisk, Wardell—Dodgers 1937.

Masters, Billy—Bills 1966-70; Broncos 1970-74; Chiefs 1975-77
May, Bill—Cardinals 1937-38.
McCormick, Dave—49ers 1966; Saints 1967-68.
Miller, Fred—Colts 1963-72; Redskins 1973.
Miller, Paul—Rams 1954-57; Texans 1960-61; Chargers 1962.
Montgomery, Bill—Cardinals 1946.
Moreau, Doug—Dolphins 1968-69.
Morgan, Mike—Eagles 1964-67; Redskins 1968.

Neal, Ed—Packers 1945-51; Bears 1951.
Neck, Tommy—Bears 1962.
Nunnery, R.B.—Texans 1960.

Oakley, Charley—Cardinals 1954.

Prudhomme, Remi—Bills 1966-67; Chiefs 1968-69; Saints 1971-72.

Quintela, Mike—Oilers, 1979-

Rabb, Warren—Lions 1960; Bills 1961-62.
Ray, Eddie—Patriots 1970; Chargers 1971; Falcons 1972-76; Sea Hawks 1976
Reed, Joe (Rock)—Cardinals 1937-39.
Reid, Joe—Rams 1951; Texans 1952.
Reynolds, M. C.—Cardinals 1958-59; Redskins 1960; Bills 1961; Raiders 1961.
Richards, Bobby—Eagles 1962-65; Falcons 1966-67.
Rice, George—Oilers 1966-69.
Robinson, Johnny—Texans 1960-62; Chiefs 1963-71.
Robiskie, Terry—Raiders 1977-
Rogers, Steve—Saints 1975
Rukas, Justin—Dodgers 1936.

Sandifer, Dan—Redskins 1948-49; Lions 1950; 49ers 1950; Eagles 1950-51; Packers 1952-53; Cardinals 1953.
Schroll, Bill—Bills 1949; Lions 1950; Packers 1951.
Shurtz, Hubert—Steelers 1948.
Stovall, Jerry—Cardinals 1963-71.
Sykes, Gene—Bills 1963-65; Broncos 1967.

Tarasovic, George—Steelers 1952-53, 1956-63; Eagles 1963-65; Broncos 1967.
Taylor, Jimmy—Packers 1958-66; Saints 1967.
Tinsley, Gaynell—Cardinals 1937-40.
Tinsley, Jess—Cardinals 1929-33.
Tittle, Y. A.—Colts 1948-51; 49ers 1951-60; Giants 1961-64.
Torrance, Jack—Bears 1939-40.
Toth, Zollie—Yankees 1950-51; Texans 1952; Colts, 1953-54.
Truax, Billy—Rams 1964-70; Cowboys 1971-74.

Van Buren, Ebert—Eagles 1951-53.
Van Buren, Steve—Eagles 1944-51.

Williams, Mike—Chargers 1975-
Wimberly, Abner—Rams 1949; Packers 1950-52.
Winston, Roy—Vikings 1962-77
Wood, John—Saints 1973.

Zaunbrecher, Godfrey—Vikings 1970-74; Packers 1975.

LSU's MVP (1927-1932)

1927—Babe Godfrey, (QB)
1928—Hank Stovall, (QB)
1929—Dobie Reeves, (HB)

1930—J. B. Luker, (E)
1931—Tom Smith, (FB)
1932—Walter Fleming, (E)

LSU FOOTBALL

1893 (0-1-0)
Coach: C. E. Coates
Captain: R. G. Pleasant

0	Tulane	34
0		34

1894 (2-1-0)
Coach. A. P. Simmonds
Captain: S. M. D. Clark

36	Natchez AC	0
6	Mississippi	26
30	Centenary	0
72		26

1895 (3-0-0)
Coach: A. P. Simmonds
Captain: J. E. Snyder

8	Tulane	4
16	Centenary	6
12	Alabama	6
36		16

1896 (6-0-0)
Coach: A. W. Jeardeau
Captain: E. A. Scott

46	Centenary	0
6	Tulane	0
12	Mississippi	4
14	Texas	0
6	Southern AC	0
52	Miss. State	0
136		4

1897 (1-1-0)
Coach: A. W. Jeardeau
Captain: E. A. Scott

28	Montgomery AC	6
0	Cincinnati	26
28		32

1898 (1-0-0)
Coach. E. A. Chavanne

37	Tulane	0
37		0

1899 (1-4-0)
Coach: J. P. Gregg
Captain: H. F. Aby

0	Mississippi	11
0	Sewanee	34
0	Texas	29
0	Texas A & M	52
38	Tulane	0
38		126

1900 (2-2-0)
Coach: E. A. Chavanne
Captain: I. H. Schwing

70	Millsaps	0
0	Tulane	29
5	Millsaps	6
10	LSU Alumni	0
85		35

1901 (5-1-0)
Coach: W. S. Borland
Captain: E. L. Gorham

57	La. Tech	0
46	Mississippi	0
11	Tulane	0
0	Auburn	28
38	LYMCA (N. O.)	0
15	Arkansas	0
167		28

1902 (6-1-0)
Coach. W. S. Borland
Captain: H. E. Landry

42	S. L. I.	0
5	Texas	0
5	Auburn	0
6	Mississippi	0
5	Vanderbilt	27
6	Miss. State	0
11	Alabama	0
80		27

1903 (4-5-0)
Coach. W. S. Borland
Captain: J. J. Coleman

16	LSU Alumni	0
33	Eagles (NO)	0
16	La. Tech	0
5	Shreveport AC	0
0	Miss. State	11
0	Alabama	18
0	Auburn	12
0	Cumberland	41
0	Mississippi	11
70		93

1904 (3-4-0)
Coach: D. A. Killian
Captain: E. L. Klock

17	La. Tech	0
0	Shreveport AC	16
0	La. Tech	6
5	Mississippi	0
16	Nashville Med	0
0	Tulane	5
0	Alabama	11
38		38

1905 (3-0-0)
Coach: D. A. Killian
Captain: F. M. Edwards

16	La. Tech	0
5	Tulane	0
15	Miss. State	0
36		0

1906 (2-2-2)
Coach: D. A. Killian
Captain: E. E. Weil

5	Monroe AC	0
0	Mississippi	9
0	Miss. State	0
17	La. Tech	0
12	Texas A & M	21
6	Arkansas	6
40		36

1907 (7-3-0)
Coach: E. R. Wingard
Captain: S. W. Brannon

28	La. Tech	0
5	Texas	12
5	Texas A & M	11
57	Howard	0
17	Arkansas	12
23	Miss. State	11
23	Mississippi	0
4	Alabama	6
48	Baylor	0
56	Havana U.	0
266		52

1908 (10-0-0)
Coach: E. R. Wingard
Captain: M. H. Gandy

41	YMGC (N. O.)	0
81	Jackson Br. NO	5
26	Texas A & M	0
55	Southwestern T.	0
10	Auburn	2
50	Miss. State	0
89	Baylor	0
32	Haskell	0
22	La. Tech	0
36	Arkansas	4
442		11

1909 (6-2-0)
Coaches: J. G. Prichard
J. W. Mayhew
Captain:R. L. Stovall

70	Jackson Br. NO	0
10	Mississippi	0
15	Miss. State	0
6	Sewanee	15
23	La. Tech	0
0	Arkansas	16
52	Transylvania	0
12	Alabama	6
188		37

1910 (1-5-0)
Coach: J. W. Mayhew
Captain: J. J. Seip

40	Miss. College	0
0	Miss. State	3
5	Sewanee	31
0	Vanderbilt	22
0	Texas	12
0	Arkansas	51
45		119

1911 (6-3-0)
Coach: J. K. Dwyer
Captain: A. J. Thomas

42	S. L. I.	0
46	La. Normal	0
40	Miss. College	0
40	Meteor AC	0
6	Baylor	0
0	Miss. State	6
6	S'western (Tex.)	17
0	Arkansas	11
6	Tulane	0
186		34

1912 (4-3-0)
Coach: J. K. Dwyer
Captain: C. S. Reily

85	S. L. I.	3
45	Miss. College	0
7	Mississippi	10
0	Miss. State	7
0	Auburn	7
7	Arkansas	6
21	Tulane	3
165		36

1913 (6-1-2)
Coach: J. K. Dwyer
Captain: T. W. Dutton

20	La. Tech	2
26	S. L. I.	0
45	Jefferson Col.	6
50	Baylor	0
0	Auburn	7
12	Arkansas	7
0	Miss. State	0
40	Tulane	0
7	Texas A & M	7
200		29

1914 (4-4-1)
Coach: E. T. McDonnell
Captain: G. B. Spencer

54	S. L. I.	0
60	La. Tech	0
14	Miss. College	0
0	Mississippi	21
14	Jefferson Col.	13
9	Texas A & M	63
12	Arkansas	20
0	Haskell	31
0	Tulane	0
163		148

1915 (6-2-0)
Coach: E. T. McDonnell
Captain: A. J. Reid

42	Jefferson Col.	0
28	Mississippi	0
14	Miss. Col.	0
7	Ga. Tech	36
10	Miss. State	0
13	Arkansas	7
0	Rice	6
12	Tulane	0
126		49

(1916 (7-1-2)
Coach: E. T. McDonnell,
I. R. Pray, D. X. Bible
Captain: P. Cooper

24	S. L. I.	0
59	Jefferson Col.	0
13	Texas A & M	0
50	Miss. College	7
0	Sewanee	7
17	Arkansas	7
13	Miss. State	3
41	Mississippi	0
7	Rice	7
14	Tulane	14
238		45

1917 (3-5-0)
Coach: W. Sutton
Captain: A. O'Quin

20	S. L. I.	6
52	Mississippi	7
0	Sewanee	3
0	Texas A & M	27
0	Arkansas	14
34	Miss. College	0
0	Miss. State	9
6	Tulane	28
112		94

1918
(no LSU football
played)

1919 (6-2-0)
Coach: I. R. Pray
Captain: T. W. Dutton

39	S. L. I.	0
38	Jefferson Col.	0
13	Mississippi	0
20	Arkansas	0
0	Miss. State	6
24	Miss. College	0
0	Alabama	23
27	Tulane	6
161		35

1920 (5-3-1)
Coach: Branch Bocock
Captain: R. L. Benoit

81	Jefferson Col.	0
34	La. Normal	0
40	Spring Hill	0
0	Texas A & M	0
7	Miss. State	12
41	Miss. College	9
3	Arkansas	0
0	Alabama	21
0	Tulane	21
206		63

1921 (6-1-1)
Coach: Branch Bocock
Captain: F. L. Spencer

78	La. Normal	0
6	Texas A & M	0
41	Spring Hill	7
7	Alabama	7
10	Arkansas	7
21	Mississippi	0
0	Tulane	21
17	Miss. State	14
180		56

1922 (3-7-0)

Coach: I. R. Pray
Captain: E. L. Ewen

13	La. Normal	0
0	Loyola	7
0	S. M. U.	51
0	Texas A & M	47
6	Arkansas	40
25	Spring Hill	7
0	Rutgers	25
3	Alabama	47
25	Tulane	14
0	Miss. State	7
72		245

1923 (3-5-1)

Coach: Mike Donahue
Captain: E. L. Ewen

40	La. Normal	0
7	S. L. I.	3
33	Spring Hill	0
0	Texas A & M	28
13	Arkansas	26
0	Miss. College	0
3	Alabama	30
0	Tulane	20
7	Miss. State	14
103		121

1924 (5-4-0)

Coach: Mike Donahue
Captain: C. C. Campbell

7	Spring Hill	6
31	S. L. I.	7
20	Indiana	14
12	Rice	0
0	Auburn	3
7	Arkansas	10
7	Ga. Tech	28
40	La. Normal	0
0	Tulane	13
124		81

1925 (5-3-1)

Coach: Mike Donahue
Captain: J. E. Steele

27	La. Normal	0
0	Alabama	42
38	S. L. I.	0
6	LSU Freshmen	0
0	Tennessee	0
0	Arkansas	12
6	Rice	0
13	Loyola	0
0	Tulane	16
90		70

1926 (6-3-0)

Coach: Mike Donahue
Captain: L. T. Godfrey

47	La. Normal	0
34	S. L. I.	0
7	Tennessee	14
10	Auburn	0
6	Miss. State	7
0	Alabama	24
14	Arkansas	0
3	Mississippi	0
7	Tulane	0
128		45

1927 (4-4-1)

Coach: Mike Donahue
Captain: L. T. Godfrey

45	La. Tech	0
52	S. L. I.	0
0	Alabama	0
9	Auburn	0
9	Miss. State	7
0	Arkansas	28
7	Mississippi	12
0	Ga. Tech	23
6	Tulane	13
128		83

1928 (6-2-1)

Coach: Russ Cohen
Captain: Jess Tinsley

46	S. L. I.	0
41	La. College	0
31	Miss. State	0
30	Spring Hill	7
0	Arkansas	7
19	Mississippi	6
13	Georgia	12
0	Tulane	0
0	Alabama	13
180		45

1929 (6-3-0)

Coach: Russ Cohen
Captain: Frank Ellis

58	La. College	0
58	S. L. I.	0
27	Sewanee	14
31	Miss. State	6
53	La. Tech	7
0	Arkansas	32
6	Duke	32
13	Mississippi	6
0	Tulane	21
246		118

1930 (6-4-0)

Coach: Russ Cohen
Captain: W. Reeves

76	S. D. Wesleyan	0
71	La. Tech	0
85	S. L. I.	0
6	S. Carolina	7
6	Miss. State	8
12	Sewanee	0
27	Arkansas	12
6	Mississippi	0
0	Alabama	33
7	Tulane	12
296		72

1931 (5-4-0)

Coach: Russ Cohen
Captain: Ed Khoury

0	T. C. U.	3
35	Spring Hill	0
19	S. Carolina	12
31	Miss. State	0
13	Arkansas	6
6	Sewanee	12
0	Army	20
26	Mississippi	3
7	Tulane	34
137		90

1932 (6-3-1)

Coach: L. M. Jones
Captain: Walter Fleming

3	T. C. U.	3
8	Rice	10
80	Spring Hill	0
24	Miss. State	0
14	Arkansas	0
38	Sewanee	0
6	S. Carolina	0
0	Centenary	6
14	Tulane	0
0	Oregon	12
187		31

1933 (7-0-3)

Coach: L. M. Jones
Captain: Jack Torrance

13	Rice	0
40	Millsaps	0
0	Centenary	0
20	Arkansas	0
7	Vanderbilt	7
30	S. Carolina	7
31	Mississippi	0
21	Miss. State	6
7	Tulane	7
7	Tennessee	0
176		27

1934 (7-2-2)

Coach: L. M. Jones
Captain: Bert Yates

9	Rice	9
14	S. M. U.	14
20	Auburn	6
16	Arkansas	0
29	Vanderbilt	0
25	Miss. State	3
6	George Wash.	0
14	Mississippi	0
12	Tulane	13
13	Tennessee	19
14	Oregon	13
172		77

1935 (9-1-0)

Coach: Bernie Moore
Captain: Jeff Barrett

7	Rice	10
18	Texas	6
32	Manhattan	0
13	Arkansas	7
7	Vanderbilt	2
6	Auburn	0
28	Miss. State	13
13	Georgia	0
56	S. L. I.	0
41	Tulane	0
221		38

Sugar Bowl

2	TCU	3

1936 (9-0-1)

Coach: Bernie Moore
Captain: Bill May

20	Rice	7
6	Texas	6
47	Georgia	7
13	Mississippi	0
19	Arkansas	7
19	Vanderbilt	0
12	Miss. State	0
19	Auburn	6
93	S. L. I.	0
33	Tulane	0
281		33

Sugar Bowl

14	Santa Clara	21

1937 (9-1-0)

Coach: Bernie Moore
Captain: A. Morton

19	Florida	0
9	Texas	0
13	Rice	0
13	Mississippi	0
6	Vanderbilt	7
52	Loyola (NO)	6
52	La. Normal	0
41	Miss. State	0
9	Auburn	7
20	Tulane	7
234		27

Sugar Bowl

0	Santa Clara	6

1938 (6-4-0)

Coach: Bernie Moore
Captain: Ben Friend

7	Mississippi	20
20	Texas	0
3	Rice	0
47	Loyola (NO)	6
7	Vanderbilt	0
6	Tennessee	14
32	Miss. State	7
6	Auburn	28
32	S. L. I.	0
0	Tulane	14
160		89

1939 (4-5-0)

Coach: Bernie Moore
Captain: Young Bussey

7	Mississippi	14
26	Holy Cross	7
7	Rice	0
20	Loyola (NO)	0
12	Vanderbilt	6
0	Tennessee	20
12	Miss. State	15
7	Auburn	21
20	Tulane	33
111		116

1940 (6-4-0)

Coach: Bernie Moore
Captain: Charles Anastasio

39	La. Tech	7
6	Mississippi	19
25	Holy Cross	0
0	Rice	23
20	Mercer	0
7	Vanderbilt	0
0	Tennessee	28
7	Miss. State	22
21	Auburn	13
14	Tulane	0
139		112

1941 (4-4-2)

Coach: Bernie Moore
Captain: Leo Bird

25	La. Tech	0
13	Holy Cross	19
0	Texas	34
0	Miss. State	0
27	Rice	0
10	Florida	7
6	Tennessee	13
12	Mississippi	13
7	Auburn	7
19	Tulane	0
119		93

1942 (7-3-0)

Coach: Bernie Moore
Captain: Willie Miller

40	La. Normal	0
16	Texas A & M	7
14	Rice	27
21	Mississippi	7
34	Georgia Navy	0
16	Miss. State	6
0	Tennessee	26
26	Fordham	13
7	Auburn	25
18	Tulane	6
192		117

1943 (5-3-0)

Coach: Bernie Moore
Captain: Steve Van Buren

34	Georgia	27
20	Rice	7
13	Texas A & M	28
28	La. Army STU	7
27	Georgia	6
14	T. C. U.	0
7	Ga. Tech	27
0	Tulane	27
124		144

Orange Bowl

19	Texas A & M	14

1944 (2-5-1)

Coach: Bernie Moore
Captain: Al Cavigga

27	Alabama	27
13	Rice	14
0	Texas A & M	7
6	Miss. State	13
15	Georgia	7
0	Tennessee	13
6	Ga. Tech	14
25	Tulane	6
92		101

1945 (7-2-0)

Coach: Bernie Moore
Captain: Andy Kosmac

42	Rice	0
7	Alabama	26
31	Texas A & M	12
32	Georgia	0
39	Vanderbilt	7
32	Mississippi	13
20	Miss. State	27
9	Ga. Tech	7
33	Tulane	0
245		92

1946 (9-1-0)

Coach: Bernie Moore
Captain: Dilton Richmond

7	Rice	6
13	Miss. State	6
33	Texas A & M	9
7	Ga. Tech	26
14	Vanderbilt	0
34	Mississippi	21
31	Alabama	21
20	Miami (Fla.)	7
40	Fordham	0
41	Tulane	27
240		123

Cotton Bowl

0	Arkansas	0

1947 (5-3-1)

Coach: Bernie Moore
Captain: Jim Cason

21	Rice	14
19	Georgia	35
19	Texas A & M	13
14	Boston College	13
19	Vanderbilt	13
18	Mississippi	20
21	Miss. State	6
12	Alabama	41
6	Tulane	6
149		161

1948 (3-7-0)

Coach: Gus Tinsley
Captain: Ed Claunch

0	Texas	33
26	Rice	13
14	Texas A & M	13
0	Georgia	22
7	North Carolina	34
19	Mississippi	49
7	Vanderbilt	48
0	Miss. State	7
26	Alabama	6
0	Tulane	46
99		271

1949 (8-2-0)

Coach: Gus Tinsley
Captain: Melvin Lyle

0	Kentucky	19
14	Rice	7
34	Texas A & M	0
0	Georgia	7
13	N. Carolina	7
34	Mississippi	7
33	Vanderbilt	13
34	Miss. State	7
48	Southeastern	7
21	Tulane	0
231		74

Sugar Bowl

0	Oklahoma	35

1950 (4-5-2)

Coach: Gus Tinsley
Captain: Ebert Van Buren

0	Kentucky	14
19	Col. of Pacific	0
20	Rice	35
0	Ga. Tech	13
13	Georgia	13
40	Mississippi	14
33	Vanderbilt	7
7	Miss. State	13
13	Villanova	7
14	Tulane	14
6	Texas	21
165		**151**

1951 (7-3-1)

Coach: Gus Tinsley
Captains: Ray Potter, Chester Freeman

13	Miss. Southern	0
13	Alabama	7
7	Rice	6
7	Ga. Tech	25
7	Georgia	0
0	Maryland	27
6	Mississippi	6
13	Vanderbilt	20
3	Miss. State	0
45	Villanova	7
14	Tulane	13
128		**111**

1952 (3-7-0)

Coach: Gus Tinsley
Captains: Norm Stevens, Joe Modicut, Bill Lansing, Leroy Labat, Jim Sanford, Ralph McLeod.

14	Texas	35
20	Alabama	21
27	Rice	7
34	Kentucky	7
14	Georgia	27
6	Maryland	34
0	Mississippi	28
3	Tennessee	22
14	Miss. State	33
16	Tulane	0
148		**214**

1953 (5-3-3)

Coach: Gus Tinsley
Captains: Jerry Marchand, Charley Oakley

20	Texas	7
7	Alabama	7
42	Boston College	6
6	Kentucky	6
14	Georgia	6
21	Florida	21
16	Mississippi	27
14	Tennessee	32
13	Miss. State	26
9	Arkansas	8
32	Tulane	13
194		**159**

1954 (5-6-0)

Coach: Gus Tinsley
Captain: Sid Fournet

6	Texas	20
0	Alabama	12
6	Kentucky	7
20	Ga. Tech	30
20	Texas Tech	13
20	Florida	7
6	Mississippi	21
26	Chattanooga	19
0	Miss. State	25
7	Arkansas	6
14	Tulane	13
125		**173**

1955 (3-5-2)

Coach: Paul Dietzel
Captains: Joe Tuminello, O. K. Ferguson

19	Kentucky	7
0	Texas A & M	28
20	Rice	20
0	Georgia Tech	7
14	Florida	18
26	Mississippi	29
0	Maryland	13
34	Miss. State	7
13	Arkansas	7
13	Tulane	13
139		**149**

1956 (3-7-0)

Coach: Paul Dietzel
Captain: Don Scully

6	Texas A & M	9
14	Rice	23
7	Georgia Tech	39
0	Kentucky	14
6	Florida	21
17	Mississippi	46
13	Okla. A & M	0
13	Miss. State	32
21	Arkansas	7
7	Tulane	6
104		**197**

1957 (5-5-0)

Coach: Paul Dietzel
Captain: Alvin Aucoin

14	Rice	20
28	Alabama	0
19	Texas Tech	14
20	Georgia Tech	13
21	Kentucky	0
14	Florida	22
0	Vanderbilt	7
12	Mississippi	14
6	Miss. State	14
25	Tulane	6
159		**110**

1958 (10-0-0)

Coach: Paul Dietzel
Captain: Billy Hendrix

26	Rice	6
13	Alabama	3
20	Hardin-Simmons	6
41	Miami	0
32	Kentucky	7
10	Florida	7
14	Mississippi	0
50	Duke	18
7	Miss. State	6
62	Tulane	0
275		**53**

Sugar Bowl

7	Clemson	0

1959 (9-1-0)

Coach: Paul Dietzel
Captain: Lynn LeBlanc

26	Rice	3
10	TCU	0
22	Baylor	0
27	Miami	3
9	Kentucky	0
9	Florida	0
7	Mississippi	3
13	Tennessee	14
27	Miss. State	0
14	Tulane	6
164		**29**

Sugar Bowl

0	Ole Miss	21

1960 (5-4-1)

Coach: Paul Dietzel
Captain: Charles Strange

9	Texas A & M	0
3	Baylor	7
2	Ga. Tech	6
0	Kentucky	3
10	Florida	13
6	Mississippi	6
35	So. Carolina	6
7	Miss. State	3
16	Wake Forest	0
17	Tulane	6
105		**50**

1961 (9-1-0)

Coach: Paul Dietzel
Captain: Roy Winston

3	Rice	16
16	Texas A & M	7
10	Ga. Tech	0
42	So. Carolina	0
24	Kentucky	14
23	Florida	0
10	Mississippi	7
30	No. Carolina	0
14	Miss. State	6
62	Tulane	0
234		**50**

Orange Bowl

25	Colorado	7

1962 (8-1-1)

Coach: Charles McClendon
Captain: Fred Miller

21	Texas A & M	0
6	Rice	6
10	Georgia Tech	7
17	Miami (Fla.)	3
7	Kentucky	0
23	Florida	0
7	Mississippi	15
5	TCU	0
28	Miss. State	0
38	Tulane	3
162		**34**

Cotton Bowl

13	Texas	0

1963 (7-3-0)

Coach: Charles McClendon
Captain: Bill Truax

14	Texas A & M	6
12	Rice	21
7	Georgia Tech	6
3	Miami	0
28	Kentucky	7
14	Florida	0
3	Mississippi	37
28	TCU	14
6	Miss. State	7
20	Tulane	0
135		**98**

Bluebonnet Bowl

7	Baylor	14

1964 (7-2-1)

Coach: Charles McClendon
Captain: Richard Granier

9	Texas A & M	6
3	Rice	0
20	No. Carolina	3
27	Kentucky	7
3	Tennessee	3
11	Mississippi	10
9	Alabama	17
14	Miss. State	10
13	Tulane	3
6	Florida	20
115		**79**

Sugar Bowl

13	Syracuse	10

1965 (7-3-0)

Coach: Charles McClendon
Captains: Billy Ezell and John Aaron

10	Texas A & M	0
42	Rice	14
7	Florida	14
34	Miami	27
31	Kentucky	21
21	So. Carolina	7
0	Mississippi	23
7	Alabama	31
37	Miami	20
62	Tulane	0
251		**157**

Cotton Bowl

14	Arkansas	7

1966 (5-4-1)

Coach: Charles McClendon
Captains: L'nard Neumann and Gawain DiBetta

28	South Carolina	12
15	Rice	17
10	Miami	8
7	Texas A & M	7
30	Kentucky	0
7	Florida	28
0	Mississippi	17
0	Alabama	21
17	Miss. State	7
21	Tulane	7
135		**124**

1967 (6-3-1)

Coach: Charles McClendon
Captains: Barry Wilson and Benny Griffin

20	Rice	14
17	Texas A & M	6
37	Florida	6
15	Miami	17
30	Kentucky	7
14	Tennessee	17
13	Mississippi	13
6	Alabama	7
55	Miss. State	0
41	Tulane	27
248		**114**

Sugar Bowl

20	Wyoming	13

1968 (8-3-0)

Coach: Charles McClendon
Captains: Barton Frye & Jerry Guillot

13	Texas A&M (H)	12
21	Rice (A)	7
48	Baylor (H)	16
0	Miami (A)	30
13	Kentucky (H)	3
10	TCU (H)	7
24	Mississippi (H)	27
7	Alabama (Birmingham)	16
20	Miss. State (H)	16
34	Tulane (A)	10
190		**144**

Peach Bowl

31	Florida State	27

1969 (9-1-0)

Coach: Charles McClendon
Captains: George Bevan & Robert (Red) Ryder

35	Texas A&M (H)	6
42	Rice (A)	0
63	Baylor (H)	8
20	Miami (H)	0
37	Kentucky (A)	10
21	Auburn (H)	20
23	Mississippi, (Jackson, Ms.)	26
20	Alabama (H)	15
61	Miss. State (H)	6
27	Tulane (H)	0
349		**91**

1970 (9-3-0)

Coach: Charles McClendon
Captains: Buddy Lee & John Sage

18	Texas A&M (H)	20
24	Rice (H)	0
31	Baylor (H)	10
34	Pacific (H)	0
14	Kentucky (H)	7
17	Auburn (A)	9
14	Alabama (Birmingham)	9
38	Miss. State (H)	7
0	Notre Dame (A)	3
26	Tulane (A)	14
61	Mississippi (H)	17
277		**96**

Orange Bowl

12	Nebraska	17

1971 (9-3-0)

Coach: Charles McClendon
Captains: Louis Cascio & Mike Demarie

21	Colorado (H)	31
37	Texas A&M (H)	0
38	Wisconsin (A)	28
38	Rice (H)	3
48	Florida (H)	7
17	Kentucky (A)	13
22	Mississippi (Jackson,Ms.)	24
7	Alabama (H)	14
28	Miss. State (Jackson, Ms.)	3
28	Notre Dame (H)	8
36	Tulane (H)	7
320		**138**

Sun Bowl

33	Iowa State	15

1972 (9-2-1)

Coach: Charles McClendon
Captains: Paul Lyons & Pepper Rutland

31	Pacific (H)	13
42	Texas A&M (H)	17
27	Wisconsin (H)	7
12	Rice (A)	6
35	Auburn (H)	7
10	Kentucky (H)	0
17	Mississippi (H)	16
21	Alabama (Birmingham)	35
28	Miss. State (H)	14
3	Florida (A)	3
9	Tulane (A)	3
235		**121**

Astro-Bluebonnet Bowl

17	Tennessee	

1973 (9-3-0)

Coach: Charles McClendon
Captains: Tyler Lafauci & Binks Miciotto

17	Colorado (H)	6
28	Texas A&M (H)	23
24	Rice (H)	9
24	Florida (H)	3
20	Auburn (A)	6
28	Kentucky (H)	21
33	South Carolina (A)	29
51	Mississippi (Jackson, Ms.)	14
26	Miss. State (H)	7
7	Alabama (H)	21
0	Tulane (A)	14
258		153

Orange Bowl

9	Penn State	16

1974 (5-5-1)

Coach: Charles McClendon
Captains: Brad Boyd & Steve Lelekacs

42	Colorado (H)	14
14	Texas A&M (H)	21
10	Rice (A)	10
14	Florida (A)	24
20	Tennessee (H)	10
13	Kentucky (A)	20
24	Mississippi (H)	0
0	Alabama (Birmingham)	30
6	Miss. State (Jackson)	7
24	Tulane (H)	22
35	Utah (H)	10
202		168

1975 (5-6-0)

Coach: Charles McClendon
Captains: Greg Bienvenu & Steve Cassidy

7	Nebraska (A)	10
8	Texas A & M (H)	39
16	Rice (Shreveport)	13
6	Florida (H)	34
10	Tennessee (A)	24
17	Kentucky (H)	14
24	South Carolina (H)	6
13	Mississippi (Jackson)	17
10	Alabama (H)	23
*6	Miss. State (H)	16
42	Tulane (A)	6
159		202

*Forfeited to LSU by NCAA

1976 (7-3-1)

Coach: Charles McClendon
Captains: Roy Stuart & Butch Knight

6	Nebraska (H)	6
28	Oregon State (H)	11
31	Rice (H)	0
23	Florida (A)	28
33	Vanderbilt (H)	20
7	Kentucky (A)	21
45	Mississippi (H)	0
17	Alabama (Birmingham)	28
*13	Miss. State (Jackson)	21
17	Tulane (H)	7
35	Utah (H)	7
255		149

1977 (8-4-0)

Coach: Charles McClendon
Captains: Kelly Simmons & Steve Ripple

21	Indiana (A)	24
77	Rice (H)	0
36	Florida (H)	14
28	Vanderbilt (A)	15
13	Kentucky (H)	33
56	Oregon (H)	17
28	Mississippi (A)	21
3	Alabama (H)	24
27	Mississippi State (H)	24
20	Tulane (A)	17
66	Wyoming (H)	7
375		196

SUN BOWL

14	Stanford	24

1978 (8-4-0)

Coach: Charles McClendon
Captains: Ch. Alexander & Thad Minaldi

24	Indiana (H)	17
13	Wake Forest (H)	11
37	Rice (A)	7
34	Florida (A)	21
17	Georgia (H)	24
21	Kentucky (A)	0
30	Ole Miss (H)	8
10	Alabama (A)	31
14	Mississippi State (A)	16
40	Tulane (H)	21
24	Wyoming (H)	17
264		173

Liberty Bowl

15	Missouri	20

1979 (7-5-0)

Coach: Charles McClendon
Captains: John Ed Bradley, Willie Teal, Rusty Brown

44	Colorado (A)	0
47	Rice (H)	3
12	USC (H)	17
20	Florida (H)	3
14	Georgia (A)	21
23	Kentucky (H)	19
19	Florida State (H)	24
28	Ole Miss (A)	24
0	Alabama (H)	3
21	Mississippi State (H)	3
13	Tulane (A)	24
241		141

Tangerine Bowl

34	Wake Forest	10

LSU VARSITY FOOTBALL LETTERMEN

A

AARON, John (RG)
Natchitoches, La., 1963-64-65
ADAMS, John Aubrey (DE)
DeRidder, La. 1976-77-78-79
ABNEY, Wilbert (E)
Slidell, La., 1945
ABRAMSON, Louis J. (Luke) (HB)
Shreveport, La., 1923
ABY, Hulette F. (Red) (T)
Natchez, Miss., 1898-99
ADAMS, Jeff (E)
Memphis, Tenn., 1946-47-48
ADDISON, Don (S)
Springhill, La., 1968-69-70
ADDY, Ken (FB)
Baton Rouge, La., 1972-73
ADSIT, John R. Jr. ( )
Decatur, Ga., 1943-44
ALBRIGHT, John G. (Jonnie) (QB)
Memphis, Tenn., 1908-09
ALEXANDER, Arnold (RE)
Bear Creek, Ala., 1954-55
ALEXANDER, Charles (TB)
Galveston, Tex., 1975-76-77-78
ALEXANDER, Dan (DT)
Houston, Tex., 1974-75-76
ALEXANDER, Glenn (T)
Rayville, La., 1969-70
ALFORD, Andrew (Andy) (LG)
Bogalusa, La., 1952-53
ALLEN, Tommy (Trigger) (TB)
DeRidder, La., 1966-67-68
ALLEN, W. D. (Bill) (T)
McComb, Miss., 1929-30-31
ALMOKARY, Joe (HB)
Oil City, La., 1930-31-32
ALSTON, Francis H. (Frank) (HB)
Logansport, La., 1927-28
AMEDEE, Lynn (QB)
Baton Rouge, La., 1960-61-62
ANASTASIO, Charles (HB)
White Castle, La., 1938-39-40
ANDERSON, Mike (LB)
Baton Rouge, La., 1968-69-70
ANDERSON, Roy Joe (FB)
Shreveport, La., 1937-38-39
ANDING, Aubrey (E)
Tyler, Tex., 1949
ANDREAS, Herman (C)
El Paso, Tex., 1930
ANDREWS, Charles P. ( )
Mer Rouge, La., 1893
ARRIGHI, J. H. (Hughes) (T)
Natchez, Miss., 1894-95-96
ATIYEH, George (DT-NG)
Allentown, Pa., 1977-78-79
ATKINSON, James S. (QB)
Ruston, La., 1896
AUCOIN, Alvin (LT)
Houma, La., 1955-56-57

B

BABERS, Bertram (Bert) (T-G)
Baton Rouge, La., 1926-27
BAGGETT, Billy (RHB)
Beaumont, Tex., 1948-49-50
BAILEY, Robert L. (Bunkie) (HB)
Bunkie, La., 1926-27
BAIRD, Albert W. (Dub) (QB)
Shreveport, La., 1916
BAIRD, Joe Garnett (Red) (T)
Shreveport, La., 1946-47-48-49
BALDWIN, Bob (C)
Fort Worth, Tex., 1955
BALDWIN, Harry (G)
Albion, Mich., 1907

BALDWIN, Marvin (T)
Lake Charles, La., 1934-35-36
BALLARD, Shelton (C)
Bogalusa, La., 1946-47
BAME, Abie A. (T)
Toledo, Ohio, 1922
BANKER, Eddie (LG)
Jennings, La., 1964-65-66
BANNISTER, Bobby (T)
Bogalusa, La., 1931-32
BARBER, Ronald J. (Ronnie) (S)
Oil City, La., 1974-75-76
BARBIN, A. T. ( )
Marksville, La., 1896
BARHAM, Garnett E. (Joe) (HB)
Oak Ridge, La., 1925
BARNES, Walter (Piggy) (T)
Parkersburg, W. Va., 1940-46-47
BARNEY, Charles (C)
Shreveport, La., 1943
BARRETT, Jack (T)
Houston, Tex., 1940
BARRETT, W. Jeff (E)
Houston, Tex., 1933-34-35
BARRETT, Woodrow (C)
San Antonio, Tex., 1940
BARRILLEAUX, Jim (LG)
Amite, La., 1968
BARROW, Edward R. ( )
Baton Rouge, La., 1899
BARTHEL, Donald R. (KS)
Rayville, La., 1979
BARTON, James (Jim) (LHB)
Marshall, Tex., 1949-50-51
BARTRAM, Dave (G)
Laurel, Miss., 1937-38-39
BASS, William (Bill) (C-LB)
Lafayette, La., 1963-64-65
BATES, Oran P. (E)
Cairo, Ill., 1903
BATES. William C. (RE)
Baton Rouge, La., 1893
BATEMAN, Joel B. (G)
Franklin, La., 1895, 1898
BAUER, Charles C. (HB)
Winnfield, La., 1907
BAUR, F. Ogden (E)
Cairo, Ill., 1937-38-39
BAZILE, Sterling (DT)
Mt. Airy, La., 1979
BEALE, L. S. (Rusty), (HB)
Baton Rouge, La., 1919-21
BEARD, James, (RHB)
Lake Providence, La., 1893-94
BENGLIS, Jim (FB)
Lake Charles, La., 1970-71-72
BENNETT, Reldon (E)
Lake Village, Ark., 1941
BENOIT, Robert L. (Rabbit) (QB)
Shreveport, La., 1917-19-20
BENTLEY, Granville D. (QB)
New Orleans, La., 1903
BERGERON, Carroll (T)
Houma, La., 1958
BERNHARD, James (T)
Baton Rouge, La., 1943-44-45
BERNSTEIN, Joe (FB)
Elmira, N. Y., 1915-16-19
BERNSTEIN, Dave (T)
New Orleans, La., 1939-40
BERON, Phil Jr. (LG)
New Orleans, La. 1952-54
BERTUCCI, Gerald (G)
New Orleans, La., 1944-45
BESSELMAN, Tom (OT)
New Orleans, La., 1970

BEVAN, George (LB)
Baton Rouge, La., 1966-67-69
BIENVENU, Greg (C)
Lafayette, La., 1973-74-75
BIRD, Leo (HB)
Shreveport, La., 1939-40-41
BLACKETTER, Gary (S)
Lake Charles, La., 1975-76-77
BLAKEWOOD, Eldridge G. (Blake) (G)
Kleinwood, La., 1922-23
BOFINGER, Bill (G)
Baton Rouge, La., 1966-67
BLASS, John P. (Jay) (DE)
Metairie, La., 1977-78-79
BOND, C P. (HB) 1910
BOND, Jimmy (E)
Bogalusa, La., 1959
BOOTH, Barrett (QB)
New Orleans, La., 1936-37-38
BOOTH, Billy Joe (T)
Minden, La., 1959-60-61
BORDELON, Kenny (DE)
New Orleans, La., 1972-73-74-75
BOUDREAUX, Wilfred (G-T)
Sunset, La., 1893
BOURGEOIS, Andy (E)
New Orleans, La., 1958-59-60
BOURGEOIS, Louis C., Jr. (C)
Franklin, La., 1921-22-23-24
BOURQUE, Hart (HB)
Gonzales, La., 1958-59-60
BOUTTE, Doug (OT)
Sulphur, La., 1973-74-75
BOWMAN, George, Jr. (QB-HB)
Hammond, La., 1932-35
BOWMAN, Sidney S. (Stinkey) (HB)
Hammond, La., 1929-30-31
BOWSER, Gregory M. (Greg) (NG)
Franklin, La., 1979
BOYD, Brad (TE)
Jennings, La., 1972-73-74
BOZEMAN, Donnie (DT-DE)
Baton Rouge, La., 1967-68-69
BRADLEY, John Edmund Jr. (C)
Opelousas, La., 1976-77-78-79
BRADLEY, Richard (Dick) (RG)
Norristown, Pa., 1948-49
BRAINARD, Pete (G)
Artesia, N. M., 1931
BRANCATO, George (LHB)
New York, N. Y., 1952-53
BRANCH, Mel (LT)
DeRidder, La., 1958-59
BRANNON, S. W. (Red) (QB)
Pollock, La., 1905-06-07-09
BRIAN, Alexis (Alex) (LT)
Montgomery, La., 1893-94
BRITT, James E. (CB)
Minden, La., 1978-79
BRODNAX, J. W. (Red) (FB-HB)
Bastrop, La., 1956-57-58
BROGAN, John E. (C)
New Orleans, La., 1901
BROGAN, Lawrence E. (G)
New Orleans, La., 1904
BROHA, Max Kent (DE)
New Orleans, La., 1976-77-78
BROOKS, Richard (Bear) (OG-OT)
Crowley, La., 1972-73-74
BROUSSARD, Billy (QB)
Jennings, La., 1973-74
BROUSSARD, Ralph A. (HB)
Abbeville, La., 1893-94
BROWN, A. D. (Andra) (G)
Laurel, Miss., 1933-34-35
BROWN, Caswell (FB)
New Orleans, La., 1951

BROWN, E. A. (Fuzzy) (HB)
Minden, La., 1929
BROWN, Gerald (Buster) (FB-P)
Richlands, N. C., 1964-65
BROWN, Harry (E)
Alexandria, La., 1931-32
BROWN, Lobdell P. (Broncho) (HB)
Baker, La., 1927-28-29-30
BROWN, Roland (HB)
Monroe, La., 1932-34
BROWN, Russell Louis (Rusty) (S)
Houston, Tex., 1977-78-79
BROWN, R. Tommy (RE)
Baker, La., 1949-51
BROWN, Samuel P. (G-T)
Carencro, La., 1893
BRUE, Darryl (DT)
New Orleans, La. 1975
BRUHL, S. Kyle (NG)
Covington, La., 1979
BRUNO, Phil (QB)
New Orleans, La., 1940
BRYAN, Jack (HB)
Starkville, Miss., 1943-44
BUCK, Gordon (Charlie) (HB)
Marksville, La., 1906-07
BUCKLES, William (C)
Memphis, Tenn., 1944
BULLIARD, Ed (LE)
St. Martinville, La., 1950-51
BULLOCK, Farris (C)
El Dorado, Ark., 1944
BULLOCK, Ray (E)
El Dorado, Ark., 1946-47-48-49
BUNDY, Charles (SE)
Gulfport, Miss., 1965-66
BURGE, Pete (E)
Poplarville, Miss., 1933
BURKETT, Jeff, (FB)
Laurel, Miss., 1941-42-46
BURAS, Leon (Buddy) (OG-OT)
Covington, La., 1973-74
BURNS, Craig (S)
Baton Rouge, La., 1968-69-70
BURKS, Michael P. (Mike) (OG)
Baton Rouge, La., 1979
BURNS, Matthew (QB)
Lake City, Fla., 1954-55-56
BURRELL, Clinton Blane (S)
Franklin, La., 1974-75-76-78
BYRAM, James E. (C)
Bossier City, La., 1900-01
BUSSE, Bert M. (T-G)
Alton, Ill., 1919-20-21
BUSSEY, Young (HB)
Houston, Tex., 1937-38-39
BUTAUD, Tommy (DT)
Crowley, La., 1971-72
BUTLER, W. E. (Bill) (HB)
Ponchatoula, La., 1929-30-31

C

CAIN, Clay (OG)
Sulphur, La., 1973-74
CAJOLEAS, Jimmy (QB)
New Orleans, La., 1937-38-39
CALHOUN, Shelby (T)
Bastrop, La., 1934
CAMBON, F. Joseph (G-T)
Dulac, La., 1893
CAMP, Ivan (C)
Haynesville, La., 1951-52-53-54
CAMPBELL, Cliff C. (Shorty) (T)
Liberty, Miss., 1921-22-23-24
CAMPBELL, Edward (Bo) (LHB)
Shreveport, La., 1960-61-62
CAMPBELL, Eugene P. (E)
Vidalia, La., 1893
CAMPBELL, Irving (T)
Fayette, Ala., 1937-38-39
CANGELOSI, Dale (CB)
Baton Rouge, La., 1971-72-73
CANNON, Billy (HB)
Baton Rouge, La., 1957-58-59

CANTRELLE, Arthur (TB)
Biloxi, Miss., 1969-70-71
CAPONE, Warren (LB)
Baton Rouge, La., 1971-72-73
CARLIN, Kent (C)
Sulphur, La., 1967
CARRIERE, Oliver P. (Ike) (QB)
New Orleans, La., 1923-24-25-26
CARROLL, Paul (T)
Lake Charles, La., 1935-36-37
CARSON, Carlos (SE)
West Palm Beach, Fla., 1977-78-79
CASANOVA, Jackie (S)
Crowley, La., 1975-76-77
CASANOVA, Tommy (CB)
Crowley, La., 1969-70-71
CASCIO, Louis (LB)
Bossier City, La., 1969-70-71
CASON, Jim (HB)
Victoria, Tex., 1944-45-46-47
CASSIDY, Ed (G)
Bogalusa, La., 1955-56-57
CASSIDY, Francis (C)
Bogalusa, La., 1940-41
CASSIDY, Steve (DT)
Baton Rouge, La., 1972-73-74-75
CAVIGGA, Al (G)
Jeanette, Pa., 1940-41-44
CHADWICK, Gene (QB)
Homer, La., 1941
CHAMBERLIN, W. Benjamin (Ben) (QB)
DeVall, La., 1897-98-99
CHAMPAGNE, Ed (T)
New Orleans, La., 1946
CHAMPAGNE, Gary (LB)
Nederland, Tex., 1971-72-73
CHANDLER, Walter B. (Teeter),
Shreveport, La., 1925-26
CHAVANNE, Edmund A. M. (C)
Lake Charles, La., 1896-97-98-99
CHRISTIAN, Mickey (DE)
Magnolia, Ark., 1967-68
CLAITOR, Otto (C)
Rayne, La., 1915
CLARK, Blythe (G)
Frenchman Bayou, Ark., 1937-38
CLARK, N. Jackson (TB)
Baton Rouge, La., 1976
CLARK, Samuel M. D. (LE)
DeVall, La., 1893-94
CLAUNCH, Ed (C)
Haynesville, La., 1943-46-47-48
CLAY, Jack T. (FB)
White Castle, La., 1924-25-29
CLEGG, Robert T. (Bobby) (LHB)
Baton Rouge, La., 1947-48
COATES, Ray (HB)
New Orleans, La., 1944-45-46-47
COCO, Walter A. (G)
Marksville, La., 1898
COFFEE, Al (SB)
Baton Rouge, La., 1970-72-73
COFFEE, Pat (HB)
Minden, La., 1935-36
COLE, F. E. (Estes) (C-G)
Franklin, Tex., 1929-30
COLE, John R. (Jack) (QB)
Bastrop, La., 1948-49-50
COLEMAN, John J. (HB)
New Orleans, La., 1899-1900-01-02-03
COLLE, Beau (LHB)
Pascagoula, Miss., 1963-64-65
COLLINS, Albin Harrell (Rip) (FB)
Baton Rouge, La., 1945-46-47-48
COLLINS, D. W. (Dan) (FB)
Shreveport, La., 1917
COLLINS, Ray (G)
Paradis, La., 1947-48-49
CONN, Bobby (CB)
Lake Charles, La., 1975-76-77
CONNELL, Allen P. (T)
White Creek, Tenn., 1924-25-26
CONNELL, George M. (C-T)
White Creek, Tenn, 1922-25
CONNELLY, Edwin M. (HB)
Houma, La., 1904

CONNER, John C. ( )
Monroe, La., 1894
CONWAY, Mike (KS)
Texarkana, Ark., 1975-76-77-78
COOK, Dave (CB)
Rayne, La., 1973-74-75
COOK, Frederick W. (Freddie) (E)
Houma, La., 1901
COOPER, Philip (Chief) (G)
Amite, La., 1913-14-15-16
COPES, Charles (FB)
Tylertown, Miss., 1950
CORE, Harvey (G)
Covington, La., 1944-45-46-47
CORGAN, Bill (B) 1943
CORMIER, Ken (LHB)
Jennings, La., 1963-64-65
CORMIER, Thomas (Skip) (DE)
Opelousas, La., 1971-72
COX, Mickey (RT)
Monroe, La., 1962-64
COYNE, Edward (Ed) (LT)
Bemis, Tenn., 1949-50-51
CRANFORD, Charles (FB)
Minden, La., 1960-61-62
CRASS, Bill (HB)
Electra, Tex., 1935-36
CRAWFORD, John Egan (G)
Liberty Hill, La., 1911-12-13
CUNNINGHAM, Ed (G)
Wilmington, N. C., 1937
CUPIT, George D. (LB)
Vidalia, La., 1976-77-78
CURTIS, Arthur M. (Jeff) (E)
New Orleans, La., 1921
CUSIMANO, Charles (G)
New Orleans, La., 1945-48-49

D

DAILY, Ron (DE)
Houston, Tex., 1972-73-74
DAMPIER, Al (FB)
Sicily Island, La., 1958
DANIEL, Loyd (OG)
Franklinton, La., 1970-71-72
DANIEL, Steve (G)
North Little Rock, Ark., 1966-67
DANTIN, Chris (TB)
Baton Rouge, La., 1970-71-72
DARK, Alvin (HB)
Lake Charles, La., 1942
DASPIT, Armand P. (HB)
Houma, La., 1895-96-97-98
DASPIT, Justin C. (HB)
Houma, La., 1895-96-97-98
DAVIS, Arthur (HB)
Pine Bluff, Ark., 1944
DAVIS, Arthur (DE-MG)
Sulphur, La., 1968-69-70
DAVIS, Brad (TB-RB)
Hammond, La., 1972-73-74
DAVIS, Grady (LHB)
Haynesville, La., 1951-52
DAVIS, R. L. (Bebee) (E-T)
Monroe, La., 1920-21
DAVIS, Tommy (FB-K)
Shreveport, La., 1953-58
DAYE, Donnie (HB)
Ferriday, La., 1958-59-60
DeCROSTA, Bob (TB)
Hudson, N. Y., 1956-57
deLAUNAY, Louis F. (Lou) (OG)
Neosho, Mo., 1976-77-78
DeLEE, Robert E. Jr. (TE)
Clinton, La., 1977-78-79
DEMARIE, John (OT)
Lake Charles, La., 1964-65-66
DEMARIE, Mike (OG)
Lake Charles, La., 1969-70-71
DENNIS, Gordon A. ( )
Shreveport, La., 1893
DENNIS, Rand (S)
Natchitoches, La., 1972-73-74
DeRUTTE, ROBERT (S)
Port Neches, Tex., 1978-79

DeSONIER, Richard (RE)
Morgan City, La., 1953
DESORMEAUX, Ronald Bill Jr. (TE)
New Iberia, La., 1976
DEUTSCHMANN, Lou (RHB)
New Orleans, La., 1953-54
DIBETTA, Gawain (FB)
New Orleans, La., 1964-65-66
DICKINSON, Wayne (SB-P)
Hattiesburg, Miss., 1970
DIDIER, Melvin (C)
Baton Rouge, La., 1944-45
DILDY, Gary (C)
Bogalusa, La., 1951-52-53-54
DIMMICK, Opie (QB-FB)
Shuteson, La., 1924-25-26
DINKLE, Gary Mitchell (Mitch) (TE)
Silsbee, Tex., 1974-75-76
DODSON, Adrian (HB)
Columbus, Miss., 1940-41
DOGGETT, Al (HB)
Homer, La., 1951-52-53-54
DOMINGUE, Rusty (LB)
Port Arthur, Tex., 1975-76
DONAHUE, Patrick Michael (Pat) (OG)
Baton Rouge, La., 1974
DOUSAY, Jim (TB)
Baton Rouge, La., 1965-66-67
DOW, Robert (SE)
Jackson, Miss., 1973-74-75-76
DOYLE, Mike (DE)
Houston, Tex., 1970
DREW, Harmon C. (G)
Minden, La., 1907-09
DRY, Ronald (RT)
Fairland, Okla., 1950
DUFRENE, Marty J. (C)
Larose, La., 1979
DUGAS, Robert W. (OT)
Luling, La., 1976-77-78
DUHE, A. J. Adam (DT)
Reserve, La., 1973-74-75-76
DUHE, Butch (QB)
New Orleans, La., 1969
DUHE, Craig (OT)
Lutcher, La., 1975-76-77
DUHON, Mike (MG)
Sulphur, La., 1964-65-66
DUMAS, Bernie (E)
El Dorado, Ark., 1935-36-37
DUNN, Lester, Jr. (FB)
Covington, La., 1979
DUNPHY, Robert Francis (Bo) (TE)
Houston, Tex., 1973-74-75
DUPONT, John M. (E)
Houma, La., 1911-12-13-14
DUPONT, Lawrence H. (Dutch) (QB-HB)
Houma, La., 1910-11-12-13
DUPREE, Sam G. ( )
Baton Rouge, La., 1893-94
DURRETT, Bert E. (E)
Arcadia, La., 1925-26-27
DUTTON, John G. (Pete) (E)
Minden, La., 1917-19-21
DUTTON, Thomas W. (T)
Minden, La., 1912-13-19
DYER, Jack (T)
Baton Rouge, La., 1965-66-67

E

EARLEY, Jim (DB)
Jonesboro, La., 1968-69-70
EASTMAN, Dan (T)
New Orleans, La., 1939-40-41
EDMONDS. Walter R. (Ray) (E)
Lyon, N. Y., 1915-19
EDMONSON, Arthur T. (Shorty) (HB)
Marshall, Tex., 1921-22-23
EDWARDS, Bill (G)
Little Rock, Ark., 1940-41-42
EDWARDS, Frank M. (Snake) (G)
Amite, La., 1903-04-05
EDWARDS, William E. Jr. (LB)
Metairie, La., 1976
EGAN, Raymond (G)
New Orleans, La., 1934
ELKINS, Brent Louis (CB)
Dallas, Tex., 1976-77-78

ELKINS, Jimmy (OG)
Crowley, La., 1970-71-72
ELLEN, Don (LG)
Monroe, La., 1963-64-65
ELLIS, Frank (T-G)
Covington, La., 1927-28-29
ENSMINGER, Steven Craig (QB)
Baton Rouge, La., 1976-77-78-79
ERDMANN, Charles (HB)
New Orleans, La., 1938
ESTAY, Ronnie (DT)
LaRose, La. 1969-70-71
ESTES, Don (LT)
Brookhaven, Miss., 1960-61-62
ESTES, Stephen Clayton (Steve) (OG)
Port Arthur, Tex., 1974-75-76
ESTHAY, Terry (LT)
Lake Charles, La., 1965-66-67
EVANS, Miller (G)
Vicksburg, Miss., 1941
EVANS, W. Morton (HB-E)
Baton Rouge, La., 1910-11-12-13
EWEN, Earl L. (Tubbo) (FB)
Bertrand, Neb., 1920-21-22-23
EZELL, Billy (QB)
Greenville, Miss., 1963-64-65

F

FAHEY, John K. (G)
Opelousas, La., 1903
FAKIER, Joe (SE)
Thibodaux, La., 1971-72-73
FAMBROUGH, Larry (FB)
Springhill, La., 1964-65
FARMER, Hermann (Red) (T)
Shreveport, La., 1936-37-38
FARRELL, William Y. (DE)
Pompano Beach, Fla., 1978-79
FATHERREE, JESSE L. (HB)
Jackson, Miss., 1933-34-35
FAY, Theodore D. (Red) (FB)
Jeanerette, La., 1923-24-25
FENTON, G. E. (Doc) (QB)
Scranton, Pa., 1907-08-09
FERGUSON, Commodore (T)
Memphis, Tenn., 1937
FERGUSON, O. K. (FB)
Woodville, Miss., 1955
FERGUSON, Pleasant L. (G)
Leesville, La., 1907
FERRER, Steve (DT-OG)
Metairie, La., 1973-74-75
FIELD, Elmer (Bubba) (HB)
Marshall, Tex., 1949
FIELD, Jimmy (QB)
Baton Rouge, La., 1960-61-62
FIFE, Robert (HB)
Waterproof, La., 1938
FLANAGAN, H. F. (Mike) (HB)
New Britain, Conn., 1916
FLEMING, Walter (Goat) (E)
Lake Charles, La., 1929-31-32
FLOOD, Martin T. (G)
Shreveport, La., 1925
FLOYD, J. C. (Red) (T-G)
Jena, La., 1915-16-19
FLUKER, H. V. (E)
Monroe, La., 1913
FLURRY, Bob (LE)
Homer, La., 1960-61-62
FOGG, Ed (LT)
Slidell, La., 1953-55
FOLEY, Art (HB)
Eugaula, Okla., 1931
FONTENOT, Ferdinand M. (FB)
Crowley, La., 1903
FORET, John (OT)
Lake Charles, La., 1971-72
FORET, Lynn (C)
Lake Charles, La., 1970
FORGEY, Charles W. M. (FB)
Berwick, La., 1923
FORTIER, Bill (T)
Jackson, Miss., 1966-67-68
FOTI, Russ (LG)
Ravenna, Ohio, 1947
FOURMY, James M. (QB)
Franklin, La., 1903-04

FOURNET, Emile (G)
Bogalusa, La., 1958-59
FOURNET, John B., (G)
St. Martinville, La., 1917-19
FOURNET, Sidney (LG)
Bogalusa, La., 1951-52-53-54
FRANCIS, Harrison (FB)
Franklin, La., 1975-76
FRANCIS, Jerome N. (DE)
Sulphur, La., 1979
FRAYER, Jack (T)
Toledo, Ohio, 1958-59
FREEMAN, G. A. (Nubs) (G-E)
Natchitoches, La., 1927
FREEMAN, G. Chester (RHB)
Baton Rouge, La., 1949-50-51
FREY, Ignatius (FB)
New Orleans, La., 1941
FRIEND, Ben (T)
Gulfport, Miss., 1936-37-38
FRIZZELL, Thos. N. (LB)
Athens, Tex., 1978-79
FROECHTENICHT, W. H. (E)
Blue Point, N. Y., 1939
FRYE, Barton (CB)
Baton Rouge, La., 1966-67-68
FRYE, Lloyd (LB)
Baton Rouge, La., 1969-70-71
FUCHS, George (G)
New Orleans, La., 1899-00-01
FUGLER, Max (C)
Ferriday, La., 1957-58-59
FULKERSON, Jack (E)
Hope, Ark., 1940-41-42
FUSSELL, Tommy (RT)
Baton Rouge, La., 1964-65-66

G

GAINEY, Jim (DE)
Hammond, La., 1971-72
GAJAN, Howard L., "Hokie" (TB)
Baton Rouge, La., 1977-78-79
GAMBLE, Harry P. (E)
Natchitoches, La., 1894-95
GANDY, Marshall H. (Cap) (T)
Negreet, La., 1906-07-08
GARDNER, Dennis (OG)
Crowley, La., 1975-76
GARDNER, Jim W. (E)
Minden, La., 1956-57
GARLAND, Joseph M. (G-T)
Opelousas, La., 1900
GARLINGTON, John (DE)
Jonesboro, La. 1965-66-67
GARY, Dexter (LG)
Kaplan, La., 1960-61
GATES, Jack (RE)
Lake Charles, La., 1960-61-62
GATTO, Eddie (T)
New Orleans, La., 1936-37-38
GAUBATZ, Dennis (C)
West Columbia, Tex., 1960-61-62
GAUTREAUX, Russell (FB)
Baton Rouge, La., 1952-53
GAYDEN, George L. (Hack) (E)
Gurley, La., 1926
GAYLE, Edwin F. (HB)
Legonier, Pa., 1893
GIACONE, Joe (HB)
Bogalusa, La., 1941-42
GIANELLONI, Vivian J. (G)
Baton Rouge, La., 1939-40
GILBERT, Jimmy (QB-DB-TB)
Bastrop, La., 1967-68-69
GILL, Audis (HB)
New Orleans, La., 1945
GILL, Reuben O. (Rube) (HB-E)
Ruston, La., 1907-08-09
GIOVANNI, Charles (Tony) (G)
Lake Charles, La., 1930-31
GLADDEN, Sterling (Buck) W. (HB)
Alexandria, La., 1919
GLAMP, Joe (HB)
Mt. Pleasant, Pa., 1942
GODCHAUX, Frank A. (QB)
Baton Rouge, La., 1897

GODFREY, Lola T. (Babe) **(QB)**
    Willington, Tex., 1925-26-**27**
GONZALES, Vincent (Vince) **(LHB)**
    New Orleans, La., 1952-53-**54-55**
GOREE, J. W. (G)
    Haynesville, La., 1938-39-40
GORINSKI, Walter (FB)
    Mutual, Pa., 1940-41-42
GORHAM, Edwin S. (E)
    Lake Charles, La., 1899-1900-**01**
GORMLEY, Jack (E)
    Tyler, Tex., 1936-37-38
GORMLEY, Richard (C)
    Tyler, Tex., 1936-37-38
GOSSERAND, M. L. (Goose) **(FB)**
    New Roads, La., 1910-11-**12**
GOODE, Burton (E)
    DeQuincy, La., 1943
GOURRIER, Samuel A. (QB-HB)
    Baton Rouge, La., 1896
GRAHAM, Durwood (C)
    Vicksburg, Miss., 1955-56
GRANIER, Richard (C)
    St. James, La., 1963-64
GRAVES, White (LHB)
    Crystal Springs, Miss., 1962-**63-64**
GRAY, Dale (LHB)
    El Dorado, Ark., 1946-47-48
GREEN, V. E. (Chick) **(FB)**
    DeRidder, La., 1914
GREEN, Winfred C. (Poss) **(HB)**
    DeRidder, La., 1913-14-**15-16**
GREENWOOD, Bobby (C)
    Lake Charles, La., 1959
GREER. Ed (QB) Minden, La., **1964**
GREMILLION, F. V. (T) 1899-**1900**
GREVEMBERG, Albert (T)
    Savannah, Ga., 1927
GREVEMBERG, Joseph H. (E)
    Savannah, Ga., 1926-27
GREZAFFI, Sammy (S)
    New Roads, La., 1965-66-67
GRIFFITH, Carroll (RHB)
    N. Little Rock, Ark., 1943-47-**48-49**
GRIFFITH, J. H. (John) (E)
    Jackson, Mich., 1905
GRIFFIN, Benny (LB)
    Baton Rouge, La., 1965-66-67
GRIVOT, Maurice ( )
    New Orleans, La., 1894
GROS, Earl (FB)
    Houma, La., 1959-60-61
GUENO, Albert J. (E)
    Crowley, La., 1901-02-03
GUGLIELMO, Al (RE)
    Lutcher, La., 1951-52-53
GUIDRY, J. W. (T)
    Opelousas, La., 1901-02-03
GUILLOT, Jerry (RG)
    Thibodaux, La., 1966-67-68
GUILLOT, Rodney (T)
    Baton Rouge, La., 1960-62
GUILLOT, Rodney (Monk) **(RG)**
    New Orleans, La., 1959-60-61
GUILLOT, Stephen Roch (Rocky) **(C)**
    Shreveport, La., 1976-77-78
GUNNELS, William D., Jr. **(DE)**
    Hahnville, La., 1977

H

HABERT, Ed (RG)
    Vicksburg, Miss., 1960-61-62
HAGUE, Perry G. (QB-HB)
    Baton Rouge, La., 1919-20
HALEY, Otis (B)
    Tyler, Tex., 1943
HALL, Fred (Skinny) (T-G-E)
    Haynesville, La., 1941-42-46
HALL, J. O. (Doc) (E)
    Lake Charles, La., 1909-10-**11-12**
HAMIC, Garland (Buddy) **(FB)**
    Crowley, La., 1961-62-63
HAMIC, Jimmy (RG)
    Crowley, La., 1965-66
HAMILTON, Andy (SB)
    Ruston, La., 1969-70-71
HAMILTON, W. J. (QB)
    Winnfield, La., 1907

HAMLETT, Bob (TE)
    Bossier City, La., 1966-67-68
HAMMOND, M. R. (Bull) **(HB-FB)**
    Jennings, La., 1910-11
HANDY, Beverly B. (Spaghetti) **(QB)**
    Monroe, La., 1907
HANLEY, William B. (Red) **(G-T)**
    Crowville, La., 1919
HARGETT, Dan (LG)
    Lafayette, La., 1960-61
HARP, James F. ( )
    Bonita, La., 1896
HARRELL, Louis (Tee-Tee) **(QB)**
    Baton Rouge, La., 1929
HARRIS, Bill (LT)
    Bossier City, La., 1953
HARRIS, Clinton (Bo) (LB)
    Shreveport, La., 1972-73-74
HARRIS, L. B. (T)
    Denham Springs, La., **1904**
HARRIS, Sulcer (HB)
    Baton Rouge, La., 1941-42
HARRIS, Wendell (HB)
    Baton Rouge, La., 1959-60-**61**
HARRISON, Pollard E. (E)
    Colfax, La., 1913
HARTLEY, Joe (T)
    St. Petersburg, Fla., 1943
HARVEY, Hugh (T-HB)
    Marksville, La. 1906
HATCHER, George R. (E)
    Clinton, La., 1927
HAYNES, Everette H. (Hinkey) **(HB)**
    Lineville, Ala., 1925-26-27
HAYNES, Fred (QB)
    Minden, La., 1966-67-68
HAYNES, George (LHB)
    Clinton, La., 1963-64-66
HEALD, Russell (OT)
    Texas City, Tex., 1971-72-73
HEARD, Holley (RT)
    Haynesville, La., 1942-47
HEARD, T. J. (Fatty) **(G)**
    Marksville, La., 1904-05
HEDGES, Lee (QB)
    Shreveport, La., 1949-50-**51**
HELM, Newton C. (Dirty) **(E)**
    Bunkie, La., 1919-20-21-**22**
HELMS, Lee (HB)
    Holmwood, La., 1926
HELSCHER, Harold (HB)
    New Orleans, La. 1941
HELVESTON, Osborn (Butch) **(G)**
    Biloxi, Miss., 1933-34-35
HEMPHILL, Fred Bruce (SE)
    Sulphur, La., 1974-75-76
HEMPHILL, Don (E)
    Bogalusa, La., 1945-46-47
HENDRICK, Bruce (QB)
    Birmingham, Ala., 1938
HENDRIX, Billy (E)
    Rayville, La., 1956-57-58
HENDRIX, John A. (Jonnie) **(HB)**
    Olla, La., 1928-29-30
HENDRIX, Sid W. (QB)
    Baton Rouge, La., 1922
HENRY Thomas J. (HB-FB)
    Alton, Ill., 1916
HENSLEY, James Craig (LB)
    Lake Charles, La., 1976-77-**78**
HERBERT Arthur W. (Doc) **(G)**
    Alexandria, La., 1916-17
HEREFORD, Robert M. **(T)**
    Lake Charles, La., 1920-**21**
HERGET, George Caldwell **(Warm-Up)**
    (E) Baton Rouge, La., 1925-**26**
HERNANDEZ, Jude B. (FB)
    Baton Rouge, La., 1978-79
HEROMAN, Alfred (LHB)
    Baton Rouge, La., 1946-47-48
HERPIN, Joseph O. (E)
    Lafayette, La., 1899-1901
HERRINGTON, James (G)
    Lake Providence, La., 1944
HEWETT, Lem F. (E)
    Lexington, Neb., 1920

HIGHTOWER, Gerald (HB)
    Arcadia, La., 1939-40-41
HILL, Jerry D. (LB)
    Midwest City, Okla., 1978-**79**
HILL, Terry (LB)
    Baton Rouge, La., 1973-**74-75**
HILLMAN, Mike (QB)
    Lockport, La., 1967-68-69
HILLMAN, William A. (G)
    Minden, La., 1906-07-08-09
HIMES, Levi A. (Lee) (QB)
    Baton Rouge, La., 1906-07-**08-09**
HINTON, Lora (TB-RB)
    Chesapeake, Va., 1973-74-**75**
HODGE, Abner A. ( )
    Natchez, Miss., 1894
HODGES, Harry (C)
    Baton Rouge, La., 1954-**55**
HODGINS, Leo M. (TE)
    Metairie, La., 1976
HODGINS, Norman (DB-SB)
    Metairie, La., 1971-72-73
HOGAN, Bill (QB-C)
    Laurel, Miss., 1939-40-41
HOLDEN, T. D. (E)
    Picayune, Miss., 1929-30
HOLLAND, Pershing (G-E)
    Plain Dealing, La., 1941-**42**
HOLLAND, Woodrow (E)
    Plain Dealing, La., 1942
HORNE, Frank (RT)
    Fayette, Ala., 1952
HOVER, Allen (E)
    Memphis, Tenn., 1948-49-50
HOWELL, Robert C. (E)
    Wilcox, La., 1903
HOWELL, Roland B. (Billiken) **(QB)**
    Thibodaux, La., 1909-11
HOWELL, William C. (E)
    St. Francisville, La., 1897
HUBBELL, Michael R. (Mickey) **(SB)**
    Metairie, La., 1978
HUCKLEBRIDGE, Robbie **(LG)**
    Bossier City, La., 1961-62-63
HUEY, James M. ( )
    Ruston, La., 1893
HUFFMAN, Alva S. (Brute) **(T)**
    DeRidder, La., 1926-27-28
HUGHES, Clyde B. (Red) **(T)**
    Baton Rouge, La., 1921-23
HUMBLE, John (C)
    Monroe, La., 1944
HUNSICKER, George R. (E)
    Shreveport, La., 1905
HUNT, Ralph (T)
    Shreveport, La., 1943
HUNTER, Guy N. ( )
    Waterproof, La., 1894
HUNTER, Louis T. ( )
    Waterproof, La., 1894
HUNTER, Robert (LE)
    Los Angeles, Cal., 1950
HURD, Roy (K)
    Covington, La., 1967
HUYCK, Philip P. (G)
    Baton Rouge, La., 1895-96-**97-99**

I

IPPOLITO, Mark A. (LB)
    New Orleans, La., 1978-**79**
INDEST, Adalphe (G)
    New Orleans, La., 1944
IVES, Clarence A. (Fatty) **(HB)**
    Baton Rouge, La., 1917-19-**20-21**

J

JACKSON, Augustus W. (Gus) **(FB)**
    LeCompte, La., 1922-23-24
JACKSON, Dalton (Rusty) **(KS)**
    Chatom, Ala., 1972-73-74
JACKSON, Steve Loran (S)
    Chatom, Ala., 1974-75-76
JAMES, Albert (T)
    Covington, La., 1940-41
JANNECK, Carl (G)
    New Orleans, La., 1943-44

JAUBERT, Jack (C)
  Lafayette, La., 1969-70-**71**
JENKINS, Darryl (QB)
  Franklinton, La., 1958-59-**60**
JENKINS, Harry (E)
  Crowley, La., 1904
JENKINS, Marvin (QB)
  Tupelo, Miss., 1939-40
JENNINGS, Joe Patrick **(DE)**
  Baker, La., 1974-75-76
JETER, Ronald (G)
  Ferriday, La., 1965-66-67
JOFFRION, A. Bush (HB)
  LeCompte, La., 1904-05
JOHNS, Levi (Chuck) (LHB)
  Rayville, La., 1953-54-55
JOHNSON, Charles (E)
  Conroe, Tex., 1938-39-40
JOHNSON, Melvin F. (HB)
  Lake Charles, La., 1912
JOHNSON, Michael K. (LB)
  Franklin, La., 1979
JOHNSON, Phil (C)
  Shreveport, La., 1965-66
JOHNSON, Ray L. (C)
  Electra, Tex., 1932
JOHNSON, William C. (OT)
  Athens, Tex., 1976-77-78
JOHNSTON, Jerry (HB)
  Waynesboro, Miss., 1956
JOHNSTON, Ronnie (HB)
  Bastrop, La., 1956
JONES, Benjamin M. (Ben) **(SE)**
  Ruston, La., 1972-73-74
JONES, Bertram H. "Bert" **(QB)**
  Ruston, La., 1970-71-72
JONES, Carroll (HB)
  Ruston, La., 1941
JONES, David (DB)
  West Monroe, La., 1966-67
JONES, Keith E. (G)
  Winnfield, La., 1915-16-17
JONES, Larry (C)
  Little Rock, Ark., 1953-54
JONES, LeRoid, E. (FB)
  Baton Rouge, La., 1977-**78-79**
JONES, LeRoyal A. (CB)
  Baton Rouge, La., 1977
JONES, Mike (OG)
  Shreveport, La., 1975
JONES, Norwood (Chubby) **(C)**
  Lake Providence, La., 1927-**28-29**
JONES, Richard (SE)
  West Monroe, La., 1965-66
JOSEPH, Jerry (DB)
  Baton Rouge, La., 1964-**65-66**

K

KAFFIE, Leopold (C)
  Natchitoches, La., 1897-98
KAHLDEN, Larry (G)
  Weimar, Tex., 1956-57-58
KAISER, Bradley (OT)
  New Orleans, La., 1975
KALIL, Emile (LT)
  McComb, Miss., 1952
KARAPHILLIS, John M. (S)
  Tarpon Springs, Fla., 1976
KAVANAUGH, Ken, Sr. (E)
  Little Rock, Ark., 1937-38-**39**
KAVANAUGH, Ken, Jr. (SE)
  Ft. Washington, Pa., 1969-**70-71**
KEIGLEY, Gerald (SB-SE)
  Greenville, Miss., 1970-71-**72**
KELLER, Joe L. (C)
  Reserve, La., 1930-31-32
KELLUM, Bill (E)
  Haynesville, La., 1945
KELLY, Angus H. (E)
  Colfax, La., 1906
KELLY, Charlie (RT)
  Natchez, Miss., 1951
KENDRICK, Herbert (T)
  Homer, La., 1939-40-41
KENDRICK, Robert (Bob) **(FB)**
  Homer, La., 1939
KENNEDY, Ralph M. (HB)
  Los Angeles, Calif., 1901-**02-03**

KENT, Gerry **(CB)**
  Jackson, Miss., 1966-67-**68**
KENT, John (C)
  Amite, La., 1931-32-33
KENNON, Robert F. (C)
  Minden, La., 1924
KHOURY, Ed (Big Ed) **(T)**
  Lake Charles, La., 1929-30-**31**
KILLEN, Logan (C)
  McDade, La., 1971-72-73
KIMBLE, DENNIS J. (S)
  Baton Rouge, La., 1977-**78-79**
KINCHEN, Gary (C)
  Baton Rouge, La., 1960-**61-62**
KINCHEN, Gaynell (E)
  Baton Rouge, La., 1958-59-**60**
KING, Bobby Joe (DT)
  Shreveport, La., 1968-69-**70**
KING, Larry (E)
  New Orleans, La., 1937
KING, Larry (FB)
  Lake Charles, La., 1955
KINGERY, Don (TB)
  Lake Charles, La., 1943
KINGERY, Wayne (HB)
  Lake Charles, La., 1945
KITTO, Armand (RE)
  New Orleans, La., 1948-49-**50**
KIZER, Roland C. (Chesty) **(QB)**
  Monticello, Ark., 1922
KNECHT, Jas. Doyle (CB)
  Natchitoches, La., 1972-73-**74**
KNIGHT, Alex A. (Butch) **(DE)**
  Baton Rouge, La., 1974-75-**76**
KNIGHT, Gene (Red) (FB)
  Bossier City, La., 1943-44-**45-46**
KNIGHT, Roy (C)
  El Dorado, Ark., 1935
KLOCK, Arthur E. (G)
  Cheneyville, La., 1912-13-**14-16**
KLOCK, E. L. (G)
  Cheneyville, La., 1902-03-**04-05**
KOBER, Jerry (E)
  Souderton, Pa., 1967-69
KOCH, David T. (OT)
  Houston, Tex., 1979
KONZ, Kenneth (LHB)
  Weimar, Tex., 1948-49-50
KOSMAC, Andrew (QB)
  Plains, Pa., 1942-45
KREMENTZ, F. B. (Freddy) **(E)**
  Baton Rouge, La., 1915-16

L

LABAT, Leroy (HB)
  LaPlace, La., 1951-52
LABRUZZO, Joe (LHB)
  Lockport, La., 1963-64-65
LAFAUCI, Tyler (OG-DT)
  New Orleans, La., 1971-72-73
LaFLEUR, Gregory L. (SE)
  Ville Platte, La., 1977-**79**
LALLY, Michael F. (HB)
  Jessup, Pa., 1908-10
LAMBERT, James (Coot) (S)
  Canton, Miss., 1967-68
LAMBERT, Sam (FB)
  Baton Rouge, La., 1895-96
LAND, Fred N. (T)
  N. Little Rock, Ark., 1944-**45-46-47**
LANE, Clifton R. (Clif) **(TE)**
  Monroe, La., 1976-77-78
LANDRY, Ben H. (T)
  Lake Charles, La., 1929
LANDRY, Henry E. (FB)
  Garyville, La., 1899-1900-02
LANDRY, M. J. (HB)
  Baton Rouge, La., 1945
LANDRY, Walter M. (Bud) **(G)**
  Westwego, La., 1921-22
LANDRY, Willard (LHB)
  Baton Rouge, La., 1945-46
LANE, Robert H. (QB-S)
  Monroe, La., 1979
LANGAN, John (C)
  Carbondale, Ill., 1957-58-59
LANGLEY, Leroy (HB)
  Jennings, La., 1932-33

LANGLEY, Willis (RT)
  Basile (Oberlin), La., 1962-**63**
LANOUX, Paul R., III (OT)
  New Orleans, La., 1974-**75-76**
LANSING, Bill (RG)
  Magnolia, Miss., 1950-51-**52**
LaSUEUR, Leon J. (G)
  Baton Rouge, La., 1902
LAVIN, Jim (T)
  New Orleans, La., 1956-**57**
LAWRASON, Charles M. **(E)**
  St.Francisville, La., 1899
LAWRENCE, Bob (LT)
  Brilliant, Ala., 1951-52
LAWRIE, Joe (QB)
  St. Petersburg, Fla., 1933-**34-35**
LAWTON, Jack E. Jr. (Jackie) **(CB)**
  Sulphur, La., 1976-77
LAY, Andrew (HB)
  Homer, La., 1944
LEACH, Joe (E)
  Shreveport, La., 1946-47
LEAKE, Sam (RT)
  Woodville, Miss., 1953
LeBLANC, Allen (T)
  New Iberia, La., 1965-66-67
LeBLANC, Danny (RHB)
  Lake Charles, La. 1962-63-65
LeBLANC, Lynn (T)
  Crowley, La., 1957-58-59
LeBLANC, Maurice (SB)
  Lafayette, La., 1966-67-68
LeBLEU, Claude A. (E)
  Lake Charles, La., 1929
LEDBETTER, Wiltz M. (G)
  Summerfield, La., 1895-96
LeDOUX, Jimmy (SE)
  Sulphur, La., 1970-71-72
LEE, David (DE)
  Bastrop, La., 1973
LEE, Felix (Buddy) (QB)
  Zachary, La., 1969-70
LEGGETT, Earl (T)
  Jacksonville, Fla., 1955-56
LEISK, Wardell (G)
  Shreveport, La. 1935-36
LELEKACS, Steve (LB)
  Angleton, Tex., 1972-73-74
LEMAK, Charles W. (TB)
  Duquesne, Pa., 1937
LEMOINE, Hampton T. (Tick) **(G)**
  Marksville, La., 1899
LEONARD, Michael B. (Mike) **(S)**
  Shreveport, La., 1974-75-76
LEOPARD, Duane (C)
  Baton Rouge, La., 1957-58-**59**
LeSAGE, Joe (QB)
  Homer, La., 1948
LESTER, Gordon (T)
  Lockhart, Tex., 1936-37
LeSUEUR, George B. (Heck) **(FB)**
  Baton Rouge, La., 1897-98-**99**
LEVY, Julius M. ( )
  Evergreen, La., 1897
LEWIS, James (LG)
  Tyler, Tex., 1943-47-48
LEWIS, John W. (Johnnie) **(E)**
  Opelousas, La., 1920-21
LEWIS, William J. (QB-HB)
  Ruston, La., 1894
LEWIS, William S. (Bill) (HB)
  DeRidder, La., 1915-16
LINDSEY, Clyde (E)
  Kilgore, Tex., 1944-45-46
LIPKIS, Bernie (C-E)
  New Orleans, La., 1939-40
LOBDELL, W. Y. (Bill) (QB)
  Baton Rouge, La., 1932-33
LOFLIN, Jim (E)
  New Orleans, La., 1946-47
LOFTIN, Billy (T)
  DeRidder, La., 1967-68
LONERGAN, Patrick M. (Pat) **(OG)**
  New Orleans, La., 1978
LOTT, Bobby (E)
  Texarkana, Ark., 1956

LOTT, Tommy (G)
  Texarkana, Ark., 1957-58-59
LOUSTALOT, Albert L. (HB)
  Franklin, La., 1903
LOUSTALOT, Matthew L. (Matt) (C)
  Franklin, La., 1923
LOUVIERE, William H. (Chick) (C)
  Houma, La., 1914
LUKER, J. B. (E)
  Alexandria, La., 1928-29-30
LUMPKIN, Mark (KS)
  Lake Charles, La. 1967-68-69
LYLE, Jim (Egg) (LE)
  El Dorado, Ark., 1948-49-50
LYLE, Mel (E)
  El Dorado, Ark., 1946-47-48-49
LYLES, William M. (Buffalo) (T)
  Leesville, La., 1904-07
LYONS, Frederick G. (QB)
  New Orleans, La., 1893
LYONS, Pat (QB)
  Midland, Tex., 1975-76-77
LYONS, Paul (QB)
  Midland, Tex., 1970-71-72

M

MAGGIORE, Ernest (LT)
  Norco, La., 1963-64-65
MAHFOUZ, Robert P. (QB)
  Lafayette, La., 1979
MAHTOOK, Robert   , Jr., (LB)
  Lafayette, La., 1978-79
MALONE, Jim (G-T)
  Reform, Ala., 1930-31-32
MAMOUDIS, Charles G. (Chuck) (FL)
  Chesapeake, Va., 1974-75
MANGHAM, Mickey (E)
  Kensington, Md., 1958-59-60
MANTON, Ronnie (G)
  Brookhaven, Miss., 1965-66-67
MARCHAND, Jerry (LHB)
  Baton Rouge, La., 1952-53
MARSHALL, Leonard A (DT)
  Franklin, La., 1979
MARTIN, C. Y. (G)
  Bowie, La., 1910
MARTIN, Curtis (SE)
  Golden Meadow, La., 1969
MARTIN, G. H. (G)
  Crowley, La., 1914
MARTIN, Jackie (FB)
  Haynesville, La., 1950
MARTIN, Steve (DT-OG)
  Houston, Tex., 1968-70
MARTIN, Wade O. (Skinny) (E)
  Arnaudville, La., 1902-03-04
MASON, C. C. (Charlie) (QB)
  Shreveport, La., 1926-27-28
MASTERS, Billy (E-SB)
  Olla, La., 1964-65-66
MATHERNE, Durel (QB)
  Lutcher, La., 1958-59
MATLOCK, Oscar (RG)
  Shreveport, La., 1936
MATTE, Frank (SB)
  Jennings, La., 1966-67-68
MATTHEWS, Lawrence R. (Tubbo)
  (FB) St. Francisville, La., 1922-23
MAY, Bill (QB-FB)
  El Dorado, Ark., 1934-35-36
MAY, William J. (Jon) (DT)
  Homer, La., 1977
MAY, Joe (HB)
  Shreveport, La., 1954-55-56
McCAGE, Samuel V. (TE)
  Baytown, Tex., 1977-78-79
McCALL, Henry L. (Mac) (E)
  Lake Charles, La., 1923-26
McCANN, John (RG)
  Baton Rouge, La., 1968-69-70
McCANN, M. G. (Mickey) (HB)
  New Orleans, La., 1927
McCARSON, Paul (HB)
  Batesville, Ark., 1944
McCARTY, Dave (T-E)
  Rayville, La., 1958-59

McCASKILL, Larry (T)
  Baton Rouge, La., 1967-68
McCLAIN, Jess (C)
  Covington, La., 1930-31
McCLAIN, Scotty (E)
  Smackover, Ark., 1957-58-59
McCLELLAND, William (RG)
  Crowley, La., 1943-44-47-48
McCOLLAM, Andrew M. (HB)
  Houma, La., 1909
McCORMICK, Dave (LT)
  Rayville, La., 1963-64-65
McCREEDY, Ed (G)
  Biloxi, Miss., 1958-59-60
McDANIEL, Orlando K. (SE)
  Lake Charles, La., 1978-79
McDONALD, Robert (LE)
  Franklin, La., 1960
McDUFF, Chas. H. (OT)
  Baton Rouge, La., 1978-79
McFARLAND, Reggie A. (HB)
  Baton Rouge, La., 1919-20-21-22
McFERRIN, Sherman S. (Mack) (G)
  Pleasant Hill, La., 1929
McHENRY, Barney G. (Mac) (T)
  Monroe, La., 1910-11
McINGVALE, Ralph C. (OT)
  Dallas, Tex., 1977
McKINNEY, Billy (HB)
  Jackson, Tenn., 1939-41
McKINNEY, Jim (QB)
  Bogalusa, La., 1939
McLEOD, James (E)
  Laurel, Miss., 1941-42-47
McLEOD, Ralph (LE)
  Beaumont, Tex., 1950-51-52
McNAIR, Dan (OG)
  Monroe, La., 1973
McNEESE, Oswald W. (E)
  Lake Charles, La., 1900-01
McSHERRY, Robert (LB)
  Monroe, La., 1967-68
MENETRE, Ralph (LHB)
  Covington, La., 1945
MERCER, John (RHB)
  Bossier City, La., 1961-62
MESSA, Rene A. (FB)
  Santiago, Cuba, 1904-05
MESSINA, Jack (G)
  Port Arthur, Tex., 1937-38-39
MESTAYER, Otto (E)
  New Iberia, La., 1914
MICHAELSON, Fred (MG-T)
  Foley, Ala., 1967-68-69
MICHAELSON, Julius (Jay) (TE)
  Foley, Ala., 1969-70-71
MICIOTTO, Charles (Binks) (DE)
  Lafayette, La., 1971-72-73
MICKAL, Abe (HB)
  McComb, Miss., 1933-34-35
MIHALICH, John (Mickey) (E)
  Lorain, Ohio, 1934-35-36
MILEY, Mike (QB)
  Metairie, La., 1972-73
MILLER, Charles (Chip) (DT)
  New Orleans, La., 1972-73
MILLER, Ben R. (E)
  Shreveport, La., 1923-24-25
MILLER, Dale (FB)
  Franklinton, La., 1971
MILLER, Fred (RT)
  Homer, La., 1960-61-62
MILLER, Herd (T-G)
  Springfield, La., 1943-44-45-46
MILLER, Paul (LT)
  Baton Rouge, La., 1950-52-53
MILLER, Willie (G)
  Minden, La., 1940-41-42
MILLET, Walter (CB)
  Pasadena, Tex., 1973
MILLICAN, Samuel (Buddy) (DE)
  Baton Rouge, La., 1968-69-70
MILNER, Guy (Cotton) (HB)
  Alexandria, La., 1936-37-38
MINALDI, Thad (FB)
  Lake Charles, La., 1975-76-77-78

MISTRETTA, Albert (T)
  Covington, La., 1943
MITCHELL, George (Gee) (G)
  Rayville, La., 1932-33
MITCHELL, Jim (E)
  Baton Rouge, La., 1952-53-56
MIXON, Neil (HB)
  Amite, La., 1931-32-33
MOBLEY, Larry (RE)
  Baton Rouge, La., 1952-54
MOBLEY, T. R. (Ray) (G-C)
  Coushatta, La., 1913-14
MODICUT, Joseph (LG)
  Baton Rouge, La., 1951-52
MONGET, Gayle (C)
  Baton Rouge, La., 1937-38-39
MONSOUR, Eli (Mike) (E)
  Shreveport, La., 1927
MONTGOMERY, William (FB)
  Murphysboro, Ill., 1942-43-45
MOORE, Charles (E)
  Chattanooga, Tenn., 1964-65
MOORE, Charles F. (SB)
  Plaquemine, La., 1964-65
MOORE, D. Haywood (G-T)
  Jonesboro, La., 1928-29-31
MOORE, Frank E. (Specks) (E)
  Douglas, Ariz., 1932-33-34
MOREAU, Kenneth R. "Bobby" (QB-LB)
  Alexandria, La. 1975-76-77
MOREAU, Doug (LE)
  Baton Rouge, La., 1963-64-65
MOREL, Tommy (SE)
  New Orleans, La., 1966-67-68
MORGAN, Mike (RE)
  Natchez, Miss., 1961-62-63
MORGAN, Paul C. (FB-HB)
  Elba, Ala. 1927
MORGAN, Sam R. (T)
  Elba, Ala., 1924-25-26
MORRIS, John E. (T)
  West Monroe, La., 1895
MORTIMER, Eugene H. (HB)
  Laurel, Miss., 1900
MORTON, Arthur (Slick) (HB-TB)
  Tallulah, La., 1935-36-37
MOSES, Phil (C)
  Sulphur, La., 1972-73-74
MULLER, J. C. (HB)
  Washington, La., 1904-05
MULLINS, William B. (E)
  Simsboro, La., 1894
MUNDINGER, Adam G. (Addie) (T)
  Baton Rouge, La., 1900-01-02
MURPHREE, Jerry D. (TB)
  Birmingham, Ala., 1977-78-79
MURPHY, Sammy (RE)
  Baker, La., 1952-53-54
MURRAY, Phil (OT)
  Franklinton, La., 1970-71-72
MYLES, Jesse J. (TB)
  Gray, La., 1979
MYLES, Lonny (SE)
  Franklinton, La., 1967-68
MYRICK, Basil (LE)
  El Dorado, Ark., 1936

N

NAGATA, Joe (HB)
  Eunice, La., 1942-43
NAGLE, John (CB)
  Gloster, Miss., 1969-70-71
NEALY, Wrendall (RE)
  Homer, La., 1951-52
NECK, Tommy (HB)
  Marksville, La., 1959-60-61
NELKEN, William ( )
  Natchitoches, La., 1894
NELSON, Manson (G)
  Ferriday, La., 1958-59
NELSON, Robert J. ( )
  Monroe, La., 1894
NESOM, Guy W. (T)
  Tickfaw, La., 1926-27-28
NEUMANN, Danny (E)
  Tallulah, La., 1961-62-63

NEUMANN, Leonard (TB)
Tallulah, La., 1964-65-66
NEVILS, Ab (T)
Lake Charles, La., 1931-32-33
NEWFIELD, Kenny (FB)
New Orleans, La., 1966-67-68
NEWELL, Edward T. J. ( )
St. Joseph, La., 1894
NICAR, Randy (DT)
Morgan City, La., 1971
NICHOLSON, Gordon B. (HB)
Baton Rouge, La., 1894-95-96-97
NICOLO, Sal (HB)
Saugus, Mass., 1952-54
NOBLET, Oren H. (Babe) (G)
Livingston, La., 1904-05-07-08
NOONAN, James (DT)
New Orleans, La., 1976
NORSWORTHY, Bill (DB)
New Orleans, La., 1968-69-70
NORWOOD, Don (E)
Baton Rouge, La., 1957-58-59
NUNNERY, R. B. (RT)
Summit, Miss., 1954-55

O

OAKLEY, Charles (FB)
Lake Charles, La. 1951-52-53
O'BRIEN, Robert (Bob) (TE)
New Orleans, La. 1964-65-66
O'CALLAGHAN, Joe (HB)
Summerville, Mass. 1952
ODOM, Sammy Joe (LB)
Minden, La., 1961
O'DONNELL, Joe (HB)
Ovett, Miss., 1940
OGDEN, Don G. (QB)
Baton Rouge, La., 1929-30
OLIVER, George (RT)
Little Rock, Ark., 1952
OLIVER, L. A. (E)
Lafayette, La.,.1901
O'QUIN, Arthur (Mickey) (E)
Shreveport, La., 1914-15-16-17
O'QUIN, Leon (QB)
Natchitoches, La., 1914
OUSTALET, Jimmy (C)
Lake Arthur, La., 1972-73-75
OWENS, Richard (Ricki) (LB)
Homer, La., 1967-68-69

P

PARDO, Diego (QB)
Panama, 1944
PARIS, Ted (C)
Leesville, La., 1954-55-56
PARKER, Enos (T)
Mobile, Ala., 1953-54 55-56
PARNHAM, Spencer (T)
Hawthorne, N.J., 1945
PEEBLES, Leo (Les) (HB)
Shreveport, La., 1928-29
PEGUES, William T. (T)
Mansfield, La., 1900
PERE, Ralph (LT)
LaRose, La., 1961-62-63
PERCY, Chaille (FB)
Baton Rouge, La., 1968-69
PERRY, Boyd (LB)
Orange, Tex., 1970-71
PEVEY, Charles (QB)
Jackson, Miss., 1946-47-48-49
PHARIS, Mike (C)
Shreveport, La., 1965-66
PHELPS, Joe R. (Polly) (QB)
Shreveport, La. 1927
PHILLIPS, Ivan J. (DT)
New Orleans, La., 1977-78-79
PHILLIPS, Marty (DT)
Baton Rouge, La., 1973-74
PICKETT, Garland (E)
Temple, Tex. 1933
PICOU, Richard (LB)
Gonzales, La., 1969-70-71
PIERCE, Spike (DB)
Baton Rouge, La., 1965

PIKE, Mike (S)
Metairie, La., 1973-74-75
PILLOW, Dudley (E)
Greenwood, Miss., 1939-40
PILLOW, Walter (TE)
Greenwood, Miss., 1963-64-65
PITALO, Alex M. (C)
Biloxi, Miss., 1950
PITCHER, James E. (Jim) (HB)
Hammond, La., 1917
PITCHER, William (HB)
Hammond, La., 1922-23-24
PITTMAN, Albert (G)
New Orleans, La., 1944
PITTMAN, J.S. (Big Pitt) (G)
Lake Providence, La., 1914-15
PITTMAN, Paul (T)
Hot Springs, Ark., 1937
PLATOU, R. (HB)
Brooklyn, N.Y., 1915
PLEASANT, Ruffin G. (QB)
Farmerville, La., 1893
POLLOCK, William M. (Judge) (T)
Bernice, La., 1908-09-10
POLOZOLA, Steve (CB)
Baton Rouge, La., 1967-68-69
PORTA, Ray (Coon) (QB)
Baton Rouge, La., 1948
PORTER, Tracy R. (SB)
Baton Rouge, La., 1979
POTTER, Ray (T)
Peabody, Mass., 1949-50-51
POTTS, John H. (E)
Baton Rouge, La., 1910
POWELL, R. H. (Bob) (T)
Quitman, La., 1929-30-31
POWELL, Tommy (RT)
Bogalusa, La., 1963-64-65
PRATHER, Trey (QB)
Shreveport, La., 1966
PRATT, George K. (T)
New Orleans, La., 1899
PRATT, Joel M. (E)
Baton Rouge, La., 1893
PRESCOTT, Aaron (RT)
Washington, La., 1893
PRESCOTT, Dickie (HB)
St. Francisville, La., 1951-52-54
PRESCOTT, Willis B. (FB)
Washington, La., 1893-94
PRESSBURG, Joel W. (G)
Baton Rouge, La., 1929-30
PRICKETT, Greg (DE)
Houston, Tex., 1975-76
T. J. PRICE (HB)
Alexandria, La., 1939
PRUDHOMME, Remi (LG)
Opelousas, La., 1962-63-64
PURVIS, Don (Scooter) (HB)
Crystal Springs, Miss., 1957-58-59

Q

QUINN, Marcus (SB)
New Orleans, La., 1977-78-79
QUINTELA, Mike (SE)
Port Arthur, Tex., 1975-76-77-78
QUIRK, Lewis A. W. (T)
Washington, La., 1894-95

R

RABB, Carlos C. (DRT)
Ferriday, La., 1966-67-68
RABB, Warren (QB)
Baton Rouge, La., 1957-58-59
RABENHORST, Oscar D. (Dudey) (QB)
Baton Rouge, La., 1921-22
RACINE, Frank (S)
Shreveport, La., 1971-72-73
RADECKER, Gary (OG)
New Orleans, La., 1975-77-78
RAIFORD, Albert (Rock) (DT-OG)
Destrehan, La., 1972-73-74-75
RAY, Eddie (FB)
Vicksburg, Miss., 1967-68-69

RAYMOND, Gregory P. (OT)
Metairie, La., 1979
REAGAN, C. R. (Jerry) (HB)
Jackson, La. 1915
REBSAMEN, Paul (QB)
Eudora, Ark., 1955
REDHEAD, J. A. (T)
Vicksburg, Miss., 1901
REDING, Joe (LT-G)
Bossier City, La., 1966-67-68
REED, J. T. (Rock) (HB)
Haynesville, La., 1934-35-36
REEDY, Frank (T)
Baton Rouge, La., 1929
REEVES, W. A. (Dobie) (HB)
Lake Charles, La., 1928-29-30
REID, Alfred J. (Alf) (FB)
Lake Charles, La., 1912-13-14-15
REID, Joseph (Joe) (C)
Meridian, Miss., 1948-49-50
REILY, Charles S. (T)
Clinton, La., 1910-11-12
RENFROE, John C. (Cherry) (HB)
San Antonio, Tex. 1927
RENFROE, John C. (QB)
San Diego, Cal., 1929-30
RENFROE, Olin (HB)
Ft. Myers, Fla., 1956
REYNOLDS, Gerald (Jerry) (LG)
Baton Rouge, La., 1947-48
REYNOLDS, M. C. (QB)
Mansfield, La., 1955-56
RHODES, H. J. (G)
Vicksburg, Miss., 1900-01-02
RICE, George (T)
Baton Rouge, La., 1963-64-65
RICE, R. E. (Red) (C)
West Plains, Mo., 1915-16
RICE, Robert (T)
Lake Charles, La., 1962
RICH, Christopher J. (Chris) (OT)
San Antonio, Tex., 1976-77-78
RICHARDS, Bobby (T)
Oak Ridge, Tenn., 1960-61
RICHARDSON, Albert J. III
Baton Rouge, La., 1979
RICHARDSON, Lyman (QB)
Shreveport, La., 1940-41-42
RICHMOND, Dilton (E)
Nacogdoches, Tex., 1941-42-46
RINAUDO, Martin (B)
New Roads, La., 1943
RIPPLE, Steve (LB)
Metairie, La., 1975-76-77
RITTINER, Chris M. (SB)
New Orleans, La., 1976
RIVERO, V. Victor (HB-E)
Monterey, Mex., 1904
ROANE, James A. (RG)
Vienna, La., 1893
ROBERTS, Henry Lee (HB)
North Little Rock, Ark., 1958
ROBERTSON, Archie Ed (FB)
Plaquemine, La., 1896
ROBICHAUX, Al (T)
Taft, La., 1951-52-53
ROBICHAUX, Mike (E)
Raceland, La., 1965-66
ROBINSON, Dwight (DB)
Ponchatoula, La., 1961-62-63
ROBINSON, Johnny (HB)
Baton Rouge, La., 1957-58-59
ROBISKIE, Terry (RB-TB)
Lucy, La., 1973-74-75-76
ROCA, Juan (KS)
Metairie, La., 1972-73-74
RODRIGUE, J. C. (Friday) (HB-FB)
Duboin, La., 1915-16
RODRIGUE, Ruffin (C)
Thibodaux. La., 1962-63-64
ROGER, Don (LB)
Garland, Tex. 1972-73-74
ROGERS, Steve (TB-RB)
Ruston, La., 1972-73-74
ROHM, Charles (Pinky) (HB)
New Orleans, La., 1935-36-37
ROMAIN, Richard (FL)
Gretna, La., 1973-74

ROSHTO, James (Jimmy) **(HB)**
Baton Rouge, La., 1949-50-**51**
ROSS, George (LB)
Lake Charles, La., 1975
ROUSSOS, George (G)
Santa Ana, Cal., 1949-50
ROWAN, Elwyn (FB)
Memphis, Tenn., 1944
RUKAS, Justin (Ruke) (T)
Gary, Ind., 1933-34-35
RUSSELL, Randy (OT)
West Monroe, La., 1971-**72**
RUSSELL, Tony (G)
Tallulah, La., 1967-68-69
RUTLAND, James (Pepper) **(LB)**
Baton Rouge, La., 1970-**71-72**
RUTLEDGE, D. H. (Don) (E)
Robeline, La., 1917
RYAN, Mike (DB)
Mooringsport, La., 1967
RYAN, Warren (Pat) (G-T)
New Orleans, La., 1908-09
RYDER, Robert (Red) (OT)
Alexandria, La., 1968-69

S

SAGE, John (T)
Houston, Tex., 1968-69-**70**
SAIA, S. J. (LB)
Baton Rouge, La., 1975-76
ST. DIZIER, Roger V. (Blue) **(E-G)**
New Roads, La., 1916-17
SALASSI, John R. (G)
French Settlement, La., **1894-95-96**
SANCHEZ, A. C. (G)
Santa Lucia, Cuba, 1914
SANDERS, Al (Apple) (C)
Baton Rouge, La., 1945-46
SANDERS, James W. (C)
Franklin, La., 1895
SANDIFER, Dan (HB)
Shreveport, La., 1944-45-46-47
SANDRAS, Jules (T)
Westwego, La., 1956
SANFORD, James (Jim) (T)
Covington, La., 1951-52
SANFORD, Joseph H. (QB)
Baton Rouge, La., 1901
SCHEXNAILDRE, Merle **(FB)**
Houma, La., 1958-59
SCHNEIDER, Edward D. (Pete) **(LG)**
Lake Providence, La., 1920
SCHNEIDER, Frederick H. (G)
Lake Providence, La., **1894-95-96**
SCHNEIDER, F. H. (Teddy) **(G)**
Lake Providence, La., 1929-30
SCHOENBERGER, George C. **(E)**
Buras, La., 1893-96
SCHROLL, Charles (C)
Alexandria, La., 1946
SCHROLL, Bill (FB)
Alexandria, La., 1946-47-48
SCHROLL, William (FB)
Alexandria, La., 1943
SCHURTZ, Hubert (T)
Pinckneyville, Ill., 1946-47
SCHWAB, Don (FB)
Thibodaux, La., 1963-64-**65**
SCHWALB, Gerald (Jerry) **(G)**
Baton Rouge, La., 1954-57
SCHWING, Ivan H. (QB)
Lake Charles, La., 1899-**1900**
SCOTT, Edwin A. (Ned) (T-L)
Wilson, La., 1895-96-97
SCOTT, E. E. (C)
Kingston, La., 1893-94
SCOTT, Malcolm M. **(TE)**
New Orleans, La., 1979
SCREEN, Pat (QB)
New Orleans, La., 1963-64-**65**
SCULLY, Don (G)
St. Petersburg, Fla., 1955-**56**
SEAGO, Ernest (Son) (FB)
Temple, Tex., 1933-34-35
SEBASTIAN, James A. (HB-E)
Spring Ridge, La., 1901

SESSIONS, Wayne (SE)
Springhill, La., 1965-66
SEIP, John J. (E)
Allentown, Pa., 1907-08-09-**10**
SHARP, Linden E. (C)
Baton Rouge, La., 1902
SHAW, Elton (G)
Kentwood, La., 1952
SHEEHY, Billy (E)
Mobile, Ala., 1956
SHERBURNE, Thomas L. **(G)**
Baton Rouge, La., 1897-98
SHIRER, Joe (HB)
New Orleans, La., 1950-51
SHOAF, James (Jim) (T)
Greensburg, Pa., 1948-49-50
SHOREY, Allen (TB)
Ruston, La., 1969-70-71
SIBLEY, Llewellyn R. (Lew) **(DE)**
Longview, Tex., 1974-75-**76-77**
SIGREST, Ed (E)
Bogalusa, La., 1944-45
SIMMONS, Charles (T)
Moss Point, Miss. 1962-64
SIMMONS, Kelly (FB)
Houston, Tex., 1975-76-77
SIMMONS, Ray (HB)
El Dorado, Ark., 1952
SIMES, Ashford (HB)
Houston, Tex., 1938-39
SKIDMORE, Claude (Skid) **(QB)**
Winchester, Tenn., 1931-**32**
SKIDMORE, Jim (Big Skid) **(T)**
Winchester, Tenn., 1930-31-**32**
SLAUGHTER, William S. **(E)**
Port Hudson, La., 1894-95-**96-97-98**
SMEDES, William C. (C)
Vicksburg, Miss., 1893-94
SMITH, Benny (Gunboat) **(E)**
Bossier City, La., 1919
SMITH, Billy (E)
Ruston, La., 1955-56-57
SMITH, Charlie (C)
El Dorado, Ark., 1950-51
SMITH, Clarence I. (HB)
Albion, Mich., 1905-06-08
SMITH, David C. (SB)
Natchez, Miss., 1976
SMITH, Glenn (TB)
New Orleans, La., 1967-68
SMITH, Guy (LE)
Marshall, Tex., 1952
SMITH, John Hugh (G)
Shreveport, La., 1936-37-**38**
SMITH, Rollis (E)
Dubach, La., 1944
SMITH, Spencer L. (OG)
Baton Rouge, La., 1976-**77-78**
SMITH, Tom (FB)
Alexandria, La., 1929-30-**31**
SMITH, Thielen (LB)
Metairie, La., 1973-74-75
SMITH, Tommy (LB)
Brookhaven, Miss., 1970
SMITH, V. E. (Bob) (HB)
Albion, Mich., 1905-08
SNYDER, John E. (Texas) **(QB)**
Georgetown, Tex., 1894-95
SOEFKER, Buddy (HB)
Memphis, Tenn., 1961-62-**63**
SOILEAU, Danny L. (FB)
Elton, La., 1977-78-79
SOWELL, Claude (HB)
Crowville, La., 1926
SPENCE, Ray (T)
Shreveport, La., 1956-57
SPENCER, Curtis (HB)
Grove, La., 1925
SPENCER, Floyd W. (E)
Grove, La., 1912-13
SPENCER, Fritz L. (C)
Grove, La., 1919-20-21
SPENCER, George B. (G)
Grove, La., 1911-13-14
SPENCER, Hugh Frank (T-G-C)
Grove, La., 1916-17

STAFFORD, David Grove (HB-**FB)**
Alexandria, La., 1919
STAGG, Jack (B)
Eunice, La., 1943-44
STAGGS, John (S)
Texas City, Tex., 1970-71-**72**
STANFORD, John T. ( )
Baton Rouge, La., 1898-99
STAPLES, Duncan P. ( )
Alexandria, La., 1894-97
STANTON, Edward J. **(OT)**
Friendswood, Tex., 1977-78
STAPLES, Jake (FB)
Calhoun, La., 1937-38-39
STAUDINGER, Louis P. (QB)
New Orleans, La., 1904
STAYTON, William D. (Judge) **(C)**
Keatchie, La., 1903-04
STEELE, John E. (Pug) (T)
Yadkin Valley, N.C., 1921-**23-24-25**
STELL, J. H. (Jabbo) (HB)
Shreveport, La., 1937-38
STEPHENS, Harold (LB)
Baton Rouge, La., 1966-67-**68**
STEVENS, Ed (HB-QB)
Picayune, Miss., 1930-31
STEVENS, Norman G. (Steve) **(E)**
Picayune, Miss., 1922-23-24-**25**
STEVENS, Norman (QB)
Picayune, Miss., 1950-51-52
STEWART, Marvin (Moose) **(C)**
Picayune, Miss., 1934-35-36
STINSON, Don (HB)
Shreveport, La., 1954-55
STOBER, Bill (E)
Rockford, Ohio, 1967-68-69
STOKLEY, Nelson (QB)
Crowley, La., 1965-66-67
STONECIPHER, Wade (E)
Haynesville, La., 1939
STOVALL, Hefley H. (Hank) **(QB)**
Dodson, La., 1927-28
STOVALL, Jerry (HB)
West Monroe, La., 1960-61-**62**
STOVALL, Lloyd J. (C)
Dodson, La., 1932-33-34
STOVALL, Robert L. (Strauss) **(C)**
Dodson, La., 1906-07-08-09
STOVALL, Rowson F. (G)
Dodson, La., 1907-08-09
STRANGE, Charles (Bo) (T)
Baton Rouge, La., 1958-59-**60**
STRANGE, Clarence (Pop) **(T)**
El Dorado, Ark., 1935-36
STRANGE, David (G)
Baton Rouge, La., 1963-64-**65**
STANTON, Edward J., Jr., **(OT)**
Friendswood, Tex., 1977-**78-79**
STREETE, Jon G. (LB)
Lake Charles, La., 1974-75-76
STREETE, Steve (OG-OT)
Lake Charles, La., 1971-72
STRICKLAND, Tom (OT)
Houston, Tex., 1972-73
STRINGFIELD, Cliff (QB)
Bogalusa, La., 1951-52-53
STROTHER, Howard (T)
Baton Rouge, La., 1945-48
STUART, Charles (OT)
Sterlington, La., 1969-70-71
STUART, Roy J. (OG)
Jackson, Miss., 1974-75-76
STUMPH, John C. (Shorty) **(G)**
New Orleans, La. 1926
STUPKA, Frank (T)
Bogalusa, La., 1934-35
STUPKA, Mike (G)
Bogalusa, La., 1958-59
SULLIVAN, Walter (Sully) **(HB)**
Hazelhurst, Miss., 1932-33-34
SWANSON, A. E. (Nip) (E-T)
Quitman, La., 1926-27-28
SWANSON, Arthur L. (Red) **(G-FB-T)**
Quitman, La., 1923-24-25
SYKES, Gene (E)
Covington, La., 1960-61-62

T

TALBOT, Edward L. (HB)
Napoleonville, La., 1912
TALLEY, Jim (C)
Houston, Tex., 1941-42
TARASOVIC, George (C)
Bridgeport, Conn., 1951
TAYLOR, Jimmy (FB)
Baton Rouge, La., 1956-57
TEAL, Willie Jr. (CB)
Texarkana, Tex., 1976-77-**78-79**
TEXADA, James C. (G-T)
Alexandria, La., 1906
THIBODEAUX, Chester B. (Benjy) (DT)
Rayne, La., 1977-78-79
THOMAS, Alvin W., Jr. (CB)
Donaldsonville, La., 1979
THOMAS, Arthur J. (Tommy) (G)
Baton Rouge, La., 1908-09-**10-11**
THOMASON, Bill (LB)
Sulphur, La., 1967-68-69
THOMPSON, Leon (TE)
Shreveport, La., 1973
THOMPSON, Steve (FB)
Winnsboro, La., 1956
THORNALL, Bill (C)
Metechin, N.J., 1942
THORNTON, Sam B. (T-G)
Pitkin, La., 1922-23
TILLY, L.R. (E)
St. Martinville, La., 1909
TINSLEY, Gaynell (Gus) (E)
Homer, La., 1934-35-36
TINSLEY, Jess D. (T)
Haynesville, La., 1926-27-**28**
TISDALE, Charles H. (HB)
New Orleans, La., 1893
TITTLE, Billy (Mgr.)
New Orleans, La., 1976
TITTLE, Y. A. (QB-HB)
Marshall, Tex., 1944-45-46-**47**
TOCZYLOSKI, Edward (QB) **1940**
TOLER, Jack ( )
Baker, La., 1943-44
TOMS, Randy (TE)
Hodge, La., 1969-70
TORRANCE, Jack (Baby Jack) (G-T-C)
Oak Grove, La., 1931-32-33
TOTH, Zollie (FB)
Pocahontas, Va., 1946-47-48-**49**
TRAPANI, Felix (G)
Donaldsonville, La., 1943-**45**
TRICHE, Philip J. (LB)
Metairie, La., 1975-76-**77**
TRICHEL, Walter S. (FB)
Natchitoches, La., 1893
TRIMBLE, Carl Otis (QB-SB)
Tallulah, La., 1974-75-76
TROSCLAIR, Milton (T)
Thibodaux, La., 1962-63-64
TRUAX, Bill (E)
New Orleans, La., 1961-**62-63**
TULLOS, Earl R. (T)
Bogalusa, La., 1943-44-45-46
TULLY, Thomas N. (OG)
Baton Rouge, La., 1979
TUMINELLO, Joe (E)
Brookhaven, Miss., 1952-53-**54-55**
TURNER, Jim (G)
Baton Rouge, La., 1962-63
TURNER, J. Michael (Mike) (LB)
Shreveport, La., 1978-79
TURNER, Win (QB)
Baton Rouge, La., 1953-54-56-**57**

U
NONE

V

VAIRIN, Kenny (E)
New Orleans, La., 1963-64
VALENTINE, Miles S. (OG)
Ft. Walton Beach, Fla., **1979**
VAN BUREN, Ebert (HB)
Metairie, La., 1948-49-50
VAN BUREN, Steve (HB)
New Orleans, La., 1941-**42-43**

VENABLE, Jack ( )
Covington, La., 1943
VENABLE, John ( )
Camden, Ark., 1951
VERNON, Benton R. (C)
Ruston, La., 1923-24-25
VICKERS, Donald G. (C)
Greenwell Springs, La., **1979**
VINCENT, Mike (LB)
Sulphur, La., 1963-64-65
VINEYARD, Hershal (Sleepy) (G)
Albertville, Ala., 1926-27
VIRGETS, Warren (E)
Baton Rouge, La., 1950-51
VOSS, Harold (T)
Baton Rouge, La., 1948-49-**50**

W

WADDILL, George D. ( )
Baton Rouge, La., 1894
WALDEN, Henry E. (E)
Marksville, La., 1913-14
WALET, P. H. (HB)
New Iberia, La., 1911
WALKER, Delmar (Del) (TB)
Baton Rouge, La., 1969-70-**71**
WALKER, Jack (HB)
Houma, La., 1936
WALKER, R. F., (Foots) (G-T)
Dodson, La., 1913-16
WALL, Benjamin B. (HB)
Alexandria, La., 1898-99
WALLIS, Lionel J. (SE)
Houma, La., 1977-78-79
WALSH, Ewell (G)
Tempe, Ariz., 1949-50
WALTON, R. H. (Tough) (T-G)
Albermarle, La., 1914-15
WARD, Steve (FB)
Baton Rouge, La., 1960-**61-62**
WARMBROD, James (C)
Belvidere, Tenn., 1936-**37**
WARNER, Ambrose D. (HB)
Robert, La., 1922-23-25
WATSON, John E (OG)
Bossier City, La., 1977-78-79
WATSON, A. Scott (S)
Pensacola, Fla., 1979
WEAVER, A. V. (Tubbo) (T)
Natchitoches, La., 1924
WEAVER, Odell (HB)
Homer, La., 1940-41
WEAVER, Otto L. (E)
Natchitoches, La., 1924-**25**
WEBB, Charles (E)
McComb, Miss., 1943-44
WEBER, S. R. (Chink) (E)
Baton Rouge, La., 1924
WEBSTER, Rene J. ( )
Jeanerette, La., 1894
WEIL, Edgar E. (FB)
Alexandria, La., 1905-06
WEINSTEIN, John (DT)
Opelousas, La., 1970
WEST, Billy (FB)
Natchitoches, La., 1949-50-**51**
WEST, Jim (SB)
Bossier City, La., 1967-68-69
WEST, Kerry L. (OT)
Pineville, La., 1979
WESTBROOK, John T. (E)
Baton Rouge, La., 1894-95-**96-97**
WHITE, Lyman D. Jr. (DE)
Franklin, La., 1977-78-79
WHITFILL, Steve (DE-LB)
Dallas, Tex., 1973-74
WHITLATCH, Blake (LB)
Baton Rouge, La., 1975-76-**77**
WHITLEY, John B. (Jay) (C)
Baton Rouge, La., 1976-**77-78**
WHITMAN, Ralph (T)
Jennings, La., 1938-39
WHYTE, Vernon ( )
Tyler, Tex., 1943
WILBANKS, T. E. (HB)
Shreveport, La., 1917

WILKINS, Ray (HB)
Homer, La., 1960-61-62
WILLIAMS, Chris A. (CB)
Tioga, La., 1977-78-79
WILLIAMS, Henry L. (E)
Baton Rouge, La., 1906
WILLIAMS, Mike (CB)
Covington, La., 1972-73-**74**
WILLIAMS, T. Demetri (DT)
Plaquemine, La., 1978-79
WILLIAMSON, Charles (Chuck) (TE)
Baton Rouge, La., 1971-72
WILSON, Barry (C)
New Orleans, La., 1965-**66-67**
WILSON, N. A. (Fatz) (G)
Shreveport, La., 1926-27-28
WILSON, Roy (E-G)
Bossier City, La., 1930-31-32
WIMBERLY, Abner (E)
Oak Ridge, La., 1943-46-47-48
WINKLER, Joe (S)
New Orleans, La., 1971-72-73
WINSTON, Roy (Moonie) (G)
Baton Rouge, La., 1959-60-61
WINTLE, James V. (Wee Willie) (QB-HB) Leesville, La., 1921-22
WOLF, Sidney K. (Izzy) (HB)
Baton Rouge, La., 1920
WOOD, John (DE)
Lake Charles, La., 1970-**71-72**
WOOD, John (E)
Lake City, Fla., 1954-55-56
WOODARD, Risdon E. (Red) (T)
Dubberly, La., 1919-20-22
WOODLEY, David E. (QB)
Shreveport, La., 1977-78-79
WORLEY, Mitch (LB-P)
Dallas, Tex., 1966
WORLEY, Wren (G)
El Dorado, Ark., 1946-47-48
WRIGHT, Mike (RT)
Sulphur, La., 1968-69-70

X
NONE

Y

YATES, BERTIS (Bert) (FB)
Haynesville, La., 1932-33-34
YATES, Jesse (E)
N. Little Rock, Ark., 1949-50-**51**
YEAGER, Rudy (T)
Philadelphia, Pa., 1951
YOKUBAITIS, Mark (LB)
Houston, Tex., 1972
YOUNG, Charles G. (T-G)
Homer, La., 1893-94
YOUNG, Jerry (G)
Lafayette, La., 1962-63
YOUNGBLOOD, Tommy (DE)
Shreveport, La., 1967-68

Z

ZAUNBRECHER, Godfrey (C)
Crowley, La., 1967-68-69
ZERINGUE, Brian (FB)
Raceland, La., 1973
ZICK, Francis (T)
Phillipsburg, N.J., 1941-42
ZIEGLER, Bob (G)
Crowley, La., 1956
ZIEGLER, Paul (G)
Crowley, La., 1954-55

SEC PLAYERS-OF-THE-YEAR

(Selected by the Atlanta Touchdown Club)

Jimmy Taylor (back) 1957
Billy Cannon (back) 1958
Roy Winston (lineman) 1961
Jerry Stovall (back) 1962

LSU FOOTBALL LETTERMEN *

1893

Andrews, C. P.
Bates, W. C.
Beard, J.
Boudreaux, W.
Brian, A.
Broussard, R. A.
Brown, S. P.
Cambon, F. J.
Campbell, E. P.
Chavanne, C. E.
Clark, S. M. D.
Dennis, G. A.
Dupree, S. G.
Gayle, E. F.
Huey, J. M.
Lyons, F. G.
Pleasant, R. G.
Pratt, J. M.
Prescott, A.
Prescott, W. B.
Roane, J. A.
Schoenberger, G. C.
Scott, E. A.
Smedes, W. C.
Tisdale, C. H.
Trichel, W. S.
Young, C. G.

1894

Arrighi, J. H.
Beard, J.
Brian, A.
Broussard, R. A.
Chavanne, C. E.
Clark, S. M. D.
Conner, J. C.
Dupree, S. G.
Gamble, H. P.
Grivot, M.
Hodge, A. A.
Hunter, G. N.
Hunter, L. T.
Lewis, W. J.
Mullins, W. B.
Nicholson, G. B.
Nelken, W.
Nelson, R. J.
Newell, E. T.
Nicholson, G. B.
Prescott, W. B.
Quirk, L. A.
Salassi, J. R.
Schneider, F. H.
Scott, E. A.
Slaughter, W. S.
Smedes, W. C.
Snyder, J. E.
Staples, D. P.
Waddill, G. D.
Webster, R. J.
Westbrook, J. T.
Young, C. G.

1895

Arrighi, J. H.
Bateman, J. B.
Daspit, A. P.
Daspit, J. C.
Gamble, H. P.
Huyck, P.
Lambert, S.
Ledbetter, W. M.
Morris, J. E.
Nicholson, G. B.
Quirk, L. A.
Salassi, J. R.
Sanders, J. W.
Schneider, F. H.
Scott, E. A.
Slaughter, W. S.
Snyder, J. E.
Westbrook, J. T.

1896

Arrighi, J. H.
Atkinson, J. S.
Barbin, A. T.
Chavanne, E. A.
Daspit, A. P.
Daspit, J. C.
Gourrier, S.
Harp, J. F.
Huyck, P.
Lambert, S.
Ledbetter, W. M.
Nicholson, G. B.
Robertson, E.
Salassi, J. R.
Schneider, F. H.
Schoenberger, G. C.
Scott, E. A.
Slaughter, W. S.
Westbrook, J. T.

1897

Chamberlin, W. B.
Chavanne, E. A.
Daspit, A. P.
Daspit, J. C.
Godchaux, F.
Howell, W. C.
Huyck, P.
Kaffie, L.
LeSueur, G. B.
Levy, J. M.
Nicholson, G. B.
Scott, E. A.
Sherburne, T. L.
Slaughter, W. S.
Staples, D. P.
Westbrook, J. T.

1898

Aby, H. F.
Bateman, J. B.
Chamberlin, W. B.
Chavanne, E. A.
Coco, W. A.
Daspit, A. P.
Daspit, J. C.
Kaffie, L.
LeSueur, G. B.
Sanford, J.
Sherburne, T. L.
Slaughter, W. S.
Wall, B. B.

1899

Aby, H. F.
Barrow, E. R.
Chamberlin, W. B.
Chavanne, E. A.
Coleman, J. J.
Fuchs, G.
Gorham, E. L.
Gremillion, F. V.
Herpin, J. O.
Huyck, P.
Landry, H. E.
Laurents, A.
Lawrason, C. M.
Lemoine, H. T.
LeSueur, G. B.
Pratt, G. K.
Sanford, J.
Schwing, I. H.
Wall, B. B.

1900

Byram, J. E.
Coleman, J. J.
Fuchs, G.
Garland, J. M.
Gorham, E. L.
Gremillion, F. V.
Landry, H. E.
McNeese, O. W.
Mortimer, E. H.
Mundinger, A. G
Pegues, W. T.
Rhodes, H. J.
Schwing, I. H.

1901

Brogan, J. E.
Byram, J. E.
Coleman, J. J.
Cook, F. W.
Fuchs, G.
Gorham, E. L.
Gueno, A. J.
Guidry, J. W.
Herpin, J. O.
Kennedy, R. M.
Landry, H. E.
Laurents, A.
McNeese, O. W.
Mundinger, A. G.
Olivier, L. A.
Redhead, J. A.
Rhodes, H. J.
Sanford, J. H.
Sebastian, J. A.

1902

Coleman, J. J.
Gueno, A. J.
Guidry, J. W.
Kennedy, R. M.
Klock, E. L.
Landry, H. E.
LeSueur, L. J.
Martin, W. O.
Mundinger, A. G.
Rhodes, H. J.
Sharp, L. E.

1903

Bates, O. P.
Bentley, G. D.
Coleman, J. J.
Edwards, F. M.
Fahey, J. K.
Fontenot, F. M.
Fourmy, J. M.
Gueno, A. J.
Guidry, J. W.
Howell, R. C.
Kennedy, R. M.
Klock, E. L.
Loustalot, A. L.
Martin, W. O.
Stayton, W. D.

1904

Brogan, L. E.
Connelly, E. M.
Edwards, F. M.
Fourmy, J. M.
Harris, L. B.
Heard, T. J.
Jenkins, H.
Joffrion, A. B.
Klock, E. L.
Lyles, W. M.
Martin, W. O.
Messa, R. A.
Muller, J. C.
Noblet, O. H.
Rivero, V. V.
Staudinger, L. P.
Stayton, W. D.

1905

Brannon, S. W.
Edwards, F. M.
Griffith, J. H.
Heard, T. J.
Hunsicker, G. R.
Joffrion, A. B.
Messa, R. A.
Noblet, O. H.
Smith, C. I.
Smith, V. E.
Weil, E. E.

1906

Brannon, S. W.
Buck, C.
Gandy, M. H.
Harvey, H.
Hillman, W. A.
Kelly, A. H.
Klock, E. L.
Muller, J. C.
Smith, C. I.
Stovall, R. L.
Texada, J. C.
Weil, E. E.
Williams, H. J.

1907

Baldwin, H. E.
Bauer, C. C.
Brannon, S. W.
Buck, C.
Drew, H. C.
Fenton, G. E.
Ferguson, P. L.
Gandy, M. H.
Gill, R. O.
Hamilton, W. J.
Handy, B. B.
Hillman, W. A.
Lyles, W. M.
Noblet, O. H.
Seip, J. J.
Stovall, R. F.
Stovall, R. L.

1908

Albright, J. G.
Fenton, G. E.
Gandy, M. H.
Gill, R. O.
Hillman, W. A.
Lally, M. F.
Noblet, O. H.
Pollock, W. M.
Ryan, W. F.
Seip, J. J.
Stovall, R. F.
Stovall, R. L.
Smith, C. I.
Smith, V. E.
Thomas, A. J.

1909

Albright, J. G.
Brannon, S. W.
Drew, H. C.
Fenton, G. E.
Gill, R. O.
Hall, J. O.
Hillman, W. A.
Howell, R. B.
McCollam, A. M.
Pollock, W. M.
Ryan, W. F.
Seip, J. J.
Stovall, R. F.
Stovall, R. L.

Thomas, A. J.
Tilly, L. R.

1910

Bond, C. P.
Dupont, L. H.
Evans, W. M.
Gosserand, M. A.
Hall, J. O.
Hammond, W. M.
Howell, R. B.
Lally, M. F.
McHenry, B. G.
Martin, C. Y.
Pollock, W. M.
Potts, J. H.
Reily, C. S.
Seip, J. J.
Thomas, A. J.

1911

Crawford, J. E.
Dupont, J. M.
Dupont, L. H.
Evans, W. M.
Gosserand, M. A.
Hall, J. O.
McHenry, B. F.
Reily, C. S.
Spencer, G. B.
Thomas, A. J.
Walet, P. H.

1912

Crawford, J. E.
Dupont, J. M.
Dupont, L. H.
Dutton, T. W.
Evans, W. M.
Gosserand, M. A.
Hall, J. O.
Johnson, M. F.
Klock, A. E.
Reid, A. J.
Reily, C. S.
Spencer, F. W.
Spencer, G. B.
Talbot, E. L.

1913

Cooper, P.
Crawford, J. E.
Dupont, J. M.
Dupont, L. H.
Dutton, T. W.
Evans, W. M.
Fluker, H. V.
Green, W. C.
Harrison, P. E.
Klock, A. E.
Mobley, T. R.
Reid, A. J.
Spencer, F. W.
Spencer, G. B.
Walden, H. E.
Walker, R. F.

1914

Cooper, P.
Dupont, J. M.
Green, V. E.
Green, W. W.
Klock, A. E.
Louviere, W. H.
Martin, G. H.
Mestayer, O. J.
Mobley, T. R.
O'Quin, A.

* In the early years of LSU football, no letters were given. Only by reading newspaper accounts of the games is it possible to determine which team members actually played, and any list drawn from such write-ups obviously might omit some who played but who were not mentioned. I have therefore included all members of the team (as best as can be determined) for the years before 1900. Thereafter the lists are of lettermen only.

O'Quin, L.
Pittman, J. S.
Reid, A. J.
Sanchez, A. C.
Spencer, G. B.
Walden, H. E.
Walton, R. H.

1915

Bernstein, J.
Claitor, O.
Cooper, P.
Edmonds, W. R.
Floyd, J. C.
Green, W. C.
Himes, L. A.
Joffrion, E. J.
Jones, K. E.
Krementz, F. B.
Lewis, W. S.
O'Quin, A.
Pittman, J. S.
Platou, R.
Reagan, J. R.
Reid, A. J.
Rice, R. E.
Rodrigue, J. C.
Walton, R. H.

1916

Baird, A. W.
Bernstein, J.
Cooper, P.
Flanagan, H. F.
Floyd, J. C.
Green, W. C.
Henry, T. J.
Herbert, A. W.
Himes, L. A.
Jones, K. E.
Klock, A. E.
Krementz, F. B.
Lewis, W. S.
O'Quin, A.
Rice, R. E.
Rodrigue, J. C.
Spencer, H. F.
St. Dizier, R. V.
Walker, R. F.

1917

Benoit, R. L.
Collins, D. W.
Dutton, J. G.
Fournet, J. B.
Herbert, A. W.
Ives, C. A.
Jones, K. E.
McKnight, O. W.
O'Quin, A.
Pitcher, J. E.
Rutledge, D. H.
Spencer, H. F.
Stafford, D. G.
St. Dizier, R. V.
Wilbanks, T. E.

1918

(no LSU football
played)

1919

Beale, L. S.
Benoit, R. L.
Bernstein, J.
Busse, B. M.
Dutton, J. G.
Dutton, T. W.
Edmonds, W. R.
Floyd, J. C.
Fournet, J. B.
Gladden, S. W.
Hague, P. G.
Hanley, W. B.
Helm, N. C.
Ives, C. A.
McFarland, R. A.
Smith, B.
Spencer, F. L.
Woodard, R. E.

1920

Benoit, R. L.
Busse, B. M.
Davis, R. L.
Ewen, E. L.
Hague, P. G.
Helm, N. C.
Hereford, R. M.
Hewett, L. F.
Ives, C. A.
Lewis, J. W.
McFarland, R. A.
Schneider, E. D.
Spencer, F. L.
Wolf, S. W.
Woodard, R. E.

1921

Beale, L. S.
Bourgeois, L. C.
Busse, B. M.
Campbell, C. C.
Curtis, A. M.
Davis, R. L.
Dutton, J. G.
Edmondson, A. T.
Ewen, E. L.
Helm, N. C.
Hereford, R. M.
Hughes, C. B.
Ives, C. A.
Landry, W. M.
Lewis, J. W.
McFarland, R. A.
Rabenhorst, O. D.
Spencer, F. L.
Steele, J. E.
Wintle, J. V.

1922

Bame, A. A.
Blakewood, E. G.
Bourgeois, L. C.
Campbell, C. C.
Connell, G. M.
Edmondson, A. T.
Ewen, E. L.
Helm, N. C.
Hendrix, S. W.
Jackson, A. W.
Kizer, R. C.
Landry, W. M.
McFarland, R. A.
Matthews, L. R.
Pitcher, W.
Rabenhorst, O. D.
Stevens, N. G.
Thornton, S. B.
Warner, A. D.
Wintle, J. V.
Woodard, R. E.

1923

Abramson, L.
Blakewood, E. G.
Bourgeois, L. C.
Campbell, C. C.
Carriere, O. P.
Edmondson, A. T.
Ewen, E. L.
Fay, T. D.
Forgey, C. W.
Hughes, C. B.
Jackson, A. W.
Loustalot, M. L.
McCall, H. L.
Matthews, L. R.
Miller, B. R.
Pitcher, W.
Steele, J. E.
Stevens, N. G.
Swanson, A. L.
Thornton, S. B.
Vernon, B. R.
Warner, A. D.

1924

Bourgeois, L. C.
Campbell, C. C.
Carriere, O. P.
Clay, J. T.
Connell, A. P.
Dimmick, O.
Fay, T. D.

Jackson, A. W.
Kennon, R. F.
Miller, B. R.
Morgan, S. R.
Pitcher, W.
Steele, J. E.
Stevens, N. G.
Swanson, A. L.
Vernon, B. R.
Weaver, A. V.
Weaver, O. L.
Weber, S. R.

1925

Barham, G. E.
Carriere, O. P.
Chandler, W. B.
Clay, J. T.
Connell, A. P.
Connell, G. M.
Dimmick, O.
Durrett, B. E.
Fay, T. D.
Flood, M. S.
Godfrey, L. T.
Haynes, E. H.
Herget, G. C.
McCall, H. L.
Miller, B. R.
Morgan, S. R.
Spencer, C. N.
Steele, J. E.
Stevens, N. G.
Swanson, A. L.
Vernon, B. R.
Warner, A. D.

1926

Babers, B.
Bailey, R. L.
Carriere, O. P.
Chandler, W. B.
Connell, A. P.
Dimmick, O.
Durrett, B. E.
Gayden, G.
Godfrey, L. T.
Grevemberg, J. H.
Haynes, E. H.
Helms, L.
Herget, G. C.
Huffman, A. S.
McCall, H. L.
Mason, C. C.
Morgan, S. R.
Nesom, G.
Stumph, J. C.
Swanson, A. E.
Tinsley, J. D.
Vineyard, H.
Wilson, N. A.

1927

Alston, F. H.
Babers, B.
Bailey, R. L.
Brown, L. P.
Durrett, B. E.
Ellis, F.
Freeman, G. A.
Grevemberg, A.
Grevemberg, J. H.
Godfrey, L. T.
Hatcher, G. R.
Haynes, E. H.
Huffman, A. S.
Jones, N.
McCann, M. G.
Mason, C. C.
Monsour, E.
Morgan, P.
Nesom, G.
Phelps, J. R.
Renfroe, J. C.
Stovall, H. H.
Swanson, A. E.
Tinsley, J. D.
Vineyard, H.
Weaver, O.
Wilson, N. A.

1928

Alston, F. H.
Brown, L. P.
Ellis, F.

Hendrix, J.
Huffman, A. S.
Jones, N.
Luker, J. B.
Mason, C. C.
Moore, H.
Nesom, G.
Peebles, L.
Reeves, W. A.
Stovall, H. H.
Swanson, A. E.
Tinsley, J. D.
Wilson, N. A.

1929

Allen, W. D.
Bowman, S. S.
Brown, E. A.
Brown, L. P.
Butler, W. E.
Clay, J. T.
Cole, F. E.
Ellis, F.
Fleming, W.
Harrell, L.
Hendrix, J.
Holden, T. D.
Jones, N.
Khoury, E.
Landry, B. H.
LeBleu, C. A.
Luker, J. B.
McFerrin, C. S.
Moore, H.
Ogden, D. G.
Peebles, L.
Powell, R. H.
Pressburg, J. W.
Reedy, F.
Reeves, W. S.
Renfroe, J. C.
Schneider, F. H.
Smith, T.

1930

Allen, W. D.
Almokary, J.
Andreas, H.
Bowman, S. S.
Brown, H.
Butler, W. E.
Cole, F. E.
Gioviani, C.
Hendrix, J.
Holden, T. D.
Keller, J. L.
Khoury, E.
Kirkpatrick, H. L.
Luker, J. B.
McLain, J.
Malone, J. L.
Ogden, D. G.
Powell, R. H.
Reeves, W. A.
Renfroe, J. C.
Schneider, F. H.
Skidmore, J.
Smith, T.
Stevens, E.
Wilson, R.

1931

Allen, W. D.
Almokary, J.
Bannister, R. M.
Bowman, S. S.
Brainard, G. R.
Brown, H.
Butler, W. E.
Fleming, W.
Foley, A.
Gioviani, C.
Keller, J. L.
Kent, J. C.
Khoury, E.
McLain, J.
Malone, J. L.
Mixon, N.
Moore, H.
Nevils, A.
Powell, R. H.
Pressburg, J. W.
Skidmore, J.
Skidmore, J.
Smith, T.
Stevens, E.
Torrance, J.
Wilson, R.

1932

Almokary, J.
Bannister, R. M.
Bowman, G.
Brown, J.
Brown, R.
Fleming, W.
Johnson, R.
Keller, J. L.
Kent, J. C.
Langley, W. L.
Lobdell, W. Y.
Malone, J. L.
Mitchel, G.
Mixon, N.
Moore, F. E.
Nevils, A.
Skidmore, C.
Skidmore, J.
Stovall, L. J.
Sullivan, W.
Torrance, J.
Wilson, R.
Yates, B.

1933

Barrett, W. J.
Brown, A. D.
Burge, D. P.
Fatherree, J.
Helveston, O.
Kent, J. C.
Langley, W. L.
Lawrie, J.
Lobdell, W. Y.
Mickal, A.
Mitchell, G.
Mixon, N.
Moore, F. E.
Nevils, A.
Pickett, G.
Rukas, J.
Seago, E.
Stovall, L. J.
Sullivan, W.
Torrance, J.
Yates, B.

1934

Baldwin, M.
Barrett, W. J.
Brown, A. D.
Brown, R.
Calhoun, S.
Egan, R.
Fatherree, J.
Helveston, O.
Lawrie, J.
May, W.
Mickal, A.
Moore, F. E.
Reed, J. T.
Rukas, J.
Seago, E.
Stewart, M.
Stovall, L. J.
Stupka, F.
Sullivan, W.
Tinsley, G.
Yates, B.

1935

Baldwin, M.
Barrett, W. J.
Bowman, G.
Brown, A. D.
Carroll, P.
Coffee, J.
Crass, W.
Dumas, B.
Fatherree, J.
Helveston, O.
Knight, R.
Lawrie, J.
Leisk, C. W.
May, W.
Mickal, A.
Mihalic, J.
Morton, A.
Nolen, M.
Reed, J. T.
Rohm, C.
Rukas, J.
Seago, E.
Stewart, M.
Strange, C.
Stupka, F.
Tinsley, G.

1936

Baldwin, M.
Booth, B.
Carroll, P.
Coffee, J.
Crass, W.
Dumas, B.
Farmer, H.
Friend, B.
Gatto, E. T.
Gormley, R.
Leisk, W.
Lester, G.
LeMak, C.
Matlock, O.
May, W.
Mihalic, J.
Milner, G.
Morton, A.
Myrick, B.
Reed, J. T.
Rohm, C.
Smith, J. H.
Stewart, M.
Strange, C.
Tinsley, G.

1937

Anderson, R. J.
Baur, F. O.
Booth, B.
Bussey, Y.
Cajoleas, J.
Campbell, I.
Clark, B.
Cunningham, E
Dumas, B.
Farmer, H.
Ferguson, C.
Friend, B.
Gatto, E. T.
Gormley, J.
Gormley, R.
Kavanaugh, K.
King, L.
Lester, G.
LeMak, C.
Messina, J.
Milner, G.
Morton, A.
Pittman, P.
Rohm, C.
Smith, J. H.
Staples, J.
Stell, J.
Warmbrod, J.

1938

Anastasio, C.
Anderson, R. J.
Bartran, D.
Baur, F. O.
Booth, B.
Bussey, Y.
Clark, B.
Cajoleas, J.
Campbell, I.
Erdman, C.
Farmer, H.
Fife, R.
Friend, B.
Gatto, E.
Goree, J. W.
Gormley, J.
Gormley, R.
Graham, R.
Hedrick, B.
Johnson, C.
Kavanaugh, K.
Messina, J.
Milner, G.
Monget, G.
Simes, A.
Smith, J. H.
Staples, J.
Stell, J.
Whitman, R.

1939

Anastasio, C.
Anderson, R. J.
Bartran. D.
Baur, F. O.
Bernstein, D.
Bird, L.
Bussey, Y.

Cajoleas, J.
Campbell, I.
Eastman, D.
Froechtenicht, W. H.
Gianelloni, V.
Goree, J. W.
Hightower, G.
Hogan, Bill
Jenkins, M.
Johnson, C.
Kavanaugh, K.
Kendrick, B.
Lipkis, B.
McKinney, J.
Messina, J.
Monget, G.
Price, T. J.
Simes, A.
Staples, J.
Stonecipher, W.
Whitman, R.

1940

Anastasio, C.
Barnes, W.
Barrett, J.
Barrett, W.
Bird, L.
Bruno, P.
Cassidy, F.
Cavigga, A.
Dodson, A.
Edwards, Bill
Fulkerson, J.
Gianelloni, V.
Goree, J. W.
Hightower, J.
Hogan, Bill
Jenkins, M.
Johnson, C.
Kendrick, Bob
Kendrick, H.
Lipkis, B.
McKinney, Bill
Miller, W.
Pillow, D.
Richardson, L.
Stell, A.
Tocaylowski, E.
Weaver, O.
Whitman, R.

1941

Bennett, R.
Bird, L.
Burkett, J.
Cassidy, F.
Cavigga, A.
Chadwick, G.
Dodson, A.
Eastman, Dan
Edwards, Bill
Evans,
Fulkerson, J.
Giacone, J.
Gorinski, W.
Hall, Fred
Harris, S.
Helscher, H.
Hightower, G.
Hogan, Bill
Holland, W.
James, A.
Jones, C.
Kendrick, H.
Lipkis, B.
McKinney, Bill
McLeod, J.
Miller, W.
Pillow, D.
Richardson, L.
Richmond, D.
Tally, J.
Van Buren, S.
Weaver, Odell
Zick, F.

1942

Ballard, S.
Barnes, W.
Burkett, J.
Crafton, J.
Dark, A.
Glamp, J.
Gorinski, W.
Hall, F.
Heard, H.

Loflin, J.
Richmond, D.
Shurtz,.H.
Worley, W.

1943

Barney, C.
Bernhard, J.
Bryan, J.
Casanova, R.
Claunch, E.
Corgan, Bill
Goode, B.
Griffith, C.
Haley, O.
Hartley, J.
Hunt, R.
Janeck, C.
Knight, G.
Lewis, J.
McClelland, Bill
Nagatta, J.
Polozola, P.
Reeder, J.
Schroll, B.
Schroll, C.
Stagg, J.
Trapani, F.
Tullos, E.
Van Buren, S.
Walker, K.
Webb, C.
Weimer, J.
Wimberly, A.
Wolf, M.

1944

Bernhard, J.
Bertucci, G.
Bryan, J.
Buckles, Bill
Bullock, F.
Cason, J.
Cavigga, A.
Core, H.
Didier, M.
Knight, G.
Land, F.
Landry, W.
Miller, H.
Pardo, D.
Rowan, E.
Sigrest, E.
Tittle, Y. A.
Trapani, F.
Tullos, E.
Webb, C.

1945

Abney, W.
Bernhard, J.
Bertucci, J.
Cason, J.
Coates, R.
Collins, H.
Core, H.
Cusimano, C.
Didier, M.
Gill, A.
Hemphill, D.
Janeck, C.
Kellum, Bill
Kingery, W.
Knight, G.
Kosmac, A.
Land, F.
Landry, M. J.
Landry, W.
Lindsey, C.
Miller, H.
Montgomery, Bill
Parnham, S.
Sanders, A.
Sandifer, D.
Shawberger, M. J.
Sigrest, E.
Strother, H.
Tittle, Y. A.
Tullos, E.
Trapani, F.

1946

Adams, J.
Ballard, S.
Barnes, W.

Bullock, R.
Cason, J.
Champagne, E.
Claunch, E.
Collins, H.
Core, H.
Eckert, W.
Gray, D.
Hall, Fred
Heard, H.
Heroman, A.
Land, F.
Landry, W.
Leach, J.
Lewis, J.
Lindsey, C.
Loflin, J.
Pevey, C.
Sanders, A.
Sandifer, D.
Schroll, C.
Schroll, W.
Shurtz, H.
Tittle, Y. A.
Toth, Z.
Tullos, E.
Wimberly, A.
Worley, W.

1947

Adams, J.
Baird, J.
Ballard, S.
Barnes, W.
Bullock, R.
Cason, J.
Claunch, E.
Clegg, R.
Coates, R.
Collins, H.
Collins, R.
Core, H.
Cusimano, C.
Foti, R.
Gray, D.
Griffith, C.
Heard, H.
Hemphill, D.
Heroman, A.
Land, F.
Leach, J.
Lewis, J.
Loflin, J.
Lyle, M.
McClelland, W.
McLeod, J.
Pevey, C.
Reynolds, G.
Sandifer, D.
Schroll, W.
Shurtz, H.
Tittle, Y. A.
Toth, Z.
Wimberly, A.
Worley, W.

1948

Adams, J.
Baird, J.
Baggett, W.
Bradley, R.
Bullock, R.
Claunch, E.
Clegg, R.
Cole, J.
Collins, H.
Collins, R.
Cusimano, C.
Gray, D.
Griffith, C.
Heroman, A.
Hover, A.
Kitto, A.
Konz, K.
LeSage, J.
Lewis, J.
Lyle, J.
Lyle, M.
McClelland, W.
Menetre, R.
Pevey, C.
Porta, R.
Reid, J.
Reynolds, G.
Schroll, W.
Shoaf, J.
Strother, H.
Toth, Z.
Van Buren, E.

Voss, H.
Wimberly, A.
Worley, W.

1949

Adams, J.
Anding, A.
Baggett, W.
Baird, J.
Barton, J.
Bradley, R.
Brown, T.
Cole, J.
Collins, R.
Coyne, E.
Cusimano, C.
Field, E.
Freeman, C.
Gray, Dale
Griffith, C.
Hedges, L.
Hover, A.
Kitto, A.
Konz, K.
Lyle, J.
Lyle, M..
Pevey, C.
Potter, R.
Reid, J.
Roshto, J.
Roussos, G.
Shoaf, J.
Smith, H.
Toth, Z.
Van Buren, E.
Voss, H.
Walsh, E.
West, W.
Yates, J.

1950

Adams, J.
Baggett, W.
Barton, J.
Cole, J.
Copes, C.
Coyne, E.
Dry, R.
Freeman, C.
Hedges, L.
Hover, A.
Hunter, R.
Kitto, A.
Konz, K.
Lansing, W.
Lyle, J.
McLeod, R.
Martin, J.
Miller, P.
Pitalo, A.
Potter, R.
Reid, J.
Roshto, J.
Roussos, G.
Shirer, J.
Shoaf, J.
Smith, C.
Stevens, H.
Van Buren, E.
Virgets, W.
Voss, H.
Walsh, E.
West, W.
Yates, J.

1951

Barton, J.
Brown, C.
Brown, T.
Builliard, E.
Coyne, E.
Davis, G.
Dildy, G.
Doggett, A.
Fournet, S.
Freeman, C.
Guglielmo, A.
Hedges, G.
Hedges, L.
Kelly, C.
Labat, L.
Lansing, W.
Lawrence, R.
McLeod, R.
Modicut, J.
Nealy, W.
Oakley, C.
Potter, R.

HOW LSU ADOPTED ITS NICKNAME

Way back in the fall of 1896, Coach A. W. Jeardeau's LSU football team posted a perfect 6-0-0 record, and it was in that pigskin campaign that LSU first adopted its nickname, **Tigers.**

"Tigers" seemed a logical choice since most collegiate teams in that year bore the names of ferocious animals, but the underlying reason on why LSU chose "Tigers" dates back to the Civil War.

During the "War Between the States," a battalion of Confederate soldiers composed of New Orleans Zouaves and Donaldsonville Cannoners distinguished themselves at the Battle of Shenandoah.

These Louisiana rebels had been known by their contemporaries as a fighting band of Louisiana Tigers. Thus when LSU entered the gridiron battlefields in their fourth year of intercollegiate football competition, they tagged themselves as the "Tigers."

It was Paul Dietzel's 1955 "fourth-quarter ball club" that helped the moniker "Tigers" grow into the nickname: **Fighting Tigers.**

Index